Social Media for Strategic Communication

Second Edition

Sara Miller McCune founded SAGE Publishing in 1965 to support the dissemination of usable knowledge and educate a global community. SAGE publishes more than 1000 journals and over 600 new books each year, spanning a wide range of subject areas. Our growing selection of library products includes archives, data, case studies and video. SAGE remains majority owned by our founder and after her lifetime will become owned by a charitable trust that secures the company's continued independence.

Los Angeles | London | New Delhi | Singapore | Washington DC | Melbourne

Social Media for Strategic Communication

Creative Strategies and Research-Based Applications

Second Edition

Karen Freberg

University of Louisville

Los Angeles | London | New Delhi
Singapore | Washington DC | Melbourne

FOR INFORMATION:

SAGE Publications, Inc.
2455 Teller Road
Thousand Oaks, California 91320
E-mail: order@sagepub.com

SAGE Publications Ltd.
1 Oliver's Yard
55 City Road
London EC1Y 1SP
United Kingdom

SAGE Publications India Pvt. Ltd.
B 1/I 1 Mohan Cooperative Industrial Area
Mathura Road, New Delhi 110 044
India

SAGE Publications Asia-Pacific Pte. Ltd.
18 Cross Street #10-10/11/12
China Square Central
Singapore 048423

Acquisitions Editor: Lauren Gobell
Editorial Assistant: Sam Diaz
Production Editor: Gagan Mahindra
Copy Editor: Colleen Brennan
Typesetter: C&M Digitals (P) Ltd.
Indexer: Integra
Cover Designer: Janet Kiesel
Marketing Manager: Victoria Velasquez

Printed in the United States of America

Library of Congress Cataloging-in-Publication Data

Names: Freberg, Karen June, author.

Title: Social media for strategic communication : creative strategies and research-based applications / Karen Freberg.

Description: Second edition | Thousand Oaks : SAGE Publishing, [2022] | Includes index. |

Identifiers: LCCN 2021009653 | ISBN 9781071852514 (paperback) | ISBN 9781071826898 (epub) | ISBN 9781071826881 (epub) | ISBN 9781071826874 (pdf)

Subjects: LCSH: Social media. | Communication. | Internet in publicity. | Persuasion (Psychology)

Classification: LCC HM742 .F739 2022 | DDC 302.23/1—dc23
LC record available at https://lccn.loc.gov/2021009653

This book is printed on acid-free paper.

21 22 23 24 25 10 9 8 7 6 5 4 3 2 1

BRIEF CONTENTS

DETAILED CONTENTS

There are *still* many perceptions of social media as a profession and career:

> Social media is a side hustle that anyone can do in their free time; you just tweet and share content.

> Social media is not hard and demanding. You can WFH and have work/life balance.

> Analytics and math? I didn't sign up for that in social media. I am a people person!

> Go on TikTok and hire someone in Gen Z as an intern. They are the experts.

> You do not need a book to learn about social media. Once it's published, it's irrelevant.

> Why go to school to study social media? Everything you need to know is on YouTube.

I am sure you have heard some of these points one time or another. So, let's address each of these points. Even as we enter a new decade, these myths and assumptions are always true. Here's a rule to always be aware of: Never assume anything, because you could be completely wrong. Social media is not a "new" field; it has become a mature, established, and vibrant profession in strategic communications. Social media professionals do more than just post content; they are in charge of creating stories, experiences, and executions that contribute to the bottom dollar for businesses. Social media professionals are the digital frontline employees of a brand, in good time and challenging ones, bringing the myth of a work/life balance to the forefront. Just because someone is young, it does not mean they are experts in the use of strategic social media platforms. However, most interns coming into the workplace are getting the training, experience, and education to be strategic in social media, which is very exciting. Plus, interns are coming into the workplace with more experiences in classes, internships, and with more of an entrepreneurship drive to their work than ever before. Yes, there are a lot of great resources on YouTube about social media, but having coursework and class activities that provide you with the ins and outs of how and why we use social media is crucial. Plus, these courses teach you all about critical thinking, creativity, and some of the fundamental skills needed to work within the industry, such as writing and research. Last but not least, there are books that can provide more of a sustainable view of social media that can build on a strategic mindset on how to approach social media.

This book aims to provide a solid and sustainable framework to help professionals, at all levels, achieve their professional goals in social media.

How did the book come about? This book has been years in the making. The overall goal of *Social Media for Strategic Communication* (SMSC) is to help rising and established professionals in the field to create a strategic mindset for social media activities, conversations, and relationships. Social media is the hub component of communication, integrating various disciplines and interweaving communities to formulate new knowledge, connections, and experiences virtually. Social media has become a rising area of focus for disciplines such as public relations, marketing, journalism, communication, computer science, and psychology among others. The profession of social media continues to be a living, breathing, and constantly adapting area of study and practice, and it deserves to have a concentration and book dedicated to not just the new shiny objects but also the strategies, behaviors, and mindset that connects everything together.

The overall goal for the first edition of this book was to set forth a foundation for understanding the strategic nature of social media. Most books that cover social media either focus only on the practice and execution or on theory. Other books skim over areas the authors are not comfortable covering. There no books that have addressed all of the aspects of social media that people want to learn about. I did not just want to write a book about social media; instead, I wanted to write THE book on social media. There has not been a universal or dedicated book that has connected all of the different facets of social media. This book hopes to achieve this and be a catalyst to help shape and change the field to be more interconnected and transdisciplinary.

This book embraces all of these challenges head on to make sure students have a comprehensive view of the strategic approach to social media. Research, practice, case studies, and insights from professionals are parts of each chapter, creating a thorough 360-degree perspective on strategic social media practices.

BEHIND THE SCENES

As I shared in the first edition of SMSC in 2018, I came to the realization a book needed to be written that encompasses all of the areas I felt were missing from other books. I felt there was a need to create a book that focused on the strategic mindset of social media while also providing the how and why aspect of what we do in social media and strategic communications. The overall goal was for this book to become a strong advocate and endorser of the social media industry as an established yet evolving area in communication.

I did not know what to expect for the first edition. The first edition was a huge success and was extremely well received when it launched in 2018. There was nothing more rewarding to hear students and educators from all over the world share their reactions and thanks for the book. Seeing my book adopted and endorsed by brands such as Facebook and Cannes Lions was also very exciting. This book also won the National Communication Association Public Relations Division PRIDE Award in 2020, making it the first social media textbook to win this award.

But as Anton Ego says in the movie *Ratatouille*, what does the chef (or in this case, author) have that is new? The answer to this question is this second edition of SMSC.

As I was finishing up my first public relations book (*Discovering Public Relations*) in 2020, I got the exciting news that a second edition of SMSC would be published. I was excited to get started working on the revisions and updates for the book. As you all know, social media has changed A LOT since the first edition came out. New platforms have come to light, along with innovative case studies, brand campaigns, and opportunities for social media professionals to take advantage of. In addition, new challenges have come to light. The amount of material to research, review, and discuss was a lot to consume. With that being said, it was a challenge

I was willing to take and embrace, which resulted in some really exciting updates for the second edition.

The first edition of SMSC was to introduce how and why we can use social media strategically in the social media industry. This was the introduction to the social media industry game. Now the second edition is here to make the rules of the social media game.

So, with a large cup of coffee in hand, my new writing buddy Mando Wade (my Australian Shepherd puppy) at my feet, and my laptop charged, I got started with the second edition of SMSC.

OVERVIEW OF *SOCIAL MEDIA FOR STRATEGIC COMMUNICATION* (2ND EDITION)

The goal of the SMSC book is to provide students with a current, integrated, engaging, and strategic focus on what social media is as a profession and industry. While most books have focused on tactical executions and finer aspects of the specific tools and platforms, this book focuses on the larger picture of creating a longstanding strategical mindset that helps students, professionals, and brands navigate the ever-changing landscape with sustainable action steps and fundamental skills that will never be outdated. SMSC is a bridge between research and practice, where students, educators, and professionals can find useful insights, best practices, and case studies to implement in their work and projects.

Chapters. All of the chapters have been updated with new case studies, examples, areas of interest, and insights from the field. However, we also added substantial new content, which made this book a bit longer than the first edition.

I am excited to have some brand new content for this second edition. We added three new chapters that address the growing changes and interests from the community in social media. Chapter 4 focuses on diversity, equity, and inclusion (DEI) in social media. This chapter was added to acknowledge the growing importance of representation and inclusion of all audiences from every background and community. Chapter 8 focuses on the rising area of influencer marketing, outlining not just what it is but how to strategically plan and execute an influencer campaign on social media. Lastly, with social media embracing the "pay-to-play" model, Chapter 9 focuses on the paid media aspect of social media.

Like the first edition, the second edition begins with the foundations of creating a strategic mindset. These beginning chapters provide an overview of how social media is both an art and a science (Chapter 1), while going forward into establishing ethical and legal guidelines for social media (Chapter 2), and proactive measures to create a sustainable and authentic personal brand (Chapter 3). Chapter 4 discusses the importance of DEI, and Chapter 5 outlines the key skills, expectations, and responsibilities that are part of the social media industry. Chapter 6 addresses the growing need to understand research, listening, monitoring, and key principles of analyzing the data coming from social media. Part II of the book focuses on understanding the strategic side of social media with campaign planning (Chapter 7), influencer marketing (Chapter 8), and paid media (Chapter 9). Chapter 10 discusses strategic writing for social media, and Chapter 11 covers audience segmentation and rise of specialized audiences such as advocates and influencers. Chapter 12 focuses on creating, managing, and curating content, and Chapter 13 connects all aspects of the previous chapters together with measurement and budget/calendar creation. Part III explores the application and where social media is practiced in the world. Specializations are highlighted in Chapters 14 and 15 with specific examples and best practices with some new specializations added, such as memes and more. Chapter 16 finalizes everything in the book while providing insights into what to look for next. Each chapter features case studies, examples, and notable takeaways (essentially, the "so what" factor). We cover relevant areas like ethics and law, DEI, social media strategies, and whether or not social media is a science or an art. The book goes into greater detail with the key components needed for effective listening and monitoring practices on social media, personal branding practices, the pros and cons of influencer and advocate marketing, budgeting (yes, social media costs money!), and outlining key areas of specialization that are integrated with social media practices.

Humans of Social Media Feature. Most social media books start off each chapter with a case study or an example of a social media campaign. This book, however, focuses on some of the leading voices and people BEHIND the campaigns, brands, and work we often reference and discuss in our books.

The Humans of Social Media feature is inspired by the Humans of New York stories, highlighting the experiences and insights of professionals leading the way for others in social media. All disciplines and roles are featured here, from public relations, brand marketing, journalism, entrepreneurship, sports, crisis communications, and analytics, to name a few. These stories, from a diverse group from different backgrounds and experiences, represent the vast array of professional opportunities in the field of social media.

In this second edition of the book, we added some additional questions to the Humans of Social Media feature (e.g., asking about marketable skills to have for social media, walkout music for presentations, etc.) and interviewed some new professionals in their roles.

I would like to thank all of the great professionals who participated in the Humans of Social Media feature, including Deirdre Breakenridge, Chris Strub, Chris Yandle, Jennifer Hartmann, Rich Calabrese, Samantha Hughey, Jeremy Darlow, Dennis Yu, Kerry Flynn, Melissa Agnes, Bella Portaro-Kueber, Adam Ornelas, Adrian Molina, Jared Gaon, Leah Schultz, Mireille Ryan, Tevin Johnson-Campion, Russ Wilde, Mark Murdock, Nick Stover, Miri Rodriquez, Carl Schmid, and Whitney Drake. I am also grateful to Natalie Uhl, Lizelle Lauron, Camille England, Nick Hartledge, Harry Quinn Cedeno, and Emily Hayes for sharing their best advice to students and future professionals who are entering the field. Thank you for taking the time to support this project and share your story with everyone.

Ancillaries and assignments. This textbook's companion workbook, *Portfolio Building Activities in Social Media,* was also very well received, and included more than 50 assignments. For this second edition, the workbook has been updated, and there are now more than 125 assignments and activities, which are categorized into different types, such as individual, group, and workshop/consultation projects.

After reading this book, students will walk away with the knowledge and understanding to not only identify what social media is, but also how to use it strategically today and in the future. Providing resources for students to apply what they have learned and read in the classroom with this book is critical. It's one thing to say you have learned all about social media, but when the rubber meets the road (e.g., when asked to apply for a social media position after graduation), this is where it matters.

The expectations continue to be high for this area of research, practice, and education, but the rewards are endless. In fact, the expectations have risen a lot more since the first edition for professionals entering the field. However, having the right experiences, insights, and opportunities to showcase work, like the activities and assignments presented in this book, will help you achieve your goals and showcase your marketable skills.

THE TEAM BEHIND THE TEAM

There was certainly a team behind this book, and this book couldn't have happened without their support. There are many people I would like to dedicate this book to. First, to my family. You were with me from the very beginning, seeing me type furiously over holidays, breaks, and times with coffee by my side and Ronnie and Rosie (our family Australian Shepherds) next to me keeping me company. Without the support, encouragement, and inspiration for this book, this project wouldn't have happened. A special thank-you as well to the new edition to my Louisville family, Mando Wade, who joined me as I was finalizing the edits to this book. Mando is also an Australian Shepherd, who of course had much to say in making sure I included plenty of Baby Yoda references (his first name is inspired by *The Mandalorian*) and Ryan Reynolds (as his middle name is in reference to his role from *Deadpool*).

I would like to thank Mom (aka the Original Dr. Freberg and inspiration to look up to as a professor) and Dad (Coach Dad from track and field days who has always been my biggest supporter of my work from being a student-athlete to being one of my biggest cheerleaders in my professor life). Look Mom and Dad, another Dr. Freberg has entered the publishing world! Luckily, this book is not going to be covering brain worms (however, if you are interested in learning more about this, check out the original Dr. Freberg's books in psychology and neuroscience). Thank you, Mom and Dad, for your constant support, encouragement, and words of wisdom throughout this journey. This book is dedicated to you both.

Major thanks to my sisters Kristin and Karla, my brother-in-law Scott, and nephew Marcus. You all provided me with constant encouragement, praise, and well wishes, and you made sure I had lots of coffee along the way. Your love and support mean the world to me!

I would like to extend a special thank-you to my predecessor and mentor at the University of Louisville, William Thompson (aka Thompson, as many U of L alums in the Department of Communication refer to him) for his help in getting me into the book business. Without William, I would not have had this wonderful publishing opportunity with SAGE.

Special thanks to the great team at SAGE (my editor Lily and the rest of the amazing team, Sarah, Staci, Vicky, Colleen, and Gagan) for your continued support and help making this second edition come to life!

I also would like to thank the great social media professors community (#SMprofs) for their constant engagement in and inspiration for the field. We are seeing more and more professors come together and dedicate time, resources, and energy toward making the field and classroom experience in social media a wonderful and relevant experience for our students. Thanks to those who have led the way in this area, including Sabrina Page, Amanda Weed, Carolyn Kim, Keith Quesenberry, Stephen Marshall, Jeremy Lipschultz, Gina Luttrell, Adrienne Wallace, Emily Kinsky, Matt Kushin, and the entire #SMprofs group. Thank you for making this a vibrant and wonderful area to teach.

I would also like to thank all of the professors and classes who made the decision to adopt my book. Thank you for your support and sharing the wonderful stories from your classes and students. I greatly appreciate it, and it means the world to me.

In addition, brands have also been super supportive and collaborative over the years for me, helping make the bridge between education and practice even stronger. Without the support of companies like Hootsuite (Hootsuite Academy), HubSpot (HubSpot Academy), Adobe (#EDUMax and Creative Campus), Chipotle, Brown-Forman, Meltwater, Agorapulse, M&Ms Chocolate, Buff City Soap, Cannes Lions, Talkwalker, and Facebook Blueprint to name a few, this task of addressing the professional gap between academia and industry would have been even more challenging. I am grateful to have had these brands collaborate with me and my classes over the years, bringing together some of the insights I have been able to share and discuss in this second edition of SMSC.

A special thank-you to Steve Latham, for your friendship and support for the Cannes Lions Educator Summit. Thank you, Nicole Goldstein, Mark Zeller, and the entire Facebook Blueprint team, for your support and dedication to educators in social media. Sebastian DiStefano and the rest of the Adobe team have been instrumental in providing the opportunities for this educator to learn, grow, and create content that is relevant and strategic for social media practices. Thank you to the entire team at HubSpot Academy for the dedication and commitment HubSpot has placed on educators to be empowered in sharing their stories and experiences in and outside of the classroom. Also, the community of #MarketingTwitter—and the great professionals who I can call friends—is the best. I am so grateful to you all for your generosity and kindness throughout these years and sharing your expertise with my students. Special thanks to Tod Meisner, Adam Ilenich, Adam Molina, Adam Ornelas, Brianne Fleming, Leo Morejon, and Julian Gamboa. You all are amazing colleagues and dear friends!

Of course, I have to give an extra special shout-out to Ryan Reynolds. Yes, that Ryan Reynolds. Thank you for continuing to be a game changer in our industry and showing students how creativity and expanding the social media horizon opens new doors, opportunities, and experiences. Thank you also for following me on Twitter and allowing me to be an honorary member of the X-Force. I will always be on #TeamRyan!

Furthermore, I want to also dedicate this to all of my current and former students. You all are what makes this worthwhile and your work, dedication, and commitment to the field is what makes this truly a remarkable and wonderful experience to give back to the field. Very proud of each and every one of my #FrebergAlums!

I hope you enjoy this book and what it offers to you in your career and classes. Please provide me with feedback and comments. I would love to hear from you all. Together, we can make social media a truly remarkable field and discipline to be in.

Best Wishes,
Karen

Karen Freberg (@kfreberg) is an associate professor of strategic communications at the University of Louisville.

She is also an adjunct faculty member for the integrated marketing communications online graduate program at West Virginia University. Freberg has presented at several U.S. and international research conferences, including in Australia, Brazil, China, Ireland, Greece, Italy, Ireland, Slovenia, Spain, Sweden, the Netherlands, and the United Kingdom. In 2019, she was appointed an associate adjunct instructor during her sabbatical in Australia at the University of the Sunshine Coast.

In addition to presenting at academic conferences, Freberg has presented at professional and trade conferences such as PRSA, Adobe Creative Campus, SXSW EDU, and Cannes Lions, and has given industry workshops and talks on social media trends and strategies to the Dallas Mavericks, Kentucky Organ Donors Affiliates, and Signature Healthcare.

Freberg is also a research consultant in social media and crisis communications and has worked with many organizations and agencies, such as Adobe, Chipotle, Facebook, HubSpot, Breeders' Cup, M&M's Chocolate, Buff City Soap, Brown-Forman, Firestorm Solutions, Hootsuite, Kentucky Derby Festival, IMC Agency, U.S. Department Homeland Security, Centers for Disease Control and Prevention, National Center for Food Protection and Defense, Kentucky Organ Donor Affiliates, and the Colorado Ski Association. As a 2015 Plank Center Fellow for General Motors (GM), Freberg worked with the public relations and social media teams forming best practices and recommendations on social media measurement strategies and influencer marketing practices.

Freberg has coordinated and advised various companies on the areas of social media pedagogy and certification programs, such as Hootsuite (Advanced Social Media Certification and #HootAmb), Meltwater (certification program and contributor), Adobe (EDUMax Thought Leader), HubSpot (education program and podcast), and Facebook Blueprint (subject matter expert).

Along with her teaching, Freberg's research has been published in several book chapters and in academic journals such as *Public Relations Review*, *Media Psychology Review*, *Journal of Contingencies and Crisis Management and Health Communication*. She also serves on the editorial board for *Psychology for Popular Media Culture*, *Corporate Communication*, *Marketing Education Review*, *Journal of Public Relations Research*, and *Case Studies in Strategic Communication*.

Freberg has been interviewed for popular press publications such as *Adweek*, *USA Today*, *USA Today College*, and *Forbes*. Freberg also serves on the executive committee for the PRSA Entertainment and Sports section and on the Technology Chapter Committee for the Commission for Public Relations Education.

Before coming to the University of Louisville, Freberg earned a Ph.D. in communication and information at the University of Tennessee, a master's degree in strategic public relations at the Annenberg School for Communication at the University of Southern California, and a bachelor of science degree in public relations at the University of Florida.

Before her academic career, Freberg was a four-time All-American in the shot put, two-time SEC Champion, and 2004 Olympic Trials finalist.

PART I

FOUNDATION FOR CREATING A STRATEGIC MINDSET

1

INTRODUCTION TO SOCIAL MEDIA

An Art and Science

Learning Objectives

After reading this chapter, you will be able to

- Define social media

- Differentiate between social media platforms

- Explain the evolution of social media over time

- Identify the main considerations for using social media strategically

- Identify the key characteristics of the science and art of social media

INTRODUCTION

Social media is no longer a "fad" that might go away; it is a profession that has matured but still has room to grow. Early on, social media was limited to college students; now, it is a powerhouse medium bringing communities together, breaking down barriers, raising awareness of issues around the world, and creating movements to spark impact. With the tap of a button, we can tweet, snap, and go live with our thoughts, perspectives, and stories for a global audience. We bypass mainstream media to create our own communities and personal identities.

Events that spark on social media can change the field to be more established, diverse, and integrated. It might seem unlikely for a cookie brand to create a movement for real-time engagement, but that's exactly what Oreo did in 2013. During the power outage at the 2013 Super Bowl, Oreo established itself as a digital legend when it tweeted, "You can still dunk in the dark." The tweet inspired other brands to interject themselves into trending events. Brands have since then tried to meet the "Oreo standard" for real time marketing, and several have come close to this, such as Aviation Gin with their famous commercial making fun of Peloton back in 2019. This catapulted the gin company (owned by actor Ryan Reynolds) into the marketing stratosphere of creative, original, and relevant brands to watch in the social and digital space.

Social media allows brands and individuals to create movements and support causes. The 2014 amyotrophic lateral sclerosis (ALS) Ice Bucket Challenge gained momentum on social media from celebrities and everyday people sharing videos of themselves dumping buckets of ice water on their heads to raise awareness for ALS (Braiker, 2014). The $115 million raised by this campaign in 2014 helped scientists discover a new gene tied to ALS (ALS Association, n.d.; Rogers, 2016). In another example, the July 2016 "Brexit" campaign—which promoted United Kingdom citizens voting to exit the European Union—succeeded in part due to social media impact (Singh, 2016). Movements around the world have become synchronous to the power of social media. The 2020 presidential campaign integrated social media across party lines and platforms to persuade audiences to vote for their candidate.

There have been many brands that have found success with utilizing a social first perspective for their strategic communication efforts. Brands such as Aviation Gin, GoFundMe, Lyft, MAC Cosmetics, Match.com, Burger King, Steak-Umm, and Chipotle catapulted their brands into the spotlight thanks to creative partnerships and innovative strategies. Aviation Gin goes against the grain (compared to other liquor brands) by investing in humorous real-time responses to current events (e.g., their Peloton commercial response and Leap Day ad). Steak-Umm unites communities with serious social issue discussions in an entertaining and snarky tone (e.g., their responses to the COVID-19 pandemic). GoFundMe positioned their brand as one that supports issues (ex. fundraising for basic needs, etc.) and their overall purpose. Chipotle gained new audiences by partnering with new communities (e.g., Fortnite and Call of Duty), influencers (e.g., David Dobrik, Mr. Beast, and more), and more. Match.com became a trending topic on social media and catapulted their brand to viral status with their marketing campaign with Maximum Effort celebrating the "match" between 2020 and Satan. Lyft creating a strong presence on TikTok by working with Generation Z audiences to create more brand and cultural awareness for the ride sharing brand. MAC Cosmetics partnered with Whalar and TikTok to create a creator-first campaign called #MoodFlip that created a viral challenge with an original challenge. Burger King, recognizing the impact of COVID-19 on small businesses and restaurants, rented out their Instagram handle for the Christmas holidays in France to support these restaurants, basically giving them free advertisement in tough economic times. As we can see here, all of these examples show the maturation growth of the social media profession, as well as how these campaigns used strategy, innovation through research principles (science), and creative executions (art) to succeed.

Social media has built on its strong foundation to become a staple in our global society. Many schools now offer courses and majors in social media, positioning it alongside marketing, public relations, communications, and more. Social media is an evolving specialization and constant focus within society that continues to expand. Brands, businesses, and universities are realizing the power social media has and how it can be applied for personal branding.

This chapter will discuss social media as a concept, profession, and specialization in the 21st century. Over the course of this book, we will discuss social media tools and the behaviors and strategies behind these tools.

Deirdre Breakenridge, Author, Professor, and CEO of Pure Performance Communications

Introduction

I've been working in public relations and marketing for 30+ years. I started my career focused on media relations and publicity. Today, I'm a chief relationship agent (CRA) and a communications problem-solver to help business professionals tackle their relationship challenges and to build credibility and trust with the public. After a 52+ week research study beginning in 2018, my work in communications also takes a FEEL first approach with a communications model focused on facing **Fears**, having **Empathy**, living with **Ethics**, and unleashing **Love** to build genuine relationships.

How did you get your start in social media?

I wish it was some great epiphany back in 2003. However, my journey began when I experienced an embarrassing situation with a client during a presentation to launch a new tech product. I was an agency owner at the time. My team and I were sharing our PR plan for the launch of load balancer product that required a new media focus.

After we wrapped up our presentation, the CEO of the company looked at me and said, "This is good, but where are all of the new media channels?" Not a good feeling when you thought you delivered the latest strategies and tactics to reach the media and other important stakeholders. From that point forward, my new media/social media research increased tenfold. By 2007, I was working on a manuscript for Financial Times Press called PR 2.0, a book to educate PR professionals on how to bridge the gap between traditional, online, and social media. I didn't

want other pros to experience that "Uh Oh" moment with their clients or executives. The "Ah Ha" moment is always much better.

What is your favorite part of working in your area of expertise in social media?

Social media is one of the best ways to build relationships when you can't meet and collaborate in person. For anyone who says you can't build a relationship through social media, I say, "You're not using social media correctly." There is an incredible amount of intelligence you can gather through social media to help you learn more about people and build a relationship. Social media levels the playing field. It's less about titles and your position and more about like-minded thinking, sharing perspectives, and passionate causes. When you take a peer-to-peer approach (companies must be more human and transparent, too), you can become a trusted resource.

What is one thing you can't live without while working in social media?

Social media is one of the easiest ways for you to connect quickly and collaborate with your colleagues, media, influencers, clients, etc. I can't live without the instantaneous interaction and how I receive answers to important inquiries within minutes. It's that quick DM [direct message] you send to an influencer to participate in a client Facebook Live interview at an industry conference. Or, it's that Facebook message to a colleague when you have a great opportunity to partner on a client account. It's also the ability

(Continued)

(Continued)

for my professional students on LinkedIn to message me after they've taken one of my video courses and want to share feedback. For me, social media has become an indispensable part of my PR and marketing toolkit that helps me to develop, maintain, and build even stronger relationships.

What is your favorite social media account (person/brand/etc.) to follow and why?

Although I really like Instagram and I think Snapchat and TikTok are where you can find Millennials and the bulk of Gen Z, I'm still addicted to Twitter. Approaching the 2020 presidential election, I found myself tapping into the Twitter feeds of several news outlets and political figures who report of the state of our affairs from foreign policy to education, the state of the economy, climate change, and health care. After all, we had a president who used Twitter to announce policy and his stream of consciousness. Because the media is there too, reporting on what's shared, it has become a go-to platform.

What is the most challenging part of working in social media?

The ever-changing media landscape poses a challenge in two ways. First, you always have to be 10 steps ahead of your customers. The media landscape is incredibly fragmented with new social media communities proliferating at a rapid pace. You must stay current on the platforms and understand how and where people connect. Of course, there is only so much time in a day and professionals are always challenged to learn and embrace newer channels.

What is your take on your area of expertise and the social media industry?

Public relations and social media go hand-in-hand. Traditionally, PR people are the storytellers. They are the relationship builders who create the bridges of good will between organizations and their publics. PR professionals are also the brand police who work tirelessly to watch, listen, interpret, maintain, and protect the brand.

Of course, social media takes your brand to new heights of awareness and offers the ability to build a larger digital footprint. At the same time, PR has to be right there communicating effectively on behalf of an organization, while maintaining a trusted reputation, wherever the company and its employees participate. Social media and PR together can propel your brand forward. When you fuse the power of community and relationships with collaborative technology, the result is stronger bonds, customer loyalty, and brand advocacy.

What do you wish you had known when you were starting out?

Don't take anything too personally, and always remember whatever happens and whatever is said may not be about you. When you have interactions with people in your personal life or throughout your career, what they say and how they react have more to do with their own personal or professional situations and what they're going through.

To my peers and younger professionals: Remove your emotional self and be more of an observer of any situation. Because social media is an important part of our lives both personally and professionally, remember that you'll collaborate with many inspiring individuals and you'll grow from those relationships. Also, keep in mind that there will be uneasy and tense interactions that make you take pause. Try to remember to step back, remove your personal emotional self, ask a lot of questions, walk in someone else's shoes, and learn from the situation.

What are three marketable skills a social media professional needs to have to work in the industry?

The first is emotional intelligence. Professionals who show up with emotional intelligence on social media will foster deeper relationships. Because they have a better handle on their own emotions, they'll be able to manage the behaviors of others.

The second skill is adaptability. Because technology and media are changing so quickly, the professionals who are flexible, quick to learn, and include new technologies into their workflow will do well.

The last skill is hands-on experience with data and analytics. Professionals who can capture and analyze data are valuable assets to an organization. They will not only be able to prove value in a social media program, but also improve brand communication based on the data they analyze and use moving forward.

Where do you go to keep up to date with trends and continue learning about social media?

As a LinkedIn Learning Instructor, of course, I'll say LinkedIn Learning is a great platform that keeps me "in the know" with communications, business, and leadership video courses. I follow industry blogs and online publications including SmartBrief, Spin Sucks, PR News, PR Daily, CommPRO.biz, HubSpot, to name a few. Podcasts are also an excellent avenue for learning with a few of my go-to shows including Maximize Your Social Influence, Social Media Marketing, and Marketing Over Coffee.

If you had to choose a song to walk out to in a presentation on social media, what would it be and why?

My song would be "Have It All," by Jason Mraz.

Deirdre Breakenridge is an award-winning public relations practitioner, educator, and author. She can be contacted via Twitter at @dbreakenridge, and her website is www.deirdrebreakenridge.com.

HOW DO WE DEFINE SOCIAL MEDIA?

Social media has been defined, classified, and conceptualized in probably a million different ways. Wherever you go, there is a new term, definition, or way of looking at social media. Every discipline wants to own the term and its definition. Every industry wants to control the duties assigned to social media. Social media is a powerful yet transdisciplinary profession, requiring an understanding of all integrated perspectives, approaches, and views.

Historically and from an academic perspective, social media combines "a wide range of online, word-of-mouth forums including blogs, company sponsored discussion boards and chat rooms, consumer-to-consumer e-mail, consumer product or service rating websites and forums, Internet discussion boards and forums, [and] microblogs" (Mangold & Faulds, 2009). Social media is about people (Marken, 2007), and the technology not only provides means for establishing and maintaining relationships but also allows users to create their own (user-generated) content to share with others in the online community (Waters, Burnett, Lamm, & Lucas, 2009).

Some of the content that individuals share with others in their online networks includes information regarding news events, updates on personal and professional achievements, and multimedia content. Social media has "amplified the power of consumer-to-consumer conversations in the marketplace by enabling one person to communicate with literally hundreds or thousands of other consumers quickly and with relatively little effort" (Mangold & Faulds, 2009, p. 361). As a result, official messages are competing for consumer attention with many other sources of information.

Some professionals classify it as a group of social networks that allow conversations and relationships to emerge. Others focus on the community aspect in which people are able to converse together in a centralized location to collaborate and initiate dialogue. All of these are key characteristics of social media, but in any case, keep in mind that this definition will need to be fluid and adaptive to the growing list of tools, features, and changes we are seeing in this particular space. For the purposes of this textbook, one way to define **social media** is that it can

> provide a personalized, online networked hub of information, dialogue, and relationship management. These new communication technology tools allow individual users and organizations to engage with, reach, persuade, and target key audiences more effectively across multiple platforms. Industry professionals, scholars, and social media users have contributed a number of different definitions and conceptualizations of the concept of social media. Some emphasize the role of social media as a toolkit that allows users to create and share content. Others focus on how social media extend Web 2.0 technologies to bring communities together. (Freberg, 2016, p. 773)

The overall functions of social media are not limited to communicating messages designed by professionals for audiences, in parallel to message construction in traditional media. In addition, social media allows users to participate to an extent not seen previously in traditional media. Increased empowerment of the individual stakeholder leads to greater feelings of control over a situation and a willingness to help others in the community, which could potentially be used by brands and corporations to engage with audiences, formulate message strategies, and evaluate their own reputation in the eyes of their online audience members.

With these new shifts in power and breakdown in barriers, brands are expected to listen and respond to stakeholder concerns in new ways. Recognizing the influence of social media provides professionals with the opportunity to use social media strategically to discover potential issues relevant to their stakeholders, to prepare for different scenarios and situations, to implement online communication strategically, and to evaluate results of communications in real time.

In addition, social media platforms serve as gateways where content and conversations are created and ignited between individuals, brands, organizations, and nations. Essentially, social media platforms provide first-impression management tools for corporations and individuals to showcase their own brands and reputations. Although individual social media platforms may be somewhat separated at times from others, they are all part of the same ecosystem. Each platform has its own features, dynamic characteristics, and community attributes, but they are integrated with the organization, brand, or individual's persona online. In addition, they are also one part of the overall communication mix of media channels that can be utilized to share information, establish communities, and formulate relationships for a brand. Earned, paid, shared, and owned media have converged to formulate this new ecosystem of communities and networks. Social media is more than just a set of tools to use; it is also a larger network of communities tied together through virtual and offline connections.

All of the various platforms that make up this social media ecosystem can be quite daunting to visualize. As shown in Figure 1.1, JESS3 and Brian Solis created an infographic outlining the conversation prism of all of the social media platforms out there for users, businesses, and organizations to take advantage of (JESS3, n.d.).

Essentially, this infographic highlights the various platforms available as well as categorizes them based on the function they serve. Note, this infographic is relatively "old" in social media standards, but the key concepts are still important. This is different from most of the other visualizations out there for social media, which focus more on the application of the social media platform rather than the specific type of platform.

Several other defining characteristics should be noted when it comes to social media. Each of these computer-based applications and platforms allows users to share and create information, disseminate ideas in various forms, share content, and respond to these pieces of content. In addition, each platform allows you to create your own personal identity with a picture or avatar. An avatar is acceptable to use on certain platforms, but most individuals use one consistent photo across all of their respective accounts online. This is done for several reasons, but a prominent one is to establish a proactive positive **online reputation.**

Figure 1.1   Social Media Conversation Prism

Source: Jesse Thomas (JESS3) / Brian Solis

In addition, there is a possibility for these pieces of content (videos, images, posts, updates, etc.) to go viral. **Virality**, or rapid dissemination of information from person to person, is one way in which news, stories, and updates reach across various networks in a short amount of time.

There are various examples of a post, update, story, or even video becoming viral. Some platforms, like Facebook, allow this to happen much more easily since the content is shared within the platform itself. In 2016, Chewbacca Mask Mom became famous when she filmed herself on Facebook Live wearing a Chewbacca mask from Kohl's (Eordogh, 2016). Her laugh became contagious, and everyone began sharing this video. It became the most watched and viral Facebook Live video ever in 2016 with over 130 million views (Eordogh, 2016). We have also seen brands get their moments in the spotlight by engaging with their biggest fans. Let's take Ocean Spray for example. When TikTok user Nathan Apodaca filmed himself on his skateboard drinking a bottle of Ocean Spray while Fleetwood Mac's song "Dreams" was playing, it became a viral hit. Not only did the challenge go viral with the CEO of Ocean Spray and Fleetwood Mac joining as well, it also reintroduced both Ocean Spray and Fleetwood Mac to a younger audience, making the song hit most of the top played music charts and having Ocean Spray bottles selling out at stores. All of this can be attributed to social media. As a result, this case study has become an iconic commercial for TikTok in showing how it all starts on their platform (the campaign is called It Starts on TikTok).

In other cases, brands have used certain platforms, such as TikTok, to go viral. E.L.F. Cosmetics found by attaching their videos to popular songs and posting them on TikTok, their products sales increased significantly (Flora, 2020). Even newspapers have gotten notoriety for their work going viral on TikTok, including *The Washington Post* with Dave Jorgenson ("21 Inspiring Brands on TikTok to Fuel Your Creative Strategy," n.d.). Jorgenson stated that the success of creating viral content for *The Washington Post* has been due not only to the type of content they share but also the nature of the platform:

> The metaphor that I use often is we've been invited to this dinner party
> by TikTok, TikTok is the host, and TikTok is a really good cook and
> they do everything right. We just got invited and we don't want to walk
> into the house and say "Hey, this is how you cook your steak." We might
> bring a bottle of wine and be like "Hey, we brought this to help make
> the meal better, and we also have some new jokes you haven't heard."
> (*"The Washington Post* Has a Surprisingly Popular TikTok Account," n.d.)

The overall fundamental use and motive behind social media has been to establish personal connections with others and tell our stories virtually. Why do we share what we share online for the world to see? What motivates us to create content for others to see? Think about the last time you used social media—what did you share? Why did you share it on a particular platform?

It's important to explore not only where you shared this information, but how and why you decided to share it with one person, a few people, or everyone in your respective communities. Sometimes, what you share, post, comment, and discuss on various social media platforms is not just for your friends but for the entire world to see. What you say on social media is public and can be used as documentation. Each action taken on social media has a specific purpose—whether we are creating the content ourselves or consuming the content to be shared with our communities. Yet we also have the power to comment on and engage with the content as we see fit.

Some fundamental characteristics make social media unique compared to other types of media platforms. First, the platforms are web- and mobile-based applications. Most of the rising applications are mobile based to fit the growing trend for more mobile capabilities without a desktop- or web-specific requirement like Snapchat, TikTok, Instagram, WhatsApp, and others have done.

Second, the power of **user-generated content (UGC)** is a prominent characteristic of why businesses and individuals like social media. UGC is content that is created directly by a user. This could be a video that you created over the holidays showcasing your zip-lining experience over the Costa Rica terrain with a GoPro camera, or even an infographic outlining the main items to bring to the Kentucky Derby, SXSW, or Coachella. UGC is not the only type of content that can be created on social media; for example, there is **branded content** (BC or brand storytelling), which a lot of businesses create. This type of content allows brands to emerge as their own media outlets and create their own content uniquely aligned with their goals, mission, and brand voice. We have seen this for various brands, especially in the entertainment industry. Take the Netflix show *Emily in Paris*, for example. The star of the show (Emily, who is played by actress Lilly Collins) works in marketing and social media, but the show has its own handle on Instagram (@emilyinparis) like the character does in the show. Why is this an effective strategy? This can help brands create advocates or brand ambassadors to help pass along these pieces of branded content (or assets) to other communities around the world. Social media provides an open and dynamic online community. Individuals and corporations can participate in various communities linked together by similar interests and backgrounds. These communities can brainstorm ideas, share perspectives, and engage in dialogue to formulate networking relationships.

For example, Hootsuite, a global social media management company based in Vancouver, Canada, has created a brand ambassadorship program for users around the world to share their stories and experiences openly and to connect with other potential users and stakeholders in social media (Photo 1.1). Other companies (such as Fast, IBM, Applegate, and Public) have similar programs to bring together fans, customers, and loyal advocates for the brand to establish a community. Adobe, for example, has created an ambassador program in two different areas of the company. Adobe Insiders, a group of professionals across the social media and marketing industry, focuses on using their platforms to share insights, stories, and experiences using Adobe products for their work. Adobe Education Leaders make up educators who are at all levels in a program that focuses on creativity, education, and bringing together ideas and perspectives in and out of the classroom.

Let's build something great together

As Hootsuite spreads its wings across the globe, we meet people who are passionate about our product. Explore our Community programs and find out how you can help bring our brand to the globe.

Hootsuite Ambassadors

Passionate about social media? So are we. That's why we invite our most passionate fans and expert users to join our Ambassador program, where they get to showcase their social media expertise and help us deliver a better product. Check out what they're up to: #HootAmb

▶ **Photo 1.1** Hootsuite Ambassador Program

Source: Hootsuite Inc., https://www.hootsuite.com/community/ambassador-program

Social media has been characterized as distinguished compared to other forms of media due to the power of its real-time content creation and the level of engagement it offers to users across many respective platforms. That said, social media provides a range of different opportunities, challenges, and experiences for users to take part in, such as the following:

- Dialogue on a one-to-one, one-to-many, and many-to-many format in real time

- New relationships, connections, and professional and personal opportunities for your personal brand

- Visual and immersive storytelling through video, live video, photos, and other multimedia content

- Providing awareness of the brand voice, story, and people behind the scenes

- Sparking creativity with communities through challenges that can go viral in popularity

- Becoming a resource for education, training, and support for the community

- Entertaining through memes and video content that capture current trends and views on topics in society

- Initiating behaviors and call-to-action statements for audiences to note

- Sending persuasive messages that are strategically targeted using advertising and personalized data

- Responding immediately to customer inquiries and providing updates on crisis situations

One of the most important things to be aware of is that the definition as well as the statistics, practices, and strategies of social media will change on a frequent basis. You do not need to have all of the answers or even know all of the platforms in play. If you try to learn every single change that happens with each platform, that will become your life as a social media professional. However, it is important to note you may be asked to come up with your own definition of social media, per se, so think about the defining characteristics, features, and overall attributes that make up this dynamic and evolving set of platforms.

HOW HAS SOCIAL MEDIA EVOLVED?

Social media is still a very young profession and industry, even though it has matured substantially over the years. At each stage, expanded sets of features have been added to meet the increasing expectations of audiences. With each new feature being implemented by one platform, others follow and sometimes take the idea and incorporate it into their own version. Google launched Google+ (RIP) to compete with Facebook. Instagram created Instagram Stories to compete with Facebook. Instagram added Reels to compete with TikTok. LinkedIn jumped on the Stories bandwagon to compete with TikTok, Snapchat, YouTube, Facebook, and Instagram. TikTok was rebranded from the success of Musical.ly. Facebook is offering a Jobs feature to compete with LinkedIn. LinkedIn offers LinkedIn Live to compete with Facebook and Twitter live video features. YouTube features Stories to compete with Facebook, Instagram, and Snapchat. Facebook bought GIPHY, which brings questions on whether or not platforms like Twitter and Snapchat can still use them. Clubhouse, the social audio platform that offers exclusive invites, has faced its own competition in the social audio space with Twitter adding Spaces, and Instagram opening up their Live Room features on the platform.

Okay, did you get that? So many different platforms competing with each other—it's essentially a digital media soap opera. Or, think of it as a battle in Game of Thrones: Social Media Edition. Every platform is out there to buy, conquer, and get as much digital real estate as possible to garner the most attention and use time.

The Current State of Social Media

Social media platforms are in constant flux and evolution, and managing the change in those platforms could become your job in addition to your other responsibilities. Keep in mind that you want to take a tier system approach to looking at social media in general. Social media platforms are divided by function and overall purpose. However, most social media platforms are indexed, edited, and revised over time, as well as categorized and searchable online through search engines. Some of the main types of social media platforms are wikis (e.g., Wikipedia), blogs (e.g., WordPress, Medium, and Blogger), video conferencing platforms (Google MeetMe, Facebook Messenger Rooms and Messenger, Zoom, BlueJeans, Microsoft Teams), collaborative crowdsourcing sites (e.g., Google Drive, Dropbox, Slack, Asana, Trello, and Box), messaging (e.g., WhatsApp, WeChat, Messenger), micro-blogging (e.g., Twitter and Weibo), live streaming (e.g., Twitch, Facebook Live, Instagram Live, LinkedIn Live, and going live on TikTok), mobile-based platforms (e.g., TikTok, Dispo, Snapchat, and Instagram), social audio (e.g., Clubhouse, Twitter Spaces, etc.), podcasts (e.g., Soundcloud, Anchor, Apple Podcasts, etc.), and business networking (e.g., LinkedIn), to name a few.

Facebook, the largest social media platform in the world, is an example of a **social networking site (SNS).** Social networking sites can be defined as "(1) web-based services that allow individuals to construct a public or semi-public profile within a bounded system, (2) articulate a list of other users with whom they share a connection, and (3) view and traverse their list of connections and those made by others within the system" (boyd & Ellison, 2008, p. 211). Using an SNS, an individual can control personal information to share with others. Users can also affiliate with businesses and large organizations that have a presence on these sites by adding them as "friends" (Boyd, 2006).

Twitter, on the other hand, allows individuals and brands to create, curate, and communicate information in real time in a limited number of characters. Twitter allows users to push content to their followers that can include textual information, hyperlinks, images, videos, and even interactive GIFs for entertainment, information, and conversation purposes. Users can also participate in chat sessions surrounding particular common interests and topics by following a hashtag, which is a keyword preceded by a # sign to allow users to track and follow certain conversations. Many corporations presently have integrated a branded hashtag to help manage their reputation (e.g., Cinnabon, Star Wars, Pixar, and Popeyes), as well as embracing user-generated hashtags from their community. Some examples of branded hashtags include #EmilyInParis (for Netflix's *Emily in Paris* show), #LifeNeedsFrosting (e.g., Cinnabon), and #VPDebate or #Election2020 (2020 Election and Debates). Corporations are able to monitor, track, and evaluate the success of a hashtag within a campaign through social media monitoring platforms and analytics using an application programming interface (API). Using API, corporations can create tools and software programs to work with Twitter. In addition, users can get content out to audiences who are not part of the community with the use of hashtags for key terms on trending topics, news items, community events, and industry-related issues.

Visual and "snackable" content forms such as Instagram and Snapchat are emerging as dominant platforms among users, particularly in the younger generations of audience members. These two platforms are constantly challenging each other with their features. Facebook tried to buy Snapchat in 2013 for $3 billion (Fiegerman, 2014), which caused the social networking giant to continue advancing Instagram (which it bought in 2012) with similar features to compete with Snapchat. Since then, Instagram has grown not only in popularity but in features that make it competitive in the social media landscape. Going live, having stickers supporting causes, raising money, and shopping capabilities are just some of the features that have been added. However, TikTok has risen in popularity as a visual and snackable content that combines music, entertainment, and culture. Creators, influencers, and brands have all flocked to the platform to capture the virality and presence the platform has among certain audiences, such as Generation Z. Other platforms are somewhat embracing a mobile yet exclusive visual experience with invitations, such as Dispo, which is a visual first platform that shares snapshots, but taking a more simplistic approach in sharing visual content. This social platform, which was founded by influencer David Dobrik and colleagues, is considered to be the "anti-Instagram", where it forces users to post pictures, but are not allowed to add a caption explaining the photo.

Make sure you are on the main platforms being discussed and highlighted in society (see Table 1.1). In this case, Facebook, Twitter, Instagram, YouTube, LinkedIn, Snapchat, and TikTok are some of the most familiar. Each of these key platforms has set forth some interesting advances and experienced changes throughout its history within the industry.

Table 1.1 Key Players in Social Media			
Platform	**Founded**	**CEO**	**Key Features**
Facebook	February 2004	Mark Zuckerberg	Profile, News Feed, Groups, Events, Video, Photos, Search, Messenger, Pages, Video Meetings
Instagram	October 2010	Kevin Systrom	Profiles, Business Pages, Layout, Boomerang, Instagram Live, Stickers (Donations, Music, Shopping, Reels), GIFs, Shopping, Live Rooms
LinkedIn	March 2003	Ryan Roslansky	Business Profiles, Pages, Groups, Lynda, LinkedIn Live, LinkedIn Stories
Twitter	March 2006	Jack Dorsey	Profile, Newsfeed, Live Video, Images, GIFs, Fleets, Spaces
YouTube	March 2005	Susan Wojcicki	Video, YouTube Red, YouTube Live
Snapchat	September 2011	Evan Spiegel	Snaps, Snapchat My Story, Live Stories, Discover, Spectacles, Lens Studio
TikTok	2012	Kevin Mayer	Feed, Challenges, Filters, Music, Effects, Live

With the key players in social media, it is important to note that each of these platforms has evolved and had some significant milestones as a company. Some have been bought, transformed, and evolved through the years. Table 1.2 presents some of the main milestones for each platform.

Table 1.2 Major Milestones for Key Players in Social Media	
Platform	**Major Timeline Events**
Facebook (newsroom.fb.com/company-info/)	• February 4, 2004: Facebook is founded by Mark Zuckerberg along with Dustin Moskovitz, Chris Hughes, and Eduardo Saverin • March 1, 2004: Facebook expands from Harvard to Stanford, Columbia, and Yale • September 1, 2004: Facebook Wall is launched • 2005: Photo uploading option is offered • April 1, 2006: Mobile is launched • February 9, 2009: Like button is introduced • September 22, 2011: Timeline is introduced • April 9, 2012: Facebook buys Instagram for $1 billion • February 19, 2014: Facebook buys WhatsApp • March 25, 2014: Facebook buys Oculus Rift • March 25, 2015: Messenger is launched • September 25, 2015: Facebook 360 video is launched • December 3, 2015: Live video for profiles is launched • February 24, 2016: Facebook Reactions is launched • June 9, 2016: Facebook 360 photos are available • October 16, 2016: Workplace by Facebook is introduced • October 8, 2018: Portal is introduced • March 2020: Facebook introduces measures and features to support small businesses impacted by COVID-19 • May 2020: Facebook purchases GIPHY for $400 million
Instagram (instagram-press.com/our-story/)	• October 6, 2010: Instagram is launched • April 9, 2012: Facebook buys Instagram • June 30, 2013: Instagram video is launched • December 2013: Instagram Direct is launched • August 26, 2014: Hyperlapse is launched • March 23, 2015: Layout from Instagram is introduced • September 1, 2015: Improvements are added for Instagram Direct • October 22, 2015: Boomerang is introduced • August 2, 2016: Instagram Stories is introduced • August 31, 2016: Zoom is introduced • January 24, 2017: Live Stories are available globally

(Continued)

Table 1.2   (Continued)

Platform	Major Timeline Events
	• August 31, 2017: Live Stories are available on the web
	• January 23, 2018: GIF Stickers are introduced
	• February 1, 2018: Type Mode in Stories is introduced
	• 2019: Instagram introduces cyberbullying, shopping, and AR filter tools
	• 2019: Instagram introduces Reels first in Brazil, and then more than 50 countries in 2020
	• May 2020: Instagram introduces Challenges
	• March 2021: Instagram introduces Live Rooms
Twitter (about.twitter.com/en_us/company.html)	• March 21, 2006: Jack Dorsey sends out his first tweet
	• March 2007: Twitter makes a splash at SXSW Interactive
	• August 2007: First Twitter hashtag is proposed by Chris Messina
	• April 2010: Promoted Tweets are launched
	• June 2010: Promoted Trends are launched
	• May 2011: Twitter buys TweetDeck
	• June 2012: Twitter receives a new design
	• January 2013: Twitter launches Vine
	• November 2013: Twitter files for initial public offering (IPO)
	• August 2014: Promoted Video is launched
	• January 2015: Direct Messages and mobile video are introduced
	• March 2015: Twitter buys Periscope
	• October 2015: Twitter launches Moments and Polls
	• January 2016: Periscope is embedded in tweets
	• November 2017: Twitter allows tweets to grow from 140 characters to 280 characters
	• 2019: Introduces bookmarks and dark mode features
	• 2020: Twitter launches Audio tweets
	• 2020: Twitter releases Fleets to audiences, adding another platform incorporating stories
	• 2021: Twitter releases Spaces to compete in the social audio space
LinkedIn (about.linkedin.com/)	• May 2003: LinkedIn is launched
	• April 2007: LinkedIn reaches 10 million users
	• February 2008: LinkedIn launches mobile version
	• January 2011: LinkedIn launches IPO
	• May 3, 2012: LinkedIn buys SlideShare
	• April 9, 2015: LinkedIn buys Lynda.com
	• June 13, 2016: Microsoft buys LinkedIn
	• 2019: LinkedIn Live is available in beta form
	• May 2020: LinkedIn Stories are available

Platform	Major Timeline Events
YouTube (www.youtube.com)	• February 14, 2005: YouTube is created and founded by Chad Hurley, Steve Chen, and Jawed Karim • November 2005: YouTube has its first million-hit video with Nike • February 2006: YouTube negotiates deal with NBC • November 13, 2006: Google buys YouTube for $1.65 billion • May 2007: YouTube launches Partner Program • June 2007: YouTube hosts presidential debate with CNN • August 2007: YouTube launches ads • August 2009: Usher and Justin Bieber video is posted • January 2010: Movie rentals are available • July 2012: Olympics are available to live stream • December 2012: "Gangnam Style" hits 1 billion views • 2014–2016: Creation of YouTube Red • April 2020: PewDiePie is the most followed YouTube account with 104 million subscribers • 2020: YouTube marks 2 billion users on the platform
Snapchat (www.snapchat.com)	• September 2011: Snapchat is initially released • October 2013: My Story is launched • May 2014: Video Chat is launched • September 2016: Snapchat is rebranded to Snap Inc. • September 2016: Snapchat Spectacles are introduced • March 2017: Snapchat files for IPO • 2017: Snapchat launches SnapMap • 2019: Snapchat launches Lens Studio
TikTok (www.tiktok.com)	• Musical.ly founded by Alex Zhu and Luyu Yang in 2014 • 2016: Music.ly claims 70 million downloads • September 2016: ByteDance merged to create new app and rebrand it • ByteDance purchased Music.ly in November 2017 for almost $1 billion • 2018: Available in 154 markets and in 75 languages • 2019: Fourth most popular app downloaded in 2019 and 800 million users worldwide • 2020: Charli D'Amelio becomes the first creator to hit 100 million followers on TikTok • September 2020: TikTok works with Oracle and Walmart for U.S. presence to not get banned • 2021: Oracle and Walmart collaboration is put on hold until further notice • 2021: Possible opportunities to schedule TikToks on platform are discussed

Sources: Facebook, Instagram, Twitter, LinkedIn, YouTube, TikTok, and Snapchat.

Who "Owns" Social Media?

Indeed, a lot of marketing professionals, PR practitioners, communication scholars, and others have discussed and proposed an argument for why their discipline should "own" social media. Everyone wants to claim ownership of the social media discipline and profession (it's almost like the Iron Throne from *Game of Thrones*), yet not every profession knows how to make the most of the emerging platforms. Each profession may know how to use social media specifically for its industry or discipline, but it may not be aware of the vast possibilities or ways in which others are using it.

There are many answers to this question, and this has arisen at many professional conferences, academic sessions, and discussions online. Some would say marketing has ownership of social media from a business and analytical standpoint. Marketing most of the time has the finances and support needed to provide businesses and organizations with the means for creating, disseminating, and analyzing the content and how well it is received. Yet some would say the platforms themselves "own" social media. Social media is not like traditional media in a way that we would classify it on the media spectrum, but there has been a shift in the "pay-to-play" model, essentially forcing users and corporations to pay for their content to be seen by the right target audience at a specific time on their platform. Both Google and Facebook have led the way in this area and have forced this transformation, which has led to this current paid content model for social media.

There is a difference, of course, between owned media platforms (e.g., blogs) and earned or shared media platforms (e.g., social media). One way to approach the difference between these types of media is to recognize that one is controlled by the user and the other is controlled by others. Blogs essentially are controlled by individual users who are given the opportunity to decide how their page should look, what content to share, and whether or not they want comments to appear. The power of control is quite prominent, and one way to think about it is like owning a house. You can do whatever you want to it. On the other hand, social media is somewhat controllable by the user or brand, but the user or brand is somewhat "renting" the space like an apartment. There are terms of service agreements to follow, and the platform has the opportunity to change these agreements, switch up the features and designs, or even shut down its services.

So, with everything being said, who "owns" social media?

The answer is no one owns social media. Social media is open for everyone to use, create, share, engage, and come together on. No discipline is the primary owner of social media. All disciplines need to collaborate and work together. Most of the time, social media is its own department, where it works with others internally and externally. The barrier of entry is minimal, and the opportunity to be part of many diverse communities has never been more accessible for professionals, businesses, and organizations.

The correct question would be who collaborates with social media, and who needs to know social media? The answer to this question is simple: Everyone works with and needs to know social media.

USING SOCIAL MEDIA STRATEGICALLY

Social media can be for personal use, but you can also use it professionally. Many times, we see how a group uses it for one community it is interacting with, but we forget how this is perceived from other perspectives. On social media, you need to find the balance that allows you to interact and create content that educates and informs your professional audiences of your level of expertise and thought leadership, but you also want to be personal enough so you are not perceived as a robot. There is a fine line between these two worlds, and that is why it is important to use social media strategically and effectively based on your own needs and expectations in the field. Each person is different—there are certain etiquette and professional guidelines to follow and review, but you have to be confident in knowing your own community, voice, and presence online. Social media is all about first impressions, and you want to make sure your name stands out for the right reasons.

Which Social Media Platforms Should I Use?

Choosing the right platforms for your role comes down to a few factors. First and foremost, you do not have to be on every single platform. As presented in Figure 1.2, Facebook still remains the most popular social media platform, followed by YouTube, WhatsApp, and Messenger. Yet, like all reports on social media, once content is published, it is out of date and has not accounted for other mobile-based platforms (e.g., TikTok) gaining traction within the community and in society.

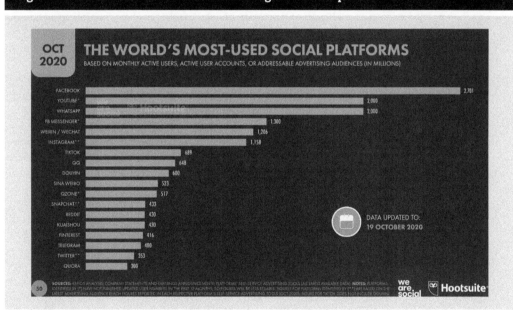

Figure 1.2   We Are Social and Hootsuite Digital 2020 Report

Source: Hootsuite & We Are Social (2019), "Digital 2019 Global Digital Overview," retrieved from https://wearesocial.com/blog/2020/04/digital-around-the-world-in-april-2020

To choose a particular platform, a social media professional must consider the following:

Audiences. Make sure to look first to where your audiences are going. Who are these individuals, and where are they having their conversations? You will of course be able to collect some information from these audiences (demographics, etc.); think about the amount of information Facebook has collected about you over the years from likes, comments, shares, and even videos watched. In addition to clear demographic points, understanding the lifestyle, opinions, interests, and behaviors (otherwise known as psychographics) of audiences is a key indicator for understanding our audiences more effectively.

Purpose. Platforms will continue to compete with each other to grab the attention and number of users from other platforms. Take the example of Facebook, which acquired Instagram for $1 billion and has transformed it into a dominant multimedia platform. Yet when Facebook wanted to buy Snapchat as well, Snapchat said no. As a result, Facebook has tried to copy various features of the mobile application for its own platform, ranging from filters on Instagram to the Messenger app. Each platform essentially has a specific function and audience in mind. Not all platforms are equal or founded on the same vision or principles. As time goes by, the competition among these brands for eyeballs and usage will only become bigger and more prominent.

For a social media professional, not only is understanding the functions and specifics of the tools important, but so is understanding the behaviors and reasons why people are using these tools in the first place. Each platform has a different overall purpose, as well as trustworthiness factor, whether it involves getting news, creating personal content, engaging in customer service, sharing negative experiences or responding to a crisis, sharing and creating stories, or initiating a call to action to drive sales, strengthen reputation, and build on an established community.

Relationships. Identifying the current state of relationships between users on social media platforms is crucial at first. Some users will be your biggest fans and want to be on every platform you are on. However, some users may just want to be on one channel with you based on your brand voice there. This has to be determined and thought out carefully to make sure you are spending the appropriate time, resources, and engagement necessary to foster these relationships as proactively as possible. When it comes to being on social media, you want a strategy in place for why you have a presence on each platform. Your network is indeed your net worth, and there is no better way to connect, engage, and proactively seek out professionals in the field. #MarketingTwitter for example is a great way to start to learn, engage, and be active in the community to meet some of the game changers in the social and digital industry.

Personality. Determining the platform you feel best establishes the personal voice for your business, organization, and even individual brand is something to consider and keep in mind. Certain platforms will feel more natural to you, but try to utilize each platform consistently to present a comprehensive brand across the board. Everyone wants the power to showcase who they are and why they are unique.

Showcasing your personality could come in a variety of different forms, from creating content on platforms like Instagram or TikTok to showing videos about various trends and daily activities (e.g., Gary Vaynerchuk and his #DailyVee shows on YouTube, or creator David Dobrik with his videos and short clips on TikTok). Other professionals in the industry showcase their personality based on the content and insights they share. Social media professionals such as Nat Balda (WhatsApp), Jenn Crim (Grand Ole Opry) share insights on what it is like to work in the social media industry for students. Jess Zafarris (*Adweek*) has created unique insights on what certain industry words mean and define them in creative and informative videos on TikTok. In addition, Brittani Warrick, a social media strategist who has helped her aunt (singer Dionne Warwick) embrace Twitter and social media for her brand, shares her strategy through visuals and threads on Twitter. Brands have to showcase their personality with content showing not only what they are doing but also what they can do to become a resource for their respective audience members. White papers, e-books, webinars, blog posts, podcasts, and even Twitter chat sessions are just some of the methods that are highlighted and expanded upon for brands.

Content. The new model for content creation and marketing on social media has shifted from just pushing content for the sake of self-promotion to becoming more personalized, interactive, and focused on storytelling. Develop the messages and pieces of content that your audiences want. The ideal situation is to think about pieces of content your audiences want, but do not realize they want, from you. This will take some additional brainstorming sessions and strategic planning in order to uncover the messages, pieces of content, and stories to showcase on social media. If you have strong content, this will allow you to become known as a resource for your **thought leadership**. Brands, individuals, and organizations can become thought leaders in their area as they continue to produce, share, and create content as a go-to resource for innovative ideas; persuade people to take action in response to their created content; and are viewed as trusted sources of information in their area. Social and digital publications such as Morning Brew, The Next Web, Fast Company, Digiday, and more are thought of as resources to get news out about trends in the industry, but many social media professionals become contributors to publications such as *Adweek*, *Social Media Today*, and *Forbes* to showcase their thought leadership and expertise on various topics in the industry.

Some pieces of content will resonate with an audience on one platform rather than another. You do not always want to post the same content across all platforms. There are some combinations that will work (e.g., Instagram and Facebook with videos), but you want to repurpose and reformat content that is designated with a particular community, platform capabilities, and purpose in mind. In addition, the content needs not only to reflect on the brand's voice but also to connect with the audience in terms of user expectations from a brand using this platform.

Innovativeness. Users want to be part of a platform that continues to raise the bar for what a social media platform should be. Responding to user audiences and suggestions is another focus these platforms have to be aware of. People have noticed that Facebook has copied a lot of its new features from other platforms like Snapchat. Yet other platforms have been willing (or at least appeared willing) to listen to their audience members' suggestions for new features. In December 2016, Twitter CEO Jack Dorsey went on social media and asked Twitter users what they would like to see in the New Year on the microblogging platform. While this came at a time when Twitter was challenged with key personnel leaving and advertisement and metrics dropping, it was better late than never. Adam Mosseri, Head of Instagram, is active on Twitter and Instagram making sure he is able to answer questions and provide updates on new features on the platform for audiences and get their feedback. One of the benefits to platforms like Twitter is the opportunity to not only get access to breaking news but also connect with the game changers in the field immediately, bypassing some of the traditional gatekeepers pre–social media.

Analytics. Data will of course be your friend when it comes to engaging with content and audiences on social media, depending on the platforms in question. You will be able to determine the time, frequency, responses, and views you will get. These data and insights will help you determine when it is appropriate to post content and share videos, and even how long a response people expect from a customer comment on social media. In addition, analytics and data will help you determine at the end how well you (or your team) did in addressing the question, challenge, or content created for a campaign. Most of the links, updates, and conversations are archived online and available for collection either through the native measurement platforms on the platform itself or through a third-party service.

Actions. After we have an idea of the audience we want to engage with based on user activity level, we can determine some of the actions these individuals take to participate in our communities online.

Ultimately, you want to take all of these important factors into consideration to determine whether or not you want to be on particular social media platforms. One way to do this is by thoroughly identifying which platforms you are currently using (inventory), determining how well they are performing (audit), and making a choice on what to do with each platform (decision action steps) as outlined in Table 1.3.

Table 1.3 Performance and Decision Action Audit	
Activity Level	**Actions**
Inventory + Benchmark Audit	• Identify key audiences and where they are in their relationship with the client (organization, business, agency, etc.) on social media
	• Identify the rationale for why they are on each platform (e.g., to be educated, consume content, gain insights, build communities, or host events and promotions)
	• Evaluate each platform to determine audience, content, relationships, analysis of brand voice, and overall purpose
Evaluation (Short-Term and Long-Term Impacts)	• Look at each platform to determine how well it is doing in terms of its KPIs (key performance indicators) and the overall health of the brand community, voice, and investment
	• Evaluate the longevity of the platforms that are aligned with the brand's mission and business objectives, and determine which platforms to keep and which ones to vote off "social media island" (aka shut down)
Decision + Action Steps	• Formulate a decision tree to determine the overall actions that need to be taken into consideration when evaluating social media platforms
	• Invest in platforms that have an established community but are growing in audiences so more resources and support is needed, or perhaps shut down platforms that are not bringing back return on investment (ROI) to the client or are no longer available
	• Determine whether some platforms are fine, so there is nothing that needs to be done
	• Set a timeline and date for when you do the evaluation and health report again for all of the platforms

Working in Social Media

Working in social media can be very exciting yet demanding, and the roles constantly change as quickly as the platforms do. Neill and Moody (2015) explored the changes and duties happening for social media strategists and discussed the various tasks, experiences, and expectations facing these professionals in their roles. These duties ranged from handling communication issues to testing emerging technologies, and even discussion of the importance of understanding the collection and analysis of data emerging from these platforms. Yet one of the growing areas of discussion about working in social media is whether or not you need to have the same principles and practices for your personal use as your professional use, which Moreno, Navarro, Tench, and Zerfass (2015) examined in their research. Professionals working in social media have a high level of usage of these platforms for the sole purpose of creating influence in their community, establishing proactive relationships, and becoming relevant influencers in their own right in their thought leadership circles.

The workload and skills necessary to succeed in the field are changing. Some underlying skills and abilities are still important for organizations looking to hire social media professionals. Writing, research, and creative execution are traditional skills seen in marketing, public relations, and other communication disciplines. However, the rising expectations of the maturing field have also allowed the expectations for young professionals entering the field to be a bit higher. Of course, this depends on the industry, business, and even company or organization in focus. There is no real set "standard" for the expectations, roles, or even qualifications. Yet, certain fundamental skills, experiences, and qualifications do need to be taken into consideration (these are discussed and highlighted in greater detail in Chapter 5).

The information we share on social media is vastly different from the capability of the original platforms. When Facebook got started in 2004, you were only able to share updates via text, but it has evolved to allow chat bots, live video, virtual reality, mixed reality, and 360-degree immersive experiences.

BRIDGING THE SCIENCE AND ART OF SOCIAL MEDIA

Social media encompasses both the research and theoretically driven work being done to explore networks, relationships, and how individuals respond and react to various messages and information online. Understanding the foundation of why people share information publicly and privately provides social media professionals with a sound view of why certain things occur without reinventing the wheel. On the flip side, exploring the creative possibilities for these insights turning into actionable steps and strategies is also important. Bridging these two perspectives together in a way that is both integrated and comprehensive is one of the most important accomplishments of a social media professional.

What Can Science Tell Us About Social Media?

Researchers who have explored social media in their work have used a variety of different theoretical frameworks to help explain and predict why certain attitudes, behaviors, and actions are taken online. These frameworks include dialogic theory (Kent & Taylor, 2016; Yang & Kent, 2014), user gratification theory (Gao & Feng, 2016), psychological empowerment theory (Li, 2016), and theory of planned behavior (Freberg, 2012). Even in social media research, there are still some challenges and opportunities for researchers to determine how to effectively measure certain concepts in the field, such as engagement (Jiang, Luo, & Kulemeka, 2016; Sisson, 2017; Smith & Gallicano, 2015). Further research in understanding these concepts, as well as how they can be strategically applied, needs to be taken into consideration. Even though social media is a source for engagement and an opportunity for users and businesses specifically, little research up to this point discusses how exactly social media fits in the overall strategy from a marketing and communications standpoint (Killian & McManus, 2015), which brings forth the growing need for a bridge between practice and research to address this.

Social media can be accomplished by looking at the scientific elements that make up the communities. It helps the strategist understand not only what is happening but also why and how things happen and evolve at any given time. The tools and methods used in traditional disciplines like marketing, education, computer science, public relations, advertising, and communication, among others, can help test and evaluate online behaviors. Social media professionals cannot rely just on the creative artistic opportunities social media allows us to use and take advantage of. Instead, we have to hone our analytical and scientific approaches and fine-tune our research skills. This will allow us to make sense of the substantial unstructured data available so we understand what is being presented and in what context it is presented. This adds to the growing expectation and need for social media professionals to have a solid research foundation and background to help them make sense of the data and apply it in a creative and innovative way.

Research. You will have to become one with statistics, Excel spreadsheets, data, and many other mathematical elements when it comes to social media. There are two parts of the equation a successful social media strategist needs to be aware of when looking at the various platforms. First, the actual information and data are collected in a systematic way from the various platforms or third parties. Also consider the physical elements that are created, shared, and constructed on social media. Social media strategists have to organize the information in ways that show us what is going on. This will help identify trends, gaps, opportunities, or even challenges that need to be addressed in a systematic and applied manner. The second element is that research comes down to a science in the systematic process in which the data are analyzed. Most of the time, the data are in raw form and need to be organized in a way that makes sense and is understandable to both the strategist and the client/organization in question.

How Is Social Media Like an Art?

While the previous sections briefly discussed the science (research- or theory-driven) aspect of social media, it is also important to note areas on the other side of the social media coin. Understanding the creative execution is an area most people associate with social media, but each platform has a strategic purpose behind each area.

Creativity. The demands of being creative today in social media are more important than ever. Without creativity, there is no buzz, excitement, or word-of-mouth conversations that spark audiences to share content. New tools, software programs, and people are coming on board with social media, which is raising the bar to take ideas that would be considered good at any other point in time to the next level. Any person can go about sharing and creating content, but content that is unique, invokes an inspired and emotional response, and can cut through the digital and irrelevant noise really makes an impact on the audience. That's what creativity does for social media. It's about not just looking at the tools or thinking creativity is all about being artistic. It is the light that shines on the brand and communities that help generate these innovative conversations through insights and data that leads them to have these great ideas. **Informed decision making** (coined by Rich Calabrese) is about taking creativity, data, and insight into account for social media. Creativity can be disseminated from the top down (organization to key publics), but there is also the co-creation aspect of creativity, where you are able to use your community to help share, brainstorm ideas, and discover content, stories, or original ways of approaching an idea. The ultimate goal is not just to have one organization or brand tell a story but also to create a spark for others to be motivated to participate and share these conversations and stories with others.

When it comes to being creative with content, certain campaigns and brands have been particularly innovative. Brands now realize that if they extend their presence by embracing their culture and popularity among their audience members, they can achieve great things. Consider Taco Bell. Taco Bell announced the opportunity to be part of their pop-up hotel in California, which would be branded in the Taco Bell logo and merchandise. The result? The fast food brand did not have any paid media to the campaign but in the campaign succeeded in multiple ways: It got more than 4..4 billion earned media impressions, more than 5,000 media stories, and 2 million Instagram posts; and the campaign's branded GIFs on Instagram stories garnered 1.2 million views (United Entertainment Group/Edelman, Taco Bell, n.d.). This was an integrated marketing campaign where the brand's drive for success was embracing the culture and showcasing it across a vast array of social media channels.

Other tactics—like creating new limited edition products to create a buzz, or generating fear of missing out (FOMO) moments—can also drive brand awareness and creativity to new heights. Going against the grain and in a space where the brand would have never been conceived before could be one direction to go. To go where no mustard company has gone before—that's what French's Mustard did with their social media brand campaign featuring French's Mustard Ice Cream. Yes, you read that correctly: mustard ice cream. Sounds delicious! The overall purpose of this campaign for French's Mustard was "to sell something familiar, make it surprising. To sell something surprising, make it familiar" (Fitzco/McCormick French's, n.d.). When promoting a product, your visual has to generate both brand awareness and message recall and recognition. The thought of mustard ice cream surprises and intrigues—pairing them together in a photo of a scoop of mustard-yellow ice cream accomplishes this even more. French's ad plays on this strange pairing with a funny twist on the old "I scream, you scream, we all scream for ice cream" line (Photo 1.2). The campaign succeeded in driving brand awareness and interest through French's partnership with Coolhaus Scoop Shop by using pop-up ice cream trucks and posting on social media (specifically on Instagram) and partnering with 18 influencers who got surprise and delight packages with the limited edition ice cream experience (Fitzco/McCormick French's, n.d.).

Creativity can be experimented with. A brand's message does not have to be delivered by the lead actors (i.e., the company itself). Supporting actors (i.e., spokespeople) can play a role as well. In fact, many sports teams and brands have used their mascots as the vehicle for testing out messages, content, and platforms.

▸ **Photo 1.2**
French's Mustard Ice
Cream Campaign

Source: French Mustard
Ice Cream Campaign
(retrieved from https://
www.mccormick.com/
frenchs/mustard-ice-
cream)

Benny the Bull, the mascot for the NBA Bulls team, is one channel through which
the professional team has put forth new ideas, content, and entertainment for their
audiences in unique ways ("Benny the Bull," n.d.). Benny the Bull is successful on
TikTok because of his constant dance moves and choreography to popular songs
and challenges. In one TikTok, Benny does the #DipAndLeanChallenge in front
of the Bulls logo, capturing the attention of TikTok users with a dance challenge
while reinforcing the Bulls brand (Photo 1.3). Although Benny is present on other
platforms, TikTok allows creativity and the emphasis on popular music and audio
tracks to make a strong connection with the audience.

Creativity doesn't always mean thinking completely outside the box when
it comes to proposing new ideas for a campaign. What it does mean is making
informed decisions based on the landscape, industry, audience, and brand through
brainstorming sessions, data analysis, and insights gathered.

▸ **Photo 1.3**
Benny the Bull on
TikTok

Source: TikTok/
@bennythebull

Storytelling. Everyone has a unique story to share. The worst thing to do is try to tell a story just like someone else's because that will not be authentic to your brand. Plus, stories that are not executed correctly will be lost in the mix. You could have the best visual effects and videographer out there, but if the execution of your story is not there, it is a waste of time.

Successful stories connect and resonate with audiences on a personal level to drive them to feel a specific emotion based on what they have seen from you. Whether via a video or post, you will make a strong connection if you tap into the emotions of an audience member. Once this connection is made, a memorable experience is added to the story, and this allows the receiver to consider what actions to take. Users may just view the piece of content, but they may also be compelled to share it with their network for others to see and experience as well.

The best person to share your story according to what best represents your personality and vision is you. All successful social media brands, companies, and professionals spend a lot of time and energy sharing their stories in creative and unique ways.

Brands and users can use storytelling effectively in several ways:

- *Allow users to be part of the experience.* Some brands allow users to get these experiences and share their viewpoint with others on behalf of the brand. Build ambassador programs, loyalty programs, and communities to gather insights, formulate relationships, and bring forth new stories into the spotlight for the brand as a whole.

- *Listen and create relevant content.* Data will be your friend when you need it to be in social media. Use data as a guide to what stories and pieces of content you feel will most resonate with your audiences. Taking the initiative to ask questions or telling your audience to do something specific (e.g., snap us back a selfie, post a picture on Instagram, etc.) allows you to gauge the user-generated content aspect but also use the buzz, insights, and data to make a more informed decision on what stories to showcase next.

- *Showcase your values.* When you are looking at brands or individuals, they may want to focus on their products and services as well as what they can offer you in terms of making a sale. Yet sometimes brands and others stand up for what they believe in and share content featuring what they want to be known for in a different way. Brands such as Patagonia and Aviation Gin have all been forward-thinking in approaching their views and perspectives as a brand on social media. Patagonia has focused their efforts in supporting the national parks, whereas Aviation Gin has been active in supporting those in their community (such as bartenders) who have been impacted by economic challenges. The consistent messaging for these two brands made their social media campaigns extremely successful from a strategy perspective.

- *Share your point of view.* Gary Vaynerchuk has become a storytelling content machine. From a personal branding standpoint, he has mastered this down to a science by consistently sharing his story and experience through videos, essentially vlogging his daily activities, and moves in a consistent and branded manner with his videographer, David Rock (otherwise known to the social media world as "DRock"). Gary also emphasizes this strongly to point out the difference between documenting and creating content. Documenting your daily activities online does not mean you are creating content; rather, it is a version of creating that focuses more on the practical aspect of sharing than on storytelling (Vaynerchuk, 2016). The difference is that documenting is creating content of who you are rather than creating content for who you want to be (Vaynerchuk, 2016).

How Can We Bridge Science and Art Effectively?

Throughout this book, you will note there is a growing need for understanding both sides of what makes social media a strategic profession and industry to work, research, and teach in. Most of the time, only one side of the coin is presented. Having a balanced approach to research and practice is not only necessary but expected by those working in the field.

Several new expectations are outlined for social media professionals to adapt to not only for their own sakes but also for their clients, organizations, businesses, and communities. Some of the following will be discussed in later chapters:

- Social media is not owned by one person or platform. It is owned by the community.

- Social media is an established field to be in. It is not easy, free, or replaceable. Social media professionals serve as the digital front door for brands. The field and profession need to garner the same respect as other roles and departments.

- Social media is more than just posting updates and taking snaps. It's a strategic mindset to embrace.

- The primary reason for social media is not to publish content to generate hype or FOMO, but to have a purpose and rationale behind it and to be a win-win for you and your audiences.

- Saying you are an expert or "guru" on social media doesn't truly show your expertise. Your work and the relationships you formulate do.

- Social media needs to shift from promoting to everyone, to fine-tuning your efforts on engaging with your audiences at the right time, on the right channel, and in the right situation.

- Quality over quantity—whether it is followers, content, or conversations—always wins.

- Social media roles will evolve, blur with other duties, and sometimes actually disappear.

- Social media is not about audiences just "seeing" your content. It's about your audience sharing and responding to your content.

- Social media is about being "social." Don't be a programmed robot.

- Social media has challenges. Which field doesn't? It has a dark side. However, we have to look at the field in a balanced perspective.

- You are what you present yourself as online. First impressions are all that count.

- People want engagement and content that resonates with them, not spam.

- Be authentic and consistent, not a constant salesperson.

- Social media is more than just content. This is surface level, and there's much more below that is planned, brainstormed, argued, and executed before the post button is even pushed.

CHAPTER SUMMARY

Social media is an evolving area of professional activities and personal relationships. These platforms will continue to evolve or, in some cases, disappear completely. This is an industry where change comes at a rapid pace and is always on the move. Social media professionals may at times feel they are "out of date" with the technologies even though they are just catching up on last week's news. There are many areas in which social media can be viewed as both an art and a science, but some fundamental aspects create bridges between these two areas. Relationships, strategy, and people are what make social media the platform, community, and industry it is today.

THOUGHT QUESTIONS

1. What is your definition of social media? What are some attributes you would assign to social media and why?

2. What are some of the biggest milestones for social media in your opinion?

3. What are the challenges and opportunities in social media? How can creativity and strategy come together?

4. Discuss why research, creativity, and practice are key parts of what makes social media prominent today.

EXERCISES

1. You enter a job interview and the human resources director asks you to define social media and answer the question, "Is social media a science or an art?" Discuss your thoughts on this and use a current campaign or case study not mentioned in this chapter as evidence to support your points.

2. You are applying for an internship with Texas Roadhouse for the summer, and the manager has asked you to come up with some potential ideas for the restaurant to use for storytelling on social media.

Provide a few suggestions for content Texas Roadhouse could consider creating that is both branded and user-generated, and include a rationale for each.

3. You have been asked to create a social media audit for a local nonprofit in town. The firm is on all of the social media platforms but does not get as much engagement on Twitter as it wants. Discuss the process you will go through in determining which platforms to use and no longer use.

REFERENCES

21 Inspiring brands on TikTok to fuel your creative strategy. (n.d.). *Wallaroo*. https://wallaroomedia.com/blog/social-media/tiktok-brands-examples-strategy/

ALS Association. (n.d.). ALS Ice Bucket Challenge spending. https://www.als.org/ice-bucket-challenge-spending

Benny the Bull. (n.d.). *The Shorty Awards*. http://shortyawards.com/12th/bennythebull

boyd, d. m. (2006). Friends, Friendsters, and top 8: Writing community into being on social network sites. *First Monday*, *11*(12), 1–19.

boyd, d. m., & Ellison, N. B. (2008). Social network sites: Definition, history, and scholarship. *Journal of Computer-Mediated Communication*, *13*, 210–230.

Braiker, B. (2014, August 14). The "Ice Bucket Challenge": A case study in viral marketing gold. *Digiday*. http://digiday.com/brands/ice-bucket-challenge-case-study-viral-marketing-success/

Eordogh, F. (2016, May 23). Why "Chewbacca Mask Mom" is the most famous haul video to date. *Forbes*. http://www.forbes.com/sites/fruzsinaeordogh/2016/05/23/why-chewbacca-mask-mom-is-the-most-famous-haul-video-to-date/

Facebook Newsroom. (2018). Company info. http://newsroom.fb.com/company-info/

Fiegerman, S. (2014, January 6). Snapchat CEO reveals why he rejected Facebook's $3 billion dollar offer. *Mashable*. http://mashable.com/2014/01/06/snapchat-facebook-acquisition-2/

Fitzco/McCormick French's (Producers). (n.d.). French's mustard ice cream. *The Shorty Awards*. http://shortyawards.com/12th/frenchs-mustard-ice-cream-2

Flora, L. (2020, May 15). E.l.f.'s TikTok strategy: Make viral songs that slap. *Glossy*. https://www.glossy.co/beauty/e-l-f-s-tiktok-strategy-make-viral-songs-that-slap

Freberg, K. (2012). Intention to comply with crisis messages communicated via social media. *Public Relations Review*, *38*(3), 416–421. https://doi.org/10.1016/j.pubrev.2012.01.008

Freberg, K. (2016). Social media. In C. Carroll (Ed.), *Encyclopedia for corporate reputation* (pp. 773–776). Thousand Oaks, CA: SAGE.

Gao, Q., & Feng, C. (2016). Branding with social media: User gratifications, usage patterns, and brand message content strategies. *Computers in Human Behavior*, *63*, 868–890. http://doi.org/10.1016/j.chb.2016.06.022

JESS3. (n.d.). *JESS3 Labs: The Social Media Brandsphere*. http://jess3.com/social-media-brandsphere/

Jiang, H., Luo, Y., & Kulemeka, O. (2016). Social media engagement as an evaluation barometer: Insights from communication executives. *Public Relations Review*, *42*(4), 679–691. http://doi.org/10.1016/j.pubrev.2015.12.004

Kent, M. L., & Taylor, M. (2016). From *Homo economicus* to *Homo dialogicus*: Rethinking social media use in CSR communication. *Public Relations Review*, *42*(1), 60–67. http://doi.org/10.1016/j.pub rev.2015.11.003

Killian, G., & McManus, K. (2015). A marketing communications approach for the digital era: Managerial guidelines for social media integration. *Business Horizons*, *58*(5), 539–549. http://doi.org/10.1016/j.bushor.2015.05.006

Li, Z. (2016). Psychological empowerment on social media: Who are the empowered users? *Public Relations Review*, *42*(1), 49–59. http://doi.org/10.1016/j.pubrev.2015.09.001

Mangold, W. G., & Faulds, D. J. (2009). Social media: The new hybrid element of the promotion mix. *Business Horizons*, *52*, 357–365.

Marken, G. A. (2007). Social media . . . The hunted can become the hunter. *Public Relations Quarterly*, *52*(4), 9–12.

Moreno, A., Navarro, C., Tench, R., & Zerfass, A. (2015). Does social media usage matter? An analysis of online practices and digital media perceptions of communication practitioners in Europe. *Public Relations Review*, *41*(2), 242–253. http://doi.org/10.1016/j.pubrev.2014.12.006

Neill, M. S., & Moody, M. (2015). Who is responsible for what? Examining strategic roles in social media management. *Public Relations Review*, *41*(1), 109–118. http://doi.org/10.1016/j.pubrev.2014.10.014

Rogers, K. (2016, July 27). The "Ice Bucket Challenge" helped scientists discover a new gene tied to A.L.S. *The New York Times*. https://www.nytimes.com/2016/07/28/health/the-ice-bucket-challenge-helped-scientists-discover-a-new-gene-tied-to-als.html?_r=0

Singh, A. (2016, December 2). Brexit campaign would have failed before advent of social media, say remain voters in new poll. *Independent*. http://www.independent

.co.uk/news/uk/politics/brexit-social-media-new-poll-failed-remain-voters-a7450911.html

Sisson, D. C. (2017). Control mutuality, social media, and organization-public relationships: A study of local animal welfare organizations' donors. *Public Relations Review*, *43*(1), 179–189. http://doi.org/10.1016/j.pubrev.2016.10.007

Smith, B. G., & Gallicano, T. D. (2015). Terms of engagement: Analyzing public engagement with organizations through social media. *Computers in Human Behavior*, *53*, 82–90. http://doi.org/10.1016/j.chb.2015.05.060

United Entertainment Group/Edelman, Taco Bell (Producers) (n.d.). The Bell: A Taco Bell hotel and resort. (n.d.). *The Shorty Awards*. https://shortyawards.com/12th/the-bell-a-taco-bell-hotel-and-resort

Vaynerchuk, G. (2016, December 1). Document, don't create: Creating content that builds your personal brand. *Gary Vaynerchuk*. https://www.garyvaynerchuk.com/creating-content-that-builds-your-personal-brand/

The *Washington Post* has a surprisingly popular TikTok account. (n.d.). *Insider*. https://www.insider.com/the-washington-post-tiktok-account-has-a-surprisingly-popular-2019-6

Waters, R. D., Burnett, E., Lamm, A., & Lucas, J. (2009). Engaging stakeholders through social networking: How nonprofit organizations are using Facebook. *Public Relations Review*, *35*, 102–106.

Yang, A., & Kent, M. (2014). Social media and organizational visibility: A sample of Fortune 500 corporations. *Public Relations Review*, *40*(3), 562–564. http://doi.org/10.1016/j.pubrev.2014.04.006TikTok/@

2

ETHICAL AND LEGAL FUNDAMENTALS IN SOCIAL MEDIA

Learning Objectives

After reading this chapter, you will be able to

- Define ethics and construct your own ethical standards for social media

- Recognize the legal and ethical consequences and challenges social media raises

- Explain key ethical and legal principles for establishing a social media policy

- Understand the ethical and legal best practices to work in social media

INTRODUCTION

To succeed in social media, we need to be aware of the underlying legal and ethical implications that guide our practices, communication efforts, and behaviors online. You may ask, "Do I really have to understand law when it comes to social media?" More than you might think. Law is a moving target—as platforms evolve, the law slowly but surely follows with new rules and regulations. It is important to understand the law to navigate the growing changes and expectations arising online.

This is true for ethics as well. You need to understand ethical practices in social media and the importance of applying those practices in your day-to-day interactions online. Many professionals face these questions in the social media field—make sure you know how you will answer and act on these questions:

- Do I care if people search previous updates (pictures, messages, blog posts, etc.) to use for job interviews?

- Do I understand the legal implications for sharing misinformation on my channels?

- Do I know (and understand) all of the terms of service (TOS) for the platforms I have a presence on?

- Do I understand what I have been willingly giving brands and platform companies over the years in terms of my personal information?

- Do I know the best practices of uncovering what is real or "fake" information being circulated on social media?

- Am I aware that while I have my account settings set to "private," they really are not?

- Do I care if I send out a tweet, story, or snap that may look "cool" online with my friends but could reflect poorly on the organization or company I represent?

- Have I assessed the risks associated with posting controversial content?

- Am I aware of the consequences of posting information that may not be true or may be misleading?

- Do I know the risks and challenges associated with the social media platform algorithms?

- Do I know what I need to do in case someone uses my profile picture to create a fake account?

- Do I know how to identify real versus fake accounts before engaging with them on social media?

- Am I aware that an update made in a spark of emotion or outrage could cause me to get suspended from my job, miss out on a job opportunity, or even get fired?

- Do I understand the impact of sharing my opinion online for the world to see, and do I understand the community, professional, and global implications toward my personal brand?

- Am I aware of the power (and risks) associated with saying something online and the effects it may have on another person?

You may be wondering how this all pertains to social media and being online. The answer is simple: Social media is not only about building an online brand, establishing paid ads or sponsored posts to generate buzz online, or even setting up a place to tell your own story. All of these are important, but fundamentally, social media is about being "social." Being social means establishing and maintaining relationships. It's an art form in itself, since users must be skilled at navigating their various relationships with colleagues, friends, peers, and community members. Relationships have layers (like onions from the movie *Shrek*); these layers are complex and constantly evolve from experiences. People have expectations when it comes to social media from a communication standpoint and how we should operate and present ourselves. Issues arise when users' expectations for the brand or profession are violated online. A lot of ethical issues could be addressed if people were aware of how their actions and behaviors might be perceived. Essentially, what we say and stand for online must be supported by our actions.

When it comes to social media ethics, it is very easy to talk about being professional, but it's a skill to consistently act ethically. This builds trust, which is earned over time. One incident can change someone's opinion of you as a person. Ethics and professionalism are at the forefront of the profession and the curriculum across various disciplines, but we are still facing an uphill challenge in teaching others how to be proactive members of society on social media.

Dr. Chris Yandle, Communication Specialist at St. Tammany Parish Public Schools

Introduction

If there were a modern definition of "nomad," I seriously might be it. I spent more than 15 years in college athletics at six NCAA Division I institutions—Southern Miss, Louisiana-Lafayette, Marshall, Baylor, Miami, and Georgia Tech. During the latter part of career 1.0, I had one foot in academia and the other foot in college athletics. It was my time in the classroom at both Baylor and later Kennesaw State where I realized my calling might be in the classroom. After being accepted into the Ph.D. program at Mercer, I was let go from my job at Georgia Tech, effectively ending my college athletics career. Now, I have a normal 9-to-5 job as the social media and digital media strategist for one of Louisiana's largest public school systems, and it has been the most rewarding thing I've done in a very long time.

What is your favorite part of working in your area of expertise in social media?

My favorite part of working in social media is definitely the creative and planning process. Many don't like planning in social media, and their idea is to post when things come up. I like looking two, three, four weeks in advance and planning for content so that we can be flexible in curating spontaneous content or sharing immediate stories that don't require days of video editing. Planning content allows us to be more "in the moment" than most people realize.

What is one thing you can't live without while working in social media?

Aside from an endless supply of iPhone cords or extended batteries, my answer is buy-in. Buy-in from the top and other outward-facing departments that social/digital touch. You can have the greatest content and a closet full of phone batteries, but if the powers that be DON'T GET "IT" or BUY YOUR "WHY," then what's the point? I assure you many people will disagree with me, but I don't 100% believe that social media is a necessity for everyone. For example, only a handful of public school districts here in Louisiana are active on social media. What does that say? It says not only do these districts not have the people resources, the time resources, or the financial resources, it also means it's not a necessity for them. YOUR WHY cannot be "because everyone else is doing it and they have 10 people posting social media content all day." That's not a strategy, nor is it a reason why to do something.

What is your favorite social media account (person/brand/etc.) to follow and why?

My feet and interests overlap into so many areas that I don't have one person above all

(Continued)

HUMANS OF SOCIAL MEDIA

(Continued)

to follow, but I have a favorite in different areas.

- Overall Branding/Thought Processes. This one is a tie between Gary Vaynerchuk (@garyvee), Jon Acuff (@jonacuff), and Simon Sinek (Facebook). Gary provides a refreshing view at things I've believed or things that I didn't understand. Simon and Jon's ideas of knowing your why have helped me to where I am today and as I am trying to look towards the future.

- Sports Media. My friend Jessica Smith (@warjesseagle) on Twitter. I think her thoughts transcend sports. What she offers is applicable to other industry across the country.

- Higher Ed Academia. Here, I suggest (aside from this book's author, of course) Dr. David Ridpath (@drridpath) and a nonacademic, ESPN's Jay Bilas (@jaybilas). Both on Twitter. Really and selfishly for me, I mention these two because they played a vital role in my Ph.D. dissertation on the lived academic experiences of NCAA Division I football student-athletes.

- Leadership. @KevinDeShazo on Twitter. Kevin gets it. I had the opportunity to meet Kevin when he was launching his social media education firm, Fieldhouse Media, and we've since become good friends. He was in the corporate world and what he learned there has been applied to his new venture, Fieldhouse Leadership.

- General. @thedogist on Instagram. My reason is simple: I have two dogs and I am a dog lover. Most days, this account makes me smile and changes the course of my day.

What is the most challenging part of working in social media?

We are in the throes of a serious nuclear arms race in the sports digital space. College teams are trying to one-up each other with graphics, video presentations, and content because it all ties back to recruiting kids. It's not necessarily about the fans anymore, and the media are a distant afterthought on social for many schools. I think schools are losing sight of what's important and instead are looking to be the next viral sensation.

Again, maybe I'm sounding like that old guy shouting "GET OFF MY LAWN" at the neighborhood kids, but I feel for some in the business, social is all about getting clicks and clickbait headlines. There's more to life than retweets, new followers, and mentions. There are bigger picture things, bigger than us, that we should focus on and use social media as the avenue to achieve those big picture ideals.

What do you wish you had known when you were starting out?

Control social, don't let social control you. We have an amazing power in our hands with our phones. We are creators and inventors. We have the power to build people up or tear people down. I think it's a power that many don't know how to use effectively. Use social media for the common good and to make a positive difference in the world. Don't let the faceless and nameless egg avatars control how you feel. That's been my biggest struggle and it continues to affect me today because I let it.

Dr. Chris Yandle is a K–12 communications professional and a recovering college athletics administrator. You can follow Chris on Twitter, @ChrisYandle.

WHAT IS ETHICS?

Ethics is a set of moral guidelines and principles that influence our behaviors and interactions. Having a set ethical code of conduct is essential when exploring how to react and respond to various situations that may emerge when we are working in social media. These guidelines help us tell the difference between what is wrong and what is right. Most of the time, people have a set of values that they hold dear and feel are important for them to follow. These ethical principles can be personal behaviors and actions, but they also translate into professional circles. All professional organizations (advertising, public relations, marketing, journalism, communications, and additional disciplines) have a professional code of ethics for members to follow when they are working and practicing in the field.

Social media professionals may face a variety of different situations while they are employed for a large corporation, media outlet, agency, or consulting firm, or even when they are part of an organization (e.g., student athletes). Access to information pertaining to personal accounts on social media sites has been discussed in the online community as well as in the court of law.

Certain behaviors are not universally accepted when it comes to social media professionals. Steph Parker (2013) discussed some of these "new deadly sins of social media."

Misappropriation. This particular sin focuses on the timing and appropriateness of jumping into a conversation that is not entirely relevant or necessary for a brand. It is all about understanding the overall context of the situation and determining whether or not you are able to be part of the conversation. For example, some brands have gotten mixed reviews on when they have (or have not) commented on various topics ranging from global pandemics (e.g., COVID-19) to social issues (e.g., racial injustice cases) to security and privacy issues for conversations on certain platforms (e.g., recording conversations and downloading contacts from Clubhouse) to leadership concerns (e.g., Wells Fargo and Tesla). It really comes into play when brands try to jump on board with a trend **(trendjacking)** on social media. The trends can be viral, such as Running Man and Crying Michael Jordan memes, among others, but there is a time and place for brands and professionals to promote themselves. This is especially true when the trending topic focuses on an emotional situation (e.g., insensitive tweets by Gap during Hurricane Sandy or by Epicurious during the Boston Marathon bombing) or global trending topics (e.g., elections, competitions, and other newsworthy events).

Abandonment. As mentioned earlier, social media is about the conversation, and you can't have success with a community if you are not actively participating in the community. Social media communities need to be built as well as maintained. Brands, organizations, and professionals must decide which platforms to be on and how invested in these platforms their communities should be. The worst thing that can happen is to jump on board a platform and then leave it before it can really be embraced. Abandonment is an extreme case, but the point is to make sure you are using a particular platform for the conversation and community. As they say, if you build it, they will come. However, if you leave, so will your community.

Manipulation. There is a time and place to ask your community to take action to support a cause, share a post or update, or even help another member of the community. Yet social media is not the place to ask your community to reach a certain number of followers so you can get paid more for speaking opportunities, which is sometimes seen in the professional social media circuit. The ultimate goal is to be yourself and present your brand in the most authentic way, and that comes from not using cheap tricks and measures to generate a false view of who you are. Be willing to share content that is relevant with your community, but respect the fact that people may or may not be influenced by what you ask them to do. That comes with trust, credibility, and a relationship.

On the flip side, you do not want to manipulate or present a false sense of community or success by using services to make it appear like your account or campaign is successful when in reality, it is not. For example, some businesses set up click-through sign-ups for a charity or donation or falsely promise to take action if you get a certain number of likes or comments/views.

Ignorance. The topic of ignorance comes with a lot of components to address, and it's important to highlight the ones most at risk of being committed by social media professionals. There is the ignorance of basic terms and practices in social media. Be aware of the main terms, jargon, and legal obligations for social media practices (e.g., asking permission to use a tweet or image for a story, or to livestream a college football game knowing you are in violation of TV rights). This goes back to knowing the Federal Trade Commission (FTC) guidelines as well as terms of service for each platform you are using for your social media practices. Then, there is the ignorance of not seeing what your community members are sharing and thus failing to respond to them. With no engagement or interaction from either side, there is a risk to the overall health of the community on social media. If people feel ignored, they will go somewhere else. View exchanges and questions not as threats but as opportunities to learn how to improve.

Monotony. Passion is a great element to connect audiences on social media, but social media professionals do not want to push the same content over and over again. Content needs to be fresh, relevant, and tied to the audience's needs and expectations. These needs and expectations change over time. Keeping a constant pulse on what is happening in the community and among the different audience groups is critical. Audiences do not want to receive updates sharing "Like our page" or "Tag three people to win this contest" because businesses and brands have been using these tactics on social media since the beginning. They want to be entertained, inspired, and motivated to share because the content they see connects with them on an emotional level. Although it can be challenging for brands to recognize, this is how audiences are presently operating, and it is going to take more time (and investment) to bring forth creative and fresh new pieces of content online. Continuing to push the same content to audiences is no longer going to cut it in the digital first world.

Narcissism. Since social media is public, what you share with the world is for everyone to see. Essentially, you are what you share, so make sure to keep that in mind. I am holding the mirror up to some of the popular influencers and creators, such as Kendall Jenner and James Charles. There is a time to personalize your brand, but you do not want to spam people with your logo, YouTube videos, and every piece of content you have ever created. Also, do not worry about how many people are following you or your ratio between follows and followers. Social media professionals have been guilty of following, and then unfollowing, a lot of people so their numbers stay up but others go down. You do not need to share your own content all the time or quote it on Twitter.

The cardinal sin for social media is buying followers. Do not do this. Quality is always better than quantity when it comes to your community. While high numbers get a lot of excitement and praise from people, qualifying you for some of those "must-follow lists" you see getting published, it's not worth it. Plus, it is very easy to find out who has real followers and who has **bots** (automated accounts to share and comment on posts) across these various platforms. A number of fake accounts and services do this, but you do not want to create a fake image for yourself—it will only damage your reputation.

Uniformity. Having a consistent image is one thing, but having the same content on every platform is another. Whereas on some platforms repurposed content is appropriate (e.g., Facebook and Instagram), this does not mean you share the exact same content all at once or in the same format. Consider the differences between Snapchat videos and Instagram videos, or the different algorithm characteristics you need to be aware of on Facebook versus LinkedIn. Plus, each platform has its own communities and expectations, so make sure to personalize these experiences across the board.

Additional Ethical and Legal Consequences and Challenges

As the platforms and social media field evolve, so do the ethical and legal consequences and challenges. Since Social Media Today author Steph Parker discussed these sins back in 2013, social media has come a long way in addressing them, but there are others of which we have to be aware as well that can influence how we conduct our business, communication, and storytelling practices. With that being said, here are some additional "deadly sins" that should be added for social media practices:

> Losing control over personal accounts to employers due to influential presence. Naturally, it is assumed that a person owns his or her own personal accounts on social media. What happens if a business sees one of their employees have an influential presence on social media—does that mean they own this personal account because the person works at the business? This is a growing legal and ethical issue as employees can become influential based on their expertise, personality, and the community they have built. This has been a focus in several cases, including the one involving wedding designer Hayley Paige. Paige, who has gained a presence in the wedding dress industry as a designer for her employer JLM Couture, lost access to her personal Instagram account to her employer JLM Couture in 2020. In March 2021, a New York judge upheld a restraining order saying Paige does not have the right to the account and Paige had "developed the account within the scope of her employment with [JLM]. Using the account to promote JLM's goods was the kind of work she was employed to perform, as it was commensurate with her position as a lead designer" (Coleman, 2021). This account sets a significant yet serious precedent for ownership of personal social media accounts in which social media professionals need to watch as future cases may come forward as more brands and businesses view ownership of popular and influential personal accounts from their employees.

Bullying. This will be discussed in more detail later in this chapter, but essentially, you want to treat others how you would like to be treated. It is very easy to hide behind the screen and vent on someone, or even try to make people feel different based on what you share with them. Establishing fake accounts, saying negative false things about people, being aggressive with hurtful messages, and sharing others' private information for the public to see are just some examples of bullying behavior.

Not giving credit where credit is due. Everyone wants to be acknowledged and praised for bringing a useful point to the discussion, sharing a great article, or even providing a great example of a campaign to a community. You want to give credit to the person who came up with the original idea—similar to citing a source in a research paper. No one likes it when someone else gets the praise and shout-outs when he or she was not the one who came up with the idea. That's not good manners. Giving praise and thanks does not cost anyone anything. In fact, it can actually be valuable and help contribute to your personal brand.

Intolerance. One of the things that sometimes happens on social media is staying within circles where common values, views, and perspectives are universal, with no differences of opinion or debate allowed. This is what it means to be "bubbled," being exposed only to one perspective and not others. As a result, when different opinions and perspectives arise, this can create some conflict and reactions online and in person. This has resulted in some places like Twitter and other platforms to attack individuals—high profile or not—for having different views than their own. Or, this gravitates others to take actions to continue to isolate themselves from others on a designated platform ranging from unfollowing, blocking, or muting accounts, to the extreme action of deactivating their account entirely. Society is diverse in many ways, including differences of opinion. By understanding and acknowledging these differences, we are better equipped to understand others and have a complete view of our society as a whole rather than just one side.

Misinformation. In a famous scene in *A Few Good Men*, Jack Nicholson says, "You can't handle the truth!" Yes, we can handle the truth, but seeking the truth online can be challenging. One of the biggest challenges is the rise of online information that is fake, not true, or purposely manipulated to look as if it were real. Why do people believe inaccurate information? Psychologists Marsh, Cantor, and Brashier (2016) study "truthiness," or the qualities of information that make it more likely to be perceived and remembered as "true." People are predisposed to believe that information is true because in most situations in life, the information we obtain is, in fact, true. Simple processes, such as including a photo or repeating a message, make a piece of information more likely to be viewed as true. Although audiences understand that some sources are more reliable than others, the source of information is usually forgotten much faster than the information itself. The science of misinformation presents several practical pieces of advice to social media professionals. Tagging information as "fake," as Facebook, YouTube, or Twitter does, is unlikely to have much effect, due to our quick forgetting of source information. Be careful about repeating myths, even though you want to "bust" them. By repeating them, you make them more memorable.

Consider the images and videos that are shared during a trending event. We have all seen the photo with the shark swimming through flooded streets following a hurricane or other disaster. This is a fake photo, but it is shared all the time. A rising trend that has occurred on social media is misleading or framing coverage to tell a certain viewpoint or perspective on a situation. One example started with a viral video that sparked global and national attention in 2019. The video featured a high school student, Nick Sandmann, supposedly confronting a Native American peace activist, Nathan Phillips, in Washington, D.C. Sandmann was wearing a MAGA hat and participating in a "March for Life" rally with fellow students, while Phillips was beating a hand-held drum and singing. The short clip made it appear that Sandmann was antagonizing Phillips while he performed, as they stood face to face (Schwartz, 2019). After the video went viral through major media outlets, an investigation reviewed all of the footage that was being shared online and through the mainstream media and found the footage did not tell the full story of events that were originally reported and shared on social media (Schwartz, 2019). It was not proven that Sandmann initiated any confrontation. Sandmann and his family sued *The Washington Post*, CNN, and other media outlets for $250 million for defamation as a result (Coffman, 2019).

We also know what audiences should be doing to avoid believing false information: Consider the source, check the author, check who is sharing the information, check the date, look for supporting sources, read beyond the headline, ask if a piece of information is a joke or satire, look for other expert opinions, and finally, consider how your personal biases might make you more or less accepting of the information.

Sharing too much. Transparency is key to building authenticity online, but there's transparency, and then there is transparency. You want to be transparent, of course, on social media, but you don't want to appear to be spamming everyone. There is a right amount of content to present across the different platforms. Yet keep in mind that not everyone may want to know what you had for breakfast or what you experienced at dinner last night at the latest new restaurant. In addition, remember that some people use social media to have conversations and a positive experience, but not to be bombarded with negativity all the time. Consider the balance between sharing your voice and point of view and how others may be responding to it.

Sparking outrage. Hell hath no fury like a social media user scorned by something he or she does not like. Have you ever been outraged by something online? Often, we vent or sometimes even try to strike up a **flame war** (a campaign to spark negativity toward the other party involved) online. We must maintain our cool and take a moment away from our keyboard before we start engaging. It is important that we collect ourselves and evaluate the consequences or effects of a particular post, update, tweet, or snap. Tea accounts, accounts that are dedicated to gossip and juicy details of online feuds, have been used to escalate influencer disagreements to enhance media coverage (Lorenz, 2019). Bots can also escalate a feud to gain publicity and attention, such as in the case of Barstool's podcast *Call Her Daddy* with Alexandra Cooper and Sofia Franklyn (Rotter, 2020). Sofia and Alexandra hosted a popular yet raunchy podcast, when Sofia's boyfriend Peter Nelson tried to obtain more money and possible new deals for the podcast away from Barstool Sports (Pomarico, 2020). This of course caused a lot of drama for everyone involved, with statements, updates, and accusations flying all over the place.

Automation. You can't really call in social media. While many tools allow you to schedule updates ahead of time, most businesses and social media professionals know of the dreaded "automated direct messages" that frequently emerge if you follow a new account online. These automated responses are impersonal and not really about connecting on a relationship basis with another person. Automation can also pose a challenge and risk if a business or professional sends automated updates when others may not want to see them (like during a natural disaster incident or breaking news). With automation, you lose the personal exchanges and conversations that make social media a great place to network and communicate. People follow you not because you are a robot, but because there is a human side to your personal or professional brand.

Going rogue. Social media is about representing yourself truthfully online. Posting opinions without permission or out of context while still representing the agency or organization of record (otherwise known as **"going rogue"**) can lead to a misinterpretation of the information shared on the platform. Historically in social media, there are many cases in which employees have gone rogue for their brands. These situations can range from actual employees of an organization or business taking control of its online account without permission (e.g., HMV in 2013) or alternative accounts being made on Twitter for government agencies (e.g., @RogueNASA or #AltNationalParkService) in 2017.

There is always a social media manager or team that may not necessarily want to go out of their positions a normal way but rather choose to leave their positions with a bang by using their social media platforms to communicate this loud and clear to the global community. Take the UK Civil Service Twitter account. During COVID-19, the Twitter account stated, "Arrogant and offensive. Can you imagine having to work with these truth twisters?" in reference to the UK government's take on lockdowns and pandemic strategies (Reid, 2020). The tweet was taken down within ten minutes but had considerable influence nonetheless. This goes to show the power of social media in a time of great debate, uncertainty, and stress.

Another type of account that comes up on social media and pushes the envelope a little bit for brands and individuals is the alternative account. **Alternative accounts** serve as a notion to resist the official voice and stories they represent. Essentially, these accounts have tried to place themselves in a position to interconnect with the official ones, but they provide an alternative perspective and offer to spark dialogue with others who may or may not agree with the official voice. A lot of risk is associated with these rogue accounts that touches on the ethical and legal lines of social media.

First, we do not know who is behind these accounts or if they are who they say they are. Some individuals on these accounts have claimed they are employees (or former employees) of these organizations, but we do not know for sure.

Second, we are not aware of the ultimate goals of these accounts or if there is an alternative motive connecting these specific social media accounts to another task at hand (cybersecurity, hacking, etc.). Although some of these accounts have large followings, we do not know if they are "real" or authentic, which brings forth the importance of having an official stamp of approval from the platform itself. For example, Facebook, Instagram, Twitter, and even LinkedIn offer verification checks to let others know this is the official account. Yet there is no guarantee who is hiding behind the screen even for these official accounts.

Third, if someone decides to create the illusion of a real account with a fake message or update, this could also be viewed as going rogue and could damage a company's reputation online and offline. For example, in response to the George Floyd protests of June 2020, NASCAR mentioned their stance on not allowing the Confederate flag at their events (NASCAR, 2020). Shortly afterward, race car driver Ray Ciccarelli stated he was going to retire from the sport due to this action. This prompted someone to create a fake response to Ray, supposedly from NASCAR's Twitter account, which was immediately shared widely before it was deemed to be fake (Photo 2.1). This is a risk not just for brands but for users as well, as rogue actions that are not true can be used to create potentially catastrophic consequences, damaging the reputation of those who were impacted.

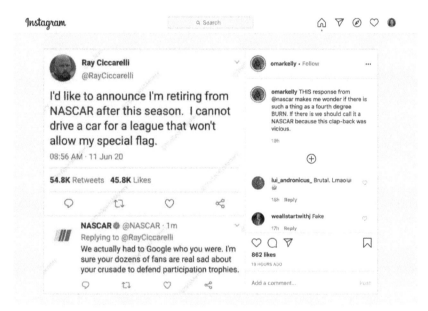

▶ **Photo 2.1**
NASCAR Fake Twitter Response to Ray Ciccarelli's Announcement

Source: Instagram / @TheSportsMemery

LEGAL FUNDAMENTALS

Terms of service agreements. Before you sign up for a social media account, be sure to review the terms of service (TOS). A TOS agreement is common for all social media accounts and platforms and is known to outline the terms and uses (or rules) dictated by the parent company (Facebook, Twitter, Instagram, etc.) for its platform. In each TOS agreement, the platform states clearly what a user (or business) can and cannot do on the respective social media site (see Table 2.1).

To create an account or profile, the user has to agree to the terms of service. Some TOS agreements range from what users are able to own and create on the site to basic requirements (e.g., Instagram states you have to be 13 years or older to use the site). In addition, some platforms (e.g., Instagram and Snapchat) state the content that is shared and created on these sites is technically owned by the platform, whereas others (e.g., LinkedIn) state that the users own the content they share and create on social media. Other listings can be viewed on the Digital.gov

Table 2.1	Current Listings of the Main Platforms' Terms of Service (TOS)	
Platform	**Terms of Service**	**Link**
Facebook	2015	www.facebook.com/terms
Twitter	2017	twitter.com/tos?lang=en
Instagram	2013	help.instagram.com/478745558852511
Snapchat	2017	www.snap.com/en-US/terms/
LinkedIn	2017	www.linkedin.com/legal/user-agreement
Pinterest	2016	policy.pinterest.com/en/terms-of-service
YouTube	2010	www.youtube.com/static?template=terms
TikTok	2019	www.tiktok.com/legal/terms-of-use?lang=en
WhatsApp	2019	www.whatsapp.com/legal/
Clubhouse	2020	www.notion.so/Terms-of-Service-cfbd1824d4704e1fa4a83f0312b8cf88

website (www.digital.gov) for other platforms as well as third-party applications frequently used on social media. Keep in mind, for all social media platforms, that TOS agreements may evolve and expand as new cases, legal rulings, and situations arise online.

Free speech on social media. Of course, traditional legal terms need to be discussed not only in relation to social media but also in how they are translated for use on each platform. For example, tweeting a rumor about another person could result in a lawsuit (Gunkel, 2015). This is an ongoing topic of conversation when it comes to what employees share on social media related to their employers and job, what student athletes share relative to their athletic teams, and even what is shared during political campaigns. Whether or not people should share their opinions online in a public forum is one part of the equation, but the other is whether people's content should be censored or only allowed on certain social media platforms. Twitter, Facebook, and others are dealing with extreme cases of people abusing their platforms (trolling, cyberbullying, making online threats, etc.). Protection and respect for free speech is necessary in a free democracy, yet while social media has become more mainstream and established as both a field and a communication channel, brands, companies, and individuals still face challenges in this particular area.

Freedom of speech on social media has been shoved into the spotlight in many ways. For example, free speech was brought to the forefront in 2020 as a result of the actions of Twitter and Snapchat regarding then President Donald Trump. In May 2020, Twitter labeled President Trump's tweets about mail-in voting as misleading in nature (Kelly, 2020). In response, President Trump argued that the social media companies needed to be regulated and suggested revoking

Section 230 of the Communications Decency Act (Myers, 2020). According to Cayce Myers of Virginia Tech University, the Communications Decency Act (CDA) of 1996 states, "The internet and other interactive computer services offer a forum for a true diversity of political discourse, unique opportunities for cultural development, and myriad avenues for intellectual activity" (Myers, 2020). Specifically, Section 230 of the CDA focuses on social media or online communication as an "interactive computer service" and states that a "website or a social media site is not a 'publisher or speaker' of content meaning that they are largely immune from liability for content posted by third parties" (Myers, 2020). In other words, Section 230 focuses on how no provider or user of an interactive computer service shall be treated as the publisher or speaker of any information provided by another information content provider (47 U.S. Code § 230, n.d.). This ruling is what has allowed YouTube to post videos, Amazon to allow reviews, and Facebook and Twitter to offer social networking and what has made social media platforms offer their features for their users and made Section 230 one of the most influential rulings to make the internet the way it is since 1996 (47 U.S. Code § 230). Essentially, if this section was revoked, it could change the way in which social media platforms and communication operate.

Following Twitter's actions, Snapchat's CEO Evan Siegel took actions to stop promoting President Trump's account on their designated platform (Wong, 2020). In contrast, Facebook and Mark Zuckerberg did not initially restrict or block President Trump's social media messages on their platform. Zuckerberg said, "I think political speech is one the most sensitive parts in a democracy and people should be able to see what politicians say. Political speech is the most scrutinized speech already by a lot of the media" (Bond, 2020b). Eventually, however, Facebook, Twitter, and the other social media platforms banned President Trump from their platforms.

Disclosure of consent. Facebook as a platform and company got into trouble in 2016 over the amount of data it was collecting on users, but it also conducted an experiment that manipulated information posted. This experiment focused on 689,000 users and whether people were feeling positive or negative about what they were viewing on their timeline (Booth, 2014). In essence, Facebook was able to manipulate and filter information, comments, pictures, and videos in users' networks to test whether or not seeing positive or negative items on their timeline had an effect on their overall state (Booth, 2014). The news of this case study sparked outrage in the public on both ethical and legal grounds because the social network did not disclose this practice or ask users if it could do this for their timelines. Universities and research firms go through the ethical process of disclosing the nature of the study (via institutional review boards, or IRBs) for all studies involving human subjects, as well as require participants to fill out an informed consent form for the study, both of which Facebook did not do (Booth, 2014). Since then, Facebook has installed measures for highlighting certain content coming from various sources and flagged others from state-run media outlets that are shared on the platform (Bond, 2020a).

Employees and Personal Branding Mishaps

Online threats and cyberbullying. What you post online can become evidence in a court of law. Many cases have focused on issues of cyberbullying, using profile pictures to create fake accounts, and even posting content that could lead to termination of your job. However, one case has become an iconic example of what can happen when employees post things on their channels that have resulted in job loss and long-term consequences. It only takes one snap, tweet, video, or comment to change your life dramatically, which this case will show.

 Justine Sacco
@JustineSacco

Going to Africa. Hope I don't get AIDS. Just kidding. I'm white!

↩ Reply   ↻ Retweet   ★ Favorite   ••• More

▶ **Photo 2.2**
Justine Sacco Case Study

Source: Twitter/ @JustineSacco

2,678
RETWEETS

1,206
FAVORITES

10:19 AM - 20 Dec 13 ♀ from Hillingdon, London

The most common reason social media users get into legal trouble is for posting inappropriate, insensitive, or egregious content. These posts can result in lawsuits, firings, and other long-term consequences. Public shaming for these kinds of posts has become one of the most negatively impactful events individuals experience today on social media.

The case involving Justine Sacco is a warning for all who believe social media privacy is still a thing. Sacco, a former public relations professional, used her Twitter account to share various personal opinions and views on all types of experiences, as well as exchanges she had with individuals.

It was not until December 2013, when she was boarding a plane from London to Cape Town (an 11-hour flight), that her world turned upside down and she became the number-one trending topic on Twitter (Waterlow, 2015). As shown in Photo 2.2, Sacco posted an update that sparked outrage online and immediately went viral, and she got thousands of new followers and people reaching out to her about this. In fact, an organic hashtag, #HasJustineLandedYet, began trending (Waterlow, 2015). Even though Sacco deleted her account and tried to get rid of the evidence, her reputation was already ruined, and the professional damage was already done. What stands out about this case is the fact that Sacco is still experiencing the consequences of the incident and has not been able to escape it.

Public shaming is not just for the moment in which a tweet, video, or update is uncovered, but it also follows the unrelenting culture of an entire community of people searching online and sharing updates (even writing posts, articles, and books) about the incident. Jon Ronson, author of the best-selling book *So You've Been Publicly Shamed* (2015), met up with Sacco for an interview and noted the impact this experience had on her as well as those who felt it was their responsibility to take her down on social media.

These are the types of incidents that the internet (and society) does not allow people to forget. However, the need for an understanding of what we can learn from this experience and when it is time to move on as a society must be addressed. The consequences of these public incidents on someone's personal and professional life are significant. We need to have a better approach to educating others about the consequences and risks before they fall into a similar situation.

In many other cases, people have been fired due to insensitive or controversial tweets and social media updates shared on their personal accounts. For example, film director James Gunn was removed from *Guardians of the Galaxy* when people saw racist comments on his Twitter account, although he was reinstated years later (Fleming, 2019). This is an example of the trend of "being **canceled**."

Cancel culture in social media attempts to

> stop giving support to [the person who posted the insensitive content]. The act of canceling could entail boycotting an actor's movies or no longer reading or promoting a writer's works. The reason for cancellation can vary, but it usually is due to the person in question having expressed an objectionable opinion, or having conducted themselves in a way that is unacceptable, so that continuing to patronize that person's work leaves a bitter taste. ("What It Means to Get 'Canceled,'" n.d.)

Other cases in which celebrities and brands have been canceled or tried to be canceled include the following:

- Equinox and Soulcycle, when it was discovered that one of their corporate leaders had hosted fundraisers for President Trump (Pathak, 2019).

- Kim Kardashian, when she introduced her shapewear line called Kimono, which people viewed as not respecting the Japanese culture (Adranly, 2019).

- George Glassman, after his tweet regarding the George Floyd protests and after several CrossFit locations said they would break away from the CrossFit brand. Glassman ended up stepping down from his role as CrossFit CEO ("CrossFit CEO Greg Glassman Quits after George Floyd Remarks," 2020).

- Actor Johnny Depp, famous for his roles in *Pirates of the Carribbean* and the *Fantastic Beasts* movie franchises, was forced to resign from his role by Warner Bros after he lost his libel lawsuit against *The Sun* (Bahr, 2020).

- Olivia Jade, a popular beauty influencer, was in the spotlight related to the Varsity Blues scandal at USC because her parents, Lori Loughlin and Mossimo Giannuli, managed to get her into the school with illegal payments. Jade eventually left the school and has tried to recover her reputation by going on Jada Pinkett Smith's popular online show *Red Table Talk*.

- Kevin Hart, after it was discovered the actor tweeted inappropriate comments on Twitter regarding the LGTBQ+ community in 2011, had to step down from his hosting duties for the 2019 Oscars (Campbell, 2020).

- Goya Products, when the CEO Robert Unanue came out to support President Trump in 2020. Social media uses across both sides of the coin attempted to cancel the brand online, but others who supported Goya encouraged others to purchase their products as a result.

- *Paw Patrol*, for one of the characters on the show (Chase) being a young police officer. The popular children's TV show on Nickelodeon has been a focal point among social justice activists during the George Floyd protests (Goldstein, 2020).

Cancel culture for brands, individuals, and organizations has continued to grow, but this phenomenon has raised some concerns related to the ramifications for someone's future and livelihood. As some have said, cancel culture has become aligned with censorship, limiting the ability to have free speech (Goldstein, 2020).

Here are some things to note about cases of being canceled (Lewis, 2019):

- Be aware of all that is being said. Have an open mind and know that the cancel culture movement on social media happens rapidly, sometimes at light speed.

- Identify the root of what started the cancel culture. Exploring who (individuals, groups, or influencers) sparked the conversation on the cancel culture movement is crucial.

- Listen, monitor, and evaluate what is being shared, said, and discussed. Being present is important to make sure you are able to control the narrative and to determine how to respond.

- Know that the canceled moment is just a moment, and that it does not define a person. Humans make mistakes, and how they respond to these mistakes is more important than ever. How brands and individuals respond can help shape the movement and intensity of the emotions to shift gears from one side of the spectrum to the other.

- Learn from the experience. Understand the takeaways from the experience, and think about what to do in any similar future events.

Social media managers can get into trouble as well, sometimes interjecting humor into a situation that not many people feel is funny. Consider the case of Houston Rockets social media professional Chad Shanks. Shanks tweeted out on the official Houston Rockets account during a game in 2013 against the Dallas Mavericks (the Rockets won 103–94), but the tweet included two emojis (one was a horse, and the other was a gun) and said, "Shhhhh. Just close your eyes. It will all be over soon" (Gaines, 2015).

The Dallas Mavericks account responded, saying that was not "classy," and Shanks immediately got fired from his position since the Houston Rockets did not want to be associated with him after the incident (Harris, 2015). Shanks responded to the firing and used his own social media platform to explain the situation.

In each of these three different cases, posting on social media resulted in a firing. Each individual involved experienced a different outcome, and while it is important to note that not all social media posting fails are equal, they all share the experience of a negative impact on a reputation or personal brand, as well as a professional brand.

Privacy. Privacy is a big issue in the social media community—where your data are stored, who has access, and whether or not platforms are following the laws related to privacy issues. Several agencies and regulatory bodies are actively involved in privacy related to social media, including the FTC. The FTC oversees a variety of elements, but when it comes to social media and privacy, it looks at whether or not the sites (Facebook, Instagram, etc.) publish how they work and what they do in terms of privacy and collecting information about individual users (Claypoole, 2014).

Two big new privacy regulations were recently approved. The first, the **General Data Protection Regulation (GDPR)**, was launched in 2018 in the

European Union. This regulation makes organizations aware of the privacy needs of their users, while also empowering users to control their own personal data and what they are willing to share with brands and organizations ("Complete Guide to GDPR Compliance," n.d.).

The second, the **Children's Online Privacy Protection Act (COPPA)**, focuses on "certain requirements on operators of websites or online services directed to children under 13 years of age, and on operators of other websites or online services that have actual knowledge that they are collecting personal information online from a child under 13 years of age" (Children's Online Privacy Protection Rule ["COPPA"], 2013). This regulation affects certain platforms that have been gaining younger users, such as YouTube and TikTok. TikTok, a platform that originated in China, has been in the news for privacy violations, especially when it comes to children's data (O'Donnell, 2020) The FTC found that TikTok "currently has many regular account holders who are under age 13, and many of them still have videos of themselves that were uploaded as far back as 2016, years prior to the consent decree" (O'Donnell, 2020). TikTok was fined $5.7 million for violating COPPA (O'Donnell, 2020).

Copyright infringement. Copyright infringement may involve the author of a work, a photographer, a videographer, a musician who created the music used in a video, TV footage, the creator of artwork, or a visual content creator. This has become a big issue related to content that is shared, created, and accessed online.

Artists have brought their concerns to both Instagram and Pinterest, ranging from their copyrighted work being shared without attribution to other media outlets creating new content based on original content without permission. A case in point was the 2020 release of Disney's *The Mandalorian*, in which the character Baby Yoda was introduced. This caused a huge spike in content, parody accounts, and unofficial merchandise surfacing for everyone to enjoy. Well, everyone seemed to enjoy the merchandise except Disney, who went after the creators for copyright infringement (Gartenberg, 2020). Disney also went after users on social media platforms such as Twitter for using GIFs from the show on their accounts ("Baby Yoda Gifs Reinstated After Star Wars Takedown Confusion," 2019). However, in this case, the GIFs were restored due to "confusion" about the situation ("Baby Yoda Gifs," 2019).

There are, of course, various things to keep in mind regarding copyright and intellectual property when you are signing up to join a social media platform. It is important to know the terms you are signing into, how much control you have over the content you create, and if any changes are made to these terms. All social media platforms have their own terms of service (as outlined in Table 2.1), but each platform has experienced trouble due to rising concerns about who "owns" the content being shared—and perhaps used for profitable means. Snapchat, for example, updated its services and advised users that while individual users have "ownership rights," Snapchat still has power to use their content since it is on the platform:

> You grant Snapchat a worldwide, perpetual, royalty-free, sublicensable, and transferable license to host, store, use, display, reproduce, modify, adapt, edit, publish, create derivative works from, publicly perform, broadcast, distribute, syndicate, promote, exhibit, and publicly display that content in any form and in any and all media or distribution methods (now known or later developed).

We will use this license for the limited purpose of operating, developing, providing, promoting, and improving the Services; researching and developing new ones; and making content submitted through the Services available to our business partners for syndication, broadcast, distribution, or publication outside the Services. (Quoted in Wood, 2015)

Endorsements (bloggers and influencers). Whether or not bloggers or **influencers** (individuals who are able to persuade audiences to take action) are getting paid for their content, images, or experiences by a brand is one of the rising legal concerns about social media. The FTC has taken actions to address this concern with bloggers, but more recently has moved on to social media celebrities and influencers. For example, DJ Khaled (an influencer on Snapchat) never disclosed whether he was getting paid by the brands that he features on his snaps (Frier & Townsend, 2016). The FTC has updated their expectations, regulations, and policies on influencers and endorsements each year to make sure everything is transparent and not misleading for audiences on social media (Zialcita, 2019). As a result, all influencers, including DJ Khaled, have to note when they are getting paid to promote or create content on social with #ad, #sponsored, or acknowledge it publicly to let their community know this is paid content.

❤ 12,196 likes

letthelordbewithyou Here you go, at 4pm est, write the below.
Caption:
Keeping up with the summer workout routine with my morning @booteauk

▶ **Photo 2.3**
Screenshot of Post by Scott Disick

Source: Instagram/Scott Disick (@letthelordbewithyou)

The FTC also has been "keeping up with the Kardashians" when it comes to following their endorsement and advertising practices. The Kardashians have come under fire for promoting items and products on Instagram without making it easy for audiences to tell whether they really like the products or it is just an ad (Maheshwari, 2016). The same goes for the Kardashians promoting certain weight loss products and skin care lines. The key trend across all these cases is that these individuals are not being honest to the public about getting paid to promote or be part of a campaign. The way in which the Kardashians have addressed this in their Instagram posts has been to add #ad to the end of the update.

The main concern here is that companies are paying (and sometimes overpaying) influencers to promote their brands, and audiences need to be aware of this. These actions have significant consequences for the brands associated with these individuals. This has sparked the updated need for influencers to disclose to their audiences whether content is a promoted post or a sponsored ad. Most of the time, the influencers will use a hashtag such as #sponsored, #ad, or #paid. While this mostly applies to images and updates, the FTC requires influencers to voice this on the screen as well as place it on the screen if they are doing a video (Frier & Townsend, 2016). For example, Antoni

Porowski, host of *Queer Eye*, on his Instagram accounts promotes paid content with his videos, but it is displayed as "Paid partnership with xyz brand." This feature from Instagram and Facebook was added to follow the FTC guidelines for influencer partnerships to create more awareness and transparency on these partnerships.

Some influencers and celebrities fail at the endorsement mentions in a big way. Scott Disick learned this lesson when he copied and pasted a note from a brand without putting it into his own words (Beale, 2016). This example shows the implications that companies need to be aware of when targeting influencers and celebrities to promote their brands. Consumers today are very aware of the true nature of an influencer's promotion, and they want these recommendations and insights to be authentic, not paid. In addition, while number of followers and size of community are important indicators to consider, they are not everything. Communities come and go, and if followers detect any misleading or fake actions by an influencer, they will leave and the influencer will no longer be prominent.

ETHICAL AND LEGAL BEST PRACTICES IN SOCIAL MEDIA

Social media offers many opportunities and resources for users to share, create, report, and communicate with each other. With each opportunity comes a unique challenge that constantly must be addressed in addition to forecasting future ethical and legal incidents that may impact social media practices. A strong ethical and legal best practice to have in social media is a social media policy, which is a document that outlines guidelines, expectations, and actions that are expected to be followed for online engagement on social media. Many corporations, businesses, news organizations, and professionals have their own respective social media policies that help guide them through their online correspondence to promote a strong brand image and community, as well as serve as a guide to prevent behaviors or actions that could spark a crisis.

One case that really put this front and center involved Domino's Pizza in 2009. In April of that year, two Domino's employees went rogue and decided to film themselves being inappropriate with the food being served. This video caught the attention of a blogger, who then went to Twitter to voice his concern. As a result, Domino's responded (actually creating a Twitter account because it didn't have one before) to reassure its customers and others about the situation (Clifford, 2009).

Social media policies are one way to set forth guidelines for behavior to be followed in the workplace. Many brands have incorporated these policies over the years and have tailored them to their own values and perspectives on social media. For example, National Public Radio (NPR) has a comprehensive social media policy outlining its expectations from employers and media outlets. Accuracy is one of the most important elements highlighted in the policy since NPR is dedicated to making sure the information presented to its media outlets is correct and verified ("Social Media," 2017).

While most organizations, corporations, and businesses have a social media policy, it is important that they share certain points of information with their employees directly but also with their audiences publicly. Having a social media policy will help educate and inform your audiences what to expect from you online. Here are some must-haves for your social media policy:

Introduction to the overall purpose of your social media policy. Outline not only why it is important to have a social media policy but also why it is important to the organization, business, media outlet, or agency you represent. Your rationale for the use of these guidelines and practices for your internal and external audience is crucial to state in this section. Make sure to personalize and frame it for the organization in question. Yet also make sure to include a statement that discusses the requirements. Education on your social media policy and guidelines needs to happen as frequently as they need to be updated. New legal and ethical scenarios that could possibly face your brand need to be addressed and added to the guidelines for your social media policy; holding workshops, online sessions, and educational meetings on the changes and revisions for the social media policy are ways to accomplish this.

Employee conduct and personal identity section. Employees are on the front lines of social media and are essentially brand ambassadors for their company, brand, or business. An employee conduct and personal identity code outlines what employees' roles are and how they are expected to present themselves professionally on social media. For example, you do not want to advocate for a client's work without disclosing you are actually working on that campaign. That's why you often see the hashtag #client being shared. The same goes for representing your role at an agency, media outlet, or business. In 2014, Humana invited its employees to use #HumanaEmployee to let their community know they work at Humana while providing some guidelines on what they can and cannot share (confidential information, passwords, personal communication, etc.).

Added section for representing the brand and following the law. Make sure your employees and everyone on board knows what they can share that helps represent the brand professionally and also what they need to be aware of from a legal standpoint. Terms of service, sharing of copyright content, disclosure of confidential information, privacy, respect for others, and obeying the laws online are just some of the things that need to be included here.

Overall tone on social media. Being respectful and professional, and not engaging in a flame war or going rogue, should also be advised. Outlining what to do to combat hacking, fix errors, address crises or threats, report fake accounts, or handle another challenge in a systematic way can help improve the situation further. Also, this provides consistent action steps that employees can take in order to identify, discuss, and handle specific situations in a timely manner.

Diversity, inclusion, and representation policies. Be inclusive for all audiences, perspectives, gender roles, and communities on social media. This is where the diversity and inclusion statements and policies from the organization, brand, or agency can be addressed and integrated into social media practices. (This is discussed more in Chapter 4.)

Protocols for early warning signs or crises. Have a clear line of communication for social media activities that are positive, but also have a plan in place in case something happens that brings forth challenges for the company, agency, or brand. Identifying policies for crisis communication is a good step toward creating awareness and expectations of these practices for all employees. How to handle challenges like crises is a skill that all employees need to learn.

Responsibility for what you create, write, and share. Be aware that what you share is for public viewing. Sometimes you will see a lot of discussion that is positive toward your client, the business you represent, or even yourself. However, sometimes you will get negative or even hateful comments directed toward you and your brand. Noting and reporting what each comment means for the brand and for yourself is important. Talking with your team or with close confidants about your situation is best. You always want to take action to make sure everyone on your team is aware of what is happening, and brainstorm solutions and responses that fall in line with your core values and principles in a timely manner. You should never be alone in handling these types of situations. Contacting your legal team with the necessary documents and evidence (screen shots, links, messages, etc.) will help in this situation as well.

Authenticity and values presented online. Your values for your organization offline need to be present and nurtured online as well. The trouble comes when there is a disconnect between how people see you online versus offline. Be true to yourself for a personal brand, but also note the impact being authentic has for your employer. Apply common sense to understanding the overall culture inside both your organization and the community with which you interact. Take time to see what others are saying, and put your best foot forward each and every time you interact with someone online. Be the better person because each conversation, interaction, and piece of content shared online contributes to the marble glass of items that make up your reputation.

CHAPTER SUMMARY

The legal and ethical landscape will continue to change and evolve for social media. We will be faced with new cases, legal suits, ethical challenges, and situations. Knowing the foundations of professional ethical conduct while also being aware of what the law says is more important than ever for social media professionals. You do not want to wait and ask for permission for certain tasks—that is too risky for the social media landscape today. Educating not only yourself, but your team, about some of these rising issues and situations on both professional and personal levels is key for success in the industry. In addition, we must understand that ethical and legal behavior comes not only from the top down but also from the bottom up. Ethical and legal practices from company leadership are expected since they contribute to the overall environment of the company and its future placement in the industry. If no standards are set, or value is not attributed to ethical or legal practices for social media at the organization, media outlet, or agency you belong to, move along to a place that does have these values. It only takes one misstep to wreak havoc on your personal brand for years to come.

THOUGHT QUESTIONS

1. Based on the reading, what is the current legal landscape in social media? What are some of the main issues to be aware of? How have you seen some of these issues play out for influencers or brands you follow?

2. Define ethics. What are some of the key principles in your code of ethics for using social media?

3. Identify current legal challenges and risks on social media. How would you address them?

4. From a legal and ethical standpoint, what are some benefits and challenges of using influencers and social media personalities on social media?

5. What is cancel culture? What are the ramifications and trends we need to know about cancel culture for social media practices? Identify two strategies that brands and users can use to navigate the social media waters if they are "canceled."

6. Identify the key elements of a social media policy. What is mandatory to include, and what three areas would you add or expand on for your social media policy?

EXERCISES

1. Write an ethical code of conduct for your own social media practices. What are some of the main concepts you feel are necessary to adhere to for your own personal conduct online? What concepts or behaviors do you feel strongly against and want to make sure to avoid on social media?

2. Influencer marketing and engaging with a large audience online has become quite the trend for businesses and brands. You have been asked to engage with influencers as part of the Kentucky Derby Festival. What would you advise the board of directors for the Kentucky Derby Festival to keep in mind when it comes to working with influencers based on FTC regulations? Write a few of these points down, and for each point, discuss how you would address it proactively and some of the risks to avoid.

3. You have been asked to create a social media policy for a local small business. The company has never had such a policy but wants to make sure its employees are aware of what they can and cannot do online. Design a one-page social media policy for the local small business based on what you feel they need to have in place for their employees on social media.

4. You have obtained an internship with a well-known YouTuber, but they have caused quite the scandal and they are now trending as being canceled on social media. Identify steps you will recommend to your boss for handling the situation.

REFERENCES

Adranly, C. (2019, November 26). What brands need to learn about cancel culture. *Adweek*. https://www.adweek.com/brand-marketing/what-brands-need-to-understand-about-cancel-culture/

Baby Yoda Gifs reinstated after Star Wars takedown confusion. (2019, November 25). BBC News. https://www.bbc.com/news/business-50545583

Bahr, S. (2020). Johnny Depp leaves "Fantastic Beasts" franchise at studio's request. *The New York Times*. https://www.nytimes.com/2020/11/06/movies/johnny-depp-harry-potter.html

Beale, T. (2016, May 20). Why Scott Disick's Instagram fail is everything wrong with influencer marketing. *Traackr*. http://www.traackr.com/blog/why-scott-disicks-instagram-fail-is-everything-wrong-with-influencer-marketing

Bond, S. (2020a, June 4). *Facebook begins labeling "state-controlled" media*. NPR. https://www.npr.org/2020/06/04/870105673/facebook-begins-labeling-state-controlled-media

Bond, S. (2020b, June 11). *Critics slam Facebook but Zuckerberg resists blocking Trump's posts*. NPR. https://www.npr.org/2020/06/11/874424898/critics-slam-facebook-but-zuckerberg-resists-blocking-trumps-posts

Booth, R. (2014, June 29). Facebook reveals news feed experiment to control emotions. *The Guardian*. https://www.theguardian.com/technology/2014/jun/29/facebook-users-emotions-news-feeds

Campbell, J. (2020, January 16). Have we taken cancel culture too far in 2020? *GQ.* https://www.gq.com.au/success/opinions/have-we-taken-cancel-culture-too-far-in-2020/news-story/0f12503dbf60071a63d7ffd5e29bcce7

Children's Online Privacy Protection Rule ("COPPA"). (2013, July 25). Federal Trade Commission. https://www.ftc.gov/enforcement/rules/rulemaking-regulatory-reform-proceedings/childrens-online-privacy-protection-rule

Claypoole, T. F. (2014, January). Privacy and social media. *Business Law Today.* http://www.americanbar.org/publications/blt/2014/01/03a_claypoole.html

Clifford, S. (2009, April 15). Video prank at Domino's taints brand. *The New York Times.* http://www.nytimes.com/2009/04/16/business/media/16dominos.html

Coffman, K. (2019, February 19). *Teen in Lincoln Memorial protest sues* Washington Post *for $250 million.* Reuters. https://www.reuters.com/article/us-usa-covington-suit/teen-in-lincoln-memorial-protest-sues-washington-post-for-250-million-idUSKCN1Q82SW

Coleman, O. (2021). *Hayley Paige suffers legal setback in Instagram account case.* https://pagesix.com/2021/03/05/hailey-paige-suffers-legal-setback-in-instagram-account-case/

Complete guide to GDPR [General Data Protection Regulation] compliance. (n.d.). https://gdpr.eu/

CrossFit CEO Greg Glassman quits after George Floyd remarks. (2020, June 10). BBC News. https://www.bbc.com/news/world-us-canada-52988959

Fleming, M., Jr. (2019, March 15). Disney reinstates director James Gunn for 'Guardians of the Galaxy' 3. *Deadline.* https://deadline.com/2019/03/james-gunn-reinstated-guardians-of-the-galaxy-3-disney-suicide-squad-2-indefensible-social-media-messages-1202576444/

47 U.S. Code § 230—*Protection for private blocking and screening of offensive material.* (n.d.). Cornell Law School, Legal Information Institute. https://www.law.cornell.edu/uscode/text/47/230

Frier, S., & Townsend, M. (2016, August 5). FTC to crack down on paid celebrity posts that aren't clear ads. *Bloomberg Technology.* https://www.bloomberg.com/news/articles/2016-08-05/ftc-to-crack-down-on-paid-celebrity-posts-that-aren-t-clear-ads

Gaines, C. (2015, April 29). The Houston Rockets fired a social media manager for sending a dumb, but harmless emoji tweet. *Business Insider.* http://www.businessinsider.com/houston-rockets-social-media-manager-horse-emoji-tweet-2015-4

Gartenberg, C. (2020, January 17). Disney is hunting down the most popular Baby Yoda toys on Etsy. *The Verge.* https://www.theverge.com/2020/1/17/21069124/baby-yoda-dolls-etsy-disney-mandalorian-copyright-takedown-enforcement

Goldstein, L. (2020, June 11). Cancel culture is the new name for censorship. *Toronto Sun.* https://torontosun.com/opinion/columnists/goldstein-cancel-culture-is-the-new-name-for-censorship

Gunkel, D. J. (2015, March 17). Social media: Changing the rules of business ethics. *NIU Newsroom.* http://newsroom.niu.edu/2015/03/17/social-media-changing-the-rules-of-business-ethics/

Harris, J. D. (2015, May 12). Houston Rockets social media manager should not have been fired after questionable tweet. *SportTechie.* http://www.sporttechie.com/2015/05/12/trending

Kelly, M. (2020, May 26). Twitter labels Trump tweets as "potentially misleading" for the first time. *The Verge.* https://www.theverge.com/2020/5/26/21271207/twitter-donald-trump-fact-check-mail-in-voting-coronavirus-pandemic-california

Lewis, A. (2019, November 15). A parent's guide to cancel culture, explained by a teenager. (n.d.). *Parents.* https://www.parents.com/parenting/better-parenting/teenagers/a-parents-guide-to-cancel-culture-explained-by-a-teenager/

Lorenz, T. (2019, May 16). How tea accounts are fueling influencer feuds. *The Atlantic.* https://www.theatlantic.com/technology/archive/2019/05/how-tea-channels-feed-youtube-feuds/589618/

Maheshwari, S. (2016, August 30). Endorsed on Instagram by a Kardashian, but is it love or just an ad? *The New York Times.* https://www.nytimes.com/2016/08/30/business/media/instagram-ads-marketing-kardashian.html

Marsh, E., Cantor, A., & Brashier, N. (2016). Believing that humans swallow spiders in their sleep. *Psychology of Learning and Motivation, 64,* 93–132.

Myers, C. (2020, June 3). *What Trump's new executive order on social media means for PR.* Institute for Public Relations. https://instituteforpr.org/what-trumps-new-executive-order-on-social-media-means-for-pr-practitioners/

NASCAR. (2020, June 10). *NASCAR statement on confederate flag.* https://www.nascar.com/news-media/2020/06/10/nascar-statement-on-confederate-flag/

O'Donnell, L. (2020, May 14). TikTok violated children's privacy law, FTC complaint says. *Threatpost*. https://threatpost.com/tiktok-violated-childrens-privacy-law-ftc-complaint-says/155755/

Parker, S. (2013). The 7 NEW Deadly Sins of Social Media | Social Media Today. (2013, 2013-09-04T04:40-04:00). Retrieved from http://www.socialmediatoday.com/content/7-new-deadly-sins-social-media

Pathak, S. (2019, September 11). #Canceled: How cancel culture is affecting brands. *Digiday*. https://digiday.com/marketing/cancel-culture/

Pomarico, N. (2020, May 19). Who is Sofia Franklyn's boyfriend, Peter Nelson? HBO exec at center of "Call Her Daddy" barstool drama. *YourTango*. https://www.yourtango.com/202034066/who-sofia-franklyns-boyfriend-peter-nelson

Reid, C. (2020, May 24). Civil Service tweet goes viral: "Arrogant and offensive. Can you imagine having to work with these truth twisters?" *Forbes*. https://www.forbes.com/sites/carltonreid/2020/05/24/civil-service-tweet-goes-viral-arrogant-and-offensive-can-you-imagine-having-to-work-with-these-truth-twisters/#7619a2173154

Ronson, J. (February 12, 2015). How one stupid tweet blew up Justine Sacco's Life. *The New York Times*. Retrieved from https://www.nytimes.com/2015/02/15/magazine/how-one-stupid-tweet-ruined-justine-saccos-life.html

Rotter, M. (2020, May 21). An official timeline of all the "Call Her Daddy" drama. *Cosmopolitan*. https://www.cosmopolitan.com/lifestyle/a32628219/call-her-daddy-podcast-drama-timeline-explainer/

Schwartz, M. S. (2019, February 15). *Investigators for diocese say Kentucky students did not initiate confrontation*. NPR. https://www.npr.org/2019/02/15/695036694/covington-catholic-teens-cleared-of-wrongdoing-by-detective-agency

Snapchat TOS. (n.d.) Retrieved from https://snap.com/en-US/terms

Social media: The NPR way. (2017, July). *NPR ethics handbook*. http://ethics.npr.org/tag/social-media/

Waterlow, L. (2015, February 16). "I lost my job, my reputation and I'm not able to date anymore": Former PR worker reveals how she destroyed her life one year after sending "racist" tweet before trip to Africa. *Daily Mail*. http://www.dailymail.co.uk/femail/article-2955322/Justine-Sacco-reveals-destroyed-life-racist-tweet-trip-Africa.html

What it means to get "canceled." (n.d.). *Merriam-Webster*. https://www.merriam-webster.com/words-at-play/cancel-culture-words-were-watching

Wong, Q. (2020, June 3). *Snapchat is the latest social network to take on Trump*. CNET. https://www.cnet.com/news/snapchat-is-the-latest-social-network-to-take-on-trump/

Zialcita, P. (2019, November 5). *FTC issues rules for disclosure of ads by social media influencers*. NPR. https://www.npr.org/2019/11/05/776488326/ftc-issues-rules-for-disclosure-of-ads-by-social-media-influencers

3

PERSONAL AND PROFESSIONAL BRANDING FOR SOCIAL MEDIA

Learning Objectives

After reading this chapter, you will be able to

- Define *personal brand* and explain the importance of establishing a community

- Understand the different types of personal brands in social media

- Discuss the key benefits and challenges of a personal brand

- Explain the skills needed to create a sustainable personal brand

INTRODUCTION

A common phrase about reputation comes from Benjamin Franklin: "It takes many good deeds to build a good reputation, but only one bad one to lose it." Today, within the social media community, not only does your reputation need to be managed and invested in, it also has to be sustainable and consistent. In many cases, reputation is the most valuable asset and brand businesses and professionals have today.

Any person, brand, or community can create an image online, but it does not mean a thing when the personality, voice, or person behind the screen does not match the person or brand presented. The importance of alignment, along with establishing a clear, consistent, transparent, and authentic voice online contributes to how we see ourselves and how we want others to perceive us at the same time. A brand is more than just having a logo, platform aesthetic, or color palette; it's about having a long-term, strategic, and creative approach to telling your story, sharing your knowledge, and navigating the field effortlessly to build connections.

Chris Strub, CEO of I Am Here, LLC

Introduction

I'm Chris Strub, working these days as the "Giving Day Guy." I partner with community foundations and other nonprofits around the U.S. to help them create massive attention spikes on social media during, and in the lead-up to, their 24-hour online giving days. My clients include The Big Give (San Antonio, TX); The Amazing Give (Gainesville, FL); Give Local York (York, PA); Midlands Gives (Columbia, SC); Give STL Day (St. Louis), and the day where it all started for me in 2016—in Dr. Freberg's neighborhood—Give For Good Louisville (KY). I'm the CEO of I Am Here, LLC, which encompasses my speaking engagements, webinar offerings, road trip marketing endeavors, and book writing, but I focus mainly on helping community-based giving days maximize their reach and impact.

How did you get your start in social media?

My first job out of college was at the local newspaper in Binghamton, NY, in the mid-2000s, when the industry was rapidly shifting from print-first to digital-first. During those transitional years, I was looked to in the newsroom as a leading voice, working closely with the publisher, executive editor, and senior digital staff to shape the paper's website and social media approach. When I started in 2006, there were still pica poles laying around on the proofreading tables—but as time passed, I became increasingly fascinated with how to properly blend the print product with our online presence. In 2011, I made the switch from the news department to the advertising department, leading the local chapter of a social commerce initiative called DealChicken. That job helped me land a role at a nearby advertising agency, where I helped grow our digital clientele from the ground up. My work with those clients helped inspire me to take the aforementioned road trips around the country in 2014 and 2015, connecting with people in person and then supporting those interactions with social media storytelling.

Looking back at all those years, I think it's important to emphasize that at each stop, I never could've really predicted where I'd be a few years down the line. A big-picture key for me, at each job, has always been to always ask "why"—and the older I get, that has evolved to asking "why not."

What is your favorite part of working in your area of expertise in social media?

I embrace the sincere authenticity of building a presence through livestreaming. You can do all the preparatory work in the world, but when you're broadcasting live, anything can happen, and viewers gain a very real appreciation for who you are. It's been a true blessing identifying and matching that synergy with the concept of 24-hour giving days, which are a natural hot spot for attention and a great way to shine a spotlight on communities of different sizes around the country.

What is one thing you can't live without while working in social media?

The obvious answer here would be the technology—my iPhones, a portable battery pack, a laptop, etc. But I've come to appreciate the immeasurable power of a human network. Social media has introduced me to, gosh, tens, hundreds of thousands of people around the world, with whom I might not share skin color, or an education level, or even a native language, but we do share the apps that brought us together. I met power influencer Ted Rubin a few years ago—wouldn't you know, he lived just a couple miles down the road here on Long Island—and he gifted me a book, and inside, he wrote to me: "Relationships are like muscle tissue: The more they're engaged, the stronger they become." The relationships that I've built, both with Ted and thousands of others, have become a vital part of what I do every day.

What is the most challenging part of working in social media?

Monetizing. It's tricky to quantify the real value of the relationships that can be built through social media, even from a personal branding perspective, and it's that much more difficult to do so from a business perspective. Livestreaming, Snapchat, etc., are built for people to connect individually or in small groups, and it is a constant challenge for businesses to utilize these networks in ways that can measurably deliver a return on the investment that executives make in their digital teams. Thankfully, after years of trial and error—lots of errors, in fact—I've found a fun, important, and profitable niche with giving days.

What is your take on your area of expertise and the social media industry?

I think I'd build off of my previous answer. Lately, businesses of all types have been focused on metamorphosing into media companies, but I think the next big evolution is to break down long-standing barriers between their own, big, shiny "brand" and the public's perception and interaction with it. Your brand isn't what you say it is; it is what the public perceives it to be. Social media provides an unparalleled opportunity for brands to capitalize on the positive sentiment its consumers have or, conversely, to meaningfully address, both at scale and individually, the negativity bringing the brand down.

What do you wish you had known when you were starting out?

I think my best advice to the next generation would be to sharply, and honestly, evaluate your biggest strengths and where you feel the most passionate, and pursue a path that will let those things shine through every single day. Don't let the world dictate where you go and what you do—you are your own boss. And don't be shy, or intimidated by follower counts. Social media is natively egalitarian, and the "thought leaders" are more accessible than you think.

What are three marketable skills a social media professional needs to have to work in the industry?

Because of my background, I have to start by saying journalistic instincts. Every aspiring social media marketer should take at least one journalism class before they graduate. You need to be able to have a feel for the news of the day and how it can impact your brand's messaging and/or how you can parlay outside occurrences into attention for your brand.

I'd also encourage aspiring marketers to grow their design skills. Even if you're not a graphic designer—I'm not—it's important to understand the balance, look, and feel of an image, document, or video production. Working at a college newspaper, magazine, or even on the yearbook can help you sharpen skills that you'll need forever.

Where do you go to keep up to date with trends and continue learning about social media?

Twitter. Having been on Twitter now for over a decade, I rely on it very heavily to keep me informed on the news of the day. I keep a close eye on who I follow and who I keep on certain Twitter lists, which allows me to maintain a healthy and valuable stream of information through that app daily. I also attend as many live events as I can, not just to keep up with the latest trends and info but to initiate new relationships and strengthen existing ones.

If you had to choose a song to walk out to in a presentation on social media, what would it be and why?

I think this depends on the type of presentation I'm giving, as well as the location and audience. More important to me than the messaging/lyrics would be the energy conveyed by the music, so something like "Sirius," by The Alan Parsons Project—yes, I'm a huge Michael Jordan fan—which really gets people's blood flowing and emotions in motion, would work for me.

Connect with Chris Strub on Twitter and Instagram, and almost every other social media platform, @ChrisStrub. His Facebook page is www.facebook.com/TeamStrub and website is www.teamstrub.com. You can get 50 States, 100 Days: The Book at www.50States100Days.com.

Courtesy of Daryll Borges at Opportunity Village

WHAT IS A PERSONAL BRAND?

People will, and always will, have a voice and presence on social media. Voices range from person to person, of course, but some are filtered to present a crystal-clear image across various platforms. Then there are those considered to have an unfiltered voice, who will say whatever comes to mind immediately and post it directly for their friends, community, and the world to see.

A **personal brand** can arise in many ways. People who are established in other fields have become examples of sustainable personal brands on social media. Dwayne "The Rock" Johnson, for example, has one of the most consistent and personable social media brands. He balances his content in a way where he shows authentic videos of himself working out or on set; yet he also interjects promotional updates and visuals for upcoming collaborations (e.g., Under Armour), movies (e.g., the *Fast & Furious* series and *Jumanji*), TV series (*Titans* and *Young Rock*), new product launches and entering new industries entirely (e.g., his tequila brand Teremana and ZOA energy drink), or Throwback Thursday pictures with family and friends. What makes The Rock stand out from other celebrities is his inter-mixture of content, storytelling, and personality, all of which will be discussed in this chapter. He emphasizes transparency and authenticity across the board. The Rock is just as likely to post a picture from a movie set with Ryan Reynolds as he is to post a video with one of his daughters as they watch his movie *Moana* (and to let you know how his daughter Tia is convinced her dad is not Maui!). As a result, in October 2020, The Rock became the most followed actor and man in the United States on Instagram with over 200 million followers (Photo 3.1).

▶ **Photo 3.1**
Dwayne Johnson aka The Rock's Instagram Promoting a New Drink Recipe Using His Company's Product, Teremana Tequila

Source: Instagram / Dwayne Johnson (@therock).

Another example of a professional who not only has a strong brand but has used it to create numerous professional and personal opportunities for herself is Robin Arzón (Photo 3.2). Arzón is the vice president and head instructor at Peloton, and she has defined herself as a leading voice in fitness. Not only is she a fitness instructor but she is also a *New York Times* best-selling author, an Adidas ambassador, and a frequent collaborator with various celebrities, including Reese Witherspoon, Jennifer Lopez (J.Lo), and Venus Williams. In fact, J.Lo partnered with Arzón on a strength workout session to release one of her songs exclusively in 2020 due to Arzón's influence in the fitness community. On her social media channels, Arzón has been strategic in her content but also presentation. For example, her brand colors are red and white, a palette that is evident on her Instagram profile as well as in the content she showcases for her IGTV series *Hustlers at Home*, a show she created during the national stay-at-home order for COVID-19.

▶ **Photo 3.2**
Robin Arzón

Source: Instagram/
@robinnyc

Some people have grown their presence based on what they have created and shared that is unique and different from others. Sure, there have been other dancers that have graced the digital stage on social media, but Charli D'Amelio took her dance talent and the power of TikTok to new heights, solidifying her personal brand on the platform (Photo 3.3). Her TikTok displays videos of her incorporating dance and music into daily life, and she weaves humor in as well, such as in her bio, which addresses her unexpected fame. She diversified her reach with her other profiles on platforms, but TikTok is where she built her brand, presence, and following. D'Amelio is also the first person who has made it to 100 million followers on TikTok, which is quite an accomplishment.

charlidamelio ✓ ⋯
charli d'amelio

[Follow]

804 Following   56.2M Followers   3.9B Likes

don't worry i don't get the hype either
🔗 merch link 🔗

videos   🔒 Likes

▷ 3.9M   ▷ 8.6M   ▷ 7.7M
▷ 10.3M   ▷ 17.5M   ▷ 17M

▶ **Photo 3.3**
Charli D'Amelio on TikTok

Source: TikTok/@charlidamelio

All three of these professionals come from different backgrounds and have different interests, but what do all three of them have in common? Let's break it down.

- Each has a distinctive voice on social media that showcases their personality while emphasizing the need for transparency and authenticity with their audiences.

- Each shares their expertise in their field (e.g., The Rock for acting, Robin for fitness, and Charli for dancing) but has extended their reach by adding personal interests and passion areas (e.g., The Rock and tequila, Robin for wellness, and Charli for certain brands).

- Each has distinctively created their own brand palette, mantra, logo, and presence on their social media accounts.

- Each has created a community online and offline, bringing together audiences from all over the world while providing value and engaging with their audiences.

- Each focuses on their story—not just the picture-perfect view of their story but their authentic story.

- Each keeps themselves in the conversation. They do not have a team posting their content on their channels; rather, it is them.

- Each has invested in their brands for the long term by making collaborations with people in other fields to solidify their standing as a brand. Essentially, they do not want to be a "one-trick pony" and only be known for one thing.

All of these points demonstrate that while each of these high-profile individuals comes from different backgrounds and perspectives, each takes ownership of their brand online through the investing time and resources, consistently engaging with their community, and staying true to who they are as a person online.

That's the power of social media as a whole. It allows us to have a personalized digital version of what we see in traditional media. Instead of journalists, editors, and reporters telling us the stories they choose to focus on, social media allows people to share relevant information about emerging trends in the industry, personal stories and experiences, and important issues related to their interests. A group of people who come together for a common cause is referred to as a **community**. Yet, while some communities will come together in support of you, others will be against you, no matter what, because of who you are. That's the nature of the business, and it is important for all of us to recognize this before we enter the social media space.

If you do not see a community out there for your personal brand, start one. This has been a principle that Adam Ilenich (Twitter) and Christina Garnett (HubSpot) have embraced and advocated for in the #MarketingTwitter Community. Sometimes a community can surround a hashtag, like what Brianne Fleming has done with tying together pop culture and marketing into #PopChat for a Twitter chat and Zoom community session meet-ups. In addition, keep in mind that people will always talk about you, so make sure to give them something positive to talk about. How you react and manage your overall tone and conduct online will determine how you are perceived. Essentially, actions speak louder than words. As your actions, voice, and dialogue grow within your community, your **influence** (the ability to persuade people to take action or listen to what you say) grows.

Influence is a powerful element for a personal brand. Influence can be beneficial for a brand when looking at an applicant or support for an employee, but it can also be (in rare cases) something that gets you fired. This is what happened to Ohio University student Tony Piloseno, who has a large following on TikTok and was hired by painting company Sherwin-Williams to create engaging content on mixing paints to reach Generation Z audiences. Not only was Piloseno successful in this, he was able to get audiences excited about mixing paint. Unfortunately, Piloseno was fired by Sherwin-Williams because he used their equipment for the videos on TikTok (T. Chen, 2020). Piloseno was immediately hired by another paint company (Florida Paints) to create content on TikTok for them (Liffering, 2020). Influence can be used for good for personal branding, and as Sherwin-Williams learned, ignoring this has gotten them painted into a corner.

All the while, we have to be aware of the fact that privacy is nonexistent. Think about the privacy settings you have set forth for yourself. Is your Facebook account private? Do you have an Instagram account for your personal brand and a separate account for your "real" friends (aka a fake Instagram account, or **finsta**)? All of these accounts may be set to "private," but there are ways to get around those settings, and brands have found how to do that. Do you feel like you can be on TikTok because your parents or employers are not there to see your content? Do you assume your content won't be collected and used for other purposes? Do you feel everyone will have the same interpretation of your content, voice, and messaging on social media?

In addition, keep in mind that the largest search engine in the world, Google, is more than just a place to search for your next latte or to book your next spring break vacation. It's a reputation management system, and it could be the first place people go to search your name. Plus, once something is posted online, even if you have deleted the content, it lasts forever. Google does not forget.

Today, it is rare to meet someone who does not have a digital presence or brand. According to Brian Solis (2012), having a digital presence is essentially a way of life nowadays, and it is not only expected but also insisted upon in certain industries. In some industries, you have to be active and engaged on certain platforms because that is where your future employers, clients, and community are located. For example, joining Twitter chats such as #HootChat, #AdweekChat, or #TwitterSmarter are some ways to get connected with others in the industry and to show what you know and can offer to the industry. Engaging in guest posts and commentary is another way to get connected. Creating long-form content in contributor roles at *Adweek* or Front Office Sports allows you to show your insights and perspectives in the field. Joining Facebook groups for related topics to network on a global scale (like Matt Navarra's The Social Geekout Group) can help build professional networking connections online while learning what professionals are concerned about in the field.

When it comes to social media, what matters is not only what you know, but who knows of you and your work online and offline. Who controls this exactly? The answer is simple: *you*. You are the one who is able to control your actions, networks, and voice, as well as the information and content you create, share, and talk about. That said, this does not happen overnight, and it takes investment, patience, and time to determine your personal brand and place in a community. For example, you must understand there are specific communities on certain platforms (e.g., Twitter) where you can engage with some of the best in the business and network with these professionals. Marketing Twitter, for example, is a great place to connect with professionals who lead, work, and support social media initiatives with brands, teams, and corporations. Professionals who are part of Marketing Twitter include Adam Ilenich (social at Twitter), Jack Appleby (creative strategy at Twitch), Kristen Nyham (social at Delta), Adrian Molina (brand manager for Aviation Gin), Adam Ornelas (social and influencer strategy for Chipotle), Matthew Kobach (social at Fast), Julian Gamboa (social at *Adweek*), and Taylor Cohen (global creative strategist for TikTok). All of these professionals engage on Twitter within this community; all are there to have a conversation and build a professional relationship with.

What exactly does it mean to have a personal brand? Personal branding is "the process of managing and optimizing the way you are presented to others" (Lee, 2015). Your personal brand, otherwise known as your reputation, is part of how people perceive you. Essentially, reputations essentially are

- Evolving

- Fragile

- Impactful

- Made up of personal brand and community

- Constantly maintained and invested in

- Formed from personal interactions

- Influenced by word of mouth, and

- Based on transparency and authenticity.

Last but not least, your reputation online is your most valued possession. Standing out from the crowd is very challenging, especially in the social media space. We are constantly competing for the moment and attention from others. This can be from our friends, but when it comes to the workplace, we are looking at how we differ from other professionals in our industry. TV reporters look at ways to stand out to grow the audience for their station, for example, and online influencers try to drive views, posts, and brands to their sites and videos as well. Brands and social media professionals are also competing for relevance and embracing the next trend in a way that gets the attention of the media and other audiences. As mentioned in Chapter 1, getting a brand to go "viral" is one thing, but going viral by getting a campaign, a new way to use a tool or platform, or a speaking engagement is another challenge facing people and brands today. In addition, competition for attention is on the rise, and we as social media professionals need to understand who we are and where we need to be to contribute to the conversation with our key audiences, our industry, and the overall global environment. That's why having a strong brand that is constantly evolving but stays relevant is crucial. This is how business is being done today.

What Are the Components of a Personal Brand?

Some form of **personality** that is unique and memorable about an individual can help bring forth a strong view toward his or her personal brand. Personality focuses on how an individual behaves, acts, responds, and communicates with people and their respective communities. Think about all of the distinctive characteristics that make you unique. What are your beliefs and views on certain topics? What is your mission statement? What are some brand values you feel make up who you are as a person and professional? What attributes would you use to describe yourself? How would others describe you? These are just some of the questions to consider. You can, of course, take a test to determine your type of personality. Whether you are a mastermind or a provider, according to Myers-Briggs (Vital & Vital, n.d.), additional layers of information make every one of us different for all the good reasons. Individual users each have a certain manner and approach, and that is what makes them unique and memorable. For example, people express certain personality traits in their own writing and views on social media, as Matthew Kobach from Fast has done on Twitter. Matthew emphasizes his need to be purposeful and strategic, yet also authentic in his Twitter posts and commentary, bringing his brand to the forefront as a leading voice in social media.

While personality is important, so is **consistency** with your personality. Taking the time to think about how you are presenting yourself in every single online and offline exchange is crucial. Yes, a strong online presence and correct, consistent handles are important, but underneath the layers of the screen and profiles, there needs to be consistency (as well as a human). Your actions sometimes speak louder than your words or profiles ever will. You may have the best profile, but if you do not interact with your community and talk *with* followers instead of *at* them, you will not be successful. Some influencers (e.g., Amy Landino and Goldie Chan) have strong followings and a lot of articles, features, videos, and praise written about their branding and voice in the community, but they also spend time interacting and engaging their followers. A social media community is like a garden: If you do not spend time to take care of it, it will no longer thrive and it will go away. Consistently providing value through engaging experiences while feeling valued as a member is the ultimate goal to create for audiences on social media.

Passion is a key part of a personal brand as well. What areas are you interested in? What hobbies do you feel are part of who you are? What topics are you interested in sharing with the world on social? Everyone has passion and interest pillars as part of their overall brand. Many professionals have passion and interest areas that are unique to their personal brand. For example, Julian Gamboa (*Adweek*) focuses on amplifying work of social media professionals who are part of #MarketingTwitter, whereas Tori Tidwell (IHG/Disney) has brought her craft and social media skills to retail with her creation of the online store Free The Edit Button, which sells social media swag for professionals. Hobbies, interests, and passion pillars amplify the human side of your personal brand.

The last part needed to create a personal brand, of course, is **expertise**. Being knowledgeable in your profession or industry makes you credible. Here, experience again comes into play: What is your role, and what have you done to receive a place in the conversation or have your insights taken into consideration? What evidence can you provide that shows your impact on a campaign, brand, or movement online? Some people use trendy, obscure titles such as "guru," "keynote speaker and influencer," "change evangelist," or "digital futurist" to make others perceive them as experts when, in fact, they are not. Identifying the fakes (and there are a lot of them out there) versus the true professionals in the field can be challenging, but it is an important step. Doing your research to identify who is true to their word online and who is "faking it till they make it" can take some time.

There are a few ways to help you identify the fakes. First, no social media professional will list himself or herself as a guru or expert. This is an evolving field, and no one is an expert in every single aspect of social media. It's changing too quickly for any of us to do that. Second, the followers professionals have listed and their actual engagement tell a different story. Quality in followers is always better than quantity, but sometimes people buy followers (or bots, defined in Chapter 2) to make it appear they have a large group of people following them when they do not. These accounts can be identified in many ways (this happens a lot on Instagram and Twitter), but next time, look at the followers' engagement in the account's last updates (tweets or pictures) and see if it is aligned. If not, then the account is using a lot of fake followers. Third, these individuals can talk a good game, but when push comes to shove, they cannot show the actual impact and results they have had on the industry and campaigns they have supposedly worked on. Fourth, these individuals like to talk broadly and not in specifics. If you talk to them about a campaign, they will give you an eagle's eye view of the overall perspectives and lessons learned, which they may have read about in *Adweek* or other publications. But, they are not able to discuss the finer details about what really works on social media. They do not have the evidence or experience to back up their points. Lastly, trying to be like someone else spells out disaster from the get-go. You have to be unique and true to yourself.

Sure, you can see what others do online and what works for them and learn from the experience, but it's an entirely different situation to try to *be* another person completely. That is not good, especially if the person has made his or her mark distinctly in the field. Gary Vaynerchuk has done this extremely well, but when he launched his daily videos (#DailyVees, #WeeklyVees, and more) and created his own movie-like videos with videographer David Rock (otherwise known as DRock), many social media professionals began to copy his ideas completely. They hired videographers for their conference presentations, used certain items to create videos so they could be on the same level as him, and even tried to establish their own store with their own branding—which is all fine and good, but in this industry, if someone else got the idea first, it's best to move on. Plus, there is a fine line between too much and too little self-promoting. You want to be your best advocate, of course, but if you overpromote yourself and really push the envelope of spamming people in your network with your content, you may not be viewed as credible. Let your experience and community speak for you.

Types of Personal Brands

After looking at the components of establishing a personal brand, the next step is to determine what type of brand you want. It is important to note these types are more like "guidelines" (like from *Pirates of the Caribbean*), or ways in which we can categorize concepts into different groups, and you may find you are a mixture of two or more types. As shown in Table 3.1, Bryan Kramer has created a typology of six different personas that focuses on types of individuals online. You can even take a quiz (ownyourline.lpages.co/what-s-your-personal-brand) to find out your type.

Table 3.1 Kramer's Typology of Online Personas		
Persona Type	**Brief Description**	**Example**
Altruist	These individuals are committed to helping others in their community. Actions speak louder than words for these individuals, but they value relationships.	**Leo Morejon** **Ryan Reynolds** **Adam Ornelas**
Careerist	These individuals focus primarily on professional advancement above their personal achievements. They are more associated with professional networks than with personal or informal ones.	**Gini Dietrich** **Reese Witherspoon** **Christina Garnett**
Early Adopter	These individuals will be the first to share something with their followers and friends and are very much dedicated to being independent from others, not so much part of the collective on social media. They are dedicated to careers and relationships.	**Brian Fanzo** **Sarah Evans** **David Armano**
Boomerang	The emphasis for these individuals is to share content to generate a reaction from others—whether a positive one or a negative one. Most of the time, the focus is not on what they really think of what they post, but on the audience's reaction.	**Robert Scoble**
Connector	The ultimate networkers, these individuals do virtual introductions and are highly engaged in making sure everyone in their community is united and knows each other.	**Deirdre Breakenridge** **Julian Gamboa**
Selective	These individuals share only relevant information with a select group of people. They are resourceful and are viewed as a resource, but they are also exclusive in their networks. Think about the "circle of trust" concept from the movie *Meet the Parents*.	**Jason Falls** **Matt Navarra**

Source: Adapted from Bryan Kramer, "6 Types of Personal Brand—Which One Are You?" *Social Media Today,* February 18, 2016. https://www.socialmediatoday.com/social-business/6-types-personal-brand-which-one-are-you

BENEFITS AND CHALLENGES FOR PERSONAL BRANDS

There is a benefit to establishing a personal brand in a way that has not been possible before. Our personality, voice, and overall interests on social media help define who we are online. There are numerous opportunities to evaluate and look at what others are doing in our industry to see where we stand. We can look at what other professionals are doing that is working, but we can determine where our competition is as well. No one person online is the exact same, so social media serves as a perfect opportunity to embrace our unique characteristics in a way that makes us both memorable and impactful in the industry.

One great thing about building your personal brand online is the power to grow your list of connections and network with professionals from all spans of the industry. Of course, you want to do your networking on certain platforms, and then use others to evolve your relationships with particular contacts. For example, most professionals first connect via Twitter or LinkedIn. Twitter allows you to connect with anyone you want to meet, and LinkedIn is all about business connections. Making a friend request on Facebook, however, has to be evaluated based on the situation and the professional contact with whom you are reaching out. TikTok is a place where people connect from all walks of life, but that could evolve and change as the platform becomes more established in the social media field as a professional platform for strategy and creative execution.

In addition to building your network, you can control and manage your own voice and community. Most of the time, personal branding is the heart of what makes a social media professional successful, but *community* (people who have come together on a certain platform, with a common interest, or in a common area online) allows you to build trust and credibility. People in your network have different backgrounds and interests, perhaps, but they are all coming together to have a conversation, share resources, or participate in a discussion on a topic that is relevant to their work. Twitter chats are a great way to help expand and even start building your personal community and network broadly. However, a trend for more opportunities through messaging applications (e.g., digital communities for sports and social media professionals on WhatsApp) have risen over the past few years to make things more conversational, less broadcast focused, and more authentic.

It takes time and energy, as well as investment, to be recognized and appreciated on social media for your personal brand. This does not happen overnight. It takes a little bit each day to reach out to others and share your point of view, being generous with your resources and knowledge and giving back to the industry. Sometimes you may do work for "free," and that is okay. Sharing tutorial videos, writing blog posts, creating ebooks, and spending time bouncing ideas around are just a few ways to contribute for free. Experience is one of the underlying assets that helps significantly when you are starting out in the business. Volunteer to help out with a social media event, create social media audits and run analytics reports for small businesses and their social media channels, or write sample posts to share with a nonprofit in your town—see what works and what doesn't. Having these experiences while taking the time to network is what makes a social media professional relevant and recognized in the field. Buying followers for vanity metrics will only create a faux presentation of your personal brand. It is very, very easy to identify the real versus fake social media presences now.

Of course, several challenges come into play for personal brands. Social media is not all flowers and roses—it can really be a tough place to be. In today's society, professionals are getting dismissed or fired left and right for what they post and share on social media.

HOW TO ESTABLISH A PERSONAL BRAND

Conduct an internal audit of who you are and where you want to go. This is the very first thing to do. We may live in a dynamic society where everyone wants to be like everyone else, but before we move forward with a personal brand, we have to ask ourselves several questions about who we are and where we want our brand to go. Consider the following questions as you work toward understanding where you stand compared to others, and what makes you unique as a person and brand:

- How would you define yourself? List five words that capture who you are.

- What are your brand pillars? What values align with who you are as a person?

- What are you passionate about?

- What are your brand colors? Choose a color palette (three to five colors) that fit your personality and looks.

- Do you have a brand logo? If not, what would it look like?

- What experiences have helped define you as a person and as a professional?

- What are your main topic areas? Identify these five areas, and list at least three people you feel would support you in these topic areas.

- How do you communicate with others? Is your voice different from group to group, or is it the same? Describe your point of view.

- How do others in your community feel about you? What consistent themes emerge?

- What is your personal mission statement?

- Who are you right now, and where do you want to be?

These are questions all professionals in the space ask to better understand who they are and what makes them unique. Asking yourself what makes you "you" is an important step in uncovering what separates you from others. Looking at what others have done to distinguish themselves is another exercise to consider when exploring how others have embraced personal branding. Here are some examples of personal branding:

- Entrepreneur Goldie Chan's brand colors are neon green and black—they're reflected even in her hair color!

- Mindy Thomas, a professional who worked in the hairdressing industry as a social media marketing professional before moving into consulting, focuses her content on reinvention, which has resulted in her podcast called *Reinventing with Mindy*.

- Vincenzo Landino shares his enthusiasm for social media strategy, marketing, and videography. These are professional topics, but he also is very active and transparent in sharing personal interests. Landino shares his personal passion for Italian cars, watches, and style since he embraces this as part of his lifestyle brand.

Keep brand image and voice consistent. The one thing employers, future clients, and the social media community will be looking for is a consistent image across all of the social media platforms you use (Patel, 2016). While you may have a centralized hub for your persona on one platform (e.g., website or blog), users may want to connect with you on other platforms and be part of your community there.

Presenting yourself in a consistent manner allows you to have more control of not only how others perceive you but also how you want to be viewed as a professional, person, and brand.

Maintaining a consistent **brand voice** (the overall tone you present in your updates and communication online) that is strong and sustainable is important as well. Are you someone who wants to be positive and upbeat? Or do you want to tell your community the way it is in a very honest and unfiltered manner? This is the time to determine what you stand for, what is important to you, and how you will go about communicating this to your audience.

There are many memorable brand voices to which we can look for guidance. For example, Gary Vaynerchuk has no time for nonsense and is at times brutally honest while also using various terms that you may not expect from the CEO of a large media company. That said, he has developed a reputation and image that show he will not sugar-coat anything online and that he will be honest about his advice and insights with his community. Is this the right approach for you to take? That depends on whether or not it is authentic and true to what you have to say. Don't try to be the next Gary Vaynerchuk or someone else. *Be the next you.* All of these profiles should be consistent not only in how you present yourself (headshot, cover page, biographical information, etc.) but also in how you present your voice and interact with the community (J. Chen, 2017). You, not anyone else, are branding yourself.

Determine your personal brand associations. It is key not only to know who you are as a personal brand, but to have **personal brand associations**, or specific attributes, events, settings, and interests you want others to recognize as going along with your personal brand and as different from others (Smith, 2016). For example, as a social media professional, you want to be associated with the positive feelings and attitudes of being approachable, generous with experiences and insights, and outgoing and positive in your offline and online interactions. Brands, organizations, and agencies could also be directly linked to your overall mission and vision statement as well as your brand voice. Once you have determined your personal brand associations, make a list of brands that follow your associations based on their values, characteristics, purpose, and campaigns.

For your personal brand, make sure your intended audiences on social media (e.g., future employers, customers, investors, and media) are able to remember you and what is unique about your brand compared to others. With social media, be sure to provide sustainable and valid reasons for why brands, professionals, and others should follow you. Is it the insights you share on a regular basis? Is it how you are consistent across all channels? Do audiences see you the same way if they meet you online or offline? Or is it the content and stories you produce via video? Consider these few reasons, but ultimately, your goal is to create positive associations and attitudes toward your personal brand that are backed up with evidence, sustainability, and valid benefits for all parties involved. When it comes to the point where only one party is winning, this could hinder the relationship and health of the community you have built around your personal brand.

Identify the strategy you will take. The end-all question a lot of people have in terms of social media and personal branding is "Can you integrate your personal brand with your professional one?" The answer is yes, and it is up to you to choose an approach that works best for you and your voice in the community.

Consider the several approaches by which you can take this perspective on your personal branding strategies into consideration. The **content strategy** basically focuses on the content that you share, create, and disseminate online for your personal and professional community. You focus on projecting an image of professionalism and consistency within your various networks (Ollier-Malaterre & Rothbard, 2015). With this strategy, you define the overall goals and objectives for your personal brand on social media. What type of content do you want to create and share? Will you share just long-form articles and blog posts for LinkedIn or other platforms, or are you more inclined to share visual content like photos, graphics, and videos on Instagram or Twitter? Are you creative and entertaining on TikTok? Or will it be a mixture of all these elements to make up an integrated yet synergetic brand across all platforms? Along with content strategy, social media professionals have to be able to identify not only the content that is being produced but how it is aligned with their brand voice and how it resonates with audiences.

The challenge with this approach is to not appear "too robotic" by just sharing professional content without providing personal intake and perspective. Instead, you may want to focus on the **audience strategy**, which centers on the relationships you have made on specific platforms (Ollier-Malaterre & Rothbard, 2015). For example, if you are connected mostly with your coworkers on Twitter or LinkedIn, you may be more professional there; on Facebook, you may present a more personal side of yourself to your friends and family; if you are connected with your coworkers on TikTok—well, they will see another side of you there as well. The risk here is that as the platforms evolve, your coworkers may turn into friends, and there may be a shift in friends going onto other platforms and mentioning how differently you present yourself. However, you may choose to approach your personal brand with a **customized strategy**, meaning you integrate the relationships on the platform you are communicating on (audience strategy) with shared content that is relevant to and consistent with your brand image (content strategy). A customized strategy takes time and investment to create, but you can easily do it.

Think about what makes you unique. Remember, each person has a unique voice, story, and experience to share. Don't think you have to be like everyone else. Embrace who you are and what you stand for—you are going to be your best advocate out there. Think about what makes singer Lady Gaga, viral TikTok skateboarder Nathan Apodaca, or viral child guitarist Nandi Bushell who they are. They all share a unique take and perspective on their content. Whether it is drinking Ocean Spray or playing a duet with Dave Grohl, they are creating content and experiences that are authentic and true to themselves. Let us think about this from an industry standpoint: Although a group of people may be in the same social media class or interested in social media as a career, all of them are different. That's what's great about this profession. You do not want to be like everyone else, so instead of looking at what others are doing, think about what sets you apart from your classmates, university, community, and industry.

There is a lot of competition out there, and thousands will try and fight their way to becoming "the expert" in a particular niche. Each expert title is similar to the Iron Throne from *Game of Thrones*—everyone wants to be there and will do whatever it takes to get there. Everyone wants to be *the* TikTok expert, best Instagram creator, or YouTuber extraordinaire, or to be first on the list for top influencers in the social media industry. Some professionals are already established in the social media field and may either support you or perhaps view you as competition. Be aware of this—being successful and talented in this area will draw both praise and criticism from those who feel threated professionally. There will be people who will like you for what you are doing, but at the same time, there will be those who will become jealous of you and will work against you.

Determine what you want to be known for. Once you determine what you want to focus on, consider what is going to be your angle. Do you want to be known as a professional who is invested heavily in one type of platform? Or do you want to be known more for your general interests in the industry and community? Are you a generalist or a specialist? What do you like reading and talking about? What are your passions and interests? While attending school or pursuing a career, we all have professional and personal interests at heart, and you will want to integrate all of these into your personal brand. There is a fine line between just enough and too much personal or professional focus for a personal brand. You want to appear to be human but also be able to showcase your professional expertise consistently.

Melissa Agnes (@MelissaAgnes) has created her own brand and hashtag (#CrisisReady) to focus on the need for awareness and education on proper social media and crisis communication training. Establishing a presence and niche in this area of the field has allowed her to obtain speaking opportunities and client work concerning this specialization. University of Florida professor and social media consultant Brianne Fleming (@brianne2k) on the other hand has created a movement that is integrated surrounding pop culture and marketing, with her Twitter chat called #PopChat, and her podcast *Making the Brand*. Both ladies have integrated hashtags to own an idea and area of expertise while strategically creating content that extends this to their audiences, helping them grow their reputation. Looking at more of a generalist approach, Scott Monty (@scottmonty) focuses on career-focused content and strategic insights in his email newsletters, videos, and blog posts that are shared across his different channels.

Keep in mind that when it comes to social media everyone wants to be famous or to be an influencer who gets millions of video views and all-expenses-paid speaking gigs at the largest corporate events. These perks are not given overnight, and it takes time and investment to reach a certain state in the field.

Once established, invest in your personal community. Once you have created your personal brand, extend your focus to the community you interact with. Sharing your insights and opinions and being a resource for others will not only help your personal brand but also solidify your place in the minds of this community. By investing in the community, you will be able to elevate your understanding of the current challenges, opportunities, and trends the community is seeing. Establishing yourself as a resource in the community does not mean sitting back and letting everyone else talk. It means being more active in absorbing information and being engaged. Take the time to share what is going on in your industry on social media, and talk about *why* you care about creating and sharing content. We all can create content, but we must also share why it is important and why we are doing it—which again not only contributes to the overall brand you have established but also helps build the human side of your personal brand.

What makes a personal brand unique and powerful is the fact that it is not a stable concept. Time and investment are needed to help it grow, but your brand is a part of you that continues to expand and develop as you move along in your career (J. Chen, 2017). As you move from internships to your first jobs, these experiences add to your personal brand and help transform you into the professional you want to be. The key is not only to put forth the investment necessary for your personal brand that will make you a marketable professional in the field but also to move forward with your personal brand rather than step backward.

Skills Needed to Showcase
Personal Brand Effectively

While the roles, duties, and platforms continue to change, some essential skills will continue to be relevant and key for social media professionals.

Research. All of the roles in social media have become more data driven and focused on the analytics of what people are saying and talking about and how to strategically transform these findings into actionable insights. Having a foundation in traditional research methods (surveys, experiments, interviews, focus groups, etc.) will still be apparent and key for social media professionals, but it is also important to be able to determine how to collect, analyze, and report specific findings on social media tools. This is probably one of the most important skills to have. Research for social media requires you to collect data and understand what the numbers and results mean but, at the same time, be creative in how you can incorporate these insights into the strategies for your role. It is important to know not only how to collect data but how to create insights that tell a story of what is happening and how these can be integrated into strategies and innovative ideas. Combining data collection with strategic insights is a powerful and important skill to showcase.

Research requires several skills. One of those skills, data analysis, is the ability to examine the data being collected. Being able to identify what is trending, why it is trending, and how to collect, organize, and report the data are also key areas of focus. While this may sound purely scientific and rigid, some curiosity and creativity should be mixed in to your data analysis. We have to look at the research and ask ourselves, "What is the 'so what'? What is happening here, and what can we take away from this research? Are there any surprises we can note and possibly use to our advantage for an idea?" This is where art comes into play with research. We want to explain what happened but also why it happened and what we can learn from the experience for the future. In addition, we have to communicate the findings clearly. Statistics and other research terms may be a bit overwhelming at times, but the main findings, the significance of each test in the experiment or study you conduct, and the overall strategic plan are essential items for social media managers to communicate.

Writing and visual content creation. As a social media professional, you must be one with writing. However, when it comes to the skills and experiences brands, corporations, and others are looking for in social media roles, it's not always just about being a strong writer; you have to be a strong copywriter as well. Sometimes you will write a caption for an image and have to evaluate whether or not this is the right way to approach the message and whether or not it really captures the brand's voice. Other times you will be asked to create video content—from a YouTube vlog to a TikTok storyboard strategy taking advantage of a challenge or song that is trending. Your audiences have to understand what you are communicating and sharing on social media platforms, and you must be aware of how they respond to each piece of content.

In addition, you need to understand not only the importance of using proper grammar and spelling but also the differences in writing for different platforms. Being able to tailor and adapt a message based on the platform, channel, audience, and situation is key. Adaptability, both in real time and with automation capabilities for social media (e.g., scheduling of posts), needs to be taken into consideration as well.

Be aware of the power of content and what it means for brands, audiences, media outlets, and others when it comes to their business operations. Creating content—whether visual or textual—is a key component when it comes to social media roles. When a small business or Fortune 500 company has an established presence on certain channels or is actively engaged in sharing content on its website (blog posts, webinars, resources, ebooks, infographics, etc.), this is part of the content component necessary for the social media professionals' toolkit. Being able to strategically align content with effective message copy that resonates with an audience is one of the most important skills employers look for in a social media professional.

When it comes to creating content, you may want to invest in and look at certain tools in order to create a sustainable yet consistent personal brand presence online. Across all of your social media profiles, you want to have a single theme, voice, and message for your audience that speaks to who you are and what you stand for as a personal brand for your community. Here are some additional tools to invest in and take a look at:

- **Canva (www.canva.com):** Canva is a great visual tool with affordable templates and social media–size configurations for you to use, personalize, and share for branding online (Photo 3.4). There are two versions of Canva to consider: the free version and Canva for Work. The paid version of the platform, Canva for Work, allows you to do more personalized tailoring and branding for your accounts and assets than the free version.

▶ **Photo 3.4**
Canva

Source: Canva/@Karen Freberg

▶ **Photo 3.5**
Adobe Spark

Source: © 2018 Adobe Systems Incorporated. All rights reserved. Adobe is either a registered trademark or a trademark of Adobe Systems Incorporated in the United States and/or other countries.

- **Adobe products (www.adobe.com).** Adobe's Creative Cloud suite is filled with many programs to help create content in different mediums and channels for social. The company offers tutorials, workshops, and walk-throughs on their products, which has led them to become an industry standard for content creation and creativity.

- **Adobe Spark (spark.adobe.com):** This app features mobile- and web-based products that allow you to create responsive pages (Spark Page), videos (Spark Videos), and posts for social media (Spark Post) in an easy and interactive manner (Photo 3.5).

- **HubSpot's Blog Ideas Generator (www.hubspot.com/blog-topic-generator):** If you work on the side of writing content (blog posts, etc.), this may be a good tool for determining topics to write about. You will want to use analytics and listen to your community to determine what people would like to read and learn from you, but this is another tool that can help you identify some possible ideas to explore in writing.

- **CoSchedule's Headline Analyzer (coschedule.com/headline-analyzer):** Headlines for blog posts or even some social media updates have to capture people's attention and help motivate your audience to click on the link or look at the post you have created. This tool will give you an idea of where your headline stands based on keywords, length, and potential to spark engagement.

- **Hemingway App (www.heminwayapp.com):** With all aspects of creating content—especially content that is written online—grammar and spelling are crucial. When constructing your posts, make sure you are communicating effectively and making the best first impression. We will discuss more about writing for social media in Chapter 10, but this tool is a good one to invest in to make sure you are communicating in the best way possible.

- **Personality Insights by IBM Watson (www.ibm.com/cloud/watson-personality-insights).** What type of messages are you sending out to people when it comes to the content you share online? One way to determine this is to analyze the text through a tool from IBM Watson that allows you to see some of the reactions people may have based on the content you are sharing online. In a way, this is a precursor to what you may want to do before you hit the "publish" button on a blog post or social media update.

- **Applications.** There are many apps that can be downloaded on your phone or tablet to help create content for specific channels (e.g., TikTok) or all platforms. Adobe Premiere Rush (YouTube, Instagram, and TikTok), Mojo (Instagram stories), Boosted (videos for Instagram, Twitter, and Facebook), and Photoshop (tablet or phone) are some great ones to add.

Data analytics and strategic application. There is a growing need not only for integrating current communication and technology practices into effective content creation but also for integrating current business practices and acumen. The tie-in between return on investment and the analytics features is also an important element. Social media platforms are filled with insights, knowledge, and connections, and professionals must be able to understand how search engine optimization (SEO) works for businesses, connections, and personal opportunities. Along with social media, SEO can help the professional and business identify where the conversations are emerging, what the networks look like, and which keywords users are searching for online. Identifying the key terms that are necessary to follow and listen to in the digital media landscape also applies to social media because, essentially, all of these channels (Facebook, Twitter, Instagram, etc.) are databases filled with information that can connect to valuable insights.

With SEO, your role as a social media professional will empower you with insights that will allow you to promote, engage, and analyze the data to determine what does and does not work. Most programs allow students to take advantage of Google Analytics to get a basic and advanced understanding of SEO for social and digital media purposes, and it might be a good program to explore so you can add this skill to your résumé.

In addition to understanding listening and SEO, be aware of the specific tools used to listen to, monitor, and engage with others online for personal branding purposes. Some of the tools used to evaluate reputation online include the following:

- **Talkwalker:** This program allows users (and brands) to sign up for mentions and analytics related to what others are saying about them online. Talkwalker offers a free search option as well as a quick search option (paid but affordable) for individuals to monitor their online presence.

- **BrandYourself:** This service allows you to determine which sites (websites, social media profiles, etc.) should be the first to appear in Google's search results to help you make the best first impression online.

- **Klear:** This is a good tool for analyzing platforms (e.g., Facebook, Twitter, and Instagram). You can look to see how you are doing on each platform, what your overall engagement is like, and what others in the same area as you are doing online.

- **Hootsuite:** Any social media management tool (including Hootsuite, TweetDeck, and Sprout Social) can be used not only to evaluate what you are sharing on your own platforms but also to see who is talking about your brand, your business, and even yourself.

- **Agorapulse:** Similar to Hootsuite, Agorapulse is a social media management tool that focuses on scheduling, posting, and reviewing content. The platform showcases a lot of great features related to analytics that can be helpful to determine the presence and reach of your content on your channels.

Customer service specialist. Many times, social media is the first place people go when they have an issue, question, or inquiry related to their day-to-day activities. Social media professionals must understand how to solve problems, address concerns, and listen to what others are saying to take advantage of opportunities and minimize challenges before they escalate into crisis situations. Understand that you are the storefront of the brand, and for the most part, you will provide the first exchange or opportunity for users to communicate with the brand. You have to be the brand's face as well as respond in the brand's voice, depending, of course, on the platform in question.

Along with customer service, there is a time and place to deal with happy customers and audience members, and then there are times when you have to deal with people who are not fans of your brand (e.g., trolls). These individuals may want to spark outrage and criticize your account to generate a flame war with your brand while trying to get 15 minutes of fame online. Most of the time, social care practices are recommended for brands to follow, but at other times, personality and creativity come into play when responding online. Brands like PlayStation, Warby Parker, Nike, and DunkAroos have all received praise for their work in formulating a strong brand personality for their channels, specifically on Twitter.

Experience and willingness to learn in social media. To work in social media, you need to be able to effectively keep up with the trends, people, brands, agencies, and media and identify the current cases and examples people are sharing in the field. Make sure you are able to confidently discuss some of these current issues and trends with your future employers or colleagues. It's essential to know not only what these trends and issues are, but how they impact the overall field as well as the community and brand you are working with. One way to keep up with the rising expectations and trends in the field is with effective monitoring of trade publications, news outlets, blogs, social media influencers, and others.

You have to be hungry for information—don't wait for someone to feed you what you need to know. Taking initiative and seeking out this information will help you in more ways than you can imagine. Spending at least 15 minutes per day to consume content (whether you are reading an article or listening to a podcast about a given subject) will transform you into a student of the industry. Learning is not only required but expected of strong social media professionals. One thing to note, though, is that no single person is an expert in one platform on social media because the platforms are constantly changing; so determine what you can bring to the table either as a **generalist** (who covers a broad overview of social media at the macro level) or as a **specialist** (who focuses on one or more particular areas of social media at the micro level).

One main way to gain experience is through internships. Getting hands-on experience in social media will allow you to practice what you are learning in the classroom and help you develop your online portfolio of work to share with your community and use for future applications. However, internships are not the only way to get experience in social media. Volunteering your expertise and time will allow you to get some real-world experience while also making a difference in people's lives. Consider volunteering for a nonprofit to help with a project or campaign, mentoring a group of young professionals excited to enter the field, a school-sponsored organization or team to manage its social media efforts, or small businesses you can consult with in your area. With experience comes the ability to manage your own brand online, which raises the next point.

Another way to continue your social media education is through certification programs. Many different brands offer these services and opportunities, and they can be listed on your résumé as continued education. Some of these include the following:

- Hootsuite Academy
- HubSpot Academy (Social Media, Inbound Marketing, Content Marketing, and free specific platform lessons)
- Agorapulse Social Media Manager School
- Facebook Blueprint

- Google Academy

- SEMRush Academy

- Muck Rack Academy

- Twitter Flight School

- Snap Focus Academy

- Pinterest Academy

- TikTok Education

While they range in topics and prices, these programs are available to help users enhance their understanding of social media and future learning opportunities.

Personal branding. Having a strong presence online that is consistent and true to yourself is very important to keep in mind when applying for positions in social media. Make sure to complete profiles for each account you are advocating and using, participate in relevant chat sessions in your industry, blog about topics you are interested in and share your point of view, and conduct your research ahead of time when you are applying for jobs. This is essential and can help separate you from the rest of the competition. Who are the main professionals in the position you are looking for, how do they present themselves online, and how could you engage with them in a conversation without meeting them first (cold calling in the social media age)? Put the extra effort into your application. Also, if you are applying to work at a highly competitive platform like TikTok, how can you stand out from the crowd? How about creating a TikTok that is reflective of your personal brand, showcases your experiences, and identifies your goals in an entertaining and strategic manner? It is about standing out from the crowd while advocating your experiences, story, and future potential in a creative manner.

Although most employers say what materials they expect you to provide when applying for a position, consider giving extra effort to make an impression by providing more than what is asked. One thing you can do is research what clients they have been working for, what projects they are working on at the moment, and what areas they focus on. Along with your application, you can provide a sample piece of work you have created in response to what you have found the employer may need to address. For example, if you are applying for a community manager job at Papa John's, you may want to propose a social care strategy outlining how you would respond to the trend of brands trying to interject their personality in newer platforms such as TikTok. Perhaps you provide a strategic brief and storyboard of sample challenges Papa John's can participate in with a list of their competitors who are on the platform; you can then propose a new creator and influencer strategy for the brand with data and insights from Klear and Papa John's competitors. What does this show the hiring manager looking at your application? You created a piece of work relevant to the social media role that was not requested, but it demonstrated your research into the position as well as your understanding of some of the situations you may face in this role.

How to detect fake personal brands. Most people on social media have the best intentions to present themselves honestly and with authenticity, some personal brands are not true to themselves or the people they represent. There are a lot of "smoke and mirrors" accounts and ways to create fake engagement to make you appear to be someone you are not on social media. The following are some ways to make sure you do not appear fake to your social media community:

- *Don't be fake.* A personal brand is all about being true to yourself. While it may be tempting to be someone else, your personality, community, voice, and brand are the components that truly make you unique and memorable. Personal branding is not all about you; it's about your community and helping others in the process. It is very tempting to try to gain "influencer" fame on social media, but if you focus too much on the shares, influencer lists, attention, and other vanity metrics, you will lose out on the value and impact you have on your community, which would be a shame to waste.

- *Don't buy followers or use bots.* It's tempting to create the appearance of being popular and influential online, but it is not worth it. Platforms like Twitter and Instagram are realizing there is a problem and are addressing this head-on. It is not worth the damage toward your credibility to have followers that are not truly engaging with your content. This is not the time to "fake it till you make it." It is very easy to find out who has real organic followers and a community and who has tried to game the system.

- *Stand by your opinions and don't always jump on the bandwagon.* If you believe in a product, company, or new platform, invest in the time and make sure you clearly articulate your views in a consistent manner. Don't tell your community to invest in a platform and then abandon it the first moment you get (remember the app Peach back in 2016?). Don't be selfish in sharing your ideas—you want to be generous and become a resource for your audiences to gravitate to and be related to your interests and areas of expertise.

- *Focus on quality rather than quantity of engagement.* We are all busy people in the world of social media, so focus on the quality of the exchanges and information you share. Don't create auto chat bots to do your sharing for you. Focus on creating and sharing information *you* (not a bot) feel is important for your audience to know and respond to. Quality exchanges and personalized feedback, messages, and conversations help contribute to who you are as a person. Think about how you communicate offline and see if you would do the same things online (e.g., broadcast messages or have someone else do it on your behalf) and see how you would feel. Would you feel valued as a member of the social media ecosystem? Probably not, so remember that social media is "social" first and foremost.

- *Understand your "virtual" brand is only as good as your offline brand.* Make sure you are the same offline as you are online. Social media may be a large global community, but it is a small world. Any disconnect or dissonance created when people meet you online and offline can result in a negative perception or impact on your personal brand.

- *Lead all interactions with action while considering the long-term implications.* You can't just "wing" a personal brand. You have to have a strategy in place for the type of content you want to share, how you want to present yourself, and what your personal brand stands for. Walk the walk with your personal brand, but have a plan in place for the long term. Don't take action until you have thoroughly evaluated all of the options and come up with a game plan.

CHAPTER SUMMARY

Establishing a personal brand on social media is one of the hardest yet most important tasks for a social media professional. Your personal brand is your most valuable asset to protect, invest in, and maintain for your community and professional career. A personal brand does not mean you have to be professional 24/7 and active all of the time. It depends on the overall scope, commitment, and goals for your social media communities. Keep in mind that creating a successful personal brand does not happen overnight. You have to put forth the time, investment, and work in order to reap the rewards in the long term. Spend a few minutes each day researching, studying, and working on your personal brand. As you interact with more people, opportunities will arise and allow you to share your perspectives with others. Volunteer at events and share your expertise with others. Offer your services to small businesses to get real-world experience. Start creating videos, writing content, and publishing it online for everyone to see and comment on. Seek out mentors for virtual introductions, but focus on the relationship first, not just the "ask" (e.g., don't ask people for a job when you just connected with them on LinkedIn or Twitter). The decision is up to you, which is one of the many great things that social media offers. In addition, you have to be your own best spokesperson. No one knows you better than you do.

Finding a signature image, voice, and place within your professional and personal social media communities (and the entire social media ecosystem) is crucial and can contribute significantly to how potential employers may perceive you. Businesses and others are finding out more clearly than ever that their key targeted audiences do not want to interact with a chat bot or receive a robotic response from an avatar online. They want to interact with people who are willing to engage with them through ongoing conversations and share valuable insights and resources, and whose in-person and online personas are consistent. Once you have a foundation under your belt with your personal brand, see how your audience is responding to your content and what you have to say. Be sure to stay consistent with how you conduct yourself, and pay attention to needs to be addressed and opportunities to take advantage of.

People have been hired and given tremendous opportunities based on the work and investment they put forth with their personal brand, and it is part of the daily duties of today's social media professionals. However, keeping a balanced perspective and mindset is always important. Although your personal brand may be important to you and your community, it does not make the world revolve around you.

THOUGHT QUESTIONS

1. Define *personal brand*. Why is having a personal brand important to working in social media?

2. Define *brand voice*. How it this a key part of a personal branding strategy?

3. Identify the differences between and importance of the content, audience, and customized strategies mentioned in this chapter. Outline an example of an account (e.g., professional, celebrity, etc.) that utilizes these strategies for a personal brand.

4. What best practices in personal branding resonate the most with you? What are some steps you will take to expand your personal brand?

EXERCISES

1. Write down a description of your personal brand. What type of personal brand do you have? What are some attributes you associate with your personal brand? What do you want to be online? What are some areas you feel you can contribute to in the community?

2. You are tasked to review the social media presence of the actress Lilly Collins (of Netflix's *Emily in Paris*). She is present and active on Twitter and Instagram, but she is looking to extend her reach to other channels. Discuss the key characteristics and brand pillars she showcases on social media, identify what type of personal brand she has, and highlight three content ideas you would recommend to her on another social media channel other than Twitter or Instagram.

3. You are applying for a remote social media internship to work with the brand Chipotle. The brand wants you to be creative in your application and show your personality, expertise, and experiences. Along with creating a résumé and cover letter, the company is asking you to demonstrate who you are as a brand. Create a video testimonial through Adobe Premiere Rush with your elevator pitch and an Adobe Spark page (using the tools available) to showcase your story on why Chipotle should hire you as a social media intern. Or, create a résumé presentation through Prezi Video. Discuss your journey, what you have to offer, what you have done on social media, and what you hope to learn from the internship.

4. Run a report on your personal brand online using the tools available. What are people saying about you online? What will you do with these insights? What are three takeaways you have?

5. What are some personal associations you have now, and where do you want to go? Outline three steps you will take to make your personal brand unique and expand your personal branding network.

REFERENCES

Chen, J. (2017, June 19). The ultimate guide to personal branding. *Sprout Social*. http://sproutsocial.com/insights/personal-branding/

Chen, T. (2020, November 18). College student behind massively popular paint-mixing TikTok page was fired by Sherman-Williams. *Buzzfeed News*. https://www.buzzfeednews.com/article/tanyachen/college-student-behind-a-massively-popular-paint-mixing

Lee, K. (2015, January 15). The 5 keys to building a social media strategy for your personal brand. *Buffer*. https://buffer.com/resources/social-media-strategy-personal-branding-tips

Liffering, I. (2020). Fired Sherwin-Williams paint enthusiast and TikTok star joins rival firm to develop new paints. *Ad Age*. https://adage.com/article/digital/fired-sherwin-williams-paint-enthusiast-and-tiktok-star-joins-rival-firm-develop-new-paints/2296991

Ollier-Malaterre, A., & Rothbard, N. P. (2015, March 26). How to separate the personal and professional on social media. *Harvard Business Review*. https://hbr.org/2015/03/how-to-separate-the-personal-and-professional-on-social-media

Patel, S. (2016, November 12). 9 Ways to use social media to build your personal brand. *Forbes*. http://www.forbes.com/sites/sujanpatel/2016/11/12/9-ways-to-use-social-media-to-build-your-personal-brand/

Rubin, T. (2015, June 11). Social ROI: Return on relationship is key. *Sprout Social*. http://sproutsocial.com/insights/return-on-relationship/

Smith, K. (2016, August 9). Exploring the identity of a brand: How to discover and measure brand associations. *Brandwatch*. https://www.brandwatch.com/blog/discover-measure-brand-associations/

Solis, B. (2012). Meet Generation C: The connected customer. *@BrianSolis*. http://www.briansolis.com/2012/04/meet-generation-c-the-connected-customer/

Vital, M., & Vital, A. (n.d.). The 16 personality types by Myers-Briggs and Keirsey [Infographic]. *Adioma*. https://blog.adioma.com/16-personality-types/

4

DIVERSITY, EQUITY, AND INCLUSION IN SOCIAL MEDIA

Learning Objectives

- Define diversity, equity, and inclusion.

- Discuss the relevance of diversity, equity, and inclusion as these concepts specifically apply to social media.

- Identify the best practices of incorporating diversity and inclusion principles in social media.

INTRODUCTION

One of the elements for social media professionals to recognize is that the field, the platforms, and the communities are coming in from different backgrounds. The benefits of having unique perspectives and stories being showcased can create huge opportunities for brands and professionals in their social media efforts. Diversity, equity, and inclusion are areas of focus in making sure each person, group, community, and perspective is represented and heard in the community.

The opportunities to reach and engage these audiences are limitless, and there are many cases in which brands have partnered with nonprofits, groups, and professionals to bring forth awareness to the vast array of diversity and inclusion components in society. This chapter will discuss what diversity, equity, and inclusion (DEI) are; how brands and platforms are incorporating DEI into their own business and communication practices; and what the best practices are to enhance DEI for social media.

Tevin Johnson-Campion, Laundry Service Community Manager

Introduction

My name is Tevin Johnson-Campion. I live in Los Angeles, California, where I work for Laundry Service as a community manager.

I graduated from the University of Louisville in 2017 where I got my B.S. in communication and tailored my studies towards public relations/social media. Upon graduating, I moved to Los Angeles to pursue a career working in the entertainment industry.

How did you get your start in social media?

I started small. I interned for a few companies running their social media so I could get a feel for the platforms and how they worked. Through this experience and also learning the best SM [social media] practices through my college courses, I was able to start running social media accounts on my own.

What is your favorite part of working in your area of expertise in social media?

I love the quickness of social media and how ever-changing it is. No day on social is like the previous. Being a creative, I crave variety and prefer to not do the same thing every day, and social media is the perfect way to do so. You have to be on top of current trends and what people are responding to. I personally work with fanbases on a daily basis, so figuring out what they are into and responding to brings excitement to my job.

What is one thing you can't live without while working in social media?

Twitter. Twitter is my entire life. I always prefer to lead Twitter strategy because I am always on the platform. Twitter has to be the quickest platform in the game right now, and it's how this generation gets its news, memes, and general information. If you can keep up with Twitter, you will be unstoppable.

What is your favorite social media account (person/brand/etc.) to follow and why?

Architectural Digest on IG and YouTube. They have a great curated brand that spans beyond just social. Everything is appealing to the eye and feels very strategic and put together without overwhelming the viewer with too many different colors. Sometimes minimalism is the way to go!

What is the most challenging part of working in social media?

The most challenging part would have to be quick turnaround times and always having to be creative with little downtime. Even the best person at their job can suffer from burnout. It's always important to set boundaries within your position and maintain your mental health, which needs to come first.

What do you wish you had known when you were starting out?

It's okay to make mistakes. As long as you are trying your best and constantly willing to learn new things, you will be okay! Most social media teams are very close and are always there to support and uplift each other. Try and learn from your coworkers as much as you can.

What are three marketable skills a social media professional needs to have to work in the industry?

1. Know every platform in and out from their strengths to weaknesses.

2. Get good at Photoshop and learn how to edit content.

3. Be sure to understand analytics. Numbers may not be your game, but it's an important quality to have.

If you had to choose a song to walk out to in a presentation on social media, what would it be and why?

"New Light," by John Mayer. It's a perfect song. Not too intense, but it serves major ear candy! The song itself is just easygoing and chill, and that's exactly how I like to be most the time. It creates the perfect space to be creative and collaborative.

Courtesy of Philip Truman

CURRENT STANDING REGARDING DIVERSITY, EQUITY, AND INCLUSION

When we talk about diversity, we are talking about emphasizing individuals' unique capabilities and recognizing differences, including race, ethnicity, gender, sexuality, culture, socioeconomic status, age, physical abilities, religion, and ideologies. Whereas some categories of difference appear to be fixed, others are more fluid, making self-identification an important consideration. Diversity recognizes individual differences with acceptance, appreciation, and respect, and fosters exploration of our differences in safe and supportive environments. Diversity issues arise when a policy or practice has a disproportionate negative impact on a particular group. Many areas of society experience frequent diversity issues, and social media is far from immune.

Diversity, equity, and inclusion (DEI) raise separate yet related challenges, and each of these areas requires improvement in the social media space. While some of these issues are housed offline, discussion of these topics can arise online to spark change, engage people in dialogue, and bring communities together to brainstorm next steps to improve the situation for all.

Several issues continue to be at the forefront of trending topics, discussions, and threads on various social media platforms. For example, gender pay inequality and lack of diversity in leadership roles within the social media industry are both growing concerns. Ethical concerns emerge as strategists tap different cultures and audiences in their campaigns to celebrate ties between their brand and diverse communities, the underlying purpose of which is to make money. There is a difference between simply voicing support for diversity and inclusion efforts and taking sincere actions. Historically, we can identify brands that have been supportive of diversity and inclusion efforts as part of their DNA, including Nike, Airbnb, and Adobe.

Nike ✓
@Nike

Let's all be part of the change.

#UntilWeAllWin

For once,
Don't Do It.

▶ 8M views   0:05 / 1:00 🔇 ↗

3:50 PM · May 29, 2020 · Twitter Media Studio

97.3K Retweets   8.4K Quote Tweets   222K Likes

○   ⟲   ♡   ↥

▶ **Photo 4.1**
Nike's Don't Do
It Message and
#UntilWeAllWin
Campaign on Racial
Justice

Source: Twitter/@Nike

Nike, as shown in Photo 4.1, is an active advocate for racial justice issues on their social media platforms. Focusing on this message of bringing awareness to racial injustice by being part of the change in society, Nike integrates its famous line "Just do it" but with a twist. "Don't do it" refers to not practicing behaviors that would negatively impact others. Nike's campaign #UntilWeAllWin focuses on the need for everyone to come together to address racial issues in society.

Adobe is actively engaged in making sure their work, both internally and externally, is inclusive and diverse for all in their product offerings, recruitment of talent, investment for training and education, and scholarships and grants to support underrepresented audiences to learn Adobe products and services. Shantanu Narayen, president and CEO of Adobe, states that "Adobe's values—genuine, innovative, involved, and exceptional—are built on the foundation that our people and how we treat one another are what make us a great company. Diversity is about valuing the unique life experience that every employee brings to work every day. Our success is dependent upon it" (Adobe, n.d.). Airbnb has been a prominent advocate of prioritizing diversity and inclusion efforts within a company culture, as evidenced by their stating that "there's no belonging without diversity and inclusion. To create a world where people can belong anywhere we must take real steps to build a workplace where everyone feels welcome and all voices are heard" (Airbnb, n.d.). Airbnb has taken this to heart, not just promoting this on their social channels and campaigns but incorporating it into actions and policies internally, as well as in their overall brand identity.

If brands are taking leadership roles in addressing diversity issues for their own audiences, why do we still see issues and challenges related to DEI efforts in social media? Because there is still much work that needs to be done to address these issues. Not all voices are being heard. Not all political perspectives and ideals are respected. Not all groups are being represented and acknowledged. Not all disabilities are being given the spotlight they need. This is why social media professionals need to be aware of the current state of DEI initiatives, as well as the steps needed to improve the circumstances for all, so that all voices, perspectives, audiences, and groups are included equally and respectfully.

In this chapter, we will carefully define diversity, equity, and inclusion and discuss how each relates to social media as a whole. Diversity in digital media is not only a core part of what social media professionals need to understand and address, but it is also essential to related disciplines and society as a whole.

WHAT IS DIVERSITY, EQUITY, AND INCLUSION?

Let's begin by talking about the differences and the alignment of each of these three terms. These terms are sometimes discussed in the same context and meaning, but they are distinct terms to understand and note.

Diversity refers to the ability to understand and appreciate attributes in others that differ from our own and from those of groups with which we identify. In social media contexts, remember that diversity is not just about creating messaging that features certain groups and representation; it is about engaging thoughtfully with target audiences who have different backgrounds. Internally, bringing colleagues' diverse experiences and perspectives to the table benefits the people creating messages and creative content (King, 2019). Though multiple components make up diversity—including race, ethnicity, age, gender, sexuality, culture, socioeconomic status, physical abilities, and ideology (including religious and political thought)—often, people striving for diversity focus on only one dimension of it. Remember: Diversity requires the consideration of more than just one of its dimensions.

Equity focuses on the commitment to provide equal opportunities to everyone without discrimination on the basis of race, color, national origin, age, marital status, sex, sexual orientation, gender identity, gender expression, disability, religion, height, weight, political thought, or veteran status (University of Michigan, n.d.). The popular Canadian show *Schitt's Creek*, starring Eugene Levy and Catherine O'Hara, had a strong equity message throughout their show promoting equal opportunities for LGBTQ+ characters. This message was shared across social media with designated content pieces such as GIFs (Canadian Broadcasting Corporation, n.d.). Their messages were featured throughout content across all of their social media channels (Canadian Broadcasting Corporation, 2019).

Inclusion is the bringing together of people with different experiences, perspectives, backgrounds, and ideas to make sure each group is representative of its audiences and the public at large. Inclusion also means educating each other on what messaging and ideas work, as well as those that do not (or that may be offensive to certain groups). Inclusion is all about understanding each other and moving forward together (King, 2019). Many brands have been active in making sure that their audiences know they are coming together for a common goal and purpose. For example, IPSY, a make-up brand, launched the #DiscoveringYourself inclusive online campaign to generate brand awareness and empowerment and to challenge the current standards of beauty (IPSY, n.d.). The brand brought together a diverse group of influencers and creators to spark the message on social media.

When it comes to DEI initiatives, it is also important to understand the various characteristics that make up DEI. Many times, professionals and brands only think of one or two aspects of what makes up DEI efforts, but in fact, there are many more. As public relations professors Regina Luttrell and Adrienne Wallace have shown in their Diversity and Inclusion wheel for PR professionals, there is a range of areas professionals need to take note of in campaigns (Table 4.1). To best engage, communicate, and listen to our audiences, we have to take into account all of these perspectives and views in our community.

Table 4.1 Diversity and Inclusion Wheel by Luttrell and Wallace		
Core Attributes		
Age	Gender	Ethnicity
Physical qualities/ abilities	Race	National Origin
Additional Attributes		
Political ideology	Marital status	Organizational role
Military experience	Job classification	Mental health/well-being
Religious beliefs	Socio-economic status	Thinking styles
Learning styles	Communication styles/skills	Geographic location
Education	Work background	Language
Personal habits	Recreational habits	

Many brands have been incorporating DEI as part of their brand mission and core DNA for their organization. These principles are usually showcased in the "About" page on a brand's website or in a designated blog post to generate awareness about the work they are doing internally within their brand and organization. The principles are then implemented in the brand's outside work with their external audiences. For example, Sprout Social, a social media management tool similar to brands such as Hootsuite and Agorapulse, has a DEI core mission within the company. They break down their DEI efforts into three categories: learn (education, training, and internal talent management), serve (making an impact on the communities in which they work), and recruit (creating a diverse pipeline of talent from different backgrounds and perspectives) (Bess, 2019).

What Diversity, Equity, and Inclusion Bring to Social Media

It is important to know what DEI principles bring to the table for social media professionals. Strong DEI principles lead to all of the following.

A more dynamic work environment. Being able to bounce around ideas with people from all backgrounds and perspectives brings forth new and innovative ideas.

Greater opportunity for more creative and effective messaging. By gaining insight and feedback from different groups, better messages will occur.

A better understanding of key topics, trends, and communities. Having insights into different practices, cultures, and experiences can help shape messaging, strategies, and insights that will create win-win situations for everyone.

New ideas and perspectives. There is a higher chance for success when looking at a campaign message, idea, or execution from different angles. It is key to have all perspectives noted to see how audience members may interpret a message one way or another. If we want to be effective in reaching key audiences in a certain group, we have to make sure we work with those who are part of these communities to make sure we are aligned with our messages and are not causing any disrespect.

Engaged audiences. If audiences see stories coming from people like themselves, they will be more likely to engage with the brand or company involved. This means if a brand or organization is promoting DEI topics and programs within their organization, their actions, team members, and social media team members (senior- to lower-level management) have to follow through.

Enhanced brand culture and online community. Everyone has a different experience, story, and voice to bring to the table—that is what makes life interesting. By showcasing these stories, experiences, and cultures online, it creates a greater level of understanding and appreciation for the world around us.

Bringing everyone together in a positive way. If we see that everyone has an equal chance to succeed, that means we can create a win-win situation for everyone.

Some of these benefits of strong DEI principles are highlighted in many corporate, brand, and platform company pages online. Many of the social media platforms not only have a strong diversity and inclusion presence, but some have designated team members and leaders who are in charge of these roles. Many brands (e.g., Twitter) have a chief diversity and inclusion officer who oversees the training, education, and DEI programming and research internally and externally for the brand. Almost all of the platforms have a designated statement for diversity and inclusion (see Table 4.2). While having a statement and DEI program is important, following through on these perspectives and statements is even more important. One issue we see related to DEI statements is that not all platforms follow through on these statements with their actions. For example, TikTok promotes a principle stating that all voices of creators and users are appreciated, but the platform has faced criticism for censorship issues among certain users (Perrett, 2020). Another issue with DEI statements is that some types of diversity are highlighted while others are not, so the statements are not as inclusive as they could be.

In summary, when it comes to DEI initiatives on social media, actions speak louder than words. This is crucial to note for practices by all parties.

Creating a Diversity, Equity, and Inclusion Program

We know it is important to have a DEI program, but how do we go about creating one? What are the must-haves for an established and sustainable program for social media practices? Here are some steps for creating an effective DEI program at all levels of a business, organization, agency, or start-up.

Have a diversity statement. A **diversity statement** for an organization is "a written explanation of its commitment to diversity, equity, and inclusion for its employees and customers. It tells stakeholders how diversity fits into your organization's mission and values" (Doeing, 2019b). As seen in Table 4.2, many brands already have their own diversity statements. However, you may be asked to create a diversity statement for your organization or company for social media.

Table 4.2 Statements on Diversity from Social Media Platforms		
	Diversity Statement	**URL**
Facebook	Diversity isn't an option. To bring the world closer together, diversity is a must-have for Facebook, not an option. Hiring people with different backgrounds and experiences helps us build better products, make better decisions and better serve our clients. We're committed to building a workforce that's as diverse as the communities we serve, and strive to provide the best possible care and resources to help all of our employees thrive—at work, in their personal life and across every life stage	https://www.facebook.com/careers/facebook-life/diversity
Twitter	Being a Tweep means a lot of things. It means *having a say* in what the future of Twitter looks like and how to get there. It means finding out who you are and what you have to offer the world. Showing up for what's important to you. It means being okay with being a work in progress, because that's the only way to keep moving forward.	https://careers.twitter.com/en/tweep-life.html
Snapchat	Millions of people from all walks of life use Snapchat every day to communicate with friends and family. It's important for us to bring the same diversity of cultures, backgrounds, and perspectives together at Snap Inc. A diverse, equitable, and inclusive culture helps people achieve their best work, be themselves, and build innovative products that serve our community. We're investing in new ways to strengthen this culture at Snap every day—through employee resource groups, internal development programs, unconscious bias training, allyship training, networking opportunities, recruiting initiatives, and more. We strongly believe that DEI is for everyone because it fuels creative excellence and innovation. We take a broad view of diversity, ranging from race and gender, to LGBTQ+, disability, age, socio-economic status, parental status, cognitive diversity, regional diversity and more. Here, all team members have a seat at the table and a voice that's heard.	https://careers.snap.com/diversity

	Diversity Statement	URL
Instagram	We bring organizations, experts, academics, and communities together to educate people about ways to have safe and positive experiences on Instagram.	https://about.instagram.com/community/programs
YouTube	From the beginning, we've always believed in the power of video storytelling to make a difference. It helps us feel deeply connected to a cause and empowered with knowledge to take action on issues we care about. YouTube is the place you can find an audience, join a community, and create impact, both online and off. People and organizations who are committed to driving positive social change belong here.	https://socialimpact.youtube.com/
Pinterest	Our mission at Pinterest is to bring everyone the inspiration to create a life they love. All over the world, people are preparing for moments big and small, from buying a new car to planning weeknight meals. Hundreds of millions of them come to us with the expectation that they may stumble across a spark they weren't even looking for. It's hard to feel inspired when you don't feel represented—online or in your workplace—and research shows that diverse teams make us more creative, diligent and hard working. When we are building products, a team of people with different backgrounds enables us to think through products, policies, and safety from all angles (for instance, how products could be abused or how they could unintentionally impact a community).	https://newsroom.pinterest.com/en/post/diversity-report-2020
LinkedIn	Our vision, to create economic opportunity for every member of the global workforce, connects everyone at LinkedIn. As we realize diversity, inclusion, and belonging for our employees, members, and customers, we get closer to achieving that vision.	https://careers.linkedin.com/diversity-and-inclusion
TikTok	Our platform exists to create joy and inspiration, and that is made better because of our diverse community of users, creators, partners, artists, and employees. It's important to us that nobody feels unwelcome, unheard, or unsafe on TikTok. We also fully acknowledge our responsibility to not simply wish for and talk about the importance of diversity on our platform, but to actively promote and protect it.	https://newsroom.tiktok.com/en-us/a-message-to-our-black-community
Reddit	N/A	https://www.redditinc.com/

Here are some elements to consider when you are writing your diversity statement:

- Have a strong headline for your diversity, equity, and inclusion program to focus on (provide definitions of DEI specifically) and what DEI means to the organization or brand you are representing. Use powerful language that is positive and clear in its approach (Doeing, 2019b). Look at Photo 4.2 to see the way in which HubSpot and Salesforce have communicated these points on the front page of their websites. These headlines are concise, personal, and focused on being welcoming and expressing equity for all who are part of their communities (Doeing, 2019b).

HubSpot	Salesforce
https://learn.g2.com/diversity-statement	https://learn.g2.com/diversity-statement

▶ **Photo 4.2**
HubSpot and
Salesforce Diversity
Headline

Source: Learning Hub,
G2.com.

- Be very specific in noting the actions, programs, and initiatives that will be part of the DEI program. Make sure to identify all groups you are including in your efforts. It is important to be clear and make sure you include all groups you want to feel represented and part of your community.

- Implement an **inclusive brand voice**. We have talked about the importance of brand voice (the personality characteristics that are articulated on social media by the company, person, or organization), but an inclusive brand voice adds an additional layer of understanding to make sure the overall tone we are using in our messages is aligned with all audiences and perspectives. When it comes to messaging, understanding the context of the platform and situation is important to consider before hitting the publish button—people may have different interpretations of your messages or content than you intended.

- Utilize a **diversity style guide** for content creation. Similar to what the Associated Press Style Guide is for journalists, a diversity style guide ensures that the writing, terms, and approaches in writing are inclusive for all audiences and content (Kanigel, n.d.). This will provide a standard for reviewing materials being shared on social media with this additional lens to make sure the content, messaging, and terms are appropriate and aligned with the brand, organization, and agency.

- Identify the core values that are part of the brand's DNA, and understand and articulate how these values connect with the programs that are being set forth in the DEI program and statement. This content can be created under the diversity statement as the **value statement**, which is "the documented beliefs and principles of your organization. It is an explanation of the fundamental things your organization holds important and is used to guide the organization and the people in it" (Doeing, 2019a). A strong value statement that supports values that tie into DEI components makes the program impactful. Plus, having aligned values is key to communicating to everyone that being inclusive and advocating for equity is not just a box to check for a brand but that it is at the root of who you are as a brand, company, or organization (Doeing, 2019a).

- Have an **action plan** to implement and execute DEI efforts. Many brands get into trouble by saying they support DEI efforts, but there are no clear action steps that will be taken to initiate these programs and steps. Making sure this is tied and updated on a regular basis online (digital and social channels) is crucial to practice. Actions, in most cases, speak louder than words.

Integrate diversity, equity, and inclusion efforts within all of your communication and business plans. While diversity, equity, and inclusion programming often exists as a separate entity within companies, agencies, and brands as somewhat of an "add-on," it should not be treated as such. If you want to do it right, DEI has to be integrated as part of the corporate and brand DNA and reflected in the communication and business efforts being implemented.

Have an inclusive marketing strategy for social media. Inclusive marketing is defined as "creating content that truly reflects the diverse communities that our companies serve. It means that we are elevating diverse voices and role models, decreasing cultural bias, and leading positive social change through thoughtful and respectful content" (Siegel, 2019). This approach acknowledges that brands, organizations, or agencies can take steps to make sure they are reaching all audiences equally and taking DEI into consideration with their messaging, content, stories, and tactics. Inclusive marketing can also be an element that makes sure that all voices—internally if the campaign is focused on employees and externally for outside audiences—are heard and noted in the campaign.

Take actions beyond just posting DEI commitments. It is one thing to say you support DEI, but actions speak louder than words. Make sure the messages, content, and efforts that are being done for DEI lead to sustainable and consistent actions. Specify the specific action steps, protocols, and programs that will be implemented and done. These messages have to be very clear and direct with no chances of misinterpretation or vagueness.

Keep up with the latest research in DEI research. Identifying the researchers and authors who are actively exploring the nature of these topics in social media is key. Develop a Twitter list of authors, researchers, bloggers, creatives, and consultants who can help provide context, insights, and opinions on what can be done to bring everyone together in an equal manner. Having these perspectives can help generate more understanding and collaboration for the team internally and externally with their audiences.

Invite speakers and consultants from all backgrounds and perspectives to give presentations and provide guidance. Learning does not stop when you graduate. Continued education and training are very important in fostering a strong commitment for DEI initiatives if done right. Sprout Social, Adobe, Adweek, and Hootsuite, to name a few, have held in-person panels and webinars on the topic of DEI to generate discussion, dialogue, and community on these various topics within their organizations and communities.

Challenges in Diversity, Equity, and Inclusion in Social Media

There are many challenges that arise in addressing DEI issues on social media proactively and effectively. Some of these challenges have been around for quite some time, while others have just recently arisen in the social media era.

- **Hiring practices.** Not only should hiring practices for entry-level positions reflect a commitment to DEI, but internship and mentorship opportunities should as well. We need to embed diversity, equity, and inclusion values into all of our corporate, agency, and organizational internal practices; we need to particularly emphasize these values when it comes to recruiting and hiring employees, creating internships, and conducting trainings and mentorship programs. Work with colleges and universities to make sure there is representation available for all students enrolled in different programs and institutions from different geographical areas. Recruit and hire across not only different groups but also locations. Most brands (including Facebook, Slack, Microsoft, and others) are allowing remote work to be the normal standard, so this is more important than ever.

- **Censorship of content on platforms.** Social media has experienced cases involving censorship. Twitter has censored certain political views, people with disabilities, and people who do not look like models. TikTok has been criticized for censorship of particular people as well. In a memo, TikTok discussed policies that told moderators on the platform "to avoid promoting 'abnormal body shape, chubby, have obvious beer belly, obese, or too thin.' The policies also specifically targeted users with disabilities, saying enforcement of such policies was not just 'limited to' people with dwarfism or with 'acromegaly'" (Perrett, 2019).

- **Bubbling, or lack of exposure to different views and perspectives.** "Agreeing to disagree" means that people can have their own opinions and still get along. With the rise of the polarization seen on social media based on certain viewpoints, this phrase has created some tension and hindered the opportunities to have discussions related to political or ideological perspectives. By not being aware of different perspectives, approaches, and experiences, individuals may be unable to understand the complete picture of what is going on, which may in turn create even more tension and missed opportunities to learn and acknowledge different points of view.

- **Lack of leadership representation**. Many brands and agencies have considered onboarding a chief diversity and inclusion officer, but most have not actually followed through. Most of the social media platforms either have a diversity statement or officer, but as far as other initiatives, that is still a work in progress. One exception is Reddit cofounder Alexis Ohanian, who took action by resigning his board member position and requesting that the board replace him with a Black candidate (*Alexis Ohanian Resigns from Reddit Board amid Hate Speech Outcry*, n.d.). As a result, Justin.TV cofounder and Y Combinator CEO Michael Seibel (a Black entrepreneur) joined Reddit's board of directors.

- **Lack of diversity in funding sources.** According to Deloitte, when it comes to technology venture efforts, 76% of the overall workforce and leadership for venture capital firms in the United States is white (Blustein, 2020). This is important to understand for social media because this impacts funding sources for entrepreneurs, start-ups, and other technology-focused brands and organizations.

Examples of Diversity, Equity, and Inclusion Efforts of Brands

When exploring some of the ways in which brands, organizations, and social media professionals have come together to bring more awareness to issues pertaining to diversity, equity, and inclusion, several brands stand out.

Sesame Street *and autism.* *Sesame Street* has been active not only in bringing forth awareness of current issues in society (e.g., racism, homelessness, poverty, differences in views) but also in raising awareness of autism. In 2019, *Sesame Street* introduced Julia, the first character to have autism on the popular children's show. The introduction of Julia's character was coordinated with Autism Speaks, a nonprofit organization focused on research and bringing more awareness to autism among families. The campaign was showcased not only on the *Sesame Street* show but on all of their social media channels as well. This case illustrates the importance of representing and raising awareness for conditions such as autism among the public. Photo 4.3 shows the collaboration between *Sesame Street* and Autism Speaks in the form of an Instagram post. The post aims to raise awareness

▶ **Photo 4.3**
Sesame Street and Autism Speaks Collaboration With Julia

Source: Instagram/ @AutismSpeaks

for how you can get screened for autism. It does this by framing autism not as a negative thing but as a new perspective to gain. The post shows Julia in a positive light, with a collage of her interests, abilities, and experiences. These autism awareness messages were creatively executed across all of the channels for *Sesame Street*, including Instagram.

Quay Australia and body positivity. One of the challenges that has emerged on social media is the pressure to look, feel, and present oneself in a certain way. Viewing Instagram might lead to the impression that only "hot skinny models" are successful on the platform. However, more brands are understanding the need to represent all audiences, including those who differ in size. This is where the body positivity movement comes into play, and Quay Australia, a sunglass brand, has made their mark in this area by partnering with one of the biggest stars in the music scene. Lizzo, who has been at the forefront of body positivity and has embraced this as part of her brand as a musician and artist, partnered with the Quay Australia as a result of their dedication and commitment to the body positivity movement. In a statement on the brand collaboration, Lizzo pointed out "Quay is different from other eyewear brands out there. They're cool and fresh, but also inclusive and attainable" (Davison, 2020). Photo 4.4 showcases Lizzo promoting the collaboration on her own accounts for her community (since she has a large following on Instagram). Collaborative campaign initiatives are a strategy we are seeing more brands take. Instead of promoting or announcing the campaign on their channels, they are allowing the other party (e.g., celebrity, influencer, creator, etc.) take the lead in announcing it to the world. In the Quay Australia Instagram post, Lizzo wears sunglasses whose design is inspired by the singer's career and life. The caption highlights Lizzo and the sunglasses design before inviting people to purchase a pair of sunglasses.

NFL and racial inequality. The National Football League (NFL) has dealt with many challenges regarding their handling of social and racial issues, specifically regarding former football player Colin Kaepernick. This has been a topic of conversation in the sports and mainstream media for years, ever since Kaepernick began kneeling during

▶ **Photo 4.4**
Lizzo and Quay Australia Collaboration

Source: Instagram/
@quayaustralia

the national anthem to peacefully protest against police brutality in 2016 (Yeboah, 2016). In 2020, protests took place around the country and the world in response to the police killings of George Floyd, Breonna Taylor, and others. Brands such as Twitter, Facebook, Nike, Michael Jordan, NBA, adidas, and others responded across their social channels. Some (such as Michael Jordan and Nike) were very specific in the actions they would take to combat racial injustice, whereas other brands did not go into specifics on what actions they would be doing. The NFL spoke out as well. The change in the NFL's messaging on racial injustice from 2016 to 2020 happened as a result of the NFL social team taking action publicly. The social media team at the NFL did not believe that the professional football organization was doing enough to respond to racial injustice, so they decided to take action without consulting the NFL leadership (Rodrigue & Jones, 2020). The NFL social media team recruited professional players to be part of a video discussing racial inequality. The team then shared the video on the NFL social media channels, personal channels of the social media team members for the NFL, and individual players' accounts. The video montage combined the individual frames of players from different teams brought together into one larger frame. The video emphasized togetherness despite separation, using the hashtag #StrongerTogether. As a result, Roger Goodell, the NFL commissioner, made a public statement that the organization had not done enough to address this issue (Rodrigue & Jones, 2020). The jury is out on the fate of the social media team members who acted without informing NFL leadership. Historically, when employees have gone rogue, they are fired by their bosses. Yet, this case does show how employees can spark a movement from within with the tap of a button.

▸ **Photo 4.5**
NFL Social Media Team Releases Players' Video on Racial Inequality

Source: Twitter/ @AJ_Curry

Equal representation and Crayola. When you think of Crayola, you might imagine the brand that produces crayons and school supplies. However, this brand has entered the world of representation by making sure everyone has the opportunity to feel included and respected in their communities online and offline. Crayola launched a new featured product to celebrate the colors of the world, showing crayons that make up all of the different skin colors of people. This move generated a lot of interest, praise, and reactions from the community. Crayola partnered with the Mob Beauty and Victor Casale, a former chemist from MAC Beauty who was able to help Crayola launch this campaign (Robin, 2020). Casale described this move as a way to help Crayola be part of the conversation in a positive way:

> While foundation ranges have come a long way, the beauty industry must be constantly innovating and pushing themselves creatively. What they can learn from the Colors of the World crayons is that the desire for inclusivity begins at a young age, and through adequate representation, children are able to feel confident, included, and important—just like an adult feels when they find their perfect shade at the beauty counter. There is always more work to do, and Crayola has been a positive voice in this valuable discussion. (Quoted in Robin, 2020)

With that being said, Crayola wanted to make sure to integrate this into their social media content strategy (see Photo 4.6). In a video format shared on Instagram, Crayola was able to introduce the Colors of the World products. The post allowed them to talk about the impact of the collaboration with the brand and to talk about the product with their community on social media.

Respect for different opinions and perspectives and **Sesame Street.** Alexa, play the song "Why can't we be friends?" As mentioned earlier in the chapter, lack of respect toward differences in opinion can hinder the conversation, community,

▶ **Photo 4.6**
Crayola and Colors
of the World
Campaign

Source: Instagram/
@crayola

or brand from moving forward. Not everyone is going to share the same opinion, and failing to acknowledge this can lead to more challenges than opportunities. Social media has been in the news for the past few years because of the influences it may have had on perceptions of political campaigns during the 2016 presidential election. However, according to a study that compared social media users from the 2012 and 2016 presidential elections, social media use had small but significant influence on misperceptions in both campaigns (Garrett, 2019). Differences of opinion and highly involved political discussions on social media have resulted in many people unfriending, unfollowing, blocking, muting, or leaving groups and connections on the platform.

One of the more successful campaigns to address this ongoing challenge on social media has been *Sesame Street*. *Sesame Street* has always been able to address challenges, social issues, and topics head on. Like introducing new characters such as Julia, *Sesame Street* created a campaign dedicated to social media called "Respect," which focuses on the acknowledgment of differences in opinions and perspectives. This campaign featured *Sesame Street* characters moderating discussions between characters from different popular shows who held opposing viewpoints from one another, such as Tyrion and Cersei Lannister from *Game of Thrones*. In Photo 4.7, Cookie Monster serves as the moderator for two characters from *Westworld* (Dolores and Bernard). If Cookie Monster can't bring us together, who can? We all agree cookies are amazing, right?

Collaborating to give voice on social media for LGBTQ creators. Many brands say they are supportive of certain groups, issues, and initiatives, but they don't necessarily take action to create any impact on these issues. One of the most important elements in effective social media practices is to make sure that all voices are amplified and represented on social media.

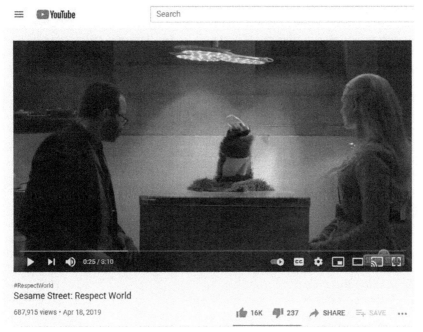

▶ **Photo 4.7**
Cookie Monster and Westworld in *Sesame Street*'s #RespectWorld Campaign

Source: Garrett (2019).

Let's explore how two brands have succeeded in collaborating with LGBTQ creators. TikTok announced their new partnership and collaboration efforts in launching their TikTok Trailblazers group, which features up and coming creators who are part of the LGBTQ community (Cohen, 2020). TikTok promoted the content each week during June 2020 (Pride Month) from the creators while also adding specific donation stickers to support charities and nonprofits who help the LGBTQ community (Cohen, 2020).

Another brand that has been working to collaborate more with LGBTQ creators is Chipotle. They have been creatively executing these initiatives in a strategic and brand-aligned manner to help spark a conversation on their platform. Chipotle partnered with *Queer Eye*'s Karamo Brown, along with other influencers to host a Lunch & Listen panel event on TikTok, while also donating to specific organizations in the community (Morillo, 2020).

Both brands have taken efforts to bring together and give a voice to creators in the LGBTQ community. These brands have also provided action steps on what they will do to support these creators and community members.

Best Practices in Diversity, Equity, and Inclusion Efforts in Social Media

As social media becomes a more established profession and field, and as it becomes more integrated into marketing, public relations, and communication practices, many elements need to be considered. When it comes to DEI program efforts, there are some universal best practices to keep in mind. Whether you work in a company with an established DEI program or a start-up business, the following practices can help you stay on top of your DEI efforts on social media.

Don't tell me, show me. In addition to having DEI statements and campaigns and posting them on social media, consider what actions should be taken to address and incorporate these perspectives. This needs to be shared, documented, and showcased for a brand that stands for these issues publicly and what will be done to sustain these efforts for the long term. Being transparent about internal programs and initiatives (such as trainings, hiring practices, and leadership decisions) is one way to go about doing this. Also, make sure to acknowledge that the DEI statement presents all diversity categories—not some—as being equally valued.

Evaluate messaging for empathy. Limiting the viewpoints of others without acknowledging what they are saying will not make things better. In fact, empathy can help us better understand and learn from each other on various topics and issues ("Guide to Inclusion and Diversity in Modern Advertising," n.d.) Taking into consideration the emotions and situations of others is often referred to as empathy marketing, which is "to establish an emotional connection with the 'brand' and embed the message in the mind of the consumer" (Tabaka, 2011). We have to understand our audiences to clearly articulate the messages we want to convey, and if we do not understand what issues are important to them, or their own experiences on the matter, we will never get the complete picture for our social media efforts. We cannot assume everything; we have to listen, educate, and reach out to better understand what we need to know and what we can do on social media more effectively.

Focus on respect. Not everyone is going to share values or think the same way. That's one of the things that makes us human. Understanding we may or may not share the same perspectives, views, or thoughts is an important element to consider both internally and externally. However, even if we disagree with the approaches, we have to be objective in making sure we listen, understand, and note these different perspectives. We have to understand the different views that are out there and how they may be shared by audiences we are trying to reach internally or externally.

Be empathic. Sometimes the best thing to do is listen. Tying in with the previous point on empathic messaging, we also do not need to rush to judgment or put out a statement before evaluating all of the facts and circumstances. Understand that everyone may come in with different experiences and may voice them publicly while expecting immediate action. Timing is an important player in all of this, but responding in a way that shows empathy, understanding, and appreciation is long lasting.

Support leadership and hiring efforts. Support can come in different forms, including emotional, financial, time, and sustainable commitment. As stated earlier in this chapter, diversity, equity, and inclusion initiatives do not always have the complete support internally to make them sustainable. Investing in DEI efforts does not happen overnight—it has to be a purposeful and long-term investment for the organization, agency, or corporation. This support is not only emotional but financial. Good programs are not free, and to fully commit to implementing strong DEI principles requires appropriate financial backing to make sure the right leadership, employees, programs, and trainings are implemented.

Invest in DEI education and training. While most of the social media certifications have addressed diversity in their courses, LinkedIn was one of the first platform brands that released their own coursework addressing diversity, equity, and inclusion topics on social media (Hutchinson, 2020). More platforms and companies that offer social media educational resources for universities and professionals (such as HubSpot, Hootsuite, and others) will likely follow suit after seeing what LinkedIn has implemented in their educational resources.

Advocate DEI beyond just a check box to click. The biggest issue that is facing DEI in the social media industry is that it is viewed as a "check box." Some brands believe that providing a statement on diversity or announcing diversity as a goal is sufficient. This is where actions speak louder than words, and this is where education and training come into play. LinkedIn and Google, for example, have designated trainings and courses that cover how to integrate these principles across their brands, and they have made these courses free for anyone to take ("4 Things We Learned About Inclusive Marketing," n.d.).

Explore inclusive hiring talent practices. Hiring bias may be something the social media industry needs to work on. This goes for the traditional areas like gender, ethnicity, and experience, and even education. Yes, having different educational backgrounds is a key part of a diverse group of social media professionals. This means recruiting from different schools of thought and programs that teach social media. Recruiting from a range of programs instead of just one or two may bring forth a wave of new talent and exciting possibilities.

Integrate different perspectives into all teamwork. Perspectives refer to the ideology a social media professional brings to the table. This is one area that has not been discussed as much in the field, but having different perspectives can improve our understanding of audiences in a more comprehensive way. For example, having a mixture of political thought on a team can produce a better understanding of how certain audiences think, feel, and react to certain messages or initiatives. To gain all perspectives and understand how audiences may interpret or respond to certain actions and messages, it is important to have diversity of thought and perspectives internally. Otherwise, the agency, company, or organization is at risk of enclosing themselves in a bubble, which can lead to missed opportunities and risks associated with not understanding the complete picture.

Let's look at another campaign that has succeeded in incorporating different perspectives. Heineken addressed this in their #OpenTheWorld campaign in 2018, which focused on bringing together people with different perspectives on a range of topics and having a conversation over a Heineken. This campaign attempted to show that even if we have opposite points of views, we can still come together and have a good conversation and experience. Heineken did this by sitting two people across from one another who shared opposing views; although we first see them as sitting opposite to one another, they are brought together to share a Heineken. The ad aimed to show that understanding different perspectives helps us to evolve, understand the world, and gain insight about ourselves in relation to others. As a result, Heineken was able to generate a lot of social media engagement around the world. The campaign became a trending topic with 324,000 engagements and 138,000 shares generated, according to Edelman ("Open Your World," n.d.). Even though this campaign is a few years old, it still reminds us that we can come together even if we have differences of opinion. We can learn, grow, and come together online and offline.

▶ **Photo 4.8**
Open Your World Campaign With Heineken

Source: Retrieved from https://www .youtube.com/ watch?v=etlqln7vT4w

CHAPTER SUMMARY

Although the social media field has embraced diversity, equity, and inclusion initiatives of late, we have a long way to go to really accomplish these principles across the board. Though diversity statements are becoming more common, relatively few agencies and companies have launched DEI programs, and many of those who have are only focusing on certain types of diversity, equity, and inclusion. If social media as a field is going to be a leader in this area, it has to invest in, support, and sustain complete DEI measures across the board. More education and training are needed in these areas. No brand, organization, or social media platform has perfected the DEI equation yet. Having statements, showing initiative and support on social media profiles, and supporting investment efforts for diversity roles in a corporation and organization are starting points, but much more work needs to be done.

Actions speak louder than words, so let's make sure the work that we post on social media channels reflects the actions we have taken and will take as the profession moves forward.

THOUGHT QUESTIONS

1. Define DEI. Why is this important for social media professionals to know?

2. What are the steps needed to create a DEI program? What is a diversity statement?

3. What are two benefits that DEI can bring to the table?

4. What are two challenges facing DEI in social media today?

5. What does it mean to have an inclusive marketing strategy? Why is this important for social media plans?

6. How can social media professionals do more in DEI in the future?

EXERCISES

1. You are interning with Reddit, and you notice they do not have a diversity statement on their website. Review all of the other platforms and what they have used for their diversity statements, and craft a diversity statement that would fit with Reddit and their brand. Once you have written this diversity statement for Reddit, review two other social media platforms and provide your edits and changes to these diversity statements.

2. You and your classmates have been brought into focus group with Under Armour, and The Rock is looking for ideas on DEI initiatives for his Project Rock line. Review what UA and The Rock are doing so far in terms of DEI, and provide three suggestions on inclusive marketing ideas they can do in the future. Provide rationale for each idea.

3. Oreo has a strong diversity statement, but they are looking to you to see what else they can do to build their core values statement to be more effective on social media. Review the core values list from G2 (https://learn .g2.com/core-values-list). Pick four values

you feel would be good to recommend to Oreo and provide a rationale for why.

4. PlayStation brings you in as a consultant and asks you to make recommendations for creating an inclusive marketing strategy for their influencer and creator campaign. Brainstorm an idea they can do in regard to inclusive marketing for this influencer and creator campaign.

5. You have been asked to create an awareness campaign to integrate DEI initiatives for Lowe's. Evaluate their current DEI efforts and how they are integrating these on their social media channels. Use the Diversity and Inclusion Wheel for PR professionals (Table 4.1) and identify five areas you will be integrating for Lowe's in this awareness campaign. Propose at least one piece of content for the brand addressing this area for each social media platform the company is on. Provide your rationale for how each piece of content aligns with the brand values of Lowe's and how it ties with the DEI area you are focusing on.

REFERENCES

4 things we learned about inclusive marketing. (n.d.). Think with Google. https://www.thinkwithgoogle .com/consumer-insights/inclusive-marketing/

Alexis Ohanian resigns from Reddit board amid hate speech outcry. (n.d.). https://sports.yahoo.com/

reddit-cofounder-alexis-ohanian-resigns-amid-out cry-to-make-room-for-black-candidate-donates-to -kaepernick-fund-serena-williams-181334683.html

Adobe. (n.d.). *Abobe for all*. https://www.adobe.com/ diversity.html

Airbnb. (n.d.). *Diversity at Airbnb*. https://www.airbnb.com/diversity/belonging

Bess, M. Y. (2019, July 17). What diversity, equity & inclusion looks like at Sprout Social. *Sprout Social*. https://sproutsocial.com/insights/diversity-equity-inclusion-at-sprout-social/

Blustein, A. (2020, June 5). Ad Tech suffers from a lack of diversity and inclusion. *Adweek*. https://www.adweek.com/programmatic/ad-tech-suffering-diversity-inclusion/

Canadian Broadcasting Corporation (Producer). (n.d.). *Schitt's Creek* GIFs and stickers. *Shorty Awards*. https://shortyawards.com/12th/schitts-creek-2

Canadian Broadcasting Corporation (Producer). (2019). *Schitt's Creek* social media. *Webby Awards*. https://www.webbyawards.com/winners/2019/social/general-social/television-film/schitts-creek-social-media/

Cohen, D. (2020, June 22). TikTok kicks off #MyPride weeklong celebration. *Adweek*. https://www.adweek.com/digital/tiktok-kicks-off-mypride-weeklong-celebration/

Davison, R. (2020, May 20). Lizzo teams up with Australian brand for bold collaboration. *Daily Mail*. https://www.dailymail.co.uk/tvshowbiz/article-8340059/Lizzo-teams-Australian-sunglasses-brand-bold-collaboration.html

Doeing, D. (2019a, May 20). Core values list: 222 Ideas to inspire your value statement. *LearningHub*. https://learn.g2.com/core-values-list

Doeing, D. (2019b, May 9). Craft the perfect diversity statement for your organization. *LearningHub*. https://learn.g2.com/diversity-statement

Garrett, R. K. (2019). Social media's contribution to political misperceptions in U.S. presidential elections. *PLOS ONE, 14*(3), e0213500. https://doi.org/10.1371/journal.pone.0213500

Guide to inclusion and diversity in modern advertising. (n.d.). *Maryville Online*. https://online.maryville.edu/online-bachelors-degrees/marketing/guide-to-diversity-and-inclusion-in-modern-advertising/

Hutchinson, A. (2020, June 4). LinkedIn offers free courses in diversity and inclusion to improve community understanding. *Social Media Today*. https://www.socialmediatoday.com/news/linkedin-offers-free-courses-in-diversity-and-inclusion-to-improve-communit/579255/

IPSY (Producer). (n.d.). IPSY redefines inclusivity with "Discover Yourself" campaign. *The Shorty Awards*. https://shortyawards.com/12th/ipsy-redefines-inclusivity-with-discover-yourself-campaign-2

Kanigel, R. (Ed.). (n.d.). *Diversity style guide: Helping media professionals write with accuracy and authority*. https://www.diversitystyleguide.com/

King, N. (2019, February 15). Making the case for diversity in marketing and PR. *Forbes*. https://www.forbes.com/sites/forbescommunicationscouncil/2019/02/15/making-the-case-for-diversity-in-marketing-and-pr/

Morillo, A. (2020, June 25). Karamo Brown is hosting a panel about LGBTQ+ pride on Chipotle's TikTok account. *Delish*. https://www.delish.com/food-news/a32970768/chipotle-karamo-brown-tiktok/

Open Your World. (n.d.). *Edelman*. https://www.edelman.co.uk/work/open-your-world

Perrett, C. (2020, March 16). TikTok memo directed censorship of users deemed ugly, overweight, or disabled, and banned users for livestreams that criticized governments. *Business Insider*. https://www.businessinsider.com/tiktok-censorship-users-deemed-ugly-overweight-or-disabled-2020-3

Robin, M. (2020, May 21). Crayola teamed up with a former MAC chemist to expand its range of skin-tone crayons. *Allure*. https://www.allure.com/story/crayola-skin-tone-crayons-extension

Rodrigue, J., & Jones, L. (2020, June 5). Inside NFL players' Black Lives Matter video, and how it forced Goodell's hand. *The Athletic*. https://theathletic.com/1857643/2020/06/06/inside-nfl-players-black-lives-matter-video-and-how-it-forced-goodells-hand/

Siegel, A. (2019, February 6). The 6 essential principles of inclusive marketing every marketer should know. *Salesforce*. https://www.salesforce.com/blog/2019/02/inclusive-marketing-equality-trailhead.html

Tabaka, M. (2011, February 28). Win customers with empathy marketing. *Inc*. https://www.inc.com/marla-tabaka/win-customers-with-empathy-marketing.html

University of Michigan, Office of Diversity, Equity & Inclusion. (n.d.). *Defining DEI*. https://diversity.umich.edu/about/defining-dei/

Yeboah, K. (2016, September 6). A timeline of events since Colin Kaepernick's national anthem protest. *The Undefeated*. https://theundefeated.com/features/a-timeline-of-events-since-colin-kaepernicks-national-anthem-protest/

5

INDUSTRY QUALIFICATIONS AND ROLES IN SOCIAL MEDIA

Learning Objectives

After reading this chapter, you will be able to

- Identify trends in the social media industry

- Differentiate between social media roles

- Explain the key responsibilities of each social media role

- Discuss best practices and expectations for applying for social media positions

INTRODUCTION

Even though social media is an established field, there are still some misperceptions of how the field works and who is behind brands engaging, creating, and innovating to move to the next level. The perception of social media professionals has evolved over the past few years. More businesses, corporations, and even individuals who want to consult are realizing the growing industry that surrounds social media to this day. The job market and roles evolve with the platforms, which means in some cases there are established platforms in the field, but in other cases the platforms have yet to be solidified. You could work in a position that has yet to be offered or created—there are numerous opportunities to break into the industry. However, in a field that is constantly in flux, workers' skills have to be adaptive. A deep commitment and dedication to learn new skills is not only expected but necessary to be relevant in the field.

Many jobs have a key role in the social media world, and each requires certain skills and a specific mindset. Picture where you would like to work. Do you see yourself

- working in a cubicle, responding in real time to customer inquiries for one primary brand?

- being a specialist in one area of the industry (e.g., creator or influencer marketing) or a generalist, where you are engaged in all aspects of social media (e.g., content creation, crisis management, social care, public relations, marketing, paid media)?

- being agile, responsive, and engaging at a moment's notice to apply what you are doing?

- being able to mentor, advise, and pay it forward to the next generation?

- being a lifelong learner and being self-taught, or someone who thrives on mentorship and collaboration?

- being your own boss and establishing your own company as an entrepreneur?

- being on the front lines of customer service and engagement for a brand online through positive and challenging times?

- working at an agency on a variety of projects, brands, and clients?

- working in a tactical, strategic, or leadership role in a company or agency?

Each role has its own set of positives, negatives, and opportunities. Candidates for social media positions need to think about what today's corporations and hiring managers are looking for. Whether you go into journalism, marketing, public relations, or another related field, hiring managers look to social media to see how you present yourself. According to *Business News Daily*, nearly 60% of employers today turn to social media to research job applicants, an increase of 11% since 2006 (Brooks, 2017).

There are different tools you can use to get an employer's attention or to look for networking and professional opportunities. You need more than just a résumé and cover letter to be marketable in today's social media industry. You'll need a personal brand and the ability to show the overall impact, presence, and connections you are able to offer. As discussed in Chapter 3, it is not only about who knows your work, but who knows you and what you can bring to the table. Influence, impact, experiences, and expertise are some of the areas to focus on building in your personal brand.

Samantha Hughey, Brand Communications Manager for Adidas

Introduction

Hi. My name is Samantha, Sam for short. I am a Western Kentucky alum and Hilltopper fan for life. I have a bachelor of fine arts [degree] where my focus was on advertising, photojournalism, and sales. I completed my master's degree in communication at the University of Louisville, where I worked as the coordinator of social media for U of Louisville's athletic department. While in Louisville, I was able to work on a few high-profile projects, such as the Thunder Lounge, the Best of Louisville, the Oaks, Taste of Derby, and the Kentucky Derby.

After my time at the University of Louisville, I relocated to Colorado Springs to work at the United States Olympic Committee. I had the incredible opportunity to live at the Olympic Training Center and work for Team USA as their audience engagement editor. It was surreal to travel to various Olympic Trials, and I still get goosebumps thinking about the fact that I was able to tweet out the first gold medal that Team USA won in the Rio 2016 Olympic Games. In November of 2016, I traded in 13 stripes for three. While it was bittersweet to put Pike's Peak in my rearview mirror, working for adidas has been a dream of mine and I couldn't be more excited to be living the #3StripeLife in the Pacific Northwest.

How did you get your start in social media?

It cannot be stressed enough how much of a visual person I am. From learning math to doodling when I have a potential concept in my mind—I have to see it and visualize it otherwise it doesn't make sense in my mind. My background has continuously been in something that had a visual aspect to it, and a lot of this goes back to the mere fact that my father is in publishing and as a child I would sit in his office talking about the covers of his magazine, and the WHY behind the image that was chosen or HOW the palette of colors was finalized.

What is your favorite part of working in your area of expertise in social media?

I tell this story often, but I do so because this is what brought me to the industry. This is why I wanted to work for adidas, and it is because of this that I love what I do and where I am now. In my bathroom there is an adidas ad. David Beckham is celebrating a victory of some sort, and these words overlay on his image: *"Impossible is just a big word thrown around by small men who find it easier to live in the world they've been given than to explore the power they have to change it. Impossible is not a fact. It's an option. Impossible is not a declaration. It's a dare. Impossible is potential. Impossible is temporary. Impossible is nothing."* That quote, that campaign, sums up the intensity of what it means to live life and the power behind those who play sports and are sports fans: There is a magic there unlike any other.

A simple answer about my favorite part of working in this realm: invoking emotions from fans (which is easier said than done). That is exactly what makes this industry so incredible—finding the why and figuring out the how is by far my favorite.

It's all about chasing your dreams. Continuing to grind. And remembering that impossible is nothing.

What is one thing you can't live without while working in social media?

Relationships keep me going. I can't live without the relationships of those at work, my family and friends, and the community I have built, the community of like-minded

(Continued)

(Continued)

people. Without these multiple components that continue to support and cheer me on, I wouldn't be where I am today. Working in this field, I cannot live without having the ability to build meaningful relationships.

What is your favorite social media account (person/brand/etc.) to follow and why?

@Starbucks, easily. And that's not just because I only managed to survive my master's program through copious amounts of their brews. It's because they built a brand, a community behind a FIVE-DOLLAR cup of coffee. They understand their consumer, and they understand how to tell a story and tell it unbelievably well. Their strategy is simple: striking photography and user-generated content. These two pieces play well into who Starbucks is as a whole and what it means when you order their coffee. Not just a product that you are buying, but rather the experience.

What is the most challenging part of working in social media?

Not enough coffee, for one. That and it takes a special person to work in sports and social media. You will have the opportunity to work with some of the best athletes in the sport, or even in the world (yeah, I fangirled HARD internally when I met Laurie Hernandez at gymnastic trials, and when I get to work with Billie Jean King I still have to pinch myself), but you have to keep it cool. You have to love the field inside and out, understand what you bring to the table, and love your role. Having the separation between your fandom and your part in the organization is critical.

What is your take on your area of expertise and the social media industry?

Everyone and everything has a story to tell—whether that be a brand, an athlete, or a product. There is some sort of beginning, middle, and end that can be told in some fashion. Executing a piece can happen in the time span for typing out 280 characters and hitting send. Then, it's on to the next thing, the newest message or the latest app that can sell what you are putting out there better. The ideology behind the production of telling an impactful story through traditional media can be a formula that is moved over to social, and it is one that should be. How does your story make sense? Are you telling it in a way that consumers are interested? Is the life span longer than a thumb swiping up on a screen?

What do you wish you had known when you were starting out?

A few things stand out to me that I wish I had known when I was first starting out in this field:

— Finding that happy medium between being yourself and fitting into your role.

— Nothing is guaranteed. This is small market and there are A LOT of qualified folks out there, but not all those people have a job within the industry. Because of that, it seems that a lot of people can be seen as replaceable or rotated out, and with the influx of interns and/or students wanting the experience, why would an organization invest in you and your talents? It's a terrible cycle. Don't take it as a reason to hang your head, but rather as a reason to grind even harder. Use it as fuel to learn more.

What are three marketable skills a social media professional needs to have to work in the industry?

1. Being adaptable: things happen, plans change, budgets decrease, a pandemic happens. You have to be willing to adapt to the new norm and come up with a new way to execute.

2. Willingness to continue to learn: social is one of those areas that remains fluid; there are constant updates and new platforms to learn and explore. Without the desire to continue pushing yourself and learning, you can miss out on a new consumer or a new way to market your good or service, and you don't want to be left in the dust,

3. Authenticity: be true to who you are and what you stand for. Don't be fake, don't be the person who is one person behind a screen and then another IRL.

Where do you go to keep up to date with trends and continue learning about social media?

I read a lot. When I say a lot, I don't mean like one book a month—I mean that my house has at least five bookshelves filled with all types of subject matter, authors, storylines, characters, and worlds. That's where I am able to truly continue to learn and hone my craft.

If you had to choose a song to walk out to in a presentation on social media, what would it be and why?

I work in sports, so it has to be hype AF! So, with that I would say "Enter Sandman" by Metallica—[it] just takes me back to game day and gets me amped. Also, I will be walking into my wedding reception to that song. A very close second would be the "Space Jam Theme Song" because that move is incredible and one of the best sports movies of all time—the OG one—with MJ (in case the new one with LeBron comes out between me answering this question and the book getting published).

Samantha Hughey is a brand manager for adidas volleyball. Her work in sports focuses on brand marketing, strategic communication, and social media strategy. She previously was the audience engagement editor for Team USA during the Rio Olympics. Samantha can be followed on Twitter at @samanthahughey, Instagram **@samanthamhughey,** *or check* **out her website at www.searching4pirates.com.**

WHO HIRES SOCIAL MEDIA PROFESSIONALS?

One major consideration when working in social media is to determine what companies you would want to work for. Social media–specific agencies operate somewhat differently than traditional corporations. Corporate settings are more structured, formal, and tied to regulations, especially if they are a publicly traded company.

Experience is the first thing that employers want to see. They will ask you how many internships, projects, work experiences, and clients you have had before you even apply for a job. You will be expected to have a virtual dossier (online portfolio) to showcase your work. Some of these can be housed on programs such as Adobe Portfolio, Adobe Spark, WordPress, Wix, SquareSpace, and many more.

Other requirements are not as obvious. For example, working in sports requires not only a strong level of sports experience but also the ability to network and engage with the sports community on social media. Meeting people—both virtually and face-to-face—is one of the most important things you can do to advance your career. These meetings do not always have to involve social media.

Not only will employers be looking at your work, but you also need to look at theirs. Here are some employer characteristics you need to assess:

Portfolio of work. First, you want to see what potential employers have already done. What awards have they won? Where are their team members speaking? Certain conferences in social media (SXSW, Cannes Lions, Midwest Digital Marketing Conference, Social Media Marketing World, CES, etc.), as well as specialized events hosted by specific platforms such as Facebook, Twitter, and Google, are well recognized. Cutting-edge professionals will not only attend but also share their knowledge in these venues in recognition of their expertise. Online portfolios are popular and the standard to have to showcase work personally and professionally. Review not only what the potential employers are doing but also their team members. See which projects, work, creative initiatives, and campaigns inspire you.

Colleagues and what they have done. Many professionals in social media today may not have specialized in social media originally but rather just fell into it. Some universities still do not offer social media classes, programs, or majors. See what the professionals in your prospective organization have done in the past and what they are continuing to do in the field.

Culture. Culture is one of the most important elements to take into consideration. Make sure you are in an environment where you can do your best work and have the opportunity to learn, grow, and contribute to the greater good for your clients. Toxic environments (unhealthy competitive natures, stealing a coworker's work, etc.) are not places you want to be. Assess the level of mentorship in the organization.

Company employee's own personal social media presence. Personal branding is not just for you as the candidate for the job but also for those who are working at the company or agency where you want to work. How are they presenting themselves on social media? What is their overall active engagement like? Do they value having a personal brand and networking within and outside of the agency? Do you know what they stand for as far as perspectives, issues, and approaches in social media?

Ethical practices and brand pillars. As we discussed in Chapter 2 on ethics and legal considerations, the values and principles of a company, agency, or partnership are areas to consider. Identifying the key elements of how people operate in practice speaks volumes to how they conduct themselves as an organization. Imagine which organizational issues have not been disclosed publicly. It's best to identify these early on to avoid going to a place that is not practicing ethical business.

Diversity and representation. Looking at the initiatives, programs, and leadership of the organization, agency, or company is also important. As discussed in Chapter 4 on diversity and inclusion, be sure to identify whether or not the place you are applying is indeed representing all different perspectives, audiences, and communities.

Organizational structure for social media. You also need to consider the organizational structure of an organization when looking at prospective positions. Is there a head or director of social media? Or is social media an "add-on" to another department? This will tell you the overall value of and investment in social media made by the organization or agency in question. Although social media as a professional area has matured, some subtle differences persist across the industries. The position you report to will let you know very quickly the skills that you need to stay with the organization. For example, if you report to the chief marketing officer, you will need to be able to tie in marketing's goals, objectives, and language for reporting and creating content. The same applies to other fields as well. In a journalism setting, for example, a social media professional needs to understand the writing, reporting, and research requirements as well as the importance of deadlines. The content produced must follow the structure and writing format necessary for a particular publication.

WHERE TO WORK IN SOCIAL MEDIA

In social media, no one designated position, brand role, or industry is universally the same. Each company has its own distinct titles, expectations, and duties assigned to designated individuals in charge of social media. However, some universal skills are required for all social media professionals.

In some cases, the social media professional will be working for multiple clients with a variety of different specializations (e.g., analytics, paid media, diversity and inclusion, creative execution and activation, content creation, and social listening). In other cases, the professional will work for one client and focus on one distinct area (e.g., influencer marketing or TikTok).

Large social media agencies. Many large social media agencies have been behind some of the largest and most effective social media campaigns for clients, brands, and corporations. Brands such as KFC, General Motors, Oreo, Wendy's, and Burger King all have agencies that work with them to focus on social media–specific efforts for their campaigns.

Most brands and corporations have an agency of record in charge of social media content, strategy, or execution of ideas. For example, Chipotle has its own agencies that partner on a wide range of initiatives on everything from engaging with farmers for the sustainability to working specifically on influencer events and campaigns such as with YouTuber David Dobrik. The same goes with most brands: They usually have an internal team in place but outsource various specialized areas within the industry (e.g., influencer marketing, etc.). Facebook worked with Whalar to tap into their expertise in influencer marketing and manage the creative execution of their student ambassador program at college campuses.

Large social media companies. Brands can also be their own social media outlets, telling their own stories about successes with their clients and campaigns. Most brands, including Sprinklr, Hootsuite, Whalar, Sprout Social, Meltwater, Agorapulse, Salesforce, Adobe, and Talkwalker, use their blogs to share case studies on what has and has not worked. Many times, these brands focus on tools that provide services, training, and education for other organizations and individuals.

Boutique social media agencies. **Boutique agencies or firms** specialize either in one aspect of social media, such as analytics, or in a specific platform channel. Conviva, a research and analytics company, empowers content creators to produce the best stories for their clients and platforms and provides advanced metrics through their measurement tools. While the agency initially specialized in the use of analytics and content creation for specific platforms, it later branched out its strategy and analytics offerings for TikTok, Snapchat, Instagram, Twitter, Facebook, and many more. Boutique agencies can offer a more specialized focus and expertise to specific tasks, channels, and strategies compared to larger agencies. Another option is to focus on agencies that are changing the game for campaigns in their creative executions and strategies. Maximum Effort, the agency owned by Ryan Reynolds, has done work that has been innovative, entertaining, and relevant for brands like Aviation Gin, Match.com, and the cookie company HighKey. New approaches and creative ideas attract talent, and while established names have created a reputation for themselves, it may be good to look at professionals and agencies that are innovating and changing the field for the future.

Small businesses or agencies. This type of employer provides many entry-level positions for social media professionals or student interns. In consultation with their college or university mentors, student interns work with small agencies and businesses to help them engage, using social media to increase their presence in the communities in which they operate. Most small agencies have few employees and serve relatively small organizations.

Self-employment (consultant, creator, influencer, entrepreneur, or freelancer). Being your own boss can be pretty cool. You can build your own business as an entrepreneur, freelance and work on projects within your specific skill set, or serve as a consultant in areas of speciality. Social media has provided many consulting opportunities. It is important to be able to identify those consultants who "get it" versus the ones who are able to play the system and appear credible when, in fact, they are not. When practicing as a social media consultant, you are your own boss, and you can pick and choose the clients with whom you work. Your cost for services (value-based fees, project-based fees, etc.) must be negotiated with your clients. Some potential clients may not see the value of consultants and their contribution to the overall business and marketing strategy using social media. To convince them of your value, provide sound evidence of your previous work (sample proposals, SWOT [strengths, weaknesses, opportunities, and threats] analysis, news sources, content graphics, etc.).

Corporations. Internal teams working within large organizations create content and stories for internal and external audiences, monitor and listen to conversations about their organizations online, and engage in proactive practices online, addressing concerns from customers with social care. Delta, Visa, NYSE, Lyft, Disney, GoFundMe, John Deere, and Hilton are just a few organizations that have established teams of social media professionals who engage, listen, and create campaigns and message strategies to resonate with their audiences on a global scale.

Nonprofits. Social media in the nonprofit sector is one of the fastest-growing areas in the field. Nonprofits provide professionals with the opportunity to share stories, create awareness of key issues, identify donors to support causes and issues, and generate momentum to support humanitarian efforts at the local, national, and international levels.

Government. Social media has slowly but surely made its way to government agencies, political campaigns, and lobby groups. Some roles have been increasing in popularity. Political and government entities, for example, now have director of social media positions (e.g., White House) or director of digital media positions (e.g., Department of Health and Human Services), as well as people in traditional communication roles such as communication specialist, social media manager, and intern.

Sports. In sports, social media is directly tied to success in fan engagement, prominence in the community and industry, and innovative trends and practices. Sports organizations were early adopters of social media in their overall organizational structure. More professional, collegiate, and youth teams recognize the need for social media professionals and teams in leadership roles due to the growing emphasis on using social media to tell stories, recap games and performances, and be the first line of building a reputation and community for a team. The size of the team working in social media for a sports organization depends on the overall structure and financial support for this endeavor, but most of the time, professionals who work in social media in sports either have a designated leadership role in this area (e.g., director of digital media strategy or director of creative media) or are assuming this role as part of an established position within the sports department (e.g., sports information director). More teams and organizations like the NFL have established head and leadership positions (e.g., director of social media), signaling the trend that social media as a profession has not only matured but gained respect for the impact it can bring to the business and the organization's communication objectives.

Media. Journalism values the importance of social media. Most writers, producers, and reporters in traditional media also engage in social media for reporting the news, updating their community and audience, and communicating with others in the industry. Reporters such as Taylor Lorenz (NYT), Kerry Flynn (CNN), and Matt Navarra (former BBC and The Next Web) fall into this category for sharing news, trends, and case studies to the masses on their established networks. This is largely a response to the fact that most users rely on social media to get breaking news and updates regarding local, national, and international events. A strong social media presence has become part of the role and duty of traditional media. Not only are journalists expected to create content and stories for their outlets, but they also have to produce and share content across multiple platforms, listen to trending topics for story ideas (data analytics), and become strong editors and creators for different categories of content.

DEFINITION OF KEY SOCIAL MEDIA ROLES

Social media roles and job titles are anything but stable, and they can be different from company to company and even among job listings in other segments of media (e.g., marketing, public relations, communications, and journalism). With social media constantly evolving, the roles and job titles are fluid as well. This section will highlight the main roles being practiced with the mindset of understanding that some skills will always be relevant and valued by employers looking to hire a social media professional. Because each industry has its own titles, it is important to review job descriptions carefully. The description of each role presented will include the underlying characteristics, responsibilities, and duties. A sample job posting for each role will also be presented and explained in this section.

Social Media Community Manager Versus Social Media Manager

The **social media community manager** role sometimes gets confused with the role of social media manager—two distinct yet related roles. There are several differences between them: A social media manager focuses on being the brand on social media, whereas a social media community manager focuses on advocating for the brand on social media. Essentially, the social media manager *is* the brand— these professionals are the ones who create content, embrace the brand voice, and answer questions as the brand. You do not see any initials or anything not distinctly connected with the brand attributed to them.

In contrast, the role of social media community manager allows a person to add a personal take on the conversation with audience members. When engaging in a conversation with United Airlines, for example, you may get a message from United, with a few initials after it identifying the social care representative and community manager responding to your inquiry. This adds a level of personal connection and a human side to the social media conversation not necessarily present in the social media manager role.

Community managers may be in charge of listening and overseeing various campaigns and initiatives on social media. One minute you may be asked to address a customer inquiry online, and the next minute you may be asked to put strategy into place for a campaign. You will wear many hats in this position, which requires skill, adaptability, and multitasking.

Table 5.1 presents a sample description of a community manager position at Twitter.

Social Media Coordinator

A **social media coordinator** focuses on the strategic planning and execution of the social media content for a brand or organization. This term has evolved over the years, from community manager to community amplification. As the field gets more established, brands such as TikTok try to distinguish the roles in a different way by giving it a new title. However, the descriptions and expectations remain largely the same with some additional lists of responsibilities (Table 5.2). As a coordinator, you are responsible for making posts and content go live on schedule across the various social media platforms. In this role, you will be responsible for ensuring not only that content goes out in the appropriate channel but that it is scheduled at the right time for optimal reach and metrics for the company. Along with ensuring posts go out at appropriate times, this social media professional has to make sure all messages are consistent with the brand message and voice. Strategy and message relevancy are two parts of the equation for the social media coordinator to reinforce and advocate for as part of a social media team.

Strong organization and planning skills are required to ensure the posts have a timing and frequency that make sense to the community in question as well as to the platform being utilized for the content. A **content calendar** outlining what

Table 5.1   Social Media Manager | Louisville City FC

Job Description

The Social Media Manager is responsible for developing, implementing, and measuring social media marketing and communications for Louisville City Football Club and its ancillary companies in order to grow and foster an engaged fan base and support business growth. Responsibilities include strategic planning, live content creation, reporting, and analysis. This role offers the opportunity for ownership of marketing programs and to contribute to the overall LouCity marketing strategy. You will be responsible for creating original content, managing campaigns, and supporting online reputation management. You should be up-to-date with the latest digital technologies and social media trends. Knowledge and experience of soccer is preferred.

Responsibilities

Create relevant, original, high-quality content on LouCity social channels in accordance with company social media policies. Create and implement a regular content schedule to engage new and current fans and support LouCity promotional priorities. Conduct reporting and analysis of social media content/campaigns and provide recommendations for future plans. Collaborate with third party partners and foundations to authentically integrate partner content in a way that is consistent with LouCity brand voice and fan interests. Collaborate with marketing and communications teams to successfully activate initiatives on social channels. Monitor social media accounts and escalate any issues in a timely fashion. Keep management informed of dynamics and changes to the social media landscape. Provide additional support to marketing team on other projects as needed. Design and implement social media strategies to align with business goals. Define and report on most important social media KPIs [key performance indicators]. Monitor and facilitate online conversations with customers. Oversee relationship with the company's social media software. Live social media at all home matches. Development of internal social media education, trainings, and tools.

Experience

Three (3) to five (5) years marketing/communications experience. Exemplary computer skills that include knowledge of Social Network mediums (Facebook, Twitter, Instagram, YouTube, LinkedIn, TikTok). Adobe Creative Suite (InDesign, Photoshop,) and Microsoft Office Suite of products.

Education, Training, and Experience

Bachelor's degree (B.A.) from four-year college or university in Social Media, Marketing or a related field. 3-5 years' experience in social media strategy, content creation, and analytics, ideally for a sports or entertainment brand. Proficient in social media management software. Experience with Photoshop and/or video editing software a plus. Demonstrated passion for social media marketing and/or the soccer industry. Detail oriented, self-motivated, able to multitask and work independently with strong organizational skills. Excellent oral, written, and visual communication skills. Analytical thinker. Creative problem solver. Experience collaborating with and leading a cross-functional team. Ability to manage multiple projects simultaneously. Proficient in Microsoft Office. Ability to provide examples of business social media accounts that you have managed. We are an equal opportunity employer and all qualified applicants will receive consideration for employment without regard to race, color, religion, sex, national origin, disability status, protected veteran status, or any other characteristic protected by law.

Source: Adapted from https://jobatic.com/jobs/amp/kentucky/louisville/louisville-city-fc/social-media-manager.html?utm_campaign=google_jobs_apply&utm_source=google_jobs_apply&utm_medium=organic

Table 5.2　Social Media and Community Amplification | TikTok

Responsibilities

- Design and execute the content strategy of social media, so as to establish the brand imagery, as well as engage the fans and other CRM [customer relationship management] responsibilities.

- Study the content trends in-app and in the market, and promote in-App contents accordingly in order to build the impactfulness and imagery of the in-App contents or creators.

- Manage the KOL [key opinion leader] pool and establish programmatic content amplification system, to increase returned users from key media platforms.

- Design offline events or other formats of interactive events, to amplify the community ambience.

Qualifications

- 3–5 years of experience in dynamic marketing practices. Experience in digital media campaign is a must. Experience in diversified formats of marketing campaign is preferred.

- High passion and good taste in music is a must. Professional knowledge about music and deep understanding of international artistic trends are preferred.

- Good data analytical skills is a must.

Source: Adapted from https://careers.tiktok.com/position/detail/6826973671748487432

content is going out at what time is crucial for the coordinator to create, maintain, and share with the rest of the team.

The coordinator works with all social media teams to make sure the messages, content, branding, and voice are consistent. As with most current social media roles, a coordinator's responsibilities will overlap with those of different team members. For example, the coordinator works with the community manager to ensure that the messages are relevant and resonate with audiences so they are able to report positive findings back to the management team during the evaluation phase. As shown in Table 5.3, the social media coordinator position for the Atlanta United FC highlights several key skills, but notice the emphasis on assisting with strategy, coordinating consistent content across the platforms, and planning to distribute this content at the right time, to the right audience, and on the right channel.

Social Media Strategist

A **social media strategist** ties in the goals and objectives for the company or client in question, and focuses on how to get these measures accomplished. This professional takes more of a manager role than a technician role, meaning he or she not only is in charge of understanding the tactical elements that go into a strong social media plan (content creation, specific tools used to create and analyze the content online, etc.) but also understands the comprehensive picture of the campaign.

Strategist roles can be centered on social media, but they can also be aimed at a particular area. Sometimes social media strategy jobs are on the creative side

Table 5.3 Social Media Coordinator | Atlanta United FC

As part of the AMBSE Media Group, the Atlanta United social media coordinator will assist with all aspects of the club's social media efforts on a day-to-day basis—including content creation, community management, one-to-one fan engagement, and strategic plan development and implementation.

This position will proactively lead, create, and manage content on Atlanta United social platforms. He or she will collaborate with and partner across all relevant departments, including content production, digital/web, video services, photography, marketing, sponsorships, community relations, and agencies to deliver and execute successful social tactics that align with Atlanta United's overall digital media strategy.

Roles and Responsibilities

- Assist in creating innovative, entertaining content (including but not limited to Facebook posts, tweets, GIFs, snaps, images, and short-format videos) to engage consumers across social channels while maintaining Falcons brand voice.

- Assist in building and aligning content strategy, team coverage, team communications, marketing partnerships, stadium news and events, and sponsored posts across all social media platforms.

- Provide coverage for both home and away Atlanta United games (may require some travel).

- Help build and manage both long- and short-term social editorial calendar.

- Drive integrated content ideation from concept to completion across all platforms.

- Together with the Atlanta United social/digital team, aggressively increase overall key performance indicator metrics across social platforms.

- Collaborate with the sponsorship and marketing teams to create engaging and valuable partnership inventory and brand integration opportunities.

- Ensure integration with all Atlanta United departments, as well as other communications, marketing, and community relations leaders across the Blank Family of Businesses.

- Monitor best practices and trends in organic and branded social media, and effectively communicate relevant news and opportunities to internal teams.

Qualifications and Education Requirements

- Bachelor's degree (required)

- One to two years' experience across multiple digital and social media functions, including strategy, digital marketing, web development, and/or a related field within a high-paced, demanding professional setting

- Agency experience (accepted)

Required Skills

- Demonstrated experience driving consumer/fan engagement across multiple social channels

- Strong writing and editing skills

- Experience with professional or collegiate sports (recommended)

Source: Adapted from MEOjobsonline.com

(such as the one listed for Netflix in Table 5.4), whereas others are on the data side (as shown for Hasbro in Table 5.5). In addition to having differences, the positions also have important similarities.

The Netflix creative strategist primarily focuses on the art side of the strategy continuum whereas the Hasbro social analytics strategist focuses more on the science side. Yet both roles are relevant to the creative integration of content, strategy, and messaging used to apply and present findings from research for the social team. While they are separate roles for these two brands, in other cases the two job titles become one; Facebook, for example, employs a strategy analyst, as shown in Table 5.6.

The social analytics strategist position at Hasbro primarily focuses on the data and analytical side of social media at the company. This role is based on a strong understanding of how to collect data and strategically apply the data to provide insights for the social team.

Content Creator

Content is king when it comes to social media. Content comes in various formats, and social media professionals are expected to be well versed in the type of content they are producing. Besides multimedia, including graphics, images, infographics, video, and animations, content can take the form of thought pieces that share resources, ideas, and research insights using white papers, blog posts, and social media updates. **Content creators** have to be able to create work that resonates with audiences. In fact, the best content creators are able to identify which stories and insights their key audiences want without knowing they want it. The range of skills needed to create these different formats of content can be challenging, combining both visual and written components (see, e.g., Table 5.7). Content that appears on social media can be long format (e.g., white papers) or short format (e.g., tweets), and often integrates multimedia and emerging media with the mix (360-degree images, virtual reality, augmented reality, etc.).

While content is an important element for the creators, context is the other part of the equation to keep in mind. Content creators have to be able to identify the overall purpose for a piece of content from a strategy standpoint and work with the coordinator, community manager, and strategist to make sure the content integrates the brand message, voice, and situation online.

Creative Director
(Multimedia, Video, and More)

This is probably one of the most in-demand jobs in social media. If you are able to create, produce, and record video content to tell effective stories, you will be in demand. Organizations are interested in people with a background in storyboarding, writing scripts, and creating demo reels that can be viewed online on YouTube, on Behance, and in other content and video creator communities (see, e.g., the creative director position at Blizzard outlined in Table 5.8). Most of the jobs listed in social media now have a multimedia component, so this is a good skill if you want to be more of a generalist. However, if you want to specialize in multimedia, be prepared to make investments in tools, software programs, and equipment.

Table 5.4   Product Creative Strategist | Netflix

The Product Creative Strategy team partners with content creators and distributors to define how their content is creatively represented on Netflix to members around the world. Our purpose is to deliver the most compelling discovery experience through artwork, video, and copy to connect our millions of global subscribers to the content they love.

At its core, the Product Creative Strategist role is grounded in creative with a strong understanding of how the Netflix product works. The successful candidate will marry a strong passion for entertainment and visual storytelling with a hearty curiosity for innovation and data, to define the creative strategy for titles within the content slate in India—working closely with internal teams and agencies to develop assets (imagery, video, text) for touch points across the Netflix product experience. If you're a fan of Indian content, this is your chance to transform how Indian storytelling is presented and discovered by millions of members around the world.

Responsibilities

Impact and success will be based on the ability to direct and produce high quality and compelling creative, and the dexterity to work seamlessly across numerous internal and external stakeholder teams. You will be required to build and maintain close partnerships with creative directors, agencies, studios and other cross-functional teams (Marketing, Content, Product) to define the creative look and feel of the India slate on Netflix. You will also be an ambassador for the member experience in India, connecting with Los Gatos–based Product and Innovation teams to be the voice of members and input to a pipeline of ongoing innovation research, testing, and design that will go toward optimizing the member experience for our subscribers.

A Typical Day Might Include

- Writing a creative brief that is grounded in data and insights derived from internal tools and partner teams.
- Working with internal and external stakeholders to source, direct, and produce compelling imagery, video, and textual assets.
- Effectively project-managing multiple title launches to ensure timely and accurate development, production, and delivery of creative assets.
- Leading onboarding meetings with studio reps and agency partners to introduce Netflix product and product creative.
- Proactively learning about latest product innovation efforts and updating cross-functional partners on the latest product features, tests, and initiatives.
- Reviewing artwork performance metrics, analyzing winning trends, and determining a path for better creative.

Qualifications

- Exceptional communicator—ability to inspire and influence, and dexterity in presenting to large/diverse audiences. Native or bilingual proficiency in speaking and writing in English and Hindi.
- Strong familiarity with business, digital media, and entertainment landscape in India.
- Strategic thinker with creative flare and project management skills: 7–10 years crafting world class creative strategy, spearheading creative direction and execution.
- Innately curious, thrives on gleaning insights from data, and able to identify creative opportunities in content and translate these into sharp creative briefs.
- Solid experience in working with creative agencies (creatives, designers, producers) and the ability to provide concise, clear, and actionable creative feedback/direction.

(Continued)

Table 5.4 (Continued)

- Proactive, fast, and flexible problem-solver with superb time, resource, and stakeholder management.
- Ability to interact meaningfully with people of diverse backgrounds, personalities, and expertise (e.g., product engineer in Silicon Valley and creative executive in Hollywood).
- Passion and curiosity toward building great product experiences for everyone.
- Self-motivated leader and strong collaborator/team player with the ability to maintain calm, make good decisions, and work with constant ambiguity.
- Understand, advocate, and embody the Netflix culture and team goals.

Source: Adapted from https://jobs.netflix.com/jobs/872007

Table 5.5 Social Media Strategist | Hasbro

At Hasbro, we are looking for people who want to explore, experiment, innovate, and create. We're changing the face of play and entertainment and looking for dreamers, doers, thinkers, and creators to come up with the best ideas. Our culture of Community, Passion, Integrity, Creativity, and Inclusion has inspired our diverse team of highly skilled, highly creative, and highly committed individuals for 90+ years and we believe the best is yet to come.

We're seeking a Sr. Manager, Data Analytics to join our Analytics and Reporting team!

The Senior Manager Data Analytics role is a business analytics leader: incumbent should be an effective communicator, naturally curious, and able to drive insights into actions that improve Hasbro's business results. Role will report to the Sr. Director, Analytics and Reporting for Hasbro North America.

This is both an internal and external facing role, that is expected to deliver analytic insights in several business domains including consumer, customer, digital, market, and share performance. Role will be a primary driver of delivering observations and recommendations that will educate and influence key business decision-making with our Account and Brand teams. Business knowledge, social, and communication skills are therefore needed, in addition to complex data analysis, to thrive in this multifunctional insights and analytics team.

This role partners with an internal business client team to own insights and analysis. Incumbent answers and anticipates critical business questions and opportunities, and delivers critical insights to the business in ways that make significant impacts.

- Collaborate and own, proactive, persistent, and efficient communication of consumable and actionable insights for business client teams.
- Tell stories with data, using a combination of data sources, including but not limited to POS [point of sale] and shipment forecast and history, NPD [new product development], promotional and media calendars.
- Lead analysis for a specific book of business—requiring a strong understanding of both demand- and supply-side trends and insights and deep appreciation for business needs.

Key Responsibilities

- Maintain deep understanding of client team's business challenges, ongoing questions, and data needs in order to anticipate and quickly respond to changes in business environment (may include sales, marketing, and operations, I.T.)
- Give analysis, observations, and insights to client teams on regular and ad hoc basis, supported by efficient, sustainable, usable self-service dashboards.

- Demonstrate brick and ecommerce POS, marketing, and NPD data to provide insight into our transaction patterns, product trends, supply chain, and inventory.

- Maintain deep knowledge on current consumer trends and insights, combined with sales and inventory data, to provide recommendations and opportunities to sales teams.

- Lead ad hoc research and analysis projects, translate business problems and questions into definable, measurable research projects.

- Effectively project lead custom research requests: working cross-functionally, compiling requirements, developing project timelines, and maintaining strong communication across all project partners.

- Find and independently lead opportunities for continuous improvement; iterating and evolving existing reporting and analysis practices for the future.

What You'll Bring

- Highly analytical, collaborative, ambitious, technical skills in a cross-functional setting

- Intrinsic curiosity and passion about data, visualization, and solving problems

- Passion for client service, and are adaptable and willing to collaborate openly with other functions

- Excellent oral and written communication skills, excellent presentation skills, with the ability to explain complicated information in a significant way

- Invite others to question the validity and accuracy of data and assumptions

- Previous experience with project management and process evaluation and design

- Experience with Tableau, Power BI, Domo, or equivalency to build impactful reports, visualizations, and interactive dashboards

- Expert level knowledge of Microsoft Excel and Microsoft Office suite

- B.A. degree required, M.B.A. preferred

- 3-5 years' experience in data analysis

Source: Adapted from MEOjobsonline.com

Table 5.6   Head of Social and Influencer Marketing, AR/VR | Facebook

At Facebook's Augmented Reality/Virtual Reality (AR/VR) organization, we're building devices and experiences that make people feel closer together. The organization includes Oculus and Portal products and other hardware, AR and VR software and content, and research and development labs. The AR/VR Marketing Communications team is seeking a bold and innovative marketing leader to drive the growth of our Oculus and Portal product portfolios through editorial content, social media, and influencer marketing channels. Ultimately, this individual is responsible for the business impact of our editorial content, social and influencer channels. Our ideal candidate will excel at team leadership, social channel strategy, content planning, channel operations, and measurement and analytics. This person is a big thinker who's more than happy to roll up his/her sleeves with the team to bring new, innovative work to our customers. They have strong cross-functional partnership skills and thrive in a fast-moving, entrepreneurial environment.

(Continued)

Table 5.6 (Continued)

Head of Social and Influencer Marketing, AR/VR Responsibilities

- Vision and Strategy: Build on holistic marketing strategy to drive growth through editorial content marketing, social media, and influencer engagement programs for current and emerging brands.
- People Management: Grow, coach, mentor, and inspire a team of social and influencer marketers to develop and execute social-first programs in support of global and regional marketing initiatives.
- Results and Impact: Partner with decision science, S&O [strategy and operations] counterparts to set key performance indicators, evaluate success against objectives and investment, and continuously optimize.
- Customer Insight: Understand our core audiences and the evolving ways they connect and create with content, media, and each other, in order to change behavior and brand perception.
- Creative Content: Partner with our creative teams and agencies to dream and deliver iterative, culturally relevant, social-first creative.
- Operations and Process: Develop, evolve, and drive processes to manage a social and influencer practice that operates in both planned and real-time moments.
- Oversee channel budgeting, resourcing, legal compliance, content planning and publishing, influencer and community engagement, moderation, and reporting.
- Tooling and Infrastructure: Oversee management of necessary tools, systems, and infrastructure required to deliver and measure social media, content, and influencer marketing programs.
- Manage new and existing partners integral for a social and influencer practice at scale.
- Cross-Functional Partnerships: Collaborate with and influence cross-functional partners in research, product marketing, integrated marketing, experiential marketing, communications, customer experience, analytics, and legal to inform social strategy, activation, and results.

Minimum Qualifications

- Bachelor in Business, Management, Marketing, or Related Support Services
- 12 or more years of experience with digital marketing, social media marketing, or content marketing
- 8 or more years of experience with team leadership or team management
- Experience managing a social and influencer marketing practice at a global consumer brand
- Experience with social media and influencer ecosystems, tools, platforms, and offerings
- Experience building and managing real-time editorial content studios
- Experience driving measurable results from social marketing at a global company
- Experience improving internal processes and creating structure within a growing organization

Preferred Qualifications

- Master in Business Administration
- Experience in the tech, media, gaming, or entertainment space

Source: Adapted from https://www.facebook.com/careers/jobs/2679169055520452/

Table 5.7 Social Media Intern | General Electric

WHAT YOU WILL LEARN AND DO

Essential Responsibilities

- Work collaboratively to support the social media team on various work assignments as identified.
- Professionally respond to consumer product reviews left on our company-owned websites as well as dealer-partner sites.
- Process consumer opt-out requests.
- Intervene and document outcomes from various chat-bot or other technology "test and learn" interactions.
- Cleanse duplicate emails or no-response required emails from the email queue to enable the team to address value-added consumer responses.
- Place orders for consumer-requested product publications and wiring diagrams.
- Scan and load product publications into electronic format for easy call center agent access.
- Resolve and document dispositions for consumer replies to email marketing campaigns.
- Send final responses to research-required escalations after answer has been identified.
- Intercept website correction requests and forward to appropriate internal contacts for resolution.

WHAT YOU NEED TO SUCCEED

Qualifications/Requirements

- Students only. Must be a current full-time student enrolled in a bachelor's or advance degree program; pursuing a marketing or business-related degree preferred
- Minimum GPA of 3.0 required
- Excellent written communication skills: grammar, sentence structure, and spelling
- Computer literate with ability to learn new applications quickly
- Positive attitude with proven ability to work well with teams
- Strong typing skills
- Dependable with strong pattern of attendance
- Must be willing to work at least 20 hrs./week; ability to work flexible hours ranging from 20–40/week is ideal
- Co-op duration of 1 year

Desired Characteristics

- Team player, collaborative style
- Self-starter, able to work independently and in team setting
- High level of enthusiasm/energy/positive

Source: Adapted from https://careers.geappliances.com/job/REQ-6248/Marketing-Coop-Social-Media

Table 5.8   Creative Director | Blizzard

We are looking for a Creative Director to help maintain and progress the brand's creative vision across multiple initiatives, including Overwatch, Overwatch 2, and our global esports league, the Overwatch League. Our team is looking for someone that exhibits a passion for design and can articulate the brand's objectives through high-quality visual content. The Creative Director seeks out opportunities to learn/grow/innovate, understands the value of process, maintains a high level of attention to detail, and is ready to play an important role within our team.

Marketing and advertising are your trade and passion but games, movies, comics, sports, and the stories that drive them are your life. Above all, we are looking for an innovative and dedicated designer and leader to help tell the story of our brands in an ever-changing media world.

Duties

Provide high-level guidance, iterative review, and approval of Overwatch related materials in all franchise extensions, ranging from traditional marketing promotional material (both print and digital) to esports stage design and broadcast graphics, with additional components of web and mobile design.

- Conceptualize and design for online ad campaigns while adhering to the visual quality of the brand.
- Solve complex visual problems and turn them into beautifully clear designed solutions that reinforce the brand.
- Lead day-to-day brand initiatives that include program logos, style guides, social media, static banner creation, community blog assets, presentations as well as help maintain asset support for our esports initiatives.
- Partner with internal/external teams to analyze provided data, help collaborate/innovate design solutions to achieve project goals.
- Maintain the visual aesthetic and spirit of the Overwatch and Overwatch League brands while maintaining your personal design perspective.
- Collaborate closely with game development team art leadership to create and iterate on style guides for franchise partners in web, mobile, marketing communications, and esports; ensure alignment as the franchise evolves visually and thematically.
- Build strong relationships with support group partners (marketing communications, esports, web/mobile, events, broadcast, and consumer products), identify key creative leaders for partnership, and further shared creative values and goals.
- Manage multiple projects from start to finish while keeping multiple stakeholders both in and out of the organization appropriately informed and engaged.
- Facilitate communications, organization, and accountability across all departments and stakeholders to ensure high-level project goals are met and ensure consistency and quality of brand representation.
- Work with creative services team to develop efficiencies within the workflow while developing Blizzard-quality creative assets.

Qualifications

- Bachelor's degree in art, design, marketing, related field, or equivalent work experience
- 8+ years of experience in creative advertising and/or marketing
- Experience managing and guiding creative employees effectively
- Demonstrated successes collaborating across departments and with external agencies
- Detailed project management skills and ability to maintain strategic view of all work
- Enjoys the challenge of growing and managing a world-class creative services team

- Proven ability to think globally and help steer regional success of Overwatch's and Overwatch League's marketing creative throughout the world
- Previous experience successfully managing creative people, including designers and copy writers
- Thinks broadly about communication challenges while helping to focus the thinking of others around clear objectives
- Has a sincere passion for branding, advertising, and storytelling as well as games, comics, movies, and media
- Exceptional verbal, written, and interpersonal communications skills for working with internal and external teams

Preferred Qualifications

- Advanced degree in related field
- Strong layout and logo design skills
- Copywriting background and advanced skill
- Broadcast media art direction experience
- Consumer product design and packaging design experience
- Illustration abilities

Source: Adapted from https://www.ivyexec.com/job-opening/creative-director/irvine/california/usa?job_id=7538837& ref=ccadz&promo=ccadz&ccuid=25656289875&ppt=eyJhbGciOiJIUzI1NiJ9.eyJzcmNfaWQiOjExNDQxNywicHBfbmFtZ SI6ImFwcGNhc3QiLCJjbGlja19pZCI6IkJ1MzFfNS10NmhHUGlxNzlXcGZYMUEiLCJlcG9jaCI6MTU5MjA3MTMyOX0 .wmWHCKgx2q_nXPrYylwx_Ldzn-k4ccAiGQ_X4JMvveU

Writer/Editor

Writing and editing content that is consistent with the brand voice for social and digital media is essential. Social media writers and editors support the storytellers, strong visionaries, and other editors. They will be working with content creators as well as coordinators to ensure their content is aligned with the content of other team members. Publishing content on a consistent basis across media channels is important not just from a textual standpoint but also in the case of other types of content (video, photos, etc.).

Diversity and Inclusion Lead

As more organizations, brands, and agencies are working toward increasing representation across all areas and audiences, more lead roles and teams are being created to address and support strategies, campaigns, and initiatives internally and externally regarding diversity and inclusion efforts (Table 5.9).

Other Social Media Roles

There are other roles to consider when exploring work in social media.

- Being a **freelancer** is one of the more popular avenues to take because of the flexibility and independence that come with choosing your own clients and projects. Freelancers tend to focus on certain types of projects and particular areas within social media, such as social media writing, content creation, videography, and social media strategic plans.

Table 5.9 Diversity and Inclusion Lead | Humana

The Diversity and Inclusion Lead develops, implements, and evaluates diversity/equal employment opportunity (EEO) and affirmative action programs to ensure compliance with government legislation and organization goals. The Diversity and Inclusion Lead works on problems of diverse scope and complexity ranging from moderate to substantial.

Responsibilities

Network Resource Group Strategy and Leadership

- Develop holistic forward-looking strategy to continuously evolve Humana's network resource groups (NRG).
- Collaborate with NRG leaders, executive sponsors and the executive Inclusion and Diversity (I&D) Council members to gain alignment on NRG strategy and goals.
- Recruit and onboard new executive sponsors and co-presidents.
- Develop approach and manage NRG/I&D summits.

Data Analysis and Metrics

- Set success measures and key performance indicators.
- Produce population snapshots and connect NRG participation to well-being, engagement, and business outcomes.
- Develop channels for information sharing, such as MS Teams, leadership calls (NRGs in the Know).
- Studies in Management partnerships, which focus on developing diverse talent at the MBA level, giving Humana an opportunity to build a stronger, more diverse talent pipeline with top talent.
- Partner with the HR college recruiting team to create recruiting strategy focused on top-tier, diverse MBA candidates.
- Represent Humana at recruiting events and manage the communication and logistics for the on-site interview pro.
- Represent the Office of I&D in external events and internal forums—panel discussions, town halls, leader training sessions, local I&D days, and requests made by key partners.

Required Qualifications

Bachelor's degree • 8 or more years of demonstrated experience in inclusion and diversity • 2 or more years of experience developing and integrating inclusion and diversity focused programs • Passion for improving inclusion and diversity across the enterprise • Demonstrated ability to connect the dots end-to-end and focus on simplifying processes and experiences • Strong presentation, facilitation, and written/verbal communication skills • Problem-solving skills and ability to proactively identify and mitigate issues • Ability to interface with multiple levels of the organization and to serve as an influence leader and a team player • Proven ability to break down silos, facilitate cross-functional collaboration, and leverage resources and opportunities across the enterprise • Proven ability to work with highly confidential information

Source: Adapted from https://joblift.com/details/979d41ff-5d1d-4ed2-95fb-babf79883761?gfj=true&utm_campaign=google_jobs_apply&utm_source=google_jobs_apply&utm_medium=organic

- **Creators** or **Influencers** market themselves to brands based on their own personal brand and the community they have been able to build. As we will discuss in the influencer marketing chapter, there are different considerations to be made based on the type of influencer someone is. Influencers have to provide their metrics and impact measures to brands to justify the payment for content, while creators work with brands and others on what content needs to be created.

- **Entrepreneurs** are their own boss, which is both freeing in not having to report to anyone but also can cause a huge amount of stress because you have to do everything yourself while not having a secure and consistent paycheck to rely on. If you do not make money, then you are not able to do the things you want to. You are on call all the time, but you get to choose when and where you want to work. However, many social media professionals (such as Victoria "Tori" Tidwell) create a side business where they are able to apply what they are practicing to selling products or services. Tori, a social media professional in Atlanta, created the store Free The Edit Button, where she creates and sells social media merchandise and swag items, such as the verified badge coffee cup and "You are on mute" sweaters.

- **Consultants** usually specialize in what they offer clients, such as creating social media plans, preparing for potential scenarios or simulations in social media crisis situations, educational and speaking opportunities based on social media expertise, and training. Consultants may be independent, but consulting agencies and firms also offer services. Both freelancers and consultants in social media must demonstrate previous work for clients and reviews of their work (e.g., testimonials and online reviews).

HOW MUCH DO SOCIAL MEDIA PROFESSIONALS GET PAID?

This is a frequently asked question in the industry. What is the going rate for social media managers (see Figure 5.1)? What about community managers? Do roles dealing with data and analytics get more resources and support? All of these questions are valid and important.

Social media roles are expanding, and they even reach department levels within organizations, media outlets, and agencies. Social media professionals play key parts in many communication, marketing, public relations, business reporting, and strategy processes. Before you start applying for internships or jobs, make sure you do your research and understand the expectations (as well as years of experience) and responsibilities for each role. It is challenging to figure out how much a professional should be making based on experience, skills, and expertise. While on some occasions a marketing, public relations, or communications professional is writing the job description, sometimes it is a human resources professional who does not know the social media industry. There are occasions where professionals and brands want everything in the job description (essentially looking for a "unicorn" candidate), or they mix up the descriptions for the role they are looking for. Essentially, you may read a description for a social media manager when, in fact, the brand hiring for the position is looking for a coordinator. That said, figuring out the salary for a position can be difficult. However, sources like Glassdoor,

Figure 5.1 Average Social Media Manager Salary

United States / Job / Social Media Manager

Average Social Media Manager Salary

$50,816

Avg. salary   Show Hourly Rate

$2,233	**$2,000**	**$1,953**
BONUS	COMMISSION	PROFIT SHARING

The average salary for a Social Media Manager is $50,816.

10%	MEDIAN	90%
$35k	$51k	$78k

Is Social Media Manager your job title? Find out what you should be paid
Use our tool to get a personalized report on your market worth. What's this?

How it works:
1. Enter city & years of experience
2. Add pay factors like skills & education
3. Find your market worth with a report tailored to you

Location:

Louisville, Kentucky

United States (change)

Years in Field/Career:

Find your market worth»

What am I worth?

Get pay report

How should I pay?

Price a job

A Social Media Manager typically makes between **$35k – $78k.**

Select your salary to compare:

$$$

$51k

$

Next, use our tool to calculate your market worth & see where you stand among peers.

Find your market worth»

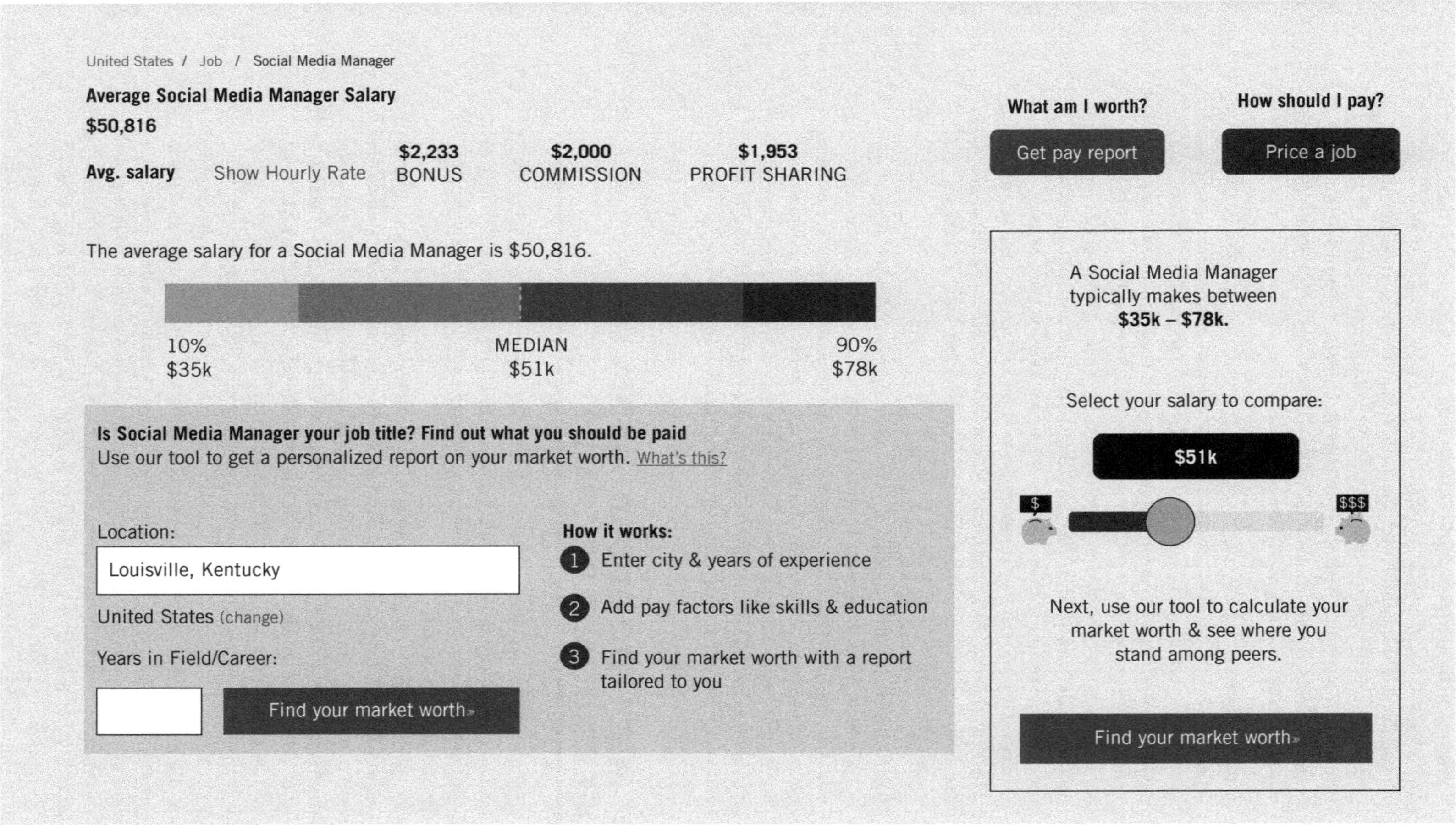

Source: https://www.payscale.com/research/US/Job=Social_Media_Manager/Salary

LinkedIn, and PayScale can help gauge where a salary should be for each social media position.

As presented in Figure 5.1, as of March 2020, a social media manager on average makes $50,816 annually. Having multiple tools, skills, and trainings under your belt should lead to a higher salary. In addition, gaining leadership experience, team coordination, and campaign executions can also help in obtaining a social media director's role. This is where a big job in salary comes forward, rewarding the candidate for the experiences. Experience and showing the work (and impact) done in social media is a key differentiator for many job candidates. For example, as shown in Figure 5.2, a social media director on average earns a much higher average salary compared to a social media manager ($71,427 vs. $50,816 in March 2020).

If you have gained several years of experience and established a reputation for yourself as a thought leader, and you have the power and presence to lead a team and formulate strategies, you might be eligible for a leadership role in social media.

Some final thoughts about working as a social media professional:

- *Relationships and networking can open up more opportunities than a résumé.* It's great to have a list of credentials related to your studies and work experience, but it's also important for the community to know who you are. Take time before applying for jobs and internships to network, collaborate, and engage with professionals online. Many professionals, especially in #MarketingTwitter, are waiting for students to reach out and connect.

- *Experience matters.* There is no magic number for how many internships, jobs, or years of experience you need to get a job in social media. Experience comes in many forms, from freelancing to working at established corporate brands. The most important thing is to show the impact and results you were able to bring to the table.

- *Show impact on résumé.* Résumés are still important to have as part of your portfolio. Yet, it is important to highlight the actual impact you made in your jobs, internships, and volunteer roles. For example, if you were to list you were a social media intern for Marvel, you may list "created content on TikTok and Instagram." However, if you were able to state "strategized and creatively executed content that generated a 50% increase in engagement on TikTok," this shows impact and your individual contribution to the role. Experience with explanation of impact and contribution is crucial to highlight.

- *Community managers have increased their presence within the industry, but the title is used in many different areas.* Social media managers, still considered to be specialized, get paid a bit more than community managers.

- *Stand out and be proud of your work.* You want to make sure you are showcasing not just the essential details everyone is expecting to see from a job candidate, but do something slightly different. Utilize a new platform and tag the brand to let them know you are applying; showcase your creativity. For example, Maggie Johnson, a graduate from the University of Louisville, wanted to work for Anheuser-Busch as part of their influencer marketing team and decided to create a TikTok video introducing herself to the brand in a visual and creative way. As a result, Maggie got the job!

Figure 5.2 Average Social Media Director Salary

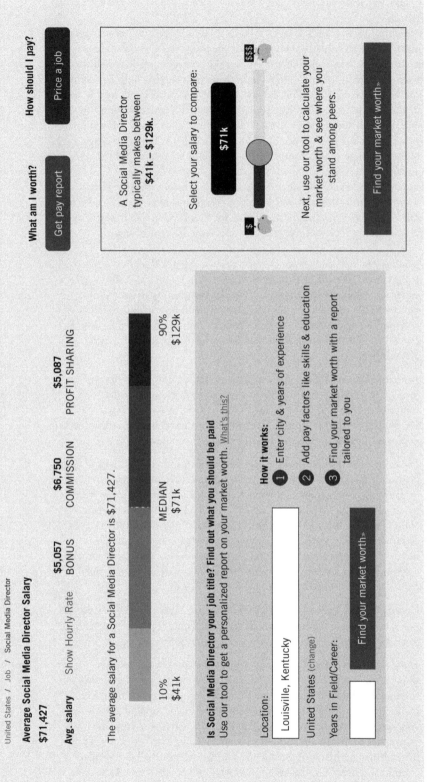

United States / Job / Social Media Director

Average Social Media Director Salary

$71,427

Avg. salary	Show Hourly Rate	**$5,057**	**$6,750**	**$5,087**
		BONUS	COMMISSION	PROFIT SHARING

The average salary for a Social Media Director is $71,427.

10%	MEDIAN	90%
$41k	$71k	$129k

Is Social Media Director your job title? Find out what you should be paid
Use our tool to get a personalized report on your market worth. What's this?

How it works:

1 Enter city & years of experience

2 Add pay factors like skills & education

3 Find your market worth with a report tailored to you

Location:

Louisville, Kentucky

United States (change)

Years in Field/Career:

Find your market worth»

What am I worth?   **How should I pay?**

Get pay report   Price a job

A Social Media Director typically makes between **$41k – $129k.**

Select your salary to compare:

$71k

Next, use our tool to calculate your market worth & see where you stand among peers.

Find your market worth»

Source: Adapted from "Social Media Specialist Salary" PayScale Inc. https://www.payscale.com/research/US/Job=Social_Media_Director/Salary

- *Show what you have done, but also what you will continue to do and how you will strive to improve in the future.* Social media is all about growing, expanding, and being adaptable. Show what you have done, but realize this is a field where you have to constantly update your skills.

- *You have to start small and work your way up in social media.* Big, high-paying jobs do not happen overnight. Take the time to hone your skills and make sure you are learning and growing as a professional. Keep in mind that this can take some time, but it is best to get the experience, establish relationships, and continue growing. Moving forward is the most important strategy.

- *It is about not only what you know but who knows you.* For some of these positions, it's all about who knows you. Invest not only in your skills but also in building networks and communities. Speak at local events, volunteer at professional functions, be a guest on blogs or webinars, and write content to share with various communities to develop your thought leadership. Building on your personal brand (as mentioned in Chapter 3) will help open doors and opportunities for you for potential collaborations, influencer or creator projects, partnerships, job offers, or speaking engagements.

- *Have a "side hustle."* If you have one job in social media, that may not be enough. Whether you are a social media manager or even leading a team, you should consider having another job on the side—or a "side hustle." This means you might have a consulting business, help invest in a start-up, volunteer to help nonprofits, build a community on a particular area or topic you are passionate about, take on side projects for videography or photography, or give paid speaking engagements at conferences and functions. It's about taking the time to create engagement not only for your personal brand but for your community.

- *Opportunities depend on geolocation as well as the industry and size of an organization.* A large global corporation like General Motors will have a different pay scale than a small business in a local college town. Take into account the cost of living and other lifestyle factors when looking at positions.

- *The more aligned the role is with management and strategy, the higher the salary will be.* When the list of responsibilities, qualifications, and experience increases, so does the salary. Do your research ahead of time with job postings and study what other sites report (Glassdoor, LinkedIn, PayScale, etc.).

- *Look at the culture of your future employer to see if you can succeed.* This is important. If you are not supported or do not have the best working environment to do your best work, it is not worth it. You want to feel your work is appreciated, supported, and acknowledged in social media. This is something to look for when interviewing and talking with other employees. Do your due diligence in your research to see how you could envision yourself working at this agency, brand, or organization. No matter how big a brand name it is, if you are not appreciated and supported, you will not be able to do your best work. Life is too short to be at a place where you are not appreciated.

CHAPTER SUMMARY

As you can see, there are many great opportunities to work in social media. The industry is still relatively new, but it has become more mainstream and established. Social media roles will continue to change: Some may go away, and new ones may be created. Social media is an ecosystem within itself, but it is increasingly being tied to other areas of communication, marketing, public relations, and media. While jobs in social media have certain required qualifications and skills, some will continue to be important (communication skills, writing, research, creativity, etc.), but others will be new. Getting a social media job is just a stepping point in your career. Focus on further developing the skills and informed insights you can bring to the table. Get as much professional experience as possible in social media to showcase what you can do. Last, but not least, continue to grow and develop. Learning does not stop when you get your social media job: It is the beginning of a lifetime of constant knowledge creation and learning.

THOUGHT QUESTIONS

1. What are some of the universal skills that are needed to work in social media?

2. What is the overall importance of having a personal brand when applying for jobs in social media?

3. What is the difference between a social media community manager and a social media strategist?

4. The numbers of consultants, freelancers, and entrepreneurs are rising in social media. What are some of the benefits of working in these roles? What are some of the challenges?

5. What are the experiences and skills that separate a manager from a director of social media?

EXERCISES

1. Identify one position you would like to pursue after this course. Describe the skills, experiences, and duties involved. Outline three steps you will do to prepare to apply for this position.

2. You have been asked to apply as a social media intern for Jeni's Splendid Ice Cream. The hiring managers are looking for not only a cover letter but also a few pieces of content you have produced on social media. Produce a visual résumé, cover letter, and video on why you are the best candidate for this position.

3. You are asked to prepare for an in-person interview and a virtual interview via Zoom with Disney. What steps will you take to make sure you are as prepared as possible? You are also asked to create a presentation on social media best practices using Prezi Video. Outline the research, questions, and answers you will have ready to go before the interview. Discuss what steps you will take *after* the interview. Prepare a presentation on Prezi Zoom you will share during your Zoom interview.

4. You are hired in your dream position working with Netflix on their social media team. The position calls for the work of the qualifications of a director of social media, but the salary represents more like a social media manager's role. Discuss the steps you will take to negotiate your salary and provide resources for your position.

REFERENCES

Brooks, C. (2017, June 16). Keep it clean: Social media screenings gain in popularity. *Business News Daily*. http://www.businessnewsdaily.com/2377-social-media-hiring.html

6

RESEARCH IN SOCIAL MEDIA
Monitoring, Listening, and Analysis

Learning Objectives

After reading this chapter, you will be able to

- Discuss the importance of research in social media practices

- Define social listening and social monitoring

- Explain the connections between listening and monitoring in social media

- Identify the key categories of metrics (basic, advanced, channel, and behavioral)

INTRODUCTION

Research is one of the most important areas of specialization within social media. Analytic results provided by businesses such as MarketCast are becoming more common and essential to social media strategy. Good data inform, educate, and validate the work social media professionals do on their respective platforms. Regardless of the industry or social media role, research insights are key.

Metrics—data collected by a social media professional in a systematic manner—allow brands to know what worked, what didn't, and what to do differently next time. Social media professionals do not want to guess or assume anything; without data and research, you would be doing exactly that.

Metrics are the numbers and points of information that validate social media's role in the larger scheme of things for a business and show senior management and key decision makers the impact of metrics on their audiences.

Researchers in social media deal with the constant challenge of keeping up-to-date on industry and platform changes as well as how to collect, analyze, and report data. Facebook changes its algorithm constantly, and platforms are always new features that make them a bit more complicated (e.g., Instagram Stories and Insights). With each new feature, there is a new way to research.

Research is one of the most demanding functions in social media. We have to understand not only how to collect data but also how to use data strategically. Social media allows you to make one first impression with your content; researching ahead of time allows you to make sure this first impression is the best it can be. Ultimately, social media research involves not only data collection but interpreting the insights into actionable strategies that are aligned with the campaign and brand. It's not how much data you have but how you use it to gather ideas, brainstorm perspectives and approaches, and execute strategies.

HUMANS OF SOCIAL MEDIA

Rich Calabrese, VP of Applied Botanics

Introduction

I am currently the vice president of Applied Botanics. Previously, I was the vice president, theatrical at MarketCast, a global research company that specializes in data science, analytics, and research to fuel fandom for media and entertainment companies, brands, and sports leagues. Prior to MarketCast, I helped lead Fizziology (a social analytics company) to acquisition (by MarketCast) as one of Fizziology's first employees.

Prior to joining Fizziology, I served in various positions in sports media, as an associate producer for Golf Channel/NBC Sports, media relations coordinator for Churchill Downs, Inc., and as a social media manager for the PGA of America. I acquired my passion for working in sports and entertainment while a student at both Ithaca College (B.S. in sports media) and the University of Louisville (M.S. in sport administration).

How did you get your start in social media?

My start in social media was actually through working in television production. While working at Golf Channel, I was an associate producer for four seasons of a reality golf show, *The Big Break*. It was in this job where I really wanted to both quantify and contextualize viewer opinions of the show from those talking about it on Facebook and Twitter. *It was almost an impossible task*, as social media data (and the understanding of it) was still very much in its infancy. This is one of the main reasons I decided to pursue graduate school, obtain social media internships while in school, and complete a comprehensive research study (master's thesis) analyzing social media consumption with college students. My first gig in social media was working on the local organizing committee for the PGA of America's 72nd Senior PGA Championship at Valhalla Golf Club in Louisville, KY.

What is your favorite part of working in your area of expertise in social media?

My favorite part of working in social media data and analytics is seeing how widely accepted the data and insights are nowadays when making business decisions. *It wasn't always this way.* As someone who was on the front lines, selling social media research to the major film studios and television networks, I've seen the change in the industry first-hand. Since I started in the social analytics industry, I've been able to provide actionable marketing strategies, via social data and audience insights that have had a significant impact on various film, TV, and brand marketing campaigns.

What is one thing you can't live without while working in social media?

My answer seems obvious for most marketing jobs these days, but the one thing I can't live without while working in social media is the internet. For social media professionals, it's essential to perform your job. For MarketCast, our proprietary technology is web-based, and I can't access our analytics dashboard to perform research and provide insights to clients without an internet connection.

What is your favorite social media account (person/brand/etc.) to follow and why?

One of my favorite social media accounts is FiveThirtyEight, Nate Silver's website, which focuses on political polling and data analysis of sports and entertainment topics. The political polling is really interesting, but I really love the sports and entertainment data studies. Whether it's analyzing data to uncover the different types of Scarlett Johansson movies, or their comprehensive March Madness breakdowns and predictions, I enjoy how they dissect different mainstream topics using data.

What is the most challenging part of working in social media?

Social media is 24/7. It doesn't just turn off when you're not using or creating content on the platform. Audiences are sharing opinions non-stop, and when opinions are shared by influencers or when news breaks that could have an impact on your team, movie, brand, etc., you have to listen, analyze, and act. That means you have to prepare for the unexpected, which means working nights, weekends, holidays.

What is your take on your area of expertise and the social media industry?

Social media insights shouldn't be the only source of information social media teams utilize to make content decisions. From an analytics standpoint, while the measurement of your fans' behaviors and opinions on social media provide amazing insight, it's crucial to synthesize your insights with other consumer research being conducted in your organization. When combined, social media insights and insights obtained from traditional research (surveys, focus groups, etc.) allow social media teams to make more informed decisions based upon their fans' observed (social media) and stated (traditional research) thoughts and behaviors.

What are three marketable skills a social media professional needs to have to work in the industry?

- Adaptability—This industry is constantly changing, be prepared!

- Problem-Solving—When things don't go according to plan, always come to the table with a solution (or two)!

- Attitude—Be an energy-giver, not an energy-taker.

Where do you go to keep up-to-date with trends and continue learning about social media?

I look to social media platforms themselves. I tend to look at what brands across various industries are doing to see what's new, interesting, and driving fan engagement (positive or negative). From there, I think critically about what those tactics are, why they chose to deploy them, and how they could be applied/not applied to work in different use cases.

If you had to choose a song to walk out to in a presentation on social media, what would it be and why?

Any song from *Jock Jams: Volume 1* – Except "YMCA."

Rich Calabrese is the VP of Applied Botanics, can be connected with on Twitter at @richcalabrese.

IMPORTANCE OF RESEARCH FOR SOCIAL MEDIA AND STRATEGIC COMMUNICATION

Research—the systematic gathering of information in a scientific and objective manner to help answer questions—is not black and white. It is a mixture of grays following a long continuum of different attributes that make it hard to determine which method, service, platform, or metrics to use. This, along with changes on the platforms, makes it difficult at times to report actual insights that help drive the bottom line for sales, revenue growth, community building, and lead generation for brands and users. Some metrics can mislead by showcasing large numbers, which can tempt brands and professionals to think things are going well when, in fact, they are not. Using data provided by platforms such as Facebook and Twitter can seem helpful, but you are taking a risk by relying on someone else's data collection.

Social media managers have to listen to what the data are saying before providing commentary on what the data mean. Content and message strategies help create stories, which then shift the waves (influencing the conversations and dialogue in the community that are meaningful and resonate with audiences) through the clutter of noise that happens on social media. Research, especially **analytics**, provides us with evidence of the impact and potential return these "waves" provide us. Did the content move the audience? Did it make an impact? Did the message truly resonate with the audience in the way we wanted it to? Without data, these waves are just entertainment for a single moment in time. However, with data, these stories have a shelf life and meaning for future implications, learnings, and practices for a brand.

Data drive the "pay to play" game for social media professionals. In order for audiences to see content in a newsfeed on platforms such as Facebook, Instagram, and Twitter, brands and others have to pay for sponsored posts, ads, or updates. Every time a sponsored post or ad comes forward, such as the brand partnership Peloton and ESPN formed for their All-Star Ride on Instagram, it was paid for by the brands participating in the partnerships. In most cases, it is easy to determine which content has been paid for. Each paid form of content is approached in a different way. One can be bought and sponsored by an entertainment channel (e.g., ESPN), while others can be sponsored by third-party endorsers and influencers, which is why #ad is attached to the content. In the Peloton and ESPN case, celebrity bike instructors for Peloton, Alex Toussaint and Robin Arzón, shared the event on their personal platforms, making them prominent influencers within this campaign partnership (see Photo 6.1). ESPN and Peloton will be able to gather not only the vanity metrics from this campaign but other advanced and business-oriented metrics that can help tell a story of the overall impact of this collaboration into behavioral action steps taken by the key audiences. Tying in the video content from ESPN to social conversations around the All-Star Rides, to brand awareness metrics from both Toussaint and Arzón, to increase search results and hits off of the Peloton's website after the ride are just some of the key items that could have resulted from this brand collaboration. Since then, Peloton has used data to formulate exclusive collaborations with celebrities such as Beyoncé (partnering with HBCUs [historically Black colleges and universities] for internship and job opportunities at Peloton, and exclusive rider series) and Shonda Rhimes for the Year of Yes Motivational class series.

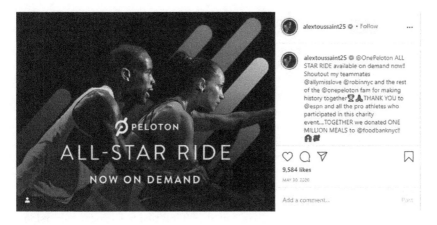

Many businesses have taken this path to present their content to audiences. Metrics that illuminate the efficacy of this content make the system possible. This illustrates the level of accountability needed to determine whether sponsored messages have an impact on the goals and objectives of campaigns and social media initiatives.

One benefit of metrics for social media platforms and third-party services is the ability to capture the essence of audiences on a level that is extremely detailed and specific. Having access to what people are willing to share about themselves on various social media platforms—what they are doing to engage, converse, and react—really drives brands, organizations, and media outlets to specific social media platforms with established marketing and advertising budgets. These insights help paint a very clear picture of users' personas (e.g., unique characteristics that make up individuals) and likes, motivational factors, and other audience segmentation characteristics to help classify them into different audience categories (demographics, psychographics, etc.). These data provide insights, which then spark creative message strategies, ideas, and targeting practices not available on other established communication platforms. Unlike traditional media, social media has allowed brands to not only explore the basic audience segments but expand their exploration to what people like, what posts and brands they engage with, and what their overall network is of trust and influence on the social media platforms. Social media professionals are able to identify more audience behaviors and actions on these platforms than with traditional media.

There is a difference between advanced metrics, such as **click-through rates** (how many times people click on a link to navigate to another website) and **behavioral metrics** (what actions people are taking on social media), and what we call **vanity metrics**, or metrics that make all of us feel really good but really do not tell us anything in the process. For example, the number of people you follow on Instagram, or who follow you, is considered a vanity metric. Behavioral metrics focus on advanced metrics, like conversions, that help tell the story of the customer journey on social media (e.g., how many people bought a product or ticket to a concert after seeing a post on Facebook). Researchers can tell more about what happened and prove that content and presence on social media led to followers' actions, which helps validate the argument for investing in social media at the senior leadership level.

Reporting vanity metrics for social media efforts does provide benefits (Dawley, 2017). Dawley (2017) suggests that businesses use vanity metrics for strategic purposes. First, identifying **followers** (people or brand accounts on social media who are keeping track of your activity on a designated platform) gives social media professionals (or brands and clients they are representing or working with) a snapshot of their potential audience members. This does not mean that followers are 100% guaranteed to view your designated content, but the advanced metrics allow you to see this in more detail. Comments and shares are also considered vanity metrics, yet they serve a purpose by informing you how actively responsive people are to your content and actions and how they feel about the content. As Dawley (2017) stated regarding social media vanity metrics, if the only reason you are reporting these metrics is to make yourself feel amazing, then they are not fulfilling the complete picture. Vanity metrics are like the movie trailer for a blockbuster film: They do not tell the whole story of the brand. When you report vanity metrics, you have to connect them back to set objectives that fulfill attitudinal and behavioral measurements. How will the increased level of comments and sentiments help the brand on social media? If it is tied to business conversions (whether or not you made a purchase based on what you were shown on social media) and email or YouTube subscriptions, then there might be a rationale for this. Essentially, vanity metrics can be included in a report, but only if they are tied to other metrics and campaign or social media objectives for a brand, person, or agency.

For example, if Aviation Gin wants to gauge whether key audience members in New York City are aware of their support for bartenders during the COVID-19 global pandemic, it may want to connect its objective of brand awareness to **mentions** or tags of the brand on social media platforms such as Twitter, Facebook, and Instagram, on their designated brand platforms, as well as having Ryan Reynolds (@VancityReynolds) share on the content on his personal channels. At the same time, Disney could review comments, ratings, and replies on its Disneyland social media accounts to evaluate the customer experience at the new *Star Wars* attraction at Disneyland Park in California. Advanced metrics tied to this, however, could be viewed to determine customer response, frequency of responses per hour, geolocation responses, and influence of users on social media.

Other cases come in the format of brand placements and sponsored content. For example, during the 2020 U.S. presidential election, the meditation application Calm went viral for having a sponsored place on CNN's media coverage for election night (Hiebert, 2020). Calm was able to not only evaluate the number of people who saw their ad placement on the election coverage but also track other social insights based on the mentions, shares, and memes that were created in response to this placement. Traditional and social media metrics and analysis are combined to get an integrated and comprehensive picture of the overall impact of this strategy.

We can gain further insight into the need for research by examining past examples, such as Jeep's efforts to increase brand awareness by working with Bill Murray. Murray, the popular actor from the movies *Ghostbusters* and *Groundhog Day*, participated in his first Super Bowl commercial ever with Jeep in 2020 (Photo 6.2). Murray reprised his iconic *Groundhog Day* role in the commercial to celebrate not only the release of a new Jeep model but also to make the connection that the Super Bowl in 2020 was held on Groundhog Day (Lacy, 2020). This commercial was not only a hit on television but also on social media. The video with Bill Murray was viewed 104,246,754 times across the Jeep brand's YouTube, Facebook, Twitter, and Instagram channels (FCA, 2020). The behavioral and attitudinal measurements related to social media (purchasing the company's products, increasing positive sentiments about its reputation online, etc.) are still to be determined.

These should allow Jeep to see if the video influenced audiences to go out and purchase a Jeep.

Many brands want to measure awareness for their products and services, and specific platforms can help accomplish this task. Consider Popeyes' Chicken Wars in 2019. The fast food chicken company used social media to let audiences know their stores were open on Sundays (creating a direct point of comparison with fast food competitor Chick-Fil-A), while also integrating message strategies to reach their audiences on both Twitter and WhatsApp (GSD&M & Popeyes Louisiana Kitchen, n.d.). The result of this campaign initiative proved extremely beneficial for the brand, as it increased their mentions, search results, and most importantly, their chicken sandwich sales. Popeyes reported that their chicken sandwich sales increased 16 times what was projected for the year (GSD&M & Popeyes Louisiana Kitchen, n.d.). This is a key purpose for research in social media. When social media professionals and their teams can use clear data and insights to demonstrate that social media efforts contributed directly to the accomplishment and overachieving of business expectations and goals, continued investment for these efforts are likely to occur.

▶ **Photo 6.2**
Bill Murray and Jeep Super Bowl Campaign

Source: Retrieved from https://www.cnbc .com/2020/02/02/jeep-recreates-groundhog-day-with-bill-murray-for-super-bowl-2020-ad .html

The amount of money being spent on research and social media is astronomical. Brands and companies are spending millions on tools and services to help collect, monitor, listen to, and analyze insights emerging on social media. As social media professionals, we have to decide which metrics are relevant to what we're trying to accomplish in our social media practices. This chapter will explore the need to do research and best practices for using research to meet goals. Contemporary social media professionals are able to listen for trends, monitor key metrics important to a company in a social media campaign, and link both science and art by using data collected in a strategic manner.

WHY DO WE NEED RESEARCH IN SOCIAL MEDIA?

Research has always been extremely beneficial for guiding practices in marketing, communication, public relations, and related disciplines and is a primary duty of social media professionals. Assessing the success of campaigns and identifying opportunities, research can provide more direction in understanding a brand's key audiences, current gaps and opportunities relative to competitors, current environmental landscapes, emerging issues or situations, and motivational factors and user attitudes.

Social media research is an increasingly important and valuable specialization among social media professionals. In most cases, research and analytics are housed in a specialized department or in a department that oversees the overall budget for social media. Social media professionals conducting or evaluating research must be able to *understand the data* that are produced. This provides a solid foundation within an organization or department by helping you evaluate the content you create. Brands and agencies are looking for professionals who understand how to collect relevant data from social media platforms, have the skills and insights to explain what the data mean, and know how to apply the results strategically. In addition, understanding research methods allows us to do a check and balance on the metrics and data collected by third-party resources and services as well as by any agencies or consultants. This checks and balances approach is necessary to ensure we are all on the same page in regard to the data collection, insights provided by the data, and ways the data were collected from the digital and social media ecosystem.

Humanizing the brand and identifying potential ideas for future content are other benefits of research (both listening and monitoring) through collecting insights online in real time. In many ways, social media platforms and channels act like an online focus group—you are able to see what people are sharing, creating, and talking about regarding your brand or company. In addition, you can ask your community a question to get their take. This input could provide feedback about a new campaign, test out new products or spokespeople, or even determine what attributes people assign to you. On other occasions, research can inform how your brand is presented and what types of engagements, content, and voice audiences are looking for in the brand. While these are mostly positive circumstances, understanding what could potentially go wrong is an additional benefit of research. Listening for early warning signs (a string of negative reviews of a restaurant on social media, users identifying an account has been hacked, etc.) could save the brand's financial standing and reputation.

As Rich Calabrese has stated, there are two types of data to consider: owned data and organic data (Table 6.1). Owned data, which are the data that you gain from the growth of your social media accounts internally and the engagement you gain through these accounts, are easily collected and managed. Organic data are the data you gather through the conversations you have outside of your accounts, which might be more difficult to access. Both types of data are key elements to collect, listen to, and monitor for all social media campaigns.

Table 6.1 Owned Data Versus Organic Data	
Owned Data	**Organic Data**
• Likes	• Volume
• Views	• Sentiment
• Comments	• Themes
• Shares	• Unique users
• Followers	• New user growth
• Date/Time	
• Interests	
• Demographics	

Source: Rich Calabrese and Applied Botanics.

WHAT ARE THE DIFFERENCES BETWEEN MONITORING AND LISTENING IN SOCIAL MEDIA?

Monitoring and *listening* are two of the most frequently debated and discussed terms in social media measurement, because they are somewhat related but have distinct differences. **Monitoring** is the systematic process of understanding, analyzing, and reporting insights and conversations on reputation, brand position, community health, and opinion of key audience members virtually. This is a systematic and sustainable area within social media measurement that focuses on key objectives and tying in metrics and key performance indicators (KPIs) to the data being collected and analyzed. This information has to be connected to current business and communication objectives within the organization or brand. **Listening** is about learning, exploring, and uncovering emerging trends, opportunities, activities, and issues that could impact the company either positively or negatively. These items can be evaluated at the surface level (e.g., vanity metrics) or more in depth (history of a customer with the brand, how engaged a customer has been with the brand, customer level of network and influence in a specific community with the brand, etc.). Monitoring practices are more reactive compared to what listening has to offer.

Both monitoring and listening are necessary for a social media campaign, department, or initiative. One cannot do just one and ignore the other. Tools, metrics, and programs can address listening and monitoring separately or in combination. Table 6.2 summarizes some of the key differences between monitoring and listening.

One of the main differences between monitoring and listening is time frame. Focused more on the long term than listening, monitoring can take place over weeks or months or even years. Monitoring is a systematic and sustainable approach to evaluating performance on social media. Social media professionals constantly evaluate standing positions and presence to see how they are received and discussed.

Table 6.2   Differences Between Social Monitoring and Social Listening

Social Monitoring	Social Listening
• Creating a systematic and sustainable program that evaluates the success or current state of a brand or person online	• Observing people's feedback, comments, questions, and inquiries in order to capitalize on emerging and innovative opportunities
• Evaluating metrics, such as mentions and trends, that could be tied to the bottom line and connected to other business and communication goals	• Evaluating sentiment, patterns, and the current state and dynamics in a community
• Using data insights to tie to strategic plans and objectives set for a campaign, business, or initiative	• Using data insights to spark ideas and creative executions for content and message strategies
• Connecting to market research and competitive analysis of the landscape (science of social media)	• Connecting to creative execution of strategies (art of social media)

Benefits of Monitoring and Listening

What are the benefits of monitoring and listening? Why are monitoring and listening important from a social media standpoint? Monitoring and listening can help the social media professional with all of the following:

- Formulating the main items we want to evaluate and monitor for our social media activities (e.g., keywords, hashtags, phrases, accounts, users, influencers, and others).

- Identifying influencers and top external channels (or accounts) driving traffic to the social media platforms.

- Evaluating which accounts, websites, brand blogs, and other external links will help show impact of word-of-mouth, but also showcase potential collaborations and partnerships to add to the community on social media.

- Analyzing and measuring key trends (positive and negative) surrounding an event, person, or brand compared to competitors and other significant parties in the community.

- Calculating the overall growth of your community audience and behavior measurements.

- Identifying how fast your audience and community is growing and comparing this to previous times in the past year. When the audience for each platform grows, this will shift the specific metrics being used to evaluate the effectiveness of the content for this audience, which leads to the next point.

- Identifying the overall responses audience members give you for your content. We learn when they are active, what type of content they are sharing, how they are mentioning you during specific times and on which platforms, and how this compares to competing accounts. These are not measurements that will stay consistent. As the audience grows or shifts for a brand on social media, these changes have to be reevaluated on a regular basis. For example, posting on Instagram on Mondays at 3 p.m. EST may have worked for a company in 2017, but in 2018, it may be Tuesdays at 10 a.m. EST due to changes emerging from audiences.

- Determining the overall tone and sentiment of the community discussing a key player in a social media plan (i.e., brand).

- Understanding our audiences and what they are responding to the most. We do not have to guess which posts, content, influencers, or accounts they are following. This information is available for us to note.

- Turning unhappy customers through proactive monitoring and interactions into loyal customers through relationship management practices.

- Understanding our audiences beyond the surface level and tying in key areas of focus (e.g., online behavior, interests, page communities, groups, influencer networks, and advocacy measures).

- Identifying any hidden risks or potential crises that could evolve based on an analysis of the community.

- Creating a sustainable measure for identifying key performance indicators that determine overall brand health, voice, and presence in the community.

- Exploring new areas and bringing back lessons learned to the team. Social media is somewhat of a "free online focus group" of ideas, perspectives, and opportunities.

- Uncovering valuable insights to help address an opportunity or a competitive gap in the strengths, weaknesses, opportunities, and threats (SWOT) analysis.

- Helping bring a strong evaluation and measurement component to our social media plan with data and insights to prove we have accomplished our set objectives.

What types of items can be monitored in social media? Social media monitoring can do the following:

- Track engagement, sentiment, and behavioral actions (e.g., shares and comments) from content across platforms over a period of time.

- Determine the best times and places to post and engage with content.

- Note what the competitors (established and emerging) are doing online and compare their operations and engagement with yours. Competitors need to be monitored based on market presence and industry. Emerging competitors who are starting out or extending into the field should be identified and tracked.

- Explore audiences' receptiveness and behavioral intentions to take action based on the messages given. Are audience members actually behaving the way we want them to based on the call-to-action statements (what we want our audience to do after seeing this message or content) we shared on social media?

- Evaluate response time for the social care team in responding and engaging with leads generated from social media conversations.

- Identify inquiries or comments that can help spark further content features for the brand.

- Discover what content actually resonates with audiences and what content and message strategies work best.

- Measure the overall health of the brand community as a whole and where current, potential, and emerging audiences are located; also, have a conversation about the brand.

- Note the official and associated keywords being used in alignment of the brand online.

You may be asking yourself why it is so important to monitor what people say and how well your organization is doing in a campaign. The answer is simple: Data equal money. To have buy-in from other departments and to retain your current clients, you need to be able to show what you have done over time. We must be able to showcase what we can provide. In addition, we need to know how well we are doing during a campaign. We may have the best intentions, but we need to understand how people are reacting to the content and promotions we share on social media. Monitoring and listening can also provide information from sources other than our brand's consumer audiences. What are our competitors talking about when they see our campaigns? What is our share of voice in the industry? We have to take all of these elements into consideration in terms of our monitoring capabilities.

Types of Metrics

Table 6.3 outlines the four categories of metrics classified in social media measurement terms. The first category is **basic metrics**. These metrics can be collected easily either from the social media channel itself or by a separate service or program. Basic metrics include *followers* (how many people are following you on a specific account), *engagement* (how many people in your community are interacting with your content), and *sentiment* (how people feel about your content—positive, negative, or neutral). Consider evaluating these basic metrics first to determine the overall scope of the community size you have (e.g., followers), how prominent you are in sharing content and how much exposure it actually gets (e.g., reach), and how people respond to your content on social media (e.g., engagement and sentiment).

The second category is **advanced metrics**, which dive into the actions and psychographics (the attitudes, behaviors, and opinions of audience members) of specific users (e.g., influencers—people who have the power to persuade others to take action [see Chapter 8 for influencers and Chapter 11 for audience segmentation for more related audiences]—and **advocates**—loyal and invested audiences who are supportive of a brand or community). These specific metrics tell a social media professional a lot about user behaviors and also about the unique characteristics of a community. Advocacy, audience engagement, and influencers are just a few metrics that can be collected and analyzed for identifying your different audience segments. These metrics are somewhat more challenging to categorize and collect, which means you may need to get specific tools to analyze these metrics (e.g., Klear for influencers) or invest in a tool that can analyze and report these metrics along with the basic metrics (e.g., Meltwater).

The third category is **channel metrics**, which are unique to specific channels. While many channels share certain basic metrics, their particular configurations also make more specific metrics useful. For example, story completion is important for Snapchat and Instagram to note, whereas retweets and favorites may be aligned with Twitter. Facebook has reactions for its updates and comments.

The last category is behavioral metrics, the most complicated yet informative metrics to collect on social media. In behavioral metrics, we explore downloads and lead generation (did the content we post on social media result in a subscription or action?). These are the metrics many senior managers and leaders want to see as a result of investment in social media. **Conversion rate** (how many clicks and actions resulted in sales divided by the number of clicks and actions taken), **amplification rate** (how much the content has been shared and viewed by others—specifically looking at shared actions like retweets [RTs] or shares on Twitter, reports, and share actions), and even **influencer impact** (how many high-profile professionals and accounts shared and engaged with the content) are just a few metrics that allow us to evaluate whether or not people took action based on what they saw on social media (a Facebook ad, an influencer campaign, a call for subscriptions to a YouTube channel, etc.).

Table 6.3 Example Metrics Used to Evaluate Social Media Campaigns and Initiatives			
Basic Metrics	**Advanced Metrics**	**Channel Metrics**	**Behavioral Metrics**
• Followers • Reach (paid or organic) • Impressions • Sentiment • Engagement • Influence • Market position • Activity (post rate, post type, post response rate, etc.) • Platform actions (likes, RTs, story views, etc.) • Votes • Shares	• Advocacy • Audience growth • Audience engagement (influencers and advocates) • Network health • Conversation reach • Time spent and content retention • Tone • Content reaction and response • Story completion rate • Share of voice • Share of conversation • Video completion rate • Share of community • Brand awareness • Customer and community retention	• Insights (reach, post engagement, targeting, etc.) • Video views • Click-through rate • Impressions • URL links (e.g., tweets) • Profile visits • Website visits • Social referrals • Percentage of visits • Visit duration	• Impact actions (download paper, get new subscribers, visit a page, etc.) • Click-through links • Amplification rate • Advocate impact • Influencer impact • Applause rate • Lead generation • Conversation rate (sales, requesting a demo, signing up for a webinar, etc.) • Saves (e.g., screenshots and repurpose) • Downloads (podcasts, videos, etc.)

A comprehensive social media monitoring and listening plan includes at least several metrics from each category, but the choices depend on the overall objectives set for the social media initiatives and which metrics best align with the goals of the social media campaign.

Implementing a Monitoring and Listening Plan

Now that you understand the differences between monitoring and listening, you are in a better position to determine the exact approach and resources you will need to accomplish your goals.

- *Responsibilities for monitoring and listening.* Determining who will be in charge of this role is instrumental in determining whether you will have the necessary resources to accomplish these tasks. Identifying key personnel (community manager, account manager, social media consultant, etc.) who will be in charge of reporting and engaging with the team or brand on this issue is also important. This is another area that can be integrated into the list of responsibilities for the team internally (or externally depending on the circumstances). Make sure those who are responsible for the listening and monitoring capabilities are aware of the objectives and overall scope of the social media practices from a business and communication standpoint.

- *Monitoring and listening training.* As with social media platforms, expectations for social media data analytics and measurement are evolving rapidly. Training on analytic tools (Hootsuite, Cision, Sprout Social, Opal, Meltwater, Agorapulse, Talkwalker, Salesforce, Facebook Blueprint, Stukent, etc.) can be very useful. Social media professionals must keep up with the latest measurement tools for monitoring and listening.

- *Outlining what you can and must listen to and monitor.* Outlining the key areas of focus before implementing a monitoring and listening plan is crucial. This will set forth a strong foundation for staying organized and current.

- *Tying in monitoring and listening practices to current business, communication, and brand objectives.* Note items that will demonstrate whether each department has accomplished its set objectives. In addition, insights can be integrated into current plans (e.g., SWOT analysis integration) as well as used to forecast trends and opportunities.

- *Using analytics and research to inform content that resonates with audiences.* In Chapter 10 ("Strategic Writing for Social Media"), you will see the importance of using data to inform the types of messages, content, and writing style that work for your brand online. Content creation does not happen on a whim all of the time, but rather it is a systematic process of evaluating the previous messages, videos, images, and updates that generated engagement and reach by resonating with key members of the community. Connecting the data to provide actionable insights for other team members and leadership can make the difference between executing and not executing the content and, in some cases, not getting the project or job. In other words, measuring and reporting content data help drive future brainstorming sessions, justification for execution, and return on investment for social channels.

- *Setting a consistent brand monitoring and listening ecosystem.* A research plan should specify the protocols for who reports the findings to whom, what is reported, what the deadlines will be, how data will be analyzed and formatted, and how the resulting reports will be shared with clients or senior management.

PLATFORM-BASED METRICS, TOOLS AND SERVICES, AND KPIS

We have discussed a number of universal, platform-independent metrics, but other metrics are uniquely defined and used for specific platforms. Once again, we can evaluate the basic, advanced, channel, and behavioral metrics aligned with each current platform. Like the platforms themselves, the metrics available on each change frequently. Thus, it is important to understand the basic underlying principles of the metrics used and to cultivate a flexible mindset.

Along with collecting the metrics from each platform, we also must explore third-party tools that are available to help collect, analyze, and report the insights gathered on each platform. Some platforms (e.g., Twitter) have been open with their application programming interface (API) with third-party tool developers, but others have not.

When evaluating individual platform and third-party tools, ask yourself the following questions:

- *What metrics is the platform already using?* Is it using only basic metrics, or is it exploring advanced metrics as well?

- *What is the payment model?* Are the tools free? Does the platform have a monthly fee? What different plans does it offer? What features does it offer? Keep in mind that data equal money, and these tools can be somewhat expensive depending on the scope and the amount of data you want to collect.

- *What data is the tool able to collect and report on?* Some tools focus on single platforms, whereas others are broader and include a variety of platforms. Some platforms provide historical data and different metrics based on location, platform, and keyword analysis. Depending on what you are willing to invest in and use, it is important to note where each tool lands in your social media budget and overview.

- *How does the platform measure each metric, and how does it calculate the results in its reports?* If a platform is not willing to share how it comes up with its influence, engagement, and other ratings, this should raise a red flag.

- *Does the platform offer training and educational opportunities?* Examining the clients of each platform, the support it gives to users, and whether or not it is willing to supply training and educational resources are other factors to consider. It's one thing to use a tool, but like all aspects of social media, tools evolve, and it is important to note the longevity of a platform based on this element.

- *How long has the platform been established in the field?* There are a number of monitoring and listening services, and you should note how long they have been part of the community, how many resources they have, what clients they serve, and in which campaigns they have participated.

- *How much does a service cost?* Most social media analytics tools are affordable, but some are designed for enterprise clients, which means they are pretty expensive. When evaluating the cost of these tools, be sure to identify their features, the type of data they are able to collect, and what you will be able to do with the data.

WHAT IS THE BRIDGE BETWEEN MONITORING AND LISTENING?

While there is a difference between listening to social media conversations and measuring the data, the bridge that connects these two areas is strategy. Creating

Table 6.4	Connection Between Monitoring, Listening, and Strategy	
Monitoring	**Listening**	**Strategy**
• Observing the wave in how it is received (reviewing the reactions people have to the content being created)	• Observing potential landscape for upcoming waves to ride on (story ideas, real-time marketing initiatives, etc.)	• Providing explanation of the wave (story or content impact) that allows it to have shelf life
• Reactive	• Proactive	• Connecting what we are going to do based on what has been collected (research) and explored (application)
• Long-term focus but open to short-term adjustments (e.g., crisis communications)	• Short-term focus with long-term implications in mind	
	• Exploring possibilities of creative executions of ideas based on established presence	• Using insights to inform and brainstorm implications, note trends, and identify gaps in the data and what they mean in social media
• Tied to sustainable goals and objectives for a brand		
• Focused more on alignment for data (science)	• Focused more on the creativity and innovativeness of the opportunity (art)	• Tying art and science together

a framework that is able to collect insights from conversations on social media (research) and turn them into applicable action steps (practice) is what strategy can bring to the table. Table 6.4 outlines the key characteristics of monitoring and listening and how strategy connects these two important areas.

TYING EVERYTHING TOGETHER WITH ANALYSIS

We need to determine the overall impact and significance of our data reports and insights for our day-to-day business and communication activities. These insights can help determine what is working and not working for an organization or business online through various social media protocols.

Good research involves coordination of monitoring and listening in addition to social research. **Social research** is conducted by applying traditional methods of research to listening and monitoring dashboards to be able to answer larger questions that cannot be addressed just by looking at dashboards like Hootsuite, Sprout Social, or even Salesforce. The ultimate goal is to integrate listening, monitoring, and strategy together under the social research umbrella while combining traditional methods (e.g., surveys, focus groups, etc.) and new methods (e.g., network analysis, social media analytics) to provide a comprehensive and integrated perspective on what is going on and what needs to be done. Essentially, social research focuses on integrating traditional and social media research to present hybrid insights that inform brands, agencies, and companies what is happening, what are the big takeaways and ideas coming from the data, and what action steps need to be taken.

As we will discuss in Chapter 7 ("Strategic Planning"), gathering insights from research is very important. **Insights** are revelations of certain truths about an audience that illuminates certain data points form the research that help drive creative strategies and formulate innovative approaches. Insights are elements that help us understand (a) certain human truths that are universal across all audiences in a community, (b) underlying emotions and feelings that drives audience members to take certain actions, (c) new perspectives that have not been implemented before, and (d) ways in which these ideas should be executed. This can range from understanding a platform audiences are gravitating to based on editing features (e.g., TikTok and MAC Cosmetics #MoodFlip campaign) to understanding audiences' need for humor after a tense year in 2020 (e.g., Maximum Effort with Match.com campaign). These are just some of the ways campaigns have integrated insights from research (listening, monitoring, and traditional research methods) that capture information that is extremely valuable to the social media professional and their team. Understanding what attitudes, motivations, wishes, and desires influences a person, community, or audience to go from one point to another is the most valuable currency for a social media initiative, which makes gathering insights the highest of priorities from the research. Without these insights, a social media plan and strategy can fall flat. However, with these insights, a social media plan can come alive and blossom into an incredible creative and experiential campaign online and offline.

Getting the most out of your research requires careful planning. First and foremost, before identifying your key metrics for analysis, you have to align them with the set objectives for your social media channels or campaign. Your goal might be to increase brand awareness, engage in more conversations online, or reduce the level of negative ratings that happen online. The metrics that you focus on have to be interconnected with the objectives you have set forth. Essentially, objectives are what you want to accomplish, and metrics and analysis represent what you actually are able to accomplish. Ideally, you should make sure these objectives follow the key specific, measurable, achievable, realistic, and time-specific (SMART) criteria.

Listening and monitoring require a social media dashboard, which is a one-stop shop program that allows you to measure, evaluate, and gather insights in one spot. Looking for the right tool to accomplish all of these goals is like finding a unicorn. There is no "perfect" tool, but what you are able to do is gather tools that can meet certain research and listening objectives for a brand's social media efforts.

An audit or request for proposals (RFP) allows brands and organizations to help their teams and agencies identify which tool is the best fit with their goals. A sample RFP is displayed in Table 6.5.

As featured in Table 6.6, there are many metrics from which to choose. Ask yourself the following questions to help decide which ones to use (Dawley, 2017):

- How does this metric connect to my objectives?

- How is the platform defining these metrics? Are they the same as the universal definition of this metric?

- How are platforms calculating the metrics?

- Is this metric really applicable to what I want to accomplish?

Table 6.5 RFP of Criteria to Evaluate Research Tools for Listening and Monitoring					
	Tool #1	Tool #2	Tool #3	Tool #4	Tool #5
Features of tool					
Number of platforms					
Types of metrics					
State of data (clean, unfiltered, etc.)					
Support for training, assistance, and education					
Work flow and functionality					
Real-time listening and monitoring					
Presentation of data					
Budget					
Budget based on (e.g., volume, data, accounts, etc.)					

- What category does this metric represent?
- How will this metric inform me about my social channels and online presence?
- Do I have the right tools (and knowledge) to collect and analyze this metric?
- Does the tool have a support team that consistently updates the tool to reflect changes based on the platforms' algorithms?
- How are these platforms, metrics, and tools evolving with the changes happening in the platforms based on their access to platform APIs?

A frequent question that arises in social media is whether or not many calculations need to be done (aka math). The answer is . . . of course. Fortunately, the formulas are straightforward. Some are consistent across platforms, but other services and tools calculate metrics based on their own algorithms. When evaluating and analyzing your data, double-check your data and reports just to make sure they are saying what you think they are saying. Some tools are focused on service-level metrics (e.g., vanity metrics) without diving into the detailed behavioral metrics we may want to add to our social media reports, case studies, and campaigns for clients and brands.

One of the main metrics to report is **social media return on investment (ROI)**. ROI is a common metric used to evaluate whether the investment (money)

Table 6.6   Metrics Available as a Function of Social Channels

	Basic Metrics	Advanced Metrics	Channel Metrics	Behavioral Metrics	Tools and Services to Use
Facebook	• Likes • Reactions • Posts (type, reach, and frequency) • Live video metrics • Messages	• Engagement • Share of voice • Conversation reach • Community • Video metrics (views, time spent on live video, completion of video, etc.) • Advertising revenue	• Likes • Reach • Page views (total views, total people who viewed, sources, etc.) • Shares • Action button • Insights • Polls • Reactions • Posts (type, targeting of audience, reach, engagement, and evaluation of promotion)	• Awareness • Percentage of visits • Page duration • Click-through rates • Impact	• Facebook insights • Talkwalker • Salesforce • Agorapulse
Twitter	• Followers • Favorites • RTs • Mentions • Number of posts • Direct messages • Polls • Audience (gender/age)	• Activity metrics on platform • Network of the community • Audience/fan base growth • Engagement • Share of voice • Influence	• Twitter Analytics • Video views • Photo views • Profile visits • Impressions • Branded hashtags • Mentions • Tags	• Click-through links • Promoted ads • DMs based on Spaces rooms	• Twitter Analytics • Keyhole • Tagboard • Hootsuite • Buffer • Sprout Social • Klear • Meltwater • Talkwalker

(Continued)

Table 6.6 (Continued)

	Basic Metrics	Advanced Metrics	Channel Metrics	Behavioral Metrics	Tools and Services to Use
		• Advocacy • Content • Multimedia content • Advertising revenue	• Spaces listening time • Replies • Live views		
Instagram	• Followers • Favorites • Posts • Reposts • Impressions • Profile views • Posts • Mentions • Saves • Comments • Direct messages • Reel views • Live room attendees	• Engagement • Content performance • Fan base growth • Influence • Views • Audience growth • Advertising revenue • Reel shares	• Views • Comments • Replies • Live views • Tags • Likes • Story views • Story insights • Story screenshots • Story hashtags • Story mentions • Story completions • Live video views • Live video view completions • Live room attendance (total and average) • Live video comments		• Klear • Keyhole • Tagboard • Brandwatch • Iconosquare • Hootsuite • Instagram Insights • Meltwater

	Basic Metrics	Advanced Metrics	Channel Metrics	Behavioral Metrics	Tools and Services to Use
LinkedIn	• Connections • Community size • Likes • Comments • Visits • Story views	• Audience growth • Content publishing metrics	• Views • Audience • Post frequency		• LinkedIn Insights
Snapchat	• Snaps sent • Snaps opened • Snaps received • Total snaps opened • Video views • Followers • Percentage of snaps opened • Chat messages sent/received	• Swipes • Story completions	• Snaps sent • Snaps opened • Snaps received • Total snaps opened • Average views of snaps • Average views of snap stories • Type of content	• Links in chats • Screen shots • Code screen shots • Reposted content	• Delmondo
YouTube	• Views • Shares • Comments • Votes	• Audience growth • Video views	• Views • Comments • Likes • Dislikes • Videos removed from playlist	• Subscribers	• YouTube Analytics

(Continued)

Table 6.6 (Continued)

	Basic Metrics	Advanced Metrics	Channel Metrics	Behavioral Metrics	Tools and Services to Use
			• Average view duration • Average view percentage • Click-through rate • Subscribers • Card impressions • Gross revenue • Playback cost per mille (CPM) • Ad impressions • CPM		
TikTok	• Views (total time watched, average time watched) • Profile views • Posts (individual) • Videos posted • Likes • Play time • Followers • Shares • Votes • Hashtags • Likes • Comments	• Traffic • Engagement rates • Audience overview • Audience territories • Trending videos • Follower activity • Sounds followers listen to • Traffic source type	• Time watched • Average time watched • Total play time • Total engagements (likes + comments + shares)	• Shares • Challenges • Collaborations • Links • Repeat views • Completion rate • Percentage of repeat views • Reach rate	• TikTok Analytics • Conviva • Tikanalytics • CloutMeter • Pentos • Analisa.io

Clubhouse	Basic Metrics	Advanced Metrics	Channel Metrics	Behavioral Metrics	Tools and Services to Use
	• Follows • Invites to room • Room duration • Attendance • Number of participants • Number of moderators	• Sentiment analysis • Engagement • Quality of hands raised • Reactions • Applauses • Shares across platforms	• Average listening time • Live room rating scale (losing to gaining listeners) duration / average • Room or Space duration of time • Total minutes listened • Average minutes listened • Max number of listeners • Scheduled rooms to attend for attendees • Quality of room	• DM connections • Clicks to room • Sales and conversions based on conversations	• Cluby (link shorter for Clubhouse) • Clubhype • Comet Events (measure rooms on Clubhouse) • Clubhouse DB

a brand or company put into a campaign accomplished the set goals and objectives. Hootsuite describes social ROI as "the sum of all social media actions that create value" (Dawley, 2017). Essentially, social media ROI can be calculated by multiplying the profit or total investment by 100 (Dawley, 2017). Social ROI is not only a metric that needs to be included to determine the overall success of the campaign you are launching, but it also helps determine

- overall stance within the industry among your key audiences,
- where you need to invest and drive your resources to in the future,
- both gaps and opportunities for future campaign initiatives, and
- the impact social media has on your bottom line as well as reputation and community relationships.

DOS AND DON'TS IN SOCIAL MEDIA RESEARCH AND ANALYSIS

Keep the following best practices in mind when it comes to social media monitoring and listening.

First, there should be *a designated person or team for monitoring and listening* to the conversations on social media. With proper training (Google Analytics, Facebook Blueprint, Twitter Flight School, TikTok Educational Platform, Pinterest Academy, Snap Focus, Hootsuite, HubSpot, etc.), team members will be prepared to not only help identify the key metrics and KPIs to track but also understand how to apply these findings to actionable steps and relate this information and how it is connected to strategy to senior management.

Second, to do the best work, social media professionals must *invest in the right tools*, especially social media management tools. As social media channels and platforms change their APIs and algorithms, the tools will have to adapt as well. Social media management tools come in different sizes, focus areas, metrics and data collection capabilities, and prices. The more data, filtering and historical capabilities, and reporting measures you want to have, the more expensive your tools are going to be. Hootsuite, Buffer, Agorapulse, Talkwalker, Sprout Social, HubSpot, Sprinklr, Zoomph, and Salesforce are just a few providers to review that cover multiple platforms. However, you may need just one tool because you are focusing on one platform for your campaign (e.g., TikTok and Analisa.io). Each system has different features, prices, and capabilities, and the social media professional in charge of monitoring and listening has to take all of these items into consideration. Presenting an RFP to each provider and seeing which one has the best package deal for a company's social media management capabilities and needs may be the best approach.

Third, social media monitoring and listening are just the beginning. It all comes down to how social media professionals *apply these insights to actionable strategies and creative executions.* Just collecting data in spreadsheets without acting on the results will collect digital dust. Look at the insights and see if any specific strategic or creative applications can be implemented. Consider what are the big "so what" moments and insights that are being gathered and collected on social media and which insights need to be explored further with additional research. These extra steps could result in creating more content focusing on certain themes or trends, or even posting content at certain times on specific channels.

Fourth, monitoring and listening need to be connected to evaluating the behaviors and actions you want your audiences to take. If you want to achieve certain goals for your organization or business (e.g., engagement and word-of-mouth), you have to *engage and talk with your audiences*. Establish a set policy and engagement protocol, though, that specifies how your team members should properly engage to best reflect your brand voice and community. This means that team members do not go off script and cause a crisis for the team and for the brand. It is very tempting to express emotion or be snarky, for example, because it is trendy and people respond to it. This could cause serious issues and drive metrics and trends about your brand in unwanted directions. Or the social media manager could fail to consider all of the different interpretations that a message might have, thus resulting in miscommunication.

Pushing content you feel is valuable is one thing, but see what happens when you listen to how your audience members respond and send them a relevant response. Whether it is a thank-you, an emoji, or a question to help drive the conversation a bit more, this helps spark a conversation with your audience, which results in engagement. Aviation Gin, Steak-Umm, and Ryan Reynolds have found that if they not only share content but also engage with their audiences on social media, the result is even more traffic and reach than if they just pushed content alone.

Last but not least, do not let vanity metrics (e.g., number of comments, follows, etc.) be clouded by spammers. A lot of bots are designated to like (e.g., like farms), share, or comment on content (e.g., bots on Instagram). Although increasing their numbers may be appealing, social media professionals have to look deeper and see if an account is real or not. Filtering out fake accounts can be time consuming, but it's necessary to see what's really going on. Some social media management platforms and services do this automatically, but it is up to the human professional to avoid inflating or misleading others with numbers.

CHAPTER SUMMARY

Monitoring and listening practices on social media have to be approached from a strategic yet creative angle to balance both the scientific process and the art of taking data and creating innovative ideas and messages. Numbers and data are not going to walk over and integrate themselves into a report by themselves. They have to be analyzed, discussed, and formatted in a way that tells a comprehensive story of where we are, where we are going, what we need to keep our eyes out for, and what we need to do on social media. Like all aspects of social media, the metrics and ways we collect, analyze, and report research findings from social media continue to evolve and change. Social media measurement and analytics make up one of the fastest-growing specializations within the field.

THOUGHT QUESTIONS

1. What is the difference between social monitoring and social listening? When is it appropriate to use each practice?

2. What is social research? How is this tied to listening and monitoring?

3. What is the difference between owned data and organic data?

4. Discuss the key best practices for monitoring and listening on social media.

5. What are the differences among basic, advanced, channel, and behavioral metrics?

6. What best practices in listening and monitoring resonate with you the most? Provide your rationale for why this is the case.

EXERCISES

1. You are working on the social media team for Buff City Soap's brand account, and the question comes up whether or not to invest in social media monitoring and social media listening to help them with their social media efforts to grow their community for their start-up soap business. Do you invest in both or just one? Provide your recommendation and rationale for your decision with three points.

2. Find an example of a nonprofit of your choice. They are looking to invest more in their research programs and are looking for advice on what metrics to analyze and focus on for their designated channels. Evaluate the vanity metrics on its social media sites (Facebook, Instagram, Twitter, YouTube, and TikTok) and discuss three ways the brand could improve these metrics. Suggest one advanced metric, channel metric, and behavioral metric it would want to track for each platform.

3. During a job interview for a social media analyst with Peloton, a question comes up about the importance of understanding metrics and KPIs related to social media brand partnerships to show the impact this has with their audience members. Outline three reasons why social media insights can help an organization like Peloton. Look at the Peloton/ESPN collaboration and see if you can find some trends looking at social and digital coverage this created as a case study to present. Tie in two business objectives the team would want to have (increase awareness, increase engagement, etc.) and what metrics and proposed tools you would recommend using to measure these.

4. You have been asked to provide insights to GoFundMe on social audio metrics and listening. You have to consider three social audio options, in Clubhouse, Twitter Spaces, and Instagram Live views. Based on these three platforms, provide a rationale for which platform to focus on, as well as outline to GoFundMe the main metrics to consider that would help their brand.

REFERENCES

Dawley, S. (2017, May 16). A comprehensive guide to social media ROI. *Hootsuite*. https://blog.hootsuite.com/measure-social-media-roi-business/

FCA. (2020, February 10). "Groundhog Day" with Jeep® Gladiator and Bill Murray is the 2020 big game's most viewed commercial on social media with 104,246,754 views. *Cision PR Newswire*. https://www.prnewswire.com/news-releases/groundhog-day-with-jeep-gladiator-and-bill-murray-is-the-2020-big-games-most-viewed-commercial-on-social-media-with-104-246-754-views-301002053.html

GSD&M & Popeyes Louisiana Kitchen (Producers). (n.d.). Popeyes—Chicken Wars. *The Shorty Awards*. http://shortyawards.com/12th/gsdm-and-popeyes-chicken-wars

Hiebert, P. (2020, November 4). Meditation app Calm was the most 2020 brand partner for CNN election coverage. *Adweek*. https://www.adweek.com/brand-marketing/meditation-app-calm-was-the-most-2020-brand-partner-for-cnns-election-coverage/

Lacy, L. (2020, April 20). Jeep brings back Bill Murray for repurposed spots. *Adweek*. https://www.adweek.com/agencies/bill-murray-returns-for-jeep-because-every-day-feels-the-same-now/

PART II

UNDERSTANDING SOCIAL MEDIA STRATEGY (CREATIVE AND SCIENTIFIC APPROACHES)

STRATEGIC PLANNING FOR SOCIAL MEDIA

Learning Objectives

After reading this chapter, you will be able to

- Identify the key components of a strategic plan

- Explain the importance of conducting a thorough background evaluation, situational analysis, and social media communication audit

- Construct a SWOT analysis

- Learn the differences between a goal, an objective, a strategy, and a tactic statement for a social media plan

- Follow best practices for strategic planning

INTRODUCTION

Social media is at the center of many conversations today. While it provides many personal opportunities to catch up with friends, check in at various locations, and share exclusive experiences with your own personal network, social media is also a powerful tool to use strategically and apply in professional settings. If professionals are not thinking social first, they are behind the curve.

On the surface, what we see online is the outcome of strategizing and hard work that takes place before content is shared. Updates, videos, and events tailored for certain communities are based on thorough research and data analyses. Research, first defined in Chapter 6, is the systematic gathering of information in a scientific and objective manner to help answer questions. As we observed in Chapter 6, research guides strategists and businesses toward actionable steps to generate awareness, cultivate relationships, engage in conversations representing multiple viewpoints and audiences, initiate changes and movements to improve business and communication practices, increase sales, share stories to spark an emotional chord with audiences, and motivate others to take action.

Strategy is an essential and an extremely valuable part of social media because strategy is a systematic plan to create an impact that wins the conversation, audience member, community, and cultural or social moment in time.

The industry has seen many strategic plans creatively executed and launched over the years. Adobe created a community among professionals from diverse backgrounds with their #AdobeInsiders group. Air Jordan used social media to announce a $100 million investment in anti-racism and education initiatives over the next 10 years. These brands have a strategy behind every post, update, and piece of content they share to achieve specific goals. In addition, every social media professional has to provide sustainable value, evidence, and impact on how

HUMANS OF SOCIAL MEDIA

Jeremy Darlow, Founder of Darlow, LLC

Introduction

Darlow is a leading brand consultant and founder of DARLOW, LLC, a brand consulting firm dedicated to helping athletes, coaches, and teams build their brands. In addition, Darlow is the former director of marketing for adidas Football and Baseball, an adjunct marketing professor, and three-time best-selling author of the books *Brands Win Championships*, a branding guidebook for college sports programs; *Athletes Are Brands Too*, teaching athletes how to build personal brands that reach beyond sports; and *The Darlow Rules*, covering Darlow's own 75 rules to becoming an elite marketer.

During and since his role at adidas, he has worked with and built marketing plans for some of the most heralded athletes, celebrities, and NCAA programs in and around sports, including Aaron Rodgers, Von Miller, Adrian Peterson, Dak Prescott, Kris Bryant, Carlos Correa, Lionel Messi, Dale Earnhardt Jr., Snoop Dogg, Kanye West, Notre Dame, Michigan, UCLA, Miami, Nebraska, Wisconsin, and Texas A&M. He lives in Portland, Oregon.

How did you get your start in social media?

My career starts and finishes with brand marketing. Along the way I've either run or managed the social media functions of the departments I've been in charge of. When I started out in brand marketing years ago, social media was just entering the picture. Back then it was MySpace, a platform I used extensively to launch video game products and brands for Ubisoft, headquartered in San Francisco, CA.

What is your favorite part of working in your area of expertise in social media?

I'm extremely passionate about brand marketing and brand building. I fell in love with the concept in college and haven't looked back. A reason for that and a key to the brand development process is storytelling. In today's digital world, there is no better place to tell a story than via social media. I've always compared marketing to a game of chess. The consumer makes a move, the brand makes a move. The consumer makes another move, the brand counters. It's that back and forth that has me hooked. That analogy has never been more relevant than today because of social media. A brand can now make changes to a strategy in real time, thanks to platforms like Twitter and Instagram.

What is one thing you can't live without while working in social media?

Inserting a brand into culture moments, without a doubt. I've always said, "It's easier to crash a party than throw a party," and these days there's at least one party a month that captures the world's attention. The great thing about a space like Twitter is that when something worth talking about happens, brands and brand managers can instantly become part of the conversation. But there's no time off now. You have to be ready for anything and everything, which keeps you on your toes and keeps your skills sharp. The moment you take your foot off the gas is the moment your competition gets a jump on a story and you're left picking up scraps.

What is your favorite social media account (person/brand/team/etc.) to follow and why?

Believe it or not, on a personal level, I stay off of social media. I'm inundated with these spaces every day because of my profession, so when I get home I like to unplug. For me, social media is strictly business.

What is the most challenging part of working in social media?

The internet doesn't forget. If you say something wrong, people will see it, screengrab it, and share it before you have a chance to take it down. There is very little room for error.

You have been active in mentoring future young professionals in social media. What has been the most rewarding experience or moment you have had in helping students of social media?

Teaching and mentoring [are] my passions. I'm not a doctor, I'm not curing diseases and I'm very much aware of that. I think that self-awareness is important. It's because of that reality that I try and find ways to use my education and experience to help in any way I can. I've found that teaching and mentoring are my way of contributing. When those young men and women that work for me move on to bigger and better things, it makes everything worth it. It truly is a rewarding feeling.

What do you wish you had known when you were starting out?

I wish I had started building my personal brand sooner.

You can connect with Jeremy on Twitter at @jeremydarlow and get his books and join his newsletter at www.jeremydarlow.com.

their investment was worthwhile from a communication, business, and reputation standpoint. In addition, to be a successful social media strategist, you have to wear many hats and embrace many roles and skill sets. For example, you must be able to

- adapt like an entrepreneur (agility is the name of the game and time is of the essence to make an impact);
- write like a novelist (tell stories that capture our minds and hearts with knowledge and emotion);

- analyze information like a scientist (understand human behaviors and motivations through taking into consideration all research perspectives);

- create like an artist (write, create content, and bring items to life in many formats); and

- entertain like a star (if it doesn't resonate with audiences, they will move on to the next thing or next rising star).

This chapter will cover the key elements that make up a strategic plan, which will tie in creative concepts and strategies and the research-based applications needed to justify each of these points.

WHAT IS A STRATEGIC PLAN?

Many steps make up the creative and systematic approach of taking an idea from research into reality, otherwise known as a **strategic plan**. A strategic plan is a systematic, thorough, concise, and illuminating document that outlines from start to finish what a brand, individual, or organization wants to accomplish to address a problem, take advantage of an opportunity, or explore potential new possibilities through experimentation. This helps the social media professional follow a set of guidelines (like in *Pirates of the Caribbean*—you've got to stick to the code) but also be able to apply these guidelines to various areas, industries, and situations. A strategic plan allows the social media planner not to reinvent the wheel but to use it as a road map and tailor it for each client and campaign. These guidelines in a social media strategic plan can be a guiding compass (similar to the one that Jack Sparrow uses in *Pirates of the Caribbean*) to navigate uncharted waters (new platforms) while bringing in fresh perspectives that are memorable and unique (owning the moment to create a viral impact that resonates with the media, audiences, and community).

Most strategic plans in marketing, business, public relations, and journalism have research as the starting point, and strategic social media plans are no different. However, before beginning the research, the brand, business, or individual needs to identify an overall purpose for the strategic plan. Are you addressing a problem (e.g., crisis) or an opportunity? What are some overall factors of the marketplace you need to consider? Do you have an opportunity to lead the way with a new platform or feature that would differentiate your brand from others (exploring and experimenting)? Do you have the support (financial and emotional) from leadership and your team to make this happen? These questions need to be addressed even before you create a strategic plan.

Strategic plans can serve a variety of purposes for social media campaigns. They can be created and launched to address an ongoing issue or problem facing a brand. For example, brands involved in crises (e.g., Boeing, Corona Beer, and Whole Foods) must have a specific plan in place to reduce the negative perceptions, interactions, and engagement on their platforms. However, strategic plans are also established to create buzz about a new initiative, raise awareness of a new product, or announce a venture on a new platform.

In today's job market, employers are looking for social media professionals who are able to think strategically and creatively while linking their proposed action steps with data. Honing these skills will help you differentiate yourself from other "social media marketers" or "social media gurus." Social media professionals create, post, and share tactical or technical elements for the social media space. Like individual trees in the forest, these actions grow, evolve, and sometimes die due to lack of investment (e.g., water is necessary for trees' survival, as are community building and interactivity for these platforms) (Photo 7.1). A strategic plan provides a road map so that the life span and direction of content is not left to chance.

A social media strategic plan doesn't just look at all of the trees in the forest, but rather looks at how the forest is connected to the mountains, lakes, and other surrounding areas. The strategic plan spans time, looking for similarities and differences compared to the past, current, and future forest. We have to be aware of the individual, unique features of each community, platform, tool, or trend—but we also have to look at the bigger picture of organizational goals and objectives at all times.

Pixabay/StockSnap

▶ **Photo 7.1**
Understanding How to View Social Media From a Forest's Perspective

COMPONENTS OF A STRATEGIC PLAN

The main components of strategic social media plans include the following categories and steps. Keep in mind that within each of these steps are specific and focused areas that need to be addressed, which will be discussed in this chapter:

- Background Information
- Brand Voice and Pillars
- Vision and Mission Statements
- Diversity, Equity, and Inclusion
- Environmental Scan Analysis
- Client or Company in Focus
- Social Media Communication Audit
- Situational Analysis and Insights
- SWOT Analysis
- Goals
- Objectives
- Key Audience Members
- Strategies and Tactics
- Evaluation
- Budget
- Calendar
- Final Recommendations and Summary

Taking a drone-like scan of the environment allows social media professionals to identify and explain insights, as well as apply them to actionable steps that combine both research (science) and creativity (art) in a structured plan for implementation.

Background Information

This is where the research (and fun) comes in. Research has to be taken into consideration not only before a campaign has started, but as an ongoing part of the process. A background research section helps the social media strategist get an idea of what has happened in the past, the main issues and challenges, and any gaps that provide opportunities and advantages. There can be creativity (along with science) in this section. Collecting the information to paint the picture of what is going on for an organization or brand in a systematic way is a big task, but by seeing what is happening and identifying the "so what" factor, you are able to use this part of the process as a spark for innovative and impactful ideas.

Brand Voice and Pillars

Brand voice, the overall tone, personality, and entity that you want to present online, is probably one of the most important elements to consider when looking at either establishing a brand from scratch or enhancing an established brand on social media. Will you be funny and engaging? Or will you have more of a professional or authoritative tone? Interns and professionals need to get into the **strategic mindset** of communicating in the brand voice rather than their own personal voice. Brand pillars are concepts or ideals that a brand has that they focus on in their content, branding, information, and community. For example, adidas has focused a lot on equality and inclusivity in their work, along with fitness, well-being, and community. On the other hand, Disney in their social media focuses on happiness and family-oriented content, so these are some brand pillars they focus on as part of their content and creative strategies.

Vision and Mission Statement

Two similar concepts, vision and mission, serve important roles within the strategic social media plan. **Vision** is the guiding principle that describes the overall goals and dreams of the organization, business, or individual for current and future activities. **Mission** describes the key elements of the overall purpose of an organization, brand, or person.

A vision statement for a social media strategic plan includes key personality characteristics that a brand, organization, or media outlet is inspired to communicate. These guiding principles and behaviors unify the brand, organization, or media outlet as its own community and help make it unique and purposeful.

Vision statements capture characteristics and principles that organizations or individuals value, which will guide their overall actions and make an impact in the community. Bridging various components in a cohesive statement, the vision of an organization or individual must tie in brand personality, key attributes, core values, and present and future behavioral intentions.

Social media professionals identify clients' unique characteristics, attributes, and future intentions, and make an assessment to determine whether these organizations and individuals are living up to the expectations and goals outlined in their vision statements. A vision should be consistent across all social media communication channels used by the client, and the social media professional determines whether relevant communities are aware of goals and aspirations in the vision statement.

Table 7.1 provides sample vision statements from several companies and organizations.

Table 7.1 Sample Vision Statements	
Company/Brand	**Vision Statement**
Peloton	• To bring immersive and challenging workouts into people's lives in a more accessible, affordable and efficient way. Peloton uses technology and design to connect the world through fitness, empowering people to be the best version of themselves anywhere, anytime.
adidas	• Our vision is . . . to enhance social and environmental performance in the supply chain, thereby improving the lives of the people making our products.
Glossier	• Our mission is to give voice through beauty, and our team is proud to work at Glossier to help democratize an industry that has forever been top-down.
Clorox	• Our mission statement is a reflection of our belief that each of our products has a meaningful impact on consumers' everyday lives. Our namesake bleach and disinfecting products help kill germs that make people sick. Burt's Bees® products address consumers' growing desire for naturally derived products. Brita® water filters make tap water taste great and help reduce bottled water waste. Hidden Valley® dressings encourage kids to eat their vegetables. And now with our acquisition of digestive health brand RenewLife®, we're able to help consumers with digestive issues with probiotics, digestive enzymes and more. We also strive to make everyday life better in the world where we do business by giving back to our communities. Whether it's contributing to disaster relief efforts through donations of Clorox® regular bleach, teaching classes at local schools or funding education, arts and culture programs, Clorox is committed to help restore, enrich and protect our communities.
Jeni's Splendid Ice Creams	• We're devoted to making better ice creams and bringing people together. It's what gets us out of bed in the morning and keeps us up late at night. We believe that you can grow a business as a community of people, with artful attention to detail and the customer experience, *and* get continuously better at the same time. That REALLY great ice cream served perfectly in a sparkling and beautiful space, with attentive and in-the-moment service (we believe service is an art) brings people together and helps them connect. And that sometimes sparks fly. And that there should be more sparks flying, generally. We like to make people feel good.
Adobe	• Creativity is in our DNA. Our game-changing innovations are redefining the possibilities of digital experiences. We connect content and data and introduce new technologies that democratize creativity, shape the next generation of storytelling, and inspire entirely new categories of business.
Warby Parker	• [Our objective is] to offer designer eyewear at a revolutionary price, while leading the way for socially conscious businesses.
KFC	• We believe in a world where educational opportunities are available to everyone, where we never give up on helping people achieve their dreams.

Sources: Peloton, adidas, Glossier, Clorox, Jeni's Splendid Ice Creams, Adobe, Warby Parker, and KFC.

The big difference between the vision statement and the mission statement is timing. While vision statements list inspiring ideals and values held presently and sustained into the future, mission statements focus on what is happening at the present moment. Mission statements characterize the fundamental level of what you are trying to be as a brand, organization, or business.

Let's look at some mission examples. Under Armour's mission is to make all athletes better through passion, design, and relentless pursuit of innovation (Under Armour, 2018). Facebook's mission is to "give people the power to share and make the world more open and connected" (Facebook, 2019). Hootsuite's motto is "Building enduring brands, one social connection at a time," and its mission statement describes how the global social media dashboard company is "not just a social relationship platform. We are not just a tech company. We are creators, innovators, and builders dedicated to revolutionizing the way you communicate" (Hootsuite, 2018). Starbucks' (2018) mission is "to inspire and nurture the human spirit—one person, one cup and one neighborhood at a time."

These memorable statements focus on the present. They are short and to the point, which is characteristic of an effective mission statement. Mission statements should be no longer than one sentence.

To prepare a mission statement for your strategic plan, ask yourself the following questions:

- Who are we?

- Who are our customers?

- What values do we stand for as a brand?

- What are our current goals?

- How can we be more inclusive?

- What insights will help drive solutions to problems and spark new ideas?

- What is our voice as a brand, and what is the voice of our community?

- What is our leadership style like?

- What is our operating philosophy (basic beliefs, values, ethics, etc.)?

- What are our core competencies or competitive advantages?

- What are our responsibilities with respect to being a good steward of our human, social, inclusive, financial, and environmental resources?

Both vision and mission statements are important components of a social media strategic plan. Without knowing core attributes, intentions for the future, and present goals, it will be difficult to identify an overall place within online and offline communities. In addition, vision and mission statements guide communication strategies, such as tone, brand voice, and which channels to use.

Diversity, Equity, and Inclusion

As discussed in Chapter 4, it is important to highlight the role diversity, equity, and inclusion (DEI) play within your company, agency, and industry. DEI is aligned with the vision and mission statements, and most organizations have a designated statement, policy, program, and team in diversity and inclusion. In matters of DEI, representation needs to be apparent, both offline and online. Having a statement is one thing, but incorporating these principles and values every day consistently becomes a much stronger statement.

Environmental Scan Analysis

An **environmental scan** helps the social media professional evaluate the current landscape within which a client or an organization operates. A number of factors contribute to this overall view of the environment.

- *Political Factors* (regulators, activism, and social issues). Political elections, social activism cases, bills and regulations from governing bodies and agencies (e.g., the Federal Trade Commission), and other governmental acts can impact a client or organization. These influences operate at the local level, the national level, and even the global level.

- *Legal Factors.* As discussed in Chapter 2 on legal implications in social media, the strategic social media plan should show awareness of key legal challenges, cases, and situations that need to be addressed or may have a future impact on the daily activities of a client or organization. Some entities are more highly regulated (military, government, etc.) than others. New laws and bills may impact how consumers interact with brands, employee hirings, citizen privacy and data collection, or the way advertisers must note whether or not posted content is promoted or sponsored.

- *Economic Factors* (e.g., cost of entry or cost to participate online). This area evaluates the current financial landscape affecting an entity, which can include spending habits on technology, information, and content creation; key trends happening in the workplace; industry hiring or layoff trends; employee satisfaction or employment trends; and financial barriers to entry.

- *Community Factors* (generational factors, social media factors, and culture). Outlining the key activities for relevant communities will form an essential part of the strategic plan. The social media professional will explore the health, presence, and engagement of a community and predict where it is going in the future. The plan should outline shifts in platform use and identify where people are getting their news. For example, as this textbook goes to press, users are gravitating to Instagram Stories and spending less time on Snapchat. Exploring the overall factors that impact the health of a community is an added component needed in the strategic plan.

- *Technology Factors* (advances, established vs. rising technologies, etc.). Evaluate the current trends, fads, platforms, and strategic practices being accepted, used, and discussed in the industry. Note the current landscape and which platforms and tools people are using to share, create, and disseminate content. Consider the overall rankings of each platform per location, community, and audience. Outline the connection between technical trends and consumer behavioral trends.

- *Social, Diversity, and Inclusion Factors.* Understand the current landscape internally and externally to identify all of the conversations, issues, challenges, and opportunities that are focused on social, diversity, and inclusion factors. Being aware of what is happening in local, national, and global societal trends and cases related to these issues is extremely important.

- *Consumer Factors* (consumer behavior trends, new uses, etc.). An understanding of key audience and generational trends should be incorporated into the strategic plan. The uses, perceptions, behaviors, and views of platforms and channels as a function of relevant audiences will need to be explored in detail.

Client or Company in Focus

The history of the organization. The history of a client organization includes the major events and key points that helped define it and shape it into what it is today. Outlining these accomplishments, and perhaps challenges, presents an opportunity to better understand where the client is today and how it reached this point. While it is important to trace the historical timeline of the client in a traditional sense, it is also necessary to outline the history of the client's social media use. Was it an early adapter on social media? Is it considered an innovator? Are its senior leaders (CEO, COO, etc.) on social media? If so, how active are they? Does the organization have a strong community focus on social media? Or is it always the very last to join a trend or platform?

Brand voice, story, reputation, and industry. Understanding the brand voice will help the social media strategist in the long term. Being able to identify the overall tone, personality, image, and unique attributes embedded within the content shared by the organization is a critical skill. For example, the voice that Four Roses Bourbon expresses on social media is quite different from the voice of Disney. Each brand has a distinct personality, allowing it to share various unique attributes and characteristics. Individuals and media outlets also have their own brand voice and characteristic ways of sharing their stories, updates, and content.

Key players and organizational structure. The strategic plan should outline the organizational structure of key players involved in social media, as well as where social media as a specialization is housed within the organization. Although social media has been established within certain companies as its own department, other organizations add social media responsibilities to the wheelhouse of skills and offerings in existing departments. Social media might be outsourced to a consultant, agency, or group of professionals. These insights will tell you a lot about the overall internal culture and whether social media is valued (or not) within the organization in question. It is useful to understand the background and experience of the social media team. Where did key players receive their education, what social media trainings and certifications have they received, and what is the overall landscape like for leadership and continued education within the organization? The strategic plan should note the likelihood of future social media education investment, and whether the level of commitment to ongoing education is a strength or weakness for the organization.

Diversity, equity, inclusion, and representation investment. An understanding of the key players and organizational structure is important, but professionals should also be aware of the current and historical state of diversity and inclusion within an organization. Programs, initiatives, campaigns, employment and recruitment data, and investment (financial, talent, etc.) attributed to these components should be analyzed and reported. Breaking down the dynamics and characteristics of each audience and cohort would be appropriate as well.

Products, services, and educational thought leadership. This factor is shared with traditional strategic plans. What main elements are being offered by the client? This is not just about goods and services but also about what the client is doing to provide educational resources or thought leadership for the community. What webinars, infographics, white papers, resource blog posts, research reports, and presentations is the client providing? All forms of promotional content can create thought leadership opportunities and educational connections with different communities.

Analysis of media channels (paid, earned, shared, owned [PESO]). For social media to be successful, it has to be aligned with the overall mission of the brand as well as the goals and objectives (and voice) of associated departments. These departments also have the opportunity to create and distribute media content on relevant channels.

The **PESO model** outlines the associated channels that can be used in social media. *Paid* media focuses on content for which an organization has paid for placement at a certain time, on a certain platform, and in front of a certain audience (Facebook ads, Instagram Stories ads, etc.). *Earned* media occurs when the content an organization shares, creates, or pitches arrives on another platform without charge (e.g., a feature on a blog post). *Shared* media is the essence of social media and how your content is distributed to others (e.g., reposted content or shared videos on Facebook and retweets on Twitter). *Owned* media is the type of content you personally own and control. Your website, blog, and internal assets are examples. For these items, you are able to control the message, updates, and the media design. Social media strategists need to outline what companies (or clients) are currently doing on each of these channels, how much they are spending, what content is going out, and how frequently they are using these channels, and conduct an analysis of their returns in terms of both financial and reputational assets. (See Figure 7.1 for a more detailed discussion of the PESO model.)

Previous campaigns and initiatives with social media. This sometimes is referred to as previous promotions or past campaigns in fields such as marketing, public relations, and strategic communications. As a social media professional, you will want to know what has been done already as far as social media campaigns and plans go. It is important to discuss the range of different campaigns that the client has implemented in the past, determine what has worked and what has not, and identify the big takeaways from these campaigns. Analyze the previous campaigns based on goals and objectives of the campaign and brand, representation (e.g., DEI integrated into the campaign content and message strategies on social media), channel(s) implemented, audiences targeted (specific persona characteristics), strategies and tactics, and evaluation of the campaign.

Different campaign initiatives can be divided into three categories: technical, managerial, and thought leadership, shown as a pyramid in Figure 7.2. Ideally, you want to have the complete picture at the bottom by adapting the technical tools first. The *technical* view of social media focuses on the specific tools that can be used immediately and is focused on the short term. These campaigns look at how we are using this new tool even though we just heard about it 15 minutes ago on

Figure 7.1 PESO 2.0 Model

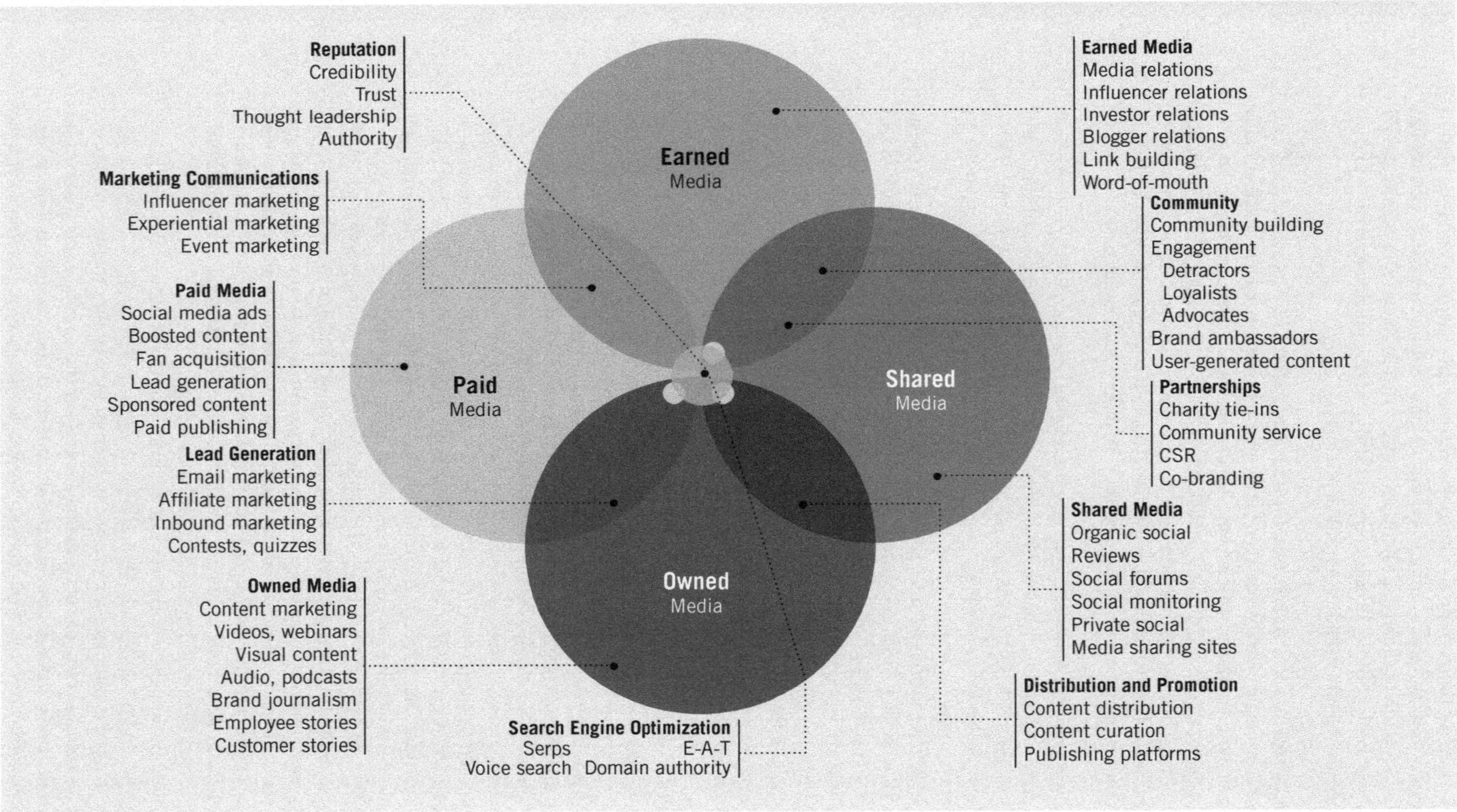

Reputation
Credibility
Trust
Thought leadership
Authority

Marketing Communications
Influencer marketing
Experiential marketing
Event marketing

Paid Media
Social media ads
Boosted content
Fan acquisition
Lead generation
Sponsored content
Paid publishing

Lead Generation
Email marketing
Affiliate marketing
Inbound marketing
Contests, quizzes

Owned Media
Content marketing
Videos, webinars
Visual content
Audio, podcasts
Brand journalism
Employee stories
Customer stories

Earned Media
Media relations
Influencer relations
Investor relations
Blogger relations
Link building
Word-of-mouth

Community
Community building
Engagement
Detractors
Loyalists
Advocates
Brand ambassadors
User-generated content

Partnerships
Charity tie-ins
Community service
CSR
Co-branding

Shared Media
Organic social
Reviews
Social forums
Social monitoring
Private social
Media sharing sites

Distribution and Promotion
Content distribution
Content curation
Publishing platforms

Search Engine Optimization
Serps   E-A-T
Voice search   Domain authority

Earned Media

Shared Media

Paid Media

Owned Media

Digiday or Social Media Today. These are very short-term blips on the radar for brands, and while you do want to use them to experiment and explore possible new tools, features, and programs, this should not be your only focus. Think about your long-term strategy. It is important to experiment and be creative in testing the waters for new tools and techniques, but this should not be the foundation for what you want to accomplish in social media.

Managerial roles and views of social media are the mid-level investment. The managerial roles and views of social media focus on building teams to work specifically on separate client accounts and projects, but the focus is tying in more strategy, higher-level brand management, and consultation on specific tools and services that will help accomplish the set business and communication objectives.

The main target for many clients and professionals, which few actually achieve, is *thought leadership*. Thought leaders share strategy, storytelling, and perspectives of the bigger picture not only of what is happening now, but what might be the case in a few years. They look at the interworkings of society, the environment, and industries that might influence what social media is doing internally and externally. Thought leaders actively contribute to the community with their insights, strategies, and experiences.

In summary, strategy and a strong foundation in the bigger picture need to come first. Tools, trends, and platforms will continue to change. Flip the pyramid model and create a sound foundation for strategy where each part is interconnected with the others and allowed to collaborate: the story, community, and brand voice of the client at the center of the Venn diagram in Figure 7.3.

Figure 7.2   Campaign Initiatives From Technical to Managerial to Thought Leadership

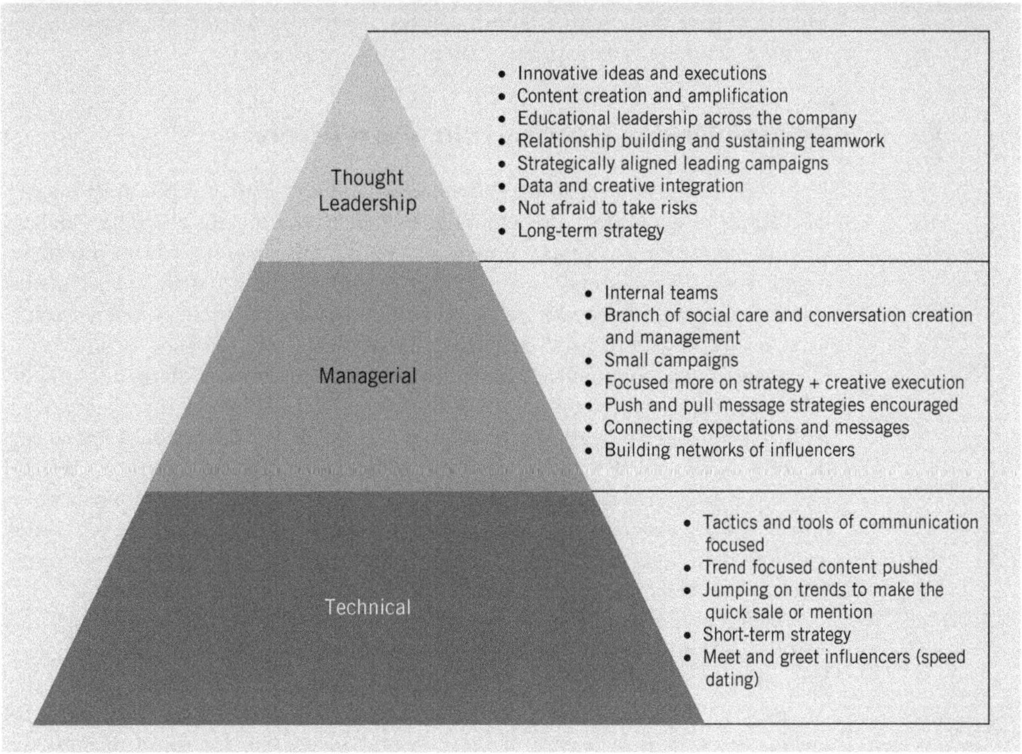

Thought Leadership
- Innovative ideas and executions
- Content creation and amplification
- Educational leadership across the company
- Relationship building and sustaining teamwork
- Strategically aligned leading campaigns
- Data and creative integration
- Not afraid to take risks
- Long-term strategy

Managerial
- Internal teams
- Branch of social care and conversation creation and management
- Small campaigns
- Focused more on strategy + creative execution
- Push and pull message strategies encouraged
- Connecting expectations and messages
- Building networks of influencers

Technical
- Tactics and tools of communication focused
- Trend focused content pushed
- Jumping on trends to make the quick sale or mention
- Short-term strategy
- Meet and greet influencers (speed dating)

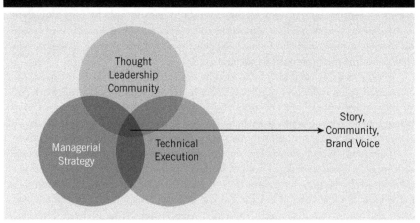

Figure 7.3 Established Influencer Relationships and Connections

Thought Leadership Community

Managerial Strategy

Technical Execution

Story, Community, Brand Voice

Many brands and accounts gravitate toward social media marketers and other influencers as part of their campaigns. Evaluate the influencers used by your client in the past. Be aware of which influencers are the real deal and which have a lot of window dressing and show-stopping antics but little substance in terms of expertise. Which brands and companies has an influencer worked with in the past on social media? Who is an influencer's agency of record? Who lists the influencer as a client or person they have worked with online? What formal or informal partnerships has the influencer formed with clients? Some of this information will be hard to obtain, but by doing the extra research into who these individuals are and what they have done with a brand, you can determine their level of knowledge, their skill level, and any gaps that may need to be addressed.

Social Media Communication Audit

Conducting a social media communication audit is one of the most important things to do before implementing a strategic plan on social media. Analyze all communication elements, content, channels, and personnel within the client organization. This should be a comprehensive evaluation of the social media tools, campaigns, influencers, online relationships, network analyses, influence and presence on platforms, voice, personnel, and players that are part of each team.

Conducting communication audits is not uncommon in marketing, public relations, and related communication disciplines. This allows us to evaluate what has been done, as well as the opportunities and challenges the organization or key personnel have failed to consider. What campaigns have and have not worked? Why? It is helpful to take a global bird's-eye view of the overall social media position of the organization. While completing this task, we will interview personnel and determine internal levels of training, organizational structure, and education relevant to social media.

When doing a social media communication audit, you need to evaluate the client's social media both internally and externally. As a social media strategist, you have to be aware of the internal culture and perhaps politics emerging within the company or brand (e.g., who has ownership of the creative assets used in social media, and who is in charge of the cost and advertising for social media?). In addition to these internal questions, social media professionals need to be aware of external factors of what the company has done, what has worked and what has not worked, and conduct a comprehensive evaluation of each platform at the technical, managerial, and thought leadership levels. This will provide a comprehensive view of where the company or brand is, and where it needs to go, on social media. Both short-term challenges and opportunities can emerge from the findings. Completing a social media audit will inform action steps and recommendations for the future.

A social media communication audit has three parts: internal social media analysis, external social media analysis, and competitor analysis. These three parts will help you determine the client's overall standing in regard to what is being created on social media and how the client compares to external audiences and others in the same market. The internal social media analysis evaluates all social media content policies, procedures, and overall interpretation elements within the organization. It covers the responsibility of the social media management and leadership culture, the level of credibility and trust toward social media within the organization, and social media education and mentorship. Some of these items will be readily available to you, but others are likely to require permission. Some relevant documents contain proprietary points of information the organization may be reluctant to share. However, the more information you receive, the stronger your strategic plan will be.

An internal analysis should outline the main leadership, including the CEO/president and other key personnel. Is the CEO on social media? What is the overall investment and commitment (financial and emotional) to supporting social media and the manager and/or their team? How active are the company's leaders online? What platforms do they use, and do they encourage their employees to use the same ones? The investment necessary for a strong social media presence comes from the top. Your strategic plan should outline present use and attitudes regarding social media as well as reactions from internal and external audiences.

The structure of the client organization will also impact its social media presence. Evaluate how social media is incorporated inside the organization, brand, media outlet, or entity in question. Where are social media functions housed within the organization? Does the organization have its own social media department like Team USA and many other organizations have? If so, to whom do the social media professionals report? Alternatively, is social media part of an established department like marketing, with the chief marketing officer reporting to senior management? For example, General Motors distributes social media functions across various departments, which all ultimately report to the CEO. Jeremiah Owyang (2010) has outlined a number of different organizational structures relevant to social media functions, such as decentralized, centralized, hub and spoke, multiple hub and spoke, and holistic (or honeycomb). An organization's social media functions can be centralized or decentralized, have multiple hubs and spokes, or be coordinated and aligned together or not.

- *Decentralized*: There is no clear organization of where social media is placed and who is in charge.

- *Centralized*: All business reports and social media efforts are dictated by one source and passed down to others (e.g., government accounts for social media like General Motors).

- *Hub and spoke*: This function focuses on a cross-functional team but is a centralized area that helps various business departments have a consistent social media presence. This is where most of the corporate brand accounts fall. Examples include athletic departments (e.g., NFL, NBA, and MLB) and brand accounts (e.g., United Airlines).

- *Multiple hub and spoke*: This is the same as hub and spoke but on a global stage (e.g., Adobe).

- *Holistic or honeycomb*: Every brand, department, and person has an opportunity to collaborate on and implement social media. Social media actions are all linear and equal (e.g., Chipotle, Pfizer, and *Adweek*).

By understanding the leadership viewpoint and the organizational structure for social media, you will be able to identify many opportunities and roadblocks facing an organization in its social activities. Tables 7.2 and 7.3 will help you evaluate the internal and the external presence for a brand and determine what actions need to be taken and what areas need improvement.

The next step in the social media communication audit is the external analysis of the social media presence. Now you are being asked to survey trends, issues, situations, and events impacting the daily activities of the client externally with relevant audiences. External communications include everything that the client sends out to its external audiences. These components include marketing, public relations, advertising, and related communication content, campaigns, and relationships. This section focuses on how an organization manages the relationships and communication channels, rather than content and strategies, externally within social media.

Table 7.2   Internal Analysis of Social Media Presence Template

	Background	Content + Rationale	Strengths + Weaknesses	Action Steps and Recommendations
Internal Communication				
Personnel + Team Analysis				
Education + Mentorship				
Diversity, Equity, and Inclusion				
Employee Social Media Policy/ Advocacy Program				
Leadership				
Brand Voice				
Analytics				

	Background	Brand Voice	Relationship/ Rationale	Content + Rationale	Strengths + Weaknesses	Action Steps and Recommendations
Platform						
Campaigns						
Influencers						
Diversity, Equity, and Inclusion						
Community Analysis						
Content Creation/ Message Analysis						
Analytics + Data						

Table 7.3   External Analysis of Social Media Presence Template

The external analysis begins with identifying the platforms on which the organization has a presence—anywhere from a few accounts to hundreds depending on the size of the organization. Listing previous campaigns on social media is also important. These campaigns could have been implemented for no apparent reason based on the research and analysis conducted, or they could have a specific focus like a social selling campaign or an influencer marketing initiative. By identifying the range of campaigns that have been launched for the organization online, you will be able to evaluate whether the campaigns represent the best options for the organization or if there is room for improvement. You can determine whether the organization is making good use of the tools at its disposal and how key audiences (media, opinion leaders, influencers, etc.) have responded.

Speaking of influencers, the external analysis piece of the strategic plan should identify the primary individuals interacting with the client. Influencers comprise a key audience segment that engages with or is the target of online content. We will discuss influencers in more detail in Chapter 8. For the purposes of the strategic plan, we should look at links between the main influencers, motivational factors for engaging with specific influencers, defining characteristics of influencers (tone of voice, personal brand, history on platform, list of personality traits, types of relationships and network connections they have, etc.), and the influencers' current relationship with the content.

The overall state and health of the client's community should be assessed. Identifying the various platforms on which a brand has a presence is critical, but so is discussing the overall nature and unique characteristics of the community on each platform. Each community has its own views, attributes, and motivational factors that make its members an important target for engagement by a specific client. Social media strategists also need to evaluate the community's share of voice in the industry, which essentially means how large a position the client plays in the overall conversation within the community. In Table 7.4, you can see the analysis of the social media content and some key components to take into account when evaluating all of the social media platforms a brand or client has used. Within this analysis, you need to list each place the client has an established presence; analyze the client's overall content, voice, and community; classify the type of organizational structure it is in; and determine who are its major influencers, its share of voice (percentage of the client's voice compared to the total number of competitors in the market), and what analytics can be collected to tell how engaged it is within the industry and community. With this information, the positives (successes) as well as any short-term or even long-term obstacles (challenges) need to be addressed. Recommendations based on these points can be provided. These steps give the social media manager a comprehensive view of what is going on with competitors, in order to identify any gaps that can be (a) the focus of the campaign, (b) the key point of messages and creation of content to be strategically executed, or even (c) a jumping-off point to brainstorm creative ideas to integrate into the social media plan.

The last part of the social media communication audit is the competitor analysis, probably one of the most important background elements in a social media strategic plan. By understanding where your competitors stand, you can determine what areas you need to address and also what factors, assets, and characteristics really define you and your client on social media.

Several steps need to be taken into consideration for this part of the process. First, make sure you are able to identify which brands, individuals, or organizations to keep your eyes on when it comes to the strategic plan. It is important to note not only who is already established in the same space but also who is rising and emerging as formidable competition. Distinguishing between who is established and who is emerging is absolutely critical. Audiences evolve and change, and we have to evaluate how we can sustain our current relationships and which groups we need to reach out to. We have to be aware of who is rising in our particular industry and market and making a name for themselves on social media. If we do not take advantage of opportunities to reach these individuals, our competitors will. Attention is the currency we are driving for in the social media industry, and without a relationship connection, this will be lost.

A thorough competitive review takes place platform by platform. The main social media platforms need to be noted here, but we also need to look in new and innovative spaces. Watch for the places where competitors are experimenting, which provides us with an idea of their overall strategy and position in the marketplace. While it is important to note which platforms competing companies are on and to observe their vanity metrics (followers, who they are following, etc.), it is more important to think about how and why they use each platform. For example, what is the company's voice on each of these platforms? What is the overall health and stability of each community the company is a part of online? Are key members of the company team engaging with others and sharing their expertise with fellow professionals (Twitter chats, virtual workshops, invited speakers, guests on podcasts, speaking engagements at high-profile events, etc.)? Has the company featured its award-winning or most notable campaigns in the past few years, perhaps at Cannes Lions, *Adweek*, and Shorty Awards? Were any of its campaigns noticed for all the wrong reasons? We need to be aware of our clients' overall relationship with their community based on what has worked for them in previous campaigns and what has not.

To the best of your ability, identify competitors' overall organizational structure using the same guidelines we followed for the internal audit. Where does

Table 7.4 Analysis of Social Media Template

Company	Platforms	Content Voice Community	Representation	Campaign Influencers	Share of Voice	Analytics	Successes + Challenges	Action Steps

Gap(s) to Address

179

social media fit for them? Are they placing social media at the same level as the rest of the companies? What do their leaders do online, or how do they view social media? Identifying these extra steps can paint a picture for competing groups of how they practice, view, and use social media as an organization.

Analytics, covered in Chapter 6, with research, not only are useful for an internal audit but also provide considerable insight as part of the competitive analysis. Most organizations work on their own or with a third-party vendor (e.g., Talkwalker, Agorapulse, or Salesforce) to collect and analyze listening and monitoring data. There is no reason you can't analyze publicly available data about your competitors, too. It is one thing to identify key competitors, but collecting and evaluating data demonstrating their online successes and failures add further depth to your competitive analysis. Evaluate brand mentions, overall influence, relationships with key influencers, individuals who are advocating for and talking about the brand the most, and how the brand content is doing compared to other brands across other metrics (share of voice, engagement, interactions, influence, etc.). For each of the sections outlined in Table 7.4, data should have a strong role in showcasing evidence of the points being made. Data, especially social media data, can serve as supporting evidence to help make a point and nudge a decision from one direction to a better one.

Collecting this type of background research is a lot of work, but the payoff in the form of your strategic plan will be well worth the time and effort expended at this stage. There are no shortcuts to this step if you wish to produce a fully informed strategic plan.

Situational Analysis and Insights

This is important to remember. Situational analysis, paired with insights gathered from research, puts the creativity in the science and the systematic rigor into the art, which brings together a well-armed analysis for the social media strategist. The situational analysis will help you organize all the data you have collected so far, setting up the overall picture of what is going on for a brand, organization, or person on social media. This section At this point in the strategic planning process, the social media strategist is able to combine the findings and takeaways discovered during the external scanning, background research, and communication audit phases. We combine all of the information, data, and insights we have collected into organized columns of information. This thorough approach plays a significant role in determining the steps that need to be taken for this strategic plan. Research is only as good as your ability to identify what is happening, why things are happening, and how you can apply findings to construct sound strategies. Organizing your research efforts can help you see the whole picture at once.

As noted in Chapter 6, insights gathered from the research are one of the most valuable things that can be included in the social media process, especially for strategic planning. Insights are revelations that illuminate the how and why audiences behave in a certain manner, which is the ultimate prize for any marketer, strategist, or communication professional. This can allow the social media strategist to look at a challenge from a new perspective, or have a light bulb effect (similar to Gru in the movie *Despicable Me*) to come up with an idea that sparks.

Insights also provide opportunities to thoroughly explore motivations and underlying truths for an audience that may bring forth solutions to issues and challenges, as well as opportunities to bring together new ideas and collaborations.

There have been many insights related to this that have been present in campaigns. For example, with adidas trying to branch out to new audiences in home gyms due to COVID-19, they sponsored specific instructors working at Peloton (like Cody Rigsby and Ally Love) to create the branded apparel line adidas x Peloton. Same can be said with rapper Jack Harlow and Papa John's. Harlow, who is from Kentucky and a fan of the pizza company, has partnered with them on several influencer initiatives, creating a win-win situation. These insights are what have helped all of these cases bring together fresh, unique, and relevant experiences to the table for audiences to remember and be inspired by. Insights are not just data points to report; they are points to inform and inspire the social media strategist and his or her team to take action.

Core Problem or Opportunity. Most strategic plans outline a single main problem that needs to be addressed in a campaign. In the case of social media, this single problem might be trying to determine how social media could help address an ongoing issue for an organization. Challenges might take the form of restoring trust within a particular community after a crisis (e.g., Jake Paul and Disney) or tying it into a larger case (e.g., SXSW [South by Southwest Film Festival] and COVID-19) or a preventable crisis (e.g., Pepsi and Kendall Jenner). Often overlooked is the need for social media plans to address new opportunities rather than just solve existing problems. A social media strategic plan might include ways to use social media to take advantage of positive relationships with a community or increase sales and exposure.

SWOT Analysis

Four main categories are involved in a SWOT analysis: strengths, weaknesses, opportunities, and threats. SWOT analyses are a traditional part of the communication and marketing campaign process, but they are essential to the social media strategic plan as well. A SWOT analysis can be used to explore and identify solutions to problems, take advantage of new opportunities and ventures, decide which steps to take to help rejuvenate a community or brand online, or brainstorm new ways of engaging online through social media. The four primary aspects of SWOT, shown in Figure 7.4, are important, but we have to form bridges between these components in a fifth, strategic implications part of the plan.

Strengths. This is where you outline in detail the strengths observed in current social media practices within an organization or for a person. For example, strengths might take the form of an established presence on certain platforms, systematic training for employees so they stay on top of the latest trends, diverse representation in leadership roles, and a collaborative environment throughout which social media is not only used but embraced.

Strengths can be divided into categories to make them easier to keep organized. For example, you could group internal resources by people, financial, or creative. Consider the overall standing of the organization's culture. A positive corporate or agency culture can lead to an environment in which employees feel comfortable sharing ideas or taking leadership roles. Culture is a strength in some cases, but it could be classified as a weakness if it holds the organization back.

Each strength must be supported by the data you have collected, which come from your social media communication audit. Construct a rationale, or a summary of each strength relative to the organization's overall mission.

Figure 7.4   SWOT Analysis Diagram

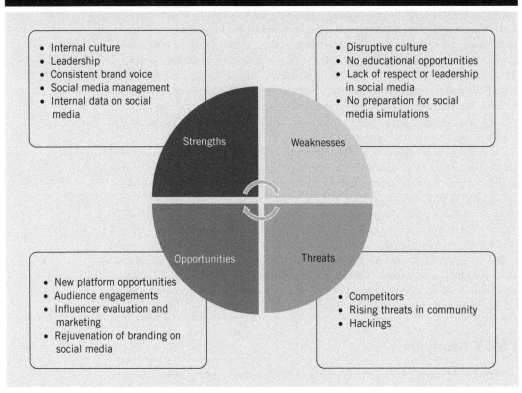

Weaknesses. Weaknesses hinder or challenge the organization's ability to accomplish its objectives and are often the complete opposite of the items listed as strengths. For example, one challenge could be a hostile leadership environment where social media is not valued. In this type of situation, employees would find it very difficult to be creative in their use of social media. Also, lack of internal resources for diversity and inclusion efforts could be a weakness for an organization, as well as lack of representation in talent and leadership roles. Another weakness could be a lack of mentorship and educational training allowing employees to keep up with the changes in social media. As was the case with strengths, you must provide evidence to support your points regarding weaknesses. The communication audit might be sufficient for these purposes, but it might also be helpful to use focus groups or your own observations of the organization's process. Analytics can also support your analysis.

Opportunities. An opportunity is a set of ideas or circumstances external to the client that can lead to new approaches and behaviors. This part of the analysis should include a list of creative ideas to promote brainstorming and to jump-start new initiatives. These ideas can take different forms. Examples include evaluating new social media strategy campaigns and trends, experimenting with new platforms or tools, reaching new audiences that have not been explored yet, and looking for new communities with which to engage. Opportunities combine the strategic insights gathered during research and the creative execution of content and stories. These insights should be supported by data, research, and observations collected during the social media communication audit and background research processes.

When it comes to opportunities, ask yourself the following questions when evaluating your client:

- What is our edge (what makes you unique compared with others)?

- What is the real competitive advantage in your industry?

- What are the opportunities to expand and partner outside of your industry?

- What has not been done yet?

- Do we want to be an explorer/leader or follower in the industry?

Threats. Threats are another classic external factor, arising from negative events affecting individuals or organizations. This part of your analysis should explore ongoing political, regulatory, environmental, and technology-driven threats. Competitors could be listed in this category if they are threatening your well-being or taking away aspects that you have built on social media. For example, Facebook has copied several of Snapchat's features and incorporated them into Instagram Stories. If you were doing a threat analysis for Snapchat, this issue would definitely be included.

Strategic Implications. The strategic implications section is a fifth component of the SWOT analysis, which looks at the "so what" factor, or why the information in the SWOT analysis is important to consider and which driving factors should be taken into consideration as the client moves forward. Strategic implications are sometimes referred to as propositions or a brand's North Star. Essentially, applying the takeaways from the situational analysis and identifying the gap of opportunity you have for your brand in addressing the opportunity and challenge in a single sentence is the ultimate goal.

This section, no more than one or two sentences long, should precisely synthesize the information gathered throughout the process of the background research and social media communication audit into a bold, clear statement summarizing the findings, what to do about them, and why they are important. This step is not always presented in other communication- or marketing-related disciplines, and including this information can differentiate you in a positive way from many other aspiring social media professionals.

Goals

Once you identify the main areas to address based on your research analysis, you are prepared to offer a broad statement that captures the overall focus of your social media initiative. You might address a rising opportunity or a significant need or issue for the client. This statement, which should be in the form of a single sentence, is the **goal statement**.

Objectives

After determining the overall focus of your social media plan, you have to set **objectives** that clearly state what you plan to accomplish. Creating good objectives is probably one of the toughest things to do when constructing a social media strategic plan or campaign. Many professionals struggle with this task, so don't be discouraged if you also find it challenging. In addition, there are many classifications of objectives to focus on, depending on the discipline. For example, marketing objectives serve the purpose of increasing profit, reaching a higher yield of customers, improving volume of sales, and gaining percentage points in market shares, among others. Others focus on engaging awareness and understanding key issues and initiatives (e.g., journalism and public relations). Social media professionals need to be aware of these and how they are tied to the social media goals for each client.

All of an organization's functions must revolve around its mission, goals, and objectives, which in turn are assessed with measurements that are definitive and quantifiable. To be effective, goals and objectives should be simple and easy to understand for everyone and linked with measurable achievements. Goals and objectives must also be updated at each planning period to ensure they are continually serving the organization's needs and purpose.

Objectives can take many different forms. For example, marketing objectives might look to increase sales, whereas public relations objectives might be to increase awareness about a campaign and restore or rejuvenate established relationships with key audience members. Social media plans can be especially challenging, because we have to consider where this plan will be housed, which professionals will be part of the team creating and launching the plan, and how we will evaluate and measure whether we have achieved our objectives.

All objectives must fulfill certain criteria, referred to as the **SMART criteria**, to be effective. Using the SMART criteria is an established way to categorize effective objectives into five different categories: specific, measurable, achievable, realistic, and time-specific. First, all objectives must be specific. This means we have to be very clear about our objectives for the social media plan. For example, we might say we are looking to increase our community on Facebook. Measurements must be aligned with what we want to accomplish, so we need specific guidance from our objectives about how much we want to increase or decrease a certain element. Measurement is helpful here and will come into play again when we look at evaluation later in this chapter.

The second criterion for objectives is that they are measurable. Objectives have to be practical in nature both in expectations and in time and resources without any issues. Social media professionals do not want to promise the world to a client or organization without fully investing in the necessary tools and resources. Setting forth objectives with a clear mindset of what an individual (or team) can handle is fair to the client and organization, as well as to those who are creating and executing the strategic plan.

Third, objectives must be achievable. This means we must be able to actually accomplish what we set out to do in the social media plan. If a client asks us to increase her followers by a million people in the span of a week, we must let the client know that that objective is not achievable.

Fourth, objectives must be realistic. Sometimes we need to have a heart-to-heart conversation with a client about this. The client may want to change the world in a day. However, it may not be realistic in the time scope for this social media plan. Having honest conversations with your clients about what is and is not realistic leads to better expectations. This is not always perceived as good news, so a certain amount of authority and poise is required for you to share these insights in a confident way.

Finally, objectives should be precise in their timing. It is only fair that the people with whom you're working on a social media plan know when they can expect objectives to be achieved.

Therefore, when implementing the SMART criteria for an objective statement, it may look something like this: to increase Aviation Gin's brand awareness among Generation Z consumers in New York City by 15% by December 2021. This objective integrates all of the components of the SMART criteria.

There is no magic number of objectives needed for a specific social media plan. The number depends on the scope of the campaign and the overall goal of the client or organization you are representing.

Key Audience Members

An essential part of a social media strategic plan is how to communicate with our audiences. Understanding the underlying characteristics, motivational factors, perceptions, social media platforms used, and how audiences use each platform are just a few of the factors that come into play. Audiences want to be talked to in a way that is personable, not promotional.

Two types of audience will be outlined in your strategic plan. **Primary audiences** are those you want to target directly and that have a meaningful relationship and connection to the client. **Secondary audiences** are supportive and potentially viewed as influencers by the primary audience members. With both types, outlining emerging audience members—or those who are not necessarily on the client's radar yet but could and perhaps should be—is very useful.

Understanding audiences means painting a picture of these groups of individuals. **Demographics** are a basic way to categorize a group of individuals and involve the basic population data that are easily collected, such as age, education level, ethnicity, and location. In social media, the description of audiences needs to be expanded much further. The more information we have about our key audiences, the easier it will be to craft effective and personalized messages to fit their motivational needs and expectations.

This is where **psychographics** come into play, where we are able to categorize audiences based on their attitudes, opinions, and values. This higher-level approach to categorization narrows down the groups into specific audiences based on psychological characteristics and attributes.

Human-to-human communication is what distinguishes successful brands in social media from those still struggling to build their community. Ignoring this principle is one thing social marketers are beyond guilty of. Instead of pushing content or playing the "pay for play" game, social media strategists need to think of people as people. Effective key messages can help captivate the brand voice as well as extend reach to the community by providing an opportunity to participate in the conversation.

Understanding your audiences plays a significant role in your ability to write key messages. Messages take time, research, and a dash of creativity to make them effective. This is probably one of the hardest tasks you'll have in social media. Each platform has its own community and brand voice, but this does not mean you should sway at all from your traditional and fundamental brand voice. Instead, you must craft the messages to align with your identity as a brand, and channel this persona and voice to the appropriate audience. The magic comes alive when you provide the right voice in the right channel to the right audience at the right time.

There are two types of key messages: primary and secondary. **Primary messages** are broad statements that you want to communicate to your key audience members. Each primary message should be simple, concise, and to the point. This is not the time to elaborate. Just one sentence long, the primary message must capture what you want to accomplish and communicate to your audiences in a limited amount of time. For example, Lego launched a campaign called Future Builders to encourage girls to be creative builders in their future dreams and careers. This campaign is revisiting their iconic 1981 campaign while modernizing the key messages, and the tag line emphasizes building community in the 21st century.

If you want to expand and elaborate on key messages, the secondary message comes into play. **Secondary messages** provide additional evidence to support the primary message. Using facts, statistics, and additional information to build on the point outlined in the primary message, these messages can incorporate evidence of what the client has already done on social media. There is no magic number of secondary messages needed to support your primary message, but you should be thorough in your explanation of these points to avoid audience confusion. A rule of thumb is the more information you can provide to guide your audience members regarding actions they should take, the better off you will be.

Strategies and Tactics

Strategy is obviously the heart of a strategic plan. However, you can have the best ideas for a social media strategic plan, but without proper execution of your strategies, nothing is gained.

Many strategies can be integrated in a specific social media plan.

- *Platform-Based Strategy*: Identifying the specific actions that will be taken on a designated platform such as Instagram, TikTok, Twitch, and more

- *Audience Strategy*: Engaging with specific audiences for the campaign across different platforms

- *Message Strategy*: Highlighting the main brand characteristics (brand values and pillars) and points that are aligned with this social media strategy

- *Content Strategy*: Identifying the type of content that will be created by the brand (owned media) and which content will be utilized by other audiences (paid media for agencies and earned media with creators, influencers, and ambassadors)

- *Insights Strategy*: Integrating insights gathered from research into actionable ideas

- *Creative Execution Strategy*: Tying in audiences with experiential offline experiences to be shared online on designated platforms

- *Influencer Strategy*: Specifically engaging with key influencers and their channels for the campaign to focus on word-of-mouth efforts to create impact and actions

- *Inclusive Strategy*: Identifying actions to make sure all audiences are represented and engaged for the campaign across platforms, making it accessible for all

Tactics are the tools and applications within social media that you will use to accomplish your objectives and fulfill your strategies. Tactics are the nuts and bolts of your social media plan. For example, using a branded hashtag is a type of tactic. An Instagram Live interview with an influencer or partnering with TikTok creators for a brand challenge is another example of a tactic. As you can see, tactics are specific and focused. Each tactic needs to be aligned with the strategy.

Managing tactics well is a way to impress employers and clients and use your creativity to stand out among your peers. Tactics allow you to experiment with new trends, tools, and platforms. At the same time, tactics must be used strategically and systematically, not just for fun. Make sure that you can support your choice of specific new tools and platforms with data.

Evaluation

This is truly the part of the strategic plan that is either overlooked or viewed as intimidating. Evaluation is the section of the strategic plan that brings in not only the value for social media strategies but also the opportunity to showcase the evidence to support the overall impact the creative and research-based strategies have accomplished in a campaign. Yes, this means there are some calculations to do. If you thought you wouldn't use any math in a social media career, you were very wrong. Measurement skills are an essential area of social media expertise. A growing specialization in social media, as discussed elsewhere in this textbook, measurement involves math, which we use to evaluate whether we have been successful in our campaigns. This does not mean a simple check in a box of "yes" or "no." Instead, we need numbers and specifics. In some cases, we can use traditional research methods, such as focus groups and interviews, to determine whether or not we have achieved our objectives. In the case of social media, we can rely on other tools and services to help answer these questions.

To determine whether or not we have achieved our objectives, we need to establish a set of **key performance indicators (KPIs).** Key KPIs should be determined *before* the social media strategic plan is implemented. KPIs not only determine what has been accomplished but inform next steps and measurements for future campaigns.

Here are some typical KPIs for social media plans. (They are discussed in more detail in Chapter 12.)

- Awareness (share of voice, tone, sentiment)

- Audience (retention rate, lifetime value, audience share of voice, influencer share of voice)

- Consideration (engagement, traffic and conversations)

- Conversion (costs per lead, sales, conversion rate of sales and leads)

We will discuss available tools and measurement methods in Chapter 12. For the purposes of the strategic plan, however, we need to outline how we will collect and interpret the data. Senior management will rely heavily on this information to determine whether or not investing in the social media plan was worthwhile. Data collection must always be transparent, and takeaways must be clearly stated. This part of the process can be challenging on a variety of levels because we have to integrate multiple sources of information into a cohesive message.

Table 7.5 Content Calendar Examples

Hootsuite

Time	Type	Topic	Post	Link
			Day 1 - Monday	
BLOG POST				
8:00 AM	NEW BLOG		Top 5 Vegan Paleo Dishes You Have To Try (You Too, Carnivores)	
TWITTER				
6:15	Club Info	Daily Class Schedule	Monday is for #MuscleMass. Get your kettlebell swing game on point.	PHOTO
11:15	Blog Promo - Paleo	Top 5 Vegan Paleo Dishes You Have To Try (You Too, Carnivores)	Vegan Paleo? It's Possible. Get the recipes here:	ow.ly/xxcerpt
11:45	Promo	#HolidayHealth	Winter is coming... share a photo of your favourite exercise for a chance to win a 10 class pass! Add #HolidayHealth to enter.	PHOTO
17:45	Blog Snippet - Paleo	Proteins	"By combining incompatible proteins, you can get complete proteins"	PHOTO
18:35	Food Tips		Dinner time! Harvest Salad with Chicken.	PHOTO
20:00	Exercise Tips	Strength Training	Moderation is key with leg extensions + Picture	PHOTO
FACEBOOK				
6:00	Club Info	Daily Class Schedule	Monday is for Muscle Mass.	PHOTO
11:15	Blog Promo - Paleo	Top 5 Vegan Paleo Dishes You Have To Try (You Too, Carnivores)	Vegan Paleo? It's Possible. Get the recipes here:	ow.ly/xxcerpt1
INSTAGRAM				
6:00	Club Info	Daily Class Schedule	Monday is for Muscle Mass.	PHOTO
14:00	Community	Member of the Month	Extra gold stars for @Casey, our member of the month. She hasn't missed a spin class since she joined!	PHOTO
			Day 2 - Tuesday	
TWITTER				
6:15	Club Info	Daily Class Schedule	The Tuesday fitness menu	PHOTO
8:15	Food Tips	Coffee	Grassfed butter, coconut oil, coffee, blend. Have you tried bulletproof coffee yet? Thoughts?	PHOTO
11:15	Exercise Tips	Strength Training	Have you visited the squat rack lately? + Picture	PHOTO
16:15	Community	#TransformationTuesday	"Half the battle is just showing up when you said you will." Dave is a huge inspiration to us all! #TransformationTuesday	PHOTO

Sprout Social

Source: Hootsuite Inc., https://hootsuite.com/education/courses/social-marketing/content/content-calendar.

Source: "4 Steps for Creating a Social Media Calendar," 2017, Sprout Social, https://sproutsocial.com/insights/social-media-editorial-calendar/.

Budget

Social media campaigns can be quite affordable or quite expensive depending on the services, tools, and programs you decide to include in the strategic plan. You must be able to account for all the resources needed for a social media plan to take place, and these resources must be itemized based on strategy. Itemized costs might include tools and services, production in creating content, data analytics tools and downloading of data, advertising and media postings on various platforms, and personnel. You might need additional freelancers, consultants, and interns on your team.

Calendar

A social media calendar has several different components. The strategies, tactics, social media placements, and evaluation and measurement components that will take place in the span of the campaign must be scheduled. This process is sometimes referred to as the customer journey landscape view. The components to be scheduled might include paid, earned, shared, and owned (PESO) media. The calendar also outlines the overall connections of the social media team with the rest of the duties and disciplines within an organization or agency.

The content calendar aligns all of the pieces of content going out at the same time on a social media platform and how they will be evaluated. Specific tools and services, such as Hootsuite and Sprout Social (see Table 7.5), allow you to create content calendars in a very simple and organized manner. Depending on the overall cost of the campaign and investment in social media, the client or senior leadership will have to determine how much they want to invest in these tools.

Final Recommendations and Summary

The final element for the strategic plan is to formulate a summary of future recommendations and themes from the strategic plan. Conclude your social media strategic plan with a summary of your findings and recommended next steps. Along with the executive summary, which is present in most social media strategic plans, the conclusion is where you provide commentary and key takeaways that you want to highlight for the client. This is an opportunity to provide additional recommendations and note suggestions for the future, allowing the social media plan to come full circle while also providing a stepping stone to the next social media strategy the organization, agency, brand, or person wants to pursue in the future.

CHAPTER SUMMARY

The strategic plan is one of the main documents a social media professional is responsible for creating. Strategic plans serve as a systematic guide to determine what has happened in the past, what needs to be implemented now, and whether or not an organization was successful in meeting its goals and objectives.

The strategic plan can spark further ideas and new possibilities. Constructing a sound plan requires both research and creativity, linking the science and art of social media as a field of study and as an element of practice. Some universal steps and categories found in the social media strategic plan are shared by plans in other fields. Other areas are unique to social media. The approach of a social media strategic plan may evolve with the channels of communication. It is up to the social media professional to determine which items to revisit, adapt, or discard when they are no longer relevant. Along with the tools of communication, social media strategic plans evolve over time and must continue to adapt to the changing expectations and needs of the industry and workplace.

Strategic plans are difficult to create and implement, but with practice and collaborative team efforts, you can learn to craft plans that lead to sound decisions and successful social media campaigns.

THOUGHT QUESTIONS

1. Why is a strategic plan important for social media? Identify three reasons why a strategic plan is necessary for a social media campaign.

2. What is the difference between a goal statement and an objective statement?

3. What are the components of a social media communication audit?

4. Identify the five concepts of a SWOT analysis. Where do strategic implications come into play for a social media campaign?

5. What different strategies can be incorporated in a strategic plan in social media, and why is each of these important?

6. What are some of the elements involving insights? What are the ways in which insights are brought into a social media strategic plan?

EXERCISES

1. While interviewing with Target for a social media job, you are asked to do a SWOT analysis of the company's social media efforts. Look at its current campaigns and channels and discuss its strengths, weaknesses, opportunities, and threats (SWOT) as a brand on social media. Then write a sentence outlining the strategic implications the company needs to note for future social media campaigns.

2. Phocus, a caffeinated, carbonated energy water drink that was created in Louisville, Kentucky, is looking to engage and build brand awareness with Generation Z about its new drink product for college students. Research the company to see what they have done so far on social media and how they are presenting themselves to Gen Z. Write two primary messages and two secondary messages for this audience. You will need to do some research regarding the characteristics of Generation Z. Then, propose one strategy and two tactics you could implement to reach this audience for Phocus. Discuss how you would evaluate the effectiveness of this campaign.

3. You are asked to do a social media communication audit for your university. Identify the internal and external characteristics of your own university as well as for three competing universities for their social media presence. In your analysis, analyze your school's diversity and inclusion statement to see if this is reflected on their social media channels. Discuss the major findings from this experience, and highlight three recommendations and actions you would recommend your university to take.

4. Fashion designer and *Project Runway* winner Christian Siriano is looking to launch a new fashion show concept that will be held in Nashville ahead of the CMA (Country Music Association) Awards. Your task is to (a) conduct an overview of Siriano's social media brand and (b) identify four new strategies (e.g., influencer, inclusive, message, and content) that will be implemented for this campaign with at least two tactics for each strategy.

REFERENCES

Facebook. (2019). *Facebook mission and vision statement analysis*. https://mission-statement.com/facebook/

Hootsuite. (2018). *About us*. http://hootsuite.com/about

Owyang, J. (2010, November 9). *Research: Most companies organize in "hub and spoke" formation for social business*. http://www.web-strategist.com/blog/2010/11/09/research-most-companies-organize-in-hub-and-spoke-formation/

Starbucks. (2018). *Our mission*. https://www.starbucks.com/about-us/company-information/mission-statement

Under Armour (2018). *Our mission*. http://www.uabiz.com/company/mission.cfm

8

INFLUENCER MARKETING

Learning Objectives

After reading this chapter, you will be able to

- Define influencer marketing
- Identify different types of influencers in social media
- Understand the steps of creating and launching an influencer campaign
- Evaluate best practices of influencer marketing

INTRODUCTION

Influencer marketing is big business, and it is only going to become bigger and more expensive for brands to participate in. According to *Bloomberg Businessweek*, brands will be expected to spend as much as $15 billion annually on influencer marketing by 2022, up from $8 billion in 2019 (Ong, 2020). This is a shift for traditional brands and others from having large media budgets for advertising and marketing and now investing it in influencer marketing. Why the shift in this investment for brands? Influencers are those who have the ability and power to motivate individuals to take some sort of action. Influencers have become an essential part of a successful social media campaign. However, not all influencers are created equal, and each has unique characteristics that distinguish one from another. To be effective, influencers practice proper etiquette and business practices, undergo media training, and follow proactive sustainable relationship management practices.

Social media professionals have engaged in discussions related to influencers over the years, examining how they are viewed as authorities in regard to views, posts, and prestige in the industry. Influencers are the ones who are able to get deals with large global brands, exclusive experiences, and opportunities to showcase their "picture-perfect" life on and offline. While these are all perks of the job, everyone can develop their overall influence. Public relations professional, social media strategist, and best-selling author Jason Falls discusses this in his work, noting how we need to focus on influence, rather than influencers. This chapter will discuss the characteristics of influencers, their role as part of a social media campaign, the pros and cons of influencer marketing, and the best practices to be noted when incorporating influencer marketing in a campaign.

HUMANS OF SOCIAL MEDIA

Adrian Molina, Senior Brand Manager for Aviation Gin

Introduction

I'm the senior brand manager for Aviation Gin, which is kind of an all-encompassing role in leading full strategy and execution for all the brand's marketing and sales efforts. Got the plane tattooed on me for job security. Ultimately a boy from the Bronx, who has always had a passion for marketing and just wants to make his mother proud.

How did you get your start in social media?

Unprofessionally, I would say wayyyy back in the days when you needed an ".edu" email address to sign up for Facebook. As the platform was still nascent, I leveraged the emerging add-ons like Events to promote fraternity parties as well as DJ gigs. Jello wrestling somehow worked. Professionally, I had a brief stint doing business development for a social media agency, which helped me shape strategy, content calendars, tone of voice, etc., on non-jello wrestling promotional things.

What is your favorite part of working in your area of expertise in social media?

It's interesting because social media is not technically my focal point heading up all marketing for the brand, but I see it as a release where I can listen to consumer feedback that would impact some sales and also engage in real time. The community Aviation has is beyond some of the most creative and passionate in the spirits industry. Very good pick-me-up if I am having a bad day.

What is one thing you can't live without while working in social media?

TweetDeck . . . hands down. I have a 20-column TweetDeck full of Boolean searches for every type of phrase that may relate to the brand. With that I can surprise and delight someone who may be wondering "what goes good with Aviator Gin?" versus direct mentions. Customer service at its finest and I wish I had that power in the real world.

What is your favorite social media account (person/brand/etc.) to follow and why?

Definitely @DesusNice. He's half of my fave podcast and late night show (Bodega Boys/Desus & Mero on Showtime) as well as a fellow Bronx Native. So A LOT of his hot takes hit me in both humor and nostalgia while also being relevant to current pop culture.

WHAT IS INFLUENCER MARKETING?

Influencers come in many different forms. Is an influencer a beauty blogger who posts their outfit of the day (OOTD) for their community on Instagram? Or a dancer who is taking to TikTok to create a viral challenge for everyone to join? Is it a social media strategist tweeting insights and takeaways about the industry? What about the teenager or kid who posts reviews on YouTube about favorite products, discussing why they do or do not like certain products? Perhaps an influencer is a marketing professional who gets on the stage to discuss a topic for which they are known, such as personal branding, live video, or Facebook marketing?

All of these individuals share common characteristics, but they differ in terms of specialization and focus. Some individuals have a substantial audience, while others are just getting started.

To influence is to have the capacity to affect something to create a memorable and sustainable impact on another person or community. An **influencer** is someone who has built an audience, naturally and over time, and who is viewed as an authority on a certain subject, practice, or perspective in online spaces. In addition, because an influencer has the trust of a community, that person can share content that persuades their audience to take a specific action. Research has explored influencers in several ways based on their personality characteristics (Freberg, Graham, McGaughey, & Freberg, 2011), professional attributes and contributions (Enke & Borchers, 2019), community engagement (Himelboim & Golan, 2019; Smith, Stumberger, Guild, & Dugan, 2017), trust (Lou & Yuan, 2019), and the role of paid media in formulating partnerships (Luoma-aho, Pirttimäki, Maity, Munnukka, & Reinikainen, 2019).

The practice of **influencer marketing** engages influencers in partnerships with aligned brands, organizations, and agencies. This approach is a growing area within the social media space. Many influencers hire various talent agencies, consultants, and teams to help them navigate the dynamics of influencer marketing. This field has evolved tremendously over the past few decades. However, influencer marketing gets confused with influence marketing, as social media strategist and author Jason Falls discusses in his podcast and book *Winfluence*. Influencer

Table 8.1 Influencer Marketing Versus Influence Marketing	
Influencer Marketing	**Influence Marketing**
• Focus on the influencer(s) involved • Influencers are used as a tactic to promote word-of-mouth communications and brand awareness • Content shared exclusively online with influencers	• Focused on the action(s) involved • Influencers are focused based on the situation involved • Content can be online but also offline with influencers

Source: Jason Falls, https://jasonfalls.com/influencer-marketing/

marketing focuses on one or more individuals to be used as a tactic to accomplish brand awareness and word-of-mouth communications on respective social media platforms, whereas **influence marketing** focuses on the action itself (influence) in persuading audiences to take action based on the relationships they have formed (Falls, n.d.). These two concepts get somewhat confusing since they are very similar, but they do have distinct differences, as highlighted in Table 8.1.

Influencers differ from opinion leaders or third-party endorsers (individuals who are not affiliated with the brand, but are part of the external audience group) in a few ways. Influencers bring their experiences, unique perspectives, and brand voices to the table, which makes it difficult to categorize them. Some influencers enjoy a strong standing based on their role and profession (e.g., sports figures, pop stars, media professionals), but for the most part, influencers are regular people with a specific interest and passion, as well as the dedication to create a name for themselves within their industry and community.

Creators can be influencers, but not all influencers are creators by trade. As far as platforms go, creators usually tend to lean toward video content, which makes YouTube as one of their top choices. Influencers today are more likely to be found on Instagram than other places, but many are gravitating to other platforms for more exposure and brand opportunities, like the Chinese based platform TikTok or video content creation platforms like YouTube. Creators focus more on what they create for their audiences to experience, enjoy consuming, and share with others, whereas influencers focus more on community building and designating themselves as an expert in a certain area, industry, or passion point. Most influencers use more than one designated platform to house their content and engage with their audiences.

Most influencers also have

- a viewpoint or perspective on social media;
- a brand voice that is consistent, unique, and memorable;
- a strong, loyal, and committed community on one or more platforms;
- a website;
- a blog;
- an engaged community;
- set brand pillars, guidelines, and expectations for payment (in the form of experiences to financial partnerships);
- social media presence (e.g., on Facebook, Twitter, Instagram, YouTube, LinkedIn, and other channels) through which they cultivate their audiences;

- an email marketing newsletter;

- a show, such as a live or recorded broadcast, a podcast, etc.;

- a YouTube channel for vlogs, tutorials, and daily videos;

- a specific platform following (e.g., TikTok, IG, YouTube); and

- a media kit (identifying key features and background pieces of their brand, previous partnerships, metrics from social and digital sites, press and publications, etc.).

Along with these tactical characteristics, influencers share some personality characteristics. The first is authenticity. *Authenticity* is a key characteristic influencers need to embrace as well as showcase on their various platforms (Charlton & Cornwell, 2019). Influencers have to be true to who they are as a brand but also be strategic regarding the brands and partnerships with whom they engage (Luoma-aho et al., 2019). If audiences view a partnership with an influencer to be true to their overall brand, the influencer will be viewed as more trustworthy and authentic to their own brand, but if the partnership is not aligned, this raises authentic and trust issues for the influencer (Luoma-aho et al., 2019). *Expertise* is another characteristic that needs to be noted. Influencers need to have expertise in some area, specialization, or focus (Zhao, Zhan, & Liu, 2018). A social media influencer is able to build upon a community that is based not only on similar interests but also a presence in establishing a voice of authority on the subject.

Expertise can come in different formats, such as the industry in which the person is working (e.g., public relations, marketing, journalism, etc.), or their craft (e.g., athletics, acting, music, etc.), or if they have a passion for a product and are invested in learning the ins and outs. For example, as discussed in Chapter 3, Dwayne "The Rock" Johnson is not only a former athlete and current Hollywood star, but he is an avid fan of tequila. He created his own brand called Teremana Tequila after spending years learning the ins and outs of how to make, market, and sell tequila. Since the launch, The Rock has been creating a community of avid tequila enthusiasts who share their first experiences with Teremana on social media, creating quite the cult following and brand awareness for both Teremana and The Rock.

Along with authenticity and expertise, *engagement* is another key characteristic influencers need to have. Engagement relates to the interactivity between the influencer and the community of which they are a part, or between the influencer and a client. Passing along advice, insights, reviews, endorsements, recommendations, and perspectives through word-of-mouth communications is a powerful way to foster strong engagement with audiences (Jiménez-Castillo & Sánchez-Fernández, 2019).

The last characteristic is *passion*. All influencers in some capacity have a passion for what they are doing or for the industry in which they work. You have to love what you do to sustain these efforts for the long term and to be able to share these perspectives openly for the audiences to grasp, listen to, and act upon. If you are not passionate about what you are doing, it will immediately come across to your audiences. Charli D'Amelio, who came to influencer fame for her dancing on TikTok and has over 100 million followers on the platform, always had a Dunkin drink (which was a Dunkin' Cold Brew with three pumps of caramel and whole milk). As a result of listening and monitoring this on social, Dunkin' decided to create and officially launch "The Charli" drink on their menu for one day, which resulted in a 57% jump in downloads in the Dunkin' mobile app and 20% daily increase in sales (Weiss, 2020).

There are many reasons why influencers resonate with audience groups, and why more brands are gravitating to working with them more often than celebrities or other paid spokespeople. Figure 8.1 is from a research that was conducted to determine what are the factors that motivate consumers and other audiences to follow and listen to influencers. As shown in the figure, one of the top reasons that they follow influencers is based on personal experience, meaning if an influencer has the opportunity to engage, interact, and have a conversation with someone, this person may be more likely to follow and stay loyal to this influencer. The figure presents research that shows the power of word of mouth communication is more effective than messages that are come from the brand directly. Based on Figure 8.1, people feel influencers are relatable, trustworthy, and, in some cases, friends they have known and viewed as an authority for years. This level of trust, authenticity, and relatability is extremely valuable for influencers to manage, sustain, and protect at all cost. Why is this the case? Because it takes only one incident to damage your reputation with your audiences after years of building a brand, community, and presence in the industry.

Types of Influencers

Not all influencers are created equally, and each has unique characteristics, demands, personality attributes, creative expectations, and attributes that make them a key audience for brands and others to evaluate. By understanding the

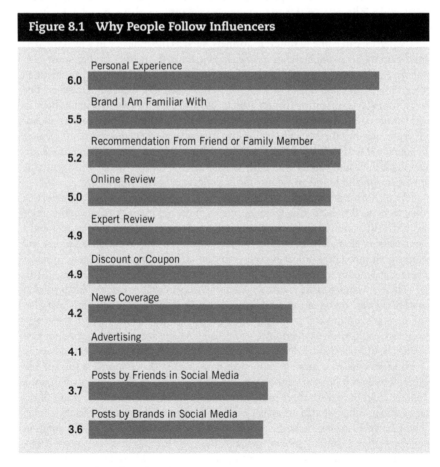

Figure 8.1   Why People Follow Influencers

Personal Experience	
6.0	
Brand I Am Familiar With	
5.5	
Recommendation From Friend or Family Member	
5.2	
Online Review	
5.0	
Expert Review	
4.9	
Discount or Coupon	
4.9	
News Coverage	
4.2	
Advertising	
4.1	
Posts by Friends in Social Media	
3.7	
Posts by Brands in Social Media	
3.6	

Source: Baer, J. and Lemin, D. (2018) CHATTER MATTERS: THE 2018 WORD OF MOUTH REPORT. Convince & Convert. Retrieved from https://www.kmosek.com/wp-content/uploads/chatter-matters-research-fall2018.pdf

nature of each of these audiences, brands and agencies are more effective in auditing, researching, and categorizing their influencers. There are several types of influencers (see Table 8.2), so let's begin with discussing the celebrity influencers.

Celebrity influencers hold a prominent status that allows them to influence others. Celebrities such as Ryan Reynolds, Reese Witherspoon, Prince Harry and Meghan Markle, Leslie Jones, and Cristiano Ronaldo are all examples of prominent celebrity influencers who have their own online spaces and channels. While each of these individuals has a strong online presence and voice in their respective industries, they may not be as credible in campaigns that are not directly related to their brands. In addition, the cost of having a celebrity influencer post or comment online, or be part of a campaign, is very high.

Mega influencers are influencers with a prominent status on social media and a broad appeal that puts them on track to reach celebrity status. These individuals shape culture and industries and make a direct impact on their communities by driving sales of products and services. These influencers may not be celebrities in the Hollywood sense, but they are prominent in their respective industries.

Micro influencers have smaller audiences than the celebrity or mega influencers and are the source of considerable contemporary buzz. These influencers have generated significant attention over the past few years because of their ability to cultivate strong communities around particular interests ("Influencer Tiers for the Influencer Marketing Industry," n.d.). They also have strong engagement rates, which is a key metric that we and our brands may look for instead of high follower counts. Some risks are associated with working with micro influencers, however. For example, they may lack brand awareness, media training, and preparation. They also have less reach than celebrity or mega influencers. However, the many benefits include higher engagement rates, lower commission costs compared to celebrities, and access to focused and niche communities. Matthew Kobach, social media strategist for Fast, would be considered to be a micro influencer in the social media space due to his growing following on Twitter and Instagram for providing valuable strategic tidbits for those in the industry.

Nano influencers, influencers with the fewest followers, have audiences even smaller than those of micro influencers. This category was first introduced in a 2018 *New York Times* article titled, "Are You Ready for the Nanoinfluencers?" (Maheshwari, 2018). As discussed in the article, nano influencers' "lack of fame is one of the qualities that make them approachable. When they recommend a shampoo or a lotion or a furniture brand on Instagram, their word seems as genuine as advice from a friend. Brands enjoy working with them partly because they are easy to deal with. In exchange for free products or a small commission, nanos typically say whatever companies tell them to" (Maheshwari, 2018). While nano influencers can be effective, one challenge is that audiences may see them as inauthentic and not a part of their community. If a community feels a nano influencer is being "bought" or has allowed a brand to take over their account for a campaign, they may not trust the influencer again.

Creators are new type of audience and a subset of influencers who create original content in their own voices for brands. They don't simply share brand-created content. Rather, they view their creativity as the most important part of their contribution to a brand. Creators want to tell a story, experiment in programming, and allow themselves to authentically integrate with a brand through the content they write. Creators and influencers are similar in many ways, but they differ in approaches and characteristics. A creator focuses more on creating and producing content for a specific platform, such as YouTube, to be shared to the masses, whereas an influencer focuses on a specific area of expertise, such as fashion or local food, across various platforms (Hakim, 2015). An example of a creator would be Roberto Blake, a YouTuber who focuses on creating videos and content tutorials based on his expertise in video content creation. Many influencers also claim to be creators because they produce videos, images, or other content that can be consumed on blogs and other online locations. What brands and organizations have to be aware of when it comes to creators is that they may be so focused on staying only to their true vision that they are not willing to compromise to create a win-win situation on the campaign. It is important to work with the creator to make sure they are comfortable with the look, feel, and perspective the campaign they are partnering with is taking, but it cannot be 100% them. It has to be a balanced partnership, and this is a challenge to be aware of when working with creators.

Memers and creators are individuals who create memes, which are pieces of content that communicate an idea, style, or behavior for a specific purpose within a particular culture, mainstream or subculture. Memes range across a variety of different types, formats, and sharing capabilities. Memes are usually humorous in nature, and they can spread virally if they capture an audience in a certain way ("10 of the Best Instagram Meme Accounts to Check Out in 2020," n.d.). Another popular meme account is Comments by Celebs (an account that curates comments of social media posts by celebs; see Photo 8.1). Sometimes, making an account that taps into popular culture, especially in the form of memes, is a way to gain traction and presence as an influencer in the industry. Comments by Celebs aggregates popular comments celebs have made on other social media accounts, which sparks both humor and entertainment for audiences. Other popular meme accounts include Captain Andrew Luck (parody account of football player Andrew Luck as if he were a soldier in the Civil War on Twitter) and Thoughts of a Dog (random thoughts of a dog that are shared on social media).

More popular memes we have seen circulated online include the laughing Michael Jordan iPad image from the documentary *The Last Dance*, Baby Yoda sipping tea, Oprah's reactions during the Prince Harry and Meghan Markle interview, and the classic Grumpy Cat (RIP).

▸ **Photo 8.1**
Comments by Celebs Instagram Page

Source: Retrieved from https://www.instagram.com/commentsbycelebs/?hl=en)

Some accounts have fallen into disrepute due to their history and reputation for taking other people's work and claiming it as their own on their respective channels (such as "f*ckjerry," which is owned by Jerry Media). Many of these accounts are paid a lot of money to post memes as a form of advertisement. For example, Ben, a teenager who goes by the username "spicymp4," was earning $4,000 or more per month by reposting memes on his Facebook and Instagram accounts. Many memers have faced challenges as a result of their postings; for example, Facebook and Instagram have sued for copyright infringement (Wellemeyer, 2019). However, 2020 presidential candidate Michael Bloomberg recruited memers to generate some interest and engagement with Generation Z audiences during his campaign, which sparked a lot of discussion related to the use of memes as political advertising, and whether or not this content would be banned by social media platforms (Lorenz, 2020b). Many memes were taken down by the platforms due to their perception of being used for political advertisements, which goes against some of the platforms' terms of use policies.

Kid influencers are one of the more popular groups of individuals hitting the social media space. Children and youth ranging from being a few years old to teenagers, have been making waves for their content on their social media platforms, particularly on YouTube. Some kid influencers are making millions of dollars a year on platforms like YouTube (Sherman, 2020). Ryan, of the YouTube channel show *Ryan's Playdate*, is the highest money maker among kid influencers, having made $26 million in 2019 with 24 million subscribers (Chmielewski, 2020).

YouTube has been the designated place for many kid influencers because of the amount of video content that is being consumed by children and youth today. In fact, the Pew Research Center reported that content featuring children gained more views on YouTube than any other content (Van Kessel, Toor, & Smith, 2019). Many of these influencers are managed either by their parents (who have control over how their image and presence appears on social media) or by an agency if they are at the point where they are gathering thousands of followers. Parents or agencies also oversee any brand partnerships, negotiations, and potential collaborations between the kid influencer and brands. These efforts can lead to more traditional brand partnerships, like merchandise, like Ryan has been able to do. Ryan has a line of clothing and products that are being sold at Target, Walmart, and other retailers (Berg, 2019).

However, the Federal Trade Commission (n.d.) has evoked the Children's Online Privacy Protection Rule (COPPA): "COPPA imposes certain requirements on operators of websites or online services directed to children under 13 years of age, and on operators of other websites or online services that have actual knowledge that they are collecting personal information online from a child under 13 years of age." This is an ongoing issue for kid influencers and their teams to address.

Lastly, there are influencers who are not even real who are making millions of dollars for endorsements. **Virtual influencers** are defined as "virtual influencers or CGI influencers as they can also be called, are *fictional computer generated 'people' who have the realistic characteristics, features and personalities of humans*" (Mosley, 2021, para. 4). These influencers are the fastest growing group of influencers (particularly on YouTube) and have an entire team of creators and brand managers behind the scenes who are part of advocating and building a strategic plan behind their virtual influencer, implementing the same process and procedures as if they were working with a human influencer (Ong, 2020). Some of the best known virtual influencers include Lil Miquela (1.6 million followers), Shudu (185,000 followers), and Seraphine (400,000). Lil Miquela has worked with brands such as Samsung and Calvin Klein, whereas Shudu has partnered on influencer campaigns for Fenty Beauty (Mosley, 2021). Seraphine was made into a playable character in the game League of Legends as part of an influencer collaboration campaign.

There are some benefits to utilizing virtual influencers, as Christopher Travers, founder of VirtualHumans.org was quoted in *Bloomberg Businessweek*: "Virtual influencers, while fake, have real business potential/ They are cheaper to work with than humans in the long term, are 100% controllable, can appear in many places at once, and, most importantly, they never age or die" (Ong, 2020).

Partnering With Influencers

Social media platforms have empowered influencers by giving them a way to foster a community, formulate a brand voice, and connect audiences with similar interests online. As an individual's community and brand voice grows, so does this individual's influence. To capitalize on this influence, influencer marketing has become a huge industry for marketing, public relations, and advertising professionals. In fact, according to a research report by *Influencer Hub*, there were 320 new influencer specific platforms that were created in the first part of 2019 alone that focus on this particular area in the social media industry ("The State of Influencer Marketing 2019," 2019).

Brands should consider a number of factors before embarking on a collaboration with influencers.

Understand the guidelines set by the Federal Trade Commission (FTC). As they say, when platforms and brands go from one community to another, the government is usually right there behind them. This is certainly true for the FTC when it comes to influencer marketing. Thanks to the vast array of cases that involve influencers who did not disclose that they were compensated for their work (e.g., Kim Kardashian, DJ Khaled, to name a couple), the FTC provided a list of guidelines for influencers to follow, such disclosing compensation from a brand, not misleading audiences, and not promoting products that are not appropriate for certain audiences. Transparency and authenticity of influencers should also be assessed carefully. Fake bots, fake amplification techniques, and other unethical and misleading practices will be easier to detect due to improved tools available to identify influencers who using such practices. Professionals have obtained more education and boosted their awareness of these issues in the industry and community.

Highlights of the FTC guidelines that are required for influencers to follow include the following (Federal Trade Commission, 2019):

- Disclose when you have any financial, employment, personal, or family relationship with a brand.

- Place the endorsement where it is hard to miss. Endorsements need to be placed on the picture or image (if shared on Instagram or Snapchat) or in the video (if the video is being endorsed).

- If the endorsement is in a live steam, the disclosure needs to be shared repeatedly throughout the stream so all audiences hear the disclosure.

- Use simple and clear language in your endorsement, along with including hashtags #ad and #sponsored in the posts and content;

- The disclosure should be in the same language as the endorsement itself.

- Do not rely only on the platform disclosure tool (e.g., paid by brand on Facebook or Instagram). Make sure to provide your own update for the disclosure to be safe.

Table 8.2 Types of Influencers

Celebrity	Mega	Micro	Nano	Memers	Kid	Virtual
• Have more than 10 million followers • Prominent in the industry • Huge reach and exposure • Trained and prepared to work with media and brands • Expensive and may not be perceived as being as credible due to payment	• Have 1–9 million followers • Specialized presence and leadership in specific industries • Effective for sponsored content • Experience working with brands and media • Somewhat expensive	• Have 10,000–50,000 followers • Highly engaged and cultivate strong community with accounts • Ability to tap into more niche and focused communities • There is a lot of benefit	• Have up to 10,000 followers • Lack of fame makes them approachable • Easy to work with for brands • Exchange is usually a small commission or free product	• Accounts sharing content for humorous purposes • Ranges as far as numbers, but most popular are in the millions of followers • Paid for advertising and driving popularity of memes • Copyright infringement issues for content	• Accounts for kids (newborns to teenagers) • Create video content that is shared and consumed by other kids • Content is managed by parents, or an agency or team • Content ranges from thousands to millions, depending on the engagement metrics • YouTube is a popular channel for these influencers • COPPA is a challenge for these influencers to address	• Influencers who are not real • Fastest growing market, especially on YouTube • Operate and act like human influencers, while creating content and establishing partnerships • No worries of dying • Remaining questions related to these influencers and the rules they must follow (e.g., FTC)

Paid amplification and measurement will be the standard. As they say, social media has become a "pay to play" kind of environment, and the same goes with influencers. Budgets need to be adjusted to make sure their content (the pieces that are part of the campaign) is amplified to reach key target audiences, as well as to increase engagement with audiences for the brand and influencer (Waller, 2020). Traditional paid measurement metrics can be used to evaluate the impact of the influencers in the campaign as far as reach, engagement, sentiment, and coverage are concerned.

Relationships need to be for the long term, not just a one-off partnership. Influencers are not just a fad tactic to use to get a boost in sales or awareness in a key market. They are becoming a more powerful and meaningful media channel for brands, and this means having a stronger and long-term influencer strategy will be essential for brands (Waller, 2020). By investing in these relationships, you are able to build upon the work of the influencer over time, and they become a strong advocate and supporter of what you are trying to do. In addition, if you are partnering with a nano influencer early on, that person may evolve and become a celebrity influencer overnight. Having this partnership and long-term focus could help drive market insights, positive engagement, and direct sales based on the work that is being supported by the brand for the influencer. In addition, brands should recognize that influencers are people as well. They have bills to pay, and they rely on the income they are able to generate from their work and collaboration efforts with brands. Many have relied on these partnerships for their livelihood, and when it is taken away due to unforeseen circumstances (e.g., the coronavirus crisis that canceled many conferences, including SXSW in 2020), the outcomes can be devastating. By formalizing these partnerships in new ways, influencers will feel more invested and tied to the brands with whom they have a long-term relationship (Waller, 2020).

Vanity metrics are out, and verified metrics will be king. The days in which influencers can talk only about how many followers they have, or their overall reach, without any substantive and verified metrics to support these claims, are over. For far too long, the industry has relied too much on these vanity metrics that have created an illusion—or in some cases even fraud—for brands and their respective communities (Waller, 2020). Metrics, such as conversion rates and brand/audience uplift studies, have to be tied directly to business, communication, and social media objectives for a campaign, and should follow the same guidelines and expectations that other media outlets have to follow.

Balance is the winning combination. A brand can't force an influencer to create content in the brand's voice, and the influencers can't create content that is only in their personal voice. There has to be a balance between the two parties. This is where a planning and brainstorming meeting between the influencer and the brand is useful. This type of meeting can be a collaborative and co-creating opportunity where each party contributes equally to the conversation. If there is one party that is not in a balanced situation, then the content and overall partnership could suffer as a result. Balance is absolutely key in this setting; by collaborating and creating content together, new approaches, stories, content, and ideas can emerge to reach different audiences and touchpoints for the influencer and brand. This approach could help create a win-win situation.

Examples of Partnering With Influencers

There are many opportunities to utilize influencers for a brand partnership or campaign. Influencers can help brands in a variety of different ways using a range of tactics to help advocate for a brand, raise awareness of a new product or service, or support the brand because they are already acting as a customer or advocate.

Here are some examples of brands that have utilized influencers effectively:

Going live. One of the companies that has utilized influencers over the years for live video has been Adobe. Adobe, one of the largest technology companies, has their own internal and external influencer cohort of 60+ influencers called "Adobe Insiders." These individuals range from creative to marketing professionals, including Lee Odden, Ian Getler, David Armano, Mellissah Smith, Ross Quintana, and Cathy Hackl. These live video sessions are done either on site at a conference such as Adobe MAX or Adobe Summit, or virtually within a specific platform like LinkedIn Live.

Being a guest on a podcast. Influencers have to make sure they are gravitating to a vast array of media outlets, including podcasts, to talk about their experiences, to share what they are able to offer as far as brand partnerships, and to be visible on these shows for increased brand exposure. Influencers like Amy Landino not only host their own podcasts, but they are frequent guests on other podcasts, talking about their brand collaborations or, in some cases, promoting their own work (e.g., Landino's book *Good Morning, Good Life*).

Creating new content for audience consumption. Brands can come together with influencers to create new content to engage with their audiences in novel ways. The campaign called the Chewy Channel was not started by the pet food company (which could have been something amazing!) but was brought on by Haribo, the gummy candy company. The company wanted to create a new way to engage with their audiences (and products) online, so it created the first streaming network for the brand. Videos and shows feature the characters of their gummy candy for the world to see through micro-show content (Barkley & HARIBO, n.d.). Another case involves Kroger, a grocery store chain that is known for their deals and prices across the United States. Kroger partnered with a group of individual creators on TikTok to bring forth new ideas for how to promote their products among college students. In 2019, Kroger partnered with four Generation Z TikTok influencers to create a brand challenge for Kroger on how they could transform their living spaces with dorm products (Kroger & 360i, n.d.). Kroger wanted to make sure they (a) researched and partnered with the right creators, (b) had a specific campaign action for the influencers to use to encourage their audiences to go to a shoppable page on Kroger's website, and (c) helped bring forth awareness of the brand to Generation Z audiences (Kroger & 360i, n.d.).

Writing a post or creating guest blog content. Influencers not only create videos and other forms of content, but they can contribute to others to extend their brand and reach new audiences and communities. For example, Chris Strub has been a frequent contributor to *Forbes*, specifically for their Giving Day and nonprofit work.

Attending and creating content at VIP events. Money is not the only thing that is motivating audiences to create content. Sometimes the most effective currency for brands to use for influencers is experiences and exclusivity. One way to generate awareness and excitement about an event or experience is to invite influencers to be a part of it. Allowing them to share events with their community may be a good way to create not only exposure but also motivation to be part of this experience and engage with the brand. Influencers can also specifically collaborate with brands to create exclusive content that is co-branded for the event, making it a win-win situation for the brand. What this essentially means is that influencers are able to create content for their social media channels that is aligned with their own work and vision while also benefitting and aligning with what the brand is trying to achieve in engaging with new audiences in a different way. When done well, it creates a very successful partnership venture for both parties. Events

such as the Super Bowl, Coachella, Emmys and Oscars, Adobe Summit, SXSW, and others utilize influencers for these types of activations and partnerships.

Providing reviews for products. Some brands send out products and services to their loyal and engaged audiences to provide opportunities to share their experiences and create their own content. For example, Cinnabon launched a campaign focused on their engaged supporters on social media, which they refer to as #BonBesties, tying in the notion that these individuals are best friends of the Cinnabon brand. For Valentine's Day, Cinnabon mailed off packages of heart-shaped minibons to these individuals with a personalized note for each (Photo 8.2). As a result, these influ-

▶ **Photo 8.2**
Cinnabon and their Valentine's Day Surprise Package for #BonBesties

encers, including the author of this book, were happy to share their thoughts about the gift on their social media channels.

Talking to the media about the brand. This is one of the more popular ways in which brands utilize influencers with whom they partner. This approach works for a particular show (such as the video news network Cheddar and Brian Fanzo, representing Wix), or a set of influencers with a particular brand (Nasdaq Live with Adobe Insiders). Influencers can be a resource by sharing their experiences with the media and what they have seen while collaborating with a particular brand or agency.

Providing a giveaway or hosting a contest for their community to create surprising and delightful experiences for audiences. This is also a frequent use of influencers for brands. Influencers are given either coupons, free products, or exclusive items they can give away to their audiences through a contest. Their community would have to like a post, follow both the influencer and the brand, and tag audiences they would want to see win this contest. Of course, proper FTC guidelines for influencers have to be followed when it comes to contests and disclosing the fact that the influencers are getting compensated for their work.

This is where Electronic Arts came into play with their Need for Speed campaign, using vlogger and influencer David Dobrik as the one to be featured in this campaign ("Electronic Arts & BEN—'Need for Speed: Heat' x David Dobrik," n.d.). Electronic Arts wanted to get excitement going around their new game "Need for Speed," so they partnered with Dobrik to generate this. Dobrik is an avid car enthusiast, so this shows the need to do research into aligning with an influencer that works with the brand in a campaign. Dobrik created a video in which he asked his audiences to design a car using the new Heat Studio app. He spoke with 10 of the designers about their designs, and then he collaborated with Electronic Arts to surprise someone with a new Lamborghini Huracán. This was all captured in the video. As a result of this campaign and partnership, it generated 8.7 million views on YouTube ("Electronic Arts & BEN," n.d.).

Creating a video or visual element for a brand as part of the campaign. The producers and filmmakers of the James Bond movie *No Time to Die* recruited Grammy award–winning artist Billie Eilish to create and perform the theme song for the movie. Not only is Eilish a talented artist, but she is a powerful celebrity influencer in her own right with millions of followers on social media. This partnership was beneficial for both parties because the movie studio provided Eilish creative freedom and power to not only write the theme song but share it first on her channels.

Launching a new product or influencer program. This is one of the more common ways in which brands utilize influencers—either creating a new separate product and partnering with influencers on the launch, or creating an influencer program to integrate influencers as part of the team and community.

The NY Jets did this when they invited 40 influencers, including Ralph Macchio and Wu-Tang Clan, to attend the team's games during the 2019 season. This allowed the team to gather new perspectives and stories and to invite audiences with high following and presence to be part of the team experience (New York Jets, n.d.) In another similar example, Starbucks partnered with Bill Nye (from *Bill Nye the Science Guy*) to introduce their new Nitro Cold Brew drink to their audiences. Nye is a popular and memorable figure in society, and Starbucks was able to create content on social media with Nye (images, videos, Reddit, GIFs, etc.) to provide awareness of this partnership and gain interest in their new drink (Starbucks & Big Spaceship, n.d.). In the ad, Nye holds Starbuck's Nitro Cold Brew

▶ **Photo 8.3**
Bill Nye × Starbucks Nitro Campaign

Source: Retrieved from https://shortyawards .com/12th/whoa-nitro

as if surprised to see the product they created is so unique, and this is what Starbucks was trying to communicate with this collaboration (Photo 8.3). Connecting the scientific element of what makes a nitro cold brew a unique coffee drink with one of the leading science thought leaders is a winning combination for both Bill Nye and Starbucks. By aligning with a traditional (or in this case, celebrity) influencer (Nye) and tying him to the Nitro Cold Brew product, Starbucks created a successful partnership with Nye.

Successes and Failures Using Influencers

In spite of these many examples of how brands have successfully implemented influencer marketing, there are, of course, situations that do not work as well. One of the biggest challenges for influencer marketing is to overcome the negative associations tied to these failures and challenges. From the Fyre Festival to Caroline Calloway, many incidents have given social media professionals and brands motivation to hit the pause button for utilizing influencers.

- **Misrepresentation.** Caroline Calloway rose to fame on social media back in 2015. The incident that made her a household name in the influencer world for the wrong reasons happened in 2019. Calloway promoted her book (for which she lost the book contract eventually) and started creating momentum to promote her Creativity Workshops to cultivate a space where anyone could learn to become an influencer

("The Biggest Influencer Fails of 2019," 2019). However, her event was so poorly planned that the result was a lot of unhappy workshop customers. Calloway had to address concerns that the event and her work were a "scam," generating significant negative media coverage ("The Biggest Influencer Fails of 2019," 2019).

- **Being a target of the cancel culture.** "Being canceled" is a phrase that emerged to refer to the essential dismissal or cutting someone out of the media or high-level status of being perceived as influential. Many celebrities and influencers have fallen victim to being canceled, including YouTube beauty influencer James Charles, comedian Kathy Griffin, and Olivia Jade. Jade, a YouTuber and influencer as well, was part of the Operation Varsity Blues crisis that hit college campuses in 2019. Jade was impacted by news that her parents, Lori Loughlin and Mossimo Giannulli, paid the University of Southern California to get her admitted to the university. Jade has since left USC, but the scandal and being canceled still follow her brand both offline and online. David Dobrik, as mentioned earlier, also was involved in being cancelled after allegations emerged from this team in 2021, and as a result, several brands like Dispo and others separated themselves from Dobrik while others reviewed their relationship with him for the future.

- **Fake influencers, followers, and bots.** Unfortunately, it is very easy to create the "illusion" of being influential. Fake bots, likes, and artificial amplification of accounts are just some of the issues found among influencers. All of these elements are misleading and fraudulent. Essentially, you do not want to take this path because it is very, very easy to detect which individuals are real and which ones have tried to create a shortcut to fame and fortune with these unethical practices. You can identify false influencers at an initial, superficial level just by looking at their publicly available metrics. For example, if individuals have 100,000 followers on Twitter, why do they only have one or two likes or favorites on their tweets? In addition, you can always look at the followers and those who comment on their work on Instagram and YouTube. There are ways to identify the bots (automated programs that do certain actions) on each of these sites. Their profiles are usually all the same, have basic information, and often comment "Like this!" or make another generic request. Another ethical issue impacting influencers is the practice of "buying" followers. This is a no-no for social media professionals, because it is easy to detect the fake profiles and who has and who has not bought an audience. False influencers also focus on the refollow–unfollow technique. The follow-to-follower ratio is constantly debated in the area of influencers and social media professionals. Some are more likely to follow their engaged audiences, but others will follow a large number of people, see who follows them back, and then immediately unfollow these same people. This helps create the illusion they have a large audience, but in reality, it upsets people when they are viewed only as a follower number to boost false influencers' ego with the size of their community. This practice is indeed looked down upon.

- **Tapping into current trends for self-gain without understanding context.** Influencers will sometimes do whatever it takes to get likes, views, and a moment in the sun for their actions, even in a time of crisis. The coronavirus (COVID-19) spread around the world in 2020, significantly impacting the way individuals do business, conduct classes, and operate in society. Specifically, this pandemic has impacted the influencer community who rely on speaking opportunities, conducting face-to-face workshops, and engaging with audiences in person. However, this has not deterred influencers from taking full advantage of the situation with their presence on their social media channels. Some influencers have taken pictures of themselves with protective masks as a way to "stay on trend." However, there are other cases in which influencers have tried to rebrand themselves as being "remote from home work experts" in their content and framing their brand around this subject area. Both examples are misleading, unethical, and not appropriate based on the context and severity of the situation. Two German influencers decided to jump on the COVID-19 mask bandwagon early in 2020 to show they were able to still enjoy social connections and travel at the same time. A post by @fitnessoskar sparked a lot of backlash since many felt the influencers were not taking COVID-19 seriously but glorifying the serious situation; the influencers were also perceived as not practicing proper social distancing measures (Photo 8.4).

▸ **Photo 8.4**
Coronavirus
Influencer Picture

Source: Instagram/
@fitnessoskar

- **Embracing the controversial angle, by any means necessary.** "Any publicity is good publicity" is a saying that has been mentioned over the years in marketing and public relations. While some say this is not true, others disagree. In fact, there are some influencers who want to be controversial because they know controversy attracts attention and makes sales. When it comes to social media, if you were to look at controversial influencers on Wikipedia, you would see Jake Paul listed. Jake Paul, a former Disney star turned YouTuber, is extremely controversial in his content and approaches online and was thrown into the spotlight when it was shown he was present during a mall looting incident in Arizona at the height of the racial injustice protests in 2020. Paul was charged with a misdemeanor for trespassing at the mall (Lorenz, 2020a), and many have acknowledged these antics by Paul as reasons to stop following or paying attention to his content (Koul, 2020). Even with attempts to "cancel" Paul, Paul continues to thrive: "He [Paul] is prolific, and despite being uninteresting, he has a rabid fandom. He could do something meaningful with his massive platform, but no. Instead, like clockwork, every few months, he does something that gets him in trouble, and he revels in it. Because to Paul, attention— good or bad— is all the currency he wants" (Koul, 2020, para. 6). At some point, there will be a point where being controversial goes too far, even by Jake Paul standards, and you not only get canceled, but you will face more significant consequences.

Steps in Creating and Launching an Influencer Campaign

There is more to creating and executing an influencer campaign than just getting influencers together and creating a campaign with them. Influencer campaigns involve planning, strategy, research, and creativity. It is important to identify the various steps that are needed to identify influencers, research their background, determine if their communities match your intended audiences, and see if there is an opportunity to co-create in a campaign. This section will identify the necessary steps that need to be taken into consideration when executing a successful influencer campaign.

Determine if influencers are needed in the campaign. Some brands want to use influencers because "everyone is using them." You do not want to use influencers just because it is a popular way to engage audiences. The team should identify a genuine need to utilize these individuals. If there is a need, a plan should be established to see if there is an opportunity to incorporate an influencer, or a group of them, in a campaign. In addition, determining if there is a budget for influencer marketing should be at the forefront of discussions and agreed conditions for a brand. If there is no budget for influencer marketing, then the conversation should be closed.

Identify influencers. Once there is an agreed upon plan to use influencers for a campaign, then a strategy needs to be set to identify influencers who would be relevant. There are many ways to identify appropriate influencers, including using influencer identification tools. Choices of a tool are influenced by budget. Brands and agencies should be aware that some tools and methods are free, but for the most part, influencer identification tools cost money, which requires a substantial budget. Table 8.3 outlines a number of free and paid methods for identifying appropriate influencers.

Evaluate evidence of influencer's community, account, and impact. Once you have identified the possible influencers to include in your social media campaign, you should next evaluate their work and evidence they have created, along with other elements. Several questions need to be addressed in order to determine the basic insights of the influencers, such as the type of influencer (based on size

Table 8.3	
Free Influencer Identification Tools	**Paid Influencer Identification Tools**
• Google (keywords search terms, blog searches, new searches, etc.) • Instagram hashtags • Blogs • Top ten lists • Twitter chats • Upinfluence • HypeAuditor	• Media monitoring (Meltwater) • Influencer-specific analytics programs (e.g., Traackr, Klear) • Social listening tools (Talkwalker, BuzzSumo)

Source: Hellenkemper, M. (2017, September 22). The 9 Steps of Your Influencer Marketing Process. *InfluencerDB.* https://influencerdb.com/blog/9-steps-influencer-marketing-process/

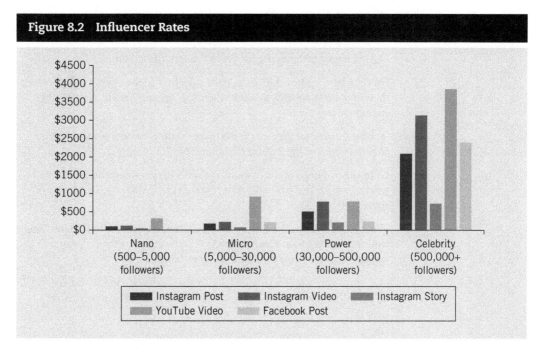

Figure 8.2   Influencer Rates

Source: Klear (2019) The Price of Influencer Marketing 2019. *Klear.* Retrieved from https://klear.com/KlearRateCard.pdf

of following and presence in the industry), their content and brand voice, and how the influencer might relate to the brand in question.

Other questions focus on the legitimacy of the influencer, for example, determining whether the influencer has a media kit. A **media kit**, a traditional form used in most public relations and marketing efforts, is a collection of material that provides a person's background to the media. In most influencer media kits, expect to find a bio, fact sheet (one-page overview of the influencer), list of platforms and their established metrics (e.g., website views, followers, engagement rate, etc.), list of partnered collaborations, metrics and key performance indicators (KPIs, which will be explained in more detail in Chapter 13) from the partnered collaborations, and **rate card** (a rate card focuses on the payment the influencer expects). Rate cards range from a campaign as a whole (mid-level commitment), a retainer (long-term campaign initiative that can last months or even years), or specific post requirements. Klear did a survey in 2019 about the cost for a specific post of content for influencers and shared their rates and findings in Image (Figure 8.2).

An influencer media kit is usually shared to interested parties via email or posted on the influencer's website.

Listed below are some questions that need to be discussed when evaluating and auditing an influencer for a social media campaign:

- Who is following the influencer? Are they following other influencers and brands?

- What is the influencer's overall brand? What is their brand voice? What values, interests, and areas of passion have they shared?

- How authentic are they perceived to be? Are they consistent across platforms?

- How are they as far as a brand fit? Do their values and interests align with your work and community?

- How engaged is their community? What are their metrics?

- Do they have a media kit? If so, what evidence do they have to showcase their metrics and previous work? Do these metrics match up with other analytics data?

- Is the influencer engaged with his or her audiences, and what are the characteristics of the audience community?

- Does the audience of the influencer align with your audience? How will you determine this based on your research using audience segmentation strategies?

- What is the influencer's history? Is the influencer professional? How long has he or she been on social media? Which brands has the influencer worked with previously on campaigns and initiatives?

- Can you afford the influencer? Is he or she a celebrity influencer or a micro influencer (an individual who is highly focused on a particular issue or area)?

- What are your overall goals? Is this partnership just an add-on, or will the partnership help achieve the KPIs you have set forth in your campaign?

Establish a relationship with the influencer. Once you figure out which influencers fit your criteria, you want to reach out to them to start the conversation. This can be done via email or directly within an influencer identification tool like Klear. You want to establish a win-win relationship with the influencer. Consider the alignment with brand values, discuss research on influencer's work and how it fits with brand's overall mission, and communicate how this could be a great collaboration for all parties. This is the time as well to discuss key expectations, rights to content, and other negotiables. Contracts between parties within the influencer marketing space are essential. These are usually done with the help of the legal team for the brand to make sure that all items are clear and legal for both parties. Items commonly included in a contract with an influencer include the following:

- **Guidelines and responsibilities for both parties.** Roles and communication practices are identified. Expectations for each party in the campaign should be clear. Guidelines for proper conduct, behavior, and communication between parties and other traditional items that are part of normal business transactions should be listed as well. A clear beginning and end date should be established.

- **Ownership of the creative rights.** An outline of who owns the rights of the work (the client or the influencer) for the campaign is required. Specify whether the influencer will be first publishing their content on their channels, and then if it is okay for the brand to repost and tag the influencer. These details need to be very clearly outlined in the contract to avoid any confusion between the parties.

- **Acknowledgement of FTC influencer guidelines.** As stated earlier, following the FTC guidelines will help prevent any issues pertaining to the influencer content, there needs to be a clear statement on the compensation which the influencer is receiving (e.g.,. free products, financial compensation, travel and access, etc.). Having an acknowledgment of these guidelines in the contract can protect both parties in case something adverse happens.

- **Creative control**. Creative control is the number one concern most influencers have when working with brands (Chaplin, 2020). This decision can determine whether or not a campaign is successful. Influencers and creators especially do not like being forced to promote something that is not directly theirs. If they have a hand in creating the content and story, that's awesome. Putting it completely into their hands is ideal, but of course, this may not always happen or be feasible for the brand or agency in campaigns. Yet, having the conversation and starting out with the fact that this is a team effort will make things go more smoothly for both parties. This has been a key best practice for YouTuber David Dobrik when it comes to brand partnerships, helping him and the brands he has worked with succeed in a number of influencer campaigns (Monllos, 2020).

- **Steps taken if agreement or deliverables are not followed.** Contracts should identify the steps to be taken if the deliverables, which are part of the contract, are not fulfilled. This protects the brand in cases in which the influencer does not follow through with the agreed upon pieces of content, actions, appearances, or other strategies that are part of the campaign. Deadlines, a list of communication channels that will be used to communicate the termination of the agreement if it comes to this point, and ramifications of the partnership are just some of the items to be included in the contract.

- **Payment of deliverables**. Compensation does not always have to be financial. In many cases, creators and influencers want experience. They create content, share their stories, and connect with their own audiences, which can then further their reach and influence factor. In addition, having the power to state they are partnering with a well-recognized entity, brand, or event can help creators and influencers in their own quest for more prominence in their respective communities. The multiple ways by which influencers can be paid for their participation will be discussed in the next section of this chapter.

- **Deliverables**. The contract includes the responsibilities, pieces of content that will be created, and other actions that the influencer agrees upon contributing for the duration of the campaign. Ideally, these items should be negotiated and discussed with the influencer prior to finalizing a contract so there is a content collaboration that reflects content that comes naturally to the influencer and is beneficial for the brand. Other details include the quantity of pieces of content to be created and when they will be launched, campaign deadlines, which assets can and should be used for the campaign, specific elements that need to be used for each piece of content to be created and executed (e.g., hashtags, campaign specific tracking website URLs, tagged accounts, etc.), and a list of attributes to use in the overall tone and presentation of the materials.

- **Wish list items**. In some cases, the brand may provide a wish list of items that serve as "recommendations or added bonuses" for the influencer to consider as he or she works on this campaign. A wish list also depends on the type of influencer involved. Most likely, celebrity influencers are not going to be doing anything else other than what is agreed upon in the deliverables, but nano influencers may appreciate the list of wish list items as inspiration for generating additional ideas for creating content and engaging with the brand during the span of the campaign.

Solidify an influencer brief and monitoring board. A brief is a one-page overview of the core elements that need to be considered in terms of the campaign, and what the influencer and brand will co-create. The brief outlines the expectations that are agreed upon in the campaign and for the contract. The brief should contain the following elements:

- Overview of the overall campaign (what this campaign is all about, the goals of the brand, and why these influencers were chosen for this campaign).

- Key metrics that will be viewed as a success in the partnership (e.g., number of new customers, traffic to website, shares and engagement, increase in sales). Outlining the key goals of this campaign with an influencer will be critical.

- Campaign deadlines and timeline to follow (when everything is due, editing and comments back to the influencer, final deliverables).

- Quantity of pieces of content (types of content to be created, where they will be posted, how they will be shared, copy that will go along with the visual elements). These need to be detailed and very clear. For example, influencers need to know not only if they have to create a blog post but if it has to be a 1,000- to 1,500-word blog post and how many images, videos, and pieces of social media content on each social media platform need to be created. Attention to the specifics (numbers, format, etc.) should be listed here.

- Specific elements to share (hashtags, specific campaign URLs) as part of the campaign and deliverables that were agreed upon in the contract.

- Key audiences being targeted for this campaign for the brand and for the influencer. Identifying key demographic, psychographic, age cohort, social media trends and behaviors, and interests will be key to highlight and share within this section of the brief.

- Overall tone, presentation, and feeling toward the content and campaign that is aligned with the brand values of the client as well as those of the influencer.

- Mandatories (information that needs to be outlined and shared to follow FTC guidelines, legal and ethical considerations for the brand and influencer, and details associated with any sweepstake, contest, or promotion for the influencer to share for a giveaway).

Launch and evaluate the influencer campaign. Once the brief is set and the influencer(s) understand the requirements and expectations for their part in the campaign, the social media professional needs to create an influencer monitoring dashboard. This is what we call "Inspect what you expect" in the social media world. These dashboards, usually created within a program like Zoomph, Talkwalker, Klear, or another influencer marketing tool, keep track of the assigned influencers who are part of the campaign, what they have shared on their social media campaigns, and their designated metrics. This allows the client to track (a) whether influencers have delivered on what they promised as far as KPIs and other metrics are concerned; (b) which content from each influencer is driving the most engagement, actions, and responses; and (c) calculations of the overall value of the posts being shared by the influencer. Photo 8.5 outlines what a sample influencer dashboard looks like from Klear.

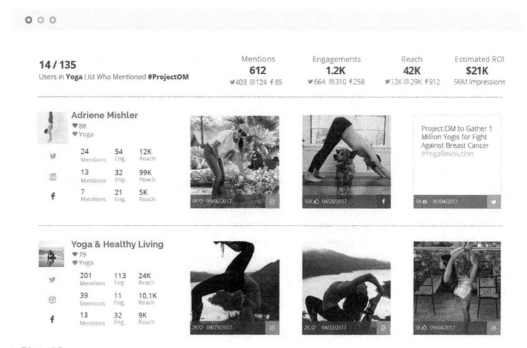

▶ **Photo 8.5**
Influencer Dashboard From Klear

Source: Retrieved from https://blog.klear.com/how-to-track-influencer-campaign/

Once you have constructed your influencer monitoring dashboard, you want to launch the campaign and evaluate the overall impact of the influencer(s) on the client, how their content is aligned toward business objectives, their earned media coverage, overall quality of their engagement and other KPIs that need to be reported, and what actions were taken based on what the influencer shared. These metrics are important to collect, analyze, and report as part of the evaluation of the influencer campaign to determine the success and impact each of these influencers have on the client and their audiences.

Payment

As the character Ron Tidwell says in the movie *Jerry Maguire*, "Show me the MONEY!" Influencers want payment, and they will be the first to say what they want and how much they feel they deserve based on their contribution to a campaign. This is always a tricky situation in which you have to determine the overall value of the work, the influencers' time commitment to the project, and overall metrics to evaluate the impact of the work for the brand. There are many ways in which influencers are paid in influencer campaigns ("Ask an Influencer," 2019). There are two categories of payment to consider: (1) through a specific channel, or (2) for a particular post or creative content. Let us discuss the payment options through specific channels first.

Most of the time, influencers want to be paid directly, which means they are the ones who negotiate and work with brands without a third-party resource. As influencers get larger in their scope, audience, and reputation, they may hire talent managers and agencies to represent them, as TikTok influencer Charli D'Amelio has done. **Agencies** specializing in influencer relations (e.g., Viral Nation, Openinfluence, and Obviously) are becoming more common. These agencies work with their clients and brands on negotiated rates and have the specific line of communication to these individuals, who may not be accessible in other ways. Another method of payment is through **multi-channel networks (MCNs),** who work with a roster of select influencers who are specific in what they offer and may add on required media fees for their services ("Ask an Influencer," 2019). MCNs frequently work with creators, particularly on YouTube, and offer specific services such as exclusive brand deals, strategies and resources for monetization of content being shared on the designated platform, and strategies to get content viewed by more audiences ("What Is A YouTube MCN & How Do They Affect YouTubers?" 2016). The last method is the **influencer marketing partnership platforms** directly, specifically influencer marketing platforms, where the influencer has to register for a specific platform and gets charged a monthly fee to get access to these platforms. Again, this may be an extra tool that influencers with more resources are able to afford, but the typical nano or micro influencer may not have these resources available to them ("Ask an Influencer," 2019).

The actual payment is made through methods based on the content influencers create. Some of these are specific to what posts they create, but others are more long-term focused:

- **Pay per post (PPP).** This is the most popular model for influencers. Based on the reach, engagement level, and overall health of their community, influencers set the different rates they have for each of their posts. For example, one Instagram feed post may cost $1,000, but it may be a different rate for an Instagram Story or blog post. The differences in these posts and content creation depend on the time that is needed to create these items (e.g., a photo will be less expensive than a video that is shared on YouTube), reach and engagement metrics for each of these platforms, and the influencer's cost for creating the content.

- **Pay per campaign.** This is a metric that is used for a particular campaign for the influencer. This is more of a long-term focused fee that covers all aspects of the campaign for the influencer. Certain agreements need to be made as far as timing, deadlines, deliverables during the span of the campaign, and costs associated with the range of content and timing to be used. These are usually negotiated with an agency or MCN for the influencer.

- **Pay per click (PPC).** For every click, view, or action taken by the influencer's community based on what they shared, the influencer gets paid. This is a typical digital metric that has been used for years for websites and blogs and is very much tied to affiliate marketing. For example, with Amazon's influencer marketing program, influencers are able to list the items they purchased from Amazon on their page. Based on whether a purchaser has viewed their feed, they are able to get payment.

- **Pay per acquisition (PPA).** This is one of the hardest methods to achieve since it forces influencers to prove they are "influential." This approach looks at how many new customers, audience members, or subscriptions were made based on what the influencer has shared. This can be anyone who makes a purchase based on what someone has shared, bought a conference ticket using an influencer link, or downloaded a new app to try out. The key thing to measure is the action and behavior that was taken by the individual based on what the influencer shared.

- **Non-monetary compensation.** This is the most common method for nano and micro influencers who are starting out and want to get the overall experience and connections with the brand. There are no financial incentives but rather access to exclusive experiences. VIP experiences, exclusive dinners and events, and free swag are some of the other forms of compensation that are used to motivate these influencers to be part of the campaign.

BEST PRACTICES FOR UTILIZING INFLUENCERS

What are the best practices for engaging with influencers? How does the professional stay up to date with the latest trends, cases, issues, and opportunities that may arise in the field of influencer marketing?

- Invest in training, education, and understanding of new and emerging influencer marketing practices. As more tools, brands, and audiences become more aware and familiar with influencer marketing, it is important to invest in the education and training needed to effectively launch and execute an influencer marketing plan and program. In addition, investing in the right tools for identifying, engaging, monitoring, and evaluating influencers in a campaign will need to be a top priority for brands and audiences to be the most effective and efficient in this area.

- Ensure that the influencers with whom you are working are relevant for your brand and community. Having the most followers does not always matter, but rather, it is important to do research to determine which influencers would have the most impact and relevance for your community. This is a key factor that influencers also have to be aware of for their own community. To matter to their audiences, influencers must anticipate and respond to what their audiences want.

- Provide an exclusive experience and partnership. It may not always be about how much you are willing to pay people to be a part of the community, but what experiences in the long term you are able to provide. People want to feel like they are getting something that not everyone else is. Being able to get information and updates first is one of the main reasons communities in social media exist. Influencers and creators must provide valuable insider information to help them stay connected with and relevant to their audiences.

- Set expectations for safety, tone, and long-term investment. Brands and influencers must be proactive in sharing policies for their collaborations and partnerships with each other to create an authentic and transparent business relationship. Both parties must outline expectations for what is acceptable and what is not and share clear statements about what will be done if policies are not followed. This helps assure audiences of their safety, the tone of their interactions, and their expectations for each other.

- Embrace consistency with partnerships, expectations, and relationships with influencers. Influencer marketing initiatives need to have a centralized purpose within not only the social media practices for a brand but for the business as a whole. Expectations, best practices, policies and guidelines, and expectations for all need to be aligned consistently. More education and training may be needed to keep everyone up to date with these initiatives.

CHAPTER SUMMARY

The influencer marketing field will continue to grow and mature not only as a key specialized area within social media but also as a component in other associated practices in marketing, public relations, and business communication settings. The expectations for doing proactive and ethical influencer marketing practice will continue to evolve as the industry becomes more established. Metrics and tools will continue to advance and become more reliable for brands and social media managers to use as a guide for identifying, engaging, and partnering with influencers. As each of the platforms evolves, and as more brands and professionals educate themselves in the influencer marketing space, this specialized field will continue to become more established and strategic in nature.

THOUGHT QUESTIONS

1. Define *influencer*. What are some attributes that are commonly associated with influencers?

2. What are the FTC influencer guidelines?

3. What does it mean to provide creative control to an influencer? Why is this important?

4. What are the different types of influencers? What makes a nano influencer unique compared to a micro influencer?

5. Identify the steps of an effective influencer campaign. What are some necessary factors to be considered by brands and influencers?

6. How are influencers compensated?

EXERCISES

1. You have been asked to be part of the new influencer team for Triscuit, and you have to identify influencers who would be good to work with. Outline the criteria you would use to evaluate the influencers you have chosen and recommended to Triscuit.

2. M&M's Chocolate has recently decided to partner with Rosanna Pansino (a popular YouTuber) for her new HBO Max show *Baketopia*. Your task as a consultant for them is to evaluate Pansino's account to see what type of influencer she is, decide what deliverables would be appropriate for her to do for M&M's, and outline the expectations for the partnership in a contract.

3. You are getting your dream job in social media for Angel City FC, a National Woman's Soccer expansion team. You are tasked to bring together a group of influencers to partner with in the LA area for Twitter, Instagram, and TikTok. Recommend three influencers and provide an analysis and rationale for each on why they would be appropriate for this expansion team. Outline content they have created and other partnerships they have formed while highlighting the cost for bringing them on board.

4. While working for Disney, you are brought into a conversation about influencer audits. You are asked what are the specific warning signs or red flags to watch out for when it comes to influencers. They have had previous interactions in this case with influencers such as Jake Paul. Identify five red flags, and give recommendations on how Disney should handle each situation with the influencer in question. For each red flag, identify a case study to illustrate how this was handled with an influencer. Make sure to provide citations and references.

REFERENCES

10 of the Best Instagram meme accounts to check out in 2020. (n.d.). *Influencer Marketing Hub*. https://influencermarketinghub.com/instagram-meme-accounts/

Ask an influencer: Product vs. payment. (2019, January 3). *Influencer Marketing Hub*. https://influencermarketinghub.com/ask-an-influencer-product-vs-payment/

Barkley & HARIBO (Producers). (n.d.). Chewy Channel. *The Shorty Awards*. https://shortyawards.com/12th/chewy-channel

Berg, M. (2019, December 18). The highest-paid YouTube stars of 2019: The kids are killing it. *Forbes*. https://www.forbes.com/sites/maddieberg/2019/12/18/the-highest-paid-youtube-stars-of-2019-the-kids-are-killing-it/#4558182238cd

The biggest influencer fails of 2019. (2019, December 17). *Traackr*. https://www.traackr.com/blog/the-biggest-influencer-fails-of-2019

Chaplin, S. (2020, January 22). Creativity vs. control: Why a clear influencer brief matters. *Talking Influence*. https://talkinginfluence.com/2020/01/22/clear-influencer-brief/

Charlton, A. B., & Cornwell, T. B. (2019). Authenticity in horizontal marketing partnerships: A better measure of brand compatibility. *Journal of Business Research*, *100*, 279–298. https://doi.org/10.1016/j.jbusres.2019.03.054

Chmielewski, D. (2020, February 8). How Ryan's YouTube playdate created an accidental (eight-year-old) millionaire. *Forbes*. https://www.forbes.com/sites/dawnchmielewski/2020/02/28/how-ryans-youtube-playdate-created-an-accidental-eight-year-old-millionaire/#b6518d43fe0b

Electronic Arts & BEN (Producers). "Need for Speed: Heat" x David Dobrik. (n.d.). *The Shorty Awards*. https://shortyawards.com/12th/need-for-speed-x-david-dobrik

Enke, N., & Borchers, N. S. (2019). Social media influencers in strategic communication: A conceptual framework for strategic social media influencer communication. *International Journal of Strategic Communication*, *13*(4), 261–277. https://doi.org/10.1080/1553118X.2019.1620234

Falls, J. (n.d.) *Influencer marketing* [Podcast]. https://jasonfalls.com/influencer-marketing/

Federal Trade Commission. (n.d.). *Children's Online Privacy Protection Rule ("COPPA")*. https://www.ftc.gov/enforcement/rules/rulemaking-regulatory-reform-proceedings/childrens-online-privacy-protection-rule

Federal Trade Commission. (2019). *Disclosures 101 for social media influencers*. https://www.ftc.gov/system/files/documents/plain-language/1001a-influencer-guide-508_1.pdf

Freberg, K., Graham, K., McGaughey, K., & Freberg, L. A. (2011). Who are the social media influencers? A study of public perceptions of personality. *Public Relations Review*, *37*(1), 90–92. https://doi.org/10.1016/j.pubrev.2010.11.001

Hakim, A. (2015, August 3). *Influencers vs. creators: How the landscape is changing*. W2O Group. https://www.w2ogroup.com/influencers-vs-creators-how-the-landscape-is-changing/

Hellenkemper, M. (2017, September 22). The 9 steps of your influencer marketing process. *InfluencerDB*. https://influencerdb.com/blog/9-steps-influencer-marketing-process

Himelboim, I., & Golan, G. J. (2019). A social networks approach to viral advertising: The role of primary, contextual, and low influencers. *Social Media + Society*, *5*(3), 2056305119847516. https://doi.org/10.1177/2056305119847516

Influencer tiers for the influencer marketing industry. (n.d.). *Mediakix*. https://mediakix.com/influencer-marketing-resources/influencer-tiers/

Jiménez-Castillo, D., & Sánchez-Fernández, R. (2019). The role of digital influencers in brand recommendation: Examining their impact on engagement, expected value and purchase intention. *International Journal of Information Management*, *49*, 366–376. https://doi.org/10.1016/j.ijinfomgt.2019.07.009

Koul, S. (2020). It's time to stop giving Jake Paul any of your time. *Buzzfeed News*. https://www.buzzfeednews.com/article/scaachikoul/jake-paul-looting-youtube-arizona-mall-protests

Kroger & 360i (Producers). (n.d.). Kroger x TikTok: #TransformUrDorm. *The Shorty Awards*. https://shortyawards.com/12th/kroger-x-tik-tok-transformurdorm-2

Lorenz, T. (2020a). Jake Paul charged in protests. *The New York Times*. https://www.nytimes.com/2020/06/04/style/jake-paul-charged-protests.html

Lorenz, T. (2020b). Michael Bloomberg's campaign suddenly drops memes everywhere. *The New York Times*. https://www.nytimes.com/2020/02/13/style/michael-bloomberg-memes-jerry-media.html

Lou, C., & Yuan, S. (2019). Influencer marketing: How message value and credibility affect consumer trust of branded content on social media. *Journal of Interactive Advertising*, *19*(1), 58–73. https://doi.org/10.1080/15252019.2018.1533501

Luoma-aho, V., Pirttimäki, T., Maity, D., Munnukka, J., & Reinikainen, H. (2019). Primed authenticity: How priming impacts authenticity perception of social media influencers. *International Journal of Strategic Communication*, *13*(4), 352–365. https://doi.org/10.1080/1553118X.2019.1617716

Maheshwari, S. (2018, November 11). Are you ready for the nanoinfluencers? *The New York Times*. https://www.nytimes.com/2018/11/11/business/media/nanoinfluencers-instagram-influencers.html

Monllos, K. (2020, March 17). YouTube star David Dobrik to advertisers: Learn to trust the creator. *Digiday*. https://digiday.com/marketing/youtube-star-david-dobrik-advertisers-learn-trust-creator/

Mosley, M. (2021, March 19). Virtual influencers: What are they and how do they work. *Influencer Matchmaker*. https://influencermatchmaker.co.uk/blog/virtual-influencers-what-are-they-how-do-they-work#:~:text=What%20Are%20Virtual%20Influencers%3F,features%20and%20personalities%20of%20humans

New York Jets (Producer). (n.d.). New York Jets influencer program. *The Shorty Awards*. https://shortyawards.com/12th/new-york-jets-influencer-program

Ong, T. (2020, October 29). Virtual influencers make real money while COVID locks down human stars. *Bloomberg Businessweek*. https://www.bloomberg.com/news/features/2020-10-29/lil-miquela-lol-s-seraphine-virtual-influencers-make-more-real-money-than-ever

Sherman, N. (2020, March 2). *The kids making up to $1m a year on YouTube*. BBC News. https://www.bbc.com/news/business-51619504

Smith, B. G., Krishna, A., & Al-Sinan, R. (2019). Beyond slacktivism: Examining the entanglement between social media engagement, empowerment, and participation in activism. *International Journal of Strategic Communication*, *13*(3), 182–196.

Starbucks & Big Spaceship (Producers). (n.d.). Whoa, Nitro. *The Shorty Awards*. https://shortyawards.com/12th/whoa-nitro

The state of influencer marketing 2019: Benchmark report [+Infographic]. (2019, February 25). *Influencer Marketing Hub*. https://influencermarketinghub.com/influencer-marketing-2019-benchmark-report/

Van Kessel, P., Toor, S., & Smith, A. (2019, July 25). *A week in the life of popular YouTube channels*. Pew Research Center. https://www.pewresearch.org/internet/2019/07/25/a-week-in-the-life-of-popular-youtube-channels/?

Waller, N. (2020, January 2). 5 Ways influencer marketing will evolve in 2020. *Ad Age*. https://adage.com/article/opinion/5-ways-influencer-marketing-will-evolve-2020/2224401

Weiss, G. (2020, September 23). Charli D'Amelio sells hundreds of thousands of signature Dunkin' Drinks, triggers 57% spike in app downloads. *Tubefilter*. https://www.tubefilter.com/2020/09/23/charli-damelio-dunkin-donuts-sales-app-downloads/

Wellemeyer, J. (2019, August 31). This teenager was making $4,000 a month reposting memes on Instagram—Until he got purged. *MarketWatch*. https://www.marketwatch.com/story/instagrams-purge-of-meme-accounts-cost-this-teenager-his-only-income-of-4000-a-month-2019-08-07

What is a YouTube MCN & how do they affect YouTubers? (2016, February 15). *Mediakix*. https://mediakix.com/blog/what-is-a-youtube-mcn-and-what-it-means-for-youtube-influencers/

Zhao, X., Zhan, M., & Liu, B. F. (2018). Disentangling social media influence in crises: Testing a four-factor model of social media influence with large data. *Public Relations Review*, *44*(4), 549–561. https://doi.org/10.1016/j.pubrev.2018.08.002

9

PAID MEDIA

Learning Objectives

After reading this chapter, you will be able to

- Define paid media

- Understand the perception of paid media compared to other types of media

- Evaluate the types of paid media components

- Understand the best practices for paid media

INTRODUCTION

Some of the many assumptions about paid media strategy include the following:

- "Social media is free! I do not need to invest anything to get people to see our content!"

- "Organic reach is still relevant and possible on social media."

- "Our ad got 7 billion impressions! It was a huge success!"

- "Social media and paid media is an area belonging to advertising professionals and no one else."

- "Paid media is an effective strategy but is too expensive."

- "I can get around the algorithm to make my content still come up without paying for it!"

Many assumptions about paid media are still circulating in the social media industry, but they are not true. Social media is indeed not free. In fact, as many have been saying for a while now, social media has become a "pay-to-play" platform where it is necessary to put money behind posts, campaigns, and experiences in order for audiences to see the content and respond to posts and messages being shared. Certain social media metrics are highlighted and framed as a success (e.g., impressions); although these metrics make us feel good, they do not show the actual impact of an ad. The times where social media is considered to be a "free" set of platforms for everyone to use are over. Social media in many ways has become more aligned with the traditional framework seen in marketing and advertising practices. Organic reach is almost nonexistent when it comes to social media. Organic reach focuses on reaching audiences without any payment backing the content to be seen by more audiences. Bypassing the algorithms of the social media platforms is neither an easy task nor a long-term strategy. Paid media also has to have a strategy. Just throwing money on bad content is not going to work. Having strong creative content and a strategy in place is fundamental to the overall success of your paid media campaign.

This is where social media was at the very beginning, but it is not the case now as more brands, professionals, and agencies are vying for the attention span of their audiences and for digital real estate. Having a paid media strategy is not as expensive as traditional media, which we will be going over in this chapter.

HUMANS OF SOCIAL MEDIA

Jennifer Hartmann, Director of Public Relations and Social Media at John Deere

Introduction

I'm the kid in school that loved poetry assignments and sentence diagramming and Shakespeare while everyone else groaned. I'm one of those people that loves to dissect everything from Super Bowl ads to political campaigns to how communication, public relations, advertising, and social media can shape the perception of a brand. As director of public relations responsible for PR, channel strategy, and social media for John Deere, I've had the privilege to turn this passion into a career with one of the most preeminent brands in the world.

How did you get your start in social media?

Several years ago, I interviewed for a marketing role at Deere that required social media experience. At that point, I had no professional experience to share. What I did have [was] a successful and active Facebook page I voluntarily created and managed for a local nonprofit. I submitted my application with links to the page, metrics on engagement and reach, and a pitch that I could do even more for Deere. I got the job!

What is your favorite part of working in your area of expertise in social media?

The ability to directly engage in real time with our customers and fans in meaningful ways.

What is one thing you can't live without while working in social media?

Social media is at its best when there's a collaborative network of talented brand, communications, and marketing colleagues working together to deliver on a unified social media strategy. Our team couldn't live without that broad cross-section of peers at Deere who make up this network. (If you're managing social for a smaller organization, lean on peers in the industry via your personal social media accounts, professional associations, or networking events to ideate and adopt best practices.)

What is your favorite social media account (person/brand/etc.) to follow and why?

I am obsessed with #AgTwitter, the self-identified community of farmers and ranchers who actively engage in agriculture-related topics and trends on Twitter. It allows me to deeply understand in real time the challenges most prevalent in the industry, customers' perception of equipment manufacturers like Deere, where they stand on a wide range of topics and issues, and how they engage, interact, and leverage the social platform.

What is the most challenging part of working in social media?

The near-impossible task of staying one step ahead of a constantly evolving, dynamic system of channels, which each have their own unique purpose, audience, and expectations.

What is your take on your area of expertise and the social media industry?

I'm probably older than most social media managers tend to be and with that comes wisdom derived from often tough but valuable lessons. A successful career in social or digital marketing is more than being a strong communicator or creator. You have to be empathetic and know how to lead, to influence others, to collaborate, to take risks, to

own your mistakes, to learn from them, and to champion others.

What do you wish you had known when you were starting out?

Your voice matters. What you think matters. Your ideas matter. Not your title. Not the amount of experience you have. Not the degree you have. Speak up. Engage in conversations. Encourage and embrace diverse thinking on your team. And never qualify that you are "just" a social media marketer or communicator.

What are three marketable skills a social media professional needs to have to work in the industry?

Empathy. Digital marketing know-how. Strong writing and communications skills.

Where do you go to keep up to date with trends and continue learning about social media?

For industry trends and strategic planning I look to professional associations like the Public Relations Society of America and Social Media.org. Day to day I turn to Twitter for inspiration from the social media, marketing, and advertising professionals I follow.

If you had to choose a song to walk out to in a presentation on social media, what would it be and why?

"Fight Song," by Rachel Platten. We have the power in all of us, personally and professionally, to make a difference. Regardless of your career path ("like a small boat on the ocean"), your contribution to the world can indeed be mighty. At the same time, one post, one story, one image can "send big waves into motion." It's on those of us in the industry to ensure that wave adds value to customers, to our organizations, and to the communities we serve.

Jennifer Hartmann is the director of public relations and social media at John Deere and founder of Royal Ball Run for Autism. Jennifer can be connected on social at @jenalyson.

WHAT IS PAID MEDIA?

It is important to clarify the main concepts being discussed in this chapter. First, **social media advertising** (or paid media) focuses on generating leads, sales, and promotional benefits that are based on the financial backing implemented for these pieces to be purchased online (Baker, n.d.). **Paid social media** is a method of displaying advertisements or sponsored marketing messages on popular social media platforms and targeting a specific sub-audience. Pay-per-click advertising, branded or influencer-generated content, and display ads are all examples of paid social media (Carmicheal, n.d.). Essentially, brands and agencies are paying to display paid components (e.g., written posts, text messages, images, videos, live streams, sponsorships, etc.) to a designated audience based on key profile characteristics. These profile characteristics range from basic demographic information (e.g., age, location, gender, etc.) to psychographic characteristics (e.g., liked pages, interests, hobbies, connections, etc.) to give the client a stronger understanding of who they are targeting and how to best frame the paid media component to get the best audience response (Gurd, 2020).

As illustrated in Gini Dietrich's PESO model (Photo 9.1), paid media is part of the overall media channel ecosystem. There is paid media for digital and social media purposes, but there are some other elements to consider here. There is pure paid media, and then there is paid yet earned media. **Paid yet earned media** falls under the caveat of being earned when you are essentially paying for content to be created, but it is not a piece of content that is coming directly from the organization or client paying for the content. Essentially, the person that is being paid is creating the content and is getting compensated for the partnership. This is where influencer marketing falls into the balance of earned yet paid media. In addition, there is **paid yet owned media**, which focuses on content marketing, webinars, and podcasts. The social media professional is essentially promoting content that they own, but they are investing in the promotion and brand awareness of these efforts. However, items that are highlighted as strictly paid media include paid ads, sponsored posts, and lead generation measures that are created, executed, and programmed out by the company or client.

Traditional elements of paid advertising have focused on how the transaction between consumer and brand through advertisement is non-personal, and there is no feedback per se for the consumer to provide to the brand. This is not the case for social media and paid media advertising. In fact, social media professionals are able to engage with audiences in real time with impressive reach and an affordable budget to boost or expand their network with online tools. One of the biggest differences between social media advertising and traditional advertising is that social media advertising is more cost-effective. As a social media professional, you are able to set a budget for the campaign and adjust the set amount within the designated platform you are using, which is quite different from traditional advertising (Baker, n.d.).

To clearly see what can be done with a budget for traditional media and how it translates to digital and social media, consider a brand given a budget for a Super Bowl ad. In 2020, the cost for a Super Bowl as was $5.6 million for 30 seconds (Monllos, 2020). This is a lot of money, and *Digiday* reported that *Ad Age* highlighted some things brands could do if they were to spend this money on digital paid media strategies rather than just traditional media. With $5.6 million, a brand could get any of the following:

- 2.8 million clicks on Walmart search ads
- One-third of a Peacock sponsorship from NBC

Figure 9.1 PESO 2.0 Model From Gini Dietrich

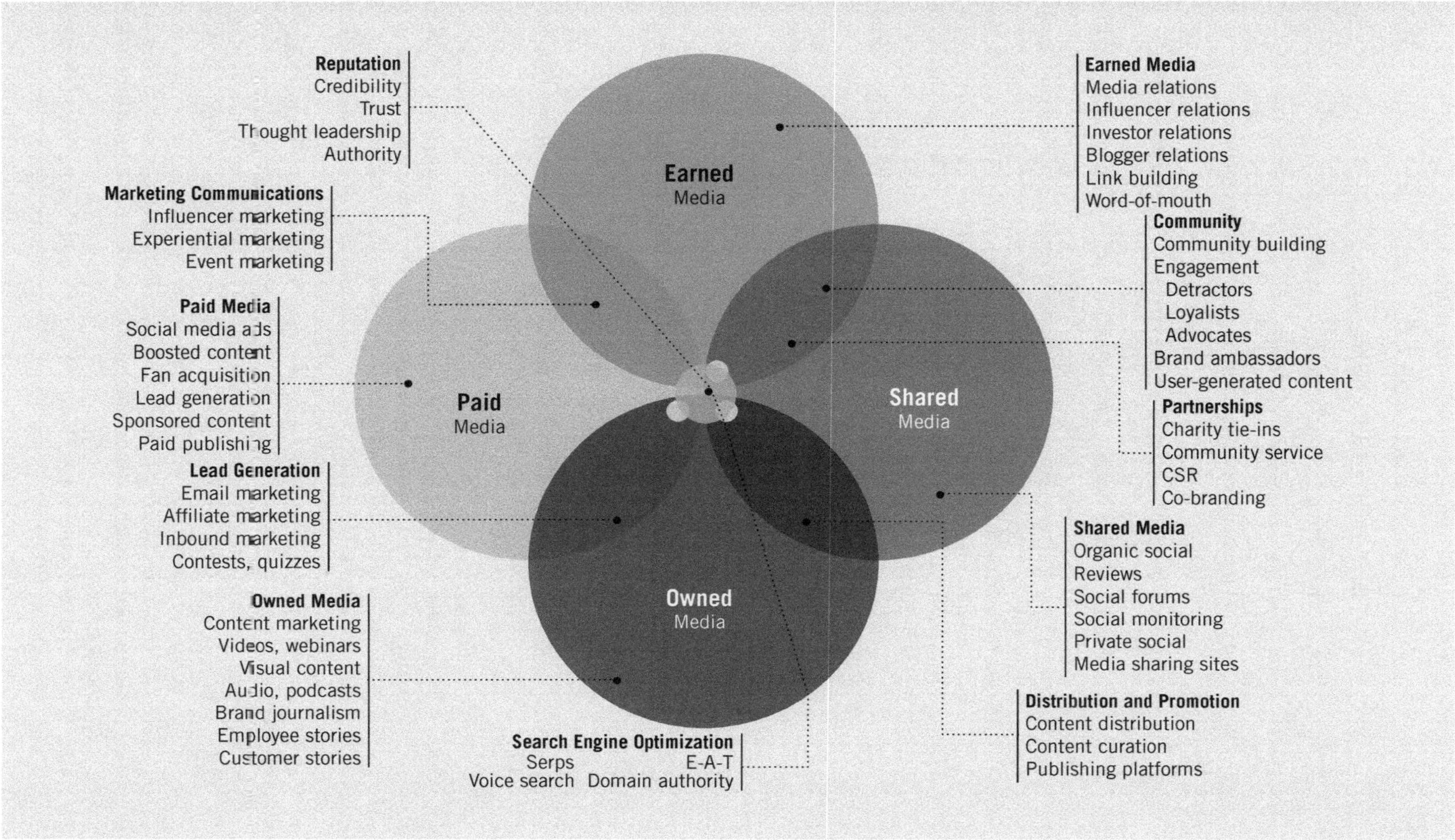

Reputation
Credibility
Trust
Thought leadership
Authority

Marketing Communications
Influencer marketing
Experiential marketing
Event marketing

Paid Media
Social media ads
Boosted content
Fan acquisition
Lead generation
Sponsored content
Paid publishing

Lead Generation
Email marketing
Affiliate marketing
Inbound marketing
Contests, quizzes

Owned Media
Content marketing
Videos, webinars
Visual content
Audio, podcasts
Brand journalism
Employee stories
Customer stories

Earned Media
Media relations
Influencer relations
Investor relations
Blogger relations
Link building
Word-of-mouth

Community
Community building
Engagement
Detractors
Loyalists
Advocates
Brand ambassadors
User-generated content

Partnerships
Charity tie-ins
Community service
CSR
Co-branding

Shared Media
Organic social
Reviews
Social forums
Social monitoring
Private social
Media sharing sites

Distribution and Promotion
Content distribution
Content curation
Publishing platforms

Search Engine Optimization
Serps   E-A-T
Voice search   Domain authority

Earned
Media

Shared
Media

Paid
Media

Owned
Media

- 862 million digital out-of-home impressions
- 16 million clicks on Instacart ads
- 37 days' worth of TikTok hashtag challenges
- 70 million impressions from Hulu pause ads
- 1.4 billion impressions on Twitter
- 560 Instagram posts by *Bachelor* stars (Monllos, 2020)

Why Is Paid Media Essential in Social Media?

All of the platforms (e.g., Facebook, Twitter, YouTube, LinkedIn, Pinterest, Instagram, TikTok, etc.) have an ad manager that focuses on bringing together various tasks to make setting up a paid media campaign easier. Paid media campaigns allow you to determine which audiences you want to reach and when you want to reach them with certain paid media components. There is a lot of control and flexibility in setting up paid media ads and other elements in a campaign. These are at the control of the user who is in charge of the ad account on the social media channel.

Before we go into the specifics related to the essential elements of paid media for social media, you also want to ask yourself the following questions:

- What is the role of paid media as part of your social media campaign?
- What paid media objectives are you trying to accomplish?
- What platforms are you looking to use in paid media on social?
- What content options for each platform will perform the best for your creative assets and target audiences?
- Who is the key audience you are trying to reach?
- What insights do you have to validate your investment and need for paid media in your social media efforts?

It is best to have answers to these essential questions before you get too deep into the details of paid media. Paid media, like all things in social, has to have a strong strategy. Many times, we see professionals focusing so much on the tactical or platform specific elements of paid media, they forget about the bigger picture. Making sure you have the bigger picture in mind will help align the right tactical elements to your content, audiences, and overall objectives for paid media.

Now, let's get into the essentials. First, the capabilities for **targeting** (focusing on audiences based on certain key characteristics only) on social media for paid media can be very effective, specifically looking at options such as age, likes, income, locations, interests, and other key demographic information. The other option is **retargeting**, which focuses on reaching people who have interacted with your content or visited your website. Retargeting allows the social media professional to reach another important key audience to engage with in their paid media strategy.

Paid media campaigns allow you to get a complete picture of the **return on investment (ROI)** for the campaign. When establishing a set budget for a paid media campaign, you want to make sure to get the most for the money you have invested in. All of the platforms' ad manager features allow you to see the revenue generated from the ad, conversions that were as a result of the campaign, number of leads generated from the campaign, and visits to the landing page for your campaign from the post on the designated social media campaign. The tracking capabilities have evolved substantially so audiences are able to get a full picture of the customer journey from the initial sponsored post directly to the purchase for the product if needed. Paid media campaigns can be very affordable. You do not need to have millions of dollars to do a paid media strategy. In fact, they can all be adjusted based on how many audience members need to be targeted and how long the campaign will be running. This is the question of the hour: Is paid media essential for social media strategic practices? The answer is indeed yes, and although the process of tracking, evaluating, and executing campaigns is very user friendly, there are some challenges to be aware of.

Like all things, there has to be a balance to how you approach paid media. There are some challenges to having to "pay to play" in order to get your content out to the audiences. A lot must be set up before a paid media campaign can be launched. Not only are the tools, training (e.g., being certified to do paid media strategies on the designated platform for agencies, etc.), and resources to create content necessary, but the quality in the creative assets (e.g., images, videos, text, etc.) needs to be strong to be included in the paid media components. Depending on the set criteria you have created for your audience, a majority of the audience may be irrelevant to or not appropriate for the campaign. This leads to wasted ad expense (money lost as a result of not engaging with the right audience) and wasted reach (reach to audiences that are not appropriate for the campaign). This is why it is critical to determine the key characteristics and attributes to list for audiences in a campaign in the set-up features in the ad manager.

Effective paid media strategies take a lot of time and attention. Posting an ad with lazy copy or **boosting a post** (putting money and ad spending on a post that is performing well to get more reach) is not enough. There has to be a strong foundation for how and why these paid media components are happening and what needs to be implemented to make sure they perform well. Creating the campaign and letting everything all hang loose is not the best strategy to have. If you build the campaign and ads, you have to check in on them and make sure they are performing in the way you want them to perform. Ignoring the elements or not investing the time to fully integrate a comprehensive strategy can lead to the campaign being ineffective for the client, which could lead to costly last-minute decisions and eat up the campaign budget.

Customers may not trust paid ad components being shown in their feed. They can also get **ad fatigue,** which is when they see too many ads in their feed or see the paid media component too early or late to do anything about it. Understanding the essence of timing, context, and approach is critical for paid media strategies to be successful in a campaign. Plus, audiences are not going to their designated social media campaigns to be interacting with brands 24 hours a day, 7 days a week. They are coming to these platforms to engage with others they know and trust, so brands and social media professionals have to know the time and place for promotion and paid media to be implemented online.

The other component that needs to be discussed is how all of these social media platforms decide what content gets presented to audiences and which pieces of content do not. The **algorithms** of each social media platform focus on the process of sorting posts in a user's feed based on relevancy instead of published time (Barnhart, 2019). Essentially, algorithms are focused on making sure audiences are seeing the content they want to see first.

Algorithms are a hot button issue for several reasons. First, there are issues with how they impact content reach. Some people see certain content come up on their feeds while others do not see that content. In addition, algorithms are presenting content that the program feels is valuable for the audience member, but they may be hiding other content. Many platform algorithms have made headlines for their constant changes (e.g., Facebook and their changes related to engagement baiting) or censorship and privacy policies surrounding the content (e.g., TikTok censoring certain content from specific audience groups). Audiences have tried to bypass the algorithm by tricking it with **pods** on Instagram. Pods are private mass groups of individuals created to let group members know when a post goes live so they can "like" the post to increase its reach and exposure. Other ways social media professionals try to get around the algorithms include tagging accounts in posts to create engagement and more reach, asking questions to audiences in posts, adding hashtags, and posting content at the right time for the platform based on the account's analytics (Barnhart, 2019).

Clearly, having a paid media strategy for a social media campaign is essential to moving forward in the industry. However, it has to be done with the right tools, education, and strategic approach. Otherwise, social media professionals will be throwing away their money with little to show for their work.

Types of Paid Media Components on Social Media Platforms

Many platforms' ad managers have similar characteristics. Some universal elements that all platform ad managers share for advertising on their designated platforms include the following:

Research to determine the platform designation for the campaign. This first step is important not only to set forth the overall purpose and goals for this campaign but also to decide which platforms to use. Will this campaign be designated on just one platform, or will it include all those available? Will the channels require paid content, or will the campaign do well with organic content? Is the target audience engaged and on this platform? Is the target audience constantly engaged here and willing to see paid media content targeting them? Do the creative assets you want to use for the campaign fit with the specific ad requirements for the platform? All of these questions have to be addressed before moving forward.

You have to designate an objective you want to achieve during your campaign. Whether it is reach, brand awareness, or conversion, there has to be a designated element you want to accomplish with this set campaign or advertisement. In most cases, all of the platforms use set objectives to frame their overall campaign paid media strategy. These three categories help determine the main things that need to be accomplished by the paid media (Newberry & McLachlan, 2020). The three objectives are **awareness** (building brand awareness and reach), **consideration** (engaging audiences to take certain actions such as going to a website or installing an app), and **conversion** (making a sale or driving offline traffic based on content). These will become prominent objectives that will be consistently present across each platform.

You need a set audience to target for this campaign or advertisement. The general public or everyone on the platform is not appropriate in this case. What is important is designating the items that capture the essence of the audiences you are targeting.

There has to be strong written ad copy. Paid media written copy is similar to traditional advertising copy: It has to be concise and to the point. Each targeted audience needs to have personalized copy that is relevant and appropriate for them. In addition to the written copy, a call to action (CTA) needs to be implemented to ask the users to take some sort of action after being exposed to the message. Swipe up for stories, click a link to a website, go here to a designated microsite, or like the post are just some types of CTAs included in most ad copy.

All ads have to have effective and relevant creative assets for formatting purposes. To have a paid media strategy, some creative assets must be used along with the written copy. This could be videos, photos, GIFs, or other visual elements. These have to be branded and of high quality to be the most effective in the paid media element for a campaign. Money does not grow on trees, yet ad managers ask you to "show them the money!" (taking a cue from the 1996 film *Jerry Maguire*), so you have to have a set budget.

Lastly, all paid media strategies across all platforms need to establish a set of metrics that will be used to evaluate the success of the ad. Depending on the ad, certain metrics will be used to evaluate the ad's effectiveness for a paid media campaign. These are all supposed to align with the designated objectives for the ad in the paid media campaign. The **click-through rate (CTR)** is the number of clicks from the ad divided by the impressions it received, making this an important metric to evaluate and determine the success of the message to take actions to go to a particular website, blog, or other online destination. **Cost per conversion (CPC)** focuses on addressing the conversion objectives (e.g., sign-ups, sales, downloads, etc.), which are calculated by dividing the amount spent for the ad by the conversions made as a result of the ad. CPC helps in deciding which ads were most effective in driving brand awareness and actions. This is a metric that many senior management and client professionals focus on. **Cost per mille/impression (CPM)** focuses on the amount paid for every 1,000 impressions received for the campaign, and this particular metric is primarily aligned with the awareness objective. **Cost per send (CPS)** focuses on the direct message costs that are being created, executed, and opened through messaging apps (e.g., WhatsApp), or message features within traditional platforms (e.g., LinkedIn and Facebook Messenger).

Platform Paid Ad Strategies and Features

Let's start by going over the platforms and their capabilities for paid media strategies. The leader in the industry for paid media strategy is Facebook. In 2020, Facebook dominated the paid media space—89% of marketers use Facebook advertising as part of their social media efforts (Zote, 2020). Facebook was an early leader in setting up their ad manager (their advertising arm for the platform where they host the ads, sponsored posts, and other paid media components to be shared on their designated platforms such as Instagram and WhatsApp). Facebook brings three ad elements brings to the table: campaigns (where all of your campaigns are housed), ad sets (if you are targeting different audiences, you will need different ads for each), and ads (the actual ads that will be created and executed on Facebook) (Stec, n.d.).

One of the many types of Facebook ads is **targeted ads**. These ads focus on a bidding system where advertisers bid on a number of ads based on their target audience, giving them a chance to have their ad run. Think about it like betting on a horse at the Kentucky Derby. You hope your horse is the winner, but you do not know for certain. Same thing when it comes to the bidding option here for targeted ads on Facebook: You have to be aware that your ad may not run, and it has to follow the rules and standards Facebook sets for ads on their platform. Targeted ads target audiences based on their characteristics and behaviors on the social media platforms. Meaning, targeted ads focus specifically on integrating data from users to incorporate into ads based on which pages people visit, where they primarily are located on the app and platform, and much more. Facebook offers many different formats for their ads to display and engage with their audiences on the platform. Formats include single images or videos, but the most popular featured format on Facebook is Carousel ads. This feature allows targeted users to be presented with a range of visuals and information rather than a single image or video ad ("Social Media Advertising & Paid Social Guide," n.d.). Experimenting through **A/B testing** (testing different characteristics in ads and copy to determine the most effective one to use in a campaign) will help determine which format to execute in the campaign. Not testing ahead of time could risk poor ad performance on Facebook or other designated platforms (Photo 9.1).

Sponsored messages are another type of paid media component on Facebook. Sponsored messages—including display ads, sponsored posts, and boosted posts— are commonly found on social media platforms between posts from accounts users follow on the timeline. The sponsored posts that appear on feeds have to have certain elements. For example, HBO Max created a sponsored Facebook message for brand awareness (Photo 9.2). The copy is there to direct audiences to sign up for access to the new service, but it also has a CTA to do this before May 27 to be able to start streaming the service. The asset used was a video showing all of the new shows, movies, and entertainment features the service offers compared to competitors.

▶ **Photo 9.1**
Facebook Ad Manager

Source: Retrieved from https://blog.hubspot .com/marketing/ facebook-paid-ad-checklist?_ga= 2.225195290.121387002 .1580754077-940436819 .1565181751

Instagram, owned by Facebook, is increasingly sought out for the promoted media components on their platform. However, in order to run ads on Instagram, the created account needs to be a business account, not a personal account. Instagram ads are structured in a similar way as Facebook ads. Ads can be created for the Instagram feed or for Instagram Stories using videos, images, filters, and lenses (which can be created and branded in Spark AR, Facebook's creative studio to create augmented reality [AR] assets). Like Facebook, Instagram ads allow you to determine the budget, length, and timing of the advertisement. However, one of the more common types of paid media on Instagram is sponsorships within brands and influencers.

Sponsorships and endorsements are not a new paid media strategy on social media, but the way they are executed, along with new partnerships for exposure and brand awareness, continues to evolve. On Instagram and Facebook, there is a designated feature called "paid partnership" acknowledging the sponsorship between influencer and brand. This is a key feature that directly resulted in making brands and influencers more transparent in their collaborations and making sure they followed Federal Trade Commission (FTC) guidelines.

▶ **Photo 9.2**
HBO MAX
Sponsored Facebook
Post

Source: Warner Bros.

Due to COVID-19 in 2020, many events were canceled, including graduation ceremonies for the Class of 2020. Many brands tried to capitalize on canceled graduations and prom for high school seniors. Chipotle focused on a sponsorship campaign to cut through the noise. They created an Instagram account called Chipotle Afterparty (Photo 9.3), which featured viral YouTuber David Dobrik inviting high school students to be a part of this experience and get the chance to win a $25,000 scholarship. Chipotle not only sponsored and partnered with Dobrik to get his reach and engagement through his channels for this campaign; they also sponsored posts within Instagram via feeds and stories to gain awareness of their event for their key audiences.

In addition to brand partnerships, there are other ways brands can come together to promote the efforts of others for free for a good cause. Many brands and agencies do work for free to support certain causes or efforts. While this is not a paid media strategy per se, it is still a part of marketing and promoting efforts that the client is working on in the hopes audiences see the content, become aware of the brand, and invest in the brand through sales or other brand marketing efforts. Many brands, such as Airbnb, did this in support of COVID-19 first responders with their posts on Instagram (Photo 9.4). While this is considered to be a partnered collaboration that's paid, it allows Airbnb to stay true to their brand voice and feature a photo of a stay while advocating for first responders and providing their community with CTA messages to donate to support this cause.

Instagram has also found success in placing ads in Instagram Stories, allowing brands to have either one photo, a series of photos, or videos integrated in between stories to reach and engage with audiences. Remember that the visual asset is the star of the show, but a CTA needs to be clearly articulated and used for these types of ads. See the Buff City Soaps ad that is presented on Instagram Stories (Photo 9.5). A clear message is presented for free two-day shipping for their products, and an easy "Shop Now" swipe-up feature allows users to immediately purchase the products within the app.

Twitter

▸ **Photo 9.3**
Chipotle Afterparty Instagram Account

Source: Instagram/@chipotleafterparty

Twitter has a strong presence when it comes to paid media strategy that is aligned with what other platforms have used in the past; Twitter also has a set of designated unique features that are relevant and appropriate for the platform, such as the following:

- Promoted tweets: promoted updates that are paid for by the company promoting the messages.

- Promoted trends: a promoted hashtag that is trending due to the financial backing of a brand, such as Star Wars for #MayTheFourthBeWithYou, or #Oscars from the Academy Awards.

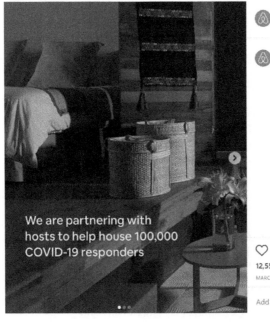

▸ **Photo 9.4**
Cause Donations (Airbnb and COVID-19 First Responders)

Source: Instagram/@airbnb

- Branded emoji: a specifically created emoji graphic that is created and paid for by a campaign like Netflix's show #EmilyInParis, NBA's #NBAFinals, or actress Leslie Jones's show #SupermarketSweep on ABC.

- Brand lifts: polls and surveys created by brands to get feedback from audiences about their brand and overall awareness. Aflac, the insurance company, uses these to get feedback from Twitter users.

- Pre-roll and promoted videos: some pre-roll ads (15 seconds or less) that appear before a video of another account (e.g., ABC, Bleacher Report, etc.) and videos that are promoted to appear in the main Twitter feed or Twitter Explore tab as a trending topic.

- Conversation cards: updates from Twitter where you have the ability to tweet which option you are supporting by clicking one of the buttons. Some range from two to four options. *Adweek* has used this feature when running their popular March Adness contest around March Madness time. *Adweek* uses Twitter conversation cards to encourage users to support their vote for the brand they support in a particular bracket session.

▶ **Photo 9.5**
Buff City Soap Instagram Ad
Source: Instagram/@buffcitysoap

Most of the time, the advertisements we see on Twitter are coming from brands to talk about their positions, services, efforts, or contributions with audiences; in other words, brands want audiences to know about what they are doing. For example, Microsoft has used Twitter to promote commercials and products, including their Super Bowl Campaign in 2018. In another example, Microsoft wanted to use a branded hashtag for Mother's Day to promote their Microsoft Teams product (a video conferencing product that is part of the Microsoft Office suite). They combined several social media paid elements that can be present in one tweet to appear in users' feeds. Some brands use the branded emoji feature as a way to put their logo and ownership on a particular product, such as Nintendo's Animal Crossing game (Photo 9.6). In all of the tweets that are created about the game, there are two sets of branded emoji hashtags: #AnimalCrossing and #ACNH. These are emojis that have

▶ **Photo 9.6**
Nintendo's Animal Crossing Game
Source: Twitter/@NintendoAmerica

been purchased as part of the brand strategy for the popular game, which allows users to use them on Twitter. Branded emoji hashtags are commonly used to create brand awareness, engagement with the online community, and hopefully, conversion to motivate audiences to purchase and play the game.

LinkedIn

LinkedIn has also done their work in formulating a paid media strategy for the platform. While most businesses and brands utilize LinkedIn ads for job postings, recruitment, and other business-oriented strategies, LinkedIn still provides a robust set of tools and features that can be utilized strategically for paid media purposes. In addition to Facebook and Instagram, LinkedIn uses the three objectives: awareness, consideration, and conversion.

One way for brands to capture targeted users' attention and actions on LinkedIn is with sponsored content ("Best Practices for Sponsored Content," n.d.). Another way is with lead generation, which focuses on generating new contacts for a brand. Lead generation allows LinkedIn to provide some ad capabilities for their platforms for businesses and social media professionals. LinkedIn's Lead Generation form allows businesses and others to utilize this feature in a seamless and tailored manner for collecting information submitted by users in the targeted audience segment. There are many opportunities to advertise and promote items, as highlighted in LinkedIn's ad manager, from job postings, new product launches, and inquiries for services.

One item tied to LinkedIn's publishing features is native advertising or sponsored posts. Native advertising is commonly used as a paid media strategy, but it is quite controversial. Essentially, native advertising is paid media content that is created in the form of an article, infographic, or video (Shewan, 2020). The reason native advertising is controversial is because publications and brands do not always disclose that these pieces of content are sponsored, creating the illusion that these pieces are objective and went through the process of research, objectivity, and other steps in proper journalism practices. Many publications, including *Digiday*, *Mashable*, and even *Forbes*, have gone this route with sponsored posts. This of course hurts the credibility of not only the publication but the brand in question. However, if the piece is disclosed properly and follows the guidelines set by the FTC on sponsored and proposed posts, these pieces have a purpose in the paid media strategy. Disclosure and transparency is of the utmost importance in native advertising.

Snapchat

Snapchat is an established presence for brands and users to create and execute ads, and it is more affordable than it was a few years ago. The ways in which Snapchat can utilize its platform from a paid media standpoint ranges from a variety of different strategies and formats ("Snapchat Ad Formats," n.d.), such as

- single image or video within the Snapchat feed for the user;
- collection ads, which showcase multiple products;
- story ads that are shown within a user's Snapchat story;
- lens AR experience (creating an augmented reality lens for users to use);
- filters for users to use as they create and share videos or photos on their account; and
- commercials within the Discovery page.

Compared to other platforms, Snapchat's strength is monetizing AR features and branded paid opportunities for brands as part of their paid media strategy. For the 2020 release of the film *Trolls*, a branded filter was created for audiences to use and share (Bain, 2020).

YouTube

YouTube's ad manager has a strong presence for businesses, users, and agencies to capitalize and showcase ads to be placed within the various features on the platform. There is prime digital real estate on YouTube, not just on the webpages and app but within the content of the videos that get viewed. Advertising on YouTube is how many creators and influencers on the platform are able to monetize their content to make a living. Several types of ads and paid media are showcased on YouTube, including the following:

- True view ads: Ads for which advertisers pay only for the number of views (when people watch or interact with the ads), which means a view can be anywhere from 12 seconds for skippable views (ads that can be skipped) or 15 to 20 seconds for ads that are non-skippable (Oetting, n.d.).

- In-stream ads: Ads that play before a user can watch the video they want to watch (Oetting, n.d.). These ads can range from being just a few seconds to 30 seconds long.

- Pre-roll ads: Ads that can play before, during, or after a video that are non-skippable and can be 15 to 20 seconds long (Oetting, n.d.).

- Video discovery ads: Ads that are presented and shown on result pages, related videos, or even the YouTube home page (Oetting, n.d.). These are similar to search results on Google for sponsored images, products, and search results (as discussed later in this chapter). This makes sense because YouTube is owned by Google, which prides itself on strong paid media strategies for keyword search results.

Pay-per-click (PPC) is a common strategy that has marketing and advertising professionals pay each time a user clicks a URL ("Pay-Per-Click Advertising," n.d.). This is a common digital marketing strategy for paid media within digital media, such as websites, blogs, and Google; PPC is also used for social media purposes. Brands essentially have the same bidding set up for their ads with search engine brands like Google, where they have to set up keywords in a bidding system called Ad Auction. This is where the marketer has to bid on keywords and key terms they want to trigger or display in their ads ("Pay-Per-Click Advertising," n.d.). For example, if a social media manager wants to see what is being created related to coffee brands, the first item that is shown on the search results is for Keurig (Photo 9.7). So, we know Keurig paid to have their website and brand placed in a prime digital real estate spot on YouTube to compete with their other competitors in the marketplace.

Pinterest

Pinterest, the visual sharing and pinning social media platform, is another place where ads are strong and present. The platform asks the ad manager to make sure their ad is focused on certain elements such as audiences, keywords, interests, placements, and demographics to be successful and effective for their audiences ("Using Ads Manager," n.d.). Pinterest focuses on the visual of course, but it also

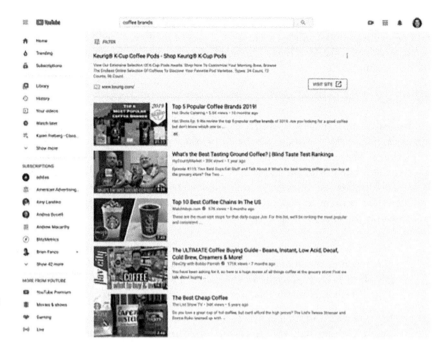

What's Your Style?

Take the Quiz

Promoted by
Wayfair.com

...

makes sure to have a strong CTA for the user to click on the image and link, ultimately creating brand awareness of the brand promoting the ad or to perhaps do business with them. Take a look at the promoted image from Wayfair about taking a quiz to determine your overall style (Photo 9.8). This interactive image is asking the user to go to a designated website (consideration) in order to engage with the brand on its website.

Tiktok

TikTok, the Chinese-based music and video platform, has entered the realm of advertising for a variety of different reasons. The exponential growth they have had among global users is one of the reasons they have established their own ad manager for brands and others to market and advertise within their mobile application ("TikTok Marketing for Beginners," 2019). While the ad manager features are still in the beta and exclusive invite-only stage, TikTok will continue building on the work that other platforms have created to set up their own robust advertising platform for more paid media opportunities. TikTok allows users to create a range of different ads, such as

- designated channels to promote content and advertisements, such as brand takeovers that take over the screen before getting the user back to their followed account content;

- influencer collaborations, where a TikTok creator or influencer creates content that appears as an ad through sponsored content (Sehl, 2020);

- brand takeovers, where the ad starts immediately after the user signs into TikTok;

- top view ads, which take over the entire screen when you first open TikTok;

- ads that appear in feed after three seconds of opening the app in the For You category (TopView);

- in-feed videos, which are videos that come up on the native news feed;

- branded effects and augmented reality (AR) content such as lenses, stickers, filters, and others that are purchased by users to add to their videos on the platform (Sehl, 2020); and

- branded hashtag challenges, which are challenges that appear on TikTok's Discovery page and which encourage audiences to participate in user-generated content (Sehl, 2020); examples include #Moodlip from MAC and Whaler, and #PepsiHalfTime from Pepsi for the 2021 Super Bowl, and Nespresso with #NespressoTalents.

Influencer marketing is one piece of the puzzle for social media, but there are audience members who are not only part of the brand community on social media but are advocates as well. Advocates are willing to put forth their name and reputation to endorse brands without the necessary financial investment an influencer may require. In addition, most audiences crave and gravitate toward sharing more user-generated content on social media. For example, Dwayne Johnson (@TheRock) has been very effective in utilizing his social media channels to promote not only his workouts and daily activities but movies as well. Entertainment brands, such as DC Comics, are encouraging their actors to create content that promotes their upcoming movies and activities, which The Rock is doing on his TikTok account. The Rock created an interactive movie of his training in preparation for his upcoming role as the Black Adam in a film of the same name, with animation and music to make the content entertaining and memorable (Photo 9.9).

▶ **Photo 9.9**
Dwayne Johnson aka The Rock training for *The Black Adam*

Source: TikTok/ @therock

Twitch

Twitch, the popular livestreaming platform that is used for gaming, has gotten into the paid media realm as well. Twitch allows players to connect with their audience through live video along with comments and Q+A sessions, creating a vibrant and interactive community.

One example of paid media is with pre-video rolls. Indeed, Twitch, the popular business job posting website created an ad promoting the notion of connection on the site between a Twitch streamer and digital artist (Carmicheal, 2020). This tied into the fact that many of the users on Twitch are young gamers, all looking for professional opportunities as they enter the workplace or apply for internships. Twitch is a unique platform on social media that does tap into the influencer marketing side of things—both on the strategic side as well as on the creative and paid side of things. Most of the paid opportunities that are showcased on their website for Twitch is dealing primarily with influencer marketing, which is key to note for aligning strategies and financial investment for a campaign.

Other ways Twitch has incorporated paid media into their overall strategy for brands to offer include the following:

- Influencer collaborations (e.g., Ninja, Guy Beahm aka DrDisrespectLive, Dr. Lupo)

- Partnerships and becoming Twitch affiliates

- Brand collaborations (e.g., Wendy's, KFC, Uber Eats, Gillette, Animal Crossing)

- Sponsorships of digital events (e.g., gaming tournaments for games like Fortnite and Fall Guys, sponsored live gaming sessions with influencers, live events for conferences, and how-to classes)

- Brand collaborations with gamers (e.g., The Rock and Xbox to promote ZOA energy drink to Twitch gamers who were fans of Xbox)

- Exclusive interviews with high-profile influencers and figure heads

- Launching exclusive digital assets to promote new products (e.g., Honda releasing their new Civic model on their gaming channel Head2Head)

BEST PRACTICES OF PAID MEDIA

With the tools, assets, and strategies to put forth strong paid media elements on social media, social media professionals should be prepared to implement and execute a strong campaign. To use paid media effectively, here are some best practices to consider:

- **Determine goals and metrics.** To have a strong paid media campaign, you, a social media professional, and your team have to determine the goals, objectives, and overall metrics you will use to evaluate whether or not your paid media strategies have been effective. Having this sound foundation will reduce the frustrations and anxiety sometimes associated with paid media. As soon as you are able to conduct the ad and ad campaign, measure the results and report them to your team, senior management, and clients. Understanding what worked, what didn't, and what are the next steps forward is crucial to an evolving and sustainable paid media strategy.

- **Learn as much as you can about your audiences.** Understand where your audiences are going not just on platforms but what other characteristics and attributes would be important to note about them. What do they like, who and what accounts do they interact with, how much time do they spend online on the designated channels, and what conversations are they having with others about your market, competition, and even your brand online? The more you understand your audience, the more effective you will be in crafting your paid media strategy and ad copy to not only resonate with them but persuade them to take actions based on your goals and objectives.

- **Let your organic posts inform your paid posts.** Let your posts that you share across your channels resonate with your audiences and see which are successful, but also recognize not all posts and pieces of content will work. Learn from these takeaways to help you move forward to future paid media posts.

- **Match CTAs to the written body copy and to overall objectives.** If you are trying to convert audiences to buy a new product, you want to use the conversion objective, not awareness. Alignment with the objectives and the CTAs for each piece of paid media content is critical to have in place so everything is coordinated. Otherwise, there could be confusion for the user; there could also be confusion when evaluating the metrics associated with the paid media placement for the campaign.

- **Get additional training on paid media for social media.** Many people who say they are Facebook ad experts or specialists in advertising on TikTok will ask you to fork over thousands of dollars for their boot camps and workshops. Most of these people have not had the necessary training, education, or experience running their own ads. If you are looking for assistance or help in continuing to learn about paid media, go to professionals with experience who have the respect from and high reputation in the industry for their work. Dennis Yu of Blitzmetrics is one such professional who has earned this reputation. In addition, taking advantage of the individual platform's educational certification programs, like Facebook Blueprint, Google AdWords, Pinterest Academy, and Twitter Flight School, among others, is also a good investment to consider.

- **Don't rely only on the metrics that are provided to by the platform.** This is the time to inspect what you expect. As platforms evolve, so do their algorithms and features. This can affect the measurement metrics for paid media components related to reach, impressions, views, and more. Being able to test and evaluate the effectiveness of paid media elements through various tools to triangulate what is really happening is a strategy that needs to be set into play.

- **Experiment with content, written copy, and frameworks.** Test, test, and test some more before putting money behind a paid media strategy. To determine what works, there has to be some testing and experimentation happening. Combine messages and different ad copy along with different visual formats to see which ones will perform the best before launching a campaign. These experiments and pilot tests will not only provide valuable insights moving forward in the campaign, but they could serve as a financial investment to save money spent on unsuccessful posts and ads. Once these paid media components are conducted and executed—whether it is a paid influencer collaboration or sponsored post—determine what worked, what didn't, and what to watch out for in the next paid media campaign.

- **Don't use the same creative assets, design, or copy for all ads.** If you are in a campaign reaching different audiences, you have to make sure to personalize the messages and copy (along with the CTAs) for each audience. Not all audiences are going to respond the same way to the messages or be stimulated into paying attention to the same visuals. Understanding the motivations, interests, and overall expectations of each audience is critical to apply individually to each target set for a paid media campaign. Assuming all audiences are going to respond the same way to an ad is a big mistake. Remember, assumptions cause issues and crises, so it is best to investigate, research, and do due diligence before moving forward. In addition, make sure the overall design of the ad is mobile first, since most social media users access their channels on their mobile device.

- **Understand the perceptions attributed to ads.** Not everyone wants to be targeted, and it is important to understand the negative perceptions people may have for brands and platforms that use their user data to target and market to them without prompts. This is a big issue for platforms like Facebook, which has been in the news for privacy and data collection concerns, including selling user data to brands for their own campaigns. In addition, there are places where users do not want ads to interrupt their activities on the social media platforms they are on. This was a big issue for Snapchat when it rose to popularity in the late 2010s, and as brands came on board with their ads and promotional content, users left.

- **Set a strong and realistic budget.** Having a realistic and sound budget for a paid media campaign is essential (Baker, n.d.). Without a budget, there is only so much a social media professional can do. Make sure to set aside a designated amount to use on specific initiatives and platforms. Results, metrics, and data are necessary to support the investment needed for the campaign. To make a budget argument to senior management, there must be data supporting the need for the budget and the investment for social. Most of these resources may come from other places that were previously used (e.g., traditional media buys) for a client. Before social media, most advertising budgets were geared toward traditional media outlets, such as newspaper ads, magazine placements, and TV spots. Digital and social media advertising was slim to none at this point. Presently, most of these budgets have reversed; in some cases, most of the advertising budget is first focused on digital first, including social media. You also want to be realistic in what you are paying for—will you be focusing on impressions or engagement? What is the overall goal and objective? The amount you need to set aside for your paid media executions on social media will depend on your answers to these questions.

- **Explore new platforms for paid media opportunities.** Some of these platforms can become saturated with paid posts and sponsored content, so it may be worthwhile to explore emerging areas to connect and engage with audiences. Getting a headstart on this can be extremely beneficial for formulating relationships with the platforms to get exclusive access to their ad manager platform, resulting in more opportunities to be highlighted and showcased as a leading example in the industry.

CHAPTER SUMMARY

Paid media is not only a component that needs to be included in traditional areas such as marketing, public relations, and advertising; it is also a key specialization and key marketable skill. Social media professionals should have evidence of paid media proficiency in their industry toolkit. The days in which there is no advertising or paid media in a social media strategic campaign are long over. In fact, the industry is going to see more paid media interconnected with all platform strategies as more brands get on board. The biggest challenge will be to not only keep up with the growing changes with platform regulations, algorithm updates, data collection concerns, and ad fatigue, but where users are going next. As users move from one platform to the next, advertisers will soon follow with their sponsored posts, ads, and paid media elements to persuade users that they need to hear from these brands.

THOUGHT QUESTIONS

1. What is paid media, and where does it fit in the overall media ecosystem?

2. What are two benefits of paid media for social media professionals? What are two challenges?

3. What are the three objectives that are universally used in paid media on platforms?

Identify one example that is associated with each objective.

4. Why is it important to know how platform algorithms play a big part for a social media campaign?

5. Identify some of the strategies of paid media that are commonly used by Instagram.

EXERCISES

1. You have been asked to create a paid media strategy for Buff City Soap, a natural ingredient soap brand, for their new store opening in Austin, TX. They have done some Facebook advertising but just boosted posts. Provide recommendations for Buff City Soap on what they could do for ads on Instagram, Twitter, YouTube, and TikTok.

2. As you are entering a new internship for Broadway NYC, and you see they have a great social media strategy plan for paid

ads on all their channels, except for TikTok and Pinterest. The internship coordinator says there is no reason to spend money on these channels for paid media. Provide your rationale for using paid media ads on these channels, and recommend at least two types of ads they could use.

3. You are part of a collaborative communication and marketing team for General Motors (GM). You are presenting a workshop on paid media and reaching

Generation Z and Generation Alpha to the team, and the vice president of corporate communication is invited to sit in. In your short presentation, provide a 3-minute mini-talk on the benefits of paid media, and highlight some paid media recommendations GM could incorporate to engage these audiences.

4. As part of a job interview for Mint Mobile, you are asked to come up with a paid media strategy for Twitter, Instagram, and Twitch. Discuss three proposed strategies and ideas you have for advertising Mint Mobile on these platforms and the associated KPIs you will be using to evaluate the effectiveness of each strategy.

REFERENCES

Bain, E. (2020, April 14). How to get the Trolls World Tour Snapchat filter—and other movie filters to try. *HITC*. https://www.hitc.com/en-gb/2020/04/14/trolls-world-tour-snapchat-filter/

Baker, K. (n.d.). The ultimate guide to mastering the basics of effective social media advertising. *HubSpot*. https://blog.hubspot.com/marketing/basics-effective-social-media-advertising

Barnhart, B. (2019, August 13). Everything you need to know about social media algorithms. *Sprout Social*. https://sproutsocial.com/insights/social-media-algorithms/

Best practices for sponsored content. (n.d.). *LinkedIn*. https://business.linkedin.com/marketing-solutions/success/best-practices/sponsored-content-tips

Carmicheal, K. (n.d.). Paid social media: Worth the investment? *HubSpot*. https://blog.hubspot.com/marketing/paid-social-media

Carmicheal, K. (2020). What is Twitch? *HubSpot*. https://blog.hubspot.com/marketing/twitch

Gurd, J. (2020, October 13). Understanding the role of organic vs paid social media. *Smart Insights*. https://www.smartinsights.com/social-media-marketing/social-media-strategy/understanding-role-organic-paid-social-media/

Monllos, K. (2020, January 20). What a $5.6m Super Bowl buy can purchase in digital media in 2020. *Digiday*. https://digiday.com/marketing/5-6m-super-bowl-buy-can-purchase-digital-media-2020/

Newberry, C., & McLachlan, S. (2020, September 9). Social media advertising 101: How to get the most out of your ad budget. *Hootsuite*. https://blog.hootsuite.com/social-media-advertising/

Oetting, J. (n.d.). YouTube ads for beginners: How to launch & optimize a YouTube video advertising campaign. *HubSpot*. https://blog.hubspot.com/marketing/youtube-video-advertising-guide

Pay-per-click advertising: What is PPC advertising? (n.d.). *WordStream*. https://www.wordstream.com/pay-per-click-advertising

Sehl, K. (2020, March 2). Everything you need to know about TikTok in 2020. *Hootsuite*. https://blog.hootsuite.com/what-is-tiktok/

Shewan, D. (2020, February 25). Native advertising examples: 5 of the best (and worst). *WordStream*. https://www.wordstream.com/blog/ws/2014/07/07/native-advertising-examples

Snapchat ad formats. (n.d.). *Snapchat for Business*. https://forbusiness.snapchat.com/advertising/ad-formats

Social media advertising & paid social guide. (n.d.). *Sprout Social*. https://sproutsocial.com/insights/topics/social-media-advertising/

Stec, C. (n.d.). How to run Facebook ads: A step-by-step guide to advertising on Facebook. *HubSpot*. https://blog.hubspot.com/marketing/facebook-paid-ad-checklist

TikTok marketing for beginners—A marketer's guide to advertising on Tiktok. (2019, May 20). *Influencer Marketing Hub*. https://influencermarketinghub.com/tiktok-marketing-guide/

Using Ads Manager. (n.d.). *Pinterest Business*. https://business.pinterest.com/en/using-ads-manager

Zote, J. (2020). Social media statistics. *Sprout Social*. https://sproutsocial.com/insights/social-media-statistics/

10

STRATEGIC WRITING FOR SOCIAL MEDIA

Learning Objectives

After reading this chapter, you will be able to

- Evaluate the importance of writing for social media

- Distinguish among content creation, content curation, and content marketing

- Identify the types of writing that are used in social media

- Understand the best practices for writing for social media

INTRODUCTION

What is the most important skill to have in social media? There are lots of answers to this question, but the one that is most valued and needed is usually not the first thing you think of. When asked what the most important skills in the social media industry are, many may come to mind, such as coding, data analysis, and even graphic design. All of these are important, but the one skill that every brand, organization, start-up, and agency needs from new hires and candidates in the social media space is writing.

Writing for social media is not rocket science. You may be intimidated by social media, but this chapter will walk you through the steps to follow not only for your own social media platforms but also for those of your client, brand, or business. Writing is the bridge that connects ideas and shares them in a strategic and relevant manner. Successful social media writers create messages that are relevant for their audiences, resonating with them on a personal and emotional level, and that at the same time are professional and aligned with the brand's mission and core attributes. The content created for social media also needs to be entertaining, which will give audiences more opportunities to remember and share what they felt and saw with others. Whether you write an update on Twitter or a long-form blog post depends on the brand, community, situation, and goal you have in mind.

HUMANS OF SOCIAL MEDIA

Leah Schultz, Director of Brand and Social Media for Twin Spires at Churchill Downs

Introduction

As the director of brand and social media at Twin Spires at Churchill Downs, Leah Schultz oversees daily social media operations. This includes social marketing strategy execution, social intelligence/analytics, social listening, paid social advertising, social care, and community management. Schultz holds a bachelor's degree in integrated strategic communication from the University of Kentucky. Connect with her on social media:

- LinkedIn www.linkedin.com/in/leahmackey

- Twitter: https://twitter.com/MackeyLeah

- Instagram: https://www.instagram.com/mackeyleah/

How did you get your start in social media?

I started in advertising sales—print (newspaper) ad sales to be exact. I lasted three months before I got fired. I hated it.

I spent the next two years at an array of résumé filler jobs that paid poorly and didn't interest or stimulate me much mentally. At one of those jobs I had randomly started a Twitter account to try to figure out if it could be a channel to drive sales (part of my job was selling birthday parties/corporate events at family fun centers across the state). I somehow stumbled across the Twitter account for Social Media Club Nashville. The account was promoting a tweet up. I thought that sounded like a great opportunity to figure

out this "Twitter thing" and maybe do some networking and score some job interviews.

Five and a half years later and I've been promoted twice. I was the Papa John's Brand Team as a Director. I managed all the social media functions, but also handled a fair amount of responsibility for overall brand strategy and calendar planning, with a heavy emphasis on creative reviews. I managed our influencer and creator program, which was a very fun adventure over the couple years. I started my new role at Churchill Downs in summer of 2020.

What is your favorite part of working in your area of expertise in social media?

My favorite part of working in the social and digital industry is creating, connecting, and curating. I love people, I love psychology, I love technology, I love learning, I love new experiences, and I love being challenged. Working in social has allowed me to put my natural curiosity to work in a virtual environment.

What is one thing you can't live without while working in social media?

Twitter. It's the first thing I look at in the morning and the last thing I look at before I go to sleep every day. There's no better way to know what is happening in the world, in the news, in culture, in entertainment, etc. than Twitter. It moves in real time with snackable bites of content with just a sentence or two.

Twitter has allowed me to meet people I never would have met IRL [in real life] and to have direct access to influencers and thought leaders.

What is your favorite social media account (person/brand/etc.) to follow and why?

Brands/Accounts

- Flex Seal, https://www.instagram.com/flexseal/, oddly popular with the millennials and Gen Z, unapologetically authentic content

- Gushers, https://www.instagram.com/therealgushers/, memes, purposefully fun and people

- https://twitter.com/ValaAfshar, Chief Digital Evangelist at Salesforce, tweets inspirational thoughts about humanity, business, tech

What is the most challenging part of working in social media?

The most challenging parts of working in social, specifically for a global QSR brand, are the pace of the industry and the pressure of how highly visible the work is.

Technology today moves at lightspeed. As soon as something is invented online or in the digital space, it seems like it's made obsolete by version 2.0 the next day. Keeping up with industry trends can be challenging.

Secondly, the visibility at scale can be daunting. There is a lot of responsibility that comes with "pressing the button." With one click of the mouse, a social media manager has the power to send a message to millions of people on behalf of a brand. This means your great work, your mistakes, and everything you say are on full display for the world to see.

In a culture that is obsessed with likes and "doing it for the 'gram'" social media managers live in an ecosystem where this is

amplified 100-fold. Here's the anxiety-inducing things we deal with daily:

- Making typos in tweets (@Jack we ever getting an edit button??)

- Trolls, Keyboard Cowboys, Grammar Police, and haters who are constantly serving up abuse, hate speech, bullying, and general negative commentary as they hide behind their screens

- Being called "the intern who makes $10 an hour"

- Newsflash: no global company has an intern making $10/hour serving as the company's mouthpiece. We are highly educated, technically skilled, and wear many hats. The stigma is real.

- Social is a 24/7/365 job. We work nights, weekends, holidays, on vacation, and when we are home sick. We are glued to our phones and laptops. We carry 35 chargers and adapters and are editing photos and videos on airplanes. And contrary to popular belief, we don't have a magic wand, a way to stop time, or the ability to turn off the internet.

- The unknown curveballs and fire drills we navigate daily are our norm. Nine times out of ten our day never goes the way we planned it. The variables are endless and the internet is a weird and unpredictable place. God speed, fellow social marketers!

What is your take on your area of expertise and the social media industry?

I've been doing social media for 11 years and the one thing I know is that I don't know anything at all. Expect the unexpected. You have

(Continued)

(Continued)

to be nimble and you have to be able to roll with the punches. The space is ever changing. I have no idea what "social media" will be in 5, 10, or 50 years.

What do you wish you had known when you were starting out?

- You are never too young to start networking. Join professional development organizations to learn new skills and meet new people.

- Keep learning. Be a sponge. No matter what industry you are in, it will not be the same in 5, 10, or 35 years. Be curious and ask questions.

- Listening, empathy, and reciprocity are the keys to success. Listen more than you speak.

- Find the intersection of simplicity, originality, emotion, and creativity. The best ideas are those that are straightforward, distinctive, emotion evoking, and inspiring.

- Gimmicks are short lived. Activate tactics for short-term wins but bet big on the long game.

- Be your biggest cheerleader and your biggest critic. Celebrate your wins and learn from your misses. Fail fast and fail hard.

What are three marketable skills a social media professional needs to have to work in the industry?

Writing, analytics, and technical acumen

Where do you go to keep up to date with trends and continue learning about social media?

- Subscribe to all the social platform's official blogs and follow the official accounts on their respective social channels.

- Subscribe to/follow top industry blogs and thought leaders.

- Complete online courses and get certified when possible (e.g., Facebook Blueprint, Twitter Flight School, Google Analytics, etc.).

- Attend conferences.

- Join groups, forums, message boards, subreddits, etc., that are focused on specific areas of interest.

If you had to choose a song to walk out to in a presentation on social media, what would it be and why?

I'm picking the ultimate hip hop pump-up song when you need to hype yourself up: "Til I Collapse," by Eminem & Nate Dogg.

IMPORTANCE OF STRATEGIC WRITING FOR SOCIAL MEDIA

Writing effectively on social media is one of the most challenging responsibilities of social media professionals. Many job postings emphasize this fundamental skill that all young professionals should have in their wheelhouse and toolkit. We sometimes forget that writing is an effective way to communicate with our audiences. To be a successful social media manager, you need to have strong writing skills along with an understanding of the six *C*s of effective writing for social media:

- Content

- Community

- Culture

- Conversation

- Creativity

- Connection

Content. Many people have a stake in creating and writing **content** for social media. Journalists use it to release breaking news to their readers. Marketing professionals use it to manage the data and metrics from their marketing campaigns. Public relations professionals use it to monitor, listen, and engage with audiences in real time to build on relationships and keep track of conversations. All of these roles have a place within the social media space, and all require creating, curating, and featuring relevant content while evaluating its effectiveness for senior management.

Social media professionals need to make sure that the content they share is relevant to their target audiences. We need to be aware of what truly matters to the audience we are trying to reach. Both primary and secondary research can help. In addition, exploring the segments of your audience (different categories and groups of individuals you want to reach in your social media efforts) might come in handy. User interests, location, type, and time on social media are some factors to review to determine the content that may be most relevant to your intended audiences. People also want to receive content that is useful. Promotional ads and updates are not always the most successful, especially for brands that go for the "hard sell" or abruptly push users to take action when there has been no transition or build-up to the relationship.

Writing skills come in various forms and include duties surrounding the importance of creating good content. You can have the best writing style, but the substance of content and information you are sharing, creating, and engaging with on social media also needs to be high in quality. These duties include editing, copy writing, and creating messages that fit the appropriate channel and audience. The content that a brand publishes and presents on social media is the first impression that audiences get online, so if the copy is filled with grammatical errors, spelling mistakes, or unrelated jargon that is inappropriate for the audience and channel, this can significantly impact the overall impression the person or company wants to make. These are just some of the reasons why excellent writing skills are so important and fundamental for today's social media professionals.

Not only must we be aware of having professional and unique content on each platform, but we also must take into consideration the differences between one channel and another when posting on them. What works on Instagram may not work on LinkedIn or as a blog post. Each post and platform needs to be evaluated based on the audience, brand, community, situation, and channel. With social media, a lot of channels need to be taken into consideration, as well as the rapid evolution of each channel. New features, algorithm and format changes, and other elements are constantly added on to these platforms, which makes it harder in some cases for social media professionals to adapt their content to fit the needs and framework dictated by these social media companies.

Brands such as Sour Patch Kids and the Colorado Rockies baseball team have built a presence for themselves in their respective industries related to what content they create, but also the captions and written updates they provide along with the content.

Community. **Community**, or a group of individuals who come together based on common interests, values, and characteristics, is part of the mix when it comes to creating content that resonates with audiences. The overall dynamics of people's interactions on social media is one of the most important factors to consider. Here are a few questions you will want to think about when you are looking at community as it relates to content.

- Do people want to receive content?
- What type of content are they expecting to see from the brand? When is it is not appropriate to share content?
- Who within the community do they want to receive content from?
- In which situations do community members expect a response or message from a brand?
- When do they want to receive content?
- Do they want engagement, or do they just want to consume content?
- What are the appropriate times and places to share content and messages with them?
- What are the responses you hope to get with your content from the community?

These are a few questions we all have to ask ourselves when looking at a community. In Chapter 6, we determined some of the monitoring and listening techniques that can be used to create and foster new ideas for messages, content, and engagement. Sometimes community is also aligned with the overall **culture** (common practices, work-life ethics and practices, professional experiences, and beliefs of a group of individuals) of the company, brand, or community in question. Etiquette, feelings and significant issues, and historical approaches that characterize how each party interacts and formulates relationships are key factors related to culture that social media writers should consider.

When it comes to community, there are many brands that have owned this space, but one brand you may not consider but should note is Slim Jim. Slim Jim, the meat stick company, had their community emerge on social media after the late Andy Hines, a meme creator. Their community, as referred to as "Long Boi Gang," where the community continues to share memes, inside jokes, and shared experiences while celebrating the meat stick products. The community, as a result, has helped Slim Jim cultivate a 1.2+ million follower base on social media across all of their platforms (Zafarris, 2021).

Conversation. **Conversation** is also important in making sure social media content resonates with key audiences. People do not want to be advertised to or promoted to all of the time. They are more likely to tune out and go on to the next thing if they feel a brand is pushing too hard with its promotional messages.

Conversation is not just responding to a post, but rather engaging in a discussion that is meaningful to both parties. Understanding the type of brand voice and writing style on social media contributes to the effectiveness of your message strategy for your audiences. Your response to a person's inquiry about your product can be either formal or snarky. It can also be humorous and evoke personality characteristics that are memorable and unique. Responding appropriately in communications that are not official social media marketing messages is an important skill. Sometimes we can anticipate these informal types of scenarios, and other times social media managers have to think on their feet, essentially, in their responses. Conversing may take some training, education, and testing to see how each social media manager would respond to each message and how far or closely aligned the responses are to the brand voice and mission.

Social care, discussed in more detail in Chapter 15 takes place when brands are able to have conversations in real time with audiences to answer questions, address concerns, or even bounce around ideas. The **creativity** involved with how these conversations arise (perhaps thanks to monitoring and listening practices) can help build memorable **connections**. Strong writers on social media should have skills to address each type of communication.

Among the many brands that haved tried to authentically engage audiences through social care and conversation practices are McDonald's and Aviation Gin. Aviation Gin has the flexibility to strike up converastions in a tone that reflects Ryan Reynolds in the brand's engagement with both fans and other brands, such as Hugh Jackman's Laughing Man Coffee (remember, we will always be part of #TeamRyan!). On the other hand, McDonald's has tapped into tying their brand into cultural events in their writing to embrace "fan truth," tying into relating with younger audiences to make a connection through their content, online engagement, and cultural moments such as their partnership with Travis Scott.

CONTENT CREATION VERSUS CONTENT CURATION

Within the overall social media strategy discussed in Chapter 7 content creation and curation are two parts of essential writing. You do not want to have 100% of one versus the other, but rather you want to provide a mixture of content that is originally created (**content creation**) and content that was published from a different source (**content curation**). Remember, whether you are looking to create content or curate content, the key for successful engagement and interaction on social media is to have good, strong content. Good content needs to be aligned with the goals and objectives set in place for a social media initiative. If the goal is to provide a sense of community and build awareness of the brand, you want to create stories integrated with videos, testimonials, and even blog posts. However, if the goal is to increase share of voice and buzz related to a campaign, you want to create content that drives home a strong call-to-action statement (share this, tweet that, use a certain hashtag, create a video, etc.). For example, the amyotrophic lateral sclerosis (ALS) Ice Bucket Challenge succeeded in creating strong content not just for the campaign in 2014 but also as the campaign continues to build momentum (Photo 10.1). The ALS Association gave audiences clear, concise, and actionable steps. In addition, organizations also create content that brings forth awareness of what resources and information might be useful for audiences to take advantage of. Cannes Lions Festival of Creativity—a global awards festival that is held every year in Cannes, France, for advertising, creativity, and digital professionals—provided updates and original content for their Lions Live virtual event in 2020 when COVID-19 cancelled the in-person event. The festival used

The ALS Association
August 1, 2016 · 🌐

[INFOGRAPHIC] The ALS Ice Bucket Challenge took us part of the way to finding a treatment and cure for ALS. Learn just how far we've come and find out how you can help take us the rest of the way. #EveryDropAddsUp

Progress Since the Ice Bucket Challenge

ALSA.ORG

▸ **Photo 10.1**
ALS Association Infographic on Ice Bucket Challenge

Source: Facebook/@The ALS Association

LIONS | The Home of Creativity ✅
@Cannes_Lions   ᵒᵒᵒ

The Lions Creativity Report of the Decade is the industry-leading resource from #CannesLions using ten years of data to benchmark creativity and effectiveness.

View the report in full here:
lionslive.canneslions.com/intelligence#L...

11:13 AM · Jul 1, 2020 · Twitter Media Studio

6 Retweets   **16** Likes

    💬   🔁   ♡   ↥

▸ **Photo 10.2**
Cannes Lions and Lions Live

Source: Twitter/@Cannes_Lions

various social media platforms such as Twitter, Instagram, Facebook, and more to distribute this content to the masses online. As shown in Photo 10.2, this was one of the first events that went completely virtual due to COVID-19, and the overall strategy Cannes Lions wanted to communicate with Lions Live was the value and additional features audiences would be getting from them, including a new research report on creativity to be cited, used, and shared within the community. Cannes Lions as a whole wanted to produce content and value for their audiences in order to enhance the overall digital learning experience for students, educators, and professionals in the creativity and media industry.

On the other hand, curation involves collecting and strategically selecting content from various sources that may be relevant for your key audiences. For example, the University of Southern California (USC) Annenberg School for Communication and Journalism might share content from another source about a fellowship or professional opportunity because this content is relevant for its key audiences on a specific platform (e.g., Twitter). This sharing in turn creates a perception among your audience members that you are not only creating original, valuable content, but also taking the time to make sure audiences get all of the information needed to make an informed decision about various possibilities and opportunities.

The overall purpose of curation is to provide your audiences with useful information that not only resonates with them but builds on their perception that your brand online is a valuable resource. That said, there should be a standard approach for deciding which resources, accounts, and outlets you would recommend as possible sources from which to share content. It may not be a common practice for a specific brand (e.g., University of Louisville) to share content from a competing school (e.g., University of Kentucky) with its audiences, but it is key to monitor and listen to your competitors on social media, just as it is important to note which brands and accounts you would share information from. Once you have a systematic approach and protocol on how to handle this, include it in the social media writing guide (discussed in the next section) as well as the social media policy maintained within a brand, organization, or agency.

UNDERSTANDING THE DIFFERENCE BETWEEN TONE AND VOICE

When creating your **brand voice** (Lee, 2014a), make sure it does not reflect your own perspective but rather the personality characteristics that are unique, memorable, and authentic to your brand. This is a challenge that can test you as a person for your personal accounts, but also when you are representing a brand online. All brands have an individual voice, characteristics, and history that make them memorable to their key audiences. The voice projected on social media must be aligned with how others perceive the company, organization, or person. Any disconnect between that perception and how people or brands share content online can result in loss of community members, business, and, in some cases, acknowledgment as a viable member of the industry.

Sometimes **tone** (Lee, 2014a) is confused with brand voice, but in a sense, they are interconnected. Tone is the overall voice characteristics you want to interject within the content you are writing. For example, do you want to sound more professional and formal when you are representing a publicly traded business, or do you want to intertwine some personality into your content by adding humor? The tone of your social media content can be tailored depending on the situation, channel, and audience in question (Read, 2017). In addition, the social media tone you convey must be aligned specifically to the characteristics of each area. The key demographics, psychographics, and location of your community (audience) will influence the overall language (professional, casual, hip, etc.) you use to accomplish your overall objectives (e.g., to create awareness, to entertain, or to educate). All of these factors are interconnected with not only the brand voice but the overall tone set for the social media brand.

Let's apply these concepts to a food example. Voice is the ice cream flavor, and tone serves as the extra toppings and sprinkles. Each voice (like ice cream) has a foundation that makes it unique and different. Vanilla ice cream has certain key ingredients, for example, but each brand (e.g., Salt & Straw, Jeni's Splendid Ice Creams, or McConnell's) has a unique twist and process for creating its products, which is analogous to establishing a brand voice. The unique combination of tone, however, is showcased in the toppings. Some people are cookies-and-cream types, and others love chocolate-covered bacon. Each topping (or, in the case of social media, tone) showcases an additional layer of the brand voice. Let's take the ice cream brands we have shared here. Salt & Straw focuses on unique flavors and collaborations but embraces a consistent warm voice as they promote their products (including their partnership with The Rock, in which they have embraced his brand voice). Jeni's Splendid Ice Creams' voice is vibrant and personable (especially with their partnerships, such as Dolly Parton), and McConnell's Ice Cream focuses on tradition and the history the Santa Barbara company has created. Both companies are in the same industry, but they position themselves differently by their products and brand voice online.

As you can see, so many different combinations can be created that no one brand uses the same voice or tone in its message strategies. The most important factor to keep in mind is to be yourself. You do not want to "force" your brand voice and persona in your written social media content if it is not authentic. This is a time not to be like everyone else but rather to separate yourself from others. Identifying the gaps in others' brand voices and the overall tone of their social media content is the name of the game. We are all unique, and we need to embrace ourselves wholeheartedly on social media without any concern about our differences. Brand voice allows us to establish a human connection online and allows conversations, relationships, and communities to be established in an authentic and true manner.

Along with maintaining a consistent and authentic voice with the appropriate tone, social media content should reflect the overall personality as well as the language of the brand or individual. What attributes do you want to display and communicate in your messages? How will you create content to show this in a certain and consistent way? What is the overall purpose and rationale for each post? Social media professionals must take all of these questions into consideration for each individual post, update, and video created and shared online.

How Do You Find Your Brand Voice in Your Writing Style?

This is an important step to consider before you start writing for social media. Before even writing up a Facebook ad or creating an Instagram Story, ask yourself the following questions to make sure you are being true in your social media messages to your personal brand or to the brand of the company for whom you work:

- How would you describe your brand (or yourself) in terms of personality attributes?

- What are some attributes that do not reflect your brand?

- How would you describe your relationships with your audiences online based on the content you share?

- How do people feel about your content?

- What is in it for your key audiences? What benefits are they getting from being part of these communities and receiving your messages?

- Who are your key audiences? What are they motivated and inspired by?

- What content, messaging, and actions do your key audiences expect from you?

- How would you describe your competitors? How do they communicate online? What is their overall tone? How would you describe their brand voice?

- What goals do you have for how your audience feels about you?

- What is the purpose for your content? How would you rate your content right now, and what are your goals for how your audience will respond to your content?

- What do you want your audience to do in response to your content?

Table 10.1 outlines the various types of content message strategies and executions that can be organized and framed within a social media writing guide. The

Table 10.1 Sample Writing Guide for Social Media

Platform	Content	Audience	Voice	Writing Style	Approaches
Facebook	Ad, video, update, live video, stories, groups	Customers, marketing pros	Engaged and interested in purchases	Professional, product/brand focused, audience focused	Have a call-to-action statement and link to a specific place
Twitter	Tweet, video, live, Fleets, spaces	Fans, media professionals	Entertainment, informative	Witty, snarky, conversational, informational, engaging	Media with specific hashtag or link to track
Instagram	Album, story, post, Reels, live, live rooms	Bloggers, influencers, fans	Community	Educational, conversational, audience focused, product/brand focused, inspirational	Short update statement
Snapchat	Story ads	Generation Z, content creators	Experiential, humorous	Audience focused, entertainment	Visual storyboard approach
LinkedIn	Pulse post, live video, stories	Marketing professionals, business-to-business customers	Informative, approachable, educational	Professional, educational	Update with key hashtags tagging keywords, and cross shares on Twitter and Facebook
TikTok	Story Challenge Live	Gen Z, marketing professionals, creators	Entertaining, humorous, educational	Mixture of professional and unprofessional (depending on the challenges)	Integrating keywords, trending hashtags, and cross shares across other platforms

255

table showcases examples of how social media managers can break down their writing content based on platform, type of content, key audiences, what voice to present and implement, what writing style to utilize, and how the writing style will be approached.

Social media managers can take several actions to engage with their audiences on social media and brainstorm ideas for content that supports the brand mission and overall voice online. Kevan Lee (2014b) of Buffer outlined 71 ways for social media managers to create content online. Specifically, he mentioned a few to consider for each platform. Table 10.2 outlines some of these suggestions for building and creating content on social media. In addition, resources like Buffer (2018) allow you to tailor posts to a specific channel and platform, which helps social media managers create the most effective content that is relevant for the audience as well as compatible with the platform format.

You also want to have a set plan to evaluate the message creation steps that already take place within the company or agency. Exploring how team members communicate with each other, with audience members, and outside of the brand are factors to consider here as well. It is important to conduct a team brand voice audit because writing in another voice (e.g., a social media community manager writing on behalf of a brand on social media) is one of the most challenging tasks for social media professionals to master. This audit can be a way to determine the overall feeling and perception of a brand voice, but you can also address and highlight this by doing research. Exploring the main attributes people associate with a brand through survey questions, focus groups, or even word clouds associated with the brand online based on social media monitoring analysis are just a few ways of identifying some of the attributes tied to a brand voice.

Along with a standard approach for social media conduct and policies, there needs to be a written and digital social media writing style guide for all social media professionals to follow, embrace, and engage in. This guide will help set forth the brand standard and overall voice online, while also ensuring that the messages attached to social media are consistent across the board. This is considered the brand standard and framework for social media professionals.

Social Media Writing Guide

Certain consistent sections need to be included in the social media writing guide. Sometimes brands will already have established a set social media writing guide, but other times one has to be set forth from scratch. Looking at the main components as follows is important for either following or perhaps creating a social media writing guide for a client, person, or business.

Content you are passionate about. This is content that you feel focuses on your strengths as a person (if you are managing a personal account) or as a representative of a professional account. If you are passionate about blogs, videos, GIFs, tweets, Instagram posts, or another type of content, discuss what makes it relevant to your cause. Most importantly, remember that it may not take as much time to create and write these pieces of content because you have such a positive association with them. It is always easier to write content that you like to create rather than content you are "forced" to create.

Content that your audience members are passionate about. This is where you will have to conduct a thorough audit of the type of content that will be

Table 10.2	Platform Characteristics and Content Writing Ideas	
Platform	**Platform Characteristics**	**Content Ideas**
Facebook	• Max character limit is 63,206, but posts that have 80 characters have the most engagement (Read, 2017). • Username is 50 characters. • Facebook Page description is 155 characters. • Facebook comments are 8,000 characters.	• Start an update with a question. • End an update with a question. • Create a list. • Add a quote from an article, interview, feature, or event/speaker. • Update with emojis. • Use an image with text overlay. • Attribute and tag other accounts. • Provide a customized URL.
Twitter	• Character limit is 280 but options are available to add images, videos, and collages, and tag users, now. • You do not always have to use all 280 characters. • Images (4) can be included. • Multimedia (e.g., video, GIFs, etc.) are also included.	• Place comments before headline. • Place comments after headline. • Include commentary + quote of tweet. • Place tweets inside the comments. • Integrate multimedia. • Conduct polls. • Attribute with tag. • Create Twitter Moments. • Twitter chats. • Twitter threads. • Create stories and announcements through Fleets. • Use Twitter threads to elaborate ongoing conversations that are more than 280 characters (use /1, /2, etc., as you see fit to complete the conversation). • Tag accounts in image or video.

(Continued)

Table 10.2 (Continued)		
Platform	Platform Characteristics	Content Ideas
Instagram	• Max character limit is 2,200 characters. • Max hashtags that can be used in a post is 30.	• Give tutorials. • Try microvisual blogging. • Offer giveaways and contests. • Ask a question + probe for engagement. • Feature products. • Share tips and tricks. • Give Q&As. • Highlight historical features. • Give interviews. • Host live concerts. • Post updates. • Go behind the scenes. • Provide storyboards (posts + Instagram Stories). • Mix up content for Stories (still images, videos, Instagram-based apps, text only, etc.). • Tag accounts in updates, stories, and albums.
LinkedIn	• LinkedIn recommendation: 3,000 characters • LinkedIn Publishing post headline: 150 characters • LinkedIn Publishing content length: approximately 120,000 characters	• Post an update. • Post an update with a URL. • Share a Pulse article. • Post an update with a video. • Post an update with an image. • Host a live streaming show with LinkedIn Live.
Pinterest	• Pinterest profile name: 20 characters • Pinterest bio: 160 characters • Pinterest username: 15 characters • Pinterest board name: 100 characters	• Share tutorials. • Share blog posts. • Upload infographics.

Platform	Platform Characteristics	Content Ideas
	• Pinterest board description: 500 characters • Pin description: 500 characters	
YouTube	• Video title: 70 characters • YouTube description: 5,000 characters • Playlist titles: 60 characters • YouTube tags: 30 characters per tag, 500 characters total	• Tutorials • Vlogs • Interviews • Informational sessions • Documentaries • Collaborations
TikTok	• App names (4–40 characters), • 150-character limit on captions • 20 keywords for TikTok • 60 seconds of content	• Challenges • Duets • Lipsyncing/Dancing • Comedy skits/dialogue reenactments • Voiceovers • Collaborations • Videos (teaching, cooking, food, workout, freeze frame, animated, etc.) • Tutorials • Walk-throughs

Source: Adapted from Dominique, J. (2020, December 15). Know Your Limit: The Ideal Length of Every Social Media Post. Sprout Social. Retrieved from https://sproutsocial.com/insights/social-media-character-counter/#linkedin

well received by your audiences and what content needs to be revamped for the appropriate platform. This content may be similar to or different from the content you are personally passionate about as discussed in the previous paragraph. If the content is the same for both parties (the person or organization and key audiences), then you are in a good position for the moment. However, if these perspectives are different, then an adjustment needs to be made. Keep in mind that these items must be surveyed on a regular basis because audiences evolve over time.

Audience and persona summary. Your audience is one of the first things to define and discuss. To write the best content, you first have to note who you will be reaching, what messages and content they want to hear, and what they are looking for in the online community. This is another way to identify the various channels of communication to focus on. You may assume your audiences will gravitate to other places and channels, but in order to fully write effective content, you have to know where they are going in order to reach them. Keep in mind that language and tone are also big factors here since different audiences will have access to these messages at different times and places, and they may want information presented

Table 10.3 HubSpot Content Template			
Content That Is Reflected in the Brand Voice	Content That Is Not Reflected in the Brand Voice	Connection Back to the Brand (Personal or Professional Voice)	Purpose and Rationale

to them in different ways. Social media professionals have to account for the various ways in which people comprehend messages across the channels. Some audience members may be more likely to respond to video, whereas others may have a preference for long-form content. Tailoring the content for the channel, audience, and situation is crucial for social media professionals to establish a strong connection with their audiences.

Branding. Along with writing great content, social media managers need to make sure that their content is informed by the art of branding. Branding is more than just slapping a logo on an image or using a specific hashtag. Instead, it encompasses the way in which a message comes across in its voice, image, community, and perception. There should be a rationale for creating the content, and it should be aligned with and connected back to the overall mission and purpose of the company, person, or organization. Content that is not aligned with the designated characteristics or perceptions of a brand could mislead audiences. Branding also translates into what messages are sent out on behalf of the brand. For example, Coca-Cola does not send out social media messages that are not representative of its overall persona or image. The company stays true to its "Open Happiness" mantra and writes content aligned with this perception. Message branding exercises to determine the types of messages reflected in the brand voice and whether they are (or are not) connected to the brand form an important component of the social media writing guide. Table 10.3 provides a template for the type of content reflected in the brand voice, the type of content *not* reflected in the brand voice, how the content is connected back to the personal or professional voice, and a purpose and rationale.

Types of Writing Styles for Social Media

For every brand and professional, a specific writing style and tone for communication is one of the most important things to solidify before executing written content. Creating a writing style guide will provide a consistent and sustainable format for writing, framing, and executing messages on various channels depending on the situation. The following are examples of the writing style approaches brands have taken to create their content (for more examples of voices on social media, see Seiter, 2012):

- Professional

- Snarky and spunky

- Product and brand focused

- Audience focused

- Inspirational

- Conversational

- Witty

- Educational

- Personality focused

- Authenticity focused

Professional (General Motors). Brands that are traditional yet consistent with their online presence treat social media like any other traditional communication channel. General Motors has one of the more professional and traditionally oriented voices on social media. The company's approach focuses on providing clear information to audience members while giving them an opportunity to interact on the account. This does not necessarily force audience members to engage but rather extends an invitation to be part of the conversation. For example, General Motors focuses on providing information about their new kid-focused initiative to introduce kids and their families to sustainability and engineering. This post provides information that may be useful for parents interested in learning more about what General Motors is doing along with educational and professional opportunities in the field. The image and copy of this image are aligned to create a cohesive and professional look, which General Motors is aiming to achieve across all of their platforms (Photo 10.3).

Most of the professionally oriented messages on social media come from corporate accounts, allowing the individual brand accounts (like Chevrolet) to showcase their personalities on social media a bit more. What is good about the General Motors style is that it is concise and appropriate for the platform, and it has a call to action to engage audiences with a question. This provides a window of opportunity and an invitation for the user to participate in the experience and conversation. The focus is to create content and a message that drives back to the

▶ **Photo 10.3**
General Motors
Instagram Post

Source: Instagram/
@Generalmotors

corporate brand mission but also extends a hand to those who perhaps want to join the conversation.

Snarky and spunky (Steak-Umm). Move over Wendy's, you may have had the crown of snarkiness for the past few years, but a new contender is in town, and it is a frozen beef company. Steak-Umm and the voice behind the brand, Nathan Allebach, provide real commentary on not only their products but politics, misinformation, and issues brands and audiences were facing during the COVID-19 pandemic. As Jay Baer (2017) points out in *Adweek*, some brands may not get the same reception as Steak-Umm or Wendy's, and posting snarky content could result in negative perceptions for a brand and even loss of trust among its key audiences.

Knowing when being snarky will work comes down to understanding the community, culture, and position within the industry for the brand. Plus, getting buy-in from leadership also needs to be accounted for when it comes to taking this approach. Feeling the burn or using the fire emoji may have some short-term success (e.g., it might get a laugh or even a mention from a high-profile account), but this approach may be difficult to maintain in the long run. People move on to the next big thing that comes along, and they will be looking at what else is trending. Building long-term relationships means focusing on the different steps needed to maintain and sustain the community on each platform. Other brands known for their personality approach include Arby's, Aviation Gin, McDonald's, and Dunkaroos.

Keep in mind that while it is appropriate to be creative and entertaining for audiences when it comes to message execution on social media, brands have to ask themselves, "What do our customers and audiences really want?" The social media management company Sprout Social found that most consumers and audiences want brands to be honest, friendly, and helpful, and being snarky was rated in last place (Morrison, 2017). Understanding what key audiences expect and want to see is an important driver of the content social media managers share, create, and execute on behalf of a brand.

Product and brand focused (E.L.F. Cosmetics). Some brands use their writing style to "stay in their lanes." These brands, such as E.L.F. Cosmetics, are innovative within their industries and among their competitors, but they stay focused on what they want to say and create, which helps their bottom line. While many may not think of TikTok as a platform that involves a lot of writing, being concise and to the point with a limited number of characters is harder than it seems. On their TikTok account, E.L.F. Cosmetics has focused on their brand messaging effectively.

Audience focused (Budweiser). One of the best brands for storytelling is Budweiser, and the company has taken a similar approach to social media. When the brand partnered with VaynerMedia for a campaign to celebrate the retirement of Derek Jeter's number (2) for the New York Yankees in May 2017, it integrated the message, content, and execution across all platforms on social media (e.g., Facebook, Twitter, and YouTube). The message was tailored appropriately for the audiences in question, and the focus was creating content that best represented the message. Different video lengths were integrated along with a specific campaign hashtag, #ThisBudsFor2. The hashtag, message, and content all resonated and told the story not just about Derek Jeter but about the experience Budweiser wanted to share with the rest of the audience, the campaign's primary focus.

Inspirational (adidas). There is a time to promote products and services, and there is a time for brands to use their writing style to enhance an idea or feeling. adidas does this very well for key message strategies on social media. During the pandemic lockdown, adidas created a series showcasing athletes working from home and encouraging their audiences to participate in challenges like #HomeTeamHero, which focused on motivating audiences to take part in the challenge to run and be active while practicing social distancing (Photo 10.4). What is unique about this campaign is that it is indeed adidas that is providing the information about their brand, but they are utilizing content from others (e.g., user generated content), which shows that the adidas community is in this together. This image could have been a branded image with the adidas three stripes logo, but the star of this post is not only adidas but the creators who have their content showcased. This post is inspirational because it highlights those who make the adidas community special, which we are seeing more brands do in their work.

▸ **Photo 10.4**
adidas
#HomeTeamHero
Campaign Challenge

Source: Instagram/
@adidas

Conversational (Cinnabon). Brands and users alike should note that social media is not always driven by sales. First and foremost, social media is about being *social*—which means striking up conversations. Interaction and two-way communication between brands and others is one way to foster relationships virtually. Several brands do this very well, such as Charmin and Hootsuite. Cinnabon, as well, not only taps into the interactive nature of social media but engages with audiences through various appropriate means, including adding their designated brand hashtag #LifeNeedsFrosting. The overall tone and framework of the content shared by the cinnamon roll company is fun and engaging and, for the most part, positive in nature. This inspires people to interact with the content, which then leads to engagement that can be monitored and tracked. Plus, their images of their products can put a smile on everyone's faces! Cinnabon in this post shows how responsive and proactive they are in addressing comments, mentions, and stories about their brand (Photo 10.5). The overall tone is upbeat and positive but also conversational in nature. When viewing this example from Cinnabon, the message does not appear it is coming from a robot but a team of human beings who are talking with people (not at them), creating a warm and inviting experience with their content. Cinnabon has done a great job in harnessing their brand voice to be consistent in their content and writing style across their channels.

▶ **Photo 10.5**
Twitter Exchange
With Cinnabon and
Buzzfeed

Source: Twitter/
@Buzzfeed; Twitter/
@Cinnabon

Witty (Taco Bell). Including humor and cleverness in your brand messages on social media can be both challenging and memorable. Taco Bell as a company has become a leader in the art of being creative yet witty in its strategies and messages, which it executes in a memorable manner aligned with the brand. This approach to crafting messages or adding wittiness to a brand voice may not work for all organizations, but social media managers may want to look at this as an opportunity to branch out to their key audiences. Taco Bell is conversational and fun on social media, but adds a layer of wit to its messages that makes the company a bit different from other brands on social media. The taco emoji campaign (#TacoEmojiEngine) was automated, but the content created to get the word out about this feature was well executed and backed by strategy and insights, which were supported by research and connected back to the brand.

Educational (Sephora). One position people can take on social media is the role of educator. Information, tutorials, resources, and additional articles that may be relevant for key audiences are a few things that brands can contribute. Sharing this type of content will help foster relationships that will extend to others referring their network to the account, which of course builds a stronger community. One brand that has done this very well is Sephora. The beauty company not only promotes its products and campaigns but creates a content calendar that allows it to schedule messages and content that educate audiences about the latest makeup trends, tutorials, and even how-tos for getting a certain look, especially on their YouTube channel. They have clear copy that highlights each video while designating keywords that come up easily if a user searches for certain videos.

Personality focused (Charmin). Some brands try to make themselves more "human" in the eyes of their key audiences. Personality-focused accounts can be either loved or despised on social media. It really all depends on how the brand is perceived as a traditional company and whether or not it has engaged in a way that is authentic, memorable, and entertaining to its key audiences. While earlier in the chapter we discussed the difference in reception to brands that are snarky and brands that are not, brands with a personality voice in their messages focus more on the positive nature of their engagement rather than trying to make others feel they have been "burned."

One brand that has been very successful in using personality is the toilet paper brand Charmin. The company is engaging and interactive and focuses on a positive tone in all of its conversations on social media.

Authenticity focused (McDonald's). When you are thinking about authenticity through social media, you may be surprised to hear the name McDonald's come up. This is a relatively recent venture for the iconic hamburger company, as the social media team has taken more of a human approach to their overall tone and writing on social media, especially on Twitter. For example, the social media manager for McDonald's tweeted out in October 2020, "It's always 'when is the McRib coming back' and never 'how are you doing person who runs the McDonald's account,'" which generated one of their most engaged posts on the platform (Beneveniste, 2020).

Along with their overall conversational tone, the brand interjects real insights, reactions, and news on collaborations with J Balvin and Travis Scott. The global fast food brand has not always taken this approach in their social media writing, but this shift has shown to be effective with their community in building their overall brand presence on social.

Common Writing Mistakes on Social Media

Many types of writing mistakes are made on social media. People write inappropriate content, produce spelling or grammatical mistakes, and share false information. Social media is still the first line of communication for a lot of people, and first impressions matter. Making a mistake or taking an approach that is not aligned with how audiences perceive you as an organization or person may lead to further consequences down the line. Here are a few pieces of advice in reaction to some common mistakes that happen on social media from a writing perspective:

- *Do not attempt to jump on the bandwagon when it is not appropriate.* There is a time and place to interject yourself into a conversation. Ever since Oreo released a tweet during the 2013 Super Bowl ("You can still dunk in the dark" when the stadium in New Orleans had a power outage), brands (e.g., GAP) have tried very hard to interject themselves into a conversation when they may not be invited, or they have not read the room. GAP found this out the hard way when they tweeted during the 2020 U.S. presidential election and had to ultimately take down their tweet.

- *Before engaging in a conversation with a trending hashtag, research the hashtag.* In 2014, for example, DiGiorno became a trending topic when it did not research the hashtag #WhyIStayed before creating a message that caused an outrage on Twitter. The #WhyIStayed hashtag was created around the serious issue of domestic violence in light of the NFL cases involving Ray Rice back in 2014. Before speaking, see what people are really talking about.

- *Evaluate the possible reactions people might have to your content (good and bad).* Before hitting post, ask yourself, "How would people react to this? What are some ways this could be misinterpreted? What are some of the things we would need to address before we send this out?" These extra steps could save brands (like Vera Bradley) a lot of grief and time. People may interpret messages differently, and you may have the right intentions, but if people feel they have been slighted at all on social media, they will come out in full force. Taking the extra time to copyedit and discuss all of these factors will be for the best in the long run.

- *An attempt to be "hip" may result in the message and purpose being misinterpreted.* While you may think it is a good idea to try to be hip or cute as a brand, it may not go over well with audiences. Understanding the role and perception of a brand's voice is crucial, and Chase learned this the hard way when they tried to embrace their humor with a poem about bank accounts. It did not go over well for the banking company, and they had to apologize for it.

BEST PRACTICES FOR SOCIAL MEDIA WRITING

Spelling and grammar are still important—and, in fact, are more important than ever—in social media. First impressions matter, and these principles are important in every channel and medium used in communication. While sometimes conversations may be informal online, it is still necessary to use proper grammar and correct spelling. No one wants to see their names misspelled online or to have information presented in a distracted manner. The same principles used in journalism (adherence to a style guide, checking facts, etc.) should not only be encouraged in social media writing practices but enforced. In other words, there is no excuse for spelling mistakes or grammatical errors in your updates.

Keep track of the best tools to support your writing. To write the best content, you have to have the right tools and services. While most social media managers use a variety of services for their social media management tools, some are specifically available to help social media managers create the best content possible before hitting the publish button. Here are a few to check out:

- *Grammarly.* This platform allows you to check your grammar and spelling online for a variety of different forms of content. From long-form content to discussion board posts, this tool helps ensure you do not make any grammatical or spelling mistakes.

- *Hemingway App.* This tool helps when you are using another program (e.g., Word) to copy and paste content from offline to online.

- *Slick Write.* This online program not only checks grammar and spelling but helps out with word associations (e.g., thesaurus). It can even check the overall word structure to make sure you are not using the same phrases over and over again or writing biased statements you may not have intended to include.

- *Trello, Basecamp, or Slack.* Having a team management platform that checks off tasks, assigns certain duties, and has the ability to communicate in real time is crucial.

- *HubSpot.* HubSpot has a blog topic generator, so if you are looking for ideas to write about and share on social media, this is a good place to start!

Brevity is the name of the game. The goal is not to squeeze the highest number of words into a single space. Sometimes, the hardest content to write is the shortest. Your messages should be concise and appropriate for the platform. In some cases, you will be asked to write short-form content (fewer than 280 characters), while in other cases, you will be asked to write long-form content (500–1,000 words). Social media professionals are expected more than ever to embrace multimedia content, or a mixture of short- and long-form content with the addition of multimedia. Whether it is a GIF, video, or infographic attached to an update, all of these elements have to be taken into consideration. Testing these messages based on the platform algorithm (e.g., Facebook vs. Twitter) is a very helpful step.

Don't force a certain writing style. Be yourself. While it is tempting to follow in the footsteps of other social media professionals and brands on social media, this may be a temporary fix to addressing key message strategies. Copying others is not viewed as authentic and true to the brand (personal or professional). To build a community and reputation on social media, brands and others have to be true to how they approach their audiences online, and a lot of this depends on how a brand creates content. No one wants to have the same writing style or brand voice on social media—this is almost like the kiss of death. The goal here is to be unique in how you present, share, and create messages using various writing and visual content that is true to who you are. We can always look for inspiration, but we have to ask ourselves, "What are other brands doing that works for them? What can we learn from how they present their content on social media? What do we have that they do not have? How can we showcase this in a sustainable way across all of our platforms and channels? How does our brand voice on social media impact our mission and vision statement as a brand?" These are just some additional questions we have to continue to ask ourselves and our team members when it comes to our writing style and content.

Put audiences first. Write content audiences not only want to share, but have to share. Make sure your content matches what the audience not only needs, but expects to see, from your brand or company on social media.

You want audiences to get the information they need in a quick manner but also to recognize that they want to experience something in return with the messages and content. **Experiential media** (where audiences feel like they are part of the conversation and community) and content that sparks emotion are more likely to be shared among audience members.

Emphasize embracing messages, not hard-sell messaging. The point of social media is to be social, not to bombard people with paid ads trying to make a quick sell. Social media is about building relationships that could ultimately turn into financial returns, but the steps (whether from a marketing standpoint or a public relations perspective) should never start off with the hard-sell message. Brands have to meet people in a place where they want to actually have a conversation. Not everyone wants to interact with brands on social media—that should be noted and interaction should not be forced. Understanding the health dynamics of a community (from monitoring and listening protocols) will inform social media professionals about when it is or is not appropriate to enter a conversation with audiences. Evaluating the state of the mood and situation will help determine which messages audiences will embrace and which messages will be discarded completely or even spark outrage among audiences.

Don't be inconsistent and confuse your audiences. Changes within a company among community managers require a smooth transition to make sure the writing style and brand voice are the same across the channels. You do not want audiences to know there has been a change within the company. Make sure your messages are not full of jargon that is commonly used in the industry but does not translate into other areas. Do not overwhelm your audiences in ways that distract them from the message. It is better to have a clear point and call to action than to distract people with a ton of emojis, visuals, and jargon all communicating different things. Keeping it simple is the name of the game.

Have a balance between your personal and brand voices. Many social media professionals maintain personal and professional accounts. One thing social media professionals struggle with when it comes to writing for their own platforms is the transition between their own personal voice and their professional voice. The purpose of writing on social media is not to make it 100% about you all of the time. You want to have a ratio of four areas when it comes to writing content:

- 25% should focus on your story and personal journey (what you are doing, where you hope to go in the future, what you can offer as a professional and person, etc.).

- 25% should focus on sharing content that may be relevant for your community or industry.

- 25% should focus on engagement (answering questions, giving shout-outs to fellow community members and brands, commenting and sharing your perspectives, etc.).

- 25% should focus on producing value and paying it forward.

Understand the differences in content and writing style based on the platform as well as the audience. Some platforms allow you to communicate visually with not a lot of text, and on other platforms short-form content (fewer than 140 characters) will not be effective or efficient for the intended audiences. For example, updates that are effective on Facebook are a bit longer than those, of course, on Twitter (63,206 compared to 280 characters), but in some cases long-form content will be necessary to explain a concept, idea, or story for an intended audience. Keeping the messages short while writing in an active voice are also elements to consider here, even with the opportunity to write longer pieces on certain platforms.

Be brief and direct. Another goal for writing on social media is not to make it a million pages long. Brevity and concise writing (which sometimes is harder) is the name of the game. Creativity in using each word for a specific purpose is important. However, you do not want to lose your audiences completely by using jargon or emojis they do not understand. We may know what they mean from the social media side of things or even from pop culture, but we have to make sure we edit and tailor our messages to be not only direct but effective. We are not all mind readers, and you do not want audience members to be confused about what you are trying to communicate on social media. Understanding the call-to-action statements highlighting what you want to do for audiences will be effective in the long term. Tell people what you want them to do based on being exposed to a certain piece of content, but also work toward giving them a direct statement about what to expect once they are exposed to this message.

CHAPTER SUMMARY

Excellent writing for social media is a fundamental task for social media professionals. Writing, like most activities and hobbies, takes time and dedication. Having the right tools and resources to create the best content is extremely important for social media managers. However, in order to become an effective writer, you have to practice writing. Posting content on behalf of a brand, agency, or person requires a strategic framework that identifies the overall brand voice, tone, and writing style to maintain across all of the platforms. Like all aspects of social media, writing style guidelines and expectations for what content should be created on each platform changes, but fundamental skills and best practices remain the same.

THOUGHT QUESTIONS

1. Why is writing considered the most important skill to have in social media?

2. What is the difference between brand voice and tone? How can they be incorporated into social media content?

3. Identify the different writing styles discussed in the chapter. Which ones do you feel are the most effective for brands? Identify a brand (that is not listed in this chapter) that has each of these writing styles.

4. What are some best practices when it comes to writing for social media? What are some things to avoid doing on social media?

EXERCISES

1. You are a social media manager for a local non-profit organization. Your colleagues have been watching some larger brands be creative with their writing style, embracing a "witty" or "snarky" approach. What are some benefits and challenges you would want to identify in this writing style for your client? Which writing style would you recommend they use?

2. You are a social media intern for Spotify. You have been asked to update a writing style guide for social media for all of their platforms (Facebook, Twitter, Instagram,

TikTok, LinkedIn, and Snapchat). What are some things you would want to have in your writing guide?

3. You are programming content to put forth in your content calendar for your local sports team, but you see a trending topic arising in your community. Participating in this trend would be appropriate for you to jump into the conversation. What steps would you want to take before participating in the conversation?

4. You are graduating and about to apply for a job with Wieden+Kennedy, the agency working with Nike, McDonald's, and P&G. They are interested in having you analyze their agency brand voice on social media. If you wanted to showcase your writing skills on social media, what pieces of content would you want to create based on the W+K brand voice?

REFERENCES

Baer, J. (2017). Brands need to ditch the social media snark. *Adweek*. http://www.adweek.com/digital/jay-baer-guest-post-brands-need-to-ditch-the-social-media-snark/

Beneveniste, A. (2020). McDonald's social media cries for help: I am more than just the McRib. *CNN Business*. https://www.cnn.com/2020/10/26/tech/mcdonalds-social-media-brands-trnd/index.html

Jackson, D. (2020). Know your limit: The ideal length of every social media post. *Sprout Social*. https://sproutsocial.com/insights/social-media-character-counter/#linkedin

Lee, K. (2014a, April 14). How to find your social media marketing voice: The best examples, questions and guides. *Buffer Social*. https://blog.bufferapp.com/social-media-marketing-voice-and-tone

Lee, K. (2014b, September 8). 71 ways to write a social media update: Specific tips to engage your followers. *Buffer Social*. https://blog.bufferapp.com/ways-to-write-social-media-updates

Morrison, K. (2017, May 16). Brands may think being snarky is cool, but consumers don't (report).

Adweek. http://www.adweek.com/digital/brands-may-think-being-snarky-is-cool-but-consumers-dont-report/

Read, A. (2017, May 18). How to craft the perfect post on Facebook, Twitter, and Instagram. *Buffer*. https://buffer.com/resources/how-to-craft-the-perfect-post-on-facebook-twitter-and-instagram

Seiter, C. (2012, August 13). 20 Great social media voices (and how to develop your own). *Marketing Land*. http://marketingland.com/20-great-social-media-voices-and-how-to-develop-your-own-18057

Wainwright, C. (2017, July 28). How to create a writing style guide built for the web [free template]. *HubSpot*. https://blog.hubspot.com/blog/tabid/6307/bid/31247/The-Simple-Template-for-a-Thorough-Content-Style-Guide.aspx

Zafarris, J. (2021, January 25). Meat and memes: How Slim Jim's Long Boi Gang surgered to 1.2 million followers. *Adweek*. https://www.adweek.com/brand-marketing/slim-jims-long-boi-gang-meat-memes/

AUDIENCE SEGMENTATION AND ANALYSIS

Learning Objectives

After reading this chapter, you will be able to

- Define audience segmentation and explain why it is important for social media professionals

- Identify audience segmentation categories and how to apply them in a social media context

- Explain the differences between influencers, ambassadors, creators, and trolls/haters

- Learn how to apply audience segmentation to campaign building

INTRODUCTION

One of the things that is very important to remember in social media is this: The more you understand and know your audience, the more effective you are going to be in reaching them, building a relationship, and creating unique experiences.

The amount of data, insights, and access to audiences is enormous on social media. However, this is only good if social media professionals are able to use these data effectively to build relationships and better understand how and why it is important to engage with each community. As noted, not all audiences are the same, and it is important to be able to segment them into different categories based on interests, behaviors, needs, and social media activities.

This chapter will discuss the importance of audience segmentation, different characteristics associated with audiences, and how to apply these strategies to campaign building in social media.

Miri Rodriguez, Head of Global Internship Program at Microsoft and Author of *Brand Storytelling*

Introduction

Born in the slums of Caracas, Venezuela, to missionary parents, I was the second of three girls and always loved writing. Our family came to the U.S. when I was 13 and we began to forge our path as immigrants in this great nation. I was blessed with scholarships that granted me a higher education and soon began my path in corporate America, dabbling in industries from banking to yachting and eventually tech, while at the same time building my personal brand. Today, I lead the Global Internship Program at Microsoft and have had the opportunity to travel the world consulting with partners and brands on the art and science of storytelling.

How did you get your start in social media?

I was quite afraid to jump on the social media bandwagon when it first began and can tell you that I have never had a personal Facebook account! I was part of a music band and in 2009 team members agreed to get on Twitter and use it as a group text platform (what did we know?). My account wasn't locked and I soon realized strangers could see my content and began to amplify and follow. I was immediately intrigued about the possibilities.

What is your favorite part of working in your area of expertise in social media?

People. It's also my least favorite (haha). Truly, social media is a place where you can find and connect with the most fascinating and brilliant personalities and there are no geographical boundaries. The same can be said about meeting negative people and haters of all kinds. I always say, social media doesn't make you a worse or better person—it just amplifies who you already are.

What is one thing you can't live without while working in social media?

My smartphone. Most of my content is in my phone and loaded through it. The convenience of being able to pop into a network, engage, and pop out is so great. I can't imagine having to engage on social through native applications.

What is your favorite social media account (person/brand/etc.) to follow and why?

So many great ones! I think it's worthwhile to say, I don't typically follow celebrities or influencers. I tend to follow people I actually know or have personally impacted me in a positive way through their content. I really love Judah Smith's Instagram account. He's my pastor in Seattle and I not only enjoy his content, but his authenticity. That is so important.

What is the most challenging part of working in social media?

I think anyone working in social media understands that one of the biggest challenges is that this is an ever-evolving platform and consumers are always a moving target. Having to reinvent yourself to keep your content fresh while at the same time keeping consistent and "on brand" is something all brands struggle with, but I also believe this is the magic of social. It keeps us on our toes and forces us to stay creative.

What is your take on your area of expertise and the social media industry?

We're only getting started with brand storytelling and social media. Brands are just beginning to scratch the surface with narrative. I'm excited to see how new technologies will introduce new ways to bring our stories to life in an immersive way and how social will enable these experiences. It's only going to get better!

What do you wish you had known when you were starting out?

To stay focused on mastering the channel where my audience is rather than trying to be relevant everywhere. Choosing a platform shouldn't be done because it's the latest sensation, but because that's where you know you will have more reach and impact with your audience. Follow your audience, not the trends.

What are three marketable skills a social media professional needs to have to work in the industry?

- Empathy (with yourself and with your audience)

- Thought-Leadership (the ability to share opinions in a way that captivates others)

- Creativity (innovation is key)

- Bonus: a thick skin (it's a tough digital world!)

Where do you go to keep up to date with trends and continue learning about social media?

I sign up for Google Alerts on the topics that matter to me. I also create lists and follow people/brands that deliver content relevant to social media latest news. Lastly, I spend a lot of time reviewing platform analytics. Data tells a great story.

If you had to choose a song to walk out to in a presentation, what would it be and why?

This is going to sound horrible, but it will be "Shoop," by Salt-N-Pepa. I just love that beat (and maybe the lyrics too)!

Miri Rodriguez is head of the Global Internship Program at Microsoft and author of the well-known book Brand Storytelling *(2020). Miri can be connected on social (Twitter and IG) at @mirirod and her book is available here:* https:// brandstorytellingbook.com/en/

WHAT IS AUDIENCE SEGMENTATION?

In social media, the goal is not to reach every single person on the planet. Rather, it is more important to focus on the quality of an audience member based on needs, expectations, products and services use, relationship, and engagement. More often than not, social media communities are more **niche** (specifically focused on a particular interest, location, or characteristic) than ever before.

Audience segmentation refers to the process of categorizing people into certain groups based on specific criteria. These criteria can be broad in nature (e.g., demographics and population data) or very specific and focused (niche) on certain characteristics (experiential, visually driven, industry and interest specific, etc.). Audience segmentation is a strategy by which companies, agencies, and brands collect information to create a profile of an audience with which they wish to engage. With insight tools for audience analysis in social media, social media professionals can be very broad in their targeting (prioritizing their audiences and whom they want to reach first) or very specific to the point where they can identify specific people to receive their messages and content. The more you segment your audience, the more focused you will be in narrowing down the people you really want to reach for a social media campaign. You don't want to reach everyone—only those who are relevant for the overall purpose of your social media activities.

Why is it important to be effective in your audience segmentation for a social media campaign? There are several reasons, but a few are especially important:

- *Being more effective in your paid advertisements on social media.* By taking the time to really home in on the various interests, behaviors, demographics, and channel engagement metrics, social media professionals will reach the right audiences, making the most of their time and financial resources dedicated to social media. Taking the time to gather the data needed to really focus on effective and efficient ads targeted to specific individuals will pay off in the end.

- *Having a clear idea of who you are reaching and what is important to them.* By understanding how audiences think, feel, and behave, social media professionals will have more insight to craft effective pieces of content as assets for their campaign initiatives, promotions, and message strategies.

- *Discovering what issues, interests, and passions that will formulate a stronger connection.* Understanding who audiences are based on demographic characteristics is just the beginning. We also have to understand what makes our audiences light up and get excited. Interested in being part of a community full of fellow marketing professionals like on #MarketingTwitter? Love sharing insights about pop culture and *Star Wars* (how cute is Baby Yoda?!) Playing with friends online with games NBA 2K or Among Us? All of these are examples tapping into different interests audiences may have.

- *Understanding the range of different touch points for each user.* Users may be engaged with a brand on one channel or on various channels. Audience members should be exposed to the same brand voice and experience across all channels in which they participate. Professionals should provide an **omnichannel approach**, which means a seamless and effortless integration of content, messages, and experiences for the user is linked to multiple communication channels. This is a growing trend for many brands, which realize that their audiences are following and engaging with them on multiple channels. All messages, content assets, and strategies need to be consistent yet tailored appropriately for each audience for each channel.

The first and foremost thing to do before actually implementing ideas for social media is to determine the target audience. Social media professionals sometimes forget that not all audiences gravitate to the same platforms for conversations, news, and information. Understanding each audience will help you develop effective key messages featuring strong points that resonate with each audience member, which will contribute to formulating strong connections and relationships.

Certain points of information to include in this analysis go beyond what is typically available in most campaigns. For social media purposes, as described in Chapter 7, we need *demographics* (basic population statistics such as gender, age, location, occupation, and education) and *psychographics* (advanced statistics that focus on the attitudes, opinions, and interests of audience members). For example, we need to know audience views of various news sources and specific motivational factors. Some individuals are motivated by financial or materialistic items (free swag, coupons shared on social media, etc.); however, others are focused on gaining connections and being part of the experience (opportunities for exclusive meetings, sponsored partnerships, VIP treatment for influencers or advocates at events, behind-the-scenes opportunities like at College GameDay, Brandweek by *Adweek*, League of Legends World Championship, NCAA tournaments, Cannes Lions, and SXSW). In addition, different platform channel segments must be considered. While Twitter, Facebook, and Instagram focus on the demographics and psychographics of their audiences, LinkedIn adds specifics about the places people work (industry size, seniority, company, etc.). TikTok, on the other hand, provides additional insights on what videos and songs followers have watched and listened to. It is also important to explore the type of user that characterizes an audience. Are the users actively creating content, or are they spectators?

Historically, there have been tools that have allowed social media managers and professionals to be able to place audiences into certain categories based on type of social media users. To assist in this type of audience analysis, Forrester created the Forrester Technographics tool in 2011 to outline and divide how people behave online (see go.forrester.com/data/consumer-technographics). Table 11.1 lists different audience categories that might appear in an audience segmentation report.

Several types of audiences are relevant to social media campaigns (see Figure 11.1). As in public relations and marketing, social media professionals consider both internal and external audiences. Internal audiences are individuals who are part of a relevant organization. These could be fellow employees, team leaders, or senior management. Even though most social media activities happen outside of the organization, it is still important to keep the internal audiences well informed. External audiences are those who are outside of the organization, including customers, brand ambassadors, influencers, opinion leaders, and competitors. Each of these audiences will have different motivational factors, attitudes, needs, interests, and social media behaviors to consider. Each audience needs a personalized and tailored approach in the construction of key messages as well as the execution of these messages and strategies. One message may not resonate with all audiences, and taking the time to personalize the messages and approaches on social media to each audience will allow you to foster stronger and more stable relationships.

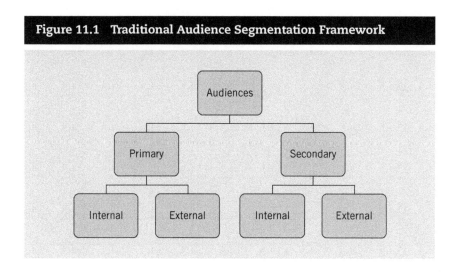

Figure 11.1 Traditional Audience Segmentation Framework

Table 11.1 Outline of Different Audience Segments Relevant to Social Media Campaigns

Demographics	Psychographics	Platform Specifics	Type of Social Media User	Social Metrics
• Age	• Attitudes	• Life stage	• Creator	• Specific digital behaviors on certain platforms
• Gender	• Behaviors	• Company size	• Inactive	• Likes/follows/interests/comments
• Occupation	• Interests	• Industry	• Collector	• Time spent on platforms
• Race	• Opinions	• Function/job	• Spectator	• Time of day/week most active and responsive
• Location	• Lifestyle	• Type of user	• Critic	• Top word associations (e.g., word cloud)
• Language preference	• Connections	• Influence and presence in the network	• Joiner	• Top bio word associations (e.g., platform bios)
• Relationship status	• Perspectives	• Connections		• Top issues and topics they are associated with
		• Community and group associations		• Content that resonates with audiences on certain platforms
		• Network and place in the community		• Device used
		• Community health and presence		• Other similar interests/brands users follow
		• Loyalty to brand		• Topics they are influential on
		• Content (visual and audio) that user has engaged with		• Other brands they are connected with
				• Other professionals (e.g., creators, influencers, etc.) they are connected with
				• Sentiment toward other brands and accounts on social media

TYPES OF AUDIENCES

Data are a social media professional's best friend when it comes to identifying key audiences and organizing them based on priority and focus. First and foremost, brands and professionals on social media must use the data collected through monitoring and listening techniques to identify the audience they are reaching on social media. Second, these results should be compared to traditional offline reports about these audiences.

The *primary audience* is made up of the individuals you want to target first. *Secondary audiences* are linked to the primary messages but are not necessarily the key audiences you want to reach at first (see Chapter 7). Instead, these could be additional audiences that help persuade and influence the particular audiences you are trying to reach. For example, if you are trying to reach Generation Z, you may want to focus on certain peer groups or influencers these individuals trust and value based on certain interests (sports, fashion and beauty, consumer and design creations, etc.). **Emerging audiences** are those you want to note as individuals, based on the monitoring and listening they do on social media; they could transform into a key primary audience. These audiences are growing in momentum based on their interactivity and engagement with the brand that may be worthy to note for the purpose of social media campaigns and initiatives. For example, brands looking to tap into the Generation Z audience may want to explore high-profile celebrity influencers such as Zendaya (as Verizon has done with the #WeNeedMore STEM campaign), James Charles (Cover Girl), Donovan Mitchell (Utah Jazz player and Spiderman Marvel shoe collaboration), and Manny Gutierrez (a male beauty blogger who has signed with Maybelline and Rimmel).

Opponents, also known as **critics**, are self-explanatory—these audiences are not the biggest fans of the brand or company you represent. Instead, they wish for negative consequences to happen to the brand. They are very active in sharing their views and how they feel about you. Some of these negative opinions could be based on previous experiences, or they could be unprovoked. These voices come from a range of different industries and types of audiences. Looking at a college sports team, for example, such as the USC Trojans (#FightOn!), one group that would be listed in this opponent category is UCLA, because the schools are academic and athletic rivals within the city of Los Angeles. However, additional audiences beyond the sports world could include fans, alums, and even other schools outside the area. In any case, it is important to note who these individuals are and how their main motivations and goals might impact the overall success and well-being of your own brand, client, or organization on social media.

Within each of these categories, social media professionals need to construct personas for each audience based on demographics, psychographics, social media behaviors, and channel action characteristics (how individuals use certain channels specifically, like connecting with friends, sharing updates, networking with professionals, etc.). These personas will help describe each audience in a way that outlines key motivational factors, similar experiences, memberships in certain groups, attitudes and behaviors, and trusted sources outside of the campaign. The more information that can be gathered about an audience, the more informed and effective a social media professional will be in crafting key strategic messages. These messages should focus on the connection that needs to be made on cognitive (sharing information, knowledge, etc.), affective (emotions and feelings that resonate with the audiences), and conative levels (calls to action, focusing on encouraging certain audience behaviors). All messages need to be personalized, tailored, and properly tested to make sure the audience in question understands and will act in desirable ways based on these messages.

COMMUNITIES, INFLUENCERS, AND CREATORS

In addition to key audiences to target in social media efforts, other sources of influence must be considered.

Communities, introduced in Chapter 10, can be hosted by individuals, groups, or brands. Online communities encompass a group of people who are invested and interested in a similar issue, brand, or area of expertise. For example, one popular Facebook group for social media professionals is the Social Geekout Community, created by Matt Navarra. This community focuses on sharing the latest updates on social media trends, issues, and campaigns, and discusses situations and challenges facing the field. Some communities are open to everyone, whereas others are more exclusive. Navarra has also expanded his community to include the Social Geekout Podcast and his exclusive social media newsletter in 2020. Communities can be created on one designated platform, or they can be multimodal, expanding their reach to other channels and outlets to engage with more audiences.

Brands can build communities to meet several goals. Some brand communities are designated for loyal customers and fans who want to become ambassadors for the brand. For the most part, they want to create communities where like-minded people can come together to brainstorm, engage, and share knowledge and ideas in a specific space. This space can be hosted within the brand's community (website, etc.) or as an extension of a specific social media site (Twitter with Twitter chats, etc.).

As mentioned earlier, many channels and platforms can be used to create and maintain a particular community for social media. Each platform is used differently, but what is important is tapping into the motivational factors driving people to specific communities and to each channel. Do they want to be educated about the latest trends in social media? This may be a case for creating videos on YouTube that explore each new trend step-by-step. Or is your audience focusing on building connections in the sports world with fellow industry leaders? If this is the case, getting active and involved on Twitter using the hashtag #SMsports (for those who practice and work in social media and sports) can be effective or even Marketing Twitter for those who work in the field. Professionals from some of the biggest brands and companies, such as GoFundMe, Twitter Marketing, Instagram, Clorox, Microsoft, PlayStation, Delta, Visa, Airbnb and more, engage with each other in this community to talk about various trends, issues, examples, and topics related to the field. Being part of these communities is not only informative for understanding current topics and trends in the industry but an excellent way to network with some of the top professionals shaping the field. Regardless of the purpose, audiences expect certain common features from each community:

- *Exclusivity.* Information and being in the know is powerful. People want to feel like they are getting something that not everyone else is getting. Having the opportunity to get information and updates first is one of the main reasons communities in social media exist. Make sure what you are providing to each community is valuable.

- *Tone.* We are all busy people, and we want to be part of communities created over time that are positive and engaging. However, some members of communities do not follow the rules, so policies for dealing with these individuals must be proactive. Expectations for what is acceptable and what is not, along with clear statements about what will be done if policies are not followed, should be emphasized across all channels and platforms populated by the community. This helps set the overall tone and expectations for the audience and community.

- *Value.* We want to be part of communities that provide value in many respects, such as relationships, professional opportunities, knowledge, and experiences. All of these will help motivate audiences to not only stay in the community but express their excitement to be part of the community with others they know. #MarketingTwitter is a community that brings together professionals who work in social media, providing value in transparent and authentic conversations. *Adweek* social media manager Julian Gamboa helped start this community in bringing people together during the COVID-19 pandemic.

- *Consistency.* People do not want to be part of communities that are all over the place. Communities need a centralized mission, goal, or purpose.

- *Sustainability.* Communities are not formed and immediately abandoned. They are constantly maintained and invested in by the hosts and main administrators. If the members of an audience know a video will be uploaded every day, they will change their behavior to make sure they are there to see it.

Table 11.2 shows some of the ways in which individuals as well as brands can use each specific social media platform to create and maintain a social media community. The third column focuses on tools for evaluating the success of engagement and interactions with each audience based on the platform.

Within each community, some individuals will have a dominant or prominent voice. Communities host a variety of different individuals, who in their own right have created their own brand and media outlet to the point where they are deemed powerful and persuasive in nature. These influencers are at the focal point of a lot of brands today. Brands and audiences have recognized that many people are gravitating to these influencers rather than to paid spokespeople. However, as discussed later in this chapter, there are challenges and benefits to engaging with influencers.

Influencers

As discussed extensively in Chapter 8, it is important to understand why these audiences are important for social media campaigns. **Creators** are a subset of influencers who focus on creating original content in their own voice for brands rather than just sharing brand-created content. They view their creativity as the most important element of their contribution to their partnership with the brand (Ingalls, 2017). **Ambassadors** are advocates for the brands, but they are perhaps not as influential and focused on reach and numbers as influencers are. Influencers are defined as people who have "the capacity of power of persons or things to be a compelling force on or produce effects on the actions, behavior, opinions, etc. of others" (Bentwood, 2008, p. 5).

Table 11.2	Platform, Audience Engagement Practices, and Tools to Measure Success Template	
Facebook	• Build a community within Facebook Groups. • Create a public profile page to manage your personal brand with audiences. • Promote your Facebook Group with relevant audience members. • Decide whether or not to make this group open, closed, or secret. • Create a Facebook show to share your ideas in real time. Schedule a time and send out announcements that audience members can save and put into their calendars. • Create branded filters for audiences to demonstrate their membership in a group, conference, or organization (e.g., Facebook frames for Facebook profiles).	• Facebook Audience Insights • Facebook Live (e.g., BlueJeans, Zoom, Switcher Studio, ReStream, or Streamyard) • Creative Suite for content to use for sponsored and targeted ads
Twitter	• Reach out and communicate with others in Twitter chats. • Possibly host/guest host a Twitter chat. • Create a branded hashtag for your community to share articles, updates, and resources. • Mix content from pushing messages to engaging (answering questions and personalizing each response). • Check in on relevant hashtags for events and professional activities. • Follow and reach out to fellow professionals.	• Hootsuite • Sprout Social • Agorapulse • Buffer • TweetAnalyzer • Tagboard • Suggested chats: #Hootchat, #SweetTalk, #Popchat, #CMWorld, #SMstudentchat, #TwitterSmarter
Instagram	• Post consistently with relevant updates and content. • Focus on emotional content to truly connect with audiences. Content that is entertaining helps the audience grow and be more informed, connect by using emotion, and so on. • Answer questions in Instagram Stories, live video, and comments on your posts.	• Canva • VSCO • Mojo • Camera+ • Adobe Lightroom and Photoshop • Adobe Spark Post and Video • Adobe Premiere Rush • Repost

	• Save Instagram stories that feature certain interests, expertise areas, experiences, and topics on your Instagram page. Create a branded title cover that is universal for your brand.	
	• Integrate messages with a strong call to action. Tag audience members, comment, follow, share, and so on—all of these actions can help build upon messages.	
	• Research potential hashtags to add to your content.	
	• Save comments you like from audiences.	
	• Reach out and comment on other posts and pictures.	
	• Host an Instagram Live session inviting others to participate or focus on a particular issue or topic you'd like to cover.	
Snapchat	• Provide content on a consistent basis that is also exclusive.	
	• Listen and respond to comments and questions. Create stories not only for you but for your audiences.	
	• Be authentic and true to your audiences.	
	• Experiment to create a personalized lens for events with Snapchat Lens.	
	• Engage in individual and group chats with audiences.	
	• Recognize that Snapchat is not like other platforms, but rather is focused on building upon a story with each new follower.	
	• Have specific points and messages you want to share with audiences. Have a call to action to get them to share content.	
TikTok	• Create original content in specific areas (e.g., tutorials, memes, voiceovers, etc.).	• Adobe Premiere Rush
	• Participate in challenges (music or others).	• Viamaker
		• Zoomerang
	• Share tips and resources to teach audiences how to do something (e.g., cooking, cleaning, couponing).	• Analisa.io
		• Quik
		• InShot
	• Showcase personality through content and point of view.	

(Continued)

Table 11.2 (Continued)		
LinkedIn	• Reach out to groups to gain access to them to be able to learn, network, and build on your knowledge base. • Create content that resonates with the interests of your audience as well as trending topics. • Acknowledge comments and thank audience members who share your work with others. • Create content relevant to the LinkedIn channels you are interested in and tag them (#) when publishing content on LinkedIn.	• LinkedIn Pulse • Canva (Graphic Post Creator) • Adobe Spark Post (Post Creator) • Adobe Premiere Rush (Video)
YouTube	• Be authentic with your audience and provide consistent content. • Create and share videos about you and your audience. • Have a call to action for your audience members to subscribe to your channel so they do not miss any updates. • Respond to comments and pin top comments at the top of your feed for others to see. • Acknowledge comments. • Reward audiences with exclusivity. • Develop exercises, timelines, and a storyboard framework for your content that resonates with audiences. • Disseminate content across other channels used by your audience.	• YouTube Creator Studio • Canva thumbnails branded for each channel • Adobe Premiere Pro • Adobe Premiere Rush
Digital Media	• Host content in a centralized resource. • Create content and recaps from events and discussions. • Create and launch webinar sessions. • Send out email newsletters for updates and resources. • Provide white papers and presentations that can be downloaded and used in the future.	• MailChimp • Constant Contact • Adobe Portfolio • Adobe Spark Page • Canva presentations

Social media influencers represent an **online persona,** or an identity constructed by an individual online that may or may not represent who he or she truly is in real life (Zhao, Grasmuck, & Martin, 2008). This type of construction using online technologies creates a new way for individuals to manage how they want to be perceived in terms of their identities and reputations (Zhao et al., 2008). Researchers need more work to conceptualize these individual influencers. For example, are these people perceived as taking the leadership role with their followers? What are some things that others say about them? How much presence do they have online and in the virtual community? Researchers and professionals in public relations and reputation management need to understand how these individuals create these influences, what attributes are assigned to them by their followers, and what makes them appear credible and trustworthy. Understanding how the social media influencer persuades others is important for organizations (Bentwood, 2008).

Influencers can be compensated in a variety of different ways. Celebrity endorsements, product placements, and statements of support are just some of the traditional ways in which influencers can be used. *Influencers, compared to celebrity endorsers who are paid spokespeople, are more relatable and viewed as a trustworthy source of information.* The primary focus of influencers is to drive conversations and build community around issues and brands that are key to their own interests and investments. This means that they are not going to promote anything that is "off their brand" and unrelated to what they are passionate about. If they do deviate from their brands, they will lose trust within their community. Authenticity and being true to who they are is extremely important. Yet, when it comes to endorsements, influencers are required to acknowledge to their community whether they are getting paid or are sponsored by the brand or another entity for their posts. In general, many audiences feel that posts tagged #sponsored or #ad are not authentic (Minsker, 2017).

Influencers have built their communities over time, not with endorsements but rather through constant social connections. These conversations emerge across different social media platforms and in different circles. Some influencers have used Snapchat (e.g., DJ Khaled and Kylie Jenner) to maintain engagement with their fans, whereas others have used Instagram (e.g., Shonduras), YouTube (e.g., Casey Neistat and Roberto Blake), or even TikTok (e.g., Addison Rae).

Influencers know who gave them their influence, and they respect and value this tremendously. All influencers know they would not be where they are without their communities and fans. Both Halsey and Casey Neistat pointed this out during their presentations at the Cannes Lions International Festival of Creativity in 2017 (Photo 11.1). Without the commitment of their fans, Halsey and Neistat would not have risen to the top of their respective professions, music and vlogging. Both of these influencers have been able to get some incredible opportunities for their brands (Neistat is now working with CNN, and Halsey's records are going platinum and she is selling out concerts).

▶ **Photo 11.1**
Ryan Seacrest Interviewing Halsey at Cannes Lions Festival

Source: Courtesy of Karen Freberg

Social media professionals must be somewhat cautious when evaluating influencers. Some individuals acting as influencers may not be presenting true information about who they really are in life, but rather may be projecting the ideal self they strive to be. In terms of personality characteristics, most research has focused on the "Big Five" factors of personality: extraversion, neuroticism,

openness to experience, agreeableness, and conscientiousness (McCrae & John, 1992; Ross et al., 2009). In a research study focusing on Facebook, Ross et al. (2009) suggested that certain personality characteristics can be associated with and attributed to individuals based on how they present themselves on social networking sites. Part of the process of creating an online persona is to determine what personality associations and attributes are being made about you and how to frame them (Gosling, Ko, Mannarelli, & Morris, 2002). People might not appear authentically, but we can still figure out their personality. We need to be able to hone in on our metrics and analytical skills to determine and identify not just those individuals who say they are "influential," but whether or not their actions and the quality of their engagements with audiences show they are truly authentic.

Audience Segmentation Tools to Find Influencers

Not all influencers are willing to engage with their audiences. This is something to expect—some individuals are only interested in promoting their work, while others wish to stay within their close network (think of it as their "circle of trust," as Robert De Niro's character states in the movie *Meet the Parents*). However, once you identify which influencers to reach and start a conversation with, make sure you are engaging with their content. Are you sharing their live videos? Are you commenting on their posts and sharing them with your audiences?

▶ **Photo 11.2**
Casey Neistat
Presenting at
Cannes Lions
Festival

Source: Courtesy of
Karen Freberg

How do brands and social media professionals identify which influencers they want to reach out to and would be relevant for their campaigns? Specific agencies and tools are available for identifying influencers based on specific interests and networks. Others can identify active members of your community, who can then become ambassadors for your brand:

- *Klear.* This tool focuses on identifying influencers on three major networks (Facebook, Instagram, and Twitter) and categorizes them on four different types of influence: celebrities, power users, casual, and novice. This tool also provides an option to home in on certain skills (sports, blogging, etc.) as well as location.

- *BuzzSumo.* This is a good tool for identifying not only audience members who have influence but what content they are driving to their networks that is rising in popularity and influence. The reports show not only the audience of the influencer but also the retweet ratio, reply ratio, and average shares on social media. With average shares, you can see how many times, on average, others are willing to share their content with their own audiences on their respective platforms (e.g., Twitter and Facebook).

- *Onalytica.* This paid service allows brands and others to map, listen, measure, and discover the most relevant social media influencers in their database.

- *Traackr.* This paid service helps identify the current list of influencers in your own network and also uncovers those who are influencing the influencers. In addition, Traackr provides ways to quantify the relationships, exchanges, and value each influencer has for your brand's campaign.

- *Talkwalker.* This paid service allows audiences to identify key members who are driving the traffic on certain key search terms.

- *Zoomph.* This enterprise platform tool calculates its own metric (Z scores) to determine who is really influencing the behavior and actions of audiences based on the audience's response to their comments.

The fact of the matter is influencers want to see you, as their audience member, value their input and content, and they are willing (or, in some cases, feel it is necessary because the information and content is so relevant to them) to share the same content with their own networks. The first step here is to show active engagement and conversation. Second is to think about ways in which you (as your own media outlet with your respective channels) create content about the influencer. Will you feature the influencer in a blog post or LinkedIn Pulse article? What about interviewing the influencer for a podcast or live show? How will you help the influencer branch out? Many influencers are looking to expand their own reach and audience, and these are ways to accomplish both your goals and the influencer's. Another way to interact with influencers is to see if you can take the conversations from online to offline. Go to events, conferences, or speaking engagements where influencers are featured. See if you can meet up with them in person.

Other ways to engage with influencers include the following:

- *Cite them in research and professional publications.* Do you have a white paper to write for a social media client? Make sure to cite influencers' work and showcase examples of what they have done for their clients. Many influencers have search engines, and programs notify them when someone has mentioned them online (Google Alerts, Mention, Talkwalker, BuzzSumo, etc.), so they will note and share this content with others.

- *Give them shout-outs during Twitter chats.* Many times, one question that comes up during professional Twitter chats is "Which influencers would you recommend that the community follow?" Share their user handles and give them a shout-out. Do this on a reoccurring basis to help establish a trustworthy relationship with the influencers.

- *Initiate conversations.* These should be natural and authentic. Reach out to influencers not just for the sake of reaching out to them but with a specific purpose in mind. State why you are contacting them and why this relationship is important. Influencers will not reach out to you directly, so you will have to take the first step to start the conversation. But, make sure you have a purpose and game plan for not only how you are going to do it but why.

- *Offer them feedback from a new perspective.* Influencers, like celebrities occasionally, may hear the same thing over and over again from people in their circles. They may also have "yes people"—people who agree with them on everything no matter what. But you can create posts and share insights from a different perspective. Think about what you can offer these influencers that is unique and has not yet been addressed. This will allow you to separate yourself in their eyes by offering something new and different. Attention is the current currency in social media in many ways, but creativity is the foundation to which people respond.

Keep in mind that some influencers are exactly how they present themselves online. These influencers truly understand the complete picture of communities and their role as influencers. Do not be surprised, however, to see some influencers behave differently in person. Some people are much more comfortable communicating with a barrier (computer screen, mobile phone, etc.) between themselves and their audience. Or, they forget how they act online and behave differently anyway.

When approaching an influencer, brands, organizations, and professionals need to ask themselves some additional questions about influencers. Campaign US interviewed WHOSAY CEO Paul Kontonis (2017) about these questions, which include the following:

- Who is following the influencer? Is the influencer engaged with his or her audiences, and what are the characteristics of the audience community?

- Does the audience of the influencer align with your audience? How will you determine this based on your research using audience segmentation strategies?

- What's the influencer's history? Is the influencer professional? How long has he or she been on social media? Which brands has the influencer worked with previously on campaigns and initiatives?

- Can you afford the influencer? Is he or she a celebrity influencer or a micro influencer (an individual who is highly focused on a particular issue or area)?

- What are your overall goals? Is this partnership just an add-on, or will the partnership help achieve the key performance indicators you have set forth in your campaign?

Identifying False Influencers

Before attempting to identify false influencers, it's important to understand what real influencers are like. There are two influencer groups. The members of one group focus on promoting themselves and presenting a certain image and lifestyle for others to aim for with their large following. Members of the other group focus on providing value, and everything they share and create is about contributing to their communities and real business (Yu, 2017).

You can identify false influencers at an initial, superficial level just by looking at their publicly available metrics. For example, if individuals have 100,000 followers on Twitter, why do they only have one or two likes or favorites on their tweets? In addition, you can always look at the followers and those who comment on their work on Instagram and YouTube. There are ways to identify the bots (automated programs that do certain actions) on each of these sites. Their profiles are usually all the same, have basic information, and often comment "Like this!" or make another generic request. An ethical issue that comes up with influencers is "buying" followers. This is a no-no for social media professionals, because it is very easy to detect the fake profiles and who has and who has not bought an audience. Yes, it is important to grow your network and gain exposure for your expertise within the community, but buying followers is a short-term solution with long-term negative reputation consequences. Quality in followers and community is always better than quantity.

False influencers also focus on the refollow–unfollow technique. The follow-to-follower ratio is constantly debated in the area of influencers and social media professionals. Some are more likely to follow their engaged audiences, but others will follow a large number of people, see who follows them back, and then immediately unfollow these same people. This helps create the illusion they have a large audience, but in reality, it upsets people when they are viewed only as a follower number to boost false influencers' ego with the size of their community. This practice is indeed looked down upon. Another emerging trend is the increased use of bots. Affordable for the most part, these bots are programmed to like, comment, and help create followers for certain accounts (Chen, 2017). Although this may result in a short-term gain from a vanity metrics perspective (lots of followers equals influence in some people's minds), it is not recommended as a long-term focus for influencers and brands. Some people fear that having an insufficient number of followers on social media will not afford them some of the professional opportunities offered to others, but this does not paint a good picture for the potential influencer. While bots may boost followership and the illusion of influence, if an account has a large following on Instagram (100,000 or more, for example) with no real likes or comments, it is easy to tell the influencer either paid for followers or used bots to create a false presentation.

Dennis Yu (2017), the chief technology officer for BlitzMetrics, outlined how to detect "real influencers" by asking relevant questions:

- Are they actually publishing their knowledge openly rather than just getting paid endorsements?

- Can they show their audiences what they can actually do?

- Does their network include fellow colleagues or other influencers who help create a mutually beneficial relationship?

- Are they focused on their numbers rather than the connections and health of their communities?

- Have they let their numbers/partnerships/internet fame get to their head and make them forget the real purpose of social media?

- Do they have the experience and are they able to show the evidence of their work through measureable results based on what they are preaching?

- Are they creating, curating, and engaging with content related to their business, or are they promoting just themselves?

These questions are relevant not only when exploring potential influencers with whom to partner on campaigns but also when thinking about your own personal brand. All of us are influential or famous to someone, so we have to be true to who we are (personal brand), and also look at our own actions within our community. A personal brand is defined by a person's actions (not numbers).

Ambassadors

Another type of audience to consider for social media are those who advocate for and promote your work based on their own personal interests and investment with the brand, agency, organization, or person in question. Individuals who leverage their own loyalty as a currency are known as ambassadors. They could be loyal customers, proud alumni and students, or engaged fans, to name a few. To create a successful ambassador program or initiative takes dedication and investment on the part of an organization, brand, or agency because these relationships must be fostered over time. Having a strong internal culture can be helpful in recruiting and engaging external audiences to be part of the community.

Hootsuite has an ambassador program that focuses on engaging professionals who not only use Hootsuite products in their work but are actively supportive of and loyal to the company. Amplify is a specific tool used to share resources and updates, allowing Hootsuite to disseminate messages, spark ideas, and share content generated by its ambassadors (Photo 11.3). The role of ambassador is often voluntary, but sometimes the title of ambassador is applied to employees. Ambassadors can be both internal and external audience members, depending on the scope and overall goal for the brand.

Yelp (2018) also has a consistent and valued ambassador program (Photo 11.4). The Yelp Elite Squad (YES!) rewards active and engaged Yelp users. To be part of this program, Yelp users must have submitted a range of well-written reviews, participate in active polling and ranking of various brands and places on the site, and have a history of engaging positively with others. Once in the program, users are part of an exclusive community where they can share their stories from their own perspective but also connect with others in the Yelp community. Along with these benefits, the currency exchanged here between the brand and its ambassadors is the authenticity of true users who believe in the mission and purpose of Yelp; exclusivity in hearing new developments, events, and openings; and ability to list themselves as ambassadors with a prominent brand recognizable by others.

Maker's Mark, which works with Doe Anderson and Taylor Cochran as the social media lead for the brand voice and strategy, is another company with an

▶ **Photo 11.3**
Hootsuite Amplify
Ambassador
Program

Source: Hootsuite Inc.,
https://hootsuite.com/
community

**From brand advocacy to social selling,
Hootsuite Amplify connects you with more people.**

What Type of Yelp Elite Are You?

Introducing Michael F. as **The Writer**

Introducing Christy A. as **The Photographer**

Introducing Chris W. as **The Adventurer**

The Writer

Sure, some people review everything, but it's not just about how many opinions you can pound out! Whether you review in haiku, max out the review character count, or detail everything, words are your thing. Do you live to write? Is Yelp your blog? Do you love sharing your experiences?

You're The Writer.

The Photographer

Sometimes it's about shooting from the hip, sometimes it's about getting the whole picture, and sometimes... it's just about the food porn. Do you capture every moment? Do you take 10 minutes to line up each shot? Do you live life through the lens?

You're The Photographer.

The Adventurer

There are reviews, there are photos, and then there's just being a total explorer. From hidden forests to brand new local hot spots, you're all about discovery. Do you love that First To Review badge? Do you barely go a week without finding new adventures? Do you come alive outside 9–5?

You're The Adventurer.

▶ **Photo 11.4**
Yelp Elite
Ambassador (YES!)
Program

Source: www.yelp
.com/elite

---

ambassador program for active and enthusiastic fans. As part of the program, specific industry perks are available, such as the chance to have your name on a Maker's Mark barrel, advance notice of special released bottles, and swag from the brand. This more traditional ambassador program is not dependent on social media, possibly due to the nature of the product (bourbon) and government regulations that limit the company's marketing and advertising to certain audiences.

These are examples of established ambassador programs, but anyone can create an ambassador program for his or her audiences. Mack Collier (2017) provided some good points to keep in mind when thinking about creating an ambassador program and how to launch it for social media strategy purposes:

Research. Use the data you are collecting to recognize the most engaged and active members of your community and what they share. Are they an authoritative voice in the community with others? When did they start engaging with the brand, and what is their overall sentiment toward you online? Identifying these individuals and evaluating whether their characteristics and personae match with your brand are important steps.

Have exclusivity. Your group should meet certain criteria and requirements for participation. This way, you can determine the audience members who are truly passionate and committed to the program versus those who are not. Similar to what Charlie experienced with Willy Wonka and the Chocolate Factory, you want to provide tests, scenarios, and potential obstacles for people to complete to determine who gets into the group and who doesn't.

Offer perks and connections to the brand directly. Sometimes brand ambassadors (like influencers) are paid, but the compensation may not be financial. These ambassadors may get other perks such as exclusives on new ideas and product launches, or even swag. The perk in many cases is the opportunity to connect with people within a brand about which you are passionate. These connections are exclusive and can be more valuable to ambassadors than financial incentives. This all comes down to what you feel ambassadors are looking for and what they value most, which can be addressed and explored through research.

Give them power to create and share content. Ambassadors are as creative as creators themselves, and you want (as a brand) to give them the opportunity to showcase this content with their networks. They may be even more effective since they are passionate and invested in the subject and brand.

Start small and grow big. You may start your group with just a few people, but as word spreads, your numbers may increase and you can start creating a group of passionate and energetic audience members who will be loyal to you.

Focus on building a lifestyle, not a product. Some ambassador programs focus primarily on the product (e.g., Maker's Mark), but there is also the need for emphasizing a certain lifestyle within the community that is relevant to the brand. Red Bull, for example, has a college ambassador program, which allows the company to build its product by partnering with fans of the product in a specific market. Red Bull has focused not just on the product but also on what the product means and represents through experiences, fun activities, and interactions with the brand directly in various settings on college campuses.

Trolls or Haters

Jay Baer wrote a book called *Hug Your Haters* (2016) focusing on how to deal with people who are not the biggest fans of your work. These individuals are sometimes referred to as trolls or haters. They are usually the accounts that comment, tag, and share your work and do not have the most positive things to say about you. Some are merely negative, but others are abusive.

Brands must ensure that they set a policy that prevents these individuals from disrupting or influencing the overall tone or dynamics of the community. Some trolls may not like certain people or brands because of what they stand for, but there could be other reasons as well. These "haters" may have had a negative experience as a customer that turned their view of the company in a negative direction. This is why social care (e.g., customer service, discussed in detail in Chapter 15) is so important on social media. Making sure you address and handle each exchange in a consistent manner could prevent relationships from turning sour. Most of the time, if people have a negative experience with a brand, the deciding factor that determines their future support of a brand is communication (or lack of it) with the brand.

Every brand has followers and audiences who do not like it for some reason, but problems result not simply from having these individuals among your audience but rather from completely ignoring them. Be aware of your trolls and what they may or may not do, but know that deleting or ignoring them completely will cause damage in the long run. One way to deal with these individuals is to make sure you have audience members who are supportive and loyal to what you have been doing on social media and as a brand and who will thus come to your defense.

As you can see from reviewing the previous sections outlining influencers, creators, ambassadors, and trolls or haters, each group is categorized based on what it is leveraging with brands and the social media community. Each audience has distinct characteristics and goals in mind when it comes to interactions and expectations from brands. Table 8.3 outlines the key differences among each of these audiences.

Table 11.3	Differences Between Influencers, Creators, Ambassadors, and Trolls/Haters		
Influencers	**Creators**	**Ambassadors**	**Trolls/Haters**
• Leverage size of audience • Paid endorsements • Access to brand and events • Brands are in control of relationship for brand voice • One-way commitment • Disclose identity and connection/ payment (Federal Trade Commission regulations)	• Leverage opportunities for creativity • Paid endorsements • Partnership • Creators are in control of creativity execution • Two-way commitment/ co-creation • Disclose identity under name or nickname	• Leverage level of loyalty and commitment • Paid endorsements and exclusive access • Ambassadors are in control of amount of participation involved • Two-way commitment/ co-creation • Disclose identity and connection	• Leverage level of outrage and anger toward brands and communities • View their negative engagement with brands on social media as a spectator sport for the world to see • Always looking for you to respond in a way that validates their views • Constant interactions and comments • More likely to participate in cancel culture antics • Tag media outlets for recognition of actions • Sometimes do not disclose identity (anonymous)

APPLYING AUDIENCE SEGMENTATION TO CAMPAIGNS

As noted, there are many audiences to consider for audience segmentation purposes for a social media campaign. Yet, some brands have seemed to master this across their audiences, like the shoe brand adidas. Adidas has been using both influencers and micro influencers (as noted and discussed along with the other types of influencers in Chapter 8) in its campaigns for the past few years, especially on social media (Joseph, 2017). Micro influencers may not have the reach of the established celebrities we commonly see in brand campaigns, such as Steph Curry for Under Armour or LeBron James for Nike. Instead, **micro influencers** have a specific focus, community, and purpose that help brand messages resonate with audiences. These specific types of influencers have a particular focus, niche, or interest they promote specifically on their social media sites (Bernazzani, 2017).

Other benefits of using micro influencers, based on research by Markerly (n.d.), include more engagement, because their communities are hyperfocused and engaged; more targeted audience bases; and better affordability. Engaging with audiences who have a decent reach yet whose content is consumed and viewed much more may be a way for brands to effectively target their focused audiences in a campaign. In addition, there are always concerns related to main influencers on the measurement front and whether or not partnering with an influencer will help achieve business goals and the measurement objectives set forth for the campaign. Instead, by using micro influencers, brands can tie into specific markets aligned with their own views and work with these individuals to make sure it's a win-win situation and the partnership is grounded on authenticity, not money.

Adidas, following the trends of other brands like La Croix, used micro influencers in a partnered effort with Glitch to promote a new set of soccer cleats. Adidas reached out to 30 players from football (soccer) academies in London not only to help promote the new product for the company but to help design and name it. This partnership was a team effort, but it was focused on utilizing the communities and power of word-of-mouth communication from each player in a way that helped create ownership of the content from the brand's side as well as the micro influencers' side.

The skill of adidas in handling its audiences is illustrated by the case of Geoffrey Blosat, a digital analyst for Zoomph and an active member of the sports and social media (#SMsports) group on Twitter. Blosat was training for his first 5K. Before and after each workout, he would take a picture and tag @adidasrunning in his posts to show the company he was using its shoes for his training. During back-and-forth exchanges over the next few weeks, adidas reached out to Geoffrey about sending him a package. The package sent included a handwritten note with a few swag items to help Geoffrey with his 5K journey (Photo 11.5). This action prompted Geoffrey to share this package from adidas not only with the community but also with the sports and social media professionals with whom he is connected on Twitter and Instagram. This community is considered very focused, but in this group, Geoffrey is an influencer in the area of social media and sports, and his posts really encouraged the community to react and reach out to adidas.

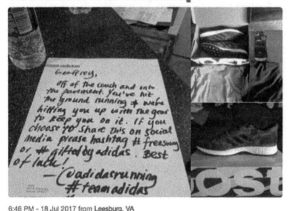

Photo 11.5
Geoffrey Blosat and adidas Running
Source: Twitter/@GeoffTBlosat

Along with the changes happening in the social media industry, social media professionals and brands have to keep their eyes on the changes evolving within their key audiences. As each generation and cohort moves along, the members of each group will have a different perception of social media and how it is integrated into their daily lives.

We cannot assume each audience is going to use or even perceive the content shared on social media in the same way, so social media professionals need to be both diligent and active in understanding the motivational factors, interests, and expectations of audience members pertaining to the brand's social media presence. In addition, new emerging audiences may come into play as a way to get messages across to other audiences, but while these audiences may still operate in a landscape like the Wild, Wild, West, some challenges, opportunities, and trends certainly need to be integrated within the social media strategy plan for both brands and professionals.

THOUGHT QUESTIONS

1. Define audience segmentation, and explain why it is important in social media practices.

2. What are some unique characteristics of powerful influencers that are relevant for social media campaigns?

3. Identify the differences between influencers, creators, ambassadors, and haters/trolls. What main concerns do brands and social media professionals need to be aware of for each type of audience member?

4. What are the best practices for working with influencers and creators? What are the best practices for working with ambassadors?

5. What are three benefits of focusing on micro influencers for a social media campaign?

EXERCISES

1. You have been asked by your internship to identify three influencers you'd recommend to be part of the campaign for the popular drink Bubly with Michael Bublé. Based on your analysis of their previous partnerships, campaigns, followers and audience, and personal brand voice, provide three reasons you would recommend these influencers to Bubly.

2. A brand asks you to be a partner in creating awareness of a new high-intensity fitness center in your town. The company is interested in generating buzz for the opening among the fitness community locally but does not know where to go to find influencers, ambassadors, or creators. Outline your recommendations based on your research and best practices in approaching each of these groups.

3. As an up-and-coming vlogger and creator, you are exploring options to partner with brands and nonprofit campaigns on social media. Outline specific metrics and information you would want to present and organize in your influencer partnership and proposal. Discuss the best practices you follow in creating authenticity with your network.

4. As part of your entry exam for consideration for a social media position, you have been asked to critique three influencers and analyze their social media accounts. Identify three things to look for.

5. You have been asked to create an influencer guide to target micro influencers for a local restaurant. What are some reasons you would suggest the restaurant implement this type of program compared to launching a general influencer campaign?

REFERENCES

Baer, J. (2016). *Hug your haters: How to embrace complaints and keep your customers*. New York, NY: Portfolio/Penguin.

Bentwood, J. (2008). *Distributed influence: Quantifying the impact of social media* (Edelman White Paper).

https://www.socialmediatoday.com/news/quantifying-the-impact-of-social-media-where-the-edelman-white-paper-got-i/496250/

Bernazzani, S. (2017, July 28). Micro-influencer marketing: A comprehensive guide. *HubSpot*.

https://blog.hubspot.com/marketing/micro-influen
cer-marketing

Chen, Y. (2017, August 1). How wannabe Instagram influencers use bots to appear popular. *Digiday*. https://digiday.com/marketing/wannabe-instagram -influencers-use-bots-appear-popular/

Collier, M. (2017, October 26). 10 things to remember when creating a brand ambassador program. *MackCollier.com*. http://www.mackcollier.com/10 -things-to-remember-when-creating-a-brand-ambas sador-program/

Gosling, S. D., Ko, S. J., Mannarelli, T., & Morris, M. E. (2002). A room with a cue: Personality judgments based on offices and bedrooms. *Journal of Personality and Social Psychology*, *82*, 379–398.

Ingalls, J. (2017, May 5). How to differentiate social media influencers and content creators. *Dash Hudson*. http://blog.dashhudson.com/influencer-marketing -content-creator-social-media-strategy-brand -marketing/

Joseph, S. (2017, July 7). How Adidas is using micro-influencers. *Digiday*. https://digiday.com/marketing/ adidas-using-micro-influencers/

Kontonis, P. (2017, August 2). 5 questions to ask yourself before investing in influencer marketing. *Campaign US*. http://www.campaignlive.com/

article/5-questions-askself-investing-influencer -marketing/1441003

Markerly. (n.d.). Instagram marketing: Does influencer size matter? http://markerly.com/blog/ instagram-marketing-does-influencer-size-matter/

McCrae, R. R., & John, O. P. (1992). An introduction to the five-factor model and its implications. *Journal of Personality*, *60*(2), 175–215.

Minsker, M. (2017). How women really feel about influencer marketing. *eMarketer*. https://www.emar keter.com/Article/How-Women-Really-Feel-About -Influencer-Marketing/1014939

Ross, C., Orr, E. S., Sisic, M., Areseneault, J. M., Simmering, M. G., & Orr, R. R. (2009). Personality and motivations associated with Facebook use. *Computers in Human Behavior*, *25*, 578–586.

Yelp. (2018). YES! Yelp Elite Squad. https://www.yelp .com/elite

Yu, D. (2017, May 5). Why I am not an influencer. *Influencive*. http://www.influencive.com/ why-i-am-not-an-influencer/

Zhao, S., Grasmuck, S., & Martin, J. (2008). Identity construction on Facebook: Digital empowerment in anchored relationships. *Computers in Human Behavior*, *24*, 1816–1836.

CREATING, MANAGING, AND CURATING CONTENT (STRATEGIES, TACTICS, AND KEY MESSAGES)

Learning Objectives

After reading this chapter, you will be able to

- Explore the overview of content marketing for social media

- Discuss the steps necessary to conduct a content audit

- Identify the four different types of media and which pieces of content work for each medium

- Understand the array of tools that are available to create written, visual, audio, and video content

INTRODUCTION

While reading this book, you have heard regularly about the growing importance of creating and managing content to be shared on social media. The common phrases heard frequently in the social media space are "content is king" and "context is queen" or a version of the two. Without strong content or the proper execution of the content, all is lost on social media. Investing in the creation and execution of content that is aligned with a brand's voice, audience, and perspective is key. In addition, it is important to create content in the format most valued by and relevant for your key audiences. Sometimes you will be creating content designated for a particular audience, and other times you will be focused on creating items that are very specific. Ultimately, we create content not just to get a higher ranking or have our audiences see something. Content essentially is anything that communicates a specific message to our audience in a designated channel.

Some brands, professionals, and organizations have established their presence and reputation based on the content they are able to share, produce, and disseminate across their networks.

Content, when strategically positioned and executed, can be the basis in helping establish a strong standing in the industry, bringing forth new opportunities to the mix. Matt Kobach of Fast has created a reputation for insightful and strong insights on the social media industry, becoming one of the most recommended follows on social media. Brianne Fleming, a University of Florida professor, has positioned herself as the go-to pop culture and marketing combination on Twitter. Roberto Blake creates tutorials on YouTube on how to launch and execute a vision for videos and other visual content pieces. Brands such as McDonald's, Ocean Spray, Nike, Disney+, and Mint Mobile are some examples of brands who have mastered the equation for having strong content that ties together brand messaging, community expectations, personality, and voice. Even students are getting a reputation for the content they share on certain platforms, such as University of Louisville student and cheerleader Terrell Cabral and his #TerrellIsFamous hashtag promoting positivity and creativity through TikTok and Instagram videos while showing his enthusiasm for Crocs shoes.

In this chapter, we discuss strategies and tactics, the importance of content marketing, and the different types of content we are creating for our social media activities. We also highlight some cases of brands and others that have used social media content effectively in their campaigns.

Adam Ornelas, Former Social Media and Influencer Strategist for Chipotle

Introduction

A marketing and strategy professional with 12 years of experience spanning across all parts of the digital marketing ecosystem, I am innately analytical and curious about people, culture, and technology and how they all intersect in products, platforms, and initiatives.

I currently sit on the digital and off-premise team for Chipotle. I lead influencer strategy, the Chipotle Celebrity Card program, and manage the marketing relationship between Uber Eats and Chipotle. I live and work in Newport Beach, CA.

Experience working with: Tony Hawk, Depop, Venmo, David Dobrik, Baker Mayfield, Diplo, Kaskade, Karamo Brown, Reebok, Airbnb, Drybar, Orangetheory Fitness, Fiverr, Red Bull, Sonos, Toms, Sling TV, Southwest Airlines, L'Oréal, HEAD, Aspen Snowmass, Scott Sports, Honor Society, 5.11 Tactical Gear, 200+ Food & Beverage Vendors in Whole Foods Market.

How did you get your start in social media?

In college, I cofounded a party and events company with a friend of mine. This was in 2010–2012, and social media was in its infancy. At the time, I worked for a radio station cluster and ran their social media. I launched our social media handles for the event company and started reaching out to influential people on campus to post about our events in return for access to artists and party perks. This was the beginning of working on partnerships and what is now influencer marketing. It paired well with my degree in political science because it tapped into my love for cultural insights, relationships, and trends.

What is your favorite part of working in your area of expertise in social media?

I love people. I love analyzing online behaviors and using cultural insights to create fun and authentic content. I work behind the scenes a lot. I am constantly seeking out and establishing relationships with talent, talent managers, agents, etc. I love being an ambassador for the brand, nurturing those relationships, and bringing them to life in meaningful ways on social media.

What is one thing you can't live without while working in social media?

My phone and laptop chargers. I keep them on me at all times. I even have back-up mobile chargers in case I can't get to an electrical outlet.

What is your favorite social media account (person/brand/etc.) to follow and why?

I love NBA Twitter as a whole. The entire twitter fandom moves fast; has the deepest, longest running jokes; makes memes faster than anyone; and is one of the most hilarious parts of twitter. I also love the Los Angeles Chargers' social media presence. They're so in tune with pop culture and create fun content.

What is the most challenging part of working in social media?

Never being able to truly turn off. Working in social media is a blessing and curse. You have to be on to be the first to know about trends. It's your job to be a culture hunter and be in the know about the latest happenings in pop culture. Because of that, you have be plugged in to social media at all times. This past year was exceptionally challenging with the pandemic, working remotely, and the current state of social unrest. Because you're constantly plugged in, you read every opinion, see every image, and feel everything that's being posted. It can be overwhelming.

What do you wish you had known when you were starting out?

I wish I had known how much time you have to invest in being online and on social media. I wish I had known how much time and attention you must sacrifice from other things to be good at your job. You are never truly off the clock. Even when you're on PTO [paid time off], you are constantly reading, sharing, and analyzing. The downside is what I just mentioned, but the upside is you build the mental muscles necessary to think and move faster than folks who didn't come up in social media. You move faster and you're less afraid to take risks.

What are three marketable skills a social media professional needs to have to work in the industry?

A genuine love and innate curiosity about people, behaviors, trends, and culture. The ability to be agile in everything you do. You've got to have a passion for people and be able to adapt to their habits, likes, and dislikes. You've got to be the front line of culture for your company. Move fast, be first, and be authentic.

If you had to choose a song to walk out to in a presentation on social media, what would it be and why?

When it comes to walkout songs, I always say, "Win the crowd over and you'll win the moment." The more niche of a song you choose, the less hyped up people will be. Therefore, I would go with ...

"Hypnotize," by The Notorious B.I.G.

People know the beat, the words, and love the energy. One of my favorites.

Adam Ornelas can be followed on Twitter and other social media platforms @TheAtomRay.

OVERVIEW OF CONTENT MARKETING

As mentioned in Chapter 7 on strategic planning, strategies are focused on how to accomplish set objectives for a campaign, whereas tactics are the nuts and bolts of a social media plan, the specific tools and pieces of content. For the purpose of content marketing, the strategies portion focuses on how content marketing can help achieve the objectives set forth through specific action steps as well as through content creation, ideation, and promotion activities. The tactics portion of content marketing focuses on the specific pieces of content (otherwise known as assets) that need to be created, distributed, and evaluated for the campaign.

It is important to discuss how strategies and tactics are key and integrated with the overall purpose of content marketing and strategies. For the most part, social media professionals have to ask themselves these questions ahead of time:

- *What communication and business objectives are the most important to consider for this social media initiative?* For every objective you need to have a purpose and goal in mind. What are the overall activities and behaviors you want the content to accomplish—to increase awareness about a new product you are launching, or to build sales leads for your business? Taking the time to outline what you want to accomplish will allow you to determine how to accomplish these goals and make sure they are aligned with the actions you take.

- *Is the content that is being showcased and implemented representative and inclusive of all audiences and perspectives?* We need to make sure we are aligning the messages and types of content we share on social media with all of the audiences we are trying to engage with. Understanding the different expectations, impressions, and interpretations of these pieces of content need to be considered. While you may view one piece of content one way, it may not come across the same way to another person.

- *What types of content really resonated with our audiences?* You want to share and provide resources on social media that your audience actually wants to see. Brands, companies, and social media professionals are all about the attention economy, and it is important to create relevant content that audiences value and appreciate. Plus, audiences today want to be entertained, which means using boring content with stock photos that are accessible to anyone may not cut it. Evaluating the messages that go along with the content is a key element to consider as well. What do you want to share with the audiences that ties into the content being presented? Evaluating the data to see what content worked before and with which audience will be helpful in brainstorming what can be done for an upcoming social media campaign.

- *Which channels have been our strongest in the past?* Evaluating the performance and growth of your audiences as well as the metrics (as outlined in Chapter 6) will enable you to see which channels are the most effective in connecting your content with the audiences. These channels may change over time, so it is key to monitor them to see if the content execution needs to be changed.

- *What channels are emerging for our brand that we need to note?* Being established on certain social media channels helps build a community, but like all things technology related, channels come and go, and new ones come up that need to be explored. Determining which ones are appropriate, sustainable, worthy of investment, and relevant for a brand are all important factors to consider. There are certainly platforms that are flashes in the pan, but there are others that have future potential for bringing back huge value and investment for the brand.

- *How much in terms of resources do we have to spend on this content execution?* This is one thing a lot of social media professionals seem to forget. The time spent creating, disseminating, and executing content effectively has to be taken into consideration. It's not about sending out a snap or posting a GIF on Twitter but rather about predicting the amount of planning, strategizing, and brainstorming needed to make sure everything is aligned.

Definition of Content Marketing and Content Strategy

Creating content for the sake of creating content is not helpful to anyone in social media. More brands and audience members are looking at new ways to make a connection, start a dialogue, and reinforce certain perceptions of the brand with the use of content creation on social media. The approach used to promote content to the masses is often referred to as **content marketing**. According to the Content Marketing Institute (2017, para. 2), content marketing is "a strategic marketing approach focused on creating and distributing valuable, relevant, and consistent content to attract and retain a clearly defined audience—and, ultimately, to drive profitable customer action." Traditionally, content marketing has been an important factor to integrate into traditional marketing practices, but it is a growing area of focus to add on to other disciplines such as advertising, public relations, and strategic communications to name a few. This concept is not new for the social media industry, but it has become an integrated tool for helping professionals determine what to create, disseminate, and share with others to accomplish certain objectives.

There are several reasons why it is important not only to share (or curate) content from other people but also to have the ability to create original content to be posted on social media. Each individual and brand has a distinct voice and perspective, and it is important to determine how and why to share these on certain social media platforms.

Other reasons to create content on social media include

- *Having strong brand awareness.* We are in the attention economy, and brands, agencies, and individuals are all trying to establish themselves in ways that separate them from others. One way to accomplish this is to think about each piece of content as an extension of your digital footprint and real estate. You control all of the content you host on your own website, but it is important to explore guest opportunities to further extend your research with other communities, industries, and partnerships. You may not have as much control or flexibility over the content you share on these other sites, but it is essential that you present a strong brand image with the content you do have and that, based on what you share, you attract new audience members to connect with and bring back to your own hosted content.

- *Ability to show and provide evidence of thought leadership.* Content marketing is not only about showing what you know but presenting it in a format that is easily consumed and shared with others. Understanding the format that audiences are looking for is part of the game, and it's about matching the right content in the right channel for the right audience.

- *Building new relationships with experiential content.* More than ever, audiences expect to be entertained and informed with the content they are presented with, and they control one of the most important currencies in social media: attention span. If a brand or organization is entertaining, that's great. But, if they are entertaining, experiential, relevant, and engaging with audiences by investing in social care (which will be discussed later in Chapter 14 under specializations), this helps build new relationships. Aviation Gin has mastered this since it had its viral commercial moment with Peloton in 2019.

- *Gaining respect and reputation in the industry as a trusted resource that produces and cultivates value to their community.* The more people see your content as consistent yet personalized for each of the designated platforms, the more they will trust the information presented and be even more motivated to become long-term readers and followers. If the content is relevant and provides helpful tips, resources, and action steps for audiences, this could be the first step in transforming a loyal audience member into an advocate for your work, which could lead to future connections and professional partnerships.

- *Tying into the search engine optimization capabilities.* In order to drive influence and your reputation online, blogs, white papers, and additional long- and short-form content could help drive traffic back to your owned media assets (media you control) as a return on investment for time and resources spent on social media. This is why whenever you post content (a blog post, white paper, update, etc.), you must do your research on the key terms so if someone comes across your content based on a search, they will see value in it and follow you on the designated platform. Using data insights along with creating relevant content is the one-two punch needed to maintain a loyal community base that consumes your content on a regular basis.

- *Providing assets to a social media campaign.* Pieces of content are often referred to as assets (items owned and created by an organization, agency, or person) to be used strategically for certain key messages and objectives in a campaign. Without these assets, the messages may fall a bit flat and lose the attention of audience members on social media.

Alignment of Content

An ultimate goal for the social media professional is to create great content. Depending on whom you ask, this could mean a variety of different things. However, great content that is successful for social media purposes is usually relevant, personal, **evergreen** (content that stays relevant for a long time and does not have to be updated as regularly as other types of content), engaging, and targeted to a specific audience with which the information and stories resonate. Creating content and putting it out there for the world to see is not the only strategy and action a social media professional should pursue. One must take multiple components into consideration when aligning content with the strategies and messages of a campaign or promotion for a brand.

First, the social media manager needs to conduct a **content audit** to determine which assets (e.g., creative, visual, audio, and written content) worked and what the takeaways were from these items in the past. Specifically, a content audit can help you determine what should be removed from a website or database of resources for a brand, identify gaps to help brainstorm future content creation opportunities, and review the overall brand voice to see if additional reviews of copy writing to improve brand voice connection and overall quality are needed (Sizemore, 2017). The first step is to collect all of the relevant pieces of content created by the company, business, or professional and analyze them based on the metrics provided.

Table 12.1 provides an overview of the template that Moz (Sizemore, 2017) provided in its recommendations, along with a few additions. The social media professional needs to categorize each asset of content based on the platform and note, according to the PESO model, whether or not it was paid (received compensation for placement or was sponsored), earned (shared without payment and done organically), shared (similar to earned but directly connected with social media), or owned (shared via a controlled platform).

The next step is to provide the context of the asset, or the URL and title, as a record of the published content to review. It is also key to outline the overall purpose of this content for the audit—what was its focus in the first place, and was it part of a specific campaign or execution by the social media manager? Metrics help the social media manager and team decide what to do with the content, and they must be tailored based on where the content was posted or hosted. For example, shares of, comments on, and inbound website traffic to a blog post may be a few metrics to consider. However, for a social media post, basic and advanced social media metrics (engagement, interactions, share of voice, reach, etc.) could be used. Each approach has to be adapted to the content and context being evaluated.

Actions focus on the larger picture of what to do with the content. For example, does a blog post need to be updated with the latest statistics, or should it stay the same because the content is still relevant? Also, social media professionals need to ask themselves what they would do with the content being evaluated in the audit. Is it still usable and relevant for the audience? Can it be updated, or should it not be used again? These are just some of the categories needed to sort the content that is still relevant for the campaign in question and the pieces that need to be set aside.

In Table 12.1, the future recommendations column notes what to keep in mind for the future. Once the content audit is complete, the social media manager and team need to discuss the key areas involved with content marketing, particularly the specialized areas and duties that help align the messages and content with the audience for a brand or organization. *Content strategy*, which primarily focuses on how and why content is created, managed, and updated for future use by the organization in question, includes the internal guidelines necessary to keep things consistent and on message (Moz, 2018; see also Chapter 7). These documents and guidelines help the social media manager (and team) ensure that all content going out on social media across the channels is consistent, aligned with the brand voice and vision, and presented in a style with which the audiences are familiar (Moz, 2018). Content marketing includes setting up a schedule for posting brand content (e.g., content calendar), promoting the content, and determining how frequently audiences will receive the content across various channels.

Table 12.1	Sample Content Audit Template						
Type of Content	Title	URL	Assets	Purpose/ Campaign Execution	Metrics	Action	Future Recommendations
Paid							
Earned							
Shared							
Owned							

Content ideation. One of the biggest challenges in social media content creation is having a strong idea. A great idea helps set the foundation for any strong content and social media campaign. The ability to see the whole picture and strategize how an idea could come alive is a necessary skill many brands and organizations look for in potential social media professionals today. Many ideas are available to choose from, but if you overlook a good idea in favor of a bad one, then you'll spend a lot of time and resources not fully capturing the potential of a campaign.

Ideas, especially good ones, do not fall from the sky. Here are some ways to generate ideas:

- *Look at what is outside of the social media industry.* Review and explore previous case studies and stories outside of social media for inspiration. Sometimes, the most brilliant idea that can be incorporated into social media was already realized, but in a different industry. Keep this in mind: Applying an idea that worked in another area to a new context and industry might be all you need. New ideas can also come about through the integration of more than one idea. Professionals can watch their competitors as well. As mentioned in Chapter 7, it is important to see what your competitors are (or are not) doing with their content. These extra steps could help generate some further discussions and ideas for creating content for the social media campaign in question.

- *See what the research is saying.* Look at what is trending (on Facebook, Google, Instagram, TikTok, Byte, Twitter, etc.), what keywords or areas are getting a lot of mentions, what the top media outlets and influencers are writing about that may be worth connecting to your brand or company, and what issues, challenges, and gaps in the industry as a whole your content could address. Use data to your advantage to identify opportunities and challenges to address with new content. Identifying these gaps and looking at how to use content created by your team to address them could be very rewarding and profitable. The strategic implications (the "so what" factor for why this is happening) are key in determining which ideas will be successful and what types of content and information to create and execute successfully for a social media campaign.

- *Categorize ideas in terms of whether they accomplish content goals.* Are the ideas helpful in providing value for the audience? Would it be relevant to create content for a particular audience? Are you producing one-of-a-kind resources people can't get anywhere else? Will the content likely motivate them to share? These are just some of the questions to ask yourself when coming up with ideas for content, because this process will not only further the brainstorming sessions but also provide a framework for how to make content even better.

- *Set up regular brainstorming sessions.* Setting aside time to brainstorm with your team will be helpful for getting different perspectives and ideas to the table. Brainstorming can be done, of course, face-to-face, but bouncing around ideas in an online setting (e.g., on intranet networks or Slack) could also be beneficial. Participants of the brainstorming session can come in prepared with a few ideas but, at the same time, encourage people to have an open mind and no preconceived view of the situation. Of course, all ideas from the brainstorming sessions should be recorded, summarized, and taken into consideration by the team along with next steps to take.

- *Find the "it" and spark.* Identify the attitudes, actions, motivational factors, desires, and interests that can capture an audience's attention. That said, there are no "bad" ideas that should be disregarded. Instead, ideas should be noted, prioritized, and then built upon by the team. Don't spend too much time on content that essentially bores you (and your audience), but rather invest in those pieces that call out to you and fit parameters for your brand (research insights, industry expectations, brand voice and community, etc.).

- *Note the reasons people like or do not like content.* It's important to look at not only why content works but also why it does not work. It could be something as simple as people having a hard time accessing the information or your presenting your content on the wrong platform. Seeing both successful and not-so-successful posts could help you identify ideas that will work and ideas to momentarily put aside.

Content strategy. The strategy component for content is simple: What are your overall goals as a brand or company, and how do you want to execute them? Vision, and staying true to your mission and brand voice, is key in making sure each piece of content, message, and asset is aligned and strategically placed on the designated platform. This also takes into account the visual presentation of the content, showcasing the voice and true nature of the brand.

To get started, social media professionals need to take the content and assets they have created, or will be repurposing and updating, and decide how to execute it on social media. As described earlier in the chapter, a thorough content audit identifying the gaps and opportunities among fellow competitors and evaluating current expectations and needs from audiences provides essential background.

Before you even get started with the creation of content, a set brand voice and style guidelines must be in place. All content and assets should share the voice of the brand, person, and account. As discussed in Chapter 10, following a writing style guide is necessary along with set protocols for promoting the content (keywords, search engine optimization tips and techniques, etc.). Other dos and don'ts for content creation and strategy execution should be clearly articulated. All members of the collaborative team should be trained on this background material, which should be included in the main social media policy distributed internally among all of the social media team members.

Delta ✓
@Delta

⊙⊙⊙

Mask on. Seatbelt on. This is the way.

But remember to keep your nose covered. That is actually the way.

9:38 AM · Jul 24, 2020 · Twitter Web App

389 Retweets   **78** Quote Tweets   **2.3K** Likes

▶ **Photo 12.1**
Delta's Twitter Account Shows Baby Yoda With a Mask

Source: Twitter/@Delta

Once you determine the current state of your content, you have to decide, as a group, where to place the content. Will you host the content on your own media platforms (blog posts, landing pages, webinars, etc.) and then share it out on social media, or will you post the content directly on social media (Facebook videos, Twitter GIFs, Instagram Stickers, TikTok, Instagram Stories, etc.) with a link back to the website? Finalize these issues to make sure your strategy is intact and your execution sound.

However, don't forget—even if you are trying to sell a product, run a fundraiser, or get fans motivated for an upcoming season, your content strategy has to have substance, and storytelling needs to be intertwined with the content being shared. The different stories that could be created (e.g., emotional journey, current landscape, humor, educational purposes, or addressing a current opportunity or problem) are ideas that could be personalized and tailored to the content, and executed in a way that resonates with the intended audience.

Many social media accounts, such as the following, have developed content that is relevant and impactful for their intended audiences (Lua, 2017):

- *Delta.* The airline company shares updates and official statements from their CEO and corporate accounts but also acknowledges the human stories and trends that are happening, like making sure to travel with a mask to protect against COVID-19. In a post tying *Mandalorian* to current events, Delta showed Baby Yoda wearing a surgical mask to prevent the spread of COVID-19 (Photo 12.1). The post used a quote from *Mandalorian* and applied it to mask-wearing.

- *Humans of New York.* The HONY Facebook account focuses on the entire story of a person showcased in an image, tying in the art of creating a story with the image and update (Photo 12.2).

- *Mint Mobile, HighKey Snacks, and Aviation American Gin.* What does a phone company, gin brand, and keto-friendly snacks all have in common? Well, the answer is Ryan Reynolds. The gin company not only shares updates and insights from one of their owners (Ryan Reynolds), but it also shares its community members, providing a range of voices and perspectives that surround the alcoholic brand. Mint Mobile creates engaging visuals with the Mint Mobile Fox icon and HighKey Snacks provides unique updates along with branded content that stands out from others on social media.

- *MoonPie and Cinnabon.* Both MoonPie and Cinnabon provide relevant content, but in different ways. These two brands interject their personalities into their social media updates to the extent that they provide value in the form of entertainment for their audiences. MoonPie delivers witty commentary related to its products, and Cinnabon interjects real-time engagement and conversations with its audiences.

- *Adweek.* Along with providing value in their articles, *Adweek* has extended its presence on social media with the establishment of webinars, Twitter chat sessions, and resources that create value and appreciation to their community.

Humans of New York
January 22 ·

"We have to keep our relationship secret. Our parents would not approve and we're not courageous enough to tell them yet. So we meet in secret three or four times per month. Since the beginning of our relationship, we've shared a diary. We take turns keeping it. Whoever has it will write down our memories. They'll also write down what they want from the other person, and how they feel misunderstood. Then every time we meet—we hand it off."

(Calcutta, India)

👍 Like   💬 Comment   ↪ Share   🌐 ▾

▶ **Photo 12.2**
Humans of New York
Facebook Page

Facebook/@Humans of
New York; Courtesy of
Brandon Stanton

- *Sour Patch Kids.* Creating engaging, visual, and bright content that reflects the fun nature of the candy brand is what Sour Patch Kids has done that has helped them generate a lot of enthusiasm on social media with their content.

- *Buff City Soap.* The "Starbucks of Soap" brand is on the rise with its beautiful visual content that brings its soap products to life on Instagram and Facebook. Tying into the strategic messaging on natural ingredients and plant-based products with strong visuals on its channels, Buff City Soaps has solidified its growth as a brand both online and offline.

- *NHL Seattle Kraken.* "Alexa, play Liam Neeson's segment in *Clash of the Titans.*" The new National Hockey League team announced their new name to pay homage to the mystical creature from Scandinavian folklore. Their content was not only aligned with its core colors and branding but was executed seamlessly through visual pieces of content across their social media channels.

There are many different ways to create content and execute it appropriately for social media channels. Yet more than just tactical items (specific pieces of content or tools to use to create and manage these pieces of content) need to be created. Social media professionals must think about both the content that will hit the surface-level goals for a brand (recognition, awareness, etc.) and the content that

Table 12.2	Specific Areas of Content to Create			
Thought Leadership	**Lead Generation**	**Visual Storytelling and Education**	**Brand Awareness**	**Outreach Efforts**
• Webinars • Courses • Tutorials • How-to guides, resources, and lists • Q&As • Research • Blog posts • White papers • Presentations • Video tutorials/ vlogs • Videos from team members and branding	• Customer service • Media kits • Promoted posts and sponsored stories • Tutorials • Testimonials • Webinars • Reviews • Email marketing • Social selling updates • White papers	• Infographics • Videos • Podcasts • Presentations • Animations • Tutorials • Testimonials • Storyboards • Infographics • Templates • Vlogs • Short-form videos	• Branded content • Conversations • Interactive media and social care • Twitter chats • Live video segments • Featured guests/ interviews • Influencer takeovers • Ambassador features • Podcast, Twitter chat, blog feature quotes	• Social media exchanges • Creator relations • Sponsorships • Media mentions • Quotes • Newsletters • Influencer relations • Blogger relations • Ambassador relations

helps with higher levels of management strategies and goals (achieving thought leadership status, changing attitudes and behaviors, enhancing reputation, etc.). Table 12.2 presents some suggestions for specific types of content that you could create to achieve certain goals and objectives. All of this content can be created and shared on social media, but some (e-books, blog posts, etc.) will need to be hosted on owned media channels.

Content promotion. You can have the best content possible, but if no one sees it and shares it with their own networks, then it is a wasted effort. Content promotion and execution in reaching out to the audience's feeds and accounts is as important as creativity in your key messages and assets.

As discussed in Chapter 11, you can identify key audience members to target regarding a specific campaign or initiative. Using tools such as Klear, Meltwater, Agorapulse, Hootsuite, Talkwalker, Zoomph, Brandwatch, BuzzSumo, and others can help you determine which audience members to reach out to based on a certain area of focus. Keep in mind, as discussed in the previous chapter, that influencers come in all shapes and sizes, so identifying not only main influencers but also micro influencers is important. To determine which influencers to potentially partner up with on a content promotion initiative, you have to examine which platforms they are on, what topics they are influential about, and what type of content (or history of content promotion partnerships) they have presented before.

Content calendar. A content calendar is an important template for keeping the content you share online organized and consistent. This shareable resource is used by social media teams to plan, organize, and coordinate all of the content going out for a brand, organization, or individual on social media.

For social media professionals, the benefits of using a content calendar are that it keeps everything organized in one single document and helps you visualize when, where, and at what time each piece of content will be distributed across the social media spaces. According to Convince & Convert (Hrach & Griffiths, 2019), a content calendar is beneficial for social media professionals because it

- helps plan out content around key dates and events in a specific industry;

- outlines which team member is responsible for each task;

- keeps everything in a single place for everyone to be on board with;

- establishes an approval process for which posts get posted, which comments need to be addressed, and overall decision tree in case things need to be escalated to a higher level during a crisis (tools like Agorapulse have features for this);

- sets up expectations for when certain content and assets need to be scheduled and/or sent out ahead of schedule (timing is essential for content calendars);

- sees where you need to add or take out content for your campaign; and

- lines up all of the content so everything is coordinated and ready to go.

Like Convince & Convert, Hootsuite (Walters, 2017) states that content calendars promote collaboration with other members of your team and save time, which is always good to keep in mind if you are working on multiple social media campaigns and projects at the same time.

To organize your content calendar, you should follow certain steps. First, determine who your audiences are. What groups do you want to reach, and where do they go for their information? Sometimes it is a good idea to create an audience persona, or a description of key audience groups you want to target based on their demographic, psychographic, and motivational factors (Walters, 2017). This will help determine what the audience members are looking for, and what content they would feel most connected with. Essentially, the more you know about your audience, the more successful you will be in discovering what they will and will not want to see come across their social media feeds.

Determining what channels your audiences are on will help inform the assets to create and distribute for the calendar. Once you look at the assets from previous campaigns and see how they have done overall, these insights will help guide the team to determine whether content should be repurposed for certain platforms, updated, or deleted. In addition, this could help the team brainstorm ideas for original content to create specifically for a campaign or initiative. So, ask yourself these questions (Walters, 2017):

- What content got the most comments, likes, and shares?

- What content got the most views and traffic?

- What content got the most reactions? Positive or negative?

- What content got the highest engagement?

- Which account generated the most engagement with the same content?

- What content was linked and referenced by others (influencers, creators, media outlets, other blogs, news, etc.)?

The content calendar should keep you on track with important dates, channel updates, and timing/expectations for how many posts, updates, and pieces of content to create for each social media platform. Particular dates (holidays, product launches, entertainment activities, sporting competitions and games, campaigns, annual events, etc.; Walters, 2017) need to be taken into account when outlining your schedule. In addition, looking at which account sends out the content on social media is an important element to consider. For example, for college or professional sports, if a team sends out a TikTok video celebrating a win, it may generate a lot of hits and hit certain engagement metrics. However, if the star player from the winning team creates a video to share out, then it may get even more. Having strong content is a fundamental component for a brand, but understanding where this content is placed transforms a winning social strategy into an iconic social strategy for brands. We are all on the same team, so this is a win-win situation for all parties.

Another point to consider is that the frequency of posting for one platform may not work for another. For example, if brands or social media professionals used Instagram like they did Twitter, the frequency would be too high. Also, taking 30 segments on Instagram Stories may be okay for a takeover but not for Instagram. Experimenting and seeing what works and what doesn't work is often helpful.

After developing the content, the next step is scheduling the content to go out on certain platforms. Determining the right timing for your content requires evaluating and examining your own data. Guidelines exist for which time and day certain posts work on each platform, but ultimately, you want to (a) analyze your own data to determine what works for your community and (b) tweak it if necessary to get better results. It sometimes comes down to experimenting and trial and error. Either way, you will gain lessons and insights for future campaign initiatives.

Sample content calendars are available from various resources like Hootsuite, Agorapulse, Sprout Social, and Buffer (Figure 12.1). Some of these brands provide free templates to download as CVS files, or they offer the content calendar feature in their platform. The content calendar should also indicate when to stop a scheduled post. For example, when a natural disaster or crisis situation happens,

Figure 12.1 Hootsuite Sample Content Calendar

Title	Author	Topic	Deadline	Publish	Time	Notes
WEEK 1						
How [New Product] Can Save You Hours of Time	Amelia Pond	product launch promotion	6/15/2017	6/19/2017	6 a.m.	
WEEK 2						
WEEK 3						
WEEK 4						

Source: Hootsuite Inc., https://hootsuite.com/community

no one wants to see a promoted post or update from a company. Some brands have learned this lesson the hard way.

- GAP got into trouble on social media when it posted a blue and red sweatshirt after the 2020 presidential election with a message about coming together.

- Snapchat shared a "Would you Rather" poll on Rihanna and Chris Brown in 2016, which sparked a lot of controversy because of the two celebrities' combative relationship.

- Corona Beer announced their new Hard Seltzer product "coming to shore" in the wake of COVID-19.

Most brands have received the message to turn off their scheduled posts during such events, but at the same time, content managers must exercise diligence and be aware of the situation on social media.

TYPES OF CONTENT MEDIA

Some basic definitions of content need to be reviewed. **Short-form content** is the content you usually see presented on social media. These short snippets of information can be consumed very quickly and effectively. A 280-character tweet with an image is just one example of short-form content. A TikTok Challenge is another form of short-form content that can be shared and consumed in other platforms. Instagram Stories, unless they are shared under highlights or as an IGTV, can also be considered short-form content. Based on the audience and the platform, this type of content is effective for expressing key messages in a short amount of time. In addition, the attention span for audiences today is much shorter than it was in the past.

Long-form content expands on a topic in greater detail and usually has a longer shelf life (and more often is evergreen content), which helps showcase the expertise, insights, and education opportunities from the brand or person writing the content. Long-form content can range from written content such as blog posts (500–1,000 words) to ebooks, webinars, research reports, and online guides, to name a few even longer forms of content. These items are posted on websites for reference and educational purposes. Long-form content also delves into much more detail with additional research (interviews with professionals, vlogs, tutorials, interviews, survey results, insights shared by experts, etc.) to inform future campaigns and education. However, long-form content is very time-consuming to read and produce compared to short-form content. The resources and time needed to be effective and thorough with long-form content is one reason why not many brands or organizations present a lot of it. Yet, effective organizations with a reputation for detailed and thorough resources are known in the industry for their insights, which helps them drive sales and customer bases.

Another type of content that can be shared over and over again because it remains relevant in social media is evergreen content. This content does not focus on the latest tools or gadgets but rather concentrates on the foundational strategies and behaviors to apply and use depending on the situation.

One model that is frequently used in social media to determine types of content to be created and managed is the PESO model, introduced in Chapter 7. The PESO model, as Gini Dietrich (2018) describes it, merges four media types (paid, earned, shared, and owned) to create an integrated media model for social media professionals to utilize in their campaigns. PESO stands for paid media, earned media, shared media, and owned media. Figure 12.2 shows the updated PESO model; what has changed is the areas that include two types of media (influencer marketing fits paid and earned media since brands pay influencers for campaigns but can also work with them for earned media purposes).

Paid media is social media advertising, or a "pay-to-play" model. The company (or advertiser/agency) is paying for the content to appear in a timeline for a certain amount of money. Examples of paid media include the following social media assets:

- Sponsored ads on Instagram Stories
- TikTok sponsored challenges
- Sponsored posts on Facebook
- Promoted tweets on Twitter
- Promoted trending hashtags on Twitter
- Snapchat ads
- Sponsored lenses on Snapchat
- YouTube ads
- LinkedIn ads
- TikTok ads, challenges, and collaborations
- Sponsored AR filters on Instagram and Facebook
- Boosted content (e.g., Facebook and Instagram)
- Paid publishing (e.g., articles, blog posts, etc.)
- Paid influencers and creators for content

On the other hand, **earned media** is often connected with public relations. Earned media is *not* controlled by brands, which in many ways makes it more trustworthy and less biased compared to other types of content. Publicity or promotion of content without paying for the content characterizes this type of media. Having strong relationships with key audiences in the media as well as influencers will help drive your messages and content out to other targeted audiences. This can be integrated with paid media, especially if influencers are compensated for their efforts, yet the overall purpose of this type of media is to disseminate the content to people with a large reach and trust level among key audiences. Earned media has a strong connection with public relations on social media, as Chipotle demonstrated with their launch of Chipotle Goods, a responsibly sourced apparel collection.

Other examples of content usually presented in earned media include the following:

- Media relations
- Influencer relations
- Ambassador endorsements
- Creator relations
- User-generated content (e.g., loyal fans, advocates, etc.)

Figure 12.2 PESO 2.0 Model

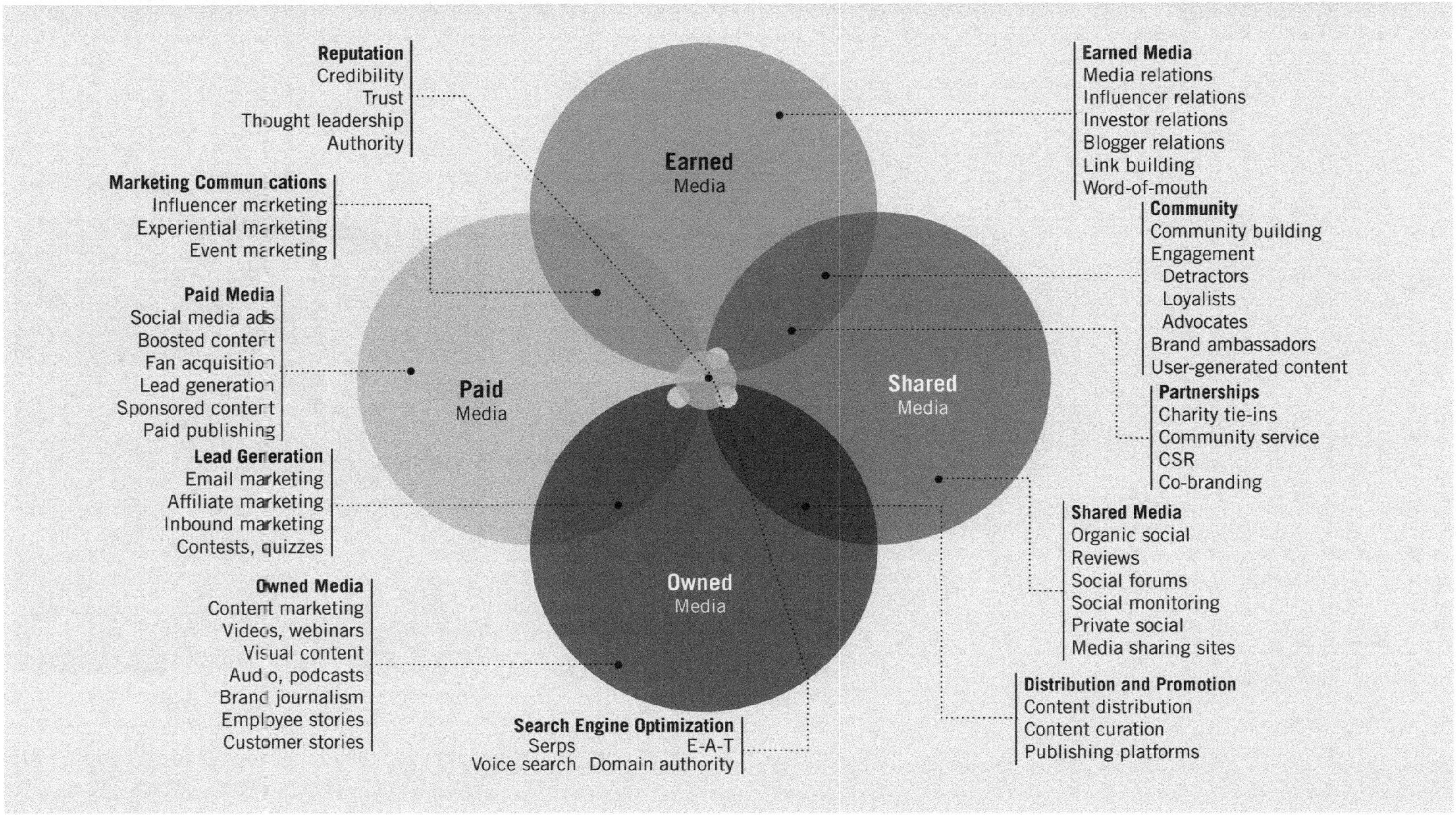

Reputation
Credibility
Trust
Thought leadership
Authority

Marketing Communications
Influencer marketing
Experiential marketing
Event marketing

Paid Media
Social media ads
Boosted content
Fan acquisition
Lead generation
Sponsored content
Paid publishing

Lead Generation
Email marketing
Affiliate marketing
Inbound marketing
Contests, quizzes

Owned Media
Content marketing
Videos, webinars
Visual content
Audio, podcasts
Brand journalism
Employee stories
Customer stories

Earned Media
Media relations
Influencer relations
Investor relations
Blogger relations
Link building
Word-of-mouth

Community
Community building
Engagement
Detractors
Loyalists
Advocates
Brand ambassadors
User-generated content

Partnerships
Charity tie-ins
Community service
CSR
Co-branding

Shared Media
Organic social
Reviews
Social forums
Social monitoring
Private social
Media sharing sites

Distribution and Promotion
Content distribution
Content curation
Publishing platforms

Search Engine Optimization
Serps
E-A-T
Voice search   Domain authority

Earned Media
Paid Media
Shared Media
Owned Media

Shared media is often associated with social media, but it is more of an interactive medium where conversations and dialogue emerge as the result of the content being shared (usually linked), which is different from earned media. In addition, shared media fosters curation and creation tied to certain trending topics, issues, and even memes (as shown with Reese Witherspoon's interpretation of the 2020 Photo Meme Challenge; Photo 12.3). This challenge was focused on bringing audiences together to share their experiences of what 2020 as a year has been, allowing some humor to what everyone was thinking. Witherspoon has utilized her social media platforms for a variety of reasons for promotional activities for her shows and her product (e.g., the clothing line Draper James), but this meme showed her humor and personalized the meme to reflect examples from each of her movies and TV work. Other examples of this are as follows:

- Facebook group shares

- Yelp, Google, and Facebook Reviews

- Messaging (e.g., Messenger, WhatsApp, WeChat, DMs)

- Twitter retweets and comments

- LinkedIn shares and linking the content in a LinkedIn update or post

- TikTok video shares

- Memes

- Slack community conversations

- Instagram pod discussions and shared endorsements

- Influencer promotions and advocacy efforts

- Advocates and ambassadors sharing content with communities

The last type of media discussed in the PESO model, **owned media**, focuses on content and the platform you control as a brand, organization, or person. This

▶ **Photo 12.3**
Reese Witherspoon and the 2020 Meme Challenge

Source: Instagram/ @reesewitherspoon

content is hosted on your own controlled media platforms such as websites, blogs, branded communities, or email newsletters. Some of the owned media content that can be created includes the following:

- Employee advocacy stories
- Testimonials
- Blog posts and resources
- White papers
- Tutorials
- Email marketing
- Customer testimonials
- Brand journalism
- Podcasts and video tutorials
- Reviews
- Ebooks

As Samuel Gentry, global social media governance and activation lead at General Motors, shared on LinkedIn, employees are great in sharing updates, news, and information on their own social media channels while also acknowledging their role with the brand for ethical and transparency reasons (usually with a hashtag like General Motors has done with #IWorkAtGM). In Photo 12.4, Gentry makes sure everyone knows on LinkedIn that he is sharing content not only for GM but as an employee of GM to create a sense of transparency with his community. This is important for brands like GM to note since audiences may not realize the person who is taking about the brand actually works for the brand. Being authentic and upfront is not only good practice for brands and social media professionals, but it is also what the Federal Trade Commission expects as far as authenticity and being transparent on endorsements and associations.

Samuel Gentry · 1st
Global Social Media Governance and Activation Lead, General Motors
3d · ⊕

"Led by LYRIQ, Cadillac will redefine American luxury over the next decade with a new portfolio of transformative EVs," #IWorkForGM

LYRIQ Show Car Leads Cadillac Into Electric Future
media.gm.com

14

▶ **Photo 12.4**
Employee Sharing Content From a Brand

Source: Retrieved from https://www .linkedin.com/feed/ update/urn:li:activity: 6697570180567986177/

TOOLS TO CREATE CONTENT

Many tools are available to help you create some amazing pieces of content (see Table 12.3). Graphic design and videography are some of the fastest-growing areas of need in the social media industry, but they are not the only considerations. Writing skills are also important but sometimes get overlooked in social media

Table 12.3	Tools to Create Content			
Written	**Audio**	**Visual**	**Graphic**	**Video**
• Blogging tools (WordPress, Medium, Blogger) • Anchor • Evernote • Google Drive • Grammarly • Hemingway App • MailChimp • Constant Contact	• Anchor • Audacity • SoundCloud • GarageBand • Evernote (for generating ideas) • Scripts (WriterDuet)	• SlideShare • Prezi • Canva • Adobe Spark Post • Giphy • Mojo • Unfold	• Adobe Spark Page • Canva • Piktochart • Alive • Camera+ • Illustrator • Photoshop	• YouTube • Adobe Premiere Pro • Adobe Premiere Rush • Final Cut Pro • Vimeo • Animoto • Zoom • BlueJeans • Adobe Spark Video

content conversations. Keep in mind, like all aspects of social media, tools to not only create content but curate it (discussed in the next section) will constantly change. Some will be open to use for free, but others will range from a "freemium" model (allowing you to download and use the service for free) to more of a paid structure. Yet, because content always needs to be created for social media purposes, it is sometimes worth it to have the right tools for the job.

- *Written.* Writing tools are helpful in not only creating content but also checking for mistakes in the content. Using Grammarly and the Hemingway App helps ensure you do not make mistakes in your writing. First impressions count, so investing in such tools will help you make everything ready to publish. In addition, other tools can help you connect on other social media channels. An email newsletter, for example, can help connect audiences back to social media and vice versa, so using MailChimp or Constant Contact for this could be useful. Also, Trello is a good tool to help you write down ideas, brainstorm with your team, and coordinate efforts regarding what needs to be accomplished by when. Osana is similar to Trello, but it comes with a different cost and additional features. Basecamp is another team collaborative tool to help coordinate tasks and responsibilities for content creation and marketing.

- *Audio.* Audio is a powerful tool to use to create content, including podcasts. Several audio tools are available, and it all comes down to which one makes you feel most comfortable. A lot of podcasts are on iTunes, Spotify, and other app-based platforms, but SoundCloud is another platform used to host podcasts for brands and professionals. Anchor allows you to create content with audio. One way to repurpose audio content is to transcribe interviews and post them, as Social Media Examiner has done with its weekly show. The company records the show and then posts a summary outlining the key takeaways from the show to be shared on its blog and then redistributed to its social media channels.

- *Visual.* LinkedIn has the ability to share presentations due to their purchase of SlideShare, which is another form of visual content. These are used for sharing information from conferences and workshops or providing simple tutorials on how to navigate or do certain activities on a platform (best tips for creating content on Snapchat or Instagram, how to create an effective TikTok video for a challenge, etc.). Visual tools help you create content that taps into thought leadership. Canva is great, for example, because it has templates for all types of content that can be formatted in any shape or size. Adobe Spark also uses various templates for its Post products, so if you are crafting updates to go out on specific social media platforms, this will be another valuable addition to your toolkit. However, more employers and companies are expecting content creators to have skills in Adobe Creative Cloud products.

- *Video and Graphic.* Having graphic design skills will make you a very marketable social media professional and content creator. However, you still must be aware of the complete picture, which means you need to have the necessary written and strategy skills. Several tools exist in this area that will make your job easier. For video, the go-to is Adobe Premiere or Adobe Premiere Rush, and if you are on mobile, Adobe Clip will help you craft short-form videos. Final Cut Pro and iMovie are helpful tools as well. Others can be used to create graphics to share on social media. Some tools are integrated within certain platforms already, such as Instagram and TikTok.

CURATING CONTENT

We have discussed the essence of content creation, but another aspect to consider is referred to as content curation. *Content curation*, according to Hootsuite, is "the process . . . of sorting through large amounts of content on the web and presenting the best posts in a meaningful and organized way. The process can include sifting, sorting, arranging, and placing found content into specific themes, and then publishing that information" (Cisnero, 2014). This is somewhat different from content creation. With content curation, you are searching for relevant articles, resources, and content from other sources you feel your audience will find relevant and useful to consume.

Some practices to note when it comes to curating the best content include the following:

- *Make it personal.* Don't just share the content on Twitter, Facebook, or LinkedIn. Tell your audience members *why* you are sharing it. This helps build a story for why you (or a brand) think it is relevant for audiences to see this content.

- *Don't rely just on sharing other people's content.* It is important to make sure everyone knows your perspectives and unique takes, not just everyone else's.

- *People gravitate toward valuable content.* If you can determine areas in which your audience wants more information, then this will help you as you search for and uncover content to share with them.

- *Content curation shouldn't take too much of your time, but it should be a factor in your daily routine.* Searching for, discovering, and sharing relevant content should not be your full-time job. Instead, it should be part of it. Taking a few minutes each day to look for items that may be good for your audiences' well-being is all it takes.

Do not share everything you can possibly get your hands on with your audiences—people do not want to be spammed with material that is not relevant to them or that they do not find useful. Be selective and have a strategic purpose for each piece of content you share, and do this in a transparent manner. This means, if you are sharing a piece of content, tell the members of your audience why you are sharing it and why it is beneficial for them to receive it. You also want to note whether or not you have any direct connection with the content (sponsored content, client work, etc.). Being transparent with what you create and share contributes to the trust the audience member puts in the content. And, as always, when you share other people's content, make sure you give them credit (tag them in the update, use their handle on social media, etc.).

Repurposing the content being shared can take many forms. For example, one way to practice content curation is to produce an email newsletter. Convina, a creative analytics agency in New York City, sends a designated email newsletter to all of its subscribers not only with updates on its live video and social analytics platforms but also with articles, updates, and news that are relevant and useful for subscribers of the email listserv. Front Office Sports has an email newsletter that hosts a variety of articles from the sports industry as well as job and internship postings. Because most of its audience members are young professionals who are still in school or have graduated, this information is extremely relevant and valuable. Some newsletters are focused on one specific feature. MEOjobs (run and hosted by Marc Oppenheim) provides a newsletter each week highlighting the top jobs and internship opportunities in social media, journalism, digital marketing, and public relations.

Other big brands, such as Orangetheory Fitness, Agorapulse, Facebook Blueprint, and Hootsuite, have designated newsletters. One of the more popular newsletters is *Morning Brew*, which provides business and technology trends and updates for professionals to follow. According to Cisnero (2014), email is the second most popular digital media marketing channel, yet it is sometimes overlooked. Integrating a newsletter into your social media content marketing strategy is an opportunity to (a) collect subscribers to connect with more professionals and build your audiences, (b) collect names into a database to provide subscribers with more updates and information on your services, and (c) provide opportunities to share content subscribers may not have seen from your other channels (blogs, social media updates, webinars, etc.).

Other strategies include private or public groups on Facebook and LinkedIn, secret groups on Facebook, and designated hashtags on Twitter to keep up with relevant content.

As for content creation, certain tools can be used to help social media professionals curate relevant content for their audiences. Some of these tools are free, and others are paid. HubSpot (Armitage, 2017) recommends the following tools for content curation activities:

- *Twitter Lists.* Creating a list for various areas of expertise (social media marketing, social selling, public relations, etc.) is one way to keep track of all of the people you want to follow for resources to share with your audiences.

- *Private communities.* Shares and endorsements that arise from communities in messaging platforms such as WhatsApp, Clubhouse, Slack, or even Discord can provide resources and information that can be shared across different platforms. Facebook groups are also a source for finding articles, reports, and information worthy to share with other community members. Matt Navarra's Social Geekout group keeps social media professionals up to date with latest news and trends happening in social media.

- *Follows on Facebook, Twitter and LinkedIn.* Follow prominent brands and people on these three social media sites, so you can bookmark and save the articles and links for future uses.

- *Nuzzel and Flipboard.* These tools have mobile apps that take the feeds you follow on social media and provide an interactive newsletter for you to read, consume, and then share on your networks. Both are free to use.

BEST PRACTICES

After reviewing the importance of content creation, strategies, tactics, and content curation, there are some best practices to follow as you head toward this area of social media. Remember and take note of these guiding principles, since they will help you plan, organize, and discover ideas to create new assets to use in a campaign, or help you find and uncover relevant work to share or use as inspiration for further ideas in your community:

- *Create content worth sharing.* As mentioned previously, you do not want to waste your audience's time. Attention is a priceless currency in social media today, and as more options and resources become available, people will go where the content, messages, and community hold their attention. Focus on quality, not quantity, in your content.

- *Look at the data and see what the numbers tell you about the content you have shared.* Data don't lie, and they can provide validation of the work being shared and created for social media and also be tied to insights that can be used to revamp the content creation aspect for a brand or person on social media. Analyze insights from the data about the reactions and receptiveness of the content shared on social media. Use data as a bouncing-off point for future brainstorming sessions, ideas, and potential strategies.

- *Invest in the time to interact with audiences to find out what they are looking for on social media.* As mentioned in other chapters, do not assume you know what audiences want on social media. It may be good to conduct some research and ask them what they are looking for. This interaction shows not only a level of community with the group but also a sense of respect for what your audiences think is valuable. Take these insights back to your team and brainstorm ways to accomplish these goals and expectations so it is a win-win situation.

- *Make the extra effort and provide more than audiences expect.* Always go beyond what is expected. If audiences find a white paper with a ton of insights and resources, they will continue to visit and come back for more. Provide more information and detail than others have done in the past to take your content to the next level. Always exceed expectations, but never go below them.

- *Edit, edit, and edit some more.* Content is under a microscope for brands and individuals, so take the time to edit, revise, review, and edit some more. However, be aware of the timing of the content to make sure it is ready to go. Perfection is always great to have, but it doesn't help anyone if the draft of a tweet or ebook is never shared and discovered.

- *Find time to write when you think you don't have any.* Research and outline some ideas and look at your peers to see what they would be interested in reading more about. Build time into your daily routine to search for content to share and items to explore for inspiration for content creation.

CHAPTER SUMMARY

This chapter covers one of the growing areas of specialization in the social media industry and an important area of focus for many young professionals entering the workplace. Content marketing, and the ability to share relevant assets that make a connection with your audiences, combines scientific and creative approaches. Without the scientific process of analyzing the information collected through monitoring and listening mechanisms in social media, social media professionals will not know which posts, updates, or traditional long-form content has worked for them and helped their community. On the flip side, without the distinct creativity of thinking outside of the box and being open to approaching content in a new way, assets and other content produced could go unnoticed and be ignored by the community. To gain momentum and help build brand awareness, trust, and credibility as a brand or as an individual, having a balanced approach to content marketing takes time, but with the proper tools, guidelines, and teamwork, the result will be a win-win within the community and for future social media efforts by the brand or social media professional.

THOUGHT QUESTIONS

1. How would you describe content marketing? Where does content marketing fit today in the current social media marketplace?

2. Define content creation. How is this relevant for social media professionals?

3. What are the challenges and opportunities content marketing can present?

4. Outline the different media in the PESO model. What are some examples of content that could be created for each type of media?

5. What are three best practices when it comes to creating and curating content for social media?

EXERCISES

1. You have been hired to create content for the Nutella Café in Chicago, but you recognize you need to do a content audit. Outline the key steps and content you will need to review for this audit. Provide three content creation recommendations you would propose in applying for this position.

2. As part of your entry exam for a new position, Tim Hortons wants you to create an editorial calendar outlining its celebration of "National Coffee Day" that will launch in the United States and Canada. Outline some recommendations for how the company should prepare for this national holiday, and come up with two ideas for content that could be created for this holiday that the company has not explored yet. Be prepared to discuss your rationale and share evidence to support these ideas.

3. You are at a networking social media event at Coachella, and you are asked by a social media strategist about your thoughts on content marketing and why it is important for social media campaigns. Write a 15- to 30-second pitch on the key benefits of content marketing, and propose an example case where it worked.

4. You are a part of a student-run agency, and you have been tasked to outline a content marketing strategy to gain awareness of your group on campus and to present to prospective agency clients in the community. Propose three items you want to create and three items (or areas) from which you want to create information. Create a sample content calendar outlining when each of these proposed items will go out and on what channels.

REFERENCES

Armitage, P. (2017, November 21). 10 content curation tools every marketer needs. *HubSpot*. https://blog.hubspot.com/marketing/content-curation-tools

Cisnero, K. (2014, August 13). A beginner's guide to content curation. *Hootsuite*. https://blog.hootsuite.com/beginners-guide-to-content-curation/

Content Marketing Institute. (2017). *What is content marketing?* http://contentmarketinginstitute.com/what-is-content-marketing/

Dietrich, G. (2018, January 4). PR pros must embrace the PESO model. *Spin Sucks*. http://spinsucks.com/communication/pr-pros-must-embrace-the-peso-model/

Hrach, A., & Griffiths, J. (2019). How to build a content calendar (plus a free template). *Convince & Convert*. http://convinceandconvert.com/social-media-strategy/how-to-build-a-content-calendar-plus-a-free-template

Lua, A. (2017, February 22). 20 creative ways to use social media for storytelling. *Buffer Social*. https://blog.bufferapp.com/social-media-storytelling

Moz. (2018). Chapter 2: Content strategy. In *Beginner's guide to content marketing*. https://moz.com/beginners-guide-to-content-marketing/content-strategy

Sizemore, E. (2017, March 22). How to do a content audit [updated for 2017]. *Moz*. https://moz.com/blog/content-audit

Walters, K. (2017, June 27). How to create a social media content calendar: Tips and templates. *Hootsuite*. https://blog.hootsuite.com/how-to-create-a-social-media-content-calendar/

MEASUREMENT, EVALUATION, BUDGET, AND CALENDAR CONSIDERATIONS FOR SOCIAL MEDIA

Learning Objectives

After reading this chapter, you will be able to

- Define what measurement and evaluation are for social media campaigns

- Explain the main components of social media measurement outlined by AMEC

- Describe the various techniques, metrics, and tools used for social media measurement and evaluation

- Identify best practices and tips for conducting effective measurement and evaluation practices for social media

INTRODUCTION

Social media is more than just creating amazing content, embracing popular and social cultural moments, sharing GIFs and memes, and formulating strategies that spark innovation and creativity. It's about analyzing the impact and success of these creative measures, which is where this chapter comes into play.

What social media professionals have to recognize is the fact that social media is rooted not only in art but also science. Similar to the discussion in Chapter 6 on listening and monitoring, measurement and evaluation help conclude the story on what worked, what didn't, and what we can learn for the future. A strong social media campaign is like a full bookshelf that has strong book ends to keep things together. One side of this social media campaign bookshelf is research, keeping things together with providing sound research and insights that can help create a strong and sustainable social media campaign. The other book end is measurement and evaluation, where everything is examined to discover the major accomplishments from the campaign. Social media professionals can't have one without the other, or the campaign (or bookshelf in this case) will not be stable and fall apart. Planning when and where content is executed, planned, and created is also an essential part for effective social media strategies. Lastly, social media is not "free" and has to have the proper respect for investment and financial support as other established areas in business and communication practices.

In this chapter, we will go over the principles and best practices for measurement and evaluation for social media, while also addressing the need to be aware of the planning that needs to take place (calendar) and respect for costs (budget) of social media campaigns.

Dennis Yu, Chief Executive Officer at Blitzmetrics

Introduction

I'm an ABC. So I'm an American-born Chinese, born in Dayton, Ohio.

English was not my first language; I learned when I was 7. I got a full ride at Southern Methodist University. School directly didn't help much, as most people will admit.

I chose finance and economics because I had a curiosity for why certain things cost what they cost. I didn't speak much English as a youngster, so I found math to be a way to communicate.

That eventually turned into competing in math contests, learning to build financial models, working with the databases that ran American Airlines, and running the internal analytics team at Yahoo. Finance and economics also naturally led me to programming, econometrics, and working with large, multidimensional data sets.

At American Airlines, I got tired of asking the information technology people to run queries for me. They took too long, and I didn't want to wait in the queue. I learned how to write JCL [Job Control Language] and SQL [Structured Query Language] myself.

How did you get your start in social media?

I started out 20 years ago at American Airlines where my mentor Al Casey, the CEO, told me to focus on my learning curve, not my earning curve. I turned down a lucrative career at Goldman Sachs and started building the company's internet presence. I was fascinated by playing with the world's largest data system. The Sabre system, owned by the American Airlines parent company, was the biggest nongovernment system out there.

Yahoo was the largest search engine while I was still at American, so I had the opportunity to analyze some outrageous behavior on the web. Facebook is the modern extension of that. Just consider how much data Facebook collects on users and also makes available to advertisers. We want not to spy on people or be creepy but to truly understand who the best customers are for a business, what content will cause them to convert, and how to assemble a system that will drive business results.

When I started marketing on Facebook in 2007, there was limited competition. I've been fortunate to have a hand in the development of some of these tools, which has given us an advantage as data-driven marketers. I expect marketers who don't live by the numbers to be stomped on by those who do.

What is your favorite part of working in your area of social media expertise?

I have a passion for observing interesting correlations and making connections. I admit that I am a numbers geek and love data, which is the reason I ended up in marketing and analytics. I follow a process called MAA, or metrics, analysis, action. This means you look at the data, understand the data, and then form your strategy based on the changes. It's one of the nine triangles we use in business, and it will help you when you are breaking down big chunks of data, or even when examining the numbers behind an ad.

What is one thing you can't live without while working in social media?

A top-notch PR team would normally charge $7,500 a month for a basic retainer, but you get that for $1, for every day you boost. "Dollar a Day" is a simple yet effective technique that we use consistently.

You need these key ingredients:

- A third-party endorsement of your skill in a particular area—not your sales literature or what's on your website

- One dollar a day, but it could be more

- An ongoing commitment to create helpful content on a daily basis, as opposed to only promotional material

- A product or service worth talking about, evidenced by happy clients, online reviews, and so on

- Patience, since generating word of mouth and influencing the press takes months

What is your favorite social media account (person/brand/etc.) to follow and why?

There are too many to count, but if you must follow one person, I am a huge fan of Mari Smith. She earned her unofficial title of the Queen of Facebook for good reason; her knowledge and strategies are rivaled by none. She's also a very down-to-earth person, full of love, and someone you can't help but smile at when interacting with her. But as I said, there are so many other great people to follow who have made great contributions to this industry.

I do my best to keep up with the continuously changing industry and try to learn from as many people as I can, including my colleagues Heather Dopson, Alison Herzog, Paul Sokol, and Jason Miller. Each of them adds a unique perspective to the world of social media, and they are all-around great people.

What is the most challenging part of working in social media?

You'd think it would be building systems, tuning complex ad campaigns, or something glamorous. But actually, the hardest struggle, *by far*, is helping people overcome fear, while the second-biggest challenge is screening clients. It's a people issue in both cases. Disguised in other forms, fear shows up as excuses, defensiveness, sickness, procrastination, and all manner of things that distract you from being successful.

The solution is a combination of three elements:

- *Checklists*—break down the big scary project into small, simple tasks.

(Continued)

(Continued)

- *Encouragement*—as a coach, not a boss, you're more interested in helping, not punishing.

- *Accountability*—measuring success against checklists and providing feedback is holding people accountable.

We also want to stop wasting time talking to unqualified prospects who only dangle the carrot in front of us to lead us along:

- Don't let just any random person book time on your calendar, and don't offer free consultations to people who don't fill out at least an intake form.

- Assemble a few packages that describe what you do in detail.

- Crank up your content marketing efforts so that all your leads are inbound. In other words, talk only to folks who come to you.

- Create a screening process to surface the good clients and filter out the bad ones.

- Have an administrator run the process. He or she can schedule, qualify, collect payments, and share basic documents.

You have been active in mentoring future young professionals in social media. What has been the most rewarding experience or moment you have had in helping students?

Mentorship is important to me because it has influenced my life time and time again. My most important mentor was Al Casey, CEO of American Airlines. I strive to provide my team members the best support I can give, answering their questions and helping them grow as marketers. If you're doing it for

the money, that's a sign something is wrong. It took me over a decade to realize that using my skills to teach young adults how to optimize digital traffic, then applied to sports teams, lead generation, and whatever, was far more rewarding. You hear a lot of people say, "Follow your dreams."

It all sounds good, in theory, especially when told by folks who are already successful and talented. "But how does this apply to me?" students say, leading to false hope and inaction. The answer is taking incremental steps in something we call "personal branding." The small steps of setting up your profile on different networks, setting up Google Alerts on things you're interested in, and writing short notes about what you observe are what counts. Perhaps you're self-conscious about your writing skills—then blog for 5 minutes a day. Sure, your initial blog posts will suck, but I promise you that you'll get way better and faster. Do this for 6 weeks straight, and you'll be surprised how far you go.

What do you wish you had known when you were starting out?

Al Casey was CEO of American Airlines and even Postmaster General—yes, he had a million employees driving around those little white trucks. He was kind enough to share his best advice with me, a poor college kid looking for a job. I wish I had heeded his words more carefully, as it would have saved me a ton of heartache, but that's a story for another time.

Focus on your learning curve, not your earning curve. Another $10,000 a year at Company A shouldn't be the reason you choose it over Company B. When you get your first real job, what you're really getting is experience and a network. In a few years, you'll be making a lot more if you're doing something you love enough to be knowledgeable about.

You can follow Dennis Yu on social media (Twitter, Facebook, LinkedIn, and Instagram) at @dennisyu. Dennis also publishes his articles and insights on his personal website, www.dennis-yu.com.

MEASUREMENT AND EVALUATION

Measurement in social media is on the rise. In fact, according to the Global Analytics Forecast Report, the global social media analytics marketplace is going to continue to increase due to the growing focus on competitive intelligence and user engagement on digital and social media platforms ("Global Social Media Analytics Market 2020-2025," 2020) Social media involves math, statistics, and numbers. These numbers are used both from a proactive standpoint, as discussed in Chapter 6, and to tell a story of what happened.

This is where measurement and evaluation come into play. Along with the creative execution of content, ideas, and stories from a visual and artistic perspective, data tell a story of how audiences reacted and responded to the data by asking the following questions:

- Did the content resonate with them?

- Did the key messages we integrated into our updates motivate them to take action like we hoped they would?

- What actions were taken in response to the content, messages, and strategies implemented and executed in the brand collaboration campaign?

- Did the influencers and creators we partnered with make the impact we expected?

- How much media and audience exposure did we get from our uniform and football team schedule unveiling?

- Who started the conversation and influenced the narrative in this crisis online?

- How many leads and sales did we accumulate in response to what we did?

- How many people signed up to our webinar with leading thought leaders?

- Did we achieve what we hoped to have achieved in our campaign?

There is an important distinction that needs to be made in the area of measurement and evaluation. **Data** are the points of information that are collected by various tools and programs, but **insights** are what connects the relevant information to tell the story on what the data are saying. These terms are used somewhat interchangeably in the industry, but they are different. For example, big data with millions of tweets and updates are great to have, but without insights, they're just big data. Insights show the "so what" factor of analysis by pointing out key learning objectives that need to be shared with others on what happened and where we need to go in the future.

Businesses, agencies, and social media professionals sometimes forget about a key step in the strategic social media process. In an eConsultancy report on social media measurement, 41% of the respondents had no idea of the financial impact of social media (Baer, 2018). This is surprising to hear, but it provides even more reason why both the surface-level metrics and the attitudinal and behavioral metrics that drive actions, relationships, and financial support are areas to cover for social media measurement and evaluation practices.

Understanding the Social Media Measurement and Evaluation Framework

Measurement and evaluation hold the key to determining whether or not we were successful in our efforts to engage our audiences, accomplish our set objectives and goals for the short and the long term (Chen, 2021), and provide value (emotionally, financially, and socially) for the intended parties. Without measurement and evaluation, social media practices would not have an end game allowing us to determine what we were able to do and whether we were successful. In addition, since social media is usually part of another department or functions within another discipline, we must provide evidence to others (e.g., senior management, colleagues, team members, clients, and the industry) to show what we were able to do. Metrics and data that show initial results as well as actionable behaviors taken as a result of social media activities are important contributions to measurement and evaluation practices. In Table 13.1, specific metrics that are most common in social media reports are listed along with the specifics on how to measure these.

Table 13.1 Key Social Media Metrics to Measure	
Social Media Metric	**Specific Metrics**
Engagement	• **Likes, comments, retweets, shares, etc.:** Individual engagement metrics like a share or a retweet add up. In a Twitter report, you'll see a total number of engagements per post or profile. • **Post engagement rate:** The number of engagements divided by impressions or reach. A high rate means the people who see the post find it interesting. • **Account mentions:** Organic mentions, like @mentions that aren't part of a reply, or tagging a brand in an Instagram story without prompting, indicate good brand awareness.
Awareness	• **Impressions** are how many times a post shows up in someone's timeline • **Reach** is the potential unique viewers a post could have (usually your follower count plus accounts that shared the post's follower counts).
Share of Voice	• **Share of voice:** Percentage of brand's voice compared to others online on a given topic.
Referrals and Conversions	• **Referrals** are how a user lands on your website. In web analytics, you'll see them broken down into sources. "Social" is usually the source/medium you'll be monitoring, and then it's broken down by network. • **Conversions** is when someone purchases something from your site. A social conversion means they visited via a social media channel and then purchased something during that same visit.
Customer Care	• **Response time:** How fast team members on the customer or social care team are in responding to messages. • **Response rate:** How many messages team members and social team members are able to address in a period of time (hour/day/week). • **Response tone and sentiment:** What was the overall tone of the responses from audiences members to the social team?

Source: Adapted from Chen (2021).

However, basic metrics tell only part of the story for measurement. More work needs to be done to tie in these metrics to key strategic communication objectives and applications. Measurement and evaluation sections are usually glossed over because they deal with numbers, data, statistics, and other elements that may not be as dazzling as the creative execution of content and stories. Without the measurement and data to show the impact of these pieces of content, however, future campaigns and resources will not be attributed to social media. The International Association for the Measurement and Evaluation of Communication (otherwise known as AMEC) has listed the various components to measure all communication functions, including social media, and how they are applied. These components and their applications are explained in Table 13.2.

Table 13.2 Application and Focus for the AMEC Framework		
AMEC Component	**Focus**	**Application**
Objectives	• Communication objectives • Media objectives • Business objectives	• Strategic planning stage after research, communication audit, and situational analysis
Inputs	• Situational analysis • Audience analysis	• Understanding the core group of people at the heart of a social media campaign and identifying the current situation and landscape
Activities	• Specific strategies and tactics to be implemented in the campaign	• Specific social media updates, assets, and tools used to create and disseminate content
Outputs	• Measuring the impact of the social media content	• Metrics designated for specific channels, platforms, and objectives • Content (e.g., updates, stories, videos, etc.) that measures the impact of these pieces of content
Outtakes	• Effects of content and messages from audiences	• Reactions • Feedback • Coverage • Recall
Outcomes	• Effects of content and messages from audience	• Reactions • Sentiment • Engagement • Feedback • Coverage • Actions taken • Increased advocacy
Impact	• How business objectives are measured and the contribution of social media	• Reputation measures • Attitude changes • Policy changes • Brand community • Advocacy

Source: Adapted from Integrated Evaluation Framework by AMEC. https://amecorg.com/amecframework/framework/interactive-framework/.

Determining whether or not a campaign initiative, idea, or program was successful is one of the most important tasks of the social media professional. In this chapter, we cover the different components needed in the measurement and evaluation stages for social media strategic practices. In addition, we highlight key areas to note when creating a calendar (e.g., customer journey) and budget (yes, social media costs money, resources, talent, and time).

Importance of Measurement and Evaluation in Social Media

Measurement and evaluation travel hand in hand in many marketing, strategic communications, and public relations campaigns. Measurement focuses on designating specific amounts that reflect change in specific objectives, whereas evaluation focuses on the assessment or value of certain actions in a campaign or strategy. They are two of the final steps to take before providing recommendations for most social media plans, programs, and campaigns.

Many professional associations (Public Relations Society of America, American Marketing Association, etc.) have presented their views on the importance of measurement and how it is tied directly to social media practices. The International Association for Measurement and Evaluation of Communication (AMEC, 2016a, 2016b) has its own framework for key areas to cover in social media:

- *Objectives.* What do you want to accomplish during the course of the social media campaign while following the requirements of the SMART criteria as discussed in Chapter 7

- *Inputs.* Who is your target audience, what is the current situation, and what resources are available to understand them? This is discussed in Chapters 7 and 11.

- *Activities.* This is the strategies and tactics portion of your social media plan. What content and messages will you be creating and disseminating to your audiences?

- *Outputs.* These are the specific metrics collected from likes, comments, reach, impressions, and engagement. How did people respond to the content you shared across all social media platforms and channels?

- *Outtakes.* What reactions and behaviors occurred as a result of the messages, content, and actions taken on social media? What actions did audiences take in response to the updates you shared? How likely were they to recall your content with others?

- *Outcomes.* How well did the audiences receive your messages? Did you change their views or attitudes?

- *Impact.* How has the organization, client, or individual been influenced and/or changed as a result of this social media campaign? These higher-level objectives contribute not just to social media protocols and actions but to the well-being of the entire organization. Examples include reputation, change in policies, or improved business practices.

This measurement framework helps organizations, businesses, and individuals manage and format the evaluation section of their social media strategic plan to identify all required variables.

Social media professionals do not just do a campaign and leave (or drop the mic on their way out the door). They must articulate clearly what they accomplished relative to their objectives, provide evidence that their efforts and the efforts of their team made this a successful initiative, and provide guidance on what indicators helped in this effort and what needs to be done in the future. This is where evaluation (gathering intel and providing an assessment explaining what happened in this program or campaign) ties back to the initial proposal in the goals and objectives components (as outlined in Chapter 7) for the social media team.

The measurement component of the SMART objectives (specific, measurable, achievable, realistic, and time-specific) is so important. Without knowing what or how much they want to increase (audience size, subscription base, awareness, engagement, etc.), social media professionals will not have clear and actionable variables to present to senior management. In addition, most of the time, senior managers want to see hard numbers that clearly illustrate the growth, impact, and results from social media for public relations, marketing, reputation, and sales. In this case, social media professionals have to connect the dots with evidence to support each of their points of insight and make recommendations and assessments accordingly.

Measurement is more than just collecting and analyzing data. As for creative execution of content, there is an art to analyzing and discovering insights gathered from the data to best tell a story of what happened and what to do for the future. This is a *measurement strategy*, which is missing from many social media campaigns. To fully integrate the importance of data analysis in social media, measurement needs to have a seat at the table along with creative content and storytelling.

To succeed in measurement and evaluation, social media professionals must be familiar with both the traditional methods of measurement (focus groups, surveys, interviews, etc.) and the new tools at their fingertips with channel (or platform) analytics (Facebook Analytics, TikTok Analytics, YouTube Analytics, TikTok Analytics, LinkedIn Analytics, Instagram Insights, Twitter Analytics, etc.) and third-party tools (Salesforce, Analisa.io, Klear, Agorapulse, Cision or Meltwater, Zoomph, etc.). Each of these methods has a specific purpose and function in the measurement and evaluation stage. Channel analytics tools show you content on the designated platform and what worked, what didn't, and how to make future improvements. Social media professionals will be able to identify the key metrics (outlined in Chapter 6) for each platform and download the data, analyze them, and integrate these findings into a social media report. In addition, you will have access to other key components like location of the source (where are the people posting from on each platform?), network (how connected are they, how interconnected are they, and are they influencers?), context and content (in what situations are they engaged with the content?), and consistency (to what extent are they engaged with the content?).

Importance of Having a Measurement Strategy

Measurement must be integrated across all areas of a strategic social media plan. It shouldn't be an add-on at the end as a checkmark to show you did it. A measurement strategy should be interwoven throughout the process. As for all aspects of social media, a game plan (or strategy) for certain actions, steps, and duties and how they contribute to the overall goal and program needs to be in place. That's why an effective measurement strategy is essential for all social media programs and campaigns. Having such a strategy will allow social media professionals to

- be better informed about their key audiences throughout the social media program and campaign journey;

- be able to execute and create effective content;

- align content, stories, and other social media updates to be executed at the right time, place, and platform;

- make each post count and be more effective in coordinating a team effort for social media;

- identify more efficiently with key audiences, influencers, and micro influencers, and discover new audiences to create relationships with (Jackson, 2016);

- note what tools work in collecting data and providing insights and which do not;

- be able to identify both opportunities and warning signs for client and campaign initiatives; and

- determine the health and well-being of community members and dynamics of the relationship they have with a brand.

As mentioned previously, measurement is as important as great content and relationships with your key audiences on social media. Evaluating social media activities is recommended for a variety of reasons (Dawley, 2017):

- You will have a better understanding of how your social media channels benefit your brand and client.

- You will have a better understanding of who is loyal to you and who is not.

- You will be able to see the overall performance of the content with and without paid support (e.g., organic vs. sponsored posts).

- You will be able to note not only the place of social media channels within the community you are engaged with but how the content spreads and is received by others (influencers, media, etc.).

- You will be able to discover which pieces of content worked well for you, as well as which did not.

- You will be able to forecast and evaluate the risks the company may face in the future and prepare for those risks.

- You will be able to determine any missed opportunities, gaps, or lessons to note for the future when it comes to social media content strategy, execution of key messages and channels, and conversations and perceptions among key audiences.

With measurement and evaluation in social media, you can address each of these points. In Chapter 6, we discussed which key performance indicators and metrics to evaluate and set forth for monitoring and listening. The same principles and metrics need to be considered for the measurement and evaluation section of a social media plan. Ask yourself the following questions:

- How do these metrics align with my set objectives?

- Are we able to measure these metrics?

- How easy is it to universally define each of these metrics?

- How easy will it be to calculate, collect, and analyze the data?

- Are these metrics universally used across different departments (marketing, public relations, strategic communications, etc.)?

- Will these metrics help in the decision-making process for future recommendations?

- Which metrics align with the outcomes set forth for the initiative and campaign?

In Chapter 7, we outlined the strategic plan for social media. It is important to evaluate objectives (the ones that you are following and for which you are using SMART criteria) to see what you want to do to achieve them. However, once you set these objectives, you must determine how and why you will be measuring and evaluating them. Measurement tools, methods, and metrics should always be set forth before a campaign or social media program is implemented. Not taking the time to do this will result in lost time and money and, on some occasions, a job loss for the social media professional.

Outcomes

Certain outcomes should be measured and reported as part of your analysis for social media. The strategic communication literature identifies three areas of outcomes to measure: cognitive, attitudinal, and conative. Although they focus on different elements, all three are key to evaluate and report when it comes to understanding what worked and what did not work in social media campaigns.

▸ **Photo 13.1**
Kroger
Implementing a Face
Mask Policy in All of
Their Stores

Source: Facebook/
@Kroger

Whether or not people were able to comprehend what you were trying to say in your messages (informational, etc.) is referred to as the *cognitive outcome*. One case that illustrates the cognitive component is Kroger's face mask policy for all of their stores (Photo 13.1). Because of the spread of COVID-19 in 2020, most stores, including Kroger, implemented a policy requiring each customer to come into their store wearing a face mask, and these messages were disseminated via the brand's social media channels. Reactions and comments were present on each of these posts, which Kroger would have to evaluate to determine the effectiveness of these messages. Each platform has unique metrics (e.g., Facebook has reactions in addition to comments and shares).

If you are telling an emotional story to inspire audiences to take action based on a brand voice, outcomes of interest will be attitudinal. *Attitudinal outcomes* focus on measuring the response to the content and audiences' feelings, perceptions, and attitudes about the content in question. For example, was the response positive? Was there a negative perception toward the brand or individual based on what was shared? Which individual(s) were driving the positive/negative conversation? What is the overall sentiment in response to the piece of content, or even more generally to the campaign? These are just a few questions to consider when exploring how to measure the reaction of audience members to the social media content presented.

Let's see how this could be applied. Planters has come to the scene with their Mr. Peanut character on social media, but in 2020, they reinvented the iconic Mr. Peanut to become "Baby Nut" to rejuvenate the brand for a newer audience. Utilizing humor and trying to connect to the younger generation of audiences, Planters used social media, specifically Twitter, to give Mr. Peanut a fresh, funny, and engaging personality. Ultimately, they aged Mr. Peanut again in time for back to school in August 2020, making the new character the age of a typical college student (Photo 13.2).

I'm officially 21, my friends! Before you ask, yes, I was just a baby. What can I say? It's been a nutty year. Now someone get this peanut a beer!

#MakeMyBirthdayNuts

▶ 383.1K views   0:01 / 0:19 ◁× ⤢

10:18 AM · Aug 11, 2020 · Twitter Web App

3.6K Retweets and comments   **6.3K** Likes

▶ **Photo 13.2**

Source: Twitter/
@Mr Peanut

Conative outcomes focus on behaviors exhibited by audience members after seeing a post on social media. As mentioned earlier, including a strong call-to-action statement in your post will allow the members of your audience to understand and know what they need to do. Conversions, or how many people were converted from regular audience members to customers or subscribers, are one metric to evaluate here. Many social media professionals like conative metrics because they show a direct action was taken based on the message shown to a particular audience member. Measuring the direct alignment of the content to the action shows the impact toward a new relationship, sale, or action as the result of the content shared and created on social media.

For example, Agorapulse has been active in both their email marketing and social media promotions, but has found a way to draw conversions and sign-ups through their Facebook initiatives, particularly in their live video sessions. Agorapulse has their own video interview series but also has launched their own virtual event called Social Pulse Summit, where they invite speakers and professionals from across different industries to speak on topics related to the Agorapulse community (Photo 13.3). While they distribute this information across their channels,

▶ **Photo 13.3**
Agorapulse's Social Pulse Summit

Source: Facebook/@Agorapulse

Agorapulse also has a dedicated website for the event for sign-ups. The content for this website is customized for each platform on social media for Agorapulse, which will be able to see all of the following:

- Which platform generated the most sign-ups

- What time and day was most effective in reaching audiences and getting people to sign up

- The source from where the most sign-ups are occurring

- Impact of shares and sign-ups based on the influencers who are advocating for the event

- Views, shares, and engagement of the event across channels

- Sentiment before, during, and after the event

- What actions audience members took after they signed up (shared the webinar, etc.)

- The number of sign-ups and additional information on each person (name, email, job, industry, etc.)

- The average response time to inquiries across channels (social care, customer relationship management, etc.)

These elements are important to collect and analyze because they will tell us what content, strategies, and channels will be the most effective in reaching our audiences to accomplish our set goals. Without these measurements, social media professionals will not know what worked, what didn't, and what tips to keep in mind for doing a similar activity in the future. Plus, these measurements and metrics are important when asking for (a) future investment for activities and (b) future investment in social media strategy and creative execution campaigns.

The three outcomes (cognitive, attitudinal, and conative) can be grouped together to formulate a comprehensive social media measurement strategy, a key component to add at the planning stages for a social media campaign or program. Measurement, as stated earlier, should be done not at the very end of the program but rather throughout the program. Table 13.3 outlines the outcomes, where

Table 13.3 Social Media Measurement Objectives

Outcome	Measurement Strategy	Measurement Metrics	Tools
Cognitive	The exposure to the message and the overall comprehension of knowledge and information being presented and evaluated by audience members	• Inquiries based on the message and information presented • Comments • Questions • Frequency of comments and responses • Response time to inquiries and responses • Looking at where and when people are coming to your site for what information	SumAll Socialbakers Simply Measured Google Analytics Agorapulse
Attitudinal	The emotional connection made based on the content, level of awareness, feelings, and perceptions of the content	• Personalized messages in response to content on social media • Sentiment and tone of shares, comments, and word of mouth • Reactions	Meltwater Agorapulse Sprout Social Brandwatch Zoomph Talkwalker Cision
Conative	The digital and offline behavior and actions taken that are a direct result of what was presented on social media	• Specific actions and behaviors taken • Advocacy efforts, ambassador endorsements, and influencer endorsements • Sign-ups • Response time • Consumption of content • Actions taken in response to content • Website and microsite traffic and analytics	Google Analytics Facebook Analytics Instagram Insights Twitter Analytics TikTok Analytics LinkedIn Analytics Pinterest Analytics YouTube Analytics Sprinklr Salesforce Brandwatch

they fall in the overall measurement strategy, and what measurement metrics are appropriate within these outcomes. Specific tools are also noted as examples of how to capture these points of data.

CALENDAR

Calendars are often used and referred to as a guide for when certain posts, initiatives, pieces of content, strategies and tactics, and research and evaluation need to happen. Not all social media campaigns are going to have the same calendar timeline. Timing affects not only resources but also placements of key messages. Most aspects of creating social media content can be created very quickly (depending on the type of content), whereas others may take longer to create, test, and execute. Along with executing content through posting on social media, a social media professional has to identify when each of their associated tactics and ideas will be implemented during the campaign. These are usually done throughout the campaign, but it depends on the overall scope and resources. Timing is everything when it comes to creating an effective and successful social media campaign.

There are other elements to consider when formulating a calendar for a social media campaign (Photo 13.4).

- *Invest in tools to help create calendars.* There are many different tools in creating calendars that are organized and professionally formatted such as Monday, Asana, Later, and more. Depending on the size of the campaign and company, investing in a professional organizing tool to help keep the campaign on track would be a worthwhile investment.

- *Work with the content team to have a content library ready for posts and updates throughout the year.* Some content pieces will be used for a campaign, but other posts can be created for specific events, themes, celebrations, and so on. Many platforms like Twitter list events and holidays to note for content purposes, which can be helpful for the social media team in brainstorming what pieces of content will go out at a given time. Tying in the content creation and strategy team with the calendar to determine the right platform, time, and type of content to execute is key.

- *Outline clear tasks and deadlines.* Having deadlines for when certain things need to happen is great, but there are many steps that need to be acknowledged before we hit the publish button. Drafts, edits, and brainstorming sessions need to be accounted for in the budget. In addition, there needs to be some resources for the social media team for giving and receiving feedback from the team in the calendar within the document or section in a customer relationship management tool. Tools such as Agorapulse and Sprinklr allow teams to comment and approve of calendar items before they are live and published.

- *Outline timing for research and evaluation.* Research and evaluation for social media is conducted throughout the campaign. Making sure to articulate and list when these steps occur in line with the other creative strategies is not only important to make the connection for the campaign, but show to senior management the ties social media has in both the science and art of strategic communications.

- *Decide what your calendar needs to track.* There are lots of different pieces of the puzzle to keep track of in a social media campaign, and being specific and thorough is the name of the game. Outlining all of the components, steps, and deadlines will be crucial to manage and keep track of. In addition, noting who on the team is responsible for what will be created, published, and executed will also be key to outline in the calendar.

- *Have protocols in place in case the calendar needs to be adjusted.* Sometimes it is necessary to hit pause on scheduled posts and campaigns (e.g., when a crisis hits). It is important to plan ahead of time and outline the duties, responsibilities, and practices that will be in place if this happens, and what adjustments need to be made. This was a lesson Planters learned when they launched their new campaign ahead of the 2020 Super Bowl but had to pause their campaign because of the unexpected death of NBA star Kobe Bryant. Tying in listening and crisis communication protocols into the calendar process and planning team is critical in making sure everyone is on the same page. Reading the room (digitally speaking) is a key part in making sure we are posting and launching content for our campaign when it is appropriate for our audiences.

▶ **Photo 13.4**
Sample Social Media Calendar From Monday.com

Source: Retrieved from https://monday .com/templates/social-media-calendar

BUDGET

Let's get a few things clear up front. Social media is NOT free. Numbers are your friend. Showing how your work in social media contributes to the bottom line is also important. Because many professionals outside the field of social media feel that social media is "easy" or can be done for "free," or even "get an intern to do it, they do not cost as much as a professional to run your social media," social media professionals need to be up front and educate others that social media can be free, but you get what you pay for. Investing in the right tools, programs, people, and content amplification will get you better results. Social media is part of a "pay-to-play" model with all of the changes emerging on each platform and their algorithms

In most cases, social media has a budget that is quite smaller than other areas in business and communication. However, there are times where there is no budget and you have to persuade team members and others to invest money in social media. This is not always the case, as social media is getting more established and more brands are investing in teams and senior roles in the area. If you do have the financial support of your employer or client to spend on social media, that is wonderful. Either way, prepare for the cases where you have to do without social media spending.

Areas to Invest in Your Budget

Throwing money at social media will not help anyone. Bad content, no matter how much money you put toward it, will still be bad content. To get the best results, you have to put forth a little bit of investment. Overall, with social media as such a developing and constant field, some questions remain about what to spend money on and how much you have to work with. Sometimes you will have extensive resources, but other times you will have only a certain amount to spend on each campaign for social media. Choose wisely and invest where you feel you need the most support to get to where you need to be for your client, brand, or agency.

Here are some areas in which to invest:

- *Tools* (content creation, content monitoring, social media measurement, staff time, etc.). You must have the right tools to do the job. For each strategy and tactic you propose for your social media program and campaign, you need a tool to help the social media team accomplish these set objectives. Some tools (as discussed in Chapter 12) are free (Canva, Adobe Spark, etc.), whereas others are not (Adobe Creative Suite, etc.). The same goes for measurement, listening, and monitoring protocols. "Free" tools are available, but they may not be able to collect all of the information needed by the social media professional.

- *People.* To be the best, you must invest in the best professionals as part of your social media team. Investing in strong candidates with great experience means you also want to look at the range of skills, experiences, and perspectives they bring to the table. Which roles do you want to fill, what duties and responsibilities will there be, and what qualifications should be outlined in your job posting and contract agreements? These different roles and teams are outlined in Chapter 5.

- *Consulting fees.* Even if you have a social media team, you may want to set aside some resources for focused projects or seek the help of experts with certain specializations. Videography, crisis communications, ideation, and augmented reality/virtual reality storytelling are just a few areas to consider. However, how many team members you want to bring in depends on your project and its social media needs.

- *Research.* Yes, research costs money, and resources should be dedicated to both traditional methods (e.g., focus groups, copy testing, interviews, and surveys) and social media methods (e.g., listening, monitoring, and reporting tools) so you can present a comprehensive view of your social media campaign and what you have been able to accomplish. Research, like social media, is not free.

- *Education (books, webinars, trainings, and certifications).* Learning does not stop in the classroom, and like the platforms themselves, measurement and content expectations and features change. Investing in education may be a top priority for your social media team. Many brands, including Microsoft,

Brandwatch, Hootsuite, Meltwater, and HubSpot, offer both free and paid certifications and webinars in which to participate. Specific platforms have their own webinars and certifications such as Facebook Blueprint (Facebook advertising, etc.), Twitter, Pinterest, Snapchat, and more. However, there may be times where specialized training (e.g., diversity and inclusion, analytics, crisis management) should also be budgeted out to help train and cultivate a culture of continued learning for talent on the social media team to be best prepared in their role.

- *Contingency plans.* When things go wrong, this usually has an impact on the overall budget. Have an understanding of what could go wrong, what tools and resources would be needed to handle problems, and what additional help and support (e.g., crisis management training and consulting) would be needed. Most of the time, 10% of the total budget is included as part of the contingency plan, but it is always safe to add to this, depending on the size of the project.

- *Promotion and sponsored content.* Because social media is a pay-to-play model, on some occasions (depending on goals and objectives) the social media manager has to boost or even pay for content to appear on someone's timeline to get it noticed. Sponsored tweets, stories, and updates come in all shapes and sizes, but tailoring the ads and posts is important. Taking advantage of Facebook's Creative Hub, for example, to determine the mock-ups of sponsored ads and posts on Facebook is a worthwhile investment of both time and money. In addition, setting up ads on the various channels to drive traffic, interactions, followers, and even leads is an important element in which to invest.

As mentioned previously, there are specific ways to budget for each platform's sponsored ads and posts to accomplish set objectives and goals for a campaign. Each platform offers designated trainings, webinars, and workshops to better familiarize social media professionals with the tools and how to create an ad based on their over-all goals. For example, Facebook and Instagram outline your overall objective and then ask you to state your marketing objective. Awareness, consideration, and con-version align for most of the set objectives of social media campaigns. Each ad that is created goes through a series of questions specific to these three categories, and at the end, social media managers have to fine-tune the specifics: who (the audience they want to target), where (the location and platform), when (the frequency and number of times people will see this ad), and how long this ad will run (depending on the amount of investment needed). Do you need to advertise on all of the social media platforms? The answer is no. It all depends on where your audience is talking about your brand and company and what types of content your audience wouldn't mind seeing if it was sponsored or promoted. Table 13.4 outlines the various ad managers for each of the major platforms.

Metrics to Consider for Budgets on Social Media

The push toward paid content in social media also needs to be addressed and discussed. When it comes to paid media and platforms, the channels range in terms of cost for their advertisements and what they charge brands and others. Most of the time, some consistent metrics can be used to evaluate social media advertising. We have covered some of these metrics in Chapter 9 already, but it is key to be

Table 13.4 Social Media Platform Ad Manager Sites

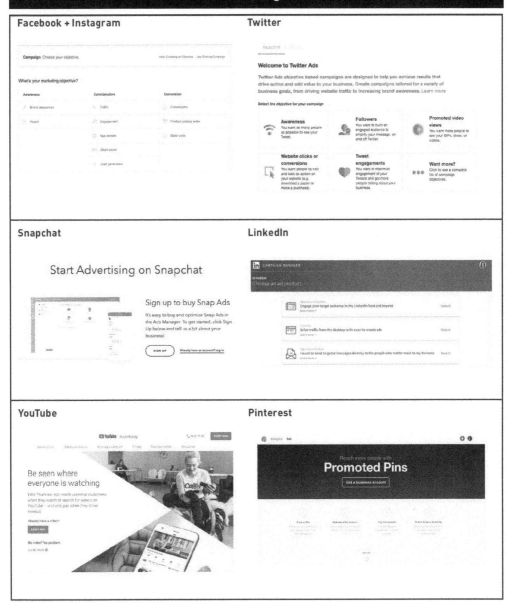

able to incorporate these into the budget to determine the level of investment in the paid media component of the budget.

Paid media (as discussed in detail in Chapter 9) has to be incorporated into the budget as a means to show return on investment for the amount spent on promotion, sponsorship, and payment for placement across different channels, and how they did in their performances.

It is important to outline the overall applications and outcomes aligned with these metrics. For example, *cost per action* (CPA) aligns more with conative outcomes because it is primarily focused on driving a certain action (or behavior in this case) by the user based on what is presented. The number of times a person likes a Facebook page, follows an account on Instagram, or swipes up on an Instagram Story will be the basis for what the advertiser will be charged for this program. *Cost per conversion* (CPC) focuses on the number of conversions made in a campaign, which is a valuable metric for marketers and others in the financial sector of a brand or agency. Showing how many people were converted into subscribers, email listserv joiners, or even new clients based on what was shared on social media, this metric is great because it can be compared across other campaigns on social media, to show the social media professional which ones were most successful in growing the customer and audience base (Paine, 2016). *Cost per engagement* (CPE) focuses on how much people reacted to the content provided for an entire campaign. CPE is the cost of the campaign divided by the total number of engagements. Keep in mind, with this metric, you also have to take into account whether or not you gave it a boost (put some dollars behind a specific post to make it perform better). The top-performing posts for a social media campaign and their associated metrics would also be a good idea to highlight here.

Table 13.5 outlines these paid metrics for social media advertising (Copp, 2016) and what to consider when setting up a social media budget.

Table 13.5   Paid Metrics to Note for Advertising in Social Media Budgets

Metric	Description	Outcome	Application and Implications
Cost per Click (CPC)	You pay the cost per click from the ad specifically.	Cognitive	• Relatively low costs help drive traffic to your site or microsite for a campaign. • These low costs also provide opportunities to create ads on different platforms. • Everyone is doing this (consider your competition; you don't want to oversaturate the audience member). • Don't just focus on getting people to click your link. Look at how much time they spend on your ad and where they go next. • Avoid large bounce-back rates (people who do not spend time on your site after arriving there).
Cost per Impression (CPI)	You pay the cost every time your ad is viewed.	Cognitive	• Get exposure on an ongoing basis. • This can be costly since you are trying to reach everyone, but conversation is not really the focus. • Impressions are not necessarily evidence that people have actually seen your ad. • This method is good if you want to drive awareness.

Metric	Description	Outcome	Application and Implications
Cost per Action (CPA)	You pay *only* for selected items for the audience member to do.	Conative	• Focus on the actions you want the audience member to take.
Cost per Conversion (CPC)	You pay only for the number of people you have converted into customers. Formula: Cost of Campaign / Total # of Conversions	Conative	• Focus on the direct line of how people became customers, based on what was presented on social media.
Cost per Engagement (CPE)	You calculate the cost per engagement for your campaign.	Attitudinal/ Conative	• Focus on the pieces of content that have the most reactions, engagements, and shares within your community. Best performing pieces of content may need a boost to get even more visibility and exposure for the campaign and program.

Consider the following elements when creating a budget for social media. These are some best practices to keep in mind at this stage of implementing a social media campaign or program:

- *Invest wisely.* Yes, like Indiana Jones, you do not want to choose "poorly" when it comes to your budget. Really evaluate the areas you need to invest in, and what tools and services you can get for free. It is better to have the right tools for the job than not be able to effectively implement your ideas.

- *Spend the money on the areas that will take the most time or with which you need the most assistance.* There are only so many hours in a day, so make sure you look at the tasks you have in play, which ones you can do effectively, and in which areas you need a little help.

A budget is part of measurement and evaluation. Most social media platforms, as stated previously, have their own measurement components to collect and analyze. In addition, to see if you have accomplished your goal in a campaign, you have to invest in successful measurement and evaluation, and because they go hand in hand with budgeting, these two areas are interconnected for strategic social media practices. Table 13.6 provides a sample checklist of items a social media professional needs to consider measuring and investing in to make a social media program and campaign successful.

Table 13.6 Sample Measurement and Evaluation Checklist

AMEC Framework	Measurement	Metrics
Objectives	Business, communication, and social media objectives	• SMART criteria (specific, measureable, achievable, realistic, and time specific)
Inputs	Audience analysis	• Location • Demographics • Network • Interests • Behaviors • Social causes • Diversity, equity, and inclusion topics • Devices • Platforms • Event/holiday targeting • Keywords • Influence • Activity • Engagement • Share of voice • Sentiment • Fans/followers/communities • Ambassadors/influencers
Activities	Customer service metrics	• Number of customer responses • Number of customer reactions • Average customer reactions rating • Views-to-comments ratio • Posts- or questions-to-comments ratio • Average response time • Average number of conversations • Follow-up survey results
Outputs	PESO (paid, earned, shared, owned) media	• Impressions • Engagement • Shares • Influence • Share of voice • Traffic • Referrals • Behaviors • Time spent on site

AMEC Framework	Measurement	Metrics
Outputs	Paid media	• Click-through rate • Cost per click • Cost per conversion • Cost per action • Cost per engagement
Outtakes	Content creation	• Engagement per content • Reactions/feedback • Sentiment • Channel/platform metrics • Advanced and behavioral metrics • Influencers and top keywords • Hashtags • Links and shares
Outcomes	Effects on target audience	• Change in attitude • Change in behavior • Increased advocacy and influence for the client • Increased outrage and cancel culture responses for the client • Increased intention to comply with messages, recommendations, and actions
Impact	Organizational and business objectives	• Sales • Donations • Contributions • Change in reputation (%) • Change in attitude (%)

FURTHER CONSIDERATIONS FOR MEASUREMENT, EVALUATION, AND BUDGET

Measurement and evaluation tasks take a large chunk of time and resources from a social media professional. Measurement of data and research should not be scary; instead, you should embrace it with open arms because it can share insights and stories and uncover gaps in opportunities not seen before. This is where the creativity of application comes into play for social media. Without insights and data, we may not have a justification or rationale for our activity on social media.

To most effectively implement a social media measurement strategy for a business, company, or individual brand, keep in mind the following tips and best practices:

- *Use plain language and avoid jargon.* Analytics, measurement, and other forms of evaluation have a lot of jargon. Covering aspects of measurement and analysis is already a bit overwhelming, so make sure you are clear, concise, and able to communicate your insights in a way that allows everyone to understand the metrics and how they contribute to the bottom line for brands both financially and in their relationships and reputation among their audience members.

- *Don't be afraid of numbers in the budget.* As mentioned many times, budgeting for a social media plan is crucial. You get what you pay for, and if your budget consists of a lot of free aspects, you may not get the quality of work and results you are looking for. Budgets are necessary because they (a) provide real actionable measures for the work you put in and what you got out of it, (b) compare spending across different channels, and (c) provide an eagle's eye view of what was spent where, what worked and performed well, what didn't work and needs to be addressed for the future, and what metrics were gained from integrating both paid media and earned media into the social media strategy (DeMers, 2017).

- *Articulate your limitations and note differences in data.* In measurement strategy and evaluation stages, like in research, you have to be up front with the limitations. This will come down to the budget restrictions for your social media efforts. Sometimes you will not be able to afford the enterprise-level measurement tools, and you will have to settle for tools that cannot capture everything. In addition, acknowledging how the data were collected, what was not collected, and whether the algorithm or formula used to calculate certain metrics is different from other tools needs to occur. This is one reason why it is important to have a range of tools for measuring social media efforts so you can see any similarities and any missing components or issues for some of these tools. In addition, it is always good to control and bring your data in-house, where you can see them first hand, versus getting the data sent to you by a third-party research tool or program.

- *Check your metrics and methods on a regular basis, and do a regular audit of the methods/tools for social media.* Set up a timeline for when you want to collect, report, analyze, and discuss findings. This shouldn't be a once-a-year type of scenario. Setting up a realistic timeline for collecting and analyzing your data also means you must audit the tools, approaches, and methods you are using for measurement and evaluation. Like all social media platforms, social media measurement tools change. Make sure you have the best tool to do the job, and this means constantly determining which tools and methods will help you accomplish your measurement strategy duties.

- *Invest in measurement training and education.* Measurement expectations constantly change along with the platforms. While many certifications out there are free, it is key to look at workshops, webinars, and other programs that can give you the tools, experiences, and applied insights to be effective and competitive in this area. Your education in measurement and evaluation should be on par with your training and resources attributed to creative execution and content creation.

- *Set forth checklists for measurement strategy and evaluation.* As Dennis Yu mentioned in this chapter's Humans of Social Media feature, you want to have a checklist of items to analyze, keywords to collect, set objectives and their associated metrics, list of tools to be used, and dates the data will be collected. Planning these steps relevant to each platform will help not only in the daily measurement activities but also in educating and preparing for new hires to join the social media measurement and evaluation team.

- *Learn from insights, and adjust when needed.* Once you have evaluated what you accomplished with your objectives and goals for your social media activities, you have to reassess and decide which items and measurement tools need to be adjusted, stabilized, or even deleted. Evaluating these insights will help you further advance the measurement strategy for the future, ensuring continued success for the social media program. Measurement and evaluation protocols should not go backward but should advance on the same innovative path as the creative content and brand storytelling on social media.

CHAPTER SUMMARY

Two areas of a social media plan that seem to be intimidating or even forgotten are the measurement and evaluation sections, including the overall budget. Both elements deal with numbers, which a social media professional should not only know but fully embrace. Insights and applying strategies from data can be extremely rewarding and make a significant difference for a brand in the long run. The same goes for a budget, because without knowing what you can do with a certain amount of resources, you may not fully understand the growing need for social media in your organization or business. Without the numbers and evidence of what has happened on social

media, the social media professional can't justify any increased support and spending capacity from senior management.

Without the numbers and evidence to support the impact, the social media campaign will dissolve. Measurement and budget are interdependent. Insights telling a story on what happened drives the support financially for social media programs. To stand out for future campaigns, social media professionals need to have the right tools to do their jobs, as well as the financial backing and support needed to educate, train, and produce sound pieces of content directly tied to the bottom line.

THOUGHT QUESTIONS

1. What is the overall purpose of measurement in social media programs? Identify three ways measurement can help social media professionals.

2. What are the three types of outcomes to measure for social media?

3. Define the key areas highlighted in the AMEC framework. What are the main

components, and what is their overall function in social media evaluation?

4. How does cost per click, cost per conversion, cost per engagement, and cost per action fit into a budget for a social media campaign?

5. What are some best practices when it comes to setting up a budget? What are the main areas to consider when creating a social media budget?

EXERCISES

1. In a job interview meeting, you hear one of the other candidates state, "Measurement is not required" in our social media duties. Provide three reasons why measurement can help, and find a social media case study where measurement was used to explain what happened.

2. You have applied for a social media internship, and you receive a face-to-face interview. You are given a task to create a social media campaign for the upcoming season of NBC's *Saturday Night Live*, but you only have $100 to spend. Discuss your recommendations for the budget, which platforms you would use, and your rationale for approaching the campaign this way on social media.

3. You are working with a campus agency and got a request to create a social media campaign to reach alumni of your university. The impact the agency wants to make is to increase its reputation among this audience group. By using the AMEC interactive framework, identify what objectives you want to set forth (communication), and what inputs, activities, outputs, outtakes, outcomes, and impact you want for your social media campaign.

4. You have been tasked to create a measurement strategy for the Make-A-Wish Foundation, which has given you certain objectives to accomplish (increase donations and awareness of its cause). List the types of outcomes Make-A-Wish may want to measure on social media, and propose an example of the social media content you would create to accomplish these objectives.

REFERENCES

AMEC. (2016a). *Integrated evaluation framework*. https://amecorg.com/amecframework/framework/interactive-framework/

AMEC. (2016b). *Social media measurement: What AMEC is doing*. https://amecorg.com/social-media-measurement/

Baer, J. (2018). Not tracking social media ROI is your fault. *Convince & Convert With Jay Baer*. http://convinceandconvert.com/social-media-measurement/not-tracking-social-media-roi-is-your-fault/

Chen, J. (2021, March 26). The most important social media metrics to track. *Sprout Social*. https://sproutsocial.com/insights/social-media-metrics/

Copp, E. (2016, December 12). Are your social ads paying off? 8 metrics you should be tracking. *Hootsuite*. https://blog.hootsuite.com/social-media-ad-metrics/

Dawley, S. (2017, May 16). A comprehensive guide to social media ROI. *Hootsuite*. https://blog.hootsuite.com/measure-social-media-roi-business/

DeMers, J. (2017, April 5). 7 reasons social media marketing is still underrated. *Forbes*. https://www.forbes.com/sites/jaysondemers/2017/04/05/7-reasons-social-media-marketing-is-still-underrated/

Global social media analytics market 2020-2025 featuring Cision, Oracle, Salesforce, IBM, and Adobe among others. (2020, August 10). *Cision PR Newswire*. https://www.prnewswire.com/news-releases/global-social-media-analytics-market-2020-2025-featuring-cision-oracle-salesforce-ibm-and-adobe-among-others-301109254.html

Jackson, D. (2016, March 30). 9 ways social media measurement can improve your marketing strategy. *Sprout Social*. https://sproutsocial.com/insights/social-media-measurement/

Paine, K. (2016, June 20). The best metrics to show off your social media efforts. *The Measurement Advisor*. http://painepublishing.com/best-metrics-show-off-social-media-efforts/

PART III

APPLICATION AND FUTURE CONSIDERATIONS

HOW SOCIAL MEDIA IS APPLIED

Exploring Different Specializations + Case Studies I

Learning Objectives

After reading this chapter, you will be able to

- Identify the areas in which social media can be applied

- Discuss how the entertainment, memes, and crisis communication, journalism fields use social media

- Explain the best practices and guidelines for social media for sports, entertainment, crisis communication, and journalism professionals

INTRODUCTION

How Social Media Is Applied

Social media is not only a field that is growing not only in research and theoretical development but also in practice. While exploring this book, you have learned to understand and appreciate social media strategy. We have discussed changes that impact measurement; understanding the various ethical and legal challenges facing the field; embracing diversity, equity, and inclusion; implementing creative execution; exploring audience analysis; and succeeding with personal branding. The foundation of strategic planning related to social media has been stressed and emphasized throughout the industry. Yet one thing missing from many cases is a clear visualization of how social media is applied, and in what industries.

Social media, as emphasized in this book, is not owned by one discipline or industry. While there may be some areas that claim this fact, the truth is that social media is part of every business, industry, and discipline. In fact, that's the beauty of social media. It is a hub form of communication, community building, and relationship management.

Part III of this book is dedicated to the specific specializations within social media. This chapter provides an overview of the different areas in which social media is applied. Best practices, campaigns, and unique characteristics are discussed and highlighted. One unique attribute characterizing this chapter is that rather than a single Humans of Social Media feature, you will find four—one for each specialization within social media. Each specialization will highlight specific expectations, examples of how to use social media for different industries, and best practices. We cover how the entertainment, sports, crisis communication, and journalism fields integrate social media into their practices, as well as some challenges, opportunities, and case studies professionals face in their respective industries.

Russ Wilde, Marketing Professional at Thuzio and President of Front Office Sports

Social Media and Entertainment

Introduction

Hello! My name is Russ Wilde, and I work on the marketing team at Thuzio and am also the president of Front Office Sports. Thuzio hosts an executive client entertainment and networking event series featuring documentary-style interviews with athletes and influencers. Front Office Sports (FOS) is a digital publication that provides insights about all things at the intersection of sports and business. Previously, I headed strategy and operations for Julius, an end-to-end influencer marketing platform leveraged by brands and agencies to identify creators and manage campaigns.

I grew up in Cranford, New Jersey, and graduated from the University of Miami in 2015 with a degree in sport administration. Fun fact: While at the U of Miami, I was a member of the debate team, which finished in the top 10 nationally in 2014!

How did you get your start in social media?

My first *real* introduction to the world of social media started in October 2014 when I joined Front Office Sports. After meeting Adam White for a salad at The Rat on campus at The U (order the no-yes fries if you're ever there!), I jumped at the opportunity to run the social media accounts for FOS.

In just 6 months, I grew the FOS follower base on Twitter from 200 to 3,000, laying the foundation for the success we have seen over the last few years. The growth of FOS can be attributed to an implemented influencer marketing strategy.

When FOS was first created, we interviewed sports business professionals about their careers with the goal of helping young professionals learn more about the industry. With that, I was able to identify professionals in the social media space with between 1,000 and 5,000 followers and asked them to be interviewed for the site. As time went on and FOS started to become a powerful brand among the #SMsports and #sportsbiz communities, we were able to interview people with 10,000 followers, then 25,000 followers, then 50,000 followers, and so on.

By interviewing these well-known, highly credible "influencers" in the industry, we were associated with them, and over time we became a highly respected publication among executives in the field. Today, we reach over 1 million digital impressions each month.

What is your favorite part of working in your social media area of expertise?

My favorite part about working with influencers is that each individual has such an amazing background and path to success. Everyone has a story, and through both FOS and Thuzio, I have always tried to showcase the stories of interesting people.

What is one thing you can't live without while working in social media?

The one thing I can't live without has to be my phone. This might be a cop-out answer, but it's 100% true.

What is your favorite social media account (person, brand, etc.) to follow, and why?

Other than FOS, anyone who follows my personal account knows that I am a huge fan of Barstool Sports (not only from a content standpoint, but from a business perspective as well). As with any comedy brand, its stuff isn't for everyone, but I love the content that

it produces day in and day out. I think I've become an even bigger fan of Barstool Sports since I started studying the media industry because its growth has been so fun to watch.

What is the most challenging part of working in social media?

The most challenging part for me is finding time to unplug. Even when I'm not "working," I'm constantly reading trade articles or scrolling through Twitter. Sometimes it's hard to take a step back and try to focus on something without thinking about what might be happening in the digital world.

What is your take on your area of expertise and the social media industry?

I'm a huge believer in media companies hiring influencers to work for them. For entities looking to create content for brand partners, it's important to have people on staff who understand how to cultivate large audiences. As display advertising continues to decrease in effectiveness (for a multitude of reasons), native advertising by way of content collaborations is the best way for media companies to monetize.

What do you wish you had known when you were starting out?

One thing that I wish I had known a few years ago is the importance of being on *all* social media platforms. For anyone in the industry, it's important to be active on different social media sites and apps so that you can think about how other people engage on the specific platforms. Whether it's Facebook, Twitter, Snapchat, Musical.ly, or House Party, it's important for people in the industry to stay on top of what's out there and actively learn how to engage on each platform because all of them are so different.

You can follow Russ Wilde on Twitter at @RussWildeJr and Thuzio at @Thuzio.

OVERVIEW OF SOCIAL MEDIA AND ENTERTAINMENT

As Russ Wilde mentioned, the entertainment world is split up into many different specializations. Thuzio works exclusively with influencers (sports, business, and entertainment celebrities) for its line of work. Entertainment is probably one of the areas where social media is a key component of any strategy for a campaign, from promoting a movie (similar to the entertainment and social media work Rich Calabrese implemented before moving to his current position) to even the work Jeremy Darlow has done with sports (which is highlighted in Chapter 7 with his consulting work).

Within the entertainment spectrum, professionals must understand how to use social media on the brand, agency, and celebrity side, as well as the consumer side. Each area of entertainment (sports, movies, gaming, fashion, etc.) has utilized social media to its advantage by raising awareness of brands (e.g., Christian Siriano and his fashion line) and by creating hype for upcoming competitions (e.g., Olympic Trials), television shows and movies (e.g., *Schitt's Creek* and *James Bond*), events (e.g., SXSW, Cannes Lions, and Comic-Con), creative activations at events (e.g., Aviation Gin at Kentucky Derby, adidas at the Super Bowl), celebrities (e.g., Gigi Hadid, Beyoncé, and Taylor Swift), and sports figures (e.g., football player Tom Brady or Olympic swimmer Katie Ledecky). Each of these brands has become its own direct media outlet where it does not have to go first to the media and then to the customers. Essentially, these brands can go straight to the community and reach followers immediately through a tweet, status update, takeover, or live video.

When it comes to entertainment social media campaigns, everything has to be tied in to the overall promotional campaign with sound business objectives and measurements. Movies are a great way to generate social media engagement and excitement among their audiences not only through movie studios but with the stars themselves. *Jumanji 2*—starring Dwayne Johnson, Kevin Hart, Jack Black, and Karen Gillin—used social media to bring awareness to the movie by having a social-first strategy. For example, leading up to the launch of the movie, the stars shot videos acting out scenes together for Halloween and Thanksgiving. This not only provided entertainment but showed the chemistry and humor among the cast members.

As mentioned previously, the entertainment industry wants to use social media strategically to help generate buzz to motivate others to take action in some way online or offline. Whether it is to download a new song or album or go to the movies or a sporting event, each of these actions can be directly tied to metrics and social media conversations. Let us look at the singer Billie Eilish. Eilish, who gained worldwide fame for her unique sound and approach to music and branding, has used her social media channels to showcase her personality, along with addressing issues that she has faced from the online community such as body image. Eilish also has used her social media platforms to release new songs and collaborations, including a song for *No Time to Die*, a James Bond movie released in 2020. Like Eilish, other celebrities use social media not only to showcase their work but to showcase their personality and demonstrate their transparency so fans can feel more connected with them.

This is somewhat different from artists who utilize social media primarily for brand image and music. Some celebrities use social media not to be constantly active and engaged but to create some mystery while also giving fans and others a chance to see a side they would not see otherwise. Taylor Swift is a master of integrating branding and reinvention with her social media channels (McIntyre, 2017). She often posts cryptic clues to upcoming announcements or releases. Sometimes she makes surprise announcements, as she did for her *Folklore* album. This message was shared exclusively on Swift's social media accounts, and not by the studios, since this provided a bigger impact and discussion with her global fanbase (Photo 14.1). This image was simple but also reflected in the overall purpose and mission of the new *Folklore* album as well as its release time for Swift (released in 2020 during the COVID-19 pandemic) and followed it shortly after with the release of *Evermore*. Swift announced *Folklore* via social media posts just hours before the album's release. Created and released during the COVID-19 pandemic, the *Folklore* album and its accompanying social media posts by Swift reflected the reinvention of Swift's image, brand, and music. This reinvention showed itself in the form of subdued black and white photos (compared with her previous color-saturated photos) and pensive captions on Instagram and Twitter. Across her channels, Swift has been able to continue reinventing her image, brand, and music with not only great visuals but powerful words that make these efforts even more impactful.

Beyoncé comes into play here with Instagram—she posts regularly, but just enough to create interest, or occasional viral content (e.g., pregnancy announcements) covered in the mainstream news (Duboff, 2016). Both Swift and Beyoncé use social media to drive attention to their brands and music, but they approach the process in different ways. Each star has her own voice, community, and view of how to use social media, but both have the same overall goal: to increase brand recognition for her work among the public and her fans and drive actions for her music and products. Additionally, both Swift and Beyoncé are dedicated to addressing issues on social media that that are important to them as well as issues their audiences are passionate about.

The entertainment industry has seen a shift not only in how events, individual celebrities, and brands are promoted but also in how these individuals engage in

▶ **Photo 14.1**
Taylor Swift and *Folklore* Announcement

Source: Instagram/ @taylorswift

the space. Entertainment professionals have to know how social media affects their work by exploring the following questions (Buchwald, 2016):

- How can social media deliver on the investment put into it?

- How can social media help create a community?

- How can professionals and teams/brands adapt to the ongoing changes?

- How does the impact of rapid change in format affect the entertainment industry?

Social media is a necessary companion tool for people watching awards shows, sporting events, and high-profile live events (Newman, 2017). Some traditional celebrities rise to the occasion and use social media to amplify their brands (e.g., Reese Witherspoon and Draper James, Michael Jordan and Air Jordan, and Rihanna and Fenty Beauty). New celebrities have arisen over the years based on what they have done with YouTube and other social media platforms. Charli D'Amelio has gone from TikTok fame to partnering with Dunkin not only for her own signature drink, but partnering with them on branded merchandise to tap into the Generation Z audience group. Rosanna Pasino and Lilly Singh both have landed their own shows (Baketopia and Late Night with Lilly Singh) as a result of their successful YouTube channels.

Social media professionals should keep the following best practices in mind when it comes to diving into the entertainment arena:

- *Identify the platforms that can best serve your brand.* Not all celebrities want to be on social media. Some will be active on certain platforms already, but others will be reluctant to join.

- *Innovation is the name of the game.* Many times when it comes to social media trends, looking at where the entertainment field is going is a good indication of how receptive certain platforms and trends will be. It also is an opportunity to stand out from the crowd in a new way if you jump on a new platform or approach quickly.

- *Content teams will be your best friend.* Behind a strong celebrity is a fantastic creative team. Move over publicists, the new team member that is key to success on social media will be a content agency. For example, movie star Will Smith has Westbrook Studios help him create his content for his channels and Ryan Reynolds has his agency Maximum Effort to help promote content for his business ventures, resulting in many professional accolades from the industry.

- *Have a strategy for all aspects.* There is a time and place for every update, picture, and action taken on social media. You want to be authentic and real for your fans and audiences, but a dash of professional branding should always be attached to the content you share. Think about ways to capture your audience members' attention and make them feel part of the community.

- *Get loyal fans and ambassadors behind your brand on social media.* These people help drive the word-of-mouth communication efforts for the entertainment business. Evaluate these individuals, see what they share and how much it impacts your own brand and network, and create relationships with them.

- Engaging fans to create memories makes social media powerful. One of the reasons people follow sports figures and entertainment stars is not only to follow what they are doing, but to have the opportunity to interact with them. Stars like Dwayne Johnson, *Deadpool* star Ryan Reynolds, and *Harry Potter* star Tom Felton hacve done this across the board with their social media accounts from engaging fans on Twitter and IG (Johnson and Reynolds) and TikTok (Felton)

- *Be aware of trolls and how they can take a toll on the celebrity.* Celebrities and any individuals in high-profile positions are well recognized on social media and thus are a target for online trolls. Being aware of the protection they may need online as well as offline is crucial. Celebrities have deleted their accounts entirely due to backlash or because of trolls.

For those in the entertainment industry, social media is a key part of engaging with fans and audiences while using the platform to showcase reach and influence. In addition, more opportunities are available for potential sponsorship and partnership deals, all key components to consider for brand marketing. Yes, even with all of these positive elements and opportunities, serious challenges need to be discussed and accounted for. Social media for entertainment professionals is a blessing or a curse, depending on how people view the array of platforms.

HUMANS OF SOCIAL MEDIA

Jared Gaon, Digital Media Planner

Memes

Introduction

Hey, I'm Jared Gaon. I'm a digital media planner based in New York City. I work at Social @Ogilvy where I help to build digital media strategy to help my clients achieve their business objectives. Outside of my day job, I spend time creating content for my Twitter account @JordanJamming, which quickly gained a following after *The Last Dance* (ESPN's docuseries about Michael Jordan) aired in the spring of 2020.

How did you get your start in social media?

I grew up as social media grew up and, like probably everyone else my age, social media has always been integral to my interactions with others. But more than that, I have always been fascinated by social media, marketing, and technology and spend much of my free time engaging with platforms, learning about the tools, and reading up on what's current in the industry.

But it wasn't until I took a chance and created something of my own that I became involved with social media content creation hands on.

In May of 2020, during the COVID-19 quarantine, I created the viral Twitter account @JordanJamming that gained over 40,000 followers in two days. I took one clip of Michael Jordan from *The Last Dance* docuseries on the team bus holding his Walkman, wearing classic over-the-ear headphones, bobbing his head and superimposed various popular songs on top of it. There was something about seeing this ruthless competitor famously known for punching teammates in practice, jam out to music that made this one-of-a-kind guy oddly relatable. To my surprise, the account took off and people really resonated with the content.

(Continued)

(Continued)

Since then, I've been maintaining the account and have had the chance to connect with others in the industry, partner with record labels, and the account was featured in several articles. While I might not be seeing the same level of engagement that I received at the start, I am still posting regularly, engaging with my audience, and testing new forms of content.

What is your favorite part of working in your area of expertise in social media?

My favorite part about working in social media and specifically on @JordanJamming is that fact that I'm creating content for something that I'm genuinely passionate about and interested in. I'm a die-hard NBA fan; I spend (probably too much) time on Reddit and Twitter following the latest basketball news. Being up-to-date on NBA trends allows me to create relevant content as a genuine member of the basketball Twitter-verse. Followers care a lot about authenticity, and in turn authentic content will perform better and garner more engagement.

What is one thing you can't live without while working in social media?

I can't live without Twitter.

It's an incredible tool to stay in touch with industry trends and the latest marketing news. Additionally, Twitter is also a great resource to network, connect with people in similar roles, and learn from others.

What is your favorite social media account (person/brand/etc.) to follow and why?

@Netflix is a must follow. They shy away from what brands generally do on social media and really have a cool and relatable personality. They meme their own shows, build up feuds with competitors like Amazon Prime Video, and retweet their followers' best Netflix related tweets. They have a finger on the pulse of social media trends and Tweet more like a friend than a brand.

What is the most challenging part of working in social media?

I feel that the most challenging part about working in social media is the "always-on" attitude. In order to be successful in the space, you need to be aware of trends and post content in a timely matter or it becomes yesterday's news. On the flipside, spending too much time on social media can be detrimental to our mental health. Try your best to stay aware and alert to find content opportunities while giving yourself a break and finding real-life ways to engage with others.

What do you wish you had known when you were starting out?

Some posts will work and some won't. Don't stress if a post doesn't achieve the engagement that you had thought it would. Instead, keep posting content and use engagement metrics to understand what content your followers prefer.

What are three marketable skills a social media professional needs to have to work in the industry?

1. Staying on top of trends: In order to create exciting and timely content, it's important to have a pulse on what's popular and what's happening today on the platforms.

2. Platform fluency: Make sure you know how to expertly use and track performance on various platforms. There are tons of YouTube tutorials that I've found super helpful.

3. Creativity: Creativity is always key—look at what's popular on social media or in your area and put your own spin on it.

OVERVIEW OF SOCIAL MEDIA AND MEMES

One of the things that Jared Gaon has shared in this Humans of Social Media feature is the rise of growing accounts based on trending topics, issues, people, and situations. Memes are not new for the online culture, but the business of memes has become more mainstream to tap into cultural moments. Memes capture humor and emotion through relatable entertainment that is shared across platforms for audience enjoyment. Many memes go viral, such as Crying Michael Jordan, Oprah during the Prince Harry and Meghan Markle interview, Grumpy Cat (RIP), Woman Yelling at Cat, Distracted Boyfriend, "Everything is fine" Dog Cartoon, and Kermit the Frog Sipping Tea. There are thousands of iconic memes to choose from; it seems as though there is a meme for every emotion and circumstance. Welcome to the age of meme creation and strategy!

As discussed in Chapter 8, memes are humorous pieces of content that comment on trends, events, perspectives, and entertainment and that spread across different online platforms. Some memes are based on experiences with a brand (e.g., Best of Nextdoor) or a moment that trended online after an event (e.g., *Last Dance*'s Michael Jordan).

Why are memes important to consider as a key specialization of business and strategy practices in social media? Memes are relatively inexpensive to create and can help build a sense of community while motivating audiences to share this content more than other types (Enthoven, 2019). If used strategically, memes can help serve as a great communication vehicle to enhance brand relevancy for a company (Enthoven, 2019).

Memes are not just for individuals—brands can get into the mix by embracing their own memes to cultivate a sense of culture and entertainment, or by participating in a meme challenge. Let's take M&M's for example. Celebrity and entrepreneur Reese Witherspoon created the 2020 Challenge in which people put together pictures representing collective feelings about each month of 2020 (see Chap. 12, Photo 12.3). The pictures show increased distress as the months go on, illustrating people's feelings about 2020. Brands saw this trending and jumped in to share their own version of the 2020 Challenge, including M&Ms (Photo 14.2). In their 2020 Challenge meme, M&M's starts the year with a group of happy M&M's characters hanging out together; in March (when shelter-in-place orders began in the United States for COVID-19), the M&M character is alone and worried.

M&M'S ✓
@mmschocolate

Pretty much. #2020challenge

JANUARY | FEBRUARY | MARCH
APRIL | MAY | JUNE
JULY | AUGUST | SEPTEMBER

9:52 AM · Aug 7, 2020   ⓘ

♡ 276   💬 89 people are Tweeting about this

▸ **Photo 14.2**
M&M's Integrating
2020 Meme Challenge

Source: Twitter/
@mmschocolate

Subsequent months show concerned or confused characters—April's yellow M&M runs away, perhaps in a dramatic attempt to social distance. June's brown M&M casts a critical look, likely a nod to the racial justice protests against police brutality that gained momentum largely in June. July through September shows the same worried character—perhaps a reference to restrictions being extended due to COVID-19.

Brands and organizations can use memes to demonstrate awareness about what to do and what not to do in certain situations. Barkbox, the popular toy and dog product monthly subscription direct to consumer (DTC) brand, used a meme to show how to properly wear a face mask. The meme shows a dog wearing a face mask in various incorrect ways and finally the right way, allowing the brand to capture the humor and messaging on the topic while using their brand voice (Photo 14.3). This strategy is an effective strategy when reacting to trending topics, which should be monitored and looked for in your social media research. Good timing as well as the integration of brand personality and voice into a meme can foster strong engagement, so it is key to be on top of what is trending and what is relevant for the brand to take advantage of.

While memes can be used for fun, there is a real monetary drive for making memes. Memers, who are popular on platforms such as Instagram, can make thousands of dollars per month (Wellemeyer, 2017). That said, memers have gotten into trouble with platforms and others for copyright issues and ownership of content, and platforms are getting more engaged in shutting down these accounts for this very reason. This will not deter other brands from embracing memes; instead, it has caused some brands to make meme production in-house. BudLight Seltzer announced they would be hiring a chief meme officer for $5,000 per month to create memes and content associated with the memes.

Best Practices for Memes on Social Media

- *Make sure your meme illustrates and supports your brand voice.* If you are trying to be cute and on point with an audience by using a meme without any consideration on how this aligns with your own brand voice, it will not only fail but you could impact the overall relationship and perception you have with your community. Best to integrate your own brand voice and personality in relation to the meme to make that connection.

▸ **Photo 14.3**
Barkbox on
Instagram With
Mask Memes

Source: Instagram/
@barkbox

- *Be aware of who owns the content and how this could result in possible ethical and legal issues.* No one wants to get sued for creating a meme without permission to use the content. Content ownership is a big topic of discussion on social media. Copyright issues have emerged on social media, and this is a big issue related to memes that can bring forth some ethical and legal issues for the person who started the meme account, or the actual meme. Best to be prepared and aware of these situations while understanding copyright regulations and rules.

- *Build a meme library and be on the lookout for emerging ones to integrate into your content strategy.* Understanding what has been done, what is trending, and which ones could be aligned with your overall content strategy is important. Personalize the meme based on the template that is used; this can be done using the tool Imgflip.

- *Understand who is behind the account and trending meme to see if they are doing it for entertainment or other reasons.* Memes can be harmless and entertaining, but they have also become a powerful tool to influence certain viewpoints and perspective under the disguise of being a meme (Stringhini & Zannettou, 2020). Specific meme factories, firms, and troll accounts have been launched to influence communities, and even political campaigns (Stringhini & Zannettou, 2020). Like news, it is important to look at memes with a critical eye.

- *There is no that rule you can't create and launch your own meme.* Who says you have to wait to start a meme trending? Brands such as Netflix, Chipotle, and celebrities (e.g., Drake and Reese Witherspoon) have done so. Why can't you?

Melissa Agnes, Founder and CEO, Crisis Ready Institute

Social Media and Crisis Communication

Introduction

I specialize in crisis management and preparedness. I'm an author and the founder and CEO of the Crisis Ready Institute. My goal and passion is helping organizations implement what I refer to as a **CRISIS READY™** culture.

How did you get your start in your field?

My mind always sees risk. It always has. Back in 2010, it struck me one day that no one was evaluating or discussing the risk of social media and real-time communication. This realization ignited a passion within me that, before that moment, I didn't know existed. At the time, I had never thought about crisis management as a "thing." But that soon changed as my new-found passion fueled the next year of me reading anything and everything I could get my hands on, on the topic of crisis management.

One early morning, about a year into my "studies," the VP of a real estate investment trust, one of our clients, called me in a panic. He told me that the company's president was in his car with a prospective investor, and they were listening to the radio reporting that one of their buildings was about to explode—which was untrue. Apparently, the story started on Twitter, and of course the company had no idea what Twitter was! So, they called me, their web strategist, to help.

I headed to my client's office and within roughly 30 minutes, we had the media correcting themselves and we had them up and running on Twitter—but more importantly, we had Twitter streamlining to their website's home page as we knew their investors would be going to their website, not to Twitter, for news and updates concerning the

incident. To make a long story short, the next day I received a call from the president of the company thanking me. He said that not only had their unit price not gone down since the day before, but it had actually gone up a cent!

So, after about a year of studying everything I could on the topic of crisis management, I had the opportunity to help a client manage a real-time, escalating issue. In those moments I learned three things:

1. I have a natural aptitude for crisis management;
2. I love it; and
3. People need it.

The rest, as they say, is history!

What is your favorite part of working in your area of expertise?

To be honest, I love every part of it. But I suppose if I must choose a favorite, it would be the value that being **CRISIS READY™** provides to organizations, every day, not just in times of crisis. For example, implementing a **CRISIS READY™** culture helps organizations foster cross-departmental collaborations and relationships, improves internal communication processes, strengthens stakeholder value, instills a mindset that looks for opportunities in all situations (especially the negative ones), and ultimately provides the brand with a quantifiable competitive advantage.

How does your field integrate social media?

Social media is an inevitable component of all crises in this day and age. On one hand, it amplifies the challenges and obstacles that organizations are forced to face in times of crisis. On the other hand, it presents unique opportunities to connect, communicate effectively, and, ultimately, strengthen relationships with key stakeholders, while managing those same crises.

What is your favorite social media account (person/brand/etc.) to follow and why?

It changes all the time. I tend to follow people and organizations that inspire me or teach me something new that I may be looking to learn. Then I move on. However, I can say that at the moment, my favorite and go-to platform is Instagram.

What is the most challenging part of working in crisis management?

All the work I do is challenging. It constantly challenges me to be at the top of my game, to continue learning and evolving, and to be the best I can possibly be for my clients. But the challenge is one of the things I appreciate the most about what I do. It keeps me on my toes, it keeps me inspired and motivated, and it keeps me excited! The most recent challenge I've undertaken is a massive mission-oriented public benefit corporation, called the Crisis Ready Institute.

What do you wish you had known when you were starting out?

It would have been nice to know for sure that it would all work out. I always knew I was on to something big; I could feel it in my bones. However, it wasn't always easy. Life as an entrepreneur comes with so many challenges and rewards. Sometimes, when I look back, I think that it would have been great to just get a glimpse of where this journey would take me.

What are three marketable skills a social media professional needs to have to work in the industry?

- Strong issue management skills are essential. The focus and achievement need to always be to come out of any negative incident with increased trust, credibility, and loyalty.

- Emotional wisdom is critical for any frontward-facing, communication, and/or leadership role.

- Adaptability is important in this day and age. Things move and evolve quickly and having the ability to be versatile and agile, always striving to be a few steps ahead of the curve, is important.

Where do you go to keep up to date with trends and continue learning about social media?

There isn't one place in particular. It's about staying in the game and staying relevant— and striving to always be a few steps ahead. The key to doing this is to continuously watch, listen, observe, analyze, experiment, engage, and to hold one's self accountable to high standards.

If you had to choose a song to walk out to in a presentation on social media, what would it be and why?

That is a difficult question for me to answer because I have a hundred favorite songs and it always depends on my mood of the moment. In this moment, at the time of this writing, I'm going to go with "Hooked on a Feeling," by Blue Swede.

Melissa Agnes can be contacted via her website (crisisreadyinstutite.com) or followed on Twitter at @melissa_agnes.

OVERVIEW OF SOCIAL MEDIA
AND CRISIS COMMUNICATION

While organizations and individuals experience many positive events and situations, negatively charged events may also distort daily activities and cause financial, emotional, and personal harm to those involved. These situations are conceptualized as crises. Crises come in various forms and can impact an organization or individual at any time. In other words, crises are significant, disruptive events that often feature a rapid onset.

Crises have been defined as events that either cause harm to or have the potential to harm an individual or organization. Whether the harm produces physical, emotional, or environmental damage to individuals and communities involved in the crisis, or damage to the corporate reputation or financial standing of an organization, the range of harm is different in each situation. Full understanding of a crisis encompasses not only the actual precipitating event but also the process or time leading from a precipitating event, including the subsequent perceptions of the crisis by various stakeholders.

While most research has been dedicated to traditional crises, social media crises are quite different depending on where they started. Tim Coombs (2013), one of the leading researchers and scholars in crisis communication, classified social media crises as acting somewhat like "zombies" compared to traditional crises. What Coombs means is that a social media crisis is an incident or triggering event (e.g., the actual crisis situation) that

- happens on social media or on a particular platform,

- rapidly spreads from person to person,

- sparks outrage and emotion online,

- spreads virally to become a traditional news story, and

- can spark from a scandal (which Coombs has labeled as a "scancis").

The biggest confusion among social media professionals regarding traditional crises and social media crises is to think they are one and the same. However, they are quite different. Social media crises are caused by certain messages, situations, and responses that emerged on the platforms themselves, whereas traditional crises usually happen offline but are discussed on social media. Natural disasters (e.g., Hurricanes Harvey and Laura), workplace or school violence (e.g., Sandy Hook or Parkland), corporate/political or social scandals (e.g., Anthony Weiner), and other traditional crises have all been covered and discussed on social media. The challenges for social media and crisis communication specialists are that (a) the technology and platforms that are used constantly change and adapt, so what can work and what can go wrong become equally important to consider, and (b) you always have to think of outside possibilities and new challenges that could emerge with each new advancement, platform, and use of a tool.

One of the things to realize is that there will always be something that is trending for the wrong reasons. Social media crises, whether they are accidents or could have been prevented, happen all the time. There are certain knowns for working in this specialization in social media. First, you will always have crises because there is always something to address and prepare for as channels and challenges emerge and evolve. Second, education and training are going to be more important than ever. Crisis communications is not just an optional skill to have for social media; rather, it is an essential skill to have, master, and implement. Lastly, when you think you have seen it all, wait. There's something that will always come up and surprise you. All I have to say is this: Murder hornets, which is something many social media managers did not have on their bingo card for 2020! Always be prepared for the unexpected surprises that may arise online and offline for social media initiatives.

Social media crises have emerged over the years for brands and others. Many brands, agencies, social media professionals, and athletic teams have had their own experiences dealing with social media crises, some recognizable. Brands and others, for example, have found themselves in some of the following unfortunate situations on social media:

- *Being cancelled on social media for what is shared or said online.* As discussed in Chapter 2, cancel culture is gripping society for various reasons and circumstances. Greg Glassman, cofounder and former CEO of CrossFit, resigned from his position due to outcry for racist comments he shared on social media. Others, such as *Vanderpump Rules* cast members Stassi Schroeder and Kristen Doute and celebrities James Charles and Ellen DeGeneres, have experienced their own cancellations due to things they did offline, but the outrage was sparked on social media.

- *Having good intentions, and audiences interpret a different meaning.* Burger King, which is known for its award-winning campaigns, was the spotlight in 2021 when they tweeted out an update on Twitter, "Women belong in the kitchen," to celebrate International Women's Day. The brand had a follow-up about the need to support women in the food industry, but audiences were outraged and reacted negatively to the post and brand. As a result, the fast food company took down the tweet and apologized publicly.

- *Taking a stand.* Lyft went viral when it responded to a passenger who was barred from Uber after coughing on the driver in San Francisco during the COVID-19 pandemic. When the passenger said she would take Lyft instead, Lyft responded on Twitter: "Although this incident did not involve the Lyft platform, the unacceptable treatment of the driver in this video compelled us to permanently remove the rider from the Lyft community. Driving in a pandemic is not easy. Please wear a mask, respect one another, and be a good person" (Lyft, 2021).

- *Making a profit during a tense situation or crisis.* The COVID-19 pandemic in 2020 rocked every country and industry. However, there were some brands that made a lot of money during this time, including Amazon, Walmart, Clorox, and Purell, to name a few. Some of these brands have given back to those impacted by COVID-19 to make sure they felt a sense of normalcy in routines (e.g., Peloton offered free access to classes for several months for those looking for fitness and meditation options), but others have not. As they say, actions speak louder than words, and history will tell which ones we can trust in the case of future epidemics.

- *Underestimating the impact of crisis history and outrage on social media.* Social media does not forget a brand that has a crisis history, and the result usually ends in more outrage online. In March 2018, United Airlines faced criticism as it was accused of putting a dog in an overhead bin during a flight from Houston to New York City (Gulliver, 2018). Amazon (employee treatment), Refinery29 (employee culture), and Pinterest (gender discrimination lawsuit) are other brands that have faced outrage on and off social media.

- *Not doing your research on the content or situation.* Trying to interject yourself into a conversation is an art form, and embracing real-time marketing or trendjacking has become quite the competition for brands to showcase relevancy. One classic case involved DiGiorno. The pizza company interjected itself into a serious Twitter conversation surrounding domestic violence with the hashtag #WhyIStayed. Instead, the company said it stayed "because there was pizza," trying to tie the conversation back to the brand (DeMers, 2016; see also Chapter 7). This did not go over well for DiGiorno, which had to respond to each tweet with an apology. In addition, Corona released their new seltzer brand during the beginning stages of COVID-19, saying it was "coming to shore," while KFC got rid of their "finger lickin' good" tagline because of the message it would be sending out during COVID.

- *Not recognizing the tone and concern expressed on social media.* Equifax announced in September 2017 a Category 5 crisis where 143 million customers had their credit impacted by hackers (Temin, 2017; also see Photo 14.4). The credit card company was not perceived to respond appropriately to this crisis, and at least from what they shared on their social media accounts, people felt Equifax was not as urgent in addressing this crisis as it should have been.

- *Not thinking about the impact of a hashtag.* SeaWorld experienced this problem during the height of the *Blackfish* scandal. The theme park wanted to start a conversation with audience members, but others immediately took over, including activists who were not too pleased with SeaWorld ("#Fail: 29 of the Biggest Corporate Brand Social Media Flubs," 2017). In addition, McDonald's wanted to do a #McDStories feature, but instead got feedback about all the negative things people experienced with the brand. These were great ideas for engagement, but the brands did not consider all of the potential ways in which people would actually use the hashtags.

In case you have not heard about the following example, it demonstrated the power of social media (specifically live video) to spark a crisis that went viral. In April 2017, a United Airlines flight became global news when passenger David Dao was forced out of his seat by Chicago airport security guards and dragged from the plane. The video of the treatment of the passenger on the Chicago to Louisville flight is very disturbing and raised outrage online and offline. This was the topic of conversation among students and professionals alike. United Airlines released a statement from its CEO regarding the situation, which caused even more negative reaction toward and discussion of the brand.

Let's talk about this a bit more. We can evaluate the case in a variety of different ways. The trigger event (or the crisis, as we call this in crisis communications) was the video of the passenger on United Express Flight 3411, but the way United responded with the CEO and the leaked email to United employees did further damage to the brand among its audiences. In addition, as Photo 14.5 shows, the initial statement shared on United's Twitter account did not go over well among key audiences and the media. How you respond and act is extremely important

Twitter

Facebook
(update with video of CEO Rick Smith)

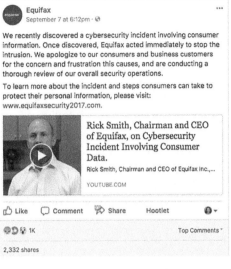

▶ **Photo 14.4**
Equifax Social Media Response to Category 5 Crisis

Source (left): Twitter/@Equifax

Source (right): Facebook/@Equifax

when faced with a crisis situation, as demonstrated here with the reputation damage available for the world to see on social media.

The response was not perceived as effective since it was viewed as generic and not displaying empathy to the situation for the audience members. An important element to consider is the fact that many people will look not only at the impacted parties during a crisis but at anyone associated with them. Associated advertisers, donors, and even the media can be called out on social media to address the situation. In fact, this happened with the United Airlines crisis. *PRWeek* (widely known as a trade publication and outlet for the public relations field) recently gave

United ✔
@united

United CEO response to United Express Flight 3411.

This is an upsetting event to all of us here at United. I apologize for having to re-accommodate these customers. Our team is moving with a sense of urgency to work with the authorities and conduct our own detailed review of what happened. We are also reaching out to this passenger to talk directly to him and further address and resolve this situation.

- Oscar Munoz, CEO, United Airlines

▶ **Photo 14.5**
United CEO Oscar Munoz's Response on Twitter

Source: Twitter/@United

Oscar Munoz its Communication of the Year Award at its annual awards banquet. The publication had a post about the case study on its website, but made no mention of giving this award to United's CEO; nor has it responded to this on social media. Eventually, after facing backlash on this issue, *PRWeek* had to release a statement as well.

Corporate or reputation crises are not the only crises relevant to social media. In fact, social media can be the means for asking for help and even reaching government authorities to save people's lives.

Several best practices can guide our responses to a social media crisis situation:

- *Create a social media component for your crisis management plan* (Keys, 2017). Constantly updating a designated section with new trends, tools, best practices, and case studies is crucial in making sure everyone is on board with the social media protocols and practices. This includes making sure a contingency plan is in place in case of certain incidents, such as a disgruntled employee trying to go rogue on the main social media platforms and locking everyone out of the accounts.

- *Set up necessary monitoring, listening, and response team strategies.* As discussed in Chapter 6, it is good to see what mentions and discussions come through that may be early warning signs, negative reviews or comments, or rising concerns that are sensitive and need immediate action. For example, many trends in a crisis start off with a hashtag, such as #DeleteFacebook, #CancelSoulcycle, or #BoycottWayfair. All of these cases brought forth the need to evaluate and determine what was happening, who started the trend, and how it evolved from online to offline.

- *Identify where the crisis first started online.* In a case involving Domino's and YouTube in 2009, two employees posted a video of themselves being inappropriate with their food on YouTube. The CEO of Domino's, J. Patrick Doyle, posted a video on YouTube to discuss how the company was going to handle this crisis situation. The brand realized, after seeing the discussion on Twitter (Domino's had to create a Twitter handle to respond to the crisis, and its first tweet was to address this situation), it had to go to the place where the crisis originated to be effective. This practice has been demonstrated across the board in other crises such as with Jake Paul being associated with looters during the protests against the police-involved death of George Floyd in 2020.

- *Write relevant content that is easy to share and easy to understand.* Provide enough clarity in what you want audience members to do in a crisis so that they understand the call to action and realize "This is important for me to follow." Social media is about dialogue, participating in the conversation, and making sure the social media professionals involved are not neglectful of or absent from a crisis. Give your community and audience members a sense of control (or self-efficacy) over the situation.

- *Take a moment and "pause" content during a crisis.* People don't want to see your promoted tweets or updates when they are searching for shelter after a natural disaster or during a traumatic event.

- *Make sure to correct any false rumors, information, or news spreading online about you or the situation.* This is an important topic. There are occasions when you have to correct the facts, let others know if images or photos from certain natural disasters or incidents are "fake," and where they can go for trusted news.

In summary, as for social media in general, crisis communication professionals working in this area are constantly bombarded with new issues, challenges, reputational risks, and opportunities to address in the industry. Keeping up with the trends in social media is one part of the equation for crisis communication professionals, but certain behaviors, message strategies, and crisis communication best practices will still be relevant to note even if the platforms change.

Kerry Flynn, Media Reporter For CNN

Social Media and Journalism

Introduction

I joined CNN in August 2019 to cover media. Prior, I reported on the relationships between marketers, publishers, and tech platforms for *Digiday.* I previously was a reporter at *Mashable,* covering tech giants and Silicon Valley culture. I also wrote for *IBTimes, HuffPost, Forbes,* and *Money* magazine. I grew up in western Massachusetts and studied environmental policy and economics at Harvard.

How did you get your start in social media?

I would say the first social networks I joined were AOL Instant Messenger (AIM) and Neopets. Those aren't traditional forms of social media from what we hear today, but I feel like it was the first time I used the internet to connect with people. I started reporting on social media when I interned at *Forbes* in 2014. Despite wanting to cover the energy business, my editor at the time saw I had a knack for using my smartphone. And well, I haven't turned back, as social media has become not just something fun to use but also a crucial aspect of our daily lives.

What is your favorite part of working in your area of expertise in social media?

My favorite part of reporting on social media has been keeping these companies accountable. Examples of that include Facebook's biases with features like the News Feed and Twitter's efforts to curb abuse. At CNN, I focus on the contentious relationship between

(Continued)

(Continued)

publishers and social media platforms. While media companies continue to use social to amplify their content, they're sacrificing more ownership of their audience.

What is one thing you can't live without while working in social media?

My iPhone—simple as that.

What is your favorite social media account (person/brand/team/etc.) to follow and why?

The team at @Square. Nick Dimichino and his team use Twitter perfectly for brands, sharing related content, offering customer support, and also joining in on conversations.

What is the most challenging part of working in social media?

Never being unplugged. I have friends in the industry who will try to take time away whether they're on vacation or just spend some time each day without their phone. The only times I'm detached from social media is while working out, in the shower, and when I'm sleeping.

You have been active in mentoring future young professionals in social media. What has been the most rewarding experience or moment you have had in helping students out in social media?

A lot of people ask me how to grow their presence on Twitter, which I always respond with "Be yourself." There's nothing better than authenticity.

What do you wish you had known when you were starting out?

I actually wish I had used social media more during college. I was so focused on my academic studies and my extracurricular activities that I didn't really take advantage of Facebook and Twitter, for example, as ways to network and build a brand earlier in my life.

What are three marketable skills a social media professional needs to have to work in the industry?

— Communication skills: You need to be good at writing, visualizing, and overall getting your message across in a succinct and effective manner.

— Fast learner: These platforms are changing all the times and new ones are emerging. You need to be willing to stay up to date and adapt fearlessly.

— Thick skin: Social media provides open communication. Even though there are terms of services and rules against harassment, you're unfortunately going to see it.

Where do you go to keep up to date with trends and continue learning about social media?

I'm a forever fan of advertising trade publications, including my former employer *Digiday* along with *Ad Age* and *Adweek*. And I follow other experts in the field on Twitter, including Taylor Lorenz, Sarah Frier, and Julian Gamboa.

If you had to choose a song to walk out to in a presentation on social media, what would it be and why?

"You Will Be Found" from the musical *Dear Evan Hansen*—it's a song about people using social media to amplify a message and garner support for a cause

OVERVIEW OF SOCIAL MEDIA AND JOURNALISM

Journalism and social media have become an integral part of what reporters, news outlets, and feature writers gravitate to for their stories, news, and community building. Social media is one of the major ways people get news today. According to the Pew Research Center, many Americans say that social media companies have too much control over the news on their sites, and that the role social media companies play in delivering news results in a worse mix of news for users (Shearer & Grieco, 2019).

In many incidents, social media is an essential part of how reporters, mainstream media, news anchors, and bloggers communicate and document their stories. Some worldwide events have captured the media's attention from the journalists' point of view, and social media has become the first stop for many audience members seeking news.

While many events have been documented on social media, several high-profile cases have used social media, from the media's perspective, to capture ongoing events. One high-profile event documented on social media was the 2020 presidential election, which garnered a lot of commentary, insights, and perspectives related to former president Trump and former vice president Biden. Other topics found on social media included the discussion of confirmed and unconfirmed messaging around COVID-19 and the protests that occurred in response to George Floyd's killing. The passing of Kobe Bryant broke first on TMZ and Twitter.

When we live in an age where the media are all about breaking the news first, we need guidelines in place to verify and then validate what messages we share on social media. In addition, we must be aware of the rise of uninformed messages that do not come from official sources (aka fake news) and how this affects the trustworthiness, credibility, and impact of the media and journalists within their communities.

The rise of misinformation, or **fake news,** is a challenge that journalists and the social media field face. Fake news is false or misleading information that is presented as truthful. Fake news is disinformation or hoaxes shared with the intent that they spread like wildfire online to shift behaviors, attitudes, or opinions offline. Disinformation (which focuses on the intention to mislead) and misinformation (false information that is attributed regardless of intent to mislead) are often associated with fake news, which circulates on social media among many platforms online. Fake news comes in various forms: Bots and trolls drive information from noncredible sites; others post fake images during disasters (e.g., the swimming shark in the street). As platforms and channels evolve, so do sinister and unethical practices to mislead audiences with online content. That said, there are some steps that journalists and others can take to assess what is factual information, and what is not. Cornell University provides tips for how to assess the legitimacy of traditional and online sources (Engle, n.d.). These tips are important not only for journalists and media professionals to know, but all members of society. **Media literacy** (the ability to analyze, access, create and evaluate media content) is more important than ever in our growing digital environment. Here are some tips on evaluating sources, adapted from Cornell University (Engle, n.d.):

- **Check the source.** Research the source to learn more about the site's mission, history, or biases. Also check the site for contact information.

- **Check the author.** Research the authors to determine if they are real and if they are credible.

- **Check the date.** Sometimes, people will post old news stories during more current events. Remember that reposting these stories does not mean they are relevant to what is happening now.

- **Check your biases.** Determine whether your own opinions or beliefs are affecting the way you interpret the news. Is the source biased, or are you reading with a biased view?

- **Check other news sources.** Some headlines are sensationalized to hook more readers. Check if other news sources are reporting on the story and if they present a more complete view of it.

- **Check the supporting sources.** See if the provided links within the story actually support what is being reported.

- **Check for satire.** Some stories are intentionally satirical. Research the author and site to determine if this might be the case.

- **Check with experts.** Use fact-checking sites to verify the information provided in the story. Some popular fact-checking sites include FactCheck.org and FlackCheck.org.

Remember that as social media evolves, new guidelines need to be incorporated in media coverage. In 2017, *The New York Times* released social media guidelines outlining practices its reporters need to follow and adhere to when reporting the news, addressing questions and comments, and engaging with their readership community. The Society of Professional Journalists (n.d.) also have guidelines and expectations presented in their social media policies, which amount to a simple instruction: Use common sense.

In addition, Reuters (n.d.) has a policy with certain requirements for its journalists to follow and be aware of on social media. Some of the overarching guidelines (fairness, asking if the story is a hoax, attribution of sources, no falsehoods, etc.) are general, but they also include specific social media guidelines (Reuters, n.d.):

- Be responsible, fair, and impartial in the stories and conversations on social media.

- Be confidential and refrain from disclosure of insider information.

- Be careful because everything stated on social media is for public viewing, but note social media can be used as a tool to improve your role in the media.

- Be proactive in making sure the sources and information shared has been vetted and confirmed.

For journalists, social media has become a way to do the following:

- *Share breaking news.* Crises and events often break on social media (in many cases, Twitter), followed by news articles on the media's site. The 2009 US Airways Hudson River crash was first reported when a bystander named Janis Krums shared a picture on Twitter (Langer, 2014). Presently, everyone who is able to document and share content is a citizen journalist. However, even in breaking news, how the story is framed can impact how people perceive or react to a situation. It is very easy to doctor or edit video or images that look real even when they are not.

- *Report news in a unique way.* Publications and news outlets are all vying for attention and reaching new audiences who may not be spending time reading a newspaper or watching cable television. Dan Jorgenson, writer and producer for *The Washington Post,* positioned the media company in a unique way by using TikTok to capture trending news items and reach a new target audience. Jorgenson and *The Washington Post* received praise for this approach, with Jorgenson saying, "The *Washington Post* TikTok takes a kind of perverse pride in its unhipness and the fact that by the time a 141-year-old newspaper stumbles upon something that's become popular on social media, its involvement is inherently comedic." As a result, the media company has gained brand notoriety and increased presence in its messaging around the world (Beaujon, 2019).

- *Home in on specialty topics to gain prominence in the field.* Taylor Lorenz, a reporter for *The New York Times,* became a must-follow for her stories on internet culture and new trends emerging in Gen Z. Lorenz uses her social media presence to discuss interesting trends happening in social media and to bring awareness to issues that need to be addressed in the field.

- *Report on stories in real time.* Providing real-time and visual content on the site of the story is one way to use social media for journalism. The media can use Facebook, Twitter, Instagram, and other platforms to play live videos and add on to their stories.

- *Offer exclusives.* To reach new audiences, many media outlets create digital- or mobile-first content, which will allow them to repurpose or even share content on different platforms. For example, *The New York Times, Fast Company,* and even *Adweek* could publish an exclusive interview but then repurpose teasers of the interview on social media platforms such as Facebook, Twitter, and Instagram in the format of short videos or even pictures.

- *Find stories.* Journalists are looking for inspiration on social media as well as information for their stories. If they see a trending topic, they pursue it to see if there is any particular light to it or if it is something to pass on. However, the days when journalists have to wait around for a source are over. The best way for journalists to do this is to ask their community on platforms such as Twitter and Instagram.

- *Engage with readers.* Reporters, anchors, writers, and other journalism professionals are encouraged to use social media to be part of the conversation, not always dictating where the conversation needs to go. Journalists engage in conversations via Twitter through direct messages, participating in a trending topic or hashtag, engaging in Twitter chats, or connecting with other professionals in the industry. *Adweek* has a regular Twitter chat that covers various topics related to their publication, bringing forth opportunities to network and connect.

Best Practices and Recommendations

Journalists, like all professionals working in social media, have some unique responsibilities and obligations to follow for their profession and the communities they serve. Here are some recommendations and best practices to follow when entering the journalism and social media industry:

- *Have a set ethical code and policy for the newsroom.* As listed in the NPR (2017) social media guidelines, it is crucial to maintain a level of professional conduct that reflects not only the role of the journalist but also the credibility of the news outlet.

- *Be aware of the new responsibilities you have as a journalist.* Not only is it important to write about the content, but journalists (print, broadcast, etc.) have to be active in distributing and promoting their content for others to see. The time and dedication needed to be part of the online conversation today is more important than ever, and the journalists who are active on social media are the more successful ones (Nicholson, 2017).

- *Be ethical, mindful, and supportive when interacting with others.* In other words, treat others how you would like to be treated. Journalism and the media have prided themselves on being objective, fair, and transparent with current events. This is important to remember on social media as well ("Social Media and Journalism," 2020).

- *Adopt the professional conduct that reflects your reputation as a media professional.* *The New York Times* updated its social media guidelines to reflect this, and spent time outlining not only some key principles for the newspaper to follow but guidelines for its reporters to follow as well (*"The Times* Issues Social Media Guidelines for the Newsroom," 2017; updated 2020).

- *Confirm and validate all information before hitting the "publish" button.* While it is tempting to be first, being able to rely on your sources and focus on fundamental journalism principles will help not only the reputation of the reporter or journalist but also the credibility of the news story. After publishing incorrect information, you may need to issue an apology and correction; if the information was false and defamatory, lawsuits could arise for the media outlet. For example, Meghan Markle and Prince Harry (the Duke and Duchess of Sussex) have sued several tabloids over the years for false information published about them and for "bullying" approaches to the couple (Foster, Kent, Lewis, & Said-Moorhouse, 2019).

- *Journalists and other media professionals not only cover cancel culture on social, but they can experience it themselves.* Some media professionals were part of the group of writers and professionals who signed the letter in *Harper's* magazine outlining the need for justice and open debate ("A Letter on Justice and Open Debate," 2020).

CHAPTER SUMMARY

Social media is practiced and integrated in a variety of different ways, as shown in Table 14.1. In many cases, it is used not only as a broadcasting tool but as a tool that helps facilitate conversations, dialogue, storytelling, and reputation management.

It is important to note that all of the professionals interviewed for the Humans of Social Media features are lifelong learners, are engaged in the community and industry they work in, and have a traditional discipline as a foundation for their work (marketing, journalism, memes, etc.). This shows how social media, though established now for several years, is still a relatively new field for degrees or even courses. This field is constantly evolving and changing, and even while taking a social media class, there is a growing expectation that while the platforms and tools may change, human behaviors, attitude and message strategy executions, understanding the community, and other core skills (e.g., research and writing) are always going to be relevant.

While each industry has its own guidelines and best practices, all focus on the tools as a channel to spark a conversation and build a community. In addition, creative education and understanding the growing nature of innovative work continue to be part of social media professionals' role and job.

Table 14.1 Social Media Content to Create and Apply in Each Specialization	
Specialization	**Content to Create**
Entertainment	• Social media updates • Strategic briefs • Social media audits • Personal brand audits • Influencer marketing plans • Influencer sponsorship packages • Analytics reports • Graphics and visual assets • Updates and social ads • Guidelines • Press releases
Memes	• Social media updates • Videos • Influencer creative execution and applications • Social media posts • Graphic and visual assets • Paid media
Crisis Communications	• Crisis plans • Statements for social media • Simulation exercises and training • Workshops • Fact sheets and background of key professionals involved in crisis • Media monitoring reports • Analytics reports • Social media listening and monitoring reports • Social care protocols (for customer services) • Message maps and strategy statements • Policies • Guidelines • Live video interviews and press conferences

(Continued)

Table 14.1 (Continued)	
Specialization	Content to Create
Journalism	<ul><li>Stories</li><li>Updates (short and long form)</li><li>Features</li><li>Articles</li><li>Exclusives</li><li>New formats for content</li><li>Informational infographics</li><li>Experiential stories (VR)</li><li>Investigative reports</li><li>Content editorial calendar</li><li>Video (live, shows, long form, short form)</li></ul>

THOUGHT QUESTIONS

1. Of the four areas covered in this chapter (sports, entertainment, crisis communication, and journalism), which profession would you want to pursue, and why?

2. What are the core best practices crisis communication professionals need to know about social media?

3. What are the similarities between sports, entertainment, crisis communication, and journalism when it comes to social media?

4. What ethical and professional guidelines do journalists and media professionals need to follow when it comes to social media?

5. What are some best practices for networking in the sports industry with social media?

EXERCISES

1. You have the choice of applying for a specialized position in social media, and the three positions offered are in entertainment, crisis communication, and journalism. Provide a brief overview of each, and explain their core differences and similarities, and which one you would be most qualified for in social media.

2. You want to produce a great portfolio of work for your social media internship application with *The Washington Post*. You believe your experience with creative short-form content in memes qualifies you for this internship. Outline some steps to take to make yourself a strong candidate for this position online. Identify three steps you will take in order to accomplish this. Discuss two work samples you will create to include in your portfolio.

3. You are working with a boutique agency specializing in entertainment and social media practices. You have been asked by your vice president to analyze the social media accounts for Ninja, the popular gamer, as he explores getting into acting. Conduct

a social media audit for Ninja, discuss three strategies you would recommend to help him with his social media accounts, and propose an idea to generate buzz for the franchise on social media.

4. You are working for a crisis communication firm, and you find out your client, Ellen DeGeneres, has become a trending topic on social media due to a significant personal scandal as well as a scandal connected to her talk show. This has become global news and created outrage for many people. Your firm has asked you to help address and respond to this crisis on its official social media accounts. Analyze the situation based on what is discussed on social media and in the traditional media, and provide a brief overview of the situation. Outline the strategies you will take to handle this crisis, what social media tools and resources you will use, and how you will evaluate these for the client.

REFERENCES

Beaujon, A. (2019, June 19). There is, in fact, a plan behind the *Washington Post*'s gloriously weird TikTok. *Washingtonian*. https://www.washingtonian.com/2019/06/19/there-is-in-fact-a-plan-behind-the-washington-posts-gloriously-weird-tiktok/

Buchwald, Y. (2016, September 17). How social media has transformed entertainment marketing. *Social Media Week*. https://social mediaweek.org/blog/2016/09/social-media-transformed-entertainment-marketing/

Coombs, T. (2013). *Crisis, social media, and zombies*. Presented at NEMO Campus Helsingborg. https://www.youtube.com/watch?v=Sospe3H9oMs

DeMers, J. (2016, May 2). The 7 worst (and most amusing) mistakes brands have ever made on social media. *Forbes*. https://www.forbes.com/sites/jaysondemers/2016/05/02/the-7-worst-and-most-amusing-mistakes-brands-have-ever-made-on-social-media/

Duboff, J. (2016, September 16). Examining Beyoncé's social-media mastery: Less is always more. *Vanity Fair*. https://www.vanityfair.com/style/2016/09/beyonce-social-media-instagram-studies

Engel, M. (2017, August 28). If J. J. Watt can do it for Houston, so can Joel Osteen. *Star-Telegram*. http://www.star-telegram.com/sports/spt-columns-blogs/mac-engel/article169850902.html

Engle, M. (n.d.). *Fake news, propaganda, and disinformation: Learning to critically evaluate media sources; Infographic: Spot fake news*. Cornell University Library. https://guides.library.cornell.edu/evaluate_news/infographic

Enthoven, J. (2019, August 7). How to use memes: A guide for marketers. *Social Media Examiner*. https://www.socialmediaexaminer.com/how-to-use-memes-guide-for-marketers/

#Fail: 29 of the biggest corporate brand social media flubs (Research brief). (2017, March 17). *CB Insights*. https://www.cbinsights.com/research/corporate-social-media-fails/

Foster, M., Kent, L., Lewis, A., & Said-Moorhouse, L. (2019). *Meghan, Duchess of Sussex, sues UK tabloid as Harry denounces "bullying" British media*. CNN. https://www.cnn.com/2019/10/01/uk/prince-harry-and-meghan-sue-uk-tabloid-gbr-intl/index.html

Gulliver. (2018, March 14). United Airlines kills another pet. *The Economist*. https://www.economist.com/blogs/gulliver/2018/03/it-s-dog-s-life

Keys, K. (2017, July 17). Are you prepared for a social media crisis? *Forbes*. https://www.forbes.com/sites/forbesagencycouncil/2017/07/17/are-you-prepared-for-a-social-media-crisis/

Langer, E. (2014, January 15). *The five-year anniversary of Twitter's defining moment*. CNBC. https://www.cnbc.com/2014/01/15/the-five-year-anniversary-of-twitters-defining-moment.html

A letter on justice and open debate. (2020, July 7). *Harper's Magazine*. https://harpers.org/a-letter-on-justice-and-open-debate/

Lyft [@lyft]. (2021, March 9). Response to passenger [Tweet]. Twitter. https://twitter.com/lyft/status/1369372936210092037

McIntyre, H. (2017, August 22). Taylor Swift has returned to social media with these cryptic videos: Is new music imminent? *Forbes*. https://www.forbes

.com/sites/hughmcintyre/2017/08/22/taylor-swift-has
-returned-to-social-media-with-these-cryptic-videos
-is-new-music-imminent/

Newman, D. (2017, April 25). Top six digital transformation trends in media and entertainment. *Forbes*.
https://www.forbes.com/sites/daniel newman/
2017/04/25/top-six-digital-transformation-trends-in
-media-and-entertainment/

Nicholson, A. (2017, September 20). How successful journalists use social media. *Cision*. https://www
.cision.com/us/2017/09/how-successful-journalists
-use-social-media/

NPR. (2017, July). Social media: The NPR way.
NPR Ethics Handbook. http://ethics.npr.org/tag/
social-media/

Reuters. (n.d.). Reporting from the internet and using
social media. In *Handbook of Journalism*. http://hand
book.reuters.com/index.php?title=Reporting_From_
the_Internet_And_Using_Social_Media

Shearer, E., & Grieco, E. (2019, October 2). *Americans
are wary of the role social media sites play in delivering
the news*. Pew Research Center's Journalism Project.
https://www.journalism.org/2019/10/02/americans
-are-wary-of-the-role-social-media-sites-play-in-deli
vering-the-news/

Social media and journalism: How to effectively reach
the public. (2020, May 11). *Sprout Social*. https://sprout
social.com/insights/social-media-and-journalism/

Society of Professional Journalists. (n.d.). *Social media
guidelines*. https://www.spj.org/social-media-guide
lines.asp

Stringhini, G., & Zannettou, S. (2020, August 15).
We analyzed 1.8 million images on Twitter to learn
how Russian trolls operate. *Fast Company*. https://www
.fastcompany.com/90540452/we-analyzed-1-8-mil
lion-images-on-twitter-to-learn-how-russian-trolls
-operate

Temin, D. (2017, September 9). Equifax: A
Category 5 cybersecurity storm. *Forbes*. https://
www.forbes.com/sites/daviatemin/2017/09/09/
equifax-a-category-5-cybersecurity-crisis-storm/

The Times issues social media guidelines for the newsroom. (2017, October 13; updated 2020). *The New York
Times*. https://www.nytimes.com/2017/10/13/reader
-center/social-media-guidelines.html

Wellemeyer, J. (2017, August 31). This teenager
was making $4,000 a month reposting memes on
Instagram—Until he got purged. *MarketWatch*.
https://www.marketwatch.com/story/instagrams
-purge-of-meme-accounts-cost-this-teenager-his
-only-income-of-4000-a-month-2019-08-07

15

HOW SOCIAL MEDIA IS APPLIED

Exploring Different Specializations + Case Studies II

Learning Objectives

After reading this chapter, you will be able to

- Discuss the key ways sports, social care, nonprofits, health care, and international campaigns integrate social media into their industries and practices

- Explain the best practices and guidelines for social media to note for social care, nonprofits, health care, and international campaigns

INTRODUCTION

As discussed in the previous chapter, there are many different areas to specialize in and focus on within a particular role (e.g., crisis communications and reporting) or industry (e.g., memes and entertainment). Social media is a core duty and area of practice that crosses all disciplines and rules, but each industry and specialization has a unique take on how to approach social media for communication and business practices. It is important to note that more areas of focus can be applied and discussed in regard to social media than can be included in one or two chapters.

This second chapter on applied social media provides an additional overview of several different areas in which social media is applied. In this chapter, we cover how sports, social care, nonprofits, health care, and international organizations and campaigns integrate social media into their practices, as well as some of the challenges, opportunities, and case studies relevant to these respective industries.

Carl Schmid, Director of Digital Strategy for Louisville Athletics

Social Media and Sports

Introduction

I grew up in Cincinnati and made the decision to attend the University of Cincinnati, majoring in architecture, but after two years in the program realized it wasn't for me and switched to sports administration. The idea of turning my love of sports in to a job was pretty enticing. One thing led to another. I got a role in the recruiting department for the Bearcats football team as a student, which became a full-time role in the football video department and eventually oversaw the social presence for UC athletics. After almost 10 years between student and employee with the Bearcats, I kept with the red and black color scheme but made the short move down the Ohio River to Louisville to join the University of Louisville Athletic Department in July 2019.

How did you get your start in social media?

I got my start as a student at Cincinnati while working in the football recruiting department. At the time the official football Twitter account wasn't an established presence and the person who had the account didn't really have the time, so I was given the "keys" to the account. We slowly built the account over the first year and a half at which point I was moved to the football video department full-time. As our assistant video coordinator, I was still creating content for and maintaining the account, while also handling video responsibilities. Game days were especially interesting as I would live-tweet the game while filming one of the angles for the coaches to review afterward.

What is your favorite part of working in your area of expertise in social media?

Hands down one of the best parts of the job is getting to know the student-athletes, tell their stories and celebrate their successes. Working with student-athletes for a good part of their collegiate career you develop a relationship with them, which makes it more rewarding when you're able to celebrate those special moments. There's also nothing like game day, covering rivalry games and the post-season. I've been lucky to cover a few conference championship teams and while it can be chaotic when the buzzer hits zero, it's so rewarding to look back on the moments that were captured/shared.

What is one thing you can't live without while working in social media?

My phone/laptop, for obvious reasons, and chargers. On a typical game day I carry three or four chargers, a wall charger, and a power strip just to be safe. I can't run the risk of my phone or laptop dying on me while trying to do my job. Oh . . . and coffee.

Favorite social media account (person/brand/etc.) to follow and why?

There are so many people that I've connected with and love to follow for their insights.

From a job perspective, SkullSparks is a fantastic resource for those in the #SMsports space as they are always shining a light on great work being done.

What is the most challenging part of working in social media?

The "always on" mentality. I always describe what I do as a 24/7/365 job that never sleeps and never stops. We have to be cognizant not only of what we are doing and trying to accomplish, but also what is going on in the world around us. Do we have something scheduled that could appear tone deaf based on a potential situation we hadn't or couldn't anticipate? On top of this, working at the department level in athletics, it's being aware of what is going on with all of our teams, tracking accomplishments/ stats, and helping with additional coverage for events like the post-season, major awards, etc.

What do you wish you had known when you were starting out?

It's OK to reach out and ask for help. When I started out it was a lot of the "one-man band" type mentality, and I put a lot of pressure to compete with schools that had far more resources that we did, which can very quickly lead to burnout. The thing with social in college athletics is that every team, program, school, etc., is all judged on the same plane no matter the amount of resources they may have behind the scenes. While our work is judged in a very public space against each other, most of the people behind the scenes are willing and ready to answer questions about how they achieved a particular piece of content. There may be a way to take their process or approach and adapt it to fit within the resources you have available at your school.

What are three marketable skills a social media professional needs to have to work in the industry?

How to create. It doesn't have to be super high-end productions, but can you bring value to a team in creating various pieces of content. Maybe it's updating a graphic template, taking a few quick photos, or even capturing video with a cell phone—all can play a vital role in a brand or account's presence.

How to write and communicate well. Copy isn't easy. Some have a knack for writing and others don't, but that's OK. Even if you're not the one writing a posting and hitting send, having a grasp on how to write and communicate well is an effective tool in the workplace when working on a team.

How to manage time and projects. There is so much going on at all times with social. The ability to manage time effectively and potentially balance a multitude of projects is something that takes time to develop but is very valuable.

If you had to choose a song to walk out to in a presentation on social media, what would it be and why?

"Lights Come On," by Jason Aldean. I tend to listen to a lot of the newer country, but feel like for a walk-out song it's gotta have some energy to it. Aldean tends to be a nice blend of country and rock, but the song also talks to the excitement of being at an event, which is how game days can feel. The usual weekdays are a bit of a grind, up early and working late, lots of coffee, but when game day rolls around, it's a totally different atmosphere.

Carl Schmid is the director of digital strategy for Louisville Athletics at the University of Louisville. He can be followed on social media @CarlSchmid and @GoCards.

OVERVIEW OF SOCIAL MEDIA AND SPORTS

The sports industry and social media have become integrated. When exploring the latest innovative storytelling and scraping techniques professionals can implement into their campaigns, some of the best and most creative examples come from the sports industry, at both collegiate and professional levels. Social media has transformed not only how people get information about sports but how people consume information, share and create stories from the team, engage with fans, and use recruiting mechanisms.

▶ **Photo 15.1**
Cody Rigsby Facebook Post on Merchandise Update

Source: Facebook/ @Cody Rigsby - Peloton

As Jeremy Darlow discusses in *Brands Win Championships* (2015) and *Darlow Rules* (2020), athletes can use social media not only for personal branding opportunities but to make a significant difference in society. Not only are these athletes role models, but they have a level of influence that brings forth awareness of important issues. Athletes with a strong social media presence include LeBron James (basketball), Donovan Mitchell (basketball), Naomi Osaka (tennis), Katie Ledecky (swimming), and Allyson Felix (track and field). Each of these athletes knows the power of their platform and how to use it strategically in their sport and beyond. In some cases, teams take advantage of social media to stand up for causes (e.g., the National Basketball Association [NBA] and National Football League [NFL] on racial justice protests), to support trends (e.g., TikTok challenges with Got Milk and Katie Ledecky and NFL football player Juju Smith-Schuster), and to give fans the chance to meet their sports heroes in person (e.g., NASCAR). Bringing together fans and sports professionals can create a lifelong memory and fan for life, online and offline.

Taking advantage of the right moment on social media can lead to future opportunities; the goal is to sustain the moment created by the initial post that captures the attention of the mass audience. In several cases, athletes, thanks to the use of their own platforms, have been able to make a difference and help others. Athletes who compete in CrossFit, for example, have used their platforms to share workouts, tips, and messages with their fans in a way that creates a true community for them online (Fitzgerald, 2017). Their ability to use social media leverage to get sponsorships from brands shows the shift in athletes becoming their own brands (Fitzgerald, 2017). At the same time, brands such as Peloton have relied a lot on social media specifically for their instructors to build their own fan base and brand, while also allowing the instructors to sell their own branded merchandise. Peloton instructor Cody Rigsby has done this with his themed bike classes called XOXO, Cody, and has translated this mantra into his own line of fitness wear with Peloton (Photo 15.1). Most of the lead generation for these purchases comes from social media, which Peloton has incorporated in not just their overall brand culture but for their instructors as well. Rigsby is very active and present on social media (particularly Facebook and Instagram) to engage with fans and let them know updates on what classes he will be teaching, as well as offering exclusive first looks for his merchandise with Peloton. With this, Rigsby has become a strong internal brand influencer for Peloton to help generate sales for their swag and merchandise, all of which fosters a strong brand community on social media.

Personal branding among athletes has become a big focus for many professionals to specialize in along with brands, such as opendorse and DARLOW, to name a couple. With the discussion in college athletics on allowing student-athletes to be able to make money off of their brand, more consultants, tools, and companies will arise to help these young professionals navigate the new social and digital world of branding and marketing themselves, which was not present or available previously until after their eligibility is over.

Athletes can come together to use their social media power in a time of crisis. J. J. Watt of the Houston Texans, currently one of the most recognizable players in the NFL, uses social media to bring awareness to and raise funds for causes in his community. When Hurricane Harvey hit Houston in 2017, Watt was quoted as saying, "To see [Houston] going through such a disaster and not be there, not be able to help, it's very difficult to have to watch it from afar and see it on TV, and look at streets that you know and you can barely recognize them under all the water" (Boren, 2017; see also Photo 15.2).

Along with other sports figures and stores, Watt reached out to his Twitter community to see if he could raise money to support the Houston community after Hurricane Harvey. Watt hoped to raise $200,000 for those impacted by the hurricane (Rapaport, 2017). In a video, he asked his online community for support; thanks to his extensive fanbase and the power of social media, he raised over $16 million. Watt's success did not go unnoticed by professionals in the social media community. In fact, many people said that this was one of the best social media campaigns of the year. It was authentic and connected to a community, and the emotional connection played out on social media to support each other was tremendous. Without social media, this support would not have gone viral. Social media can also be used to raise awareness and inspire action for specific events. One example of this is the NBA and Women's National Basketball Association's (WNBA's) posts about the racial injustice protests in 2020. Both sporting organizations put forth statements on social media along with messages from their teams on this issue.

▶ **Photo 15.2**
J. J. Watt's Twitter Account for Hurricane Harvey

Source: Twitter/ @JJWatt

Using social media platforms to take a stand on a position they believe in has become a trend among athletes at all levels—collegiate, professional, and retired—in the sports industry.

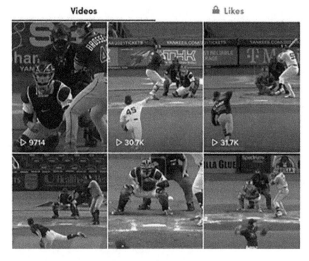

▶ Photo 15.3
Tampa Bay Rays on TikTok

Source: TikTok/ @rays

Sports teams are ahead of the game when it comes to using new tools and platforms for content purposes. For example, the NFL not only embraced TikTok as part of their overall social content strategy, but they created a separate section of their NFL Social Lab site that showed their audiences what they were creating and how it reflected their overall brand voice ("NFL TikTok," n.d.). Football is not the only sport to capture attention on TikTok. The Tampa Bay Rays, a Major League Baseball team, created quite the following for their in-game and off-game commentary on TikTok to entertain and connect with their audiences. Most of the content is micro recaps of big moments that happened with the Rays in their quest for the 2020 World Series, which they ultimately lost to the LA Dodgers. However, in an age where audiences are consuming vast amounts of micro content off of their feeds, this allows audiences to get a glimmer of not only what baseball is like but also what the Tampa Bay Rays are doing online. TikTok for Tampa Bay Rays and other teams, also allows personality and brand voice to come loud and clear, as shown in their bio. In Photo 15.3, the Tampa Bay Rays showcase short clips of player highlights during the game, which has the potential of not only entertaining current fans of the team but reaching new audiences for the baseball team on TikTok. There may be others who may want to call themselves the CEO of Savage TikTok!

College teams can bring a unique angle to social media to place them in the spotlight. One college team that excels in innovation and creative storytelling is Clemson Athletics. Under the leadership of Jonathan Gantt and assisted by Jeff Kallin and a group of interns, Clemson transformed the intersection of sports and social media (otherwise known as #SMsports). Other schools, such as USC, Florida, Michigan, and Ohio State, have embraced their creativity on social and even added specific roles within the athletic department, for example, director of creative services or director of creative strategy.

When it comes to sports and social media, we sometimes have to take a moment to breathe. There is constant pressure to be innovative and creative despite limited resources. It is important to keep a realistic perspective about your role, understand we are all human, and remember that it's okay to not be on social media every minute of every day.

Best practices to consider when exploring a career in sports and social media include the following:

- *Network online and offline.* Volunteer at your local university and with its sports teams, or even a club sport. You will get experience, which is key for sports and social media, and this could lead to future opportunities. Connect with great organizations like Front Office Sports (@frntofficesport) and participate on Twitter with fellow professionals using the #SMsports hashtag. Twitter is the Rolodex for networking and connecting with sports. Follow, reach out, and build these positive connections. Write content, share content, and participate in the community by sharing valuable insights and perspectives.

- *Invest in skills and training.* In many cases, a small team manages social media for a sports team. It could be a few professionals, or just you. Invest in all of the skills you can in order to create, disseminate, and analyze content. You must have a passion, of course, for sports, but you also want to see what other skills you can bring to the table. If you work for a sports team, reach out to local high schools and universities to see if any volunteers and students would like to help out.

- *Understand the field of social media is extremely competitive, so be creative in standing out with your work and experiences.* Sports is more than covering sporting events and athletes in the 21st century. Professionals need to be graphic designers, copywriters, videographers, storytellers, and even crisis managers. Experience matters, and doing the bare minimum for a job posting or internship opportunity is not going to cut it. Going beyond what is expected in a creative and impactful manner is the name of the game. You must be your best advocate and let your work (and social media presence) tell the story.

- *Don't go for the hard sell with teams for opportunities.* Offer what you can bring to the table when it comes to sports. Reach out to the teams for volunteer work and start small, and work to take your talents to the next level. Don't assume just because you are a fan you will get a job. Instead of telling sports teams why you need them, let them know what you can do with your experience and expertise.

- *Don't become starstruck or distracted when around high-profile stars, athletes, and coaches.* You have a job to do in social media, and you can't be a distraction to your fellow colleagues, fans, and team by getting a selfie with a celebrity or sports figure. You need to take a moment, collect yourself, and remind yourself of your job. Yes, many aspects of sports are glamorous and exciting, but at the end of the day, certain duties and expectations need to be met, and these can't be done if you are distracted.

In summary, looking at the sports industry for inspiration is one way to brainstorm new ideas, but don't forget to keep building on the creative social media education practices established in other areas. There are certain professionals and teams to review, follow, and engage with online to start a conversation with them about their work, but also follow what they are doing to continue to push the envelope in creative and strategic executions on social media. Here are some professionals to follow and add to your network in the sports industry:

- Jonathan Gantt (@Jonathan_Gantt) of Clemson Athletics
- Jessica Smith (@warjesseagle) of Stewart Haas Racing
- Kelly Mosier (@kmosier42), head of programming at Hudl

- Russell Houghtaling (@digital_russ), associate athletic director for ideation at Oregon State University

- Reva Labbe (@sorevawaslike) of ESPN and College GameDay

- Kyle Benzion (@LantaBenzion) of the Atlanta Falcons

- Adam White (@FOSAdam) of Front Office Sports

- Jeff Kallin (@CUJeffKallin) of Clemson Athletics

- Stuart Drew (@studrew1) of the Miami Dolphins

- Justin Karp (@jskarp), director of social media for NBCSports

- Matt Ziance (@MattZiance), social media for NBCSports and NBC Olympics

- Chris Littmann (@chrislittmann), director of content and platform strategy for NASCAR

- Nick Marquez (@Quezzymoto) of Facebook and Instagram College Partnerships

- Will Yoder (@WillYoder), sports partnerships at Instagram

A list of sports and social media resources is also provided in this book's companion workbook *Portfolio Building Activities in Social Media*.

Whitney Drake, Manager at General Motors

Social Media and Social Care

Introduction

By day I work at General Motors in operational excellence looking for efficiency and cost-savings opportunities, and by night I'm wife to an engineer and mom to twins. I studied communication at Michigan State University and received my master's in integrated marketing communications from West Virginia University. Throughout my career, I have had the opportunity to work with great brands such as Procter & Gamble, 3M, T-Mobile, Children's Place, Budweiser, and Ford. I'm fortunate enough to be bringing my experience to the next generation by teaching both at Wayne State University

and online at West Virginia University. I call "Pure Michigan" home, but try not to let the grass grow and enjoy traveling as much as possible.

How did you get your start in social media?

I started my social media journey at Ford when I ran its media and internal communication website.

What is your favorite part of working in your social media area of expertise?

I love the fact that social media is always changing and requires us to use both the art and science parts of our brain.

OVERVIEW OF SOCIAL MEDIA AND SOCIAL CARE

As Whitney Drake discussed, social care has become an integrated part of contemporary social media duties. It is about not only providing creative executions of campaigns but also fostering and maintaining existing relationships among members of an online community. At first glance, since customer care is an important relationship-building and communication practice, many assume it is part of the duty and responsibility list for public relations and strategic communications. However, others say it belongs to marketing because it involves reputation management, data, and sales.

Keith Quesenberry (2016) proposed in the *Harvard Business Review* that social care should not be in the hands of a marketing department. Sometimes, it actually needs its own department, which happens to be the case for General Motors. At General Motors, the separate social care department works with marketing, data marketing, public relations, communications, and other associated departments within the brand.

While social care may look like a simple yet overwhelming task for an organization or brand to accomplish, some actions can be taken to create a social care program for an organization of any size. With reputation and relationships on the line, social care must be a top priority for all brands, organizations, and even individual professionals. Quesenberry (2016) offered clear steps for setting up a proactive social care program for businesses and social media professionals, including the following:

- Establish a team of professionals trained in customer relationship management tools to address all aspects of social media information effectively, consistently, and in a timely manner.

- Create designated responsibilities and training protocols for customer service duties for each team member; have protocols in place to make sure the brand voice is consistent among team members and in conversations online, and for how to evaluate and report these conversations.

- Assign specific tasks for certain employees and how they will participate in each conversation online. Have a reporting protocol in place to keep everyone on the team informed with each transaction.

- Establish key performance indicators (KPIs) to determine success or failure for customer service on social media. After measuring these KPIs, draft a report to outline these metrics (e.g., influence of customer, response time, average response time, sentiment of conversation, shares, conversions, and other key relationship and behavioral metrics).

Social care has risen to become one of the most important specializations in the social media industry and has been defined in various ways, including as "social customer service." However, social care is more than just customer service. Social care is a "more robust approach to understanding social care positions this approach to communication via social networks as more than simply an interaction with customers, but rather an experience where key stakeholders, reaching far more than only customers, develop strong perceptions of a brand's credibility, reputation and, ultimately, cultivate loyalty" (Kim & Freberg, 2020, pp. 2–3). As Hyken (2017) mentioned in *Forbes*, social care is the new marketing for professionals, because a great experience with a brand not only impacts the individual interacting with the brand specifically but also provides an opportunity for the individual to share this experience with others. Taking the time to respond makes a world of difference to people, and it is an expectation for brands to not only respond to customers but do so in a timely manner. Customers and other members of the online community want to make their lives easier by engaging with a brand online—getting their questions answered or having their situation addressed—in a professional and seamless manner. Investing in the right policies, training, and tools for providing a responsive customer service experience for customers will help brands in many ways.

Strong customer service and a social care program can help brands by

- making it easy for customers to get on with their business and perhaps spend more money in the process since they had a good customer service experience, and

- understanding it's not only the products people are concerned about but the experience. A great experience will motivate people to come back and do business or engage with your content more. A negative experience not only will create unhappiness, but could spark outrage in the community, leading to a negative impact online for your reputation.

Brands, individuals, agencies, and other organizations usually post a statement on their website in a social media section (or occasionally under media or press relations) regarding how responsive they are online. In addition, many brands use chat bots (artificial intelligence that is programmed to respond appropriately to certain questions). Even though brands such as Southwest Airlines use messenger bots to engage with audiences, saving time and streamlining the process, a delicate and human touch is also necessary for engaging with audiences.

Facebook is not the only place where customer service happens. In many cases, customer service occurs on a completely different platform. While all social media platforms have a protocol for handling certain situations, the go-to place (especially in certain markets and industries) for inquiries regarding customer service questions is Twitter. In fact, the number of customer service requests and interactions on Twitter from 2015 to 2017 increased by 250% (Frumkin, 2017).

While many brands have chat bots or automated forms of communicating with audiences, this is just one online method for sharing the work they do to take care of audiences in a time of need. One customer representative at Delta was able to help a family with a special needs child before they were scheduled to fly, and as a result, they created a stronger brand relationship. Delta not only responded to the family but provided the special needs child with an Elmo toy and a mask. This moment happened online, but because of the Delta employee's kindness, the family shared it on social. In response to the Delta representative's kindness, the family wrote the following:

> I was speaking with an employee named Sarah about an upcoming flight. I explained that my son has special needs and is very nervous about surgical masks because of his many surgeries over the years. She helped me understand that there are options in regard to mask design, and she has actually made some for her family. I asked if she had ever seen any with Elmo on them as he is my son's favorite. She wasn't sure, but gave me some guidance on where to look. About a week later, I received a package. To my surprise, it was a note from Sarah with masks for our family, along with a very special Elmo one for my son! I was floored that she (1) actually made and sent them to us and (2) remembered my son's name and how important Elmo was to him. I could go on and on, but I wanted to take a few minutes and make sure that you know the value that Sarah brings to people as well as to a total stranger on the phone. I'm very blessed to have met her.

Delta reposted this message on Facebook, adding "Even in uncertain times, stories like this remind us that the kindness of a stranger can make all the difference." This is just another form of social care that social media professionals need to consider.

Taco Bell is another example of a brand that listens and takes note on what needs to be done to address a concern or issue on social media. When social media professional Alexa Heinrich wrote in an *Adweek* commentary about their lack of closed captions on one of their product announcements featuring their CEO, they responded with a new video and update thanking Alexa for letting them know. This shows the brand is listening, and acknowledging what audiences are saying by taking action to address these points in a timely manner. These social care practices will help establish sustainable and strong relationships on and offline for the brand.

Several brands have been praised for their strong customer service engagement over the years, including Southwest Airlines, GoFundMe, JetBlue, and Slim Jim. Each social media platform serves as a front door for the brand on social media, so investing in the training and procedures and developing a culture of proactive customer relations measures will reward brands more than just financially—it can be instrumental to increasing brand loyalty and advocacy for customers, leading to more endorsements and returns over the long term.

Best Practices for Social Care

Social care is a delicate and strategic area of specialization within the social media field, and as discussed in this section, some brands and organizations have succeeded in addressing needs and conversations online. Others have not been as successful. Keep the following best practices in mind when working with brands to implement social care engagement practices:

- *Invest in customer service.* To be the best in social care, this is a must. Investment into social care takes many forms, but tools for monitoring, responding to, and listening to social media are always part of the equation. A robust customer relationship management tool can streamline the conversations and metrics for a brand, which will help in reporting and strategy sessions. In addition, training team members to know not only the social media tools used for customer service but also how to respond professionally and on brand is important. These items take both time and money, but what is your brand's reputation worth in the end? It's priceless, and because customer service presently drives business, it is a necessary investment.

- *Realize there are people behind the screen for social care teams.* Yes, we have all had challenging days that make us think the world is going to end, but the people behind the brand's social media handle are humans as well. We do not know what is going on in their lives, so kindness and empathy for both parties is very important to remember.

- *Remember that timing is crucial.* Most platforms indicate how long the team will take to respond to your inquiry, and this is an important element to measure and note as part of the overall perception audiences have about how committed a team is to responding to questions or concerns online.

- *Be present and engaged on the same channels as your audiences.* This means having a presence on social media platforms and conversing with the individuals who mention you on social media—whether via tagging or @ your handle. You want to have a timely conversation. One update and response back can mean the world to audience members.

- *Have templates in place for responses and inquiries, and try to make these personalized.* Do not use automated responses. Everyone can see through this and would perceive it as not being transparent. As part of the social media team representing the brand, make sure you make a positive first impression and your exchange starts off on the best foot possible, especially if the other party is emotional. While bots may be the way of the future, taking the extra time to tailor the brand's exchange on social media makes a difference. While technology changes, as humans, we still crave human interactions.

- *Recognize that you do not have to be in every conversation.* Being on social media and working in the field is a 24/7 job, but this does not mean you have to be actively engaged *all* the time. Be aware of what topics you want to jump on, but also be aware of when it's best to sit back and listen. There is a huge amount of pressure to be active on social media, but constant engagement is not always the best approach. Yes, you may experience a lot of fear of missing out (FOMO), but it's not worth it to update, share, or create something that allows others to perceive you negatively.

- *Listen and understand the situation and context.* One of the most important elements of social care is understanding the situation the other person (or group of people) is in. Empathy goes a long way in handling this, so make sure you listen to what else is going on. For example, do not make light of a crisis situation or tragedy. In this context, you have to be responsive and professional, yet aware of the emotions tied to the situation.

- *Don't let your own emotions get the best of you at the risk of the brand's reputation on social media.* We are all human, but a brand's account is not the place to interject your own emotions. Do not create a crisis situation when a problem can be handled in an appropriate way. Take a deep breath and reach out to your fellow social media team members to get their take. Respond in a way that you wouldn't mind seeing in a screen shot. Always take the high road, even if the other member of the conversation does not.

Bella Portaro-Kueber, Founder and Creative Director of Bella Vita

Social Media and Nonprofits

Introduction

My name is Bella Portaro-Kueber. I'm a social media marketer that started a boutique marketing company called Bella Vita Media in 2010. I'm not only a creative director but a content creator because of my joy for bringing brands to life through the power of words and images. I'm also a freelance writer, blogger @ Bella of Louisville, and an entrepreneur with start-up companies that provide my daily life with beautiful scenery of curiosity for the unknown changes that take place every single day.

How did you get your start in social media?

I started as a community manager for an event company and a design firm. This was when social media began to appeal to businesses to harness its powers into today's superhuman force. It has been a wild ride to grow with social media as it happens. It evolves every single day; therefore, it never becomes redundant.

What is your favorite part of working in your area of expertise in social media?

When I first started developing voices for brands and nonprofits. While I still love doing both, my evolving area of expertise is market activation and elevation. I work with brands that are going into new markets, and I help them sort through the wild world of "Influencers" and the smoke and mirrors that exist within that realm; I use three forms of auditing to give my diligent advice to prevent ROI fraud.

(Continued)

HUMANS OF SOCIAL MEDIA

What is one thing you can't live without working in social media?

My phone and I go everywhere together. Social media requires constant contact. You could have a full-blown PR crisis in under five minutes, and your phone is your savior to keep you connected to what the buzz online is. While PR is a different engine than social media marketing, it's still an important component that marketers must be aware of. Marketers should never live in fear for a client or a brand we work for because we're their cheerleaders. Our messages are positive and impactful, while our minds must be balanced to listen to the chatter about the brand.

What are three marketable skills a social media professional needs to have to work in the industry?

1. Consumer knowledge: Your job is marketing a brand to others. Therefore you must have a laser-sharp mind about what consumers think, need, feel, and want.

2. Storytelling: Almost everything we've learned in life stems from stories. Pull components from every story method you've heard and observe what made them stay with you. It's a form of art, which requires you to be an artist who can understand and share.

3. Creativity: Instead of creating ads for brands that tell consumers what they need, change it up and make it about what consumers are thinking.

What is your favorite social media account (person/brand/team/etc.) to follow and why?

Social media is a trunk full of treasures, isn't it? Each Instagram account that I love has different components that make them my favorite. I love @InfluencersInTheWild for comedic relief. @TravelAndLeisure to feed my wandering desires. @TheDodo because I love their mission and I'm obsessed with fur-baby videos. They make life better.

Where do you go to keep up to date with trends and continue learning about social media?

I'm currently a student at West Virginia University in the graduate program for integrated marketing communications. The knowledge I learn from the program broadens my horizons daily. When I'm not in class, I love reading online and print publications based on marketing, public relations, and tech developments. I loved "Social Media Week" when conventions were still a thing pre-COVID. Times are changing, and I'm planning on attending more conferences digitally to stay creative and continue evolving with social media.

What is the most challenging part of working in social media?

The incredible part of social media is also the worst thing about social media: You're always connected. COVID-19 gave everyone across the world a moment to stop and breathe. I won't lie; I was grateful for the break and the ability to take a step back and absorb how we can do better. We can be connected and step away from our job. Putting that into practice is hard now that the world is opening back up, but if you really want to overcome that challenge, you must give yourself screentime regulations and follow them.

If you had to choose a song to walk out to in a presentation on social media, what would it be and why?

"Dangerous," by Big Data. The lyrics are all about how major corporations in the United States use data to understand consumers. It stores the data where we can analyze it and monetize it if we're the collector. As marketers, data provides truth.

OVERVIEW OF SOCIAL MEDIA AND NONPROFITS

Nonprofits have used social media very successfully due to its history as an affordable yet effective means to communicate and engage with audiences. Many successful nonprofits are some of the most followed on social media for their creative campaigns, executions of key issues, and innovative uses of new tools and platforms. Some are also effective in creating strong stories across all of the social media platforms. Top-ranked social media accounts for nonprofits include the National Geographic Society, TED Talks, NPR, WikiLeaks, the Museum of Modern Art, Metro United Way, and World Wildlife Fund. Sprout Social (Johnston, 2017) listed several goals for nonprofits to note when it comes to integrating social media into their organization:

- Community engagement and education

- Brand building and reputation management

- Program recruitment

- Fundraising

The shift from a "pay to play" mentality has impacted nonprofits significantly, which means they have had to be a bit more creative in their uses of resources and tools to break through the noise and connect to their key audiences and donors. However, nonprofits must produce creative content that will motivate others to donate and engage with them on social media. According to Sprout Social (Johnston, 2017), nonprofits should think about the following questions:

- *What problems do people have in their own lives when trying to live out the values they share with your organization?* Listen to and monitor what others say on social media, and also conduct your own research by conversing with audience members. What are some problems and challenges facing the community that you could address? What are some areas needing solutions? Think about how these challenges could turn into opportunities for the nonprofit to address and fill gaps.

- *What tips or tools can you give people to make their lives easier?* Nonprofits are not only looked to for support in handling certain key issues and challenges but also expected to provide resources for education, training, and community building. What pieces of content could be created to help foster a strong culture of education and helping others? What tools could be useful and relevant for audiences relative to their community?

The COVID-19 pandemic created many challenges for non-profit organizations. Those with certain social media strategies pre-COVID had to adjust their practices once the virus became widespread. According to *Fast Company* (Conrardy & Post, 2020), some new practices for nonprofits included the following:

- *Asking* "What is my organization doing differently to help people and communities respond and recover?"

- *Rethinking angles for stories about the nonprofit.* Draft stories that lean on grit, resilience, and the ways in which the pandemic has caused you to evolve your approach for the good of the people your organization serves. Inspirational stories always get audiences to think differently about organizations doing well in their space.

- *Focusing on taking specific actions on certain issues.* Talking about an issue is one thing, but what are you actually doing? What are you doing specifically about important social, environmental, and industry-related issues in your community? What are you doing specifically to address the needs of your audiences? Specifics and action steps are needed more than ever.

Two ways that nonprofits have actively tried to engage and encourage others to take part in their campaign efforts on social media are crowdsourcing and crowdfunding. **Crowdsourcing** is the process by which groups of individuals come together to provide their insights based on a call to action from an organization, a brand, or even an individual. **Crowdfunding** (using sites like GoFundMe) allows people to come together for a specific cause and raise funds to support an issue or organization. While some third-party tools and sites are dedicated to fundraising, some of the major platforms (e.g., Twitter and Facebook) give people the power to donate directly online to specific organizations through an update as well as in a live video session.

One of the most successful crowdfunding campaigns happened in 2014, when people participated in the Ice Bucket Challenge to raise funds to support research by the ALS Association. This campaign was started by Pete Frates to raise awareness of amyotrophic lateral sclerosis (ALS), or Lou Gehrig's disease. Dumping a bucket of ice over your head and calling out people who needed to take on this challenge next became a viral sensation around the world and also one of the biggest fundraising efforts using social media ever. The results were huge, with $220 million to support ALS research raised by over 2 million people participating in this challenge on social media (Chowdhry, 2015). The ALS campaign gained global attention and brought in many people to share, create, and discuss the disease on social media. The campaign was praised for its strategic implementation of certain social media platforms, including Facebook, which led to the Ice Bucket Challenge's receiving the 2015 "Facebook for Good" award (Peterson, 2015). Plus, the ALS campaign emphasized the importance of a strong message and opportunities for audience members to feel compelled to take action. Action steps were not just sharing the URL or donation page to support the research but, rather, creating personalized content in a form of a video to share with family, friends, and others in specific platforms.

Ultimately, as a nonprofit, make sure specific messages and content appear on social media that tie back to the communication plan for the nonprofit. Social media integration for nonprofits should be not an add-on but rather a key part of raising awareness about the efforts of the organization, telling the story of the nonprofit's efforts in its communities, and documenting the return of impact on these communities to create transparency.

Many great nonprofits have done significant work in addressing the needs, issues, and challenges facing society with social media. A few have used social media not only strategically but also creatively in various formats and situations to gain traction for their causes. One nonprofit that has used social media especially strategically and effectively is the Movember Foundation. Founded in 2003 to support the issue of men's health, it started in Australia with the overall purpose of encouraging men to grow out their moustaches in the month of November to raise awareness of men's health (Augure, 2017; see also Photo 15.4). Many brands have partnered with Movember and its cause, including Harry's and TOMS. Surprisingly, Movember has had success not just in the month of November but all year long (Anderson, 2017). Movember has not only empowered users to create content on their own social media channels (e.g., the ALS Association) but also integrated influencers (e.g., YouTuber Kian Lawley) into its campaigns to trigger awareness and shares on social media, which ultimately has continued to be a success for the foundation and cause (Anderson, 2017).

Nonprofits can also bring awareness on certain topics such as autism, which is what *Sesame Street* and Autism Speaks did with the launch of their new character, Julia. As we learned in Chapter 4, which focused on diversity, equity, and inclusion, Julia is the first autistic character on *Sesame Street* and was the focal point of this PSA (public service announcement) campaign. The nonprofit Autism Speaks is focused on bringing more awareness to parents and families about autism and how to get tested, so this collaboration allowed the nonprofit to get more exposure and awareness to a larger audience and mainstream. The campaign was about bringing awareness not just to autism but also to the screening process parents should consider for their children since many do not test for autism until later in life (Paynter, 2019).

▶ **Photo 15.4**
Movember on Instagram

Source: "Instagram Profile Page"; Movember https://www.instagram.com/movember/?hl=en

Another important element that makes a foundation successful in raising awareness of its issue is a branded hashtag, a searchable term that aligns with the name of the foundation. Nonprofits have either done this with their own hashtag for their own organizations, or they have tied hashtags into related issues and challenges. Some hashtags that have gained traction for supporting certain issues include the following:

- World Wildlife Fund's (WWF's) #NoBuildChallenge campaign focused on bringing Fortnite players' attention to the depletion of Earth's natural resources. The campaign asked the players to play through the game without exploiting any natural resources. WWF also asked players to share their experiences on the players' social channels and to livestream the experience via Twitch.

- Charity Water brought global awareness to clean water access. Charity Water uses their social media channels to raise awareness and bring forth stories of their contributions to making sure everyone has access to clean water.

- The John Wayne Cancer Foundation's #ShowYourGrit campaign is a call to action to support the fight against cancer with courage, strength, and grit.

- WWF's #Connect2Earth campaign focused on raising awareness of Earth's resources and asked audiences to tag others to turn their lights out at a certain time to celebrate Earth Hour.

- The Salvation Army's partnership with Chris Strub promoted the #FightForGood campaign (raising awareness of the Christmas holidays in November 2017 through social media efforts). Strub used YouTube, Instagram, and Twitter to share his story and videos with the community to try and raise $10,000 for the Salvation Army.

Best Practices for Nonprofits

As for other specializations within social media, there are some universal best practices to be aware of, but others are specifically unique to the environment and challenges facing nonprofits. If entering the field of nonprofit work with social media, keep in mind some of these best practices:

- *Don't rely on either email or social media—they need to be balanced.* Many times, nonprofits want to go all in for nonprofit social media efforts, and other times, email is their golden ticket to donors' contact information. The best of both worlds is to have a balanced approach. You want to have touch points with each of your audiences on social media, but you also want to connect with them on other channels to continue the conversation.

- *Have responsibilities, duties, and a team in place for social media.* Content creation and reporting are just two responsibilities that need to be in place. However, someone who is specialized in paid ads, fundraising, and sales may also benefit the team by creating messages, content, and a fundraising sales funnel. This will help the nonprofit to connect the dots to move an audience member from being a new member of the community to a donor.

- *Spend the time to really focus and target your messages, channels, and audiences.* You may not have the resources for all of the tools used in the industry, so be creative in choosing the ones to invest in. Think about where your audiences are going based on the reports and data you collect on each social media channel. You may have to shift your messages and strategies to address these evolving changes. Also, make sure to spend time asking which types of content need to be created and which platforms will be the most effective.

- *Allow people the opportunity to share their stories.* If you are able to create stories that allow users to feel comfortable and empowered to share their own stories on social media, then it is a win-win situation for all. Stories that showcase connections, emotions, and personal experiences are more effective (and relatable) for audiences. To accomplish this, you must guide users through how you want them to share these stories and consider what call-to-action statements you want to communicate with them.

Mark Murdock, Director of Social Media for Kindred Healthcare

Social Media and Health Care

Introduction

I grew up in a really small town in middle Tennessee. Sitting with headphones on—in my room, in my closet, in the car—was my escape from feeling isolated.

As a kid, I really wanted to be a DJ. By 14, my mom was driving me to my first job as a DJ on a local station. I eventually branched out into marketing/promotions and got involved with the social media aspect of the job. I've worked on brands including Kindred Healthcare, McDonald's, Big O Tires, the Kentucky Lottery, and CafePress.

How did you get your start in social media?

Before social media was really blowing up, I mentioned in a meeting that no one was taking advantage of the Facebook pages that we had at our company. Sometimes, you don't know what you are volunteering for; it chooses you.

What is your favorite part of working in your social media area of expertise?

Social media changes so often that you have to stay connected to it to be successful. It's like always-on continuing education. I love thinking about how to utilize content pillars, value propositions, and content strategies to express a company's mission. Making connections with people is what I do best.

What is one thing you can't live without while working in social media?

Other than the computer that lives in my pocket and by my bedside, it's my amazing coworkers. Some people have to do this job all by themselves, and I'm really fortunate to have terrific coworkers and friends who enjoy the work just like I do.

What is your favorite social media account (person, brand, etc.) to follow, and why?

I love @jasonfalls not only because he is my friend but also because he is *hilarious*. I love @generalelectric and everything it does. And I love @NASA, because it illustrates the amazing work of humankind traveling to the heavens.

What is the most challenging part of working in social media?

Social media being used to divide our society is hard to ignore.

(Continued)

HUMANS OF SOCIAL MEDIA

You have been active in mentoring future young professionals in social media. What is the most rewarding experience you have had in helping students?

I hired a student from your [Karen Freberg's] class.

What do you wish you had known when you were starting out?

I wish I had had a colleague who brainwashed me into starting a career in social media earlier. I still have a part-time radio shift, but this was the best career move for me.

Mark Murdock is the director of social media for Kindred Healthcare. Before working with Kindred, Mark worked with brands such as CafePress, Four Roses Bourbon, and McDonald's. Mark can be connected with on Twitter at @heyitsmurdock.

OVERVIEW OF SOCIAL MEDIA AND HEALTH CARE

For health care purposes, social media can provide an avenue where patients, customers, and other community members come together. Health care professionals should be aware of several opportunities related to social media. For example, social media offers a lot of benefits for patients to interact with doctors and other patients (participating in virtual support groups, asking questions about doctors, obtaining recommendations for services, etc.) in a virtual community setting (Belbey, 2016a). These conversations could then be shared, repackaged (with patient permission, of course), and used to demonstrate people's stories and experiences with certain health care entities.

There are many benefits for health care professionals as they venture into the world of social media (Newberry, 2020), such as the following:

- Raising awareness of emerging health concerns that may be important for audiences to know.

- Providing information and updates related to health concerns as Mayo Clinic has done with COVID-19. In August 2020, Mayo Clinic reinforced their commitment to providing reliable information via an Instagram post, stating "Remember you can find the latest news and most reliable information about #COVID19 on the #MayoClinic website, including what you need to know to keep yourself and your family safe."

- Building a community online that can trust the information being shared from a credible source.

- Creating educational materials and additional information that will be helpful in reducing levels of uncertainty about health issues.

- Listening and monitoring current concerns, challenges, and opportunities that have a direct impact on the reputation of the health organization or institution in question to formulate strategic plans and effective messages to audiences.

There are many challenges at the intersection of social media and the health care industry. First, the health care industry is heavily regulated (Mack, 2017) and extremely complex. The industry has to follow strict guidelines outlined by government agencies such as the Food and Drug Administration and the Health Insurance Portability and Accountability Act. Health care professionals must demonstrate that they are supervising the activities of all parties at their organization who have access to patient information as well as other legal issues pertaining to patient privacy and legal cases involving patients, doctors, and hospitals (Belbey, 2015). Another challenge that faces many health care professionals involves state and federal privacy laws, which limit how much interaction and engagement they can have on social media with patients (Belbey, 2015). These organizations and health care providers have to be careful, because if they are found to have disclosed information about patients online on social media, they could face significant fines (Belbey, 2015).

A second struggle for the health care industry and social media is patient privacy. Data protection is the primary focus for many health care professionals, and as new tools and communities are always coming up, social media raises many big issues related to privacy. Privacy could be compromised in many ways for the health care industry—ranging from employees posting pictures of patients and their families during their time at a certain facility to even broadcasting without permission the information and stories of patients who have come to use the health care facilities. Other important factors to consider when it comes to social media and the health care industry relate to the growing use and prominence of online reviews and ratings. Many different sites are used to curate reviews, including Reputation.com and Facebook check-ins. Other online review sites allow health care professionals to determine what people are saying about the facilities, clinics, doctors, and hospitals they oversee. Reputation management has become a key area of responsibility for social media professionals working in the health care industry. Online reviews can either hinder or enhance the overall reputations and perceptions of doctors, nurses, patients, and others working in the health care system.

A third struggle is the rise of misinformation and fake news related to certain topics and issues in the health care industry (e.g., COVID-19, vaccines, etc.). Anyone can post an update online, and it is very easy to present false information that looks credible. Remember to clarify and cite credible health sources in the updates being shared across the various social media channels.

Social media has been implemented and incorporated into universal business plans of health care entities in many ways. For example:

Hospitals. Hospitals and clinics have been very successful in implementing various campaigns over the years. St. Jude Children's Research Hospital (2016) uses its social media channels to tell stories about their medical care, research, and events at their facilities.

Clinics. One of the best examples of social media education and resources for professionals in the industry comes from the Mayo Clinic, one of the best in the industry for its social and digital media efforts. The organization has strong brand recognition and a dedicated social and digital innovation team that helped establish the Mayo Clinic Social Media Network (otherwise known as #MCSMN) for its own team members and others outside of the organization. Social media is embraced at the leadership and mission levels, and the Mayo Clinic also promotes innovation within its organizational culture (Pennic, 2014).

Nonprofits. Nonprofits in the health industry have an active social media presence, especially when bringing together news related to certain diseases. *Black Panther* actor Chadwick Boseman's passing away in 2020 from colon cancer increased public awareness of the disease. The American Cancer Society and the Colon Cancer Coalition have actively posted information on the risks and symptoms of colon cancer, as well as where people can go for more information. As a result, the American Cancer Society wanted to make sure to honor Boseman's legacy and challenge with colon cancer with this Instagram post, quoting Boseman about contributing to society and having a purpose (Photo 15.5). A brand interjecting themselves into a conversation on the death of a celebrity is tricky, but the American Cancer Society managed to post an appropriate message on the loss of Boseman. The post on Instagram was well received and appreciated by their community members.

▶ **Photo 15.5**
American Cancer Society's Instagram Post on the Death of Chadwick Boseman

Source: Instagram/ @americancancer society

Insurance Companies. When you think of insurance companies, you may not be aware of the creative social media partnerships formed within the industry. Insurance companies such as Aflac are also innovative with their partnerships with other brands. Aflac has done various campaigns over the years, including partnering with current head football coach Nick Saban of the University of Alabama. By partnering with Saban, Aflac not only taps into an influencer in the sports community but also allows Saban to share the spotlight to discuss the range of services Aflac offers in their insurance coverage programs. Progressive Insurance and their character Flo have also been active on social media with their social care practices and with bringing to life a fictional character for the brand. Flo has her own presence on social, including a Twitter profile where her quirky and fun personality can be displayed in relatable tweets. With this strategy, Progressive is able to connect with Flo's followers consistently without it feeling like an insurance advertisement.

Another insurance company that that has raised the standards for employee advocacy efforts is Humana. Humana, which partnered with the employee advocacy platform company Dynamic Signal, effectively implemented a brand ambassador and employee advocacy program for its employees on social media (Stein, 2016). The primary focus for Humana was to promote health information, not necessarily sales ("Employee Advocacy," 2018). Employees could help with recruiting (engaging with potential job seekers), social selling (e.g., chatting about the services offered by the insurance company), reputation management (the people behind the logo are in many cases what people look for in a brand besides goods and services), and sharing news about the organization with others (Belbey, 2016b). Humana's goal was to encourage employees not only to share updates on their internal social networks (which they had been doing) but also to do more posting and engagement on behalf of the company on public platforms like Facebook, LinkedIn, and Twitter (Stein, 2016).

Best Practices for Health Care Professionals

Best practices for working in a social media capacity are especially important in a highly regulated industry such as health care. Again there are some universal characteristics to note, but others are uniquely dedicated and specific to the health care industry:

▶ **Photo 15.6**
Flo on Twitter

Source: Flo from Progressive (2015, September 3) Still can't find the last piece [Tweet]. Retrieved from https://twitter.com/itsflo

- *Invest in a legal and public health education.* With the need to understand what federal and state laws and federal agencies say about privacy for patients, anyone working in social media must be aware of these factors and how they impact the role of social media professionals. While you may have a dedicated understanding of social media, you must be aware of the context and industry in which you are working. Education related to legal and public health regulations will help you determine what can and cannot be shared and posted on social media, which will then help in avoiding potential crises.

- *Be aware of what you can and cannot say on social media.* Because the health care industry is so regulated, you must be aware of what you can't say as well as what you can. For example, if someone checks into a hospital and says he has had a terrible experience, the social media manager can't say, "We are sorry" because that means the hospital is responsible and could be sued. The same goes for inquiries about patients, and privacy is a huge issue in the health care industry. Know the industry and government policies and regulations for yourself, but ensure that the entire team of professionals with access to the social media profiles is also up to speed. Training into what to post and what not to post should be a universal educational opportunity for everyone, not just those who work in social media, in the health care industry.

- *Recognize that listening and timing of protocol response are crucial.* Have a template and policy outlined for how to report anything that comes up on social media. Planning, along with legal and professional protocols, will help prevent and prepare for many issues that may arise on social media. Be aware people use social media to vent about patient experiences, document their experiences at a hospital (e.g., live video and online reviews), and even become outraged and try to make a photo, video, or situation go viral. You must have strong crisis communication skills to address, prevent, and react to any situation that may spark online, and understand how this could impact your reputation.

- *Turn your employees into advocates.* As shown with Humana, employees can be encouraged to share their experiences on social media. Stories, information about events, and education about related topics in the industry are just some of the areas that can be covered and shared by employees. Create training sessions, workshops on best practices, polices, and a calendar for content to be shared on social media, and create a leadership board for most active users internally. By building an advocacy culture, the internal environment can become appropriate to share with the rest of the world.

HUMANS OF SOCIAL MEDIA

Mireille Ryan, CEO of Social Media Marketing Institute

Social Media and International Campaigns

Introduction

My name is Mireille Ryan, CEO of the Social Media Marketing Institute, founder of the Social Media Marketing Awards and Social Media Marketing Summit, and award-winning entrepreneur.

I am absolutely passionate about social media. All the skills I have learned in the digital marketing space are as a result of needing to learn how to use it in my own companies.

This passion for social media led to me to establish the Social Media Marketing Institute, a membership, education, and professional development organisation for the social media industry.

How did you get your start in social media?

I fell in love with social media when I used it to grow my fitness business around Australia.

By understanding the demographics of my audience and using targeted Facebook ads, I was able to launch my business in another state without ever going there. I then used Facebook groups to keep connected with that audience. When people saw the success I was achieving, they started to ask me to help them with their social media and I loved helping them so much, I decided to leave the fitness industry to work in social media full-time.

What is your favorite part of working in your area of expertise in social media?

Through the Social Media Marketing Institute, I love that I can throw a spotlight on and highlight, through the Social Media Marketing Awards, all the exceptional work being done by amazing social media marketers. A lot of the time they are helping their clients or companies to gain attention, all whilst working behind the scenes.

What is one thing you can't live without while working in social media?

One thing I couldn't live without is Canva. I love that Canva makes my design skills look good and I use it every day, particularly for social media.

What is your favorite social media account (person/brand/etc.) to follow and why?

My favourite brands would have to be Nike and Dove. I love their storytelling.

What is the most challenging part of working in social media?

I find the most challenging part is how you are always "on" with social media. Social media is not just 9 a.m. to 5 p.m. I manage many clients' accounts and have also helped manage a community of over 1 million people and you are always needing to be responsive no matter the time of day. The pressure that can come with that can be tiring.

What do you wish you had known when you were starting out?

People are so amazing and will help you if you ask. When I started out, I tried to do everything myself. By understanding that you can ask people for help and even ask your online community, people are just so generous, particularly when they understand your passion. That is why I also try to give back whenever I can.

What are three marketable skills a social media professional needs to have to work in the industry?

1. I think you need to be a good copywriter and storyteller so you can make your content engaging and relatable.

2. Understanding the customer journey as a social media marketer needs to engage at all different parts of this journey.

3. Understanding what the data are telling you to help you shape your strategy, get more out of your advertising, and achieve success for your client or business.

If you had to choose a song to walk out to in a presentation on social media, what would it be and why?

"Girl on Fire," by Alicia Keys. I think it encapsulates the passion I have for what I do. I definitely always dream big and believe things can be achieved.

Mireille Ryan is the CEO of the Social Media Marketing Institute in Australia and can be followed on social @mireilleryan.

OVERVIEW OF SOCIAL MEDIA AND INTERNATIONAL CAMPAIGNS

Social media is a worldwide platform. In many circumstances, the same platforms are universal and consistent across different countries. This is why festivals and conferences such as the Cannes Lions International Festival of Creativity are so important for social media professionals to attend to learn, grow, and understand the different ways to use social media in strategic communications. International awareness also leads to knowledge of additional platforms to explore and possibly incorporate into the social media ecosystem.

Social media around the world has grown exponentially and will continue to do so. According to We Are Social and Hootsuite (Kemp, 2020), there are about 3.96 billion active social media users; of those active on social media, a majority of them (99 percent) access these platforms via their phones. It is key to understand the rise of and reliance on social media from a global stage to get information, create content, share stories, and embrace unique digital experiences. Some platforms that are commonly used in one country may not be used as much in other places. New platforms are emerging as powerhouse outlets to compete with established platforms. New challenges and regulations (e.g., GDPR [General Data Protection Regulation] policies, censorship, privacy and freedom of speech concerns) on these platforms also need to be considered.

Here are some of the things to consider when working in social media at the international level:

Handling various crises and challenges. Disney+ released the live action film *Mulan*, which got rave reviews from audiences for its presentation and ties to the original animated film. However, lead actress Liu Yifei's comments supporting the Hong Kong police led to calls to boycott the film globally from pro-democracy advocates around the world ("Mulan: Why Disney's Latest Reboot Is Facing Boycott Calls," 2020).

Fer Machado ✓
@fer_machado123

As we reopen our restaurants post lockdown, BK France welcomes everyone who was anxious for our food! More great stuff from our talented #BurgerKing France team and @BUZZMAN_TIME. #marketing #advertising

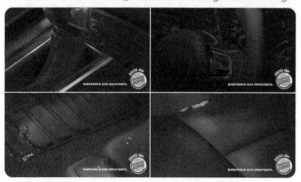

6:48 AM · Sep 3, 2020 from Miami Beach, FL · Twitter for iPhone

31 Retweets   **17** Quote Tweets   **219** Likes

▶ **Photo 15.7**
Burger King in France

Source: Twitter/
@fer_machado123

Acknowledging the current state of affairs with audiences. Many brands at the international level understand they are reaching not only one audience group but many different communities, countries, and cultures. There are unified experiences everyone can relate to, such as COVID-19 and its challenges. However, some brands interject themselves into situations to relate to their audiences on social. Fer Machado—former chief marketing officer at RBI and current CMO of Activision, worked with brands such as Burger King and Popeyes—posted about the reopening of Burger King in France. This tweet shows the various ways in which Burger King's food may end up in someone's car since the only way to get their food during the lockdown was through drive-throughs (Photo 15.7).

Impact of visuals tied to raising awareness. One campaign that generated a lot of interest, shares, and intrigue was Australia's "Meet Graham" campaign, which focused on increasing awareness about road safety in Australia. An artist created Graham to show how he would be the only person who could survive the effects of road trauma. The video introducing Graham went viral, and as a result, the campaign won the Grand Prix prize in the health category at Cannes Lions in 2017 (Nudd, 2017).

Raising awareness about serious causes. Social media can be used internationally to raise awareness about issues in specific nations and countries.

Brands, with the help of influencers and strategic partnerships, can come together and share stories on social media. Amarula (2017), a South African cream liquor company, partnered with WildlifeDirect on a global campaign called "Don't Let Them Disappear" to raise awareness of the declining elephant population. The company enhanced awareness of this issue by using influencer marketing (Photo 15.8). Amarula partnered with six Instagram influencers and Dr. Paula Kahumbu in the Amboseli National Park in Kenya to create awareness about elephant conservation. Amarula, known worldwide for its logo that features the elephant—one of the "big 5" animals and the most severely threatened in southern Africa—used social media to generate more awareness for this cause and presented ways for others to help address the growing crisis. This campaign integrated influencer marketing with cause-related marketing to address an issue tied with the brand, country, and community on social media on a global stage.

▶ **Photo 15.8**
Amarula Instagram Influencer Post for Elephant Conservation Social Media Campaign

Source: Instagram/@amarula_official

Sharing stories to spark creativity. Personalization (tailoring the content and created messages that truly resonate with intended parties) and allowing audiences to create and share what they have done is a global characteristic of social media. Personalization and opportunities to be unique give audiences the chance to create and share their stories in a way that generates an authentic connection with a brand and its intended audiences. LEGO, the popular toy company, has fully embraced their creativity in their campaigns and on social media (LEGO, 2016). In their "Level Up Your Imagination" campaign, LEGO aimed to spark creativity among children in Europe with Kronkiwongi, targeting audiences in Taiwan and China. In their "Rebuild the World" campaign, LEGO promoted creativity on a global level for all ages (Photo 15.9). LEGO has done an exceptional job in consistently communicating and creating content that resonates across all audiences, cultures, and communities.

Rising global platforms. When considering international campaigns in social media, professionals have to recognize other channels that are unique and prominently used in other countries. China, for example, uses designated apps more often than traditional social media channels (due to government censorship and blocking of main social media channels such as Facebook). In China, social

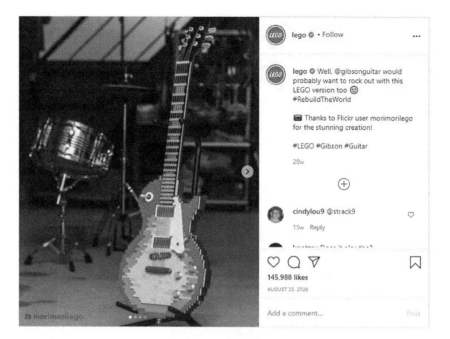

▶ **Photo 15.9**
LEGO
#RebuildTheWorld
on Instagram

Source: Instagram/
@lego

media sites such as Weibo (similar to Twitter) are used more frequently. This perspective is universal—go to the platform that the audience is going to, and make sure you understand the similarities and differences in these platforms and integrate these practices strategically in both the content and message strategy for the brand. TikTok, formerly known as Musical.ly and currently owned by ByteDance, has grown in popularity and presence in the global community. TikTok is the first social media platform from outside of the United States to become a global sensation, and it has brought new opportunities and challenges (Spangler & Spangler, 2020). Many people expressed concern about TikTok's censorship and data privacy. Several countries, including India, Australia, and the United States, have had discussions on whether to ban the platform in their countries. In response, TikTok launched a global campaign titled "It Started on TikTok," showing users from around the world using TikTok to spark creativity and entertainment and highlighting the most viral trends, challenges, and cultural experiences that started on the platform (Spangler & Spangler, 2020).

China has become a rising force in the social media world for their designated platforms. China has several to note, including WhatsApp, TikTok, WeChat, and Weibo. WeChat is a messaging app with games, shopping, and financial services. WhatsApp, owned by Facebook, has been used for a lot of different types of campaigns over the years; they launched their first global campaign in Brazil in 2020 to show that it is more than just a messaging app and how it can do what other platforms can do (Handley, 2020)

Weibo, China's answer to Twitter, is a micro-blogging platform. Weibo operates and is formatted like Twitter, and users can update and share visuals (photos, GIFs, videos, etc.). While the Weibo audience is not the same size as WeChat's, a significant number of users (550 million) do use the platform. Weibo has been used for many different campaigns, including fashion and influencer campaigns with JNBY. JNBY, an influential designer in China, created a video series called Persona Liberation, which focuses on common identities among women from different backgrounds. The campaign launched ahead of JNBY's 2020 autumn/fall campaign (Wu, 2020),

Best Practices for International Campaigns

Social media provides many opportunities, challenges, and lessons for the global community. Each country has its own designated media, legal, and political landscapes, so it is important to tailor our social media practices to follow these elements. Best practices for operating on the social media global stage include the following:

- *Know the country-specific rules and regulations applied to social media.* It is important to understand the different rules, regulations (e.g., GDPR), and practices that are acceptable and not acceptable for social media practices in different places. These can evolve and change quickly, so staying on top of these trends and updates is critical.

- *Learn the culture, people, food, and history.* Like being a student of social media, it is important to understand, appreciate, and embrace the culture of the country for which you are designing social media. Be aware of what makes the country unique and how this uniqueness is showcased on various social media platforms. Conduct research to determine the major media outlets, influencers, brands, companies, and accounts on social media to get a feel for the country's own voice and presence.

- *Choose platforms appropriate for the audiences and goals in mind.* Similar principles discussed so far often apply to international platforms. The most dominant global platforms may not be the most appropriate. Having a large audience is great, such as in the expanding WeChat, but WeChat is not necessarily the best channel for reaching a certain audience or building more engagement with a community.

- *Open your eyes to new platforms outside of your country.* While we sometimes focus only on what is happening in our own communities and countries, it is key to also look at how social media is being implemented across the world and what new messaging apps, social media communities, and sites are created each and every day. Be aware also of current social media trends in the country of origin. Look at research and reports that cover these trends. WeAreSocial and Hootsuite are good resources for this.

- *Understand the importance of culture and unique platform characteristics and expectations.* It is important for social media professionals to understand that whereas some universal practices are consistent across cultures and communities, other unique characteristics will need to be addressed and acknowledged. Going into a new country and online community with the assumption that what works in your country will work in another will not go over well. Research the current social media landscape, cultures, media expectations, and age cohorts so you understand both the differences and similarities.

- *Be aware of any universal challenges across all social media platforms.* In all cases, even international ones, social media still raises concerns that are consistent around the world. Privacy, legal issues, political climates, and understanding the implications of data and how data can be applied are just a few examples. Yet, by embracing these challenges across the board and having these universal discussions in the social media community, we will see we are all in the same boat as social media professionals and can solve these challenges together.

The specialty areas needing social media professionals are diverse, as we have seen in this chapter for sports, social care, nonprofit, health care, and international campaigns. Each of these areas has its own challenges and obstacles, whether financial, government regulations, customer expectations, or different media and political landscapes. Each area provides opportunities for social media to do great and wonderful things for relevant communities (Table 15.1). While differences exist across these sectors, there are more similarities and opportunities for social media professionals. Social media is a truly global community, channel, and industry and will continue on this projection. This chapter shows that social media professionals can break down barriers to share stories, insights, and expertise with the rest of the world and community.

Table 15.1   Social Media Content to Create and Apply in Each Specialization

Specialization	Content to Create
Sports	• Social media updates • Strategic briefs • Social media audits • Personal brand audits • Personal brand templates (graphics, images, video) • Influencer marketing plans • Influencer sponsorship packages • Analytics reports • Graphics and visual assets • Updates and social ads • Guidelines • Press releases
Social Care	• Social media updates • Code of Social Media Ethics • Customer service policies and procedures • Customer service templates and social media updates • Protocols in responding to customer inquiries • Social media posts • Graphic and visual assets
Nonprofit	• Giving Days (live video) • Fundraising plans • Workshops • Fact sheets and backgrounds of organization and key players • Social media listening and monitoring reports • Social care protocols (for fundraising)

Specialization	Content to Create
	• Message maps and strategy statements
	• Policies
	• Guidelines
	• Social media updates
	• Infographics
	• Video
Health Care	• Stories
	• Updates (short and long form)
	• Features
	• Articles
	• Exclusives
	• Content editorial calendar
	• Fundraising posts
	• Videos
	• Infographics
	• Microsites
International	• Stories
	• Updates (short and long form)
	• Features
	• Articles
	• Exclusives
	• International social media updates and briefs (different languages and accounts)

THOUGHT QUESTIONS

1. What are the core best practices for social care?

2. Discuss the main social media challenges and opportunities for nonprofits.

3. What are some of the unique elements to note when it comes to social media and health care practices?

4. What are the major similarities and differences in social media practices around the world?

5. What are some of the challenges sports and social media professionals need to be aware of for social media?

EXERCISES

1. You are volunteering for the Salvation Army, and you have been tasked by your supervisor to create a social media campaign to raise funds during the holidays. However, your supervisor's boss does not feel social media could help out in this area. Write why you feel social media is beneficial for nonprofits and outline a strategic social media plan you could propose for this fundraising campaign.

2. While working at a hospital in the social media department, you see a rise of check-ins from patients and families rating their experiences. Some of them are positive, and some of them are negative. What course of action will you take?

3. You are about to do a study-abroad internship, and you have the choice of working in social media in either China, Australia, or South Africa. Evaluate the current social media landscape in each country, and discuss one campaign using a designated social media platform you like. Evaluate and note the current social media trends highlighted for this country in the We Are Social and Hootsuite global social media report.

4. You are joining the NASCAR social media team where you are expected to keep up with the driver's social media presence and discuss potential collaborations. You have been assigned to Kyle Bursch and Bubba Wallace. Discuss each driver's presence on social media and make three recommendations on potential brands, organizations, and companies they could partner with based on their position in the sport.

REFERENCES

Amarula. (2017, August 8). Amarula launches new campaign to save African elephants on World Elephant Day. *Cision PR Newswire*. https://www.prnewswire.com/news-releases/amarula-launches-new-campaign-to-save-african-elephants-on-world-elephant-day-300500800.html

Anderson, M. K. (2017). Welcome back, Movember: Why this viral campaign is still so successful. *HubSpot*. https://blog.hubspot.com/marketing/movember-data-viral-campaign

Augure. (2017, July 12). 10 communication campaigns about Movember. https://augure.launchmetrics.com/resources/blog/movember-communication-campaigns

Belbey, J. (2015, January 21). How healthcare can use social media effectively and compliantly. *Forbes*. https://www.forbes.com/sites/joannabelbey/2015/01/21/how-healthcare-can-use-social-media-effectively-and-compliantly/

Belbey, J. (2016a, January 31). Is social media the future of healthcare? *Forbes*. https://www.forbes.com/sites/joannabelbey/2016/01/31/is-social-media-the-future-of-healthcare/

Belbey, J. (2016b, November 17). Is social media and "employee advocacy" possible within regulated industries? *Forbes*. https://www.forbes.com/sites/joannabelbey/2016/11/17/is-social-media-and-employee-advocacy-possible-within-regulated-industries/

Boren, C. (2017, August 28). Houston sports stars leverage social media to help victims of Hurricane Harvey. *The Washington Post*. https://www.washingtonpost.com/news/early-lead/wp/2017/08/28/as-harvey-rages-on-clint-capela-and-j-j-watt-harness-the-power-of-social-media-to-help-houston-residents/

Chowdhry, A. (2015, August 26). Remember the Ice Bucket Challenge? Donations from the $220 million campaign enhanced ALS research. *Forbes*. http://www.forbes.com/sites/amit chowdhry/2015/08/26/remember-the-ice-bucket-challenge-donations-from-the-220-million-campaign-advanced-als-research/#6b655460692b

Conrardy, A., & Post, W. (2020, August 31). The essential nonprofit fundraising guide for the rest of 2020. *Fast Company*. https://www.fastcompany.com/90545201/the-essential-nonprofit-fundraising-guide-for-the-rest-of-2020

Employee advocacy drives healthcare social media outreach. (2018). *Ragan's PR Daily*. https://www.prdaily.com/Awards/Special Edition/615.aspx

Fitzgerald, K. (2017). K. (2017, August 3). With social media savvy, CrossFit athletes help grow sport. *USA Today*. https://www.usatoday.com/story/sports/2017/08/03/crossfit-games-social-media-savvy-athletes-help-grow-sport/538856001/

Frumkin, T. (2017, January 18). The 6 most important customer service stats for 2017. *Conversocial*. http://www.conversocial.com/blog/the-7-most-important-customer-service-stats-for-2017

Handley, L. (2020, February 20). *WhatsApp chooses Brazil to launch its first major ad campaign*. CNBC. https://www.cnbc.com/2020/02/20/whatsapp-chooses-brazil-to-launch-its-first-major-ad-campaign.html

Hyken, S. (2017, April 22). Social customer care is the new marketing. *Forbes*. https://www.forbes.com/sites/shephyken/2017/04/22/social-customer-care-is-the-new-marketing/

Johnston, A. (2017, July 24). A strategic guide to social media for nonprofits. *Sprout Social*. https://sproutsocial.com/insights/nonprofit-social-media-guide/

Kemp, S. (2020, January 30). Digital 2020: 3.8 billion people use social media—We are social. https://wearesocial.com/blog/2020/01/digital-2020-3-8-billion-people-use-social-media

Kim, C. M., & Freberg K. (2020, June). Enhancing organizational public relationships: Using social care as a strategy to develop trust, authenticity, and credibility. *Public Relations Journal*, 1–12.

LEGO (Producer). (2016). LEGO Kronkiwongi. Shorty *Awards*. http://shortyawards.com/8th/lego-kronkiwongi

Mack, H. (2017, February 28). How social media can impact healthcare in the right—and wrong—ways. *MobiHealthNews*. http://www.mobihealthnews.com/content/how-social-media-can-impact-healthcare-right---and-wrong-ways

Mulan: Why Disney's latest reboot is facing boycott calls. (2020, September 4). BBC News. https://www.bbc.com/news/newsbeat-54024810

Newberry, C. (2020, March 30). How to use social media in healthcare: A guide for health professionals. *Hootsuite*. https://blog.hootsuite.com/social-media-health-care/

NFL TikTok. (n.d.). NFL Social Lab. https://www.nflsociallab.com/nfl-tiktok

Nudd, T. (2017, June 18). "Meet Graham" wins the first Grand Prix of the 2017 Cannes Lions. *Adweek*. http://www.adweek.com/creativity/meet-graham-wins-the-first-grand-prix-of-the-2017-cannes-lions/

Paynter, B. (2019, July 23). Julia, Sesame Street's autistic muppet, stars in new public service ad. *Fast Company*. https://www.fastcompany.com/90379912/julia-sesame-streets-autistic-muppet-has-a-new-campaign-to-help-teach-parents-about-autism

Pennic, J. (2014, February 17). 5 reasons why Mayo Clinic dominates social media in healthcare. *HIT Consultant*. http://hitconsultant.net/2014/02/17/5-reasons-mayo-clinic-ominates-social-media-in-healthcare/

Peterson, T. (2015, June 15). Ice Bucket Challenge, "Like a Girl" take top honors in Facebook Awards. *Ad Age*. http://adage.com/article/digital/ice-bucket-challenge-top-facebook-s-studio-awards/298983/

Quesenberry, K. A. (2016, April 19). Social media is too important to be left to the marketing department. *Harvard Business Review*. https://hbr.org/2016/04/social-media-is-too-important-to-be-left-to-the-marketing-department

Rapaport, D. (2017, September 2). J. J. Watt has raised more than $17 million for Hurricane Harvey relief. *Sports Illustrated*. https://www.si.com/nfl/2017/09/02/jj-watt-hurricane-harvey-relief-fundraiser

Spangler, T., & Spangler, T. (2020, August 18). TikTok launches biggest-ever ad campaign as its fate remains cloudy. *Variety*. https://variety.com/2020/digital/news/tiktok-advertising-brand-campaign-sale-bytedance-1234738607/

St. Jude Children's Research Hospital. (2016, October 25). *St. Jude and more than 70 leading brands ask consumers to #GiveThanks while they shop this holiday season during St. Jude Thanks and Giving campaign*. https://www.stjude.org/media-resources/news-releases/2016-fundraising-news/st-jude-thanks-and-giving-thirteenth-year.html

Stein, L. (2016, August 16). Highly regulated industries try employee advocacy on social. *Ad Age*. http://adage.com/article/agency-news/dynamic-signal-helps-highly-regulated-brands-social/305407/

Wu, W. (2020, September 4). The winners and losers in China digital marketing this week. *Jing Daily*. http://jingdaily.com/loreal-and-jnby-call-on-womens-empowerment-for-china-digital-marketing/

16

WHAT DOES THE SOCIAL MEDIA WORLD HAVE THAT IS NEW?

Learning Objectives

After reading this chapter, you will be able to

- Understanding the current state of social media

- Identify emerging trends to note for the future in social media

- Explain best practices and next steps for continuing to learn about the science and art of social media

INTRODUCTION

Congratulations! You have finished all but this last chapter of *Social Media for Strategic Communication*! You know every single thing you need to know about the field—you are done learning! This means you, a social media expert, can now take the social media world by storm and embark on a career of charging millions of dollars for your social media content.

Well, not quite. In fact, there are no experts. This is a field where you will (and always) be a student of the profession because it is constantly evolving and adapting to new trends, communities, and expectations.

Although many professionals deem themselves experts in the social media field, they are only experts for a particular moment social media's existence. Social media is constantly changing, so an expert in Facebook's algorithm today may not be an expert tomorrow if the algorithm changes. Do we have influence over what Mark Zuckerberg decides to do next with Facebook? No. What do you do if you are in a situation where your entire presence online is dedicated to a platform that gets banned, as happened to TikTok? Yikes—do you have social media insurance or should we call Farmers Insurance to see if they can help? Do we have the opportunity to tell Jack Dorsey, CEO of Twitter, how to make sure false information doesn't occupy everyone's timelines? Or perhaps we can finally convince him Twitter needs an edit button. Wait a second—let me send him a direct message. Can we tell Instagram we want everything to be in chronological order and not be inundated with promoted ads and posts all the time? Perhaps we can just create a story with our plea to make changes happen.

Although we cannot be experts, we can continue learning to be adaptive and responsive so we can continue the momentum we have built in our understanding and practices of social media. Algorithms, case studies, and creative approaches will change. Social media, unlike other fields, embodies unique challenges and opportunities that will continue to grow as the channels evolve. As channels change, so do expectations and best practices. This is the nature of social media: We are operating in rented space. Rules, formats, expectations, and features will constantly change. We have to be agile, adaptive, and willing to learn on the go. Social media allows us to continue learning, growing, and expanding our viewpoint, which ultimately benefits us as we can see how we have evolved over time.

As they say in *The Mandalorian*, "This is the way."

HUMANS OF SOCIAL MEDIA

Nick Stover, Shark Jockey Digital Social Media Professional

Introduction

Social media helped me earn every professional job I've had in my career. From general manager for a professional sports team, to chief marketing officer for a health care company, and now as an entrepreneur serving clients in multiple industries, I can point to social media's influence on every role. Social media is still a very new industry that is changing faster than most people and companies are accustomed to. Everyone I speak with asks how they can improve their social media presence in order to get ahead of competitors or put their message in front of more people than before. Currently, this is what I help multiple companies and agencies achieve. My company, Shark Jockey Digital, guides businesses through oceans of questions related to social and digital marketing as they race to improve their online sales.

How did you get your start in social media?

When I was working on a master's of science in sport management at the University of Tennessee from 2004 to 2006, social media was not an everyday term. There was very little mention of it in classes or textbooks. The jobs and internships I held with sport organizations did not require or ask me to consider how social media could impact its revenue or support. This gap was where I found an opportunity to research and talk about something I thought would be very important to the future of every sport organization in the world.

What is your favorite part of working in your area of expertise in social media?

I think many businesses and marketers spend a lot of time trying to find one magical funnel or a single viral video to point to as evidence of social media success. As someone who has worked within large businesses as an employee and on the agency side, I see a lot of problems that arise when emphasis is placed on short-term wins. My favorite part of what I do within this industry is to build bigger programs and processes that help companies grow.

My favorite part of this practice is the lightbulb moment that occurs in meetings where I show a business owner or marketing professionals how techniques being used by other industries could disrupt their own. This is especially powerful when I am able to show how it is possible to track ROIs and ROAs for the client once the program is activated.

What is one thing you can't live without while working in social media?

The constant advancement of the smartphone industry is probably the most important thing related to social media today. I would not be able to make a living in the social media industry without having a new(ish) smartphone in my hand most of the time.

What is your favorite social media account (person/brand/etc.) to follow and why?

I grew up in Columbus, OH and one of the first real-world work experiences I had was during high school when I interned for the Columbus Crew of the MLS [Major League Soccer]. I have always played soccer and began following both the team and the entire league closely during its first season, 1996, before social media became mainstream.

What is the most challenging part of working in social media?

There are two big challenges about working in social media that I fight to overcome almost every day. First, there is a term from the sports world known as "armchair quarterback." I think everyone who has ever spent any significant amount of time on social media is able to develop some thoughts on what makes the "best" type of social strategy.

The second challenge is common in many industries, but it is seems to be even more prevalent in social media because of the speed at which news occurs. It is extremely important and difficult to keep up to speed with the latest trends and effective techniques.

What is your take on your area of expertise and the social media industry?

I love that the social media industry is spread across more networks and platforms than ever before. Some of the businesses I work with have expertise in one or more areas of social media. But we are at the point where it is impossible, or at least prohibitively expensive, for any single person or business to claim to be an expert at all of social media.

What do you wish you had known when you were starting out?

After using social media to earn many different roles in multiple industries, I've discovered there are a couple different keys that I wish I had learned earlier in my career. The most important thing is that almost every company really only cares about how increasing social media efforts will impact their bottom line.

The second thing that has taken me years to understand is how to entice others into wanting more. Too often, young people (myself included) want to prove they know a lot or have a lot to offer.

The third thing every person should know is that the reason social media exists is that it is a database. If you are in the social media industry, you should do everything possible to attack your database constantly.

What are three marketable skills a social media professional needs to have to work in the industry?

My view on this might be a little different because I have a much more entrepreneurial mindset now than I did when I was employed as a director of social media. Currently I manage social media for several companies and hire others to do the same for clients. In the past I would say hard skills are most important.

If you had to choose a song to walk out to in a presentation on social media, what would it be and why?

I like the song "God's Gonna Cut You Down," by Johnny Cash. Aside from being sung by one of my favorite musicians, I think its lyrics could probably be applied in a lot of different ways to people on social media.

CURRENT (SO FAR)
STATE OF SOCIAL MEDIA

Social media will continue to be a field in which technology, communities, and humans interact with each other in ways based on knowledge sharing, relationship management, and engaging in networks within certain communities and functions. Sarah Evans, founder and CEO of Sevans Strategy, demonstrates the continued evolution of social network communication by platform and by strategic use (see Table 16.1).

Most of the time, people assume the most popular and current channels being used are social media, but that is not necessarily the case. We can always make assumptions about where people will go next, but in order to make official judgments on this, we have to look at the data and determine where exactly people are. The same goes for when to post on each designated platform as well. Best post timing recommendations may be appropriate in some cases, but not always. Understanding what works for a brand and its designated community on social media has to be approached on a case-by-case basis. We also have to look clearly and honestly at the "thought leaders" who are driving the changes, best practices, and insights influencing the field. Do they really have the experience and expertise to comment on the overall success of these strategies, or are they more focused on the paycheck they receive to be on the stage showcasing work that is being done by others? The real game changers and thought leaders are the ones doing the work rather than preaching it at a conference.

There are many new topics for conversation that need to be addressed and acknowledged as we evaluate the current state of affairs for social media. First, messaging continues to be a powerful medium for social media, but it is sometimes overlooked by the public broadcasting social media channels. These messaging channels and apps (e.g., WhatsApp, Messenger, and others) are often referred to as dark social, because these types of media are private and unmonitored or hard for social media professionals and brands to track (Hong, 2017). This raises another issue and challenge for users when brands discover how to automate conversations and program interactions with their audiences using chat bots. Chat bots are programs designed to simulate human conversation with certain actions, and they are frequently used to handle customer service inquiries and questions. Although these chat bots can handle certain questions, human communication and correspondence are still needed. This, of course, may impact the trustworthiness and authenticity needed to build social media relationships. These programs may be helpful in certain situations but not others. While the temptation of using a tool for the sake of using the tool is great, understanding the context and being empathic about how others perceive it is even more critical. Authenticity matters most, especially to Millennials and Generation Z when it comes to social content.

Second, well-being and digital wellness are growing topics of concern when it comes to audiences spending a lot of time consuming and creating online content. The blurred line between online and offline interactions can be challenging to manage, especially for social media managers who see the good and bad perspectives of their field. Social media managers and professionals are the digital front-line professionals defending and advocating for a client across platforms, and this level of responsibility affects one's mental and physical health. The discussions around these issues are becoming more transparent and accepted in the social media community, yet more work needs to be done. Balance and perspective are crucial for social media professionals.

Table 16.1 Social Network Communications by Sarah Evans

Twitter	TikTok	Facebook	LinkedIn	WhatsApp	Pinterest	Snapchat	Instagram	Reddit	YouTube
Ads	Ads	Ads	Ads	Broadcast lists	Boards	Add friends	Activity feed	Ads	About
Bio	Bio	Comment	Articles	Calls	Comment	Add URL to snap	Boomerang	Cakeday	Ads
Chats	Comment	Events	Business profile	Chats	Daily Inspiration	Bitmoji	Business account	Crosspost	Call-to-action in video
Spaces	Direct message	Fundraisers	Comment	Groups	Follow	Bounce	Carousel	Downvote	Channels
Direct message	Hashtags	Groups	Events	Message	Home feed	Chat	Comment	Share	Comment
DM groups	Influencers	Live (Facebook)	Groups	Profile	Influencers	Discover	Contact	Subreddit	Create
GIFs	Like	Mentions	Hashtags	Stats	Mention	Geofilters	Follow	Upvote	Discussion
Follow	Post	Message groups	Like	Updates	Messages	Lens	Hashtags	Karma	I like this
Favorite	Search	Messenger Kids	Live (LinkedIn)		Pin photos	Filters	Like	Message	I dislike this
Hashtags	Share	Pages	Messaging		Pins	Live stories	Live	Moderator	Live
Lists	Trending videos	Post	Post		Profile	My Story	Location	Submit a link	Pinned comment
Mentions		Private message	Pro		Promoted by	Multisnap	Messages		Playlists
Periscope/ live		Questions	Profile		React	Our Story	Pinned comment		Profile
Polls		Share on profile	Recorded video message		Saved	Replay	Profile		Replay
Photo, video		Stories	Share		Sponsored	Snap	Live Room		Share
Search		Tag	Tag		Topics	Snap camera	Promote		Subscribers
Reply		Watch parties	Trending topics			Snapchat score	Promotions		Subscriptions
Threads						Snapcode	Group messages		Trending
Trending topics						Snap map	Reels		
Tweet						Snappables	Reply		
						Stickers	Save		
						Subscriptions	Share		
							Sponsored		
							Stories		
							Screenshot		

Let's look at what remains the same in social media and what will continue to change as we look to the future. The definition of social media that was given in Chapter 1 still applies to what we are currently experiencing in the field of social media, but there will be a time when we must be adaptable (and receptive) to the growing changes in the field as well as how we conceptualize it. Social media professionals today are actively changing the field as we speak, and we have to be fluid and understand this is the way things operate in this field. Chapters 1 through 6 (covering the art and science of social media, ethical and legal foundations, DEI [diversity, equity, and inclusion], personal and professional branding, industry qualifications, and research) provided a solid foundation for the consistent skills and concepts needed to go into strategic communications and the field of social media.

Chapters 7 through 13 covered strategic planning, influencer marketing, paid media, strategic writing, audience segmentation, creating and curating content, and measurement and evaluation. These chapters provided a bit more specialization within the systematic planning and creative execution protocols needed to build on the foundations set for the field. Chapters 14 and 15 (exploring the application of social media) showed the different areas of specialization you can go into, including entertainment, sports, and health care.

The opportunities are endless in social media. This is where a lot of the momentum is. New approaches, case studies, and practices continue to evolve within areas of specialization. Who would have considered some of these specialized areas becoming mainstream even a few years ago? It is not a question of whether or not to think digital first. We *have to* embrace and always think digital is first for what we do in strategic communications. If we do not act and think digital first, we are not going anywhere.

While the opportunities grow in social media, the future allows us to experience our own challenges. With platforms such as Facebook, Twitter, Instagram, Snapchat, and others allowing access to their application programming interfaces and metrics, this raises issues not just about whether this is a "pay-to-play" situation but more about to what extent. This is where we are today in social media practices. Chapter 9 ("Paid Media") emphasized the importance of investing in content, talent, and programming to make sure our messages get to our intended audiences. Facebook, LinkedIn, and Google have mastered the pay-to-play model for their social media channels, which has created a drive to other platforms where organic reach is still possible. One of the reasons TikTok drew so many users was due to the extremely high level of exposure to audiences from around the world, without primary focus on paid media strategies. However, while TikTok brings new challenges, social media professionals have to advocate for the investment and respect they need from their organization and team members so they can do their jobs.

Other technology- and social media–related trends emerging for social media professionals range from basic content suggestions (e.g., social video) to more advanced tools that encompass the overall digital sphere in society (e.g., voice and automated intelligence). Here are some of the trends we may need to be on the lookout for.

- *Voice search* (Amazon's Alexa, Apple's Siri, Google, and eMicrosoft's Cortana). Our devices are interconnected not just with our platforms but with every facet of our lives. We can access information directly through these devices just by using our voice. Artificial intelligence can be both proactive and reactive in nature, and we have to think about how this will impact and work in our daily lives. We are seeing more integration of voice in our daily lives, even on social media platforms. We have to be able to integrate mobile, social, and voice together in a seamless and relevant manner for our own purposes and for those of our audiences.

- *Disruptive efforts to mislead or unethically influence actions that are not real.* Whereas many brands and professionals are true and honest in their practices and how they present themselves on social media, others are not so much. Misleading fake accounts and bots are created every day to fool users into thinking they are real accounts. The ultimate goal is to persuade audiences to do, think, or feel certain things based on what is presented, even if the information is not true. This is an epidemic that continues to plague social media, but in order to combat it, we first have to know what we are looking for. For example, StopTheTroll.org is a great tool that tests you on your overall understanding of identifying real or fake accounts. As the platforms get more advanced, these fake accounts will continue to become more sophisticated. Strengthen your critical thinking skills to evaluate which accounts are real and which ones are fake.

- *Rise in non-fungible tokens (NFTs).* These are coming into the digital and social space with a bang. NFTs are considered to be a unit of data on a blockchain that represents a unique digital item. These digital items can be anything related to videos, art, audio clips, or other assets. NBA has gotten into NFTs for key moments and videos of some of their players in the game, like Michael Jordan or Lebron James dunking a basketball. However, the most expensive NFT to date was $69.3 million for *Everydays: The First 5000 Days*, created by famed digital artist Mike "Beeple" Winkelmann (Phillips, 2021).

- *Advocacy marketing.* Influencer marketing (see Chapter 8) is one piece of the puzzle for social media. Advocates are audience members who are not only part of the community for a brand on social media but are willing to put forth their name and reputation to endorse brands without the financial compensation an influencer may require. However, there are influencers who really do persuade audiences to act, and there are those who are artificial in nature, meaning, they bring nothing to the table other than providing the world their aesthetic.

- *Ephemeral content.* While social video is becoming more and more prevalent, the content is short lived, mobile first, and only accessible for 24 hours. If audiences know a video is only available on Snapchat, Instagram, TikTok, or other similar apps for a certain amount of time, they will come. However, the content and experience still need to create a true comprehensive experience for the audiences.

- *Social media brand protection.* It is important to have an offensive strategy when it comes to social media, but we should also build up protocols to protect the reputation and community for a brand on social media. The rise of rumors, false information, and negative actions taken by threatening parties all have to be acknowledged and planned for in a social media strategy. The threats and risks associated with these actions can directly impact attitudes, behaviors, and communities online. No brand or platform is invincible.

Social media as we see it today is constantly changing, and no one is an expert. Everyone is operating with best guesses on trends and what will be relevant next, and these are just "guidelines," to quote *Pirates of the Caribbean*. The roles, investment, and responsibilities will soon change and of course blur together. The job postings shared for brands, agencies, and organizations are framed much differently compared to others posted earlier in the same year.

With every year that passes, more "influencers" and "keynote speakers" come up to showcase their brands and what they can do for others. Everyone is a media company with a large microphone. However, though social media has been around now for some time, it's not necessarily in its infant stage. It is more in the late teenager/young adult stage. Social media professionals are still trying to advocate (and sometimes shout) their relevancy to the world with each of their platforms—trying to one-up each other with how many conferences, clients, and speaking engagements they can take on. This is all fine and good, but those who are trying to make a difference and have new experiences and ideas may be left in the dust. Thus, young professionals not only have to be part of this community but must bring forth a game plan along with their microphone. This field is still in the Wild West, where everyone wants a piece of the pie or gold mine out there with relationships, influence, and community. The risks associated with misunderstanding audiences and what they are looking for can be detrimental for a brand and can cause additional challenges down the line.

Yet, not all is lost. With each year that passes, the social media space becomes more civilized and structured to the profession's needs. We are seeing a growing need for the congregation of all like minds related to the science and art of social media strategy. The social media industry needs everyone to come together to discuss, brainstorm, and collaborate to make sure all of the research questions, challenges, and opportunities are addressed together in a comprehensive and thorough manner.

FUTURE TRENDS AND DIRECTIONS

The million-dollar question you will be asked wherever you go in social media is What does the social media professional have that is *new*? What next trend do we need to jump on and address? What shiny new tool or platform do we need to put thousands of dollars into?

These questions are not so simple, but they shouldn't be intimidating. New tools and technology platforms will always arise in the business, but it all comes down to this:

- Is this technology sustainable? If so, for how long?

- Is this trend innovative and able to provide value?

- What is the overall life span of this new technology? Will it be mainstream or limited to a particular industry?

- What is the overall case for investing in this tool? What is our rationale for using this tool or platform in addition to the resources we already employ?

- What can we do with this tool to enhance our story and content for our audiences?

- Do we have the investment (financially and in leadership) to move forward with this technology?

These are some of the questions that need to be raised. Buy-in both financially and in leadership is crucial to be aware of and note for the future. Sometimes, it is not the social media professional who makes the call but the CEO or supervisor. That said, there needs to be a discussion around how to apply new advances. Technology is changing so fast that it is hard to keep up, but some technology advances not only are sustainable but continue to grow in prominence within the industry.

Two indicators to note when it comes to investing in new tools and platforms for social media purposes are virtual reality and augmented reality. Virtual reality is one of the more guaranteed technology investments not just for professional practices but for understanding how audiences want to interact with the digital and real space, while also creating their own experiences with these new tools. **Virtual reality (VR)** can be defined as "a three-dimensional, computer generated environment which can be explored and interacted with by a person. That person becomes part of this virtual world or is immersed within this environment and whilst there, is able to manipulate objects or perform a series of actions" (Virtual Reality Society, 2017). When it comes to VR, its growing prominence as a mainstream media channel for consumers and brands alike is a key element. In fact, by the end of 2020, the number of VR headsets reached 82 million users, marking a nearly 1500 percent increase from 2017 (Becker, 2020).

Brands sometimes use VR technologies to showcase their innovation to audiences. For example, Lowes was an early adopter of VR when they developed their Holorom, which allows customers to immerse themselves in the virtual space of their home to determine how their renovations will look before making decisions in real life (Becker, 2020).

How does VR connect with social media? Essentially, social media and VR combined make up what is defined as social presence, which Facebook has defined as "authentic and lifelike collaboration between people and colleagues in a virtual setting" (Hackl, 2020). The sense of belonging and fulfillment in an online community that recreates the offline social experience is what makes social presence in VR so powerful. In the times of isolation due to unrest and a global pandemic, people seek a sense of connection and normalcy. One way to achieve this is through immersion experiences. Essentially, social presence allows users onto a platform, let's say Facebook Horizons, to have the ability to manipulate virtual objects, engage in conversation, and create virtual social contact experiences with friends and family (Hackl, 2020).

VR can be used strategically and aligned with the work of social media professionals in several ways:

- Experiential storytelling for brands and consumers
- Representation and education with audiences
- Role playing (Hackl, 2020)
- Awareness and activism on issues and topics of interest
- Health communication and training
- Crisis communication training and response measures
- Education
- Impact of cause-related marketing

VR can be used to purposely interject a user into an experience, tapping into more of the emotional cues and responses that may result. This is one of the more prominent and strategic ways social media professionals, along with others, allow users to get inside the story, experience the moment, and walk away feeling impacted in some way.

A related trend, **augmented reality (AR)** sometimes gets confused with VR, but it is slightly different. Essentially, according to Azuma (1997), AR allows programmers to create both real and virtual elements so the individual user is able to interact with both. As Hofmann and Mosemghvdlishvili (2014) stated in their work, AR is different from VR because AR is "a view of physical, real world, but supplements it with layers of digital elements" (p. 266).

Although AR is often aligned and integrated with VR, AR can provide unique benefits for social media professionals (Griffin, 2020), such as

- *Branded filters.* We have seen these from Spark AR with Facebook and Instagram Lens, but Snapchat also offers AR filters that allow customers to create and share their own filters. Brands have created many filters over the years for campaigns. To promote their films, Marvel and DC created the infamous taco face filter that went virtual. Branded filters and lenses create an entertaining experience for users and empower them to share the filters with their community. This promotes word-of-mouth marketing, implementation, and brand awareness objectives that many brands are measuring and evaluating in their campaigns.

- *Try before you buy.* AR filters allow you to try products virtually before you hit the buy button. Sephora offers an AR feature where customers can try makeup on virtually before purchasing anything. Prada's virtual experience allows people to visit store and exhibition locations and to explore clothes and accessories. Transforming the traditional shopping experience into an interactive online shopping experience is very attractive for those who do not want to shop at a traditional store.

- *Immersive experiences.* Consider this: What would make you more likely to share a video? Would you share one that just shows up on your news feed, or one that allows you to interject yourself as part of the video? AR filters and lenses allow you to be part of the experience, and when you share your filter on your platforms, you are at the center of the content and story.

Many brands have embraced AR in their campaigns. One example is Champs Sports, which is the first athletic lifestyle brand to take advantage of Snapchat's SnapML technology in which customers can "try on" shoes using AR lenses (Cohen, 2020). This strategic partnership illustrates the benefits of AR filters fulfilling audience needs to try on items before purchasing them. Another example is Home Depot. The home improvement store, like Lowe's, was early on the train for the AR features when they launched their Project Color app for users in 2015 (Forsey, n.d.), which allows users to see what the paint would look like in their home before purchasing the product at the store. The app has since been updated to include how other objects (e.g., furniture, home décor and products, etc.) look as well (Forsey, n.d.).

Streaming services have entered the AR game as well. When Netflix's popular show *Stranger Things* released their latest campaign, Netflix partnered with Snapchat to integrate a series of *Stranger Things*–themed lenses fans could wear around their house (Forsey, n.d.). Not to be outdone by one of their main streaming competitors, Amazon has their own AR integration for promoting their popular show *The Boys*. Amazon released an AR game called Baby Laser Tag, based on the second season *The Boys*, where fans can play a shooter-style game that aligns itself with the overall tone of the show (Kulp, 2020).

Some brands do AR collaborations to promote events and products at the same time. As in social media, one consistent theme we see in the AR space is the power of collaborations. The same can be said with what Burger King and the MTV Video Music Awards (VMAs) did in 2020 ("Burger King Delivers Immersive AR Experience During VMAs," n.d.) The burger chain had viewers scan a QR code that activated an AR experience to show The King (Burger King's mascot) and rapper Lil Yachty announce through the AR experience that they would be appearing together on the red carpet for the VMAs. Not only did users get to hear Lil Yachty perform his song "Top Down" in the AR experience, but they got a free Whopper and were entered into a chance to win free Whoppers for a year and tickets to the 2021 VMAs ("Burger King Delivers," n.d.).

These are just some of the ways in which AR is integrated within social and strategic communication campaigns. However, there are many different ways to create an AR experience for audiences, such as the following:

- *Virtual tours.* A virtual tour allows people to learn about certain locations (e.g., traveling) and see historical notations for significant landmarks.

- *Education.* Information is provided on a topic in a new format that is entertaining and interactive for audiences.

- *Collaborations.* As discussed, AR can serve as an outlet for partnerships to bring forth new opportunities to create engaging experiences for everyone to participate in.

- *Paid partnerships.* The rise of virtual paid media and ads through AR will continue to skyrocket as more people use the technologies. Keep in mind that wherever consumers go, marketers and advertisers will soon follow. If the experience is beneficial and entertaining for the user, then it may be appropriate. If not, it will be all for nothing. Lenses, filters, and games are some of the types of paid media partnerships that will continue to grow in popularity.

- *Storytelling and personal branding.* As a result of updates to platforms like Bitmoji and Snapchat, people can create their own avatars to showcase emotions and their own stories.

These new specializations are "current," and we do not know the longevity of these platforms or how they will evolve. In some cases, a new form of technology (e.g., Google Glass) emerges but is not successful because developers did not anticipate audiences' perceptions, behaviors, and attitudes (e.g., toward wearable technologies). These technologies may be great tools, but some are ahead of their time. AR glasses have been implemented by Google and Microsoft, and Apple and Facebook are even getting to be part of the conversation. Is the technology ready for mainstream use? Is society ready for this new type of wearable technology? Time will tell.

Some rising platforms become dominated by larger ones with powerful brands. Meerkat, a popular live streaming app, faced this challenge when going up against Periscope, the live streaming app Twitter eventually bought. Twitter bought Vine, which resulted in the founders of Vine creating Byte, which is Vine 2.0. The actions Twitter took with Vine made way for the rise of TikTok, even with the bans it received from countries such as Australia, India, and the United States and the news of Oracle formulating a partnership for U.S. operations with TikTok.

There are lessons to keep in mind. First, be wary of emerging platforms about which people say, "This is going to change the industry!" Sure, for the moment. Keep in mind, audiences move on very quickly to the next trend, tool, or case study. The attention span is extremely short. Social media has come to the point of maturation where the larger brands such as Google, Facebook, or others will make a purchase of the platform to integrate it into their own platforms and tools. Second, the social media landscape will continue to change and evolve. Platforms try to outdo each other. Platforms add unique features others have claimed they are the only ones to have. Look at what happened with stories, live video, and short musical clips. Snapchat's Stories were the first, and then Instagram, Facebook, and LinkedIn jumped on board. Facebook and Twitter had live video, but LinkedIn followed with their own features that are offered only through third-party partners. TikTok has been popular with Generation Z with their musical challenges and collaborations, and Instagram added Reels. The list goes on and on, making it an entertaining thing for social media professionals to witness.

What is important, though, is investing in ongoing education and training for what may emerge, which will tell us why and how a new technology is relevant for an organization and what steps to take to determine whether it is worthy to invest in.

Failure to invest in education and training relevant to emerging tools due to the limited time and resources available for some brands and professionals could cause a "virtual technology desert" for audiences. Like food deserts, **virtual digital technology deserts** provide limited access and opportunities to stand out in the industry, and the resulting community is limited. In addition, future applications and tools have to be analyzed and guided based on where the audiences are going. If your audience is baby boomers, you will need to invest in one subset of tools that might be different from tools used for an audience made up of Generation Z. It is also important to acknowledge the importance of looking ahead at emerging age cohorts, such as Generation Alpha (individuals born in the 2010s), and see what steps you and your team can take to prepare as this group becomes a primary audience to engage with. Each cohort consumes, creates, and shares information differently on social media, and this will have to be monitored, studied, and implemented on a regular basis. Ultimately, where to go next and what content to create has to be a unified decision by everyone involved in strategy and creative execution.

Strategies on Staying Relevant in the Future of Social Media

With all of these updates, changes, and advances in the industry happening every day, it may be overwhelming and challenging, to say the least, when it comes to staying up to date with every aspect of the industry. Staying relevant and engaged with social media is a challenging task. In a constantly evolving, changing, and shifting field, how does a social media professional continue to stay relevant? Many professionals, students, and professors have asked themselves this question. Instead of worrying about the advancement of tools, look at the advancement of your actions and behaviors to make sure you stay relevant.

Here are some ways to accomplish this task and continue to stay relevant:

- *Treat your understanding of the profession like a sport or hobby*. Olympians do not start training for their sport the day before the trials. They train every day and invest time and energy to better understand their sport. You need to take the same approach. Do a little bit each day. This means reading up on a few blog posts and white papers, or even reading a new book on the subject. Schedule and watch a webinar or live video show session once every couple of weeks.

- *Follow people as well as media accounts.* The professionals highlighted in this book's Humans of Social Media feature are some people you may want to follow and connect with. Media accounts will come and go, but those who are actively engaged in the business will not move around as much. The future stars and influencers are going to be employees who are behind the scenes of some of the biggest brands on social media. These people include Adrian Molina of Aviation Gin, Adam Ornelas from Chipotle, Nick Martin from Hootsuite, Kristen Nyhan of Delta, Katie Perry (no, not the singer!) of Public, Christina Garnett of HubSpot, Musa Tariq of GoFundMe, Julian Gamboa of *Adweek*, and Reva Labbe of College GameDay. Also, follow the professionals who are active in contributing to #MarketingTwitter. See? You now have a few amazing professionals who are at the top of their game to follow on social media. (You will thank me later!)

- *Focus on outlining a few online accounts you trust and that provide good content.* In addition, follow a few people who are specialists in their field or on a particular platform. For example, Chris Strub focuses on nonprofits and social media. Alexa Heinrich focuses on accessibility on social media. Roberto Blake shares insights on content creation on YouTube. Matt Navarra breaks news and updates on social media trends. Jeremy Schumann of Instagram shares insights focused on brand strategy on social media. Both Lindsay Fultz of Whalar and *The Influencer Code* author Amanda Russell share insights and best practices for campaigns and influencer marketing. Amir Zozoni shares insights on sports and social media analytics. Amanda Goertz shares insights on social strategy. Follow a few of these professionals to get up-to-date information related to specific niches, so then you have an idea of what is going on, what is relevant, and how to apply this information to your role.

- *Be an active participant.* It's not only what you know about social media that matters but who knows you. The best way for you to get known in social media and gain opportunities in the industry is to be an active participant. This means participating in Twitter chats, commenting and engaging with others online through various platforms (e.g., Twitter and LinkedIn), and creating content you feel provides value to the community. Join communities to share your perspective (e.g., if you like sports, #SMSports is for you; if you are more on the marketing side of things, engage with pros in #MarketingTwitter). Don't be a shadow to the conversation. Listen to the conversations and learn from others. Be the light that shines new perspectives while providing value to others. Who knows, if you use this strategy, you may get a follow or response from Ryan Reynolds.

- *Don't be intimidated or have imposter syndrome when working in social media.* It can be very intimidating to see what others are doing and to feel like you are not doing enough. This happens to everyone. There are many people in the industry who share their own struggles with this, while others hide it from the rest of the world. There are a lot of people who talk a good game about how "big" they are in the industry, but they are just making CO_2 and nothing else. Be your best advocate while being humble at the same time. Let your experience, expertise, and insights shine. Your work and perspective will speak for itself.

- *Do an audit of your skills and personal brand every few months.* We are all evolving as professionals, and we want to make sure we set goals for what we want to accomplish and achieve in the industry. Set forth a few professional social media goals you want to achieve (be featured in a guest blog post, be interviewed for a podcast, speak at a virtual or in person conference on social media, be invited to do a keynote, etc.). Analyze what you have done and what you need to do, and list the steps you will take to achieve those goals. With the technology and platforms changing so much, it is necessary to conduct this audit on a regular basis so it is not completely overwhelming.

- *Find a mentor.* Find someone in the industry you want not only to connect with but, more importantly, to learn from. See if people are willing to share their experiences with you, provide guidance and advice, and help you get your start in the industry. As the famous line goes, we all stand on the shoulders of giants, and we all need a little help to get to where we need to go.

Students to Students: Advice From the Social Media Classroom Seat

When it comes to social media, there are certain things to expect. Professors or professionals can share their own experiences, but when advice comes from peers in a social media class, different insights emerge.

Certain aspects of social media are universal, but students are in the position not only to embrace knowledge and understanding of the tools and concepts but to apply them in real-life circumstances in and out of the classroom. The students featured here are recent and soon-to-be graduates who were enrolled in a social media class and wanted to pass along some of their own perspectives and words of wisdom to the future generation of social media professionals entering the workplace.

Have a learning mindset. Lizelle Lauron (@letstelllizelle), the social media coordinator for the Dallas Mavericks, shared her words of wisdom on what to keep in mind when entering the workplace. Lizelle graduated in 2013 with a degree in communications with a sports administration minor from the University of Louisville.

My advice for future students is to always be in a learning mindset. In my profession, people trust those who put their noses down and grind. So many times we come across interns who have this amazing opportunity to impress us in the NBA but only want to take selfies on the court.

Present new ideas! Show how the company, organization, or whomever can improve because of your ideas. That's how you make yourself valuable. In social media, anyone can "tweet, Instagram, or post on Facebook." Start conversations with "I saw in the past we've done this, so what do you think about this?" or "I've noticed others doing this, but I think if we did this, it would work better for us!" If you have the drive to show growth, change, engagement, and impressions for your company, people will see you as a team player!

Use social media to create opportunities. Camille England, a current student studying social media and strategic communication at the University of Louisville, shares her advice on what she feels is the best thing about social media: creating opportunities for yourself.

Being a student in the social media world has been one of the most rewarding experiences.

Don't get me wrong, there are many long nights and unreasonable amounts of coffee, but I wouldn't change it for anything. One of the best ways to learn in this industry is to experience it first-hand. Confidence is key and will get you far! One tip for success is to have a presence in your community; reach out to small local businesses that could use some help with social media, and present your ideas to them. Another tip for success is to reach out to social media managers, content creators, or other fellow social media junkies. It is very surprising to see how excited some people are to share what they love with you and others! I have learned so much just by reaching out to people and asking questions; always ask questions. Most importantly, establish your brand and utilize your own social media accounts to reach out to others. Creating a personal brand is one of the key steps in entering the social media world. Showcasing your work and using your personal account as a "guinea pig" will allow you to gain more knowledge and exposure. Who knows, you may find your first social media job on Twitter.

Understand the strategic side of social media.

Nick Hartledge, a senior majoring in communication at the University of Louisville, who has worked with class clients such as Louisville Bats and Chipotle, shares his insights on what students need to be aware of as they move forward in the social media profession.

For social media, understanding the impact of each and every single message that is sent to the user in a post or advertisement is crucial. This includes pictures, words, videos; anything and everything that the social media user can perceive as having meaning. Knowing the message you are seeking to portray to the target audience will allow for better communication between you, as a social media specialist, and the social media user. Additionally, crisis situations can be avoided by understanding what is being said, in what context, through which media, and to whom it is being said. Focusing on these four aspects will assist in proper communication with your target audience. You may wonder how aspects like these are identified. Understanding the message also means doing the proper research on every aspect of a campaign. Research is how you identify the aforementioned "four aspects" and much more that will help build your understanding of the message being sent to the target audience. The better the research, the better you can understand the message, the better the communication will be.

Diversify your knowledge. Natalie Uhl, who is the digital content coordinator at the University of Louisville, focuses on how it is crucial for students to continue to move forward, not backward, in their understanding and perspectives on social media.

To students entering the social media industry: Diversify your knowledge, be confident, and have fun. Whether it's the ability to edit stunning images or write captivating copy, everyone has strengths when it comes to content creation. Understanding how each element works together will allow you to develop effective messages, whether you're a one-person show or working as a part of a team. All aspects of social media content have to work together across platforms to ensure that the brand voice doesn't become disjointed. The emojis and hashtags used, the visuals created, and the cadence of writing all need to work together to develop an impactful brand presence.

Not every piece of content you create will be great—and that's okay. Don't doubt yourself. Each time a piece of content flops, take it as an opportunity to learn. Every failure and success helps you to understand your brand's audience a little bit more. While some tactics will work for one brand, they may not work for yours. To keep your message from becoming stagnant, you have to be willing to take calculated risks. Not everything can be planned, and sometimes the best content comes from an idea sparked at the least expected time, or in a situation that you couldn't anticipate (think Oreo's famous blackout tweet).

Social media is an inherently creative field. Even in a serious situation, thinking creatively will allow you to develop a message that triggers a response. Regardless of the topic, don't take the social out of social media. Your job isn't to push content; your job is to produce engagement that helps to reach your brand's ultimate goals.

Watch for rising trends and new platforms and always continue to learn. After all, social media is an ever-evolving field. If you're not adapting, you're moving backward.

Harry Quinn Cedeno, a graduate of the University of Louisville who comes from Panama, discussed how photography and his passion allowed him to choose the medium that best fits his perspective and story.

After spending couple of years doing my general education courses in Panama, I transferred to University of Louisville to finish my degree. I spend almost two semesters figuring out what I enjoyed most. I tried industrial engineering and marketing, but they didn't click. When I took strategic communications and social media, then I knew. I was done with my communication degree in summer of 2020 after doing my internship at Vimarc.

In 2016 I bought my first camera and at the moment I didn't know it was going to be the reason I enjoyed so much digital marketing. Since learning about the world of strategic comms, I have taken my knowledge and I apply to my photography. In other words, I have work on my personal brand. What I recommend to students is to take some passion (or idea, it can be a business idea) and choose a medium where you can share it. You can write about it on a blog, become an immediate source of info in Twitter, or show off your new product/service on Instagram. Whichever scenario it is, you will learn what role fits you best or which one you would like to do. It can be that you enjoy coming up with strategies to produce more engagement, maybe your PR skills are the beauty of your new business, or you create engaging content as I do. The benefit of having something personal like a blog, Instagram, or website is that you will not want to stop learning at class. You will go home and do more research. You will see how the top brands do it and similar brands on your level do it also. You will understand that influencers are necessary and have a critical function in this industry, or that boosting content is not a taboo or waste of money. As a photographer, I chose the path of creating social media content for brands. This is how I branded myself in social media. I would reach out to different businesses and try to land a deal. Besides knowing how to take photos, I knew all this stuff about social media like Facebook ads. I would include this knowledge as recommendations in my proposals in order to get the opportunity of doing this too. I am currently living in Panama and although I work in my family business, I am the social media manager and content creator for a local specialty coffee business.

Emily Hayes (@emceris), a graduate of the University of Louisville with a degree in communication, has some additional suggestions and recommendations. Emily interned with Power, a digital and advertising agency in Louisville, and is currently working as a marketing coordinator for AMD Studios in Austin, Texas.

My best advice for any student in social media is to never assume you know it all. Social media is an ever-evolving landscape; platforms die out, tools change, and trends fade all the time. But you know how you can navigate this? Be an active participant and student in your field! Try out the latest and greatest, talk to your fellow students, and attend your classes so you know the basics like the back of your hand. Always be on the lookout for the exciting ways social media is evolving around you and how you can become a part of it! Best of luck out there, and know we're all rooting for you.

FINAL WORDS OF WISDOM AND RECOMMENDATIONS

As we finalize this chapter and book, there are some parting words of wisdom to share with the future generations of social media professionals. Let's call them #Frebergisms of social media! These are items I share with my own students, as they embark on their own journeys in social media. Keep in mind that some things will remain true in spite of ongoing changes. The behaviors, actions, and communities formed are based on human behavior. That said, social media continues to be owned not by one person but by the community.

The community decides where people make connections and whether they continue online or offline. Social media is more than just taking selfies and sharing updates. As discussed in this textbook, it takes a social media strategic mindset to understand, comprehend, and apply insights from the community to provide the best experience for everyone. The rise of **human interaction marketing (HIM)** is also apparent; it is a strain of relationship management with the strategic purpose of the health and longevity of the relationship being the currency exchanged. It may be tempting to focus on the here and now, but do not forget the long-term implications and benefits. Social media is indeed instantaneous, but always think about the ramifications and connections that can be made in an instant and how these could transform into roadblocks or opportunities down the line. Social media, with the help of screenshots and Google, does not forget.

In this book, you learned some of the fundamental skills necessary for working in the social media field. However, there are some other aspects to keep in mind as you enter your next phase of working in social media:

- *Be ambitious and embrace what you are passionate about.* Take every opportunity you see in front of you and go for it. These opportunities—whether internships or jobs—will not drop into your lap. They will have to be pursued with passion (the next skill listed here) and thinking outside of the box. There are many, many opportunities to pursue in social media. If you do not like what you are doing, figure out what you do like and pursue that area of interest. You may encounter some challenging roadblocks, gatekeepers, and obstacles, but if you are willing to put forth the time and investment, you'll eventually meet your goals.

- *Show initiative.* Opportunities and networking connections do not appear out of thin air. They come from you—yes, you!—taking the initiative to reach out. Send out an email to a professional colleague. Connect with someone with a personalized LinkedIn message. Tweet and DM a social media professional online who works for an agency you admire. What is the worst thing that can happen? You may not get an answer, but at least you tried. But, what is the *best thing* that could happen? You make new exciting opportunities for yourself.

- *Be persistent.* The industry is big enough for everyone to carve out an area of expertise and build a community. Sometimes you may feel certain people (influencers, etc.) dominate the field, or you may think, "This discipline owns social media" and try to provide roadblocks to keep it a closed circuit. Ultimately, if you provide great content, excellent resources, and a unique perspective to share with others, you have a place in the social media community. The social media community and industry as a whole is huge, and it is constantly evolving.

- *Have balance.* Social media will always be there, so it's okay to have a life. Yes, there is a "hustle" mentality, and you do have to invest time and energy—but do it in a smart way. Embrace the digital breaks as a way to brainstorm ideas, gain new perspectives, and actually have a life outside of social media. Certain audiences have the appearance of being online 24/7, but ask yourself, can I sustain this, and even if I can, do I want to? Each person may have different answers to and interpretations of these questions, so do what you feel fits with your overall goals and future directions.

- *Always be a student.* Learning does not stop in the classroom, so you will always need to be a student of the field and learn from others. In addition, you may be called upon to educate others and help them get their start in the field. Embrace the role as an educator and mentor—be a resource for others if they have questions about what the field entails. We are all in the same boat together, and the more we share and help others, the better the field will be.

- *Learn from failures and embrace Plan B.* We sometimes see everyone bask in the light of successes and notable accomplishments, but this is just one side of the coin. To get there, a lot of unsuccessful ventures, ideas, and projects first crash and burn. This happens in all aspects of life, including social media. For every yes, you will hear a lot of nos. Keep in mind that no is just one answer. No, this idea or initiative will not be good for our industry. No, we do not have the time or energy to educate everyone about social media. No, we do not have the resources to get this particular program or tool to do social media this way. No can mean a lot of things, and there are different layers of no to consider. No, this is never going to happen ever in this lifetime. No—as in not yet. Get used to hearing the word *no* a lot, but don't give up. You may have to pursue Plan B. Plan B or even updated versions of your original plan might be better in the long run. Sometimes, people say no so you can come back with something better for them to review.

- *Never settle.* Mario Armstrong, TV host and entrepreneur, is a great example of a professional who has never settled on his dream and accomplishments. He wanted to create the first Facebook Live TV talk show, and he did just that, and called it the *Never Settle Show*. The same principles apply here with social media. Never think you have done all that it takes to be successful. Each chapter and experience is a level up, but you have not reached the top of the potential you can bring to the table for your businesses, organization, and individual accomplishments.

- *Pay it forward.* Being kind does not cost a thing, and if you are willing to share your perspective, resources, and ideas with others, the benefit to you will be tremendous. Our industry needs more mentors, and with the knowledge and insights you have gained from this book, I hope you embark on a mentorship journey to help others in social media. Provide workshops, offer tutorials, and consult on topics you are passionate about and have expertise in.

CHAPTER SUMMARY

The social media and strategic communications road has come to an end, but the conversation has not. This is just the beginning, and social media is an evolving journey that embraces the entire community.

The power with which we can use technology to break down barriers in both time and location is unlike anything we have experienced before. For those just entering the workplace—whether it is right after graduating from school or embarking on a new career path—social media has a lot to offer as far as opportunities and challenges. It is important to always have a balanced perspective of the field. It is indeed the giver of pain and delight.

We need to learn to strategically use each of the social media tools to best tell our stories, engage proactively with audiences, use data to inform on what is really happening in the network through scientific measurements, and be inspired to create experiences and memories online that could last a lifetime. Having a strategic mindset that is agile, creative, and scientific is the key to success in all arenas on social media. This is truly one of the most exciting times to be working in and learning about social media.

As the author of this textbook, I wish you all the best in the journey you have taken through these chapters. I hope this book has been helpful in guiding you to create a strategic mindset in social media. I hope it serves you well for the future social media endeavors you encounter and face along the way. There will be challenges, but as in all aspects of life, there will also be opportunities. You just have to find them—especially if they are hard to see and hiding from you. This is a time to fully embrace the social media field with both arms and run with it. Age does not matter; we can all learn from each other and provide insights that can help society, the industry, and our local and global communities.

The possibilities are endless, and all it takes is that first step. This first step may be intimidating, but you are not alone.

Let's take the first step together in this exciting new social media journey.

THOUGHT QUESTIONS

1. What best practices and tips about social media resonated with you the most? Explain your rationale.

2. After reviewing this textbook, what future trends and applications do you want to learn more about in social media? What are two action steps you will take to better understand these new trends?

3. Some say that while the tools and platforms change, some best practices and strategies remain the same. Do you agree? Discuss your perspective on this statement.

EXERCISES

1. You are asked to write a post for your local agency about the top five trends that will be relevant for the next year. Research online and see what experts are talking about on the major media outlet networks for social media (*Digiday*, *Social Media Today*, *Adweek*, etc.) and highlight which ones to watch out for and why.

2. You have been asked to be a mentor to a high school senior who wants to attend your college. You share that you are taking a social media class, and the high school student is curious about what this means exactly and what the social media industry is like. What tips and best practices would you recommend to the student? Outline three tips and list three things you will do as the student's mentor to pay it forward to the future generation of social media professionals.

3. Based on your reading of this textbook, what areas within social media would you like to specialize in? This can be a designated role or a particular industry. Outline five steps you will take in order to get a job or internship in this field.

4. You come home for a visit with family and friends, and share that you want to work in social media. Your best friend from high school says anyone can work in social media by watching YouTube videos and hearing what thought leaders have to say on subjects in their keynote speeches. Discuss how you would approach this statement based on your experience reading this textbook and your other studies.

REFERENCES

Azuma, R. T. (1997). A survey of augmented reality. *Presence: Teleoperators and Virtual Environments*, 6(4), 355–385.

Becker, B. (2020). 10 VR marketing examples to inspire you in 2020. *HubSpot*. https://blog.hubspot.com/marketing/vr-marketing-examples

Burger King delivers immersive AR experience during VMAs. (n.d.). *Mobile Marketer*. https://www.mobilemarketer.com/news/burger-king-delivers-immersive-ar-experience-during-vmas/584459/

Cohen, D. (2020, September 18). Champs Sports adds Snapchat AR try-on lens to refresh your game campaign. *Adweek*. https://www.adweek.com/brand-marketing/champs-sports-adds-snapchat-ar-try-on-lens-to-refresh-your-game-campaign/

Forsey, C. (n.d.). 8 innovative & inspiring examples of augmented reality in marketing. *HubSpot*. https://blog.hubspot.com/marketing/augmented-reality-examples

Griffin, T. (2020, January 8). How augmented reality can boost social media marketing. *Forbes*. https://www.forbes.com/sites/forbestechcouncil/2020/01/08/how-augmented-reality-can-boost-social-media-marketing/

Hackl, C. (2020, August 30). Social VR, Facebook Horizon and the future of social media marketing. *Forbes*. https://www.forbes.com/sites/cathyhackl/2020/08/30/social-vr-facebook-horizon--the-future-of-social-media-marketing/#5f93802a5b19

Hofmann, S., & Mosemghvdlishvili, L. (2014). Perceiving spaces through digital augmentation: An exploratory study of navigational augmented reality apps. *Mobile Media & Communication*, 2(3), 265–280.

Hong, J. (2017, November 21). The importance of dark social is rising—here are some tips on how to track it. *Social Media Today*. https://www.socialmediatoday.com/news/the-importance-of-dark-social-is-rising-here-are-some-tips-on-how-to-trac/511358/

Kulp, P. (2020, September 10). Amazon rolls out AR shooter game to promote *The Boys*. *Adweek*. https://www.adweek.com/creativity/amazon-rolls-out-augmented-reality-shooter-game-to-promote-the-boys/

Phillips, D. (2021). The 10 most expensive NFTs ever sold. *Decrypt*. https://decrypt.co/62898/the-10-most-expensive-nfts-ever-sold

Virtual Reality Society. (2017). *What is virtual reality?* https://www.vrs.org.uk/virtual-reality/what-is-virtual-reality.html

GLOSSARY

CHAPTER 1

Branded content (BC): Content that is created by a business for the purpose of establishing ownership and consistency in brand identity and reputation.

Informed decision making: A term coined by Rich Calabrese of Fizziology that focuses on taking creativity, data, and insight into account for social media practices.

Online reputation: The collective perception of attributes assigned to an individual or brand based on digital and social media activities, actions, and conversation exchanges.

Social media: A personalized, online networked hub of information, dialogue, and relationship management. These new communication technology tools allow individual users and organizations to engage with, reach, persuade, and target key audiences more effectively across multiple platforms. Industry professionals, scholars, and social media users have contributed a number of different definitions and conceptualizations of social media. Some emphasize the role of social media as a toolkit that allows users to create and share content. Others focus on how social media extends Web 2.0 technologies to bring communities together.

Social networking site (SNS): Online service that allows audiences to create a profile and build online connections with other users and brands on the platform.

Thought leadership: Being acknowledged by others in the community for having expertise and experience in the industry and specific skills, insights, and knowledge.

User-generated content (UGC): Pieces of content created directly by a user.

Virality: Rapid dissemination of information from person to person; one of the ways in which news, stories, and updates reach across various networks in a short amount of time.

CHAPTER 2

Alternative accounts: Serve as a notion to resist the official voice and stories they represent.

Bot: A social media account that is automated to share and comment on posts.

Canceled: The action others take to stop giving support or stop reading, promoting, or advocating for a person or brand's work.

Children's Privacy Protection Act (COPPA): An act that protects children under age 13 by requiring online services to disclose what information and data they are collecting on these audiences.

Ethics: A set of moral guidelines and principles that influence our behaviors and interactions.

Flame war: An emotional and long argument streamed through a series of online messages that are focused on personal attacks and voicing outrage to a specific person or parties.

General Data Protection Regulation (GDPR): Regulation that makes organizations and individuals aware of the privacy needs of their users, allowing them to take control over what they are willing to share.

Going rogue: Going against the norm of expectations of society while initiating behaviors that are considered to be out of norm or against social, personal, and professional expectations; going off script on social media without permission and not in an official capacity.

Influencer: Individual who is able to persuade audiences to take action; someone who has built an audience, naturally and over time, and is viewed as an authority figure on a certain subject, area, or perspective in the online space.

Trendjacking: When brands try to jump on board with a trending topic, event, or situation on social media to generate buzz about their own brand and interject themselves into the conversation; for example, Oreo in the "Can Still Dunk in the Dark" tweet from 2013, or MoonPie and Hostess Cupcakes during the 2017 solar eclipse.

CHAPTER 3

Audience strategy: Creating content that focuses on the relationships that you have made on specific platforms.

Brand voice: The overall tone and format in which you present your updates and other forms of communication.

Community: A place where a group of people with similar interests come together online.

Consistency: Doing the same behaviors and actions over time to build trust.

Content strategy: How you go about sharing specific assets online depending on the audience, platform, and community related to your personal brand.

Customized strategy: Integrating specific pieces of content to send out related to your personal brand based on the relationships on the platform you are communicating on (audience) while sharing content that is relevant and consistent with your brand image (content strategy).

Expertise: Having knowledge and authority in a certain area of social media.

Finsta: A fake Instagram account where you post "real" (aka "just for your friends") pieces of content for no one else to see.

Generalist: Someone who knows a lot about a lot of things at the macro level of social media but does not have expertise in one area.

Influence: The ability to shift people to take action or listen to what you have to say on social media.

Passion: Topics and areas of interest that motivate and make you advocate these to others.

Personal brand: The collection and strategic process of crafting and sustaining a specific image in hopes of establishing a clear advantage in the minds of collective audiences online and offline.

Personal brand association: Specific attributes, events, settings, and interests you want others to recognize as going along with your personal brand.

Personality: Characteristics and attributes that are unique, memorable, and aligned with your personal brand.

Specialist: Expert in one specific area of social media at the micro level.

CHAPTER 4

Action plan: Plan to outline the steps, best practices, and guidelines to promote DEI (diversity, equity, inclusion) initiatives.

Diversity: The ability to understand and appreciate attributes that differ from our own and from those of groups with which we identify, yet are found in other individuals and groups.

Diversity, equity, and inclusion (DEI): Concepts that raise separate yet related challenges and areas requiring improvement in the social media space.

Diversity statement: "A written explanation of its commitment to diversity, equity, and inclusion for its employees and customers. It tells stakeholders how diversity fits into your organization's mission and values" (Doeing, 2019b).

Diversity style guide: A guide that highlights the key terms and practices in ensuring diversity.

Equity: Equal opportunities for everyone without discrimination on the basis of race/ethnicity, color, national origin, age, marital status, sex, sexual orientation, gender identity, gender expression, disability, religion, height, political thought, weight, or veteran status.

Inclusion: The act of bringing together people with different experiences, perspectives, backgrounds, and ideas to make sure each group is representative of its audiences and the public at large.

Inclusive brand voice: The ability to include all audiences and represent all perspectives in tone and presence in brand messaging on social media channels.

Value statement: "The documented beliefs and principles of your organization. It is an explanation of the fundamental things your organization holds important and is used to guide the organization and the people in it" (Doeing, 2019a).

CHAPTER 5

Boutique agencies or firms: Agencies or businesses that specialize either in one aspect of social media, such as analytics, or in a specific platform channel.

Consultant: Specialist who provides counsel and advice on social media–specific projects and campaigns.

Content calendar: Document that outlines, defines, and structures what pieces of content need to be created and disseminated at specific points in time and on which channels for a brand, organization, or individual.

Content creator: Someone who is well versed in the ability to create pieces of work that resonate with audiences.

Creator: Professional who is hired based on his or her creative works that generate excitement and interest among audiences.

Diversity and inclusion lead: Lead roles and teams created to address and support strategies, campaigns, and initiatives to promote and increase diversity and inclusion internally and externally.

Entrepreneur: Person who is their own boss in their own business.

Freelancer: Someone who is paid on a project basis for specific creations and products.

Influencer: Person who has the ability to persuade audiences to take actions based on their expertise, personality, and presence in the community offline and online.

Social media community manager: Professional who can add a personal take on the conversation and engagements with audience members.

Social media coordinator: Professional who focuses on the strategic planning and execution of the social media content for a brand or organization.

Social media strategist: Professional who ties in the goals and objectives for the company or client in question and focuses on how to get these measures accomplished.

CHAPTER 6

Advanced metrics: Calculations that dive into the actions and psychographics (attitudes, behaviors, and opinions of audience members) of specific users (e.g., influencers and advocates).

Advocate: Someone who shows support, appreciation, and dedication across all digital and social channels publicly.

Amplification rate: Average number of shares per post across a specific platform.

Analytics: Structured calculation of data and statistics collected from online sources to produce scientific and actionable insights.

Basic metrics: Metrics that can be collected easily either from the social media channel itself or by a separate service or program.

Behavioral metrics: The measured calculations of the actions users take that are connected to specific strategic initiatives on social media and communication objectives.

Channel metrics: Specific calculations that are unique to specific channels.

Click-through rate: Rate at which people click to navigate to another website from your site.

Conversion rate: Percentage of users who initiate a specific behavior based on what is shown and presented to them on social media.

Followers: Individuals or brand accounts on social media that are keeping track of your activity on a designated platform.

Influencer impact: Percentage of users who actually initiate an action or behavior based on what the influencer has shared.

Insights: Revelations of certain truths about an audience that illuminates certain data points from the research that help drive creative strategies and formulate innovative approaches.

Listening: Focused activities on social media to learn, explore, and uncover emerging trends, opportunities, activities, and issues that could impact a company, individual, or brand either positively or negatively.

Mention: Naming and tagging a brand handle and name on social media.

Metrics: Data collected by a social media professional in a systematic manner.

Monitoring: The systematic process of understanding, analyzing, and reporting insights and conversations on reputation, brand position, community health, and opinion of key audience members virtually.

Research: The systematic gathering of information in a scientific and objective manner to help answer questions; one of the primary duties of social media professionals.

Social media return on investment (ROI): Common metric used to evaluate whether the investment (money) a brand or company put into a campaign accomplished the set goals and objectives.

Social research: Applying traditional methods of research to listening and monitoring dashboards, to be able to answer larger questions that cannot be addressed just by looking at dashboards. This is the ultimate goal to integrate listening, monitoring, and strategy under the social research umbrella.

Vanity metrics: Metrics that are pretty to view and report but do not necessarily impact the business objectives or bottom financial line of organizations and individuals.

CHAPTER 7

Brand voice: Overall tone, personality, and entity that you want to present online.

Demographics: Basic way to categorize a group of individuals, involving the basic population data that are easily collected, such as age, education level, ethnicity, and location.

Environmental scan: Assessment that helps the social media professional evaluate the current landscape within which a client or organization operates.

Goal statement: Broad statement that captures the overall focus for your social media initiative.

Key performance indicators (KPIs): Indicators determined before the social media strategic plan is implemented that not only determine what has been accomplished but inform next steps and measurements for future campaigns.

Mission: Key elements of the overall purpose of an organization, brand, or person in the respective spaces.

Objective: Clear statement of what you plan to accomplish—probably one of the toughest parts of constructing a social media strategic plan or campaign.

PESO model: Model, created by Gini Dietrich, that focuses on outlining the key components of media for social media such as paid media (P), earned media (E), shared media (S), and owned media (O). (See individual definitions in Chapter 12.)

Primary audience: People you want to target directly and who have a meaningful relationship and connection to the client.

Primary message: A broad statement that you want to communicate to your key audience members; it should be simple, concise, and to the point.

Psychographics: A way to categorize audiences based on their attitudes, opinions, and values.

Secondary audience: People who are supportive and potentially viewed as influencers by the primary audience members.

Secondary message: Message that provides additional evidence to support the primary message; using facts, statistics, and additional information to build on the point outlined in the primary message, secondary messages can incorporate evidence and additional information regarding what the client has already done on social media.

SMART criteria: An established way to categorize effective objectives into five different categories: specific, measurable, achievable, realistic, and time-specific.

Strategic mindset: Communicating in the brand voice rather than one's own personal voice.

Strategic plan: A systematic, thorough, and aligned document that outlines from start to finish what a brand, individual, or organization wants to accomplish to address a problem or opportunity or to explore potential new possibilities through experimentation.

Strategy: How you will go about accomplishing set objectives and the heart of the social media strategic plan.

Tactics: Tools and applications within social media that you will be using to accomplish your objectives and fulfill your strategies; the nuts and bolts of your social media plan.

Vision: Characteristics and principles that an organization or individual values, which will guide its overall actions and make an impact in the community; vision statements bridge various components together in a cohesive statement, tying in brand personality, key attributes, core values, and present and future behavioral intentions.

CHAPTER 8

Agencies: Business organizations that serve multiple clients while offering specific services and expertise.

Celebrity influencers: Influencers who hold a prominent status that allows them to influence others.

Creators: Subset of influencers who create original content in their own voices for brands.

Influence marketing: A practice that focuses on the action itself, rather than on the individual influencer, in persuading audiences.

Influencer: Someone who has built an audience, naturally and over time, and who is viewed as an authority on a certain subject, practice, or perspective in online spaces.

Influencer marketing: Marketing that engages influencers in partnerships with aligned brands, organizations, and agencies.

Influencer marketing partnership platforms: Where the influencer has to register for a specific platform and gets charged a monthly fee to get access to these platforms.

Kid influencers: Children and youth, ranging from a few years old to teenagers, known for their content on their social media platforms, particularly on YouTube.

Media kit: Traditional form used in most public relations and marketing efforts, is a collection of material that provides a person's background to the media.

Mega influencers: Influencers with a prominent status on social media and a broad appeal that puts them on track to reach celebrity status.

Memers: People who create memes, which are pieces of content that communicate an idea, style, or behavior within a particular culture (mainstream or subculture) to convey a specific purpose.

Micro influencers: Influencers that have smaller audiences than the celebrity or mega influencers and are the source of considerable contemporary buzz.

Multi-channel networks (MCNs): Networks that work with a roster of select influencers who are specific in what they offer and may add on required media fees for their services.

Nano influencers: Influencers with the fewest followers, have audiences even smaller than those of micro influencers.

Pay per acquisition (PPA): Approach that looks at how many new customers, audience members, or subscriptions were made based on what the influencer has shared.

Pay per campaign: Metric that is used for a particular campaign for the influencer. This is more of a long-term focused fee that covers all aspects of the campaign for the influencer.

Pay per click (PPC): For every click, view, or action taken by the influencer's community based on what

they shared, the influencer gets paid for this particular view and action.

Pay per post (PPP): Based on the reach, engagement level, and overall health of their community, influencers set the different rates they have for each of their posts.

Rate card: Focuses on the payment the influencer expects.

Virtual influencers: Also called CGI (computer-generated imagery) influencers; fictional computer-generated "people" who have the realistic characteristics, features, and personalities of humans.

CHAPTER 9

A/B testing: Testing different characteristics in ads and copy to determine the most effective one to use in a campaign.

Ad fatigue: Fatigue audiences feel as a result of seeing too many ads in their feed or seeing the paid media component too early or late to do anything about it.

Algorithms: Focused on making sure audiences are seeing the content they want to see first on a designated platform.

Awareness: Building brand awareness and reach.

Boosting a post: Putting money and ad spend on a post that is performing well to get more reach.

Click-through rate: Number of clicks from the ad divided by the impressions it received, making this an important metric to evaluate and determine.

Consideration: Engaging audiences to take certain actions like going to a website or installing an app.

Conversion: Making a sale or driving offline traffic based on content.

Cost per conversion (CPC): Focuses on addressing the conversion objectives (e.g., sign-ups, sales, downloads, etc.).

Cost per mille/impression (CPM): Focuses on the amount paid for every 1,000 impressions received for the campaign; primarily aligned with the awareness objective.

Cost per send (CPS): Focuses on the direct message costs that are being created, executed, and opened through messaging apps (e.g., WhatsApp) or message features within traditional platforms (e.g., LinkedIn and Facebook Messenger).

Paid social media: Method of displaying advertisements or sponsored marketing messages on popular social media platforms and targeting a specific sub-audience.

Paid yet earned media: Falls under the caveat of being earned when you are essentially paying for content to be created, but not a piece of content that is coming directly from the organization or client paying for the content.

Paid yet owned media: Focuses on content marketing, webinars, and podcasts.

Pay per click: For every time a person clicks on a link to go to a website or additional destination, payment is due from the advertiser to the publisher.

Pods: Private mass groups of individuals created to let group members know when a post goes live so they can "like" the post to increase its reach and exposure.

Retargeting: Technique that focuses on reaching people who have interacted with your content or visited your website, allowing the social media professional to reach another important key audience to engage with in their paid media strategy.

Return on investment (ROI): The return on the financial support you put forward in a campaign or advertisement.

Social media advertising: Lead generation, sales, and promotional benefits that are based on the financial backing implemented for these pieces to be purchased online.

Targeted ads: Feature that focuses on a bidding system where advertisers are able to bid on a number of ads based on their target audience, essentially giving them a chance to have their ad run.

Targeting: Technique focusing on audiences based on certain key characteristics such as age, likes, income, locations, interests, and other key demographic information.

CHAPTER 10

Brand voice: Strategic position for a brand to express specific attributes through written and visual exchanges interconnecting the brand culture and community.

Community: Group of individuals who come together based on common interests, values, experiences, and characteristics.

Connection: A valued relationship individuals or brands could have that could link them together based on an experience, similar interest, or other valued activities.

Content: Anything that is published and presented on social media; pieces of original work that are distributed and consumed by audiences.

Content creation: A mixture of content that is originally created.

Content curation: A mixture of content that was published from a different source.

Conversation: The exchange of words between two individuals or among a group of individuals online.

Creativity: Approaching situations, ideas, and concepts in a unique and imaginative manner that resonates with audiences.

Culture: Common practices, work life ethics and practices, professional experiences, and beliefs of a group of individuals.

Experiential media: Content that immerses audiences in the story and channel.

Tone: Overall voice characteristics you want to interject within the content you are writing.

CHAPTER 11

Ambassadors: Individuals who advocate and promote your work based on their own personal interests and investment with the brand, agency, organization, or person in question.

Audience segmentation: Process of categorizing people into certain groups based on specific criteria, which can be broad in nature (e.g., demographics and population data) or very specific and focused (niche) on certain characteristics (e.g., experiential, visually driven, or industry and interest specific).

Creators: People who can be useful because of the talent of their creative insights and strategy.

Emerging audience: Group that is gaining traction to become a prominent community to reach.

Niche: Specialized focused area or community surrounding a common interest, location, or characteristic.

Omnichannel approach: Seamless and effortless integration of content, messages, and experiences for the user that is linked to multiple communication channels.

Online persona: Summation of all of the characteristics and attributes assigned to a person by engaged audiences in online networks; an identity constructed by an individual online that may or may not represent who he or she truly is in real life.

Opponent/critic: Person who does not have your best interest at heart and demonstrates this either publicly or secretly online.

CHAPTER 12

Content audit: A thorough overview of the key characteristics and features of content to determine what worked and what did not in a social media campaign.

Content marketing: "A strategic marketing approach focused on creating and distributing valuable, relevant, and consistent content to attract and retain a clearly defined audience—and, ultimately, to drive profitable customer action." (Content Marketing Institute, 2017, para. 2).

Earned media: Content that is sometimes connected with public relations but not controlled by brands, which in many ways makes it more trustworthy and less biased compared to other types of content.

Evergreen content: Information that is created that continues to be relevant regardless of when it was first published.

Long-form content: Content that is designed for consumption over a period of time.

Owned media: Content and the platform you control as a brand, organization, or person.

Paid media: Social media advertising, or a "pay-to-play" model, in which the company (or advertiser/agency) pays for the content to appear in the timeline for a certain amount of money.

Shared media: Content that is associated with social media, but more of an interactive medium where conversations and dialogue emerge as the result of the content being shared.

Short-form content: Concise content that is consumed less than a minute.

CHAPTER 13

Data: Points of information that are collected through use of various tools and programs.

Insights: What connects the relevant information to tell the story on what the data are saying.

CHAPTER 14

Fake news: False or misleading information that is presented as truthful.

Media literacy: The ability to analyze, access, create, and evaluate media content.

CHAPTER 15

Crowdfunding: The practice of raising money online with the help of social media community outreach and advocacy efforts in small and large donations.

Crowdsourcing: The practice of collecting information, asking for assistance, and reaching out to the community for help to solve a problem or address an opportunity online in a centralized space.

CHAPTER 16

Augmented reality (AR): Both real and virtual elements created by users and programmers so the individual user is able to interact with both.

Human interaction marketing (HIM): A strain of relationship management, with the strategic purpose of the health and longevity of the relationship being the currency exchanged.

Virtual digital technology desert: Limited access and opportunities to stand out in the industry, putting the resulting community at a disadvantage.

Virtual reality (VR): A digital and real space in which users interact, while also creating their own experiences.

INDEX